Albany Unravelled

ALBANY

UNRAVELLED

Published by Bonfire Books,
753-755 Nicholson Street
Carlton North, VIC 3054, Australia
info@bonfirebooks.org
www.bonfirebooks.org

Copyright © Steffan Silcox & Douglas R.G. Sellick 2023
Steffan Silcox and Douglas R.G. Sellick assert their right to be known as the authors of this work.

Foreword Copyright Peter Spearritt & Stephen Foster
Postscript Copyright Graham Seal

ALL RIGHTS RESERVED
No part of this publication may be reproduced, stored in a retrieval system, or transmitted in any form by any means electronic, mechanical, photocopying, recording or otherwise without the prior written consent of the publishers.

ISBN 978-0-6457768-2-9

A catalogue record for this book is available
from the National Library of Australia

The publishers wish to thank Jason Beer for his assistance

Cover image: *HMS Chatham & Discovery*, Scrimshaw by Mr Gary Tonkin, Fellow of the Marine Arts Society of Australia and founding Chairman of Maritime Heritage Society of Albany.

A Note on the Text: Every endeavour has been made to locate the original primary source for the information that is provided in this book. If earlier documentation can be found that challenges The Historical Record presented here, then please share with the authors and the Albany History Collection Co-ordinators. We have attempted to provide an unembellished accurate record of Albany's historical development from 1791-1927 and in doing so present a document that can withstand peer scrutiny. To ensure accuracy we have submitted the manuscript to recognised and acknowledged historians for their feedback. We have followed the spelling and punctuation of the original extracts, altering them only when it seemed essential to do so for the sake of clarity for the reader. We have reproduced the writer's own spelling of proper and place names: where the modern version is so different as to be unrecognisable, we have used brackets to clarify. Some omissions of some passages from the original text may have occurred for the sake of brevity and these have been denoted by a series of dots in the text.

ALBANY UNRAVELLED

A History of Albany on King George's Sound
1791 to 1927.

Using Primary Written Source Material that
Extends and Corrects
The Historical Record

Steffan Silcox with Douglas R.G. Sellick

Albany 2023

For Family and Friends.

Compiled as a tribute to those who have contributed in a meaningful way to the Albany and King George's Sound Historical Record.

CONTENTS

Foreword *i*
Preface *ii*

Introduction *1*

Chapter 1
A Meeting of Cultures – The Early Reports
Overview *7*
George Vancouver and William Broughton *8*
Matthew Flinders *9*
Thomas Nicholas Baudin *9*
Phillip Parker King *10*
Jules Sébastien César Dumont D'Urville *11*
Edmund Lockyer *12*
Isaac Scott Nind *14*
Thomas Braidwood Wilson *15*
Alexander Collie *16*
Death of Mokare *16*
Winds of Change *18*
Anne Camfield and *Annesfield* *21*
Tommy King *22*
Daisy Bates *23*
Closing Remarks *24*

Chapter 2
Early Visitors to King George's Sound
Global Overview *25*
George Vancouver and William Broughton *26*
Thomas Manby *29*
Archibald Menzies *30*
Bruny D'Entrecasteaux *32*
Whalers and Sealers *32*
Matthew Flinders *34*
Thomas Nicolas Baudin *37*
Convict Ship *Emu* *40*
Phillip Parker King *40*
Jules Sébastien César Dumont D'Urville *43*
Closing Remarks *46*

Chapter 3
From Cantonment to Settlement
Overview *47*
Correction to The Historical Record *47*
Cantonment at King George's Sound *49*
Edmund Lockyer and Joseph Wakefield *52*
New South Wales Report on The New Settlement *57*
Joseph Wakefield *58*
George Sleeman *60*
Thomas Wilson *61*
Collet Barker *64*
Thomas Bannister *66*
James Stirling *68*
Alexander Collie *69*
Richard Spencer *73*
George Grey *76*

Patrick Taylor *77*
Edward John Eyre and Wylie *81*
Albany Snapshot 1841 *84*
Closing Remarks *84*

Chapter 4
Selection of Early Visitor Impressions of Albany
Overview *85*
Reports and Traveller's Tales *85*
Carl Von Hügel *86*
Charles Darwin *89*
Anthony Trollope *91*
Mary Mackillop *92*
The Prince George of Wales and The Prince Albert Victor of Wales *93*
Henry Archibald Lawson *97*
Mark Twain *99*
Herbert Clark Hoover *100*
Harry Furness *100*
Eastern Colony Newspaper Impressions of Visitors *100*
Travellers' Remarks *105*
Margaret Walpole *108*
Other Visitors of Note *110*
Closing Remarks *111*

Chapter 5
The Vexatious Issue of Convict Labour
Overview *113*
Global Update *113*
Convict Past *114*
Anti-Transportation Movement *119*
Closing Remarks *126*

Chapter 6
Whaling
Foreign Whaling Around King George's Sound *127*
Settler Forays in Whaling *128*
Closing Remarks *130*

Chapter 7
The Development of the Town's Education Facilities
Overview *131*
The Need for a School *131*
Political Adversaries and State Aid *134*
Government School Board Established *140*
Infants, Primary and High Schools *142*
Roman Catholic School Development *145*
Christian Brothers *146*
Church and Private Grammar Schools *147*
Closing Remarks *151*

Chapter 8
Catering for Albany's Spiritual Needs
Overview *153*
The Church of England *153*
Church of St John the Apostle and Evangelist *154*
The Roman Catholic Church *156*
Scots Presbyterian Church *157*
Wesley Methodist Church *158*
Closing Remarks *159*

Chapter 9
Significant Town Infrastructure
Overview *160*
Global Update *160*
Quarantine Facilities *161*
Lighthouses *168*
Telegraph *173*
Telephone Exchange *177*
Albany to Perth Road *178*
The Administration of Albany *180*
Closing Remarks *181*

Chapter 10
The Great Southern Railway Network Unfolds
Settlement Comes to Life *182*
Anthony Hordern and the Albany to Perth Railway *182*
City of New Albany *185*
Hordern's Vision Unfolds *187*
Closing Remarks *190*

Chapter 11
Royal Mail and the Albany Post Office
Overview *191*
Royal Mail and the Advent of Steam Ships *193*
A Purpose-Built Post Office *195*
For Want of Service *195*
The Last Mail Coach *196*
Mysterious Alcove Under the Old Post Office *197*
Closing Remarks *198*

Chapter 12
Health Facilities and Development of the Albany Hospital
Need for Hospital Facilities Identified *199*
Agitation for Better Facilities *200*
1922 Royal Commission *203*
Closing Remarks *203*

Chapter 13
The Provision of Amenities in the Town
Overview *204*
Water Supply *204*
Sanitary Issues *209*
Street Lighting *212*
Electrifying the Town *215*
Closing Remarks *216*

Chapter 14
Golden Era of Steam Ships 1851-1900
Overview *217*
Arrival of Steam Ships *217*
P&O Working the Sound *217*
Excitement in the Town *218*
Coaling Depot *218*
P&O Shareholders Meeting *224*
Facilities to Service the Ships *224*
Jetty Structures *224*
P&O Floating Dock *226*
Closing Remarks *228*

Chapter 15
The Imperial Defence of King George's Sound
Setting the Scene *231*
Albany Defence Rifles *233*
Russian 'Scare' *234*
Fortress Albany *237*
The Boer War *240*
Hail Columbia! The U.S. Navy's Great White Fleet *245*
Japanese Naval Squadron Visits *252*
Closing Remarks *252*

Chapter 16
Albany At War and its ANZAC Connections
The Great War 1914-1918
1914 Departures for War *253*
The War at Home *259*
Wartime Military Wedding *260*
Arrival of Hospital Ships and the Wounded *260*
Anti-German Feelings *262*
The Returned Soldiers and Sailors Imperial League *262*
Albany War Memorials *264*
Notable Post-War Visitors *265*
A Royal Visit *266*
Arrival of British Naval Squadron and HMS Hood *267*
Church of England Anzac Day Dawn Requiem (1930) *269*
1931 Parish Pilgrimage *271*
1937 Anzac Day Wreath Laying in the Sound *271*
The 1938 Famous Summit Photograph *272*
Commemoration of the First Anzac Day 1916 *272*
Visit by Sir Rider Haggard *274*
Origin of the Word Anzac *275*
Closing Remarks *276*

Chapter 17
Development of Notable Private Commercial Interests
Overview *277*
Reporting the News *277*
Newspaper Development in The Town *279*
The Albany Despatch Newspaper *281*
Booming Hotel Industry *281*
Breweries *293*
Bakers *294*
Transport *296*
First Aeroplanes to Grace Albany's Sky *298*
Albany Baths *299*
Albany Chamber of Commerce *301*
Brothel Incident *302*
Albany Zoo *303*
Chinese Market Gardens *303*
Gold Find *304*
Albany Woollen Mills *306*
Closing Remarks *308*

Chapter 18
Buildings of Historical Significance
Overview *309*
Octagonal "Chapel" *309*
Anglican Church of St John the Apostle and Evangelist *310*
Roman Catholic Church of St Joseph and Convent *310*

Government Cottage: The Rocks *310*
The Old Farm - Strawberry Hill *311*
Albany Mechanics Institute and Town Library *312*
Headmaster's House *313*
Commissariat Store *313*
Albany Town Hall *314*
Convict Depot and Gaol *316*
Cabman Shelter and Women's Refuge *317*
The Residency *317*
Albany Courthouse *317*
Albany Co-Operative Store *318*
Albany Cottage Hospital *319*
Matthew Cull House *319*
Hillside House *319*
Pyrmont House *320*
Wollaston House *320*
Norman House *320*
Camfield House *321*
The Mount *321*
Patrick Taylor Cottage *321*
A Snapshot of the Town 1840s to the Early 1900s *322*
Closing Remarks *323*

Chapter 19
Celebrations and Entertainment
Overview *324*
Albany Week and The Albany Season *325*
Queens Victoria's Jubilee Celebration *328*
First Agricultural Show *329*
Cinemas *330*
Albany and the Federation Issue *332*
British Empire Day *335*
Albany Centenary Celebrations of 1927 *335*
Reaction to Western Australia's Centenary Celebrations *337*
Outdoor Leisure Pursuits *340*
Closing Remarks *347*

Chapter 20
Conclusion *348*

Postscript *350*

Appendix 1
A Short Chronology of The King George's Sound (1791-1927) *351*
Appendix 2
Military Commandants, Government Residents & Magistrates *354*
New South Wales and Western Australian Governors *355*
Appendix 3
The 39th Regiment of Foot in Australia *355*

Index *357*
Bibliography *365*

Acknowledgements *368*

About the Authors *369*

Photographs

Centenary Celebrates, 21st January 1927.	6
Candyup Homestead	78
Cricket Match circa 1890 on Parade Street Grounds	111
Government School Albany 1900, Stirling Terrace	141
Roman Catholic Convent and School circa 1890's	146
St John's Church Nineteenth Century	155
Point King Lighthouse	169
Albany Railway Station Nineteenth Century	186
Royal Mail Coach	194
Albany Boer War Contingent	241
Great White Fleet	246
HMS Hood	268
Albany Woollen Mills 1921	307
Matthew Cull House	319
The Mount	321
Albany Floaters Football Team 1902	347

Maps

Map of Port Roi George 1791.	25
Map of South Western Australia showing land grant to Anthony Hordern	183
Map of Railway Routes from Albany to Mt Barker and Denmark	190
Map of proposed new Colony centred on Albany Secession Petition in 1900	333

Illustrations and Scans

Book "Centenary of Western Australia Albany 1827-1927".	6
Albany Menang Woman and Child by Robert Neill 1843.	7
Albany Menang Man by Robert Neill 1843.	7
Vancouver's ship Discovery by Gary Tonkin [Albany Mace Project].	27
Aboriginal Fish Traps on the French River [The Kalgan].	42
Princess Royal Harbour by Robert Neill 1842	83
Postcard of Portrait of Henry Lawson	97
Point King Lighthouse 1890	168
1851 Town Seal as found on City of Albany Mayoral Chain	180
Albany Post Office Building, Stirling Terrace	195
New Albany Cottage Hospital	202
Japanese War Squadron	252
Banner for first Edition of King George's Sound Observer	279
Handwritten list of approvals for 1850 Liquor Licences	285
Octagonal Chapel in Albany History Collection, Town Library	309
St John's Church by J. Campbell	310
St Joseph's Covent by E. Bracey	310
Government Cottage	311
Mechanics Institute	312
Town Hall	314
Convict Depot and Gaol by E. Bracey	316
The Residency by E. Bracey	317
Patrick Taylor's Cottage in Albany History Collection.	321

Advertisements and Insignias

Royal Arms of George III	iii
Bailye's Railway Hotel, 1912	289
London Hotel, 1912	290
Weld Arms Hotel, 1912	291
York Hotel, 1912	292
Southern Brewery Company, 1890	294
J.F.C. Greeve and Son, Bakery	295
A series of Advertisements 1890-1912	301
Insignia of 39th Dorchester Regiment of Foot 1825	355

FOREWORD

Why is Albany a name readily recognised by many Australians, but visited by relatively few? Many people have a rough idea that is it located on the southern coast of Western Australia, and they may be confused about its pronunciation—it is Al-bany, not All-bany.

Albany was better known in the 19th century than the 21st century. As this book explains, by the 1880s Albany had established itself as Western Australia's pre-eminent port, the first and last Australian port for all large ocean-going mail steamers, taking on coal and provisions before embarking, if heading for the northern hemisphere, on their long voyage. British, French and American ships were a regular sight in the port. Albany also served as the main port for the WA goldfields, bringing new sources of revenue with the 1893 discoveries in and about Kalgoorlie.

The hundreds of documents assembly in this book demonstrate that Albany remained a thriving regional city in the 20th century, with its rail and port connections servicing a wide agricultural hinterland. Residents from Perth could travel to Albany by ship or rail, enjoying its equitable climate, its sea breezes a refreshing change from the harsh summers that beset the state's capital. In the 1920s school children were most likely to learn about Albany because of its key role as a staging point for troops and horses to head to fight for Empire in the Great War. Other than that Albany has rarely figured prominently in national news, though closing the last whaling station in the southern hemisphere in 1978, did receive attention.

With the rapid growth in national and international tourism, Albany started to lose out as a holiday destination to intensively marketed places, especially if they offered direct air routes from the eastern states and glamorous accommodation. By 2018/19, the last year for pre-pandemic statistics, Broome got over seven times Albany's 50,000 international visitors, and over three times Albany's 440,000 domestic visitors, most of whom came from Perth, just four hours' drive away.

As this book demonstrates, Albany has a long and complex history, much of which can be read into its landscapes, from the magnificent King George's Sound to its rich Indigenous, port and whaling heritage. Generations of historians, journalists and travel writers made little or no acknowledgement of prior Indigenous occupation, especially in cities and towns. When such recognition did happen it usually treated the Indigenous inhabitants as part of the prehistory of the 'settlement'. In recent decades new research has led to an appreciation of the rich and complex history of Indigenous land management techniques, while locality studies have revealed the ongoing Indigenous presence in all our urban settlements. Albany is no exception to this, as the documents included here demonstrate.

Douglas Sellick and Steffan Silcox have put in a prodigious amount of effort in assembling these documents, along with explanatory commentary. Both authors live in Albany and manage to convey their fascination with its rich history. They have gone to great pains to check some of the key claims about Albany's history, often taken for granted by generations of historians, not always going back to the original sources. So, this book will stand as a well-researched collection for many years to come.

If you are planning on visiting Albany, its spectacular coastal setting and majestic landscapes will not disappoint. But you will gain a better understanding of what you are looking at, not least the profusion of heritage properties, if you have a copy of this book with you.

Peter Spearritt	**Stephen Foster**
Emeritus Professor in History	Adjunct Professor
School of Historical and Philosophical Inquiry	School of Humanities and the Arts
University of Queensland	Australian National University

PREFACE

"Those who cannot remember the past are condemned to repeat it."
George Santayana. (Philosopher)

As the published collection of articles pertaining to Albany and King George's Sound are quite extensive and disparately housed this often makes the task of finding and sequencing material and events difficult to achieve, except perhaps for the most selfless of historians. However, the opportunity to read original documentation and manuscripts (primary sources) unadulterated by the opinions of others provides a clearer perspective on events, particularly as they inform Albany's historical evolution.

The material used in preparing this manuscript has been garnered from a wide variety of sources, each characterised by its immediacy in respect to the occurrence of the event it reports. It is maintained that such an approach will enhance and strengthen the reader's general understanding of the event, unimpeded by the vicarious misrepresentation of others, collectively contributing to the town's unique history. Nonetheless, every effort has been made to source and select documents that contain the essential evidence to allow for the reader to interpret events from their perspective and personal prejudice.

In making selections among the many thousands of pieces of primary documentation it was realised that we could ourselves inadvertently distort some reporting of events of historical value just through omission. Such an issue is always present when attempting to manage, in an unbiased way, events as represented in the general Historical Record. Many thousands of articles, documents and transcripts contiguous with the time have been sourced in selecting what we believe are appropriate to include in this work. Be that as it may, in some cases only pertinent extracts from the available documents have been included because of the length of the original article or report. The reference for each of the included articles, correspondence and reports have been detailed in footnotes that will enable the interested reader or student to source the full documentation if desired.

While the material could have been arranged in chronological order, we have chosen instead to group the documentation into thematic categories that have then been chronologically presented to make the narrative more coherent for the reader.

Changing The Historical Record

As indicated, this work presents defining moments in Albany's Imperial, Colonial and Federation history through the presentation of real and rare glimpses of King George's Sound culled from autobiographies, despatches, letters, diaries, telegrams, newspapers, periodicals and publications found in libraries, special collections and archives in London, Windsor, Edinburgh, Boston, Yale, Princeton, Washington DC, Cape Town, Sydney, Canberra, Perth and of course Albany. In completing this research, it has always been our intention to let the town's history stand on its own, without embellishment. Consequently, many of the myths and inaccuracies that have crept into The Historical Record of the town have been exposed and addressed.

Albany was not Incorporated as a Municipal Town until 1851, then on 1st July 1998 it was gazetted a City. The town's unique journey is well worth recording. On the 24th January 1871, the District Roads Act, 1871 came into effect and 18 road districts were formally established covering the whole colony. This Act was followed by the Municipal Institutions' Act, 1871 which came into effect on 21st February 1871, that created six extensive municipalities (in additional to Perth) at Fremantle, Guildford, Bunbury, Busselton, Geraldton and Albany. At this time the Municipality of Albany was extended to include the Plantagenet Region as well.

Albany was once often disparagingly referred to as a "Sleepy Hollow". A cognomen that it held until 1890 when the Imperial Government in London decided to establish a permanent fortress and garrison overlooking King George's Sound, to protect The Colony of Western Australia, together with the British

Empire's Indian Ocean and Asian trade routes. It was envisaged that fortress Albany would become "a sort of Gibraltar" for The British Army, The Royal and Merchant Navies on the Australian continent.

The selection of the period between 1791 and 1927 is an important timespan in Australian history. Albany's story and foundation unfolds through the initial actions back in Imperial London and then to Colonial Sydney. In following Albany's history, we are better able to know and understand "how, when and why" the first British settlements came into existence on the western side of New Holland. Unfortunately, with the passage of time and the degradation of memories The Historical Record has sometimes been hijacked through poor research practices and a mischievous element of myth making. Past events and recollections then have become muddled to the extent that historical accuracy morphs into unrecognisable tales.

It is indeed unfortunate that the wonderful and unique history of Albany's evolution from The British Army Cantonment to Settlement, to town and now city has been dogged by these local myths which are very hard to extirpate. Myths born of flimsy evidence and assertions that crumble on closer examination. In researching the town's history by referring to primary source material whenever possible it came as no surprise to discover that many of these myths and simple historical errors of fact concerning Albany's foundation had been made and then perpetuated over the years by amateur history writers. Accordingly, the opportunity was taken in this work to correct The Historical Record in the hope that it will benefit future researchers and writers.

This work is by intention a documentary in the form of an anthology made up primary sources and pioneering encounters of a great diversity of people and the town's history. Their stories are central to our understanding and appreciation of Albany's history and heritage. Reading these early first-hand eyewitness encounters allows for the extra-ordinary history of Albany to unfold. What is presented is a picture of a remote corner of the then British Empire as exciting and colourful as that of the great frontiers in North America, India and Africa. These exciting and often adventurous stories become a valuable and now permanent literary and historical resource for the present-day reader, whether they be student, resident, traveller or tourist.

Albany's European story begins with Captain George Vancouver taking Possession of the area for Britain in 1791 and then continues with later exploration of the hinterland at King George's Sound. The work provides a unique insight into the meeting of Indigenous and European cultures. These interactions are particularly noted for their more amicable nature and the lack of violence in its immediate vicinity than were witnessed by way of example, in many other parts of Western Australia during the Nineteenth and early Twentieth Centuries. Consequently, Albany provides a unique insight into the meeting of Indigenous and European cultures. Also, news of the two wonderful natural harbours, The Princess Royal and Oyster, first reached Sydney and then quite rapidly London early in 1792, during a period representing the last four decades of the Hanoverian Georgian and early Victorian periods of British and Australian history.

Interestingly as George III, George IV and William IV all shared the same Royal Coat of Arms until Queen Victoria's accession to the throne in 1837 when the new Royal Arms were gazetted and then was extensively used until 1901 by Empire and Colonial officials on all Royal Proclamations. In Albany only two relics appear to have survived from the Hanoverian period: parts of the fabric of Sir Richard and Lady Spencer's dwellings on Strawberry Hill, on the site of the first military farm, now called The Old Farm administered by The National Trust. The other is the Hanoverian Royal Cipher or Monogram on the gun barrel of a cannon situated alongside a replica of the New South Wales Government brig *Amity* dry-docked near the Albany Western Australian Museum on the original shoreline of Hanover Bay in The Princess Royal Harbour. Much of the site of Hanover Bay has been reclaimed in recent times and is now occupied by the ANZAC Peace Park and a busy road and railway line.

The pervasive belief in Albany is that Major Edmund Lockyer and Captain Joseph Wakefield read out an official Proclamation at the time of establishing the military cantonment is incorrect. The actual happenings on that day were definitively recorded by Major Lockyer himself in his journal and subsequent reports to Governor Darling. A proclamation did not take place because the senior British Army Officer was not given the requisite Signed and Sealed Order authorising him to do so on behalf of the Governor of New South Wales, nor was he required to. This "Proclamation" event did not take place and it is foolish to pretend it did. London and Sydney knew that Vancouver and Broughton had already claimed the area for King George the Third. After careful research and enquiry, no reference to such a document or occasion has been found in any index or file in The Historical Records of Australia, The Historical Records of New South Wales, the National Archives of Australia, the State Records Offices of New South Wales and Western Australia, The Historical Records of the British Army, The Edmund Lockyer Papers in the Mitchell Library, Sydney or the National Archives of the United Kingdom at Kew. This is one local history myth that can and should be dismissed. It did not happen and the continued promulgation of this myth is not helpful or appropriate, perpetuating a major error in The Historical Record.

Another example which has caused misunderstanding in local affairs is a recorded speech made by a local historian on Thursday March 12th 1936 on the occasion of the unveiling of a granite monument on Residency Point to commemorate the arrival from New South Wales of a British Army detachment of the 39th (Dorsetshire) Regiment of Foot at King George's Sound in 1826 and the raising for the second time of the British flag officially in 1827. The following is an extract from the exuberant end of that speech:

It is fitting that we should be reminded that here on this spot on a memorable Sunday, 109 years ago, the British flag was hoisted to the accompaniment of cannon booming a royal salute of twenty-one guns and the whole of Australia west of 135o East longitude was then formally and solemnly claimed as the possession of the British Crown.

When this part of the speech is compared with Major Lockyer's account of events on Sunday 21st January 1827, the difference is so profound that the reader could be forgiven for thinking that there are two separate events being discussed. Nevertheless, this extravagant misrepresentation has been accepted without question and frequently deployed in subsequent local histories and even printed in The Western Australian Historical Society Journal and Proceedings, Volume 2 for 1936. It has remained uncorrected until now.

Yet another persistent local myth that gained some popularity concerns the misuse of "Frederickstown" or "Frederick's Town" as the initial place name for the town. Such a name was never gazetted as a place name for the settlement at King George's Sound. Major Lockyer failed in his attempt to name his Cantonment after Field Marshall The Prince Frederick, The Duke of York & Albany, the Commander-in-Chief of the British Army. Known to many as "The Grand Old Duke of York". This failed attempt at naming was because the Governor of New South Wales, General Ralph Darling, did not acknowledge or respond to the Major Lockyer's suggested designation of "Frederick's Town". The matter was not followed up by Edmund Lockyer who had hurriedly returned to Sydney early in 1827 to assume a future career in private enterprise after selling his army commission.

We have enjoyed immensely the innovative research which has underpinned this Historical Record of Albany. Likewise, we hope readers will be surprised and delighted at the amount of new information unearthed and arranged to show how the town evolved in its first hundred or more years. The happenings, together with important new biographical details and appendices, of contemporary newspapers extracts relevant to the first rules and regulations of local government will combine to enhance the history not only of Albany but Western Australia as well.

Albany's story does not need to be embellished. This old garrison town and port is undoubtedly one of the most significant maritime, military and ecclesiastical sites in all of Australia. We hope that this book and its content add to, and when necessary, correct The Historical Record of Albany's early development in the period 1791 to 1927.

Steffan Silcox & Douglas R.G. Sellick
Mid-Winter 2023

INTRODUCTION

It is not imaginable to such as have not tried, what labour an Historian is condemned to: He must read all, good and bad, and remove a word of rubbish before he can lay the foundation.
John Evelyn to Samuel Pepys. 28th April 1682.

A conscious decision has been made to rely on written eyewitness accounts and other primary sources whenever and wherever possible in reporting significant Albany events over the period 1791-1927. One advantage of insisting on these premium accounts is that it makes for authenticity in reporting. This is because such accounts are not just based on a supposition; rather they can be derived from participants in the actual event, people who can say I was there when it happened, whether in the role of an active participant, traveller, professional newspaper reporter or a by chance a bystander. It is maintained that eyewitness accounts are perceived as being more accurate and truthful because they are spontaneous, often subjective, unlike reconstituted history written well after the event has occurred and based on filtered secondary or vicarious made-up experiences.

Further, wherever possible reports are included that could be dated and referenced precisely.

The historian must acknowledge the importance of providing an accurate account of historical events in order to understand history honestly, not-withstanding that at times it may hold some unpalatable truths; and that the presentation of an identified reality may be distasteful and, unfortunately, some may be offended by it accordingly. It is crucial that the language, particularly as it applies to The Historical Record, is used correctly as a means of communication.

Mythologies are not truths; they mislead and can distort factual history often embroidering it. When populist myths evolve truth can be altered. In researching this work, we have encountered several such myths that have evolved with the story of Albany's development. No apology is made for confronting these myths directly in this work.

When constructing a local history record it is vital that any assertions made can stand up to scrutiny and detailed examination. It is a discipline where one cannot have a laissez-faire or presumptive attitude to available evidence.

In using primary sources, inferences, therefore, can be based on verifiable evidence, often contiguous with the event being described. By verifiable evidence, we mean concrete factual reporting based on participant observations which other historical researchers can access to check for accuracy. Sometimes experience has shown that it is not easy to distinguish a fact from a widely shared illusion. Consequently, the best that can be done is to recognise that a fact is a descriptive statement of reality which, historians, after careful examination and cross-referencing and checking, can agree in believing to be accurate. It is argued that each historical statement and conclusion represented is the most reasonable interpretation of the available historical evidence. Nonetheless even given this effort to present the material as sourced there may still be challenges to its accuracy. Such challenges are welcomed if the source of that challenge is based on verifiable and time pertinent evidence.

Unfortunately, memories can result in certain facts getting mixed up, with names misspelt or confused, dates wrongly transcribed, events and happenings either misinformed or at times most likely exaggerated. Recalling such memories is a difficult task at the best of times especially for those recording them post facto, some years later, without access to primary source materials. Such inaccuracies recorded are not necessarily done intentionally. Therefore, it is important to appreciate that aspects of daily life around Albany described at times by various people with perhaps ancestral links within the town, or later correspondents and writers often remain a source of many of the myths associated with the district that have evolved. Accordingly, by returning to the primary source material relating to the events included in this work we believe that part of our mission in correcting The Historical Record of Albany has been fulfilled.

Historians, by the nature of their research, must retain an ethically neutral stance. However, to be ethically neutral, no aspect of historical inquiry is too sacred to explore, and in so doing sometimes revered myths are destroyed and some cherished values subsequently challenged.

History can be written from many different viewpoints, consequently the interpretation of facts is always open to dispute. Linking these facts into a sequential narrative moreover becomes a challenge, especially as people come to the evidence available with a different interpretation. Inevitably, all historians and those interested in the past, prone to adjusting history according to personal prejudices and beliefs. To what extent then can we claim to be bias-free in our endeavours? Given a surfeit of primary sources to choose from, the very act of selecting one piece over another calls into question the concept of bias. That is why every attempt has been made to select from a cross-section of available accounts and records, to give a flavour and at times perhaps an alternative view of what happened at that time by those present or participating in it.

The events presented give expression by a variety of people, some known, many unknown, who caused history to be made or were the actual eyewitnesses responsible for recording it in the first place. It has been necessary to adopt the persona of historical detectives setting out in search of accuracy and then weighing the fresh historical and literary evidence for its relevance to the topic. Rare books, autobiographies, telegrams, local and international newspapers, personal papers, periodicals and journals held in special collections including as far afield as London, Edinburgh and Windsor in the United Kingdom, Princeton, Yale, New York and Washington in the United States, Wellington New Zealand, Sydney, Melbourne, Canberra, Perth and of course Albany have been examined in constructing this work. In many cases the material found has been resurrected from these sources, much of it had vanished from public view, therefore what is reproduced in this work appears perhaps for the first time in an Albany based history.

As this work is not meant to be an encyclopaedia, and given the selected narrative is not meant to be a definitive collection with accompanying critical analysis, it should be seen for what it is, personal accounts and relevant documents which otherwise would be inaccessible to many interested in Albany's Historical Record. This anthology of collected writings is meant to speak for itself, as a selection of first-hand impressions which are intended to give the reader a sense of continuity over the passage of time and through it, an insight into the gradual development of Albany. Most importantly, the many documents that have been included have been allowed to speak for themselves in the hope that the reader will be surprised and delighted at the amount of new information relevant to Albany that has been unearthed and presented.

Many attempts at presenting local histories are based on unverifiable evidence, so much so that often the assertions that are made do not stand up to closer examination or scrutiny and therefore end up becoming local folklore and myths. It will be of no surprise to many readers to discover that a number of these myths are borne out of simple historical errors of fact that have been perpetuated over the years. Consequently, every endeavour has been made in this work to correct them. For example, as indicated earlier, this work outlines for the first time in written form, the correct version of Albany events relevant to its place name, its foundation and the first commemoration of Anzac Day from 1916 to 1937. The first myth concerning the Royal Duke whose title is honoured in the main street and city's name was H.R.H Prince Frederick, Duke of York and Albany, a point sometimes confused in some historical writings.[1]

Another error of interest noted in some extant historic reporting concerns the evolution of the name of Albany itself. The placename in everyday use, even after Captain James Stirling RN, the new Governor of the Territory of Western Australia, officially named the settlement Albany in 1831, was consistently 'King George's Sound', 'The Sound' or "The Princess Royal Harbour" and in some cases 'the Camp'. Frederickstown was never used in private letters, on maps, or in any official dispatches to and from Sydney and London. These, and many other identified errors in the town's Historical Record are challenged in this work and evidence presented to refute them.

Included in the work are touching and sympathetic reports of the Indigenous people of King George's Sound, distilled from the first 'on the spot' learned observations to be made by those early visitors to the

---

[1] Royal Archives at Windsor Castle. Also, recorded in Royal Register for his baptism on 14th September 1763.

area that would later receive international attention in the published reports and subsequent articles and books they have written.

It is recognised that human memory can be notoriously fallible, hence events and observations not recorded at the time are to an extent not dependable. Conclusions drawn or based on informal recollections may be very misleading and reliance on these can result in the rise of myths concerning an event, for they invariably expose the prejudices of the writer or observer masquerading as historical facts. Given that mankind's memory is an imperfect tool, communities will often remember events the way they prefer them to be remembered, rather than as they eventuated. It is important, therefore, that an event be recorded as quickly as possible, otherwise, its record will be significantly impacted by prejudice, personal preferences, nationalistic feelings, expediency and afterthoughts that together can distort it.

Another classic example of an error in the extant Historical Record relates in part to a couple of memorial plaques installed on monuments [now removed] on Mt Clarence acknowledging The Reverend Arthur White, (Anglican Rector, Army Padre and also Chaplain to the RSL) and the Albany Dawn Service. Unfortunately, for those interested in historical fact the information contained on the plaques misrepresents his actual involvement in the Gallipoli Campaign events of 1915 and subsequent years. Research evidence indicates that the very first civic and military ANZAC Day Service was conducted in the auditorium of the ANZAC Hostel in Cairo, Egypt, in 1916. Albany citizens first commemorated the war dead drawn from across the district in 1916 with a civil service in the Albany Town Hall and later at Lawley Park. In 1930 the Albany branch of the Returned Services League (RSL) revamped the format for their own ANZAC Day commemoration based on the agenda used for the Cairo service.

Padre White was Rector of St. John's Church in Albany and in 1930 celebrated a dawn Eucharist. This event was held on the 25th April at six a.m. 1930. This service was a very solemn event and was then followed by a wreath-laying at the War Memorial adjacent to the church. It was in 1931, that following the Parish Dawn Service in St. John's Church that some members of the community climbed to the summit of Mt Clarence to remember all those who had passed by Albany and not recorded on local war memorials.[2]

Secondly, the two troop convoys were comprised of a number of ships not only *'from around Australia,'* as the plaque informs its readers, but also ships from New Zealand which unfortunately were not mentioned. Further, Padre White did not conduct a service *"as the convoy waited to depart";* as he was a busy priest member of the Bush Brotherhood of St Boniface at the time and was not assigned to Albany. He joined the army in 1916 after securing permission to do so.

So, to be clear on this point and to correct The Historical Record that with time has been distorted by some writers. Therefore, it is important to note Padre White did not conduct Australia's first ANZAC dawn service at the summit of Mount Clarence in Albany in 1914, 1916 or 1923.[3] The first ANZAC dawn service relevant to Albany was conducted by Padre White in St. John's Church, Albany at dawn on ANZAC Day, Friday 25th of April 1930 and not at the summit of Mount Clarence.[4]

A further illustration can be made using again issues relating to the ANZAC Historical Record and by enhancing the overall perspective of the significance of the troop departures from Western Australia. While the emphasis for ANZAC commemorations tends to focus locally on Albany and the departure of the convoy into the Indian Ocean, it is often overlooked that on October 31, 2014, the departure of the first two ships of the first convoy to leave Australian soil carrying troops from South Australia and Western Australia to fight in World War I occurred from Fremantle.

Albany was the main point of departure for New Zealand and Australian troops drawn from other states and territories, the majority of Western Australian troops and a contingent of South Australian troops, however, departed from Fremantle on October 31, 1914, on the ships *Medic* and *Ascarius* accompanied by

---

[2] The full account of this event as it transpired is contained in Chapter 16 of this work and is fully referenced at that time.
[3] Mount Clarence was named after the Duke of Clarence, later to become George 1V; Mount Adelaide was named for his wife.
[4] Ibid

the Japanese warship *Ibuki*. On 3 November 1914, the two Fremantle ships joined up with the Albany convoy at sea in the Indian Ocean to form the greatest military convoy the world had known.

Historians are well aware of just how vulnerable the whole texture of what we call facts can be. Consequently, no shortcuts must be taken when researching and adding to The Historical Record. The most reliable witness that testifies to the passage of time must be history itself. An important ingredient in writing a history, therefore, is hard work underpinned by detailed and unvarnished research.

A common frustration encountered when checking the accuracy of second hand or vicarious revelations or recollections is finding an original source that can verify a claim that is or has been made. For example, such an issue arose when fact-checking a claim made in the pamphlet "*Early Memories of Albany*" by Mrs A.Y. Hassell who asserted that due to the shortage of stores and concern of whaling and sealing ships seeking provisions, even though these were quite irregular, that:

> *At one time stores was so short that the women and children were put on Green Island and provided with a small rowing boat. Tents were securely pitched, and all the remaining stores were placed there. A flagstaff was planted, and the women were instructed to keep the lantern burning by night and the flag flying by day and to arm themselves. They were also told to row over to Vancouver's well for water after dark, for the natives rarely moved about at night.*[5]

When fact-checking the claims made by Mrs Hassell in this instance several issues are immediately evident. The first is related to the geography of the areas in question. The distance between Green Island and Vancouver's well in Frenchman's Bay is in excess of 8 nautical kilometres, and from Green Island in Oyster Harbour, it would need to be accessed through the Emu Point channel across the Sound to Vancouver's freshwater well. A stiff row at the best of times. Further, to do this at night would have been a treacherous journey indeed. However, perhaps this matter can be resolved when it is noted in other documentation that Emu Point itself was often confused with Vancouver's Peninsular during the early years of the colony. There was also a limited supply of fresh water accessible at Emu Point.

The second is the isolation of Green Island from where the troops and other members of the settlement were located at the Cantonment in The Princess Royal Harbour, some seven kilometres distant. Initially, Green Island was the main source of vegetables for the settlement as much of the soil around the camp itself was not of sufficient quality to promote early agricultural endeavours. Later an area which is now known as the Government Farm was cultivated and became the main source of vegetables for the population at large. Donald Garden reports that Lieutenant Sleeman had found the journey from the settlement to Green Island both "tenuous and dangerous." Therefore, common sense would mean that it would not have been an ideal haven to relocate the women and children away from the protection of the settlement in the early months as claimed by Mrs Hassell.[6] The action as described by Mrs Hassell therefore would have only been feasible if some members of the military had been relocated to the Emu Point area, however, no such detachment of troops was noted to this area in available documentation recorded at the time.

Thirdly, Green Island is very small (approximately 160 metres by 60 metres), it is virtually a rocky outcrop with little area for growing and cultivating vegetables; the garden established by Major Edmund Lockyer and his successor Captain Joseph Wakefield would have occupied available cultivating ground leaving little area for tents and people habitation. Green Island also is easily accessed by small whaleboats and so would not have provided a substantive sanctuary from rogue whalers or sealers.

Fourthly, the first two women to join the settlement, Mrs Anne Wood and Mrs Sarah Wood, were both wives of soldiers posted to the Cantonment. They arrived in the colony in May 1827, some months after *Amity*'s first venture into King George's Sound and after the military had established a foothold and accommodation at Residency Point. The soldiers were by this time in accommodation at an area adjacent to Residency Point, the Parade Ground, so placing their wives on Green Island would in reality have not been a feasible action.

---

[5] Mrs A.Y. Hassell. *Early Memories of Albany*. Albany Advertiser. circa 1910.
[6] As reported in D. Garden. (1977). *Albany: Panorama of the Sound from 1827*. Nelson.

Finally, and most importantly, there is no record in either Major Edmund Lockyer's, Captain Joseph Wakefield's or Lieutenant George Sleeman's or for that matter any of the commandant's despatches or reports emanating from King George's Sound at the time alluding to such an evacuation or action. Given the sense of urgency associated with such an evacuation, and the very detailed despatches emanating from the colony during these early years one would expect to read something of this action accordingly.

Unfortunately, accounts such as those of Mrs A.Y. Hassell, written some 84 years after the settlement was established create a situation where fact-checking is indeed warranted, however with a paucity of original documentation about this incident it is difficult to verify the claims that are made; therefore, we must use reasoned judgement about the veracity of the claim. Another issue that then arises is that if a Historical Record takes the statements made by Mrs Hassell as fact and subsequently, they are shown not to be, myths can evolve and be perpetuated. For example, in *The Albany Advertiser* of 22nd December 1928, some 100 plus years after the founding of the settlement, reproduced Mrs Hassell's account verbatim thus adding credibility to what in fact could be a flawed premise in the first place, therefore, extending the myth.

It is recognised that individual perceptions and national perspectives inform a dynamic collection of facts and fiction, fantasy, heroic legend and changing community aspirations. Further, more often than not one historical event can be viewed, explained and understood differently by different scholars.

Every care has been taken in selecting topics for inclusion in this book and each has been chosen to include subject matter that pertains to Albany's past that is of historical importance and, therefore, worth preserving for the public interest. The subject matter is of course very reliant on the event being of such public interest as to warrant reporting at the time. At all times in reporting on the events, items selected for inclusion in this tome were evaluated within the parameters of available evidence acknowledging our responsibility to ensure that The Historical Record is understood and accurately interpreted, ensuring that the perspective of each event is maintained. However, as historians, it is also important to recognise and acknowledge that in making the selection of items and extracts for inclusion in this work, we are ourselves exercising a form of personal bias into the process. Our motivation is based on a belief that the items selected will be of lasting interest to the reader and will ensure the maintenance of an accurate Historical Record accordingly.

Some of the initial explorers of King George's Sound were inspired by scientific and imperial enthusiasm at home, in particular biological, anthropological and geographical interests. Others were motivated by political and economic reasons. Historians today are indeed indebted to the reports and journals left to posterity by these early visitors to Albany's shores.

In presenting a research work of this nature there is an obligation to offer a synthesis of The Historical Record for the inquisitive person, and in doing so keeping the public and future generations aware of the paradoxes and complexities in the town's history and consequently, its significance in providing an insight into a peoples' understanding of their culture and heritage.

Why This Period in Albany's History?

A conscious decision has been made to concentrate on the period 1791-1927, as it was during this period that the unique character of the town of Albany as we now know it was forged. In doing so it is also acknowledged that there was a significant Aboriginal history that had developed over the many millennia preceding 1791. However, as a decision was made to concentrate on the readily accessible 'written' Historical Record this established and also significantly limited the earlier stated research parameters.

Secondly, post 1927 The Historical Record showed far less seismic development when compared to the period in question. Except perhaps for the development of better medical and industrial facilities, the end of whaling industry (1978), cyclone Alby (1978), the amalgamation of the Albany Town and Albany Shire (1998), the centennial commemoration of the Great War convoy departures along with the opening of the ANZAC interpretive centre (2014) Albany's history post-1927 has been gradual with the town's evolution in part mirroring aspects of Western Australia's growth into the entity now seen today.

Why Now?

In every generation, historians have been influenced by events in the stated Historical Record, with new lines of possible inquiry, and the interpretations of their age. Furthermore, identified inaccuracies in The Historical Record require correcting and with the Albany Bicentennial, it was decided that this event provided the perfect opportunity to do this.

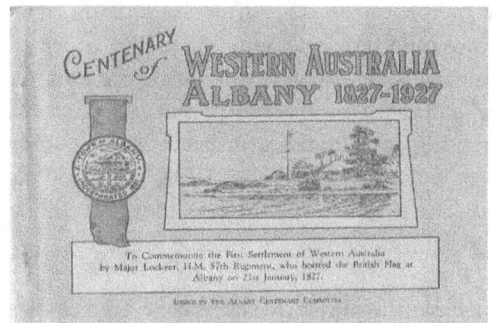

A commemorative booklet celebrating Albany's Centenary on 21st January 1927.

A further point of interest to note is that Albany's Centennial celebrations took place in 1927 and not 1926. Further, that the sesquicentennial celebrations (150 years) occurred in 1976 and not 1977, some 99 years later than those of the Centenary.

On Saturday, 22nd January 1927 the then King, George V remembered his two visits to Albany in 1881 and 1901, and on its Centennial sent to the Governor Sir William Campion a message of goodwill which read:

I am much interested to know today celebrates the Centenary of the settlement of Albany. My first experience of Albany was in May 1881, when serving on HMS Bacchante and again 25 years ago. The Queen and I will never forget the kindly reception accorded to us on our unexpected landing on that occasion. On this happy commemoration, we gladly send our best wishes to the inhabitants for their happiness and prosperity.[7]

The *Western Mail* of Thursday, 27th January in an article titled *Albany's First Century*, informed its readers of the celebrations held that day in the town.

Albany concludes today the celebration of its Centenary. Time has moved swiftly since Major Edmund Lockyer unfurled the Union Jack on Residency Point and reserved all of Australia for the British race. The years have seen the peopling and cultivation of vast lands then the domain of the Aboriginal and the kangaroo, the rise and fall of gold mining and the concentration of population and commerce north of the port with an anchorage fit for a fleet. The formal founding of the colony was reserved till 1829, but in 1827 Western Australian history within the British Empire really began. Albany may gaze with parental eyes upon the rest of Western Australia. Concerning the wonderful period of progress during the last 30 years, Albany can justly say, "I began this". In much of that prosperity, Albany has not shared as fully as was its due. In some measure, the pull of vested interests at the capital and Fremantle caused this...[8]

As indicated, we intend to provide for the public record a comprehensive primary documented synthesis of resources to enable and encourage and stimulate future studies associated with this town's fascinating history, especially where the record is now silent. [9]

---

[7] *The Western Mail*. Perth. 27th January 1927.
[8] Ibid
[9] *The Western Mail*. Centenary Number. 1929

CHAPTER 1
A MEETING OF CULTURES – EARLY REPORTS

EARLY EUROPEAN CONTACT WITH THE INDIGENOUS PEOPLES OF KING GEORGE'S SOUND 1801-1831

"We acknowledge the traditional inhabitants of the land, the Menang peoples of King George's Sound"[1]

Overview

The Indigenous culture of the area did not concern itself with recording its history in a conventional sense, that is by writing it down; for example, as a chronological narrative representing what occurred in the past. The Aboriginal peoples of the Sound, the *Menang* peoples did, however, have a strong oral tradition, and tended to weave together events of the distant and more recent past, interweaving both mythology and history together. It has been in more recent times that we have come to appreciate their story and recorded them for posterity.[2] However, in keeping with our approach of only recording eyewitness accounts or records of interviews with participants made at the time during the period 1791-1927, we have not gone down the path of including oral story-history accounts.

Drawing of Aboriginal woman at King George's Sound by Robert Neil 1843[3]

There have been some remarkable interactions reported between the Aboriginal peoples and early European visitors to King George's Sound. Most were very positive and peaceful as the records of the early Europeans (particularly French and British) indicate. However, this same perspective cannot be attributed to early interactions with the whalers and sealers from predominantly America, along with escaped European convicts from Sydney and Van Dieman's Land. These interactions were not so positive or peaceful and it is quite clear that atrocities were committed by them against the Aboriginal people, not only of the Sound but also along the south coast of Australia in general. Major Edmund Lockyer's report (presented in some detail further on) detailed his concerns with regards to the mistreatment of the Indigenous inhabitants by the whaling fraternity.

Drawing of Aboriginal man at King George's Sound by Robert Neil 1843[4]

---

[1] Menang, also spelled Minang or Mineng or Mirnong, are an Indigenous Nyungar people of southern Western Australia

[2] Those interested in pursuing Menang and Nyungar oral histories are initially referred to the Mirnang Waangkaniny Albany Region Dreaming Stories that can be found at:
http://www.aweandwonder.com.au/mirnang-waangkaniny

[3] Attached to a copy of letter to Sir George Grey, Chancellor of the Dutchy of Lancaster and Under-Secretary of State for War and the Colonies. Scottish Records Office. GD18/354/4.

[4] Attached to a copy of letter to Sir George Grey, Chancellor of the Dutchy of Lancaster and Under-Secretary of State for War and the Colonies. Scottish Records Office. GD18/354/4.

It is evident from the early eyewitness accounts that a local *Menang* leader, *Mokare*, gave significant assistance to those Europeans involved in establishing a military Cantonment at King George's Sound. [5] *Mokare's* assistance to the likes of Major Lockyer, Captain Wakefield, Dr Wilson and later Dr Barker and Dr Collie can be seen in the same light.[6] His assistance was invaluable in helping establish trust and a cultural understanding of the *Menang* Aboriginal people and their way of life during this period. Contiguous reports made during the early years of the settlement are reproduced at this point to give an initial flavour of the nature of these interactions between two vastly different cultures, that of the early Europeans and the *Menang* peoples of King George's Sound.

George Vancouver; Commander of *Discovery* Lieutenant William Broughton, in Command of the Armed Tender *Chatham* -1791

Commander George Vancouver and Lieutenant William Broughton were British Royal Navy officers, navigators and hydrographers. They are best known for their exploration of the shores of the southwest coast of Australia and in particular their momentous visit to King George's Sound which Vancouver named. Although they did not have direct contact with the local Aboriginal inhabitants of the Sound, Vancouver's report did included reference to living conditions and a supposition of their way of subsistence based on habitation artefacts they encountered during their stay. Vancouver recounted:

October 16th, 1791

It would now remain to say something of the human species, the inhabitants of this country, but as we were not so fortunate to procure an interview with any of them, all that can be advanced on this subject must be founded on conjecture or nearly so, and consequently very liable to error; it may, however, not be acceptable to state such circumstances as on the spot occurred to our observation.

The natives appeared to be a wandering people, who sometimes made their excursions individually, and at other times in considerable parties; this was apparent by the habitations being found single and alone, as well as composing tolerably large villages. Besides the village I visited, Mr Broughton[7] discovered another about two miles distant from it of nearly the same magnitude; but it appeared to be of a much later date as all the huts had been recently built and seem to have been very lately inhabited. It was situated in a swamp, which might probably have been preferred to a higher and firmer land for convenience of water. One or two huts of a larger size were also observed; the rest were precisely of the same description with those in our neighbourhood. The larger trees in the vicinity of both villages had been hollowed out by fire, sufficiently to afford the shelter that these people seem to require. Upon stones placed in the inside of these hollow trees, fires have been made……

No one species of furniture or utensil was discovered in any of the houses; the only implements seen, were pieces of sticks intended as spears, rudely wrought, and the operation of manual labour upon them but slightly discernible. The bark was stripped off, and the thickest end, after having been burnt in the fire, was scraped and reduced to a blunted point, on one of which some blood was still found adhering.

---

[5] In the journals and reports that have been accessed in respect to this book there are many different spellings for Mokare. These include Mokkarre, Mawcarrie, Markew and Makkare, however, for consistency in this document we have maintained the more common spelling of Mokare so as to minimise any confusion.

[6] Mokare was instrumental in encouraging active Aboriginal - European liaison in the new settlement. He was the son of an Aboriginal elder of the Menang tribe of the Nyungar people. This tribal group lived in and around the King George's Sound area. Mokare's first contact with Europeans may in fact have been with sailors from the French *Astrolabe*. He appears in the reports of not only Major Edmund Lockyer and surgeon Mr Isaac Scott Nind, but later on also in those of Dr Thomas Braidwood Wilson, Captain Collet Barker and Dr Alexander Collie. When the British settled in the district Mokare acted as a guide and tracker assisting exploratory endeavours of the likes of those mentioned. There are some who believe that he may have been the Aboriginal man referred to as 'Jack' in the reports of Captain Phillip Parker King in 1821, although this cannot be confirmed.

Mokare was a frequent visitor to the settlement and provided great deal of information to the early settlers about Aboriginal beliefs and customs. He appears to have been constantly in the company or settlers and was the Aborigine who resided in accommodation with Dr Nind, medical surgeon on *Amity*. Mokare gave outstanding assistance to the settlement contingent at the time in both a capacity as translator and as an early guide into the hinterland.

[7] Lieutenant William Broughton was selected to command *Chatham*. He received his appointment on 28th December and joined his ship on 1st January 1791

... it may naturally be inferred that the land principally supplies their wants, or hunger would long since have conducted them to such excellent resources. This opinion is supported by the extreme shyness of the feather creation, and the wildness of the quadrupeds, whose footing, and other signs of their being at no great distance without obtaining any sight of them, sufficiently proved that they were constantly pursued. As nothing further occurred worthy of any particular notice, I shall conclude my remarks on this country. [8]

Matthew Flinders; Captain of the sloop *Investigator*.
Explorer and Hydrographer - 1801-1802

Flinders was able to garner from his contact with the Aboriginal peoples during his initial interactions that traditionally, on an annual basis, the Nyungar families of the area would gather around the area bounded by the Sound for summer fishing activities. Consequently, given the time of year of his arrival at King George's Sound, it was fortuitous that Matthew Flinders and crew members of *Investigator* were as it turned out well-positioned to contact Menang peoples at this time. He noted that a brisk trade took place, iron (axes and knives) for Aboriginal artefacts. His notes of the 23rd of December 1801 recorded several observations. First, Flinders' overall impression of the local inhabitants of the Sound:

It was with some surprise that I saw the natives of the east coast of New South Wales so nearly portrayed in those of the south western extremity of New Holland. These do not, indeed, extract one of the upper front teeth at the age of puberty, as is generally practised at Port Jackson, nor do they make use of the Woomera, or throwing stick; but the colour, the texture of their hair, and personal appearance are the same; their songs run in the same cadence, the manner of painting themselves is similar; their belts and fillets of hair are made in the same way and worn in the same manner.

The short skin cloak, which is of kangaroo, and worn over the shoulders, leaving the rest of the body naked, is more in the manner of the natives living at the back of Port Jackson, than those who inhabit the sea coast; and everything we saw confirmed the supposition of Captain Vancouver, that they live more by hunting than fishing. None of the small islands had been visited, no canoes were seen, nor was any tree found in the woods from which the bark had been taken for making one. They were fearful of trusting themselves upon the water; and we could never succeed in making them understand the use of the fishhook, although they were intelligent in comprehending our signs upon other subjects. [9]

Flinders also observed the reaction of the Aboriginal people to some quaint European military procedures:

I ordered the party of Marines onshore to be exercised in their presence. The red coats and white crossed belts were greatly admired, having some resemblance to their own manner of augmenting themselves; and the drum, but particularly the fife, excited their astonishment; but when they saw the beautiful red and white men, with their bright muskets drawn up in a line, they absolutely screamed with delight. Nor were their wild gestures and vociferations to be silenced but by commencing the exercises, to which they made the most earnest and silent attention. Several of them moved their hands, involuntarily according to the motions; and one man placed himself at the end of the rank, with a short staff in his hand which he shouldered, presented, grounded as did the Marines their muskets, without I believe knowing what he did. [10]

Thomas Nicholas Baudin; Commander of the French corvettes *Geographe* and *Naturaliste* 1803

An encounter between the French Europeans and the Indigenous peoples of the area was recorded in the journals of the Post-Captain Thomas Nicholas Baudin when his corvette *Geographe* was at anchor in King George's Sound in February 1803. He recorded in his journal the following observations:

22nd February 1803.

While exploring the environs of the stream just mentioned, we found two rather peculiar and interesting monuments erected by the natives, if only one could discover the reason for them. The first was seven or eight feet from the stream, on a piece of bare ground that was three feet in circumference and surrounded by finely tapered spears painted red at the tip. There are eleven in all. Parallel with this trophy, on the other side of the stream,

---

[8] From George Vancouver. *A Voyage to the North Pacific Ocean and Round the World on the years 1792 - 1795 in Discovery Sloop of War.* London. 1795.
[9] Flinders, M. *A Voyage to Terra Australis.* London. 1814.
[10] Ibid.

was a plot of ground similar in shape and with the same number of spears. But they seem to be guarding the passage to the right bank from the left, just as those on the left seem to be guarding it from the right. Several people thought that the spears had been painted red with blood, so we took one out to examine it better and realised that this colour had been achieved with eucalyptus resin.

Everyone tried to guess what these monuments could be, and we reasoned in various ways. My opinion is that they are two graves in which lie two warriors of different tribes, buried there either after a private battle between themselves or after some more general fighting, and seemingly still to defy one another after death. I would not let anyone defile these graves and remove the spears that decorated them, in order that any Europeans who would reach this place may draw the conclusions upon it that their imagination may suggest. However, I did put two medals and some glass beads on each one.

And on 27th February 1803 he continued:

At about three in the afternoon, we sighted Captain Raisonnet's boat returning, and he reached the ship around six o'clock.[11] He had occasion to communicate with the natives, who showed that they were not savage and were the first to give an example of their friendly attitude, for they put their weapons aside before approaching the men from the boat. The latter did the same with theirs and then mingled with them. The two parties made themselves understood as well as possible by signs and spent the greater part of the day together on very good terms, except that the natives would not allow anyone near where they had put their wives, of whom there were three. They themselves were five in number. They made no difficulty about eating and drinking all of that was given them and feasted handsomely off the sailor's cooking. The men had forgotten to take in the boat the presents that I normally had for natives when we could communicate with them, so they gave them just the buttons off their coats, which were greatly prized, some handkerchiefs and a few rough, old jackets, which they did not like so much.[12]

Phillip Parker King; Commander of the *Mermaid* -1821

Captain Phillip King visited the Sound on three separate occasions (the last to reprovision with water before returning to England) and he established an excellent rapport with the Aboriginal people of the area on his second visit. His first tour of the area did not result in direct contact although he identified evidence of the Sound's Indigenous inhabitants.

His first actual encounter with the Indigenous peoples of King George's Sound was on December 21st, 1821 when he was in command of *Bathurst*, at which time biscuits were traded for Indigenous artefacts. This visit is of particular importance to the history of Albany because the contact made with the Indigenous peoples of the area, along with the very detailed descriptions left by Captain King of their various artefacts and language played a major role in later European and Aboriginal interactions. King recorded in his journal:

As soon as we passed the bar, three other natives made their appearance on the east side who upon the boat going to that shore to lay out the kedges, took their seats in it as unceremoniously as a passenger would in a ferry boat, and upon returning to the brig, came on board and remain with us all afternoon, much amused with everything they saw, and totally free from timidity or distrust…

As soon as the brig was secured, two of our visitors went ashore, evidently charged with some message from the other native who stayed on board, nothing hostile was expected… After an absence of an hour, our two friends returned, when it appeared that they had been at their toilet, for their noses and faces had been freshly smeared over with red ochre which they pointed out to us as a great ornament…. They had, however, put off the garments which we had clothed them and resumed their mantles… Each brought a lighted fire stick in his hand… on returning on-board we desired the native who remained behind to go ashore to his two companions, but it was with great reluctance that he was persuaded to leave us.

---

[11] Captain Raisonnet had been placed in charge of the schooner *Casuarina* which Baudin had earlier purchased in Sydney in 1801.
[12] *The Journal of Post Captain Nicholas Baudin, Commander-in-Chief of the Corvettes Geographe and Naturaliste. Assigned by order of the Government to 'a Voyage of Discovery'*, London 1809. Translated from the French by Christine Cornell, Adelaide 1974.)

Whilst on board our people had fed him plenteously with biscuits, yams, pudding, tea and grog, of which he ate and drank as if he were half-famished, and after being crammed with this strange mixture and to very patiently submitting his beard to the operation of shaving, he was clothed with a shirt and a pair of trousers and christened 'Jack' by which name he was afterwards always called and to which he readily answered. As soon as he reached the shore, his companions came to meet him, to hear an account of what transpired during their absence, as well as to examine his new habiliments, which as may be conceived had affected a very considerable alteration to his appearance and at the same time the change created much admiration on the part of his companions, it raised him very considerably in his own estimation...[13]

Jules Sebastien-Cesar Dumont d'Urville; Commander of the *Astrolabe* -1826

It was Captain Jules Sebastien-Cesar Dumont d'Urville in *Astrolabe* who provide the next record of an encounter with the Indigenous tribes of the King George's Sound. Captain d'Urville, while cruising along the coast arrived at King George's Sound in October 1826 and in an act of friendship had permitted a small group of Aborigines to board his ship *Astrolabe* for a visit. As was his habit he recorded these interactions in some detail in his log of the voyage:

Sunday 8th October.
I steered the boat towards a place on the banks of the harbour where the sailors had assured me, they had seen smoke. It was a sure indication of the presence of natives with whom I wanted to speak. Assuredly, it wasn't long before we saw a fire close to the shore and soon after a human figure appeared covered by a single hide. Soon this savage (it was one of them) advanced resolutely towards us, but as he came nearer his cockiness seemed to leave him and, even as I tried to persuade him by making signs, and when I dared to offer him a piece of bread he remained uncertainly by the boat. He ate hungrily, this act producing without a doubt a great effect on his imagination because having lost his suspiciousness he started to laugh, dance, sing, and calling out to his friends. He readily climbed into the boat without fear where he conducted himself very decently ...

He was a man about 40 years and well-made, he had thin arms and legs as are the inhabitants of New South Wales, he had absolutely the same colouring, the same features and the same ways as those Islanders. He was 5'2" tall, flat nose and it was pierced, he had big and beautiful teeth, he had whiskers and a long beard from his chin, his hair was not fuzzy. ...

On board he never lost his joviality and confidence, everybody overwhelmed him with friendliness, soon he was loaded with gifts that made him very happy at first and then he became embarrassed having to keep them. The wind blew briefly during the whole of the evening and it was impossible to take him back to shore. He took his lot happily and had a marvellous sleep onboard, no doubt he never had as good a bed made of sail and tarpaulin in his whole life. During the night we saw a fire on the shore, and I guess indicated that it had been lit by his tribe.

Wednesday the 11th, 1826.
The natives continued to be very peaceful; I was told that they had already brought three children to the camp, infallible proof of their confidence and good dispositions.

Thursday 12th, 1826.
At about nine-thirty in the morning, accompanied by de Lauverge and de Simonet [two seamen] I disembarked on the long Sandy Beach [Middleton Beach] and went along towards the woods [Strawberry Hill area]; about half a mile or a bit more from the shore in a place sheltered from the westerly winds I came across some huts. One of them was well preserved, it looked like a beehive with a radius of three to four feet sliced into two by vertical separation. Its structures consisted of thin branches, as for a roof, it was covered by grass-tree leaves. The ruined frames of four or five others remained. In front of the first one, there was a stone that had been used to grind the ochre which is used by the natives for their toilet (and body decoration).[14]

---

[13] Phillip Parker King. *A Survey of the Intertropical Coasts of Australia.* Vol.1 pp.11-19 and Vol.2 pp.119-158. 1827.
[14] Jules S-C Dumont d'Urville, *Voyage of the Corvette L'Astrolabe 1826-1829.*
A translation from the French by The Department of Lands, Perth (n.d) from an account in two volumes to *The South Seas by Captain, later Rear Admiral Jules D-C Dumont d'Urville of the French Navy to Australia, New Zealand and Oceania. 1826-1829.*

Captain d'Urville's scientific expedition and general observations of King George's Sound made at that time were enhanced by the quality observations of several members of the cohort of the French scientific community who accompanied him. In particular, Louis-Auguste de Sainson [a draughtsman] and Midshipman Jean Rene Constant Quoy, both of whom contributed diary extracts that D'Urville's was later able to incorporate into his own published work, *Two Voyages to the South Seas*.[15] Their observations and interaction with the Aboriginal people of King George's Sound are insightful. From de Sainson's notes as reproduced in d'Urville's book:

> *It is a strange destiny that gathers around the same heart fire such different inhabitants of our globe. We were involuntarily reflecting thus and would have continued in the same vein had our hosts not diverted us from it.*
>
> *Being a little preoccupied with philosophical ideas, they were obedient to whatever physical impressions were influencing them at the moment. Their bright expressive eyes observed us with curiosity and roved all over us. Their hard-thin hands alternatively touched our clothing and our skin and every word we uttered amazed them and provoked laughter. One of the natural ways to start a conversation with them was to tell them our names and learn theirs. A lot of repetition was necessary before they managed to articulate words for which their vocal organs seemed inadequate...*
>
> *You can well imagine that these tries did not take place without a lot of noise and laughter. They hardly got to know our names before they wanted to tell us theirs all at once... a man who was still young and who seem to have taken a fancy to M. Guilbert was called Mokare; he had an open face and was more lively than any of his comrades.[16]*

An extract from Midshipman Quoy's notes gives further insight into these initial interactions between the European and Indigenous cultures at King George's Sound:

> *The inhabitants of King George's Sound, like all the beach dwellers of new Holland, are not numerous and are divided into small tribes, each of which appears to comprise about 20 persons at the most. We have never seen them all together. The largest group with which we had contact contained scarcely 12 to 15 men and a few children from 10 to 12 years old who could follow them on their daily rounds. The women were never with them; and we have reason to believe that, through fear or jealousy, they carefully conceal them. It seems that women live a fair distance from the seaboard.[17]*

Edmund Lockyer: Soldier and Civil Servant - 1826 to 1827

On November 9th, 1826, Major Lockyer (57th Regiment) was dispatched by Governor Ralph Darling of New South Wales with Captain Joseph Wakefield in command of a detachment of the 39th Regiment of Foot and a number of convicts aboard the brig *Amity*.[18]

The *Amity* arrived at The Princess Royal Harbour, on Christmas Day 1826. While Major Lockyer spent only three months in the settlement, his detailed reports to Governor Darling were again insightful and provided an excellent perspective of some of the early European interactions with the Aboriginal peoples of the area. Extracts from his letter to Governor Darling pertaining to these first contacts indicated (punctuation as per his original report):

> *Wednesday 27th December 1826.*
> *A boat [longboat] was dispatched at daylight and after breakfast, I proceeded on shore with Lieutenant Festing[19] to examine the upper part of the harbour...* (The aim was to survey a possible site for the settlement). *Captain Wakefield and Mr Nind were, as well as myself and Lieutenant Festing armed with each a double-barrel gun; a ships musket was also sent on shore with the watering party, which I should have considered almost unnecessary; wishing to reach a point of land at the head of the harbour on which a thick*

---

[15] *Two Voyages to the South Seas*: Volume 1. *Astrolabe*, 1826-1829.
[16] Ibid.
[17] Ibid.
[18] Lieutenant-General Ralph Darling was the Governor of New South Wales from December 1825 to October 1831.
[19] Lieutenant Colson Festing of the Royal Navy was in command of the colonial brig *Amity* tasked with transporting Major Lockyer's establishment to King George's Sound.

scrub with tolerable sized timber appeared to grow, I proposed to Lieutenant Festing that we should keep to the shore until we reached that spot (near where Residency museum stands today), Captain Wakefield and Mr Nind having struck up into wood on the side of the hill [Parade Street playing fields]; *on getting near this point, I saw a Native come out; when he discovered he was seen, he spoke to someone in the wood, then another came out and immediately two more.*

I made signs for them to approach, which they did instantly without the least hesitation; they saw Lieutenant Festing and myself both armed, they left their spears in the wood where I am certain there were more natives: a large fire was now burning at the head of the harbour, and shortly after we saw a very large smoke about ten miles on the hills to the south west, but I did not suspect anything wrong as these four shook hands, which they appear to understand to be friendly; after a mutual salutation, two of them made signs they would go to where the brig was and two remained with us; they were four fine young men all painted and their hair clubbed and daubed all over with red ochre and fish or seal oil as described by Captain King; whether it was appropriate signal for war or not, we could not tell; the two that remained with Lieutenant Festing and myself walked with us into the wood, and, on being asked where kangaroo was to be found, they pointed, and saw us shoot several black cockatoo expressing their admiration when they saw them fall, though I had the precaution not to discharge more than one barrel, as I was well aware that these people have always spears at hand: as it was now near one o'clock, I was anxious to know the result of the visit of the boat (longboat) *to the island* (to Michaelmas Island) *and communicated the same to Lieutenant Festing, saying I would go again down to the shore of the harbour and return that way to the place where the boat would come for us: and one of the natives went with me, the other remained with Lieutenant Festing.* [20]

Major Lockyer and his second in command Captain Joseph Wakefield had separated in their exploration around the area of Mount Melville, nevertheless, both parties always remained within sight of each other.[21] On returning to the shoreline Major Lockyer's consideration had been drawn to where *Amity* lay at anchor. While resting at this location his attention was drawn to the approaching longboat, he had sent to Michaelmas Island. As he moved to the landing place of the longboat, he saw several Aborigines gathered on the hill above him [Mount Melville]. His report takes up the story at this stage:

… I saw seven or eight natives crossing over the rising ground and coming down to the seaside where I was: on their approaching, the native who was with me called out to those who were coming, and was answered in an authoritative manner to come away, and he left me without saying a word; as they passed me, I looked and tried to stop them, it was no use, their looks convinced me that there was something wrong, and, on getting to where Lieutenant Festing was, I expressed myself to him to that effect; he said he also tried to speak to them, but they would not stop, and he immediately enquired with his servant where I was, I was remaining on the rock to watch them pass me, he then acquainted me that four of these natives the boat had bought back from the island, and that one of them on getting to the shore and meeting his companions made very significant complaints and showed his neck, that had four or five deep scars as if from a sharp instrument, a sword or cutlass: we then proceeded to the spot, where the boat was repairing, and had passed the watering place about fifty yards above us; we found our friend 'Jack' the native with the carpenter repairing the boat and we sat down on a rock waiting the return of the boat from the ship, when a prisoner came running up saying the natives had attacked the watering party and was spearing the people; 'Jack' instantly ran off, and, on getting up and going around, I saw the smith [blacksmith] *Dennis Dineen, standing in the water with three spears sticking in him, and on mustering the people found no other person was hurt, the natives had crept down through the bush and would probably have speared every man, had not one of them got up to go into the water to bathe, and saw the natives on the bank above fixing their spears: and he called out to the people below to run: as soon as they threw their spears, they all ran away except one man who picked up his spear and threw it twice; four of them were those brought from the island….*[22]

Major Lockyer had rightly concluded that the natives that had been returned in the longboat had in fact been marooned on Michaelmas Island and he suspected that sealers or whalers who worked the area had

---

[20] Major Edmund Lockyer to Lieutenant-General Ralph Darling, Governor of New South Wales, 1827. "*Historical Records of Australia*", Series lll, Vol. 6, Library Committee of the Commonwealth Parliament 1921 – 1923.
[21] At this stage Captain Joseph Wakefield of the 39th Regiment of Foot was second in command at the Cantonment. He assumed command of the outpost in April 1827 upon Lockyer's departure.
[22] Ibid.

been the responsible party to this injustice. It was unfortunate, according to Major Lockyer, that instead of taking the rescued men to the ship where they could have been interrogated by him, they were instead landed on shore and immediately took the bush to join other members of their tribe. The resulting hostilities that were reported, when seen in the light of these observations, were attributed by Lockyer as payback for the crimes perpetrated on these men by the sealers and whalers. His report relating to the injuries of Blacksmith Dineen and his subsequent actions indicated:

> ....*from the serious nature of the wounds, I am very doubtful of this unfortunate man's recovery: as we had not given any cause for so what we considered an unprovoked attack, I could not count for it until I got on board when I was informed that, on the boat reaching the island, they saw four natives under a rock who did not speak until pointed to, when they got up, and Mr Wheeler, from not having arms in the boat, did not like approaching; and the natives, on seeing the boat about to pull off fell on the knees and made sad lamentations fearing the boat did not intend taking them off. Mr Wheeler ran the boat in and took them off bringing them to the vessel where they should have been detained until I returned, as it would be extremely desirable to have endeavoured to have learnt their story and how they got on the island, and if any inhuman wretches had placed them thereafter there after getting into the harbour; they were anxious to get on shore; on reflecting that these people had made this attack in consequence of the injuries they had received, I gave positive orders that no retaliation should take place on our side except in absolute self-defence, I'm certain with proper precaution nothing further will occur.*[23]

Isaac Scott Nind: Surgeon on *Amity* -1826 to 1830

While Dr Isaac Scott Nind, Surgeon attached to *Amity* and under the command of Major Lockyer had a very troubled and interesting relationship with the Cantonment's leadership, his detailed report to the Royal Geographical Society in London provided a first-hand and very extensive account of the Indigenous peoples of the district. His work titled a *Description of the Natives of King George's Sound (Swan River Colony) and Adjoining Country*, was read to the society on 14th Feb. 1831. Some extracts of this reading are reproduced:

> *The natives of King George's Sound differ little in their general appearance from the Aborigines of the neighbourhood of Sydney. They are of middle stature, slender in their limbs, and many of them with a protuberant abdomen.*

> *The only article of dress used by them is a cloak of kangaroo skin, reaching nearly to the knee; it is worn as a mantle over the shoulders and is fastened at the right shoulder with a rush, by which the right arm is left free and disencumbered. They are seldom seen without their cloaks, which in rainy weather are worn with the fur outwards; some of them, however, are so scanty, that the wearer may be almost considered in a state of nudity, particularly the children, for their cloak is but a mere strip of skin. The larger skins, which are procured from the male kangaroos, are appropriated to the women... The other articles of dress are the noodle-bul, or waistband, armlets, and head-dress. The noodle-bul is a long yarn of worsted spun from the fur of the opossum, wound round the waist several hundred times. A similar band is also worn occasionally round the left arm and the head.*

> *The single men, who are called man-jah-lies, ornament their heads with feathers, dogs' tails, and other similar articles, and sometimes have the hair long and bound round the head. The women use no ornaments, or noodle-buls, and wear their hair quite short; but the girls have sometimes a fillet of worsted yarn round the neck, which is called a woortill. Both sexes smear their faces and the upper part of the body with red pigment (paloil) mixed with grease (animal fat and oils), which gives them a disagreeable odour. This they do, as they say, for the purpose of keeping themselves clean, and as a defence from the sun or rain. Their hair is frequently matted with the same pigment. When fresh painted, they are all over of a brick—dust colour, which gives them a most singular appearance.*

> *Every individual of the tribe, when travelling or going to a distance from their encampment, carries a fire stick, for the purpose of kindling fires, and in winter they are scarcely ever without one under their cloaks, for the sake of heat. It is generally a cone of Banksia grandis, which has the property of keeping ignited for a considerable time. Rotten bark, or touchwood, is also used for the same purpose. They are very careful to preserve this, and will even kindle a fire (by friction, or otherwise) expressly to revive it.*

---

[23] Ibid

Those families who have locations on the sea-coast quit it during the winter for the interior; and the natives of the interior, in like manner, pay visits to the coast during the fishing season. Excepting at these times, those natives who live together have the exclusive right of fishing or hunting upon the neighbouring grounds, which are, in fact, divided into individual properties; the quantity of land owned by each individual being very considerable. Yet it is not so exclusively his, but others of his family have certain rights over it; so that it may be considered as partly belonging to the tribe. ….. As the country does not abound in food, they are seldom stationary, removing, according to the time of the year, to those parts which produce the articles of provision that may be in season. During the winter and early spring, they are very much scattered; but as summer advances they assemble in greater numbers.

During the summer and autumn months, the natives derive a large proportion of their food from fish. They have no canoes, neither can they swim, in both of which points they differ materially from all other parts of the Australian continent with which we are acquainted. They can, therefore, only catch those fish that approach the shores or come into shoal water. They have neither nets, nor hook and line, and the only weapon they use is the spear, with which they are very dexterous. In the mouths of streams or rivers, they take large quantities, by weirs made of bushes, but the most common method is pursuing the fish into shoal water, and spearing them, or as they lie basking on the surface. During calms, they walk over the mud and sand-banks, in search of flatfish, which are easily detected while lying at the bottom. At night, too, they light torches of grass-tree, and thus see the fish at the bottom, apparently asleep, when they very readily spear them. By these methods, vast quantities are taken, but it can only be done in dead calms. Another common method is to sit on a rock, motionless, and occasionally throw into the water pieces of limpet, or other shellfish, keeping the spear underwater until the bait is seized by a fish, when they are almost certain of striking it.

In the autumn, when the smaller species of fish approach the shores in large shoals, they surround them and keep them in shallow water upon the flats until the tide falls and leaves them when they are easily speared, and very few escaped. For this purpose, they use a very small spear, without a barb, and throw it by hand; should it so happen that the tide does not sufficiently fall to enable them to take the fish, they gather bushes, and plant them around so thickly, as to enclose them when they are speared at leisure.[24]

Thomas Braidwood Wilson: Royal Navy Physician -1829

The colony was indeed fortunate that one of its earliest visitors was Dr Thomas Braidwood Wilson, who among his many skills as a surgeon possessed a very keen interest in exploration and had demonstrated some expertise as an amateur anthropologist. His work titled *Narrative of a Voyage Around the World* is regarded by many historians as providing perhaps one of the most detailed and insightful observations of King George's Sound and the fledgling colony. While more of Dr Wilson's observations will be explored later in this historical narrative his early encounters with the local Aboriginal population and his friendship with Mokare, in particular, are worth noting. Mokare provided Dr Wilson, as well as later European explorers, in particular, Dr Collie and Captain Barker, with a great deal of information about Aboriginal beliefs and customs. Wilson wrote:

During my short stay, it is not to be supposed that the information I acquired, concerning the natives, could be very extensive. I may, however, state that in personal appearance, they have a decided resemblance to the Australian brethren [Eastern colonies], and their weapons are also similar. They all wear a covering of Kangaroo skin, with the fur next to the skin…. They are far from being destitute of intelligence: on the contrary, they appear very acute. Several of them reside constantly in the camp, where they are treated with kindness.

That they have a right of soil, is quite evident. The land about the settlement belongs to Mokare's brethren. Their food principally consists of fish, which they spear in shallow places, as they never (appear to) venture above the knees in water, with their own will; and it is a strange and singular fact, that none of them seems to swim. They have nothing in the shape of canoes; nor do they ever cross any river, except at the mouth, which is usually very shallow; or higher up, where a tree may have accidentally fallen across and formed a bridge.

---

[24] *Description of the Natives of King George's Sound (Swan River Colony) and adjoining Country.* Written by Dr Scott Nind and communicated by Robert Brown Esq., F.R.S. Read 14th February, 1831.

> *They also derive sustenance from kangaroos, iguanas (monitor lizards), and in the proper season, from young parrots, bird eggs, etcetera., and they seem to be fond of sucking cones of various kinds of banksia, which are in great abundance on this part of the coast. They have been, and continue to be, on the best terms with the settlers……. and by judicious management, and a good understanding a friendly feeling has been established, which has not yet been, nor likely to be, interrupted.* [25]

Alexander Collie: Albany's First Government Resident—1831 to 1832

Dr Alexander Collie was a Royal Navy surgeon and botanist who journeyed to Western Australia in 1829, where he gained a well-earned reputation as an explorer and Colonial Surgeon. He had a very positive relationship with the Menang leader Mokare. His letters, journals and observations of the Aboriginal peoples are quite extensive, with a selection of them are reproduced here:

> *A salutary regulation as in existence on my arrival [1831] at King George's Sound forbidding the natives taking their spears into the settlement, yet this, although still enforced, did not prevent occasions, squabbles and some skirmishing among themselves, and trivial irritations and misunderstandings with us. The origin of their own quarrels was difficult to ascertain, but it was clearly seen they were quick and violent in resenting conceived insults from one another, and sufficiently sensible of mall treatment from us. Nor was the full appreciation of the value of our friendship enough to make them cover their temporary umbrage at supposed affronts…*
>
> *All ages and sexes were among our visitors, or perhaps with more propriety our posts, as we certainly had come into their country and set ourselves down at, if not in, their homes and upon their territories. The male part of the natives extended their stay in the settlement often till after dark, especially if biscuits and tea were held out to them to join in the native dance or, as this more frequently called corroboree, from the Sydney name. The women almost invariably left before nightfall and occupied the more distant bivouac; whilst the young men and those who had left their families at a distance betook themselves only to the adjoining Grove.*
>
> *Mokare asked and obtained leave to accompany his fellow countrymen for two or three days, but did not return for twelve or fourteen, and excused his breach of promise, which I shewed him was improper, by adducing the entreaties of the other natives to remain with them - in treaties which, in every probability, were strongly backed by his success in killing kangaroo, and consequent abundance of a favourite food; for although the meals of biscuit, beef, (salt), cabbage and rice with tea may be very acceptable to the uncultivated palates of the savage, still there can be no marvel excited by the wish to gratify their old habits by gorging on fresh kangaroo…*
>
> *There are, probably, many reasons why they select the winter, the rainy and windy season for hunting the kangaroo. It is likely that in stormy weather the animals lie closer than in fine. They are less likely amidst the howling of the tempest to hear any in inferior noise; in the pursuit, the wet grass and moist surface present so slippery a footing that they cannot bound in running with the same effect when the ground is dry and firm. Their tracks too can be more easily perceived by the grass and shrubs shaken of their watery drops.*
>
> *Kangaroos are also obtained by the natives in great numbers by enclosing or encircling a tract of ground frequented by these animals, and gradually contracting the enclosure or circle, driving all before them until so closely beset that they make a rush to escape between the enclosures, and a speared as they approach…* [26]

As indicated Dr Collie's Journals are extensive and well worth continued study, unfortunately, space does not permit their full disclosure at this point in the narrative.

Death of Mokare[27]

It is important at this point in this reporting to relate aspects in Dr Collie's journal of the passing of his friend and assistant Mokare, for whom he had great regard and deep affection:

---

[25] Thomas Braidwood Wilson. *Narrative of a Voyage Around the World*. London, 1835.
[26] Collie, A. Aborigines of King George's Sound. *The Perth Gazette*. July-August 1834.
[27] The gravesite of Mokare was located at the corner of Collie and Grey Streets which is an area now occupied by City of Albany Town Hall area.

> *...Mokare complained of indisposition and was taking some mercurial preparations under injunctions not to expose himself when he walked off to the bush on the morning of 22nd June – a day which for rain and wind was not surpassed during the whole winter... Nakina [Mokare's eldest brother] followed in a few days, and neither returned until the end of July, when Mokare was labouring under such organic disease and was so much reduced in flesh and strength, as to preclude all hope of recovery. He died on 9th August in the state of delirium. The previous night, he had complained that there were too many persons and too much noise in the kitchen, I took him into my own sitting-room; he was then still strong enough to walk with slight support. A suitable fire was made for him, and he disposed himself upon it in a semicircular form upon a mattress, so that as little as possible should escape him. I am not aware that any race of savages is so dependent on fire for their existence and comfort as that of this part of New Holland. If they have any idols it is entitled to the highest honours amongst their divinities.*
>
> *Mokare passed a quiet night, and someone having come to the door at daylight, he called me by name. Soon after this Nakina came in, and both having spoken a few minutes in the usual tone... I heard Nakina earnestly calling, Mokare, Mokare, and putting an emphasis on his words half entreating half urging which made me approach them from my bedroom. I saw Mokare sitting with his back against the wall and then Nakina earnestly leaning down to his face. The latter raised himself as I advance and direct my attention to Mokare's eye... I took Nakina aside, warned him of the approaching fatal issue, and signified he should send for some others of the natives. He received the intelligence, which indeed he had evidently anticipated, with a settled sorrowful bloom, I made a few grown-up natives that are about the settlement are acquainted with the same timings... Mokare seemed sensible the greater part of the time, being in occasionally delirious and but for a few seconds noisy.*
>
> *At 2 pm Nakina, still watching him he made a slight turn with his head and apparently looking adieu to all around, his large dim eyes rolled back under their swarthy lids to be forever veiled in darkness.*
>
> *When Mokare died I endeavoured to make Nakina understand that if he would prefer having the corpse laid out like a white man, I would have done it, but he either did not comprehend me or wished the native mode to be continued. He signified that he should, be buried on the following day, till which time he left the corpse in my care...*
>
> *The grave was traced out by Nakina, – an oval about four feet by three feet nine, but the more laborious process of digging was executed by white men with European tools, to the no small satisfaction of the natives in attendance, to whom it must be both tedious and laborious....*
>
> *Nakina had bought a spear and throwing stick (meerr) belonging, perhaps, at least appropriate to, the deceased, and after taking off the knob and flint of the throwing stick and placing them over the middle of the north edge of the grave along with fibres and resin that had served to fasten them to the extremities of the meerr, he stuck one end of the latter in the ground at the head or east end of the grave but a little on the south side, and having broken the spear about a foot from the blunt extremity, so that the two parts still remained attached, and bent them nearly a right angle, he laid the spear along with the grave with the broken end touching the throwing stick and the point directed to the west, resting on the horns of the cresentic (sic) mound. A cape of kangaroo skin which Mokare had worn, was carried by Nakina in the funeral procession, and placed on the head of the grave, partly underneath the branches and partly concealed....*

During the period from Vancouver's 1791 visit up to Dr Collie's tenure as Resident Magistrate in 1831-32, interactions with sealers and whalers aside, it would appear from the written reports available that the Europeans who visited the Sound or from those living in the settlement that the Menang Aborigines of the area had become reconciled to the presence of intruders, and since the settlers appeared to have remained close to their settlement and were at this time posing no perceived threat to their immediate hunting grounds, nor were they trespassing where the women and children were gathered, a generally amicable trust relationship had endured.

Interestingly the reports also indicate that over these first few years of contact the Europeans attempted to gain the confidence and friendship of the local inhabitants through the exchange of gifts. However, over time the nature of these gifts changed from the simple medallions and coinage of Vancouver's interactions

[1791] to food and trade by the time of Phillip King [1821]. Major Lockyer engaged in trade that mainly centred on iron tools, especially tomahawks, along with blankets and flour among other items of particular interest to the Indigenous peoples.

The amity between the cultural juxtaposition of European and Aboriginal peoples was well illustrated in the reports emanating from the colony in the public record as this 1833 article illustrates:

> *The Natives in the district of King George's Sound have hitherto lived on the most friendly terms with the Residents in that quarter, whose number at present does not exceed 80 persons; and from all the other accounts which have been received, including the Report of that meritorious officer Captain Charles Sturt, of the 39th Regiment, who has seen more of the natives of Australia than any other gentleman living, we may fearlessly assert, that if the future settlers allow the natives to pursue their fishing occupations on the coast, unmolested, and treat them with humanity, by fulfilling the moral law of "doing unto them as they would be done unto" they would not only secure their attachment but take an important step in the work of their civilisation.*[28]

Winds of Change in the Relationships Between Aborigines and Europeans

Sadly, the state of amity and mutual acceptance between the European settlers and the Aborigines of King George's Sound, was not to last, as was the case in the colony generally. An article in *The Perth Gazette and Journal* of 1841 indicates that the amicable relationship between both the European and Aboriginal inhabitants of the Sound was beginning to fray:

> *From information lately received from King George's Sound by the overland mail, we learn that the tranquillity of that neighbourhood, as regards the natives, has been disturbed; a circumstance sincerely to be regretted, as for many years it has been a subject of remark, that the natives of that district were singularly peaceable and well disposed towards the whites. Our intelligence of the commencement of the affray is rather imperfect, but we believe it had its origin in some petty larceny case on the part of a black, who was subsequently apprehended, but in the attempt to take him prisoner a boy was speared. This led to a pursuit of the offenders and it is said that some of them were shot. The story runs on to the removal of the captured prisoner to Albany. On the way, a native witness, who was taken in charge to secure his evidence, endeavoured to escape, when he was fired at, and it is supposed dangerously wounded. The prisoner was safely lodged in the jail at Albany to take his trial; but the witness's evidence, if he can be found, we suspect will be reluctantly given. We merely relate these events as they have been repeated to us, not relying implicitly on the accuracy of the statements, - that an affray with the natives has occurred cannot be doubted, but we hope it will not prove so serious as at present reported. The line of road to the Sound has been travelled over repeatedly by various persons and not a single instance of molestation or offence has been committed by the natives; the mail cart also passes through monthly without the slightest obstruction, it is to be lamented, therefore, as we before observed, that the peace of these tribes has been disturbed.*[29]

And another article along similar lines from *The Port Phillip Patriot and Melbourne Advertiser*:

> *A very good understanding seems, generally speaking, to exist between the blacks and the colonists at King George's Sound, owing chiefly to the institution of a native constabulary and the care taken to conciliate the different tribes. Some recent occurrences had, however, endangered the continuance of this good feeling. A party of natives had stolen several knives from a stockman in the employ of Mr J. Hassell, Esq., in the vicinity of King George's Sound: the theft was detected and restitution being demanded the knives were given up, but on the unfortunate man's turning to leave the camp, one of the blacks launched a spear at him which penetrated his back close to the right side, and so severely injured him that, after lingering in great agony for three days, he died. The murderer was immediately given up and taken to the Sound to await his trial. A black fellow who was a witness to the perpetration of the murder was also apprehended and given over to the custody of some soldiers to be taken to jail, but on the way thither, he attempted to escape and was shot by one of the guards. Much blame was attached to the soldiers, who, it was alleged, had been very negligent, and it was feared that though the natives acknowledged the justice of the punishment expected to be inflicted on the murderer, they would take the earliest opportunity of avenging the death of the other.*[30]

---

[28] *The Perth Gazette and Western Australian Journal*. 19th October 1833.
[29] *Ibid.* 20th November 1841.
[30] *The Port Phillip Patriot and Melbourne Advertiser*. 15th November 1841.

A similar take of the account was provided in Perth newspapers:
> *We regret to say that we have received accounts of the spearing of a lad by the natives at the Sound. - the first occurrence of the sort that we have heard of in that neighbourhood; the particulars appear to be these: - On 26th September last, about 40 natives came to Mr Hassel's farm, at Kendenup, and two or three entered the house and stole some knives. A lad of the name of Charles Newell, in the employ of Mr Hassell, followed them and, after some bickering, obtained possession of the articles. As he was turning to go back to the house, a spear was thrown at him, which, entering near the backbone, penetrated in a slanting direction nearly through his body. The lad immediately fell, and the natives decamped into the bush. An express was sent to Albany, a distance of 40 miles, for Dr Harrison. Previous to the doctor's arrival, Mr Hassell had, with some difficulty, extracted the spear. In the meantime, another messenger was sent for the detachment of soldiers stationed near Mount Barker, about 10 miles distant, and on their arrival, they succeeded, with the aid of some friendly natives, in capturing the native that threw the spear. They were afterwards surrounded by a large body of between 500 and 600 men, and demonstrations were made to rescue the prisoner, but on a shot being fired into the air, they retired to some distance, and the soldiers and natives brought the prisoner along with them to King George's Sound, although apprehending an attack on the way. The culprit is a lad about 20 years of age, and he admits throwing the spear but says he was incited by others, who would have speared him if he had not done it. He has been committed to gaol for trial. Dr Harrison, on his arrival at Albany, reported that he entertained hopes of the lad's recovery, although the wound is a very dangerous one. This is the largest body of natives that have been heard of assembled at one point, and there can be no doubt of the fact, as the number of men was sworn to before the magistrates.*[31]

A significant impact on the traditional Aboriginal peoples' way of life was the commerce associated with kangaroo hunting. The population of kangaroos, a significant food mainstay for the Aboriginal population at King George's Sound was impacted by extensive hunting of the animal. It is noted that in 1847 close to 8000 kangaroo skins were exported from the settlement and by association, traditional Aboriginal hunting grounds.

The colony's government had established a position titled *Superintendent of Natives* as part of its administration in 1832. The role was subsequently known by various titles throughout the nineteenth and twentieth centuries: Superintendent of Natives (1832-1838), Protector of Aborigines (1839-1849), Guardian of Aborigines (1849-1857), Guardian of Aborigines and Protector of Settlers (1857-1887), Aborigines Protection Board (1887-1897), and Chief Protector of Aborigines (1897-1936).

In October 1841 Governor John Hutt recommended Revett Bland for appointment as *Protector of Aborigines* for his:
> *"thoughtful knowledge of the native character, acquaintance with their languages, great firmness combined with mildness of temper, long experience as a Magistrate, and a high reputation for integrity and respectability which gives him considerable influence among both the colonies and the native population of the York district."* Under his stewardship, it was reported that relations between the Aboriginals and settlers had a greatly improved, and that *"he was praised for developing good feeling and mutual confidence"*.[32]

Bland as Protector of Aborigines visited Albany in 1842 and more than likely he also accompanied Major Frederick Irwin and Mr Singleton and others on an overland trip from King George's Sound to the Vasse River in January of that year.

The annual report of the Protector of Natives 1846 addressed to the Colonial Secretary, Perth, and tabled in January 1847, provided a perspective of his office on the relationship between settlers and the Aboriginal peoples of King George's Sound:
> *Sir,*
> *I beg to furnish you with particulars of affairs connected with the Natives in my district, this being the usual period for sending in the report for His Excellency's consideration.*
> *I am happy to state that nothing of a very serious nature has occurred during the past year, to disturb the good understanding existing between the settlers and the Aborigines...*

---

[31] *The Inquirer and Commercial News.* Perth. 20th October 1841.
[32] *Correspondence of E.C.D. Keyser.* The Albany History Collection, Albany Town Library.

> *Having passed the last three months of the year at King George's Sound, I can report favourably of the conduct of the natives there during that period, and of the general good feeling of the inhabitants of the place exhibited towards them; two or three cases of cattle stealing occurred in the early part of the year. Some of these offenders have been brought to trial, the others have absconded to the Toolbrunup Mountains. As there are no mounted Police in that district, it is uncertain when they will be apprehended.*
>
> *The natives frequenting the country through which the road passes from here to Albany, a distance of 240 miles, with but three stations upon it, are very well behaved, and I have not heard of their ever-molesting travellers, who occasionally pass singly the whole way. I will mention a recent instance of their being quietly disposed: a few months since a solider from the Kojonup station lost his way, and after wandering about for five days unarmed, and without food, he at last came upon a party of natives, strangers to him, who treated him with great kindness, and having built him a hut, and supplied him with plenty of such provisions as they had, they took him home the next day, to the no small gratification of himself and comrades. To encourage this good feeling, I distributed a quantity of flour amongst about forty natives I found near that station, at the same time explaining to them my motive for so doing.*
>
> *I still continue to supply, in cases of necessity, with food and medicine, such natives as require medical treatment, and are unable to provide for themselves; it is, however, only in extreme cases, that they will consent to submit to medical treatment.*
>
> *Considerable inconvenience has almost yearly arisen to the settlers from the practice of natives setting fire to the country, to assist them in hunting, smoking animals out of hollow trees, &c.; and from the extraordinary dryness of the climate in the summer season, the grass when once ignited burns to an extent, and with a rapidity impossible to check, these fires are frequently accidental; many are caused by the carelessness of the settlers themselves, and I have no doubt that the natives occasionally wilfully set fire to the country for the purpose of annoying the settlers. To address the latter cases, a legislative enactment is necessary, as I believe the law at present existing will not apply to these cases, I have, however, entered more fully into this subject in my letter of the 2nd March.*
>
>
>
> *I have the honour to be*
> *Sir,*
> *Your obedient servant.*
> *R.H. BLAND*
> *Protector of Natives[33]*
>
>

The local press in this period persisted in carrying several stories from around the Western Australian colony about settler issues with Aboriginal inhabitants. Again in 1851, there was much hype surrounding a murder that took place in Jerramungup, to Albany's North and further issues with Aboriginal detainees in the goal. The Albany correspondent, for *The Inquirer* newspaper, wrote:

> *A shepherd who has come in from the station at Jerramungup, says that the natives are killing the sheep and robbing the huts in a wholesale way, carrying off bags of flour, &c. The native prisoners in Albany Gaol, five in number, made an attempt to escape the other day, while at work on the Gaol premises, but by prompt assistance, they were all secured in a short time. They are a determined set of villains, as will be seen by the following statement made by one of them to the jailor, which he forwarded to the visiting magistrates. There are two of them for murder. Although in gaol five months, and the others two months, they have not been brought to trial. They think that death is staring them in the face, which makes them regardless of what they do to affect their escape.*
>
> *The prisoner Coran has informed the jailor that the four native prisoners having been foiled in the attempt to make their escape, had concerted a plan, while at work, on any opportunity that might present itself, for disabling the jailor, by striking him with their grabbing hoes or tools, and then to make their escape. Coran was afraid to tell the jailor for fear he should let the other prisoners know. They threatened to strangle Coran in the night-*

---

[33] Luisa Daniele, 'Bland, Revett Henry (1811–1894)', *Australian Dictionary of Biography*, National Centre of Biography, Australian National University, https://adb.anu.edu.au/biography/bland-revett-henry-3013/text4411, published first in hardcopy 1969, accessed online 7 March 2021.

time if he divulged any of their plans. Great responsibility rests with the magistrates in ordering prisoners previous to trial to go out at all. A keeper is only justified in firing in self-defence if one or two should attempt to escape: he cannot leave his party to go after them; he may fire at them, and if he kills, he will have to stand the consequences. He should be borne blameless under such circumstances.[34]

European and Aboriginal relationships were seen as such an important issue for the colony that consequently, in 1871 the Western Australian Legislative Council appointed a Select Committee with terms of reference to report "and devise means for the systematic protection of Aborigines."[35]

Anne Camfield and "*Annesfield*" House

Anne (Annie) Camfield had travelled to Western Australia under the auspices of the Church of England Colonial and Continental Church Society of London. She later married Henry Camfield who in 1847 was appointed Resident Magistrate at Albany. Camfield House (also known as "*Annesfield*") was constructed in 1852 as a residence for them. Anne was concerned about young Aboriginal children and with the assistance of The Reverend John Ramsden Wollaston the Imperial Chaplain of King George's Sound wrote to the Colonial Secretary noting that the Camfield's new house had space to let, and that Anne was willing to take six children into her house. Wollaston was able to secure a grant from the then Governor Charles Fitzgerald to assist the endeavour. Another building constructed in 1858 was a purpose-built schoolhouse designed to house more Aboriginal children. The school continued under the auspices of John Wollaston and Anne Camfield and was focused on the education of Aboriginal children with the specific aim to 'integrate' them into European society.

Annie Camfield's report of 1868 was subsequently presented and summarised for the Select Committee. The preamble to a report on the Annesfield Native Institution in Albany of 1868 delivered by Annie Camfield, outlined to a large extent the clash of cultures that was beginning to emerge in the Albany settlement as it was elsewhere in the state at this time.[36] Her report indicated:

The natives of Australia are capable of great improvement, but it will be in some generations hence that much good will be visible, and there must be a great extension of the means now in operation.

We are too much inclined to look upon the civilisation of this people as a hopeless work because so little good is apparent from the efforts that have already been made, but multiply the means, have institutions in each district, instead of having only one or two in the whole colony, and these left to the working (and hard-working) of a very few individuals, and the results will then be more encouraging.

To wean them from their wild habits and to give them a little insight into the comforts of civilisation, together with teaching them some of the simplest but most important Truths of the Gospel, is as much as can at first be done. "Rome was not built in a day": nor did Englishmen rise from the condition described in the early parts of English history, to the high state of civilisation which they have now attained, in one generation. So, to expect that the Aborigines may be raised at once from their present wild state into that of a perfect civilisation is simply to expect what only a miracle could produce. Doubtless, it is with the power of God to place them on an equality with the most refined and intellectual, at once. The creator of all, he could make all equal, if he saw fit. But he works by means and we whom his providence has placed in this country are the means to affect the salvation of the Aborigines, in the same way as the Roman Christians were sent by and wrought so much for our Saxon ancestors in early times…

It was from an irresistible feeling that something ought to be attempted, that the result might be ever so small, that the Annesfield institution was commenced. It was begun privately with one child for six months when a favourable answer was received to an application to the government to support six children. It's now been in operation nearly 16 years, the one child in question having been received into the house June 21st, 1852…

---

[34] *The Inquirer and Commercial News*, Perth. 9th April 1851.
[35] Kimberly, W. B. *History of Western Australia*. Perth. 1897.
[36] Mrs Annie Camfield's report is quite extensive and as such excerpts are reproduced here to give a flavour of its content.

Three of these five girls have been married and they have each comfortable little cottage (and they bake beautiful bread as I have been told) and wash, and cook, and all that is necessary in the little household. What I have always urged is more than ever essential, viz.; – an institution in the colony to receive the boys and girls as they become old enough to work profitably, and where they can marry and live happily and usefully. Until such an institution is established, the amount of good done will be very small. Institutions of this kind, under judicious management, would in a few years be self-supporting.

There are at present in the school 19 Aboriginal and half-cast children, besides three white children, orphaned or deserted by the mother. These, of course, are not on the Government list, and maintenance.
Annie Camfield[37]

Unfortunately, while Mrs Camfield professed an interest in helping the young Aboriginal girls of the settlement as part of her Christian duty and a desire to better prepare them for integration into white society, her bias may well be demonstrated by her unflattering general comments about Aboriginal women and her subsequent advocacy for the removal of children, an early insight views perhaps held by many of the European at this time:

There is not in nature, I think, a more-filthy loathsome, revolting creature than a native woman in her wild state… a native woman is altogether unlovable.[38]

As has been mentioned earlier it is beneficial for a historian to have access to eyewitness statements of events to help capture and add fabric the sentiments of the time. In 1932 Captain James Sale, then living in retirement, was inspired by the interest shown in his work concerning several aspects of the history of Albany to set down his memories of the people of the town in 1936, those with whom he grew up and with whom he associated nearly all his life. Fortunately for The Historical Record Captain Sale conveyed his early eyewitness accounts to paper. Here is a snapshot of his involvement in helping transport Aboriginal children out of the town when *"Annesfield"* closed with the remaining children sent to Perth to be taught in Bishop Mathew Hale's school:

The Resident Magistrate prior to Sir Alexander Campbell was Mr Camfield. He was the principal of a school for the education of native children and turned out some fine handy boys and girls. In 1871 the natives were drafted to Perth under the care of the Miss Trimmer who afterwards became Mrs Captain Thomas. I was selected to accompany Miss trimmer and we took the native boys and girls to Perth in two large vans, one for the boys and one for the girls.[39]

Tommy King

In 1890 a Menang Elder, Tommy King petitioned Queen Victoria, indicating that his people had been disposed from their land and that their traditional way of life had been forever altered as a consequence. Tommy King, along with a small group of Menang men dressed in traditional war paint presented their petition to the Governor of Western Australia, His Excellency Sir William Cleaver Robinson on the occasion of his visit to Albany in October of that year. His request for basic supplies for his people formed a part of the petition he presented. *The Albany Observer* published the petition for its readers:

To His Excellency Sir William Francis Cleaver Robinson, K.C.M.G., etc.
May it please your Excellency,
I Tommy King, on behalf of the few remaining aboriginals of Albany, approach your Excellency with submission and profound respect, welcoming you to our native shores. We would humbly remind your Excellency that in the year 1829 all this country belonged to my tribe, of which I, at this date, would have been the Chief, but that Her Most Gracious Majesty the Queen was pleased to take it from us. Since that time, we have been gradually deprived of our hunting grounds and nearly all our kangaroos have been killed by the white men, and we are now in extreme poverty and a deplorable condition. Therefore, on this occasion when all the white men are rejoicing at Her Most Gracious Majesty having given over our land to a Constitution, we would humbly ask Your Excellency to give us something that we may rejoice. A bag of flour, a box of tea, a bag of sugar, and

---

[37] Included in Nicolay, Charles Grenville. "*Handbook of Western Australia*". Perth: Richard Pether, Govt Printer 1880.
[38] As reported in D. Garden. *Albany: Panorama of the Sound*. Nelson. 1977. And also in CSO, 482/111 527/54
[39] Captain James Sale 1936 remarks reported in *The West Australian*, Perth. 7th March 1936.

> *some tobacco would make us all very happy, and if Your Excellency will issue an order to Sergeant Cunningham to procure us these, we shall be very pleased and remain Your Excellency's most obedient servants.*
> *Signed on behalf of the Aboriginals of Albany.*
> *Tommy King.*

The paper went on to indicate that the petition was taken as read and continued with the following report of how Tommy King addressed a remonstrance to His Excellency using the following terms:

> "*Blackfellow have land, white fellow come take it away; blackfellow hear about 'sponsible Cantonment, ought to have something give blackfellow buy flour, tea, sugar, plenty bacca.*"

> *His Excellency promised that the matter should be seen into and referred him to the Government Resident.*[40]

Daisy Bates

Daisy May Bates became an Australian icon, universally respected for her work with Indigenous populations across Australia. She was often referred to in various newspapers as an amateur anthropologist. She is particularly remembered for her recording of Australian Aboriginal culture and society during the Nineteenth Century. Bates had become interested in the Aboriginal Australians for their own culture and general way of life. The Australian author Alan Moorehead wrote:
"She was not an anthropologist but she knew them better than anyone else who ever lived..."[41]

On the 17th February Daisy May O'Dwyer entered into a bigamous marriage with John Bates. This was eleven months after her marriage in England to Harry Harbord Morant, better known as 'Breaker' Morant. After coming across an article on the treatment of Aborigines in Australia she was able to negotiate a correspondent arrangement with *The Times* in London.

In all, Bates devoted 40 years of her life to studying Aboriginal life, history, culture, rites, beliefs and customs. She researched and wrote on the subject while often living in a tent in small settlements from Western Australia to the edge of the Nullarbor Plain, including settlements in South Australia.[42] Given the strains in relationships that had begun to eventuate due to European encroachment on their lands and culture, Bates was convinced that Aborigines were a dying race. She believed that her mission, therefore, was to record as much as she could about them before they disappeared. She recorded in her diary:

> *As the years passed, I was more and more convinced that it was impossible to leave these people, to be deaf to their appeal for human kindliness… So savage and simple, so much astray and so utterly helpless were they, that somehow, they became my responsibility…*[43]

In May 1908 Daisy Bates gave a lecture on Western Australian Aborigines at the St. John's Church Hall in Albany, and from later accounts it was well received and reported on as this extract from The *Albany Advertiser* on the 13th May 1908, attested:

> *West Australian Aborigines. –*
> *A most interesting lecture on the Aborigines of Western Australia, their origin and customs, was delivered to a large gathering in St John's Hall on Monday night by Mrs Daisy Bates, a lady who is at present visiting Albany in the interests of a book on the subject she is preparing at the insistence of the government. Mrs Bates is an enthusiast in questions affecting the natives and has practically given a lifetime to making herself acquainted with their laws and characteristics, even to sharing camp life with them for a period, and she not only is able to speak the language but is admitted by the blacks themselves to the mysteries of their inner life. Thoroughly well versed in her subject and a fluent speaker, Mrs Bates, unaided by lantern views or exhibits, kept her audience thoroughly interested for a couple of hours. She first of all discussed the origin of the Australian Aborigines and quoted scientific writers to demonstrate their connection with races in more northern latitudes. Next, she reviewed*

---

[40] *The Albany Observer.* 23rd October 1890.
[41] Alan McCrae Moorehead, was a war correspondent and author historical books, most notably two books on the nineteenth-century exploration of the Nile, *The White Nile* (1960) and *The Blue Nile* (1962). Australian-born, he lived in England, and Italy, from 1937.
[42] *The West Australian*, Perth. 7th March 1936.
[43] Bates, D. *The Passing of the Aborigines.* William Heineman, London. 1938.

their social organisation, class divisions and laws, including interesting reference to the records and traditions of different tribes. All their laws, she said, were based on their own standard of right and wrong and they were just to a degree, although superstition in the form of a belief in evil spirits influenced them largely. Mrs Bates detailed the methods of domestic life and explained the different tribes and that sorcery was to be found in everyone, with very similar customs and beliefs. The disposition of the race was analysed, and the occupations and amusements were not passed over…

Arch Deacon Louche introduced her and thanked her on behalf of those present for her very able discourse.[44]

The issue for Western Australian Government, which now had responsibility for the welfare of the original inhabitants of the colony and the Aboriginal peoples dispossessed by the intrusion of European settlement and associated clash of cultural expectations, was complex and has long vexed successive administrations. As a traditional hunter-gatherer society, the Aboriginal population declined through the loss of traditional hunting grounds due to the encroachment of the settler-farmer. The subsequent prohibition of their regular activity of setting fire to the bush in order to regenerate food sources around the settlements meant that they had become alienated from the land. Consequently, by 1850's a culture of dependency upon the European settlers had evolved. Except for the outliers like Nind, Grey, Collie and Moore, etc., in general only few colonists were able to truly perceive the strengths and positive aspects of Aboriginal culture. Furthermore, despite the best of intentions in terms of education and socialisation the opportunity was rarely provided to the Aboriginal peoples to truly integrate into the life of the settlement.

Early attempts at Europeanising the Indigenous population of the area focussed primarily on education and training for domestic service and the workforce in general. Anne Camfield's report to the Legislative Council's 1871 Select Committee in fact used this outcome along with marriage as a key performance indicator of success of her native school venture in Albany.

Closing Remarks

Historians today are indeed grateful to the detailed early recorded information about the Aboriginal people of the King George's Sound area, the Menang people, and in particular about their traditional way of life and practices. A selection of extracts has been reproduced to give a flavour of the way Aboriginal and European interactions evolved with time in the new settlement. Extensive recorded observations by people such as Surgeons Nind and Wilson and Government Residents Barker, Collie and Grey among others have together through their writing added significantly to The Historical Record in respect to extant Aboriginal culture. However, it must also be acknowledged that the efforts of the earlier European scientific and geographical exploration leaders' collectively through their first-hand knowledge and observations provided a foundation upon which these later 'amateur anthropologists' were able to gain insight into this very ancient Indigenous culture of King George's Sound. The likes of Vancouver, d'Urville, King, Baudin, Freycinet and Flinders recorded considerable amounts of cultural information which provided an important insight into the Menang culture. It is important to remember that the Aboriginal people had inhabited the South West of Australia, including the King George's Sound area, for many thousands of years prior to this European contact.

Further, The Historical Record also has been enriched in part to the information that was conveyed to these early visitors and settlers by Mokare, the Aboriginal leader and later guide who developed a close relationship with each group and willingly shared his knowledge of the land, its natural resources and the rich cultural practices of his people. Mokare was described in all early documentation as a man of significant skill and intelligence. A number of explorers were indeed fortunate to avail of his skills when venturing into unchartered territory.

---

[44] *The Albany Advertiser.* 13th May 1908.

CHAPTER 2
EARLY VISITORS TO THE SOUND

"... On my passage into this ocean I visited a small part of the southwest coast of New Holland, and there discovered one very excellent port, which I have honoured with the name of King George the Third's Sound. As I think from its situation, the fertility of the country, with Oyster Harbour, seas &c., it may be worthy of some further attention..."
Captain George Vancouver RN, to Captain Arthur Phillip RN,
Governor of New South Wales October 1792.

Global Overview

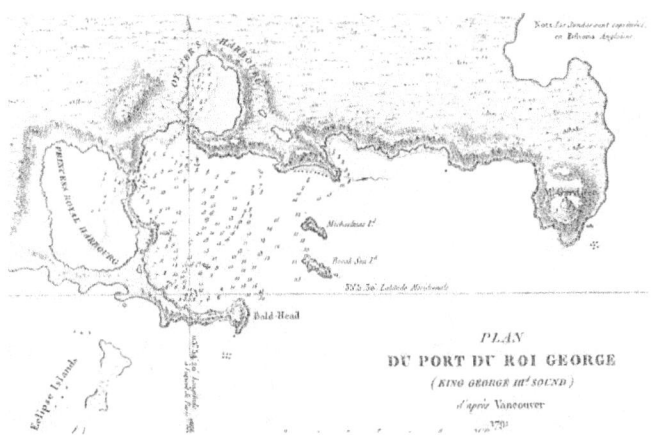

It is appropriate before introducing the early European visitors to King George's Sound in the period 1791-1826, (prior to the creation of the Cantonment in the area), to position the initial seafaring exploratory activities to the area within a timeline of some of the more significant later Eighteenth and early Nineteenth Century global events in order to get a better understanding of what was happening, historically at this time.

In France there had been a major revolution with the monarchy being overthrown in 1792, leading to the subsequent declaration of the First French Republic. Louis XVI was subsequently guillotined in 1793. Later in this decade saw the rise of Napoleon Bonaparte and under his leadership, a number of scientific exploratory journeys were undertaken, as for example, that of Captain Thomas Nicholas Baudin (1803) of which more will be revealed further on.

In America George Washington (1789-1797) was the president at the beginning of the decade, to be replaced through a peaceful transition of power to first John Adams (1797-1801) and then subsequently to Thomas Jefferson in (1801-1809), James Madison (1809-1817) and then James Monroe (1817-1825). It was under Thomas Jefferson's presidency that several scientific expeditions across the North American continent were undertaken, most notably by Captain Merriweather Lewis and Lieutenant William Clarke (The Corps of Discovery Expedition of 1804 -1806).

During the first decades of the Nineteenth Century, Spanish South America gained its independence from Spain, commencing with Paraguay (1811) through to Ecuador (1830) and finally Peru (1836).

In Great Britain, George III was on the throne and at war with France (the Anglo-French War: (1793-1802). It was part of the French Revolutionary Wars which evolved into the Napoleonic Wars (1803-1815), a series of conflicts that at one time or another involved most European powers at the time.

Some of the most significant, and beautiful, discoveries in the history of natural science exploration along the south coast of Australia, and around the King George's Sound, occurred during the period of the late eighteenth and most of the nineteenth centuries. Navigators, explorers, along with naturalists and artists together helped to create a fascinating record of their discoveries. Some scaled great heights of personal endurance and discovery and, by adding in their own way to the historical record they helped create a resource that has allowed the historians and researchers of today to revisit those earlier discoveries. In terms of voyages of discovery, the saga of HMS *Beagle* and Charles Darwin's work is perhaps one of the most famous voyages in terms of a truly global perspective, especially given the quality of the scientific record that was maintained by him.

By the latter half of the Eighteenth Century and into the Nineteenth, the organisation of expeditions improved considerably as more often they were sponsored or initiated by various governments. For example, Vancouver's voyages to Australia and North America were conducted under the auspices of the British Royal Navy and the Admiralty. As a consequence, they established a more exacting and rigorous scientific approach when recording naval history, particularly in respect to aspects relating to hydrography and navigation. Written records and drawings by the artists who accompanied the likes of Matthew Flinders on the voyage of *Investigator* to the south coast of Terra Australis provide an invaluable source of information about the nation's earliest inhabitants, the biology of the regions and the country's geography. Likewise, from Albany's perspective, many of the French voyages of scientific exploration to New Holland's south coast also have provided genuine insight into aspects relating to the King George's Sound and its Indigenous population pre-European settlement.

Extracts from several such voyages and explorations have been selected to provide a flavour of the nature of the country and its people before the establishment of the Cantonment at King George's Sound by Major Edmund Lockyer and Captain Joseph Wakefield in 1826.

It is recognised at this point that the first acknowledged European to sail in the vicinity of King George's Sound but did not land was Pieter Nuyts in 1627. Nuyts sailed around the southern coast of Western Australia and across the Great Australian Bight in the *Gulden Zeepaardt*. Nuyts's log of the single encounter he made on the south coast was very vague and the coast not closely surveyed. He presumed that the land was less than favourable and the Dutch subsequently showed no interest in settling the barren coastline outlined in his report.

This particular history narrative starts with the Royal Navy Officers Captains George Vancouver and William Broughton who made a point of taking Possession of the area for the Great Britain and also stayed for some weeks exploring King George's Sound along with an experienced botanist Lieutenant Dr Archibald Menzies RN, who assisted them in their endeavours.[1] It would be a fair statement to make that a significant contribution to Albany's initial European Historical Record was made by those involved in Vancouver and Broughton's 1791 explorations.

It is appropriate, therefore, to use Vancouver and Broughton's voyage and expedition as the starting point for this Historical Record.

George Vancouver and Lieutenant William Broughton – Royal Naval Officers - 1791

THE KING having judged it expedient, that an expedition... of the north-west coast of America... should be immediately undertaken for acquiring a more complete knowledge than has yet been obtained...
Phillip Stevens, the Secretary of The Admiralty to George Vancouver RN,
Commander of HM Sloop *Discovery* at Falmouth 8th March 1791.

George Vancouver RN, started his career as a Midshipman on *HMS Resolution*, for Captain James Cook's second voyage (1772–1775) searching for *Terra Australis*. During Cook's third voyage (1776–1780), he served on *HMS Resolution*'s companion ship, *HMS Discovery*.

Commander George Vancouver received his commission for a significant exploratory venture from the British Government on 15th December 1790, and immediately took command of *Discovery*. He was accompanied on this voyage by Lieutenant William Broughton RN, who had command of the *Discovery's* armed tender *Chatham*.[2] Among his many exploits as a Captain in the Royal Navy Vancouver is best known for his qualities as an explorer, navigator and hydrographer, particularly in respect to his 1791–95 expedition, at which time he also charted the North American continent's north-western regions. It was in 1791 that he visited the southwest coast of Australia. Upon his arrival at King George's Sound, he began a process of mapping the area and naming some of its key features. He took formal Possession of '*all the land*

---

[1] Dr Archibald Menzies was gazetted as a Lieutenant for this journey. This was a common practice of the Admiralty.
[2] Lieutenant William Broughton RN was selected to command *Chatham*. He received his appointment on 28th December and joined his ship on 1st January 1791.

on behalf of the crown' at what is now known as Point Possession on the south entrance to The Princess Royal Harbour.³

"THE DISCOVERY"
Vancouver's Sloop - King George III Sound

For Lieutenant William Broughton *Chatham* was his first command. Previously while exploring the North American continent, he was tasked with charting the islands of Queen Charlotte Sound in British Columbia, Canada and in acknowledgement of his endeavours Vancouver named the Broughton Archipelago in his honour. It was Broughton in *Chatham* who was the first to enter King George's Sound.

Vancouver, Broughton and a large party of selected officers spent a total of two weeks in the port area at which time they named some significant local geographical landmarks, including Cape Howe, Eclipse Island, Bald Head, Breaksea Island, Seal Island and Oyster Harbour. ⁴ Vancouver's Admiralty record indicates that he announced that:
This port, the first which we had discovered, I honoured with the name of King George the Third's Sound, and this day being the anniversary of Her Royal Highness Princess Charlotte Augusta Matilda's birth, the harbour behind Point Possession I called The Princess Royal Harbour. ⁵

From his ship's log, Vancouver the first recorded European to glimpse the area incorporating King George's Sound and Oyster Harbour indicated that:

[A] port, round the high rocky bluff point, soon represented itself, into which the Chatham was directed to lead, and, by four, was sufficiently advanced to determine on its eligibility. The weather by this time had become thick and rainy, with much thunder and lightning; but as the surroundings continued regular, we stood into the port, and passed the high rocky bluff point in thirty fathoms of water; directing our course close along its shore, which is a high nearly perpendicular cliff; the sounding suddenly shoaled to 12 fathoms, and gradually decreased afterwards, until abreast of the second white sandy beach; where we anchored in six fathoms of water, having a clear bottom of fine white sand.

The *Chatham* the first ship into the Sound, ensured that it was a safe harbour for *Discovery* to follow. Vancouver's log continued to provide the details:⁶

Thursday 29ᵗʰ September 1791.
A continuation of the thick weather prevented our seeing about us until Thursday, which being delightfully serene and pleasant, discovered our situation to be very snug and secure in a spacious Sound ... The high rocky bluff point forming the south-west extremity of the Sound, which, from its smooth appearance, and being destitute of verdure, obtained the name Bald Head; a high rocky island in the entrance, which, from a beaten appearance by its opposition to the sea, obtain the name of Breaksea Island... a small high island called Seal Island, being a great resort of those animals, [lay to the] *north...*

And to the north west was an extensive white sandy beach; which promising success to the seine [fishing net], *a boat was dispatched with Lieutenant Peter Puget on a fishing party. After breakfast, accompanied by Mr*

---

³ It is of interest to note that our research has led us to the conclusion that this was the first time on Australian soil that the National Anthem of that time, "God Save Our Gracious King" was played, along with western music, the fife and drums of the Royal Marines.
⁴ Sketch courtesy of Gary Tonkin from his drawings for the Albany Mace Project.
⁵ Intelligence had reached town of the death of her Majesty Charlotte Augusta Matilda, The Princess Royal of England, and Dowager Queen of Württemberg, on Monday the 6th instant. Her Majesty, who was the eldest daughter of George the Third, was born on 29ᵗʰ September, 1766. She married on 18ᵗʰ May 1797, Frederick, late King of Württemberg, who died on 30ᵗʰ October, 1816, leaving no issue.
⁶ Captain Vancouver's log book from *Discovery* is missing from the British National Archives at Kew. It is believed that he may have borrowed the log to complete the book he was writing on his voyages and did not return it.

Broughton in the Chatham's cutter, Mr [Archibald] Menzies[7], Mr Whidbey and myself, proceeded in the yawl, first to attend the success of the fishermen, and then to examine if the Sound would afford a more eligible situation than that which we now occupied. The seine was hauled on the third sandy beach from Bald Head with little success. A stream of fresh water drained there through the beach, which, although nearly the colour of brandy, was exceedingly well tasted; by this stream was a clump of trees, sufficient to answer our present want of fuel. At the borders of this clump was found [the] most miserable human habitation my eyes ever beheld, which had not been long deserted by its proprietor, as on its top was laying a fresh skin of fish, commonly called leather jacket, and by its side was the excrement of some carnivorous animal, apparently a dog. The shape of the dwelling was that of half a beehive, or a hive vertically divided into two equal parts, one of which formed the hut, in height about three feet, and in diameter, about four feet and a half; was however constructed with some degree of uniformity, with slight twigs of no greater substance than they used for large baker's baskets: the horizontal and vertical twigs formed intervals from four to six inches square, and the latter sticking a few inches into the earth, which securely fixed it to the ground.

This kind of basket hut was covered with the bark of trees, and small green boughs; its back was opposed to the North West winds whence we concluded those to be the most prevailing winds; just within its front, which was open the whole of its diameter, a fire had been made, but excepting the skin of fish before-mentioned, there were neither bones, shells, nor any other indication on what its poor inhabitant had subsisted. The reflections which naturally arose on seeing so miserable a contrivance for shelter against the inclemency of seasons were humiliating in the highest degree; as they suggested, in the strongest manner, the lonely condition of some of our fellow creatures, rendered yet more pitiable by the apparent solitude and the melancholy aspect of the surrounding country, which presented little less than famine and distress.

The shores consisted either of steep naked rocks or a milk-white barren sand, beyond which dreary boundary the surface of the ground seemed covered by a deadly green herbage, with here and there are few grovelling shrubs or dwarf trees scattered at a great distance from each. This very unfavourable appearance may not, however, originate from the general sterility of the soil, since it was evident, as far as we could traverse the sides of the hills, that the vegetation had recently undergone the action of fire; the largest of the trees have been burnt, though slightly; every shrub had some of its branches completely charred, and the plants lying close to the ground had not escaped without injury. Thus, entertaining no very high opinion of the country, but in the hope of meeting with some of the wretched inhabitants, we proceeded along the shores of the Sound, to the northward, to a high rocky point, and obtained the name of Point Possession; and, on reaching the summit, we gained an excellent view of the Sound in all directions. When on board we had supposed that the Sound branched into three arms, but it now became evident that they were only two. One, immediately behind this point, which is also its southern point of entrance, extended in a circular form, about a league across, bounded by a country much resembling that before described, though producing more trees, and with the verdure of a livelier hue, and approaching nearer to the water's edge. The other, lying about 3 miles to the northeast seemed almost as spacious, though its entrance appeared very narrow. The surrounding country in its neighbourhood presented a far more fertile and pleasing aspect. Nearly in the centre of that harbour was an island covered with the most beautiful herbage, and instead of the naked rocks and barren sands that composed the coast of the Sound, the cliffs which bounded these shores seem to be of a reddish clay, and the general texture or character of the soil appeared to be more favourable to the vegetable kingdom, as from the summits of the hills to the water side was seen a stately and luxurious forest.

The necessary observations being made at this station the British colours were displayed and having drank his Majesty's health, accompanied by the usual formalities on such occasions, we took possession of the country from the land we saw north-westward of Cape Chatham, so far as we might explore its coasts, in the name of his present Majesty, for him and for his heirs and successors. This port, the first which we have discovered, I honoured with the name of King George the Third Sound and this day being the anniversary of her Royal Highness Princess Charlotte Augusta Matilda's birth, the harbour behind Point Possession I called The Princess Royal Harbour, which with the Sound which formed Point Possession into a peninsula, united to the main by a very narrow barren sandy beach. Here although we could not discover the least trace of it having at any time being the resort of natives, yet in every part where we stayed, were seen the same effects of fire on all vegetable productions.

---

[7] Dr Archibald Menzies was surgeon-naturalist on the *Discovery*. *Banksia Menzieii* was named in his honour. Although gazetted as a Lieutenant Surgeons were always called Mr in the Royal Navy.

The ceremony of taking possession being finished, we found a passage, narrow and shoal for some distance, into the north-eastern harbour; where a bar was found to extend across its entrance, and which there was only three fathoms of water... In our way out of this harbour, the boats grounded on a bank we had not before perceived; this was covered with oysters of a most delicious flavour, on which we sumptuously regaled; and, loading in about half an hour, the boats for our friends on board, we commemorated the discovery by calling it Oyster Harbour...
Tuesday, October 11, 1791.
Tuesday being more favourable to our purpose, though the wind was still adverse, we weighed and turned out of the Sound. Whilst we were getting under weigh (sic), I caused to be deposited at the hut near the watering-place some beads, knives, looking-glasses, and other trinkets, as a compensation to its solitary owner, should he ever return, for the wood, we had cut down, and deprived him of; and to commemorate our visit, near the stump of one of the trees we had felled, in a pile of stones raised for the purpose we attracting the attention of any European, was later left a bottle sealed up, containing a parchment and on which were inscribed the names of the vessels, and the commanders; with the name given to the Sound, and the date of our arrival and departure. Another bottle, containing a similar memorandum, was likewise deposited on the top of Seal Island, with a staff erected to conduct any visitor to it, on which was affixed a medal of the year 1789. Those who may meet with the staff will most properly discover the bottle hidden near it. This precaution was here taken, on the presumption that Seal Island was entirely out of reach of the inhabitants, which might not be the case where the first bottle was secreted.[8]

Thomas Manby on *Discovery*

The journal account of Thomas Manby a Midshipman on *Discovery* captured the moment that *Chatham* entered The Princess Royal Harbour and later when Captain Vancouver took formal possession of King George's Sound in the name of His Britannic Majesty:[9]

We spent the night standing off and on and at daylight the land extended from N.W. to N. E. Sail was made and we stood in for the shore. The land had a very barren appearance with high mountains in the east country. Immense quantities of whales were seen in every direction. The Chatham was sent to head and kept close in with the land. About noon she made the signal for having discovered a harbour, but on her near approach approved mistake...

A breeze sprung up about noon with which we stood along the coast...an opening was seen bearing NNE, which gave us great hopes of a harbour. We instantly bore up for it and made the Chatham the signal to lead in. At 4p.m he made the signal that the port steered for was eligible and at 5p.m. we entered the very spacious and extensive harbour, and soon after anchored in six fathoms, almost entirely landlocked.

It being nearly dark when we came to, we waited with impatience for the returning day, which gave us a prospect by no means disagreeable. Captain Vancouver, accompanied by some of the offices, left the ship at 8 a.m. to examine the head of the sound, and I proceeded with two boats in search of water and to haul the same. The first article was procured by sinking a cask near a small spring not far from the ship and pretty tolerable success attended my fishing expedition, as provenced nearly sufficient to serve the whole ship's company...

In the evening Captain Vancouver returned, having found the most excellent harbour 5 miles up the sound on the west point which they landed and took possession of the country for His Majesty in the usual form, from whence they proceeded in the examination to the eastward and in about 2 miles from the above-mentioned harbour they found another of considerable extent. This obtained the name of Oyster Harbour from the great quantities of oysters found in it... about the centre of this harbour is a small island covered with exceeding find the due from which should've taken the name Green Island.[10]

---

[8] From George Vancouver. *A Voyage to the North Pacific Ocean and Round the World on the years 1792 - 1795 in Discovery Sloop of War*. London 1798.
[9] Thomas Moore Manby was a British naval officer who fought in the French Revolutionary and later Napoleonic Wars and later rose to the rank of Rear Admiral. He was a Midshipman when he sailed with Captain George Vancouver and Captain William Broughton on their voyages of exploration to Terra Australis in 1791.
[10] Thomas Manby. *Journal of the voyages of the HMS Discovery and Chatham* 1798.

Archibald Menzies - 1791

Secret. Lord Grenville, HM Principal Secretary of State having transmitted to us a Copy of Instructions... which has been proposed by Sir Joseph Banks & given to Mr. Menzies the Botanist... you are to accommodate him with a boat for the purpose of pursuing his researches at the several Places which may be visited at all times...
The Lord Commissioners of The Admiralty, Whitehall, London to
Commander George Vancouver RN, 8th March 1791.

We sail tomorrow...it is intended to touch on some part of the West Side of New Holland...
Dr Archibald Menzies RN, Cape Town, 10th August 1791.

Dr Archibald Menzies RN was appointed as naturalist to accompany Captain Vancouver on his 'Voyage Around the World' on HMS *Discovery*. Later in the voyage, Menzies took over the role of ship's surgeon. Sir Joseph Banks had provided to Menzies very specific details and a guide to collecting and protecting the specimens he gathered during his visits. This was provided in a very detailed, 13-page memorandum titled *Draught of Instructions for Menzies*.[11] His instructions included directing Menzies to investigate the various flora and fauna. Banks had indicated to Menzies that he was to:

...make careful notes of what sorts of beasts, birds and fishes are found in each place and ... the places where seals or whales are found in abundance...[12]

Extracts from the Journal of Archibald Menzies during his time at King George's Sound, The Princess Royal Harbour, Oyster Harbour and on the King and Kalgan Rivers provides a valuable insight into the flora of the area as it was in late 1791. (All spelling and capitalisation as per his original manuscript):

29th September
...We embarked in the Boats & proceeded to the northern parts of the Sound, where we found a small inlet communicating with a large basin or harbour & landing on its west point of the entrance we ascended a small eminence from which we had a full view of the Basin & a considerable tract of the country beyond it, the west side of it, in particular, was pleasantly diversified with groves of trees & valleys forming a rich & picturesque prospect boldly drawn by nature's manly pencil, but the inland country seemed covered with one continued forest of trees. Here we dined – drunk our most gracious Sovereign's health & took possession of the country in his name, in consequence of which the place obtained the name of Point Possession.

I met here with the Gum Plant of Botany Bay – Metrosideras & a variety of other plants in full bloom & found that the place had been recently burnt down here & there, particularly about the stems of the Gum Plant which bore its marks more than any other.

From this place we again embarked & coasted along the shore in our Boats to the North East side of the Sound, where we found another narrow inlet opening into a commodious [Oyster] harbour especially for small vessels — We landed on a small green island in the middle of it wholly covered with rank grass particularly a species of Bromus that reached up to our middles as we walked through it, & no doubt owed its luxuriance in a great measure to the rich manure left by birds & marine Animals which frequent the Island.

We saw the appearance of a large rivulet [Kalgan River] on the north side of this harbour & went in the pinnace to explore the entrance of it but met a flat running a long way offshore on which we grounded & prevented our landing. This disappointment however was amply recompensed by its leading to the discovery of some fine oysters which induced us to examine other parts of the harbour & found that the flat banks everywhere were covered with long grass among which were oysters in abundance. ... we afterwards returned on board where we arrived late in the evening with our cargo & well pleased with a discovery which offer'd such regaling refreshment during our stay.

---

[11] *Draught of Instructions for Mr Menzies*. In the State Library of NSW. In collection of Banks Papers held by the library, Catalogued as Series 61 item 4.
[12] Kieza. G. *Banks*. Harper Collins. 2020.

30th September.

... I afterwards pursued my excursion up the mountains & by noon gained the summit, where I had a fine prospect of the Sound, its islands, harbours & inlets, & to the northward of these a long extent of the country covered with verdant wood as far as the eye could reach. To a contemplative mind this prospect was by no means uninteresting for if we may judge of the fertility of the country in general from the luxuriance of vegetation in many places, we may pronounce the tract within our view capable with a little labour of sustaining thousands of inhabitants with the necessaries as well as the comforts of life, though at this time it appeared destitute of any.

...From this place I descended to a small bay on the opposite side of the ridge where I found the Orpium antiscorbuticum or wild celery & brought some of it on board to be used as greens. On the sand along the shore, we saw the tread of an animal as large as that of a Newfoundland dog but could form no conjecture what animal it was. In the evening, I returned on board with my attendants loaded with plants of various kinds & well satisfied with the day's excursion.

1st October.

On the 1st of October I accompanied Lieutenant Broughton who with some of his officers were going to examine the eastern side of the Sound – We set out pretty early in his boat – passed the two islands in the entrance of the Sound & arrived in a small bay near the outer point of the opposite shore where we landed & finding a delightful stream of fresh water we were induced to stop & take some refreshment, & while the boat's crew were getting it ready, we made a little excursion inland, and though this spot appears much exposed to the entrance of the Sound yet it was cover'd with a vast variety of shrubs & other low plants, many of them in full bloom & entirely new. Of these, there were several species of the genus Banksia & also of the genus Mimosa. We traced this brook some way up the valley from which it issued a task of no little labour on account of the density & luxuriancy of its crop of brushwood & long grass which made it difficult to penetrate. There were also two kinds of low trees here the one a Banksia & the other a Myrtus – the latter regaled our nostrils with its diffusive aromatic fragrance.

... We left one of our servants here to conduct them after us while we continued our route, & soon after came in sight of some small Lakes on which we saw some curious ducks – I shot one of a dark grey colour with wattle pendulous from the underside of its bill which induced me to name it Anas carunculata...

4th October.

...After leaving this place we soon passed Point Possession & enter'd the opening leading to the [Princess Royal] Harbour... We walked along the shore to a point about 3 or 4 miles further on where we found the wretched remains of a deserted village scattered about in the skirts of a small wood – Some of the Huts had been occupied not many months back, but the greatest part of them appeared old & dismantled.

These huts were about six & twenty in number separated a little distance from one another & formed somewhat like bee-hives with a large opening on one side which faced to the South West in all of them – They were between 3 & 4 feet high & about the same in Diameter at the bottom & in two instances we observed double ones, that is, two huts join'd together with one opening or door common to both

We left looking-glasses, beads, fish-hooks & other trinkets in some of the best huts that in case any of the natives came here before our departure these little things might impress them with a favourable idea of us & induce them to visit the Vessels...

7th October.

On the 7th of October, I accompanied Capt. Vancouver & Lieut. Broughton with some of the Officers in two boats to examine the termination of Oyster Harbour. We set out in the morning & towards noon arrived at the further end of it where we found a large rivulet [Kalgan River] empty'd itself & winded back into a delightful country which afforded a most charming prospect diversified with pastures & woodlands & little eminences rising with a very gentle ascent to the verge of very distant hills. The valley through which the rivulet winded appear'd exceedingly pleasant & inviting, for its banks were here & there bordered with extensive plains & meadows which seem'd to afford easy access into the country for a considerable way ... We here also met with several ant hillocks of an obtuse conic form somewhat like the habitations of the natives but infinitely more curious in their structure & formation – They were made of a kind of tenacious mud or clay which had acquir'd such a degree of hardness by exposure to the weather that it was a very difficult task to break any of them down. And we saw parrots, parquets & a few smaller birds but by no means a numerous variety.

9th & 10th October.
There is a small conspicuous island in the Sound covered with verdure which obtained the name of Seal Island on account of a number of these animals frequenting it. On the top of this island, a bottle was left sealed up & enclosing the date of our arrival departure &c and another of the same kind was left at a conspicuous place near to the watering-place, where there were also some garden seeds scattered about, but we fear the luxuriance of the native productions will soon choke them up & prevent there ever coming to any perfection or useful purpose.

In short, the inland country of this part of New Holland has a delightful & promising appearance & we, therefore, conceive it an object well worth the attention of the government in a more particular investigation of it, as it offers fair to afford an eligible situation for a settlement which on account of its nearness & easy access to our settlements in India possesses peculiar advantages not to be derived from the opposite shore.[13]

Bruny D'Entrecasteaux - French Naval officer - 1791

A note is made at this point of the expedition of Captain Bruny d'Entrecasteaux, who while in the area of the Sound in 1791 had sailed passed it on the way to Van Dieman's Land and then the Pacific. Bruny d'Entrecasteaux was in command of *la Recherche* and *l'Esperance* and had been tasked by the French Government with both locating the explorer Jean-François de Galaup, Comte de La Pérouse, and, within given time constraints, to map the southern coast of New Holland. He departed Brest in France on 28th September 1791.

His initial orders were to sail via the Cape of Good Hope to the south coast of Australia from Cape Leeuwin to the east and then to the Pacific. While the object of his task was, importantly to search for the missing navigator La Peruse, he was also tasked to make scientific discoveries and surveys on the way. At the Cape of Good Hope, he was informed that some items of clothing and other objects of French origin had been found in the Admiralty Islands in the Pacific, so he decided to make straight for that location. While refreshing his ships and crew along the south coast near King George's Sound he made detailed survey charts of aspects of the southern coast in the Esperance region. However, due to unfavourable winds, d'Entrecasteaux sailed past the entrance to King George's Sound (which had not been named at that point) without realising its harbour potential. Consequently, he missed an opportunity to add his name to the illustrious contingent of Naval personnel who contributed to Albany's Historical Record. [14]

Whalers and Sealers - 1800 – 1850

In the twenty years between 1792 and 1826, it is estimated that at least 60 American whalers plied the Australian coastline in search of whales.[15] Nine years after Vancouver's voyage to New Holland the British whaling industry acted on his subsequent report of King George's Sound taking particular note of the potential for whale hunting in the area. Two whaling boats owned by the London merchant and whaling ship owner, Daniel Bennett, *Elligood* with Captain Christopher Dixon at the helm and *Kingston* under the command of Captain Thomas Dennis used Vancouver's reports as a guide and followed in his footsteps to King George's Sound. While in the locality of the Sound they managed to kill and process three whales. Only scant information can be detected from *Kingston*'s log book, yet in many respects, in the endeavours of these whalers the origins of the first European whaling industry plied along the coast of Western Australia is presented.

The *Kingston* and *Elligood* were instructed to sail to New Holland to hunt for whales, and to examine King George's Sound, then proceed along the Western coastline to Shark Bay and the northwest coast before returning via Madagascar and southern Africa to England. The task took two years to complete. On the

---

[13] Extracts from *The Journal of Archibald Menzies during his time at King George's Sound, The Princess Royal Harbour, Oyster Harbour and on the King and Kalgan Rivers. 29th September – 11th October 1791.* Additional MS 32647, Department of MSS, The British Library, London.
[14] Hulot, E.B. *D'Entrecasteaux 1737-1793.* France, 2019.
[15] Thomas Dunbabin gives a very detailed inventory of some of these whaling ships in his article titled: A New Light on the Earliest American Voyages to Australia. In *The American Neptune*, 1950.

return journey, Captain Dixson and nine of his crew died from scurvy and were buried at sea between New Holland and Madagascar.

It is also worth noting that given the apparent abundance of both seals and whales along the south coast of Australia, from King George's Sound to Van Dieman's Land in the east and the ready market for pelts and whale oil, later on, proved to be a thriving industry for American and French whalers. Central to both of these geographical points is Kangaroo Island and it is here that many of the sealing and whaling fraternity co-habited. Among the inhabitants were a cadre of escaped convicts, ships' deserters and a variety of felons with the island offering them a haven for their activities both lawful and unlawful.

An article by William Nairn Clarke in *The Perth Gazette* of October 8th 1842 related to the activities of one such band of sealers. A summary of which gives an indication of the type of nefarious activities rogue sealers and whalers were reputed to have been engaged in:

'Anderson' [Jack] arrived in the fledgling King George's Sound colony aboard the American whaling vessel **Vigilant** *in 1826. While the crew were drinking ashore, a fight broke out and a man was killed. Accused of murder, Anderson and several crewmates fled in a small vessel and hid out in the Recherche Archipelago, approximately 400 kilometres to the east of King George's Sound*

Anderson and his fellows established an encampment on Middle Island in the archipelago, as it was one of the few islands with a source of fresh water and was heavily populated by both Australian sea lions and New Zealand fur seals. They are reputed to have supplemented their sealing income by robbing vessels travelling between King George's Sound and the east coast colonies. They are also said to have murdered Indigenous men and abducted their women.

According to another 1842 report, there were continued complaints received by the Governor Darling of the lawlessness and pirate activities of some of these sealers. The infamous exploits of one such sealer, 'Black' Jack Anderson were of particular note:

One of the most daring of these people was a man of colour of the name of Anderson, and lawless as these men were, they looked up to him with a sort of dread. Anderson usually carried a brace of pistols about him, knowing that he held his life by a very precarious tenure. By persevering, he had amassed a considerable sum of money, and usually kept one or two black women to attend on him and minister to his wants, when not engaged in sealing[16].

Anderson was eventually murdered by his fellow 'pirates'.

As an aside, there was a report in *The Gazette and Western Australian Journal* of 1835 of an interesting narrative concerning the escapades of two English youths who were shipwrecked and spent some time with sealer Anderson:

On 9 August last, two English lads, named James Newell and James Manning, reached King George's Sound from the mainland opposite to Middle Island, after experiencing the most bitter privations for nearly seven weeks on the main, and about two years on the islands in Spencer's Gulf. The account given of the perilous adventures runs thus:

They sailed from Sydney in August 1833, in the schooner **Defiance**, *laden with provisions for trading with the sealers on the islands of the southern coast of Australia, and then bound to King George's Sound and the Swan River, commanded by Mr George Meredith. They were wrecked in September of the same year on Cape Howe Island. They went in a whaleboat with the commander, one man, and native woman, to Kangaroo Island; the remainder of the crew of the schooner (six men) determined to make for Sydney, and accordingly started in another whaleboat: they never heard what became of them. They did not reach Kangaroo Island until February 1834…*

In September 1834, a black man, named Anderson, arrived at Kangaroo Island, in a boat, from Long Island, with another black man, named John Bathurst. Manning and his companion took a passage with them to Long Island… There was another whaleboat on the island, with four men in her… in November,… the people in this later boat caught five native women from the neighbourhood of Port Lincoln; they enticed two of their husbands into the boat, and carried them off to the island, where, in spite of all remonstrance on the part of

---

[16] William Nairn Clarke. *"Remarks Respecting the Island of the Coast of South West Australia."*. *The Perth Gazette and Western Australian Journal*. 8th October 1842.

> *Manning, they took the native men in Anderson's boat round a point a short distance where they shot them, and knocked their brains out with clubs.*
>
> *Manning believes they still have the women in their possession... Another native endeavoured to swim to the island, to recover his wife but was drowned in the attempt... on 3 June, Anderson, at the solicitation of Manning, and his fellow traveller, James Newell, landed them on the mainland, but would not give them a charge of powder. They subsisted briefly on limpets, and on roots of grass; but were sometimes, for several days, without little or nothing to eat. They found at all times sufficient water, although they never left the neighbourhood of the coast.*
>
> *They arrived at Henty, Oyster harbour, on 9 August, reduced almost to skeletons, and having almost lost all power of articulation. It is interesting to know, that these lads owe their safety entirely to the humane treatment they met with from the natives of the White Cockatoo, Murray, and Will -men tribes... they nursed, fed, and almost carried them at times, when, from weakness, they were sinking under the sufferings. This is a return which could scarcely have been expected from savages, who have no doubt been exposed to repeated atrocities, such as those we have related in the previous narrative.*
>
> *The habits of the men left on the islands to the southward, by whaling, or sealing vessels, have long borne the character given them by Manning and Newell; it appears, therefore, deserving of some consideration by what means their practices can be checked...*[17]

Captain George Sutherland, Commander of the Brig "*Governor Macquarrie* [sic]," of Sydney, 1819 describes the scene on Kangaroo Island at the time:

> *There are no natives on the island: several Europeans assembled there; some who have run away from ships that traded for salt and others from Sydney and Van Dieman's Land, who were prisoners of the crown. These gangs joined after a lapse of time and became the terror of ships going to the island, being little better than pirates. They are complete savages, living in bark huts like natives, not cultivating anything, but living entirely on kangaroos, emus, and small porcupines and getting spirits and tobacco in barter for the skins which they lay up in the winter season. They dress in kangaroo skins without linen and wear sandals made of seal skins. They smell like foxes. They have carried their daring acts to an extreme, venturing on to the mainland in their boats and seizing on the natives, particularly the women, and keeping them in a state of slavery, cruelly beating them on every trifling occasion; and when at last some of the marauders were taken off the island by an expedition from New South Wales, these women were landed on the main [sic] with their children and dogs to procure a subsistence, not knowing how their own people might treat them after so long an absence.*[18]

Matthew Flinders 1801-1802

Commander Matthew Flinders RN, in *HMS Investigator* (Renamed from *HMS Xenophon* and refitted for scientific surveys) recorded a detailed encounter with the Aboriginal people of King George's Sound. He had used his time in the area to replenish his supplies before continuing his voyage to Sydney. He was commissioned to lead a scientific expedition on this voyage charged specifically by the British Admiralty to explore the hitherto unknown and uncharted regions of the southern coast of *Terra Australis*.[19]

On 28th January 1802, he made a landing in Fowler Bay, South Australia, and in early February he entered the mouth of Spencer Gulf. On 8th April 1802, the French corvette *Le Geographe* was sighted, part of a

---

[17] *Perth Gazette and Western Australian Journal.* 3rd October 1835.
[18] J.S. Cumpston. *Kangaroo Island 1800-1836.*
[19] The name Australia was specifically applied to the continent for the first time in 1794 by two botanists George Shaw and Sir James Smith writing of "*The vast island, or rather continent, of Australia*" in their travelogue *1793 Zoology and Botany of New Holland*, and then by James Wilson including it on a 1799 chart. The name *Australia* was popularised by the explorer Matthew Flinders, who pushed for it to be formally adopted as early as 1804. When preparing his manuscript and charts for his 1814 *A Voyage to Terra Australis*, he was persuaded by his patron, Sir Joseph Banks, to use the term *Terra Australis* as this was the name most familiar to the public. Flinders did so but in a footnote, he wrote:
> *Had I permitted myself any innovation on the original term, it would have been to convert it to AUSTRALIA; as being more agreeable to the ear, and an assimilation to the names of the other great portions of the earth.*

scientific expedition to the area under the command of Captain Nicholas Baudin and he and Captain Flinders exchanged information amicably at a point that he named Encounter Bay, South Australia.

Flinders visited King George's Sound on 8th December 1801 and relied heavily on the charts prepared by his compatriot Captain Vancouver from his visit some 10 years previous in navigating its waters. Flinders arrived in Sydney on 9th May 1802, having completed the task given to him by the Admiralty in London.

On his return to England in 1810 Flinders commenced work on a book about his travels. He subsequently completed the text of the book "*A Voyage to Terra Australis*" but sadly had passed away before the book's publication in 1814. Matthew Flinders was the first writer and explorer to use the name 'Australia' consistently, and as a result, the name was gradually adopted for the greater continent. Australia's early European history is indeed well informed by the efforts of Matthew Flinders and his very capable recording of events. Aspects of his journal pertaining to the King George's Sound area are indeed well documented:

Wednesday, December 9, 1801.

King George's Sound had been chosen as a proper place to prepare ourselves for an examination of the South Coasts of Terra Australis, and I sought to make the best use of the advantage it might furnish. The first essential requisite was a place of secure shelter, where the masts could be stripped, the rigging and sails put into order, and communication had with the shore, without interruption from the elements; but this, from Captain Vancouver's chart and description, I did not expect the outer Sound to afford. The facility of quitting The Princess Royal Harbour, with such a wind as would be favourable for prosecuting the investigation of the coast, induced me to far prefer it to Oyster Harbour as to make it the first object of examination; and in the morning, after we had sounded round the ship and found her so placed as to require no immediate movement, I went in a boat for the purpose, accompanied by the master and the landscape painter; the naturalist and some other gentleman landing at the same time, to botanise in the vicinity of Bald Head.

Seal Island, where we stopped in passing, is a mass of granite, which is accessible only to its western end, as represented in Mr Westall's sketch[20]. After killing a few seals upon the shore, we ascended the hill to search for the bottle and parchment left by Captain Vancouver in 1791; but could find no vestiges either of it or other staff or pile of stones; and since there was no appearance of the natives having crossed over from the main, I was led to suspect that a second ship had been here before us.

At Point Possession, on the south side of the entrance to The Princess Royal Harbour, we had a good view of that extensive piece of water. Wood seemed not to be abundant near the shore; and therefore, a projection two or three miles to the southwest, which was covered with trees, first attracted my notice. The depth of water going to it was, however, too little for the ship; nor was there any fresh stream in the neighbourhood. Some person, but not Captain Vancouver, had nevertheless been cutting wood there; for several trees had been felled with an axe and saw. Not far from thence stood several bark sheds, like the huts of natives who live in the forest behind Port Jackson, and forming what might be called a small village; but it has been long deserted...

Thursday 10th December 1801.
...As I proposed to make a new survey of King George's Sound, we landed to take a set of angles upon the small central island; the same which Captain Vancouver describes as covered with luxuriant grass and other vegetables; and where he planted vine cuttings, water-cresses, and the seeds of various fruits. There were no remains of these valuable gifts, although nothing indicated the island to have been visited since this time; and, to our disappointment, the vegetation upon it now consisted of tufts of wiry grass, and a few stunted shrubs, supported by a thin layer of sandy soil, which was everywhere perforated with rat holes.

From the island, we rowed in various directions, sounding the harbour; but the boat could seldom approach the shore within a cable's length, of the eighth part of a mile. On the southwest side, there were two small steams, in one of which the water was fresh, though highly coloured. Returning to the entrance, we landed on the east side, and found a spot of ground six or eight feet square, dug up and trimmed like a garden; upon it was lying on a piece of sheet copper, bearing the inscription: 'August 27, 1800. Chr. Dixson - ship Elligood*', which solved the difficulty of felled trees and the disappearance of Captain Vancouver's bottle...*

---

[20] William Westall (1781 - 1850) was a topographical artist assigned to the expedition.

Saturday 12th December 1801.
The wind continuing foul for going into The Princess Royal Harbour, a wooding party was sent next morning to a bight around the north side of the entrance, where the wood was found to split better than at some other places. Another party went to the same place with the launch, to haul the seine; but the wind coming round to the eastward, the boat was recalled, and a kedge anchor and hawser put into it. We then weighed, and ran into the harbour under topsails; and at eleven anchored in seventeen feet upon the muddy ground, at one-third of a mile from the shore under the highest hill…

So soon as the ship was secured, I landed with the naturalists; and after fixing a place for our tents, ascended the highest hill to take angles. Amongst other objects, I perceived in the bearing of N 87° 20' W, two distant pieces of water, at the back of the bight near West Cape Howe; whether they were lakes or an inlet of the sea, could not be distinguished. Our tents, under the guard of a party of marines, were set up this evening; and in the morning, the observatory and instruments were sent on shore, under the care of Lieutenant Flinders [this was Samuel Flinders, the younger brother of Matthew Flinders] *who had undertaken to assist me in performing the office of astronomer.*

Wednesday 23rd of December, 1801.
I formed a party on the 23rd, consisting of the officers of the ship, the scientific gentleman, and others, amounting to 13, well-armed and provisions for two days, in order to visit the lakes behind West Cape Howe. We walked along the shore to the north-western extremity of Princess Royal Harbour, where several small runs of freshwater were found to drain in from peaty swamps, striking from thence into the country in the western direction, we had not advanced far when a native was seen running before us; and soon afterwards an old man, who had been several times at the tents, came up, unarmed as usual. He was very anxious that we should not go further and acted with a good deal of resolution in first stopping one, and then another of those who were foremost. He was not able to prevail; but we accommodated him so far, as to make a circuit around the wood, where it seemed probable his family and female friends were placed. The old man followed us, hallooing frequently to give information of our movements; and when a parakeet was shot, expressed neither fear nor surprise but received the bird with gladness; and attended with some curiosity the reloading of the gun.

Our course for the lakes led us through swamps and thick brush woods, in which our new acquaintance followed for some time; but at length, growing tired of people who persevered in keeping a bad road in opposition to his recommendation of a better, which, indeed had nothing objectionable in it, but that it led directly contrary to where our object lay, he fell behind and left us. We afterwards took to the skirts of the sea-coast hills and made better progress; but were obliged to re-cross the swamps and force our way through a thick brush, before reaching the eastern lake.

This piece of water was found to be one mile and a half east and west and one mile in-breath and appeared to receive the drainings from the numerous swamps round about. In coasting round the north side, to reach the southwestern lake, we were stopped by a serpentine stream, upon which were two black swans; but they took flight before we could get near to shoot them. After following the windings of this rivulet, some distance to the north-west without being able to pass over, we struck inland towards the skirt of some rising hills; and crossed the stream early enough to walk a mile to the south-west before sunset; when the convenience of dry ground, with wood and water at hand, induced us to halt for the night.

Thursday 24th of December, 1801.
On Thursday morning, we reached the southwestern lake and found it to be larger than the first. Its water was brackish, which bespoke a communication with the sea; and as there was no certainty that this communication might not be too deep to be passed, it was thought prudent to give up the intention of proceeding to the seaside; and our steps were retraced across the rivulet and around the northern lake. We then struck southward and ascended the hills to the top of the cliffs facing the sea; from whence I had an opportunity of seeing the bight near Cape Howe, and the form of the lakes; but no water communication was visible between them.

Our course homeward was pursued along the sandy ridge at the back of the cliffs, where the want of water was as great, as a super-abundance had been in the land going out. Towards sunset, when Princess Royal Harbour, was still some miles distant, the natural history painter became unable to proceed further, being overcome with the labour of the walk, with excessive heat, and with thirst. To have detained the whole party in a state of sufferance would have been imprudent; and Mr Brown and two others having volunteered to stay, we left them to the scanty remains of our provisions, and pushed forward to the tents, which we reached at eight o'clock. At midnight we had the pleasure to see our friends arrive, and the preparation made for sending to their assistance, at daybreak, become unnecessary.

The country through which we passed in this excursion, has but little to recommend it. The stony hills of the sea coast were, indeed, generally covered with shrubs; but there was rarely any depth of vegetable soil and no wood. The land slopes down gradually, behind these hills; and at the bottom, water drains out and forms of a chain of swamps extending from Princess Royal Harbour to the lakes. Here the country is covered with grass and brushwood, and in the parts that are a little elevated there are forest trees; nevertheless, the soil is shallow and unfit for cultivation.

Wednesday 30th of December, 1801.
On the 30th, our wooding, and the watering of the ship were complete, the rigging was refitted, the sails repaired and bent, and the ship unmoored...

Monday 4th of January, 1802.
On the fourth, a fresh gale blew from the westward and prevented me from moving the ship. A bottle, containing a parchment to inform future visitors of our arrival and the intention to sail on the morrow, was left upon the top of Seal Island; and the wind having moderated next day, and the weather become finer, though still squally, we then made sail out of King George's Sound, to prosecute the further examination of the coast.[21]

Thomas Nicolas Baudin—1803

The French scientific expedition under the leadership of Post-Captain Nicholas Baudin was quite extensive and consisted originally of two corvettes *Geographe* and *Naturaliste*. The captains under Commander Baudin's command were Louis-Claude de Saulses de Freycinet and Jacques Félix Emmanuel Hamelin; in time both of whom went on to name many geographical features along the Western Australian coastline.

A third ship, the *Casuarina* was purchased in Sydney, New South Wales and joined the expedition because Baudin had realised that *Géographe* could not venture into the shallower waters along the Australian coast that were to be part of the intended survey. The *Casuarina* was placed under the command of de Freycinet. In April 1802, Captain Baudin met Captain Matthew Flinders at the afore-mentioned Encounter Bay Esperance and exchange charts with him before continuing towards King George's Sound, which he reached on 17 February 1803. Earlier *Naturaliste* had proceeded back to France with a significant cargo of scientific zoological specimens that had been collected at that point in the voyage.

Of particular interest in The Historical Record of Albany at this time was the French encounter with a United States whaler *Union* (Captain Isaac Pendleton) at a place that Baudin named Port des Deux Peoples (Two Peoples Bay). It was Captain de Freycinet on board *Casuarina* that in fact made this encounter.

While Baudin's contact with the area was very brief his crew were able to note the existence of fish traps in Oyster Harbour and other natural features of the area. His journal relates his exploration of King George's Sound in some detail:

February 17, 1803
... During the morning the breeze was occasionally very weak and, in spite of our closeness to the anchorage, we were more than once afraid of not reaching it before dark. However, the wind increased a little at sunset and we entered it, passing between Seal Island and the mainland in order to anchor abeam of the cove in which the watering-place mentioned by Vancouver is to be found. At eight o'clock, reckoning ourselves opposite it, we dropped a bower in seventeen fathoms, with a bottom of muddy sand, and immediately moored across, for the

---

[21] Flinders. M. *A Voyage to Terra Australis*. London, 1814.

weather did not look promising. We also unrigged our top gallants for the night and everything was done for the maximum security of the ship…

February 18, 1803.

At daybreak on 18 February, we put our boats out. One was immediately dispatched to reconnoitre the watering-place and the other was employed in the establishment of our observatory on a reasonably pleasant island lying northwest by north of the ship. When the boat returned from the watering-place, I was informed that it was very good and easy to access. Ten casks were found there belonging to the Casuarina, which we knew to be in one of the two ports, for she had informed us of her arrival ahead of us buy a flag placed on the summit of Seal Island. As early as the preceding day we had told her of our own arrival by a cannon shot fired during the night. She had replied to it with several flares which had indicated that she was in the Port de la Princesse Charlotte [The Princess Royal Harbour].

At about eight o'clock we sighted that ship's boat and shortly after, her commander, Citizen Freycinet, arrived.

… Immediately after, I set off in my boat to visit the watering-place myself and see if it was convenient as reported. After examining it, I found it was indeed so and straightaway established our tents there, one being for our sick men, then numbering four, and the other for the naturalists…

February 20, 1803.

On 20 February I dispatched two boats: one for a period of six days and the other for ten. The one I put under Citizen Ransonnet's command, with ten-day supplies, was to visit the section of coastline between Vancouver's Mount Gardner and d'Entrecasteaux's Bald Island. Citizen Ransonnet was the bearer of the following orders and instructions:

> *"I am in trusting you, Citizen, with a command of my large boat to explore the portion of the coast between Vancouver's Mount Gardner and d'Entrecasteaux's Bald Island. It seems to me that it is particularly useful to know it in detail, as it offers a view of various inlets which could hold resources or a haven in bad weather for future navigators in these regions.*
>
> *Generals d'Entrecasteaux's and Vancouver only saw the coast from a distance; you are going to examine it closely and with scrupulous attention. You will enter all the inlets long it and explore each one in detail. If, as I might be inclined to believe, you find some ports there, you are to survey them, taking soundings and determine as exactly as possible the points that form the entrances.*
>
> *As you have only 8 or 10 leagues of coast to explore, eight or ten days should be more than sufficient for this work. That is why you should be back by then. You will not proceed east of the eastern point of Bald Island and will limit yourself to the reconnaissance of the bay to the north of it. Take the greatest care of your boat and avoid all things that could endanger it."*
>
> *Greetings Nicholas Baudin.*

I placed midshipman Baudin [no relation to Captain Baudin] *into the second boat and gave him the following instructions:*

> *"Citizen, you are to take command of the large working longboat, in which Faure, the geographer, is to go. You will make a complete tour of the bay and of the two ports that we are now in, starting with the one to the northwest of our anchorage as far as Mount Gardner. As Citizen Faure is to survey them, you are to take him to the places that he indicates or to those that appear to merit particular attention. You will not forget to sound wherever you go and, and above all, at the entrance to each port. In the one called Oyster Harbour, there should be a bar over which there is only 3 fathoms depth. You will ascertain whether this information is correct or not.*
>
> *Pay the greatest attention to the safety of your boat and avoid carefully all that could endanger it. You are not to stop on board the Casuarina, which is beached in the Havre de la Princess Charlotte, so as to not waste your time on useless visits. Your boat will be provided with six days supplies, but, if possible, you are to return before consuming them all, for I do not think Citizen Faure's work should require that length of time."*

Having dispatched the two boats just spoken of, I ordered half the crew to send their linen and hammocks ashore to be washed in the reservoirs that I had built for that purpose. Four men from the crew were specially instructed to do this work. In the afternoon we began taking on our water and brought twenty-five casks-full aboard. The little boat, sent fishing on Vancouver's Seal Island, returned with only eight or ten fish of the parrot-fish variety so far as the shape was concerned, but very good to eat. No seals were found there, which leads me to think they have a particular season of the year for frequenting these regions.

February 21, 1803.

As the weather was fine on 21 February, I left the ship at half-past five in the morning in order to see the Havre de la Princess Charlotte and Oyster Harbour for myself. For this visit, I used my private boat which holds only five men, including the one steering, and this enabled me to be my own guide…

I went first to the island upon which our observatory is placed and visited Citizen Bernier. This island has no name on Vancouver's chart, although it is pleasant and more densely wooded than the others. After two hours with Citizen Bernier, I proceeded to the Havre de la Princess Charlotte following the line of the shore. The entrance to this port is possibly a mile across and is large and easy. But a ship like ours would have to scud before the wind, as tacking is hardly possible in the fairway. One must, for preference, coast the port side since the starboard one has much less water…

The Havre de la Princess Charlotte seemed commodious to me and appeared to offer good shelter for storm-battered ships in need of urgent repairs; but although water is not lacking there, it is not so good, nor so easily obtained as in the place where we are. Furthermore, there are only two or three places around the entire harbour with clumps of trees suitable for use by ships of a certain size. The transport of the wood is made difficult by the extent of a shoal that forms a border around the bay and dried up in great swamps roughly 1 ½ miles off shore. At that distance, the Casuarina was in no more than 1 foot of water at low tide.

After examining this port, I proceeded to Oyster Harbour, continuing along the coast… The large beach at the head of the bay is formed by low, sandy land; but inland, the mountains are high and well covered by what look to be big trees. Upon reaching the port's entrance, the northern side of which is formed by a projecting sandy headland [Emu Point], *and the southern by some fairly high terrain, we ran in for the middle of the channel to take soundings. With the tide out, we found the depth to be between 12 and 13 feet, so when it is in, I do not think there can be more than 14 or 15 there. The port appears to be a commodious and well-enclosed place; however, we soon saw that it was not without shoals and that in order to visit it frequently, it is most necessary to know them. Having run aground two or three times and re-floated ourselves, we went ashore where our large boat was with Citizen Faure, to whom I had entrusted in more detailed reconnaissance than the one I was doing myself.*

Since it was growing late when I arrived, we spent the rest of the day and the night there, taking care only to keep our boats afloat overnight so as to be able to make a tour of the harbour the following day and visit every section of it. The large boat had been to the island that Vancouver named Green Island and the men were extremely surprised to find there none of the seed that he had planted. The only greenery was provided by two or three patches of scrub. The rest of the island, which is very small, was covered by a type of very fine, yellowish grass. It seems that this quantity of it must have been injurious to the germination of the seed or, more likely still, that the great hordes of ants there destroyed it as it came up…

Immediately after dinner, we set off again up the river. I was planning to go far enough along to find freshwater, but we were barely a mile further on when we found little water and the passage shut off by dikes that the natives had constructed in the form of locks. These dikes were built at each side of the river, in the middle of which was an island, by means of natural rocks coming out from either bank. But in the places where there were none and which had been hollowed out by the current, the natives had placed stones which, arranged skilfully and symmetrically side by side, are proof that they are not without intelligence. Until then we have found nothing less than six fathoms, and it was with great regret that we saw ourselves halted in the middle of our excursion.

Citizens Faure and Bailly, who had been put ashore in order to observe the subsequent course of the river, reported that it appeared to be obstructed only in the place where we were and that beyond the two dikes in view it seemed to be just as deep and navigable as we had found it so far. At this juncture the large boat arrived, having got afloat and followed us a long way behind. I decided to use this reinforcement to carry my boat over the dikes, and the operation was accomplished much more easily than I had expected. When it was across, we re-embarked and went on further three-quarters of a mile, until six new dikes, each higher than the one before, completely shut off our passage and obliged us to return the way we had come. The water was still salty and the speed of the current was half a knot.

As before, we went ahead on foot and again saw no obstruction on the other side of the dikes. However, as the river winds considerably, we could not see very far. We noticed that these later locks were built with even more intelligence than the earlier ones. We could make out several embrasures in them, the opening of which was broader on the side of the incoming tide, while on that of the outgoing one, it was so narrow that seems rather difficult for the fish, easily brought in on the tide to get out.
Obliged to go back, we are again carried our boat over to the other side of the dikes crossed earlier and thought of our return, for the night was beginning to fall.

February 28, 1803.
The botanists were very pleased with the collections that they made. From what he has told me, Citizen Leschenault appears to have gathered roughly 200 new species of plants that were unknown to him and as many varieties within the species. Guichenot, the gardener is no less satisfied and has even more specimens.

I think that Citizen Peron, too, will be able to write a volume on worms and molluscs. He has one or two cases of broken shells, for in several places along the shore one can shovel them up. These, he claims, should help him establish the period at which New Holland must have risen from the floor of the sea…

March 1st 1803.
At about half-past four on 1 March the weather promised well and the offshore breeze started up with a slight catspaw from north variable to the north-west, so we prepared to sail and hove short. We then hoisted the topsails and got underway with all sails set.[22]

Convict Ship Emu - 1815

The convict transport ship *Emu* had a very interesting history. Forty-nine female convicts had previously embarked on the ill-fated *Emu* 1812 which was seized by an American privateer the *Holkar* during the American – British War (1812-1814). A load of convicts on the seized ship were put off at St Vincent, Cape Verde Islands, where they languished enduring great privations for eleven months until they were later found almost naked and starving.

The *Emu* was on-sold as a prize of war. However, later in 1815 it was again purchased by British interests and returned to transporting of convicts to Australia. It moored to refuel with water at Emu Point in King George's Sound at the peninsular that extends into the entrance of Oyster Harbour. This geographical feature is most likely named after the visit of this ship and not after the bird of that name.[23]

Phillip Parker King – 1818

On January 20th, 1818, Captain Phillip King RN, made his first visit to King George's Sound and Oyster Harbour, using the latter as his base camp to refurbish and fettle his ship *Mermaid*. He was tasked to undertake the first complete hydrographical survey of the coast of New Holland. Interestingly, a participant in this exploration was one Midshipman John Septimus Roe who went on to considerable acclaim for his later work as Western Australia's first Surveyor-General. King used the entrance to Oyster Harbour, the current Emu Point channel, as a mooring. In his log he indicated:

---

[22] The Journal of Post Captain Nicholas Baudin, Commander-in-Chief of the Corvettes *Geographe* and *Naturaliste*. Assigned by order of the Government to '*A Voyage of Discovery*'', London 1809. Translated from the French by Christine Cornell, Adelaide 1974. (Courtesy Libraries Board of South Australia.)
[23] Hook, E. *Journey to a new life: the story of the ships Emu in 1812 and Broxbornebury in 1814, including crew, female convicts and free passengers on board*. Pyramid Hill. 2014.

> *It was convenient for our purposes, as wood was abundantly procured close to our water holes which we dug at the edge of the sand within 30 yards of the vessel so that the people employed in these occupations could be protected against the Aborigines by the proximity of the cutter without preventing the necessary repairs to the riggings being carried on at the same time by the remainder of the crew on board.[24]*

During *Mermaid's* replenishment, Midshipman Roe used the opportunity to explore Oyster Harbour on foot, at which time he noted the sighting of several Aboriginal fish traps. In respect to the fishing exploits of his crew King recorded:

> *Oyster Harbour is plentifully stocked with fish… we were not successful with a hook-on account of the immense number of sharks that were constantly playing about the vessel… A few fish were taken with the seine which we hauled on the eastern side of the small central island.[25]*

Captain King's report that his first visit to King George's Sound was insightful and extracts of this dialogue are represented here:

> *20th of January, 1818.*
> *Oyster harbour.*
> *On the 20th, at daylight, we were close to Bald Island, and in the afternoon took up an anchorage in King George the Third's Sound, between Seal Island and the first sandy beach, at the distance of half a mile to the eastward of a flat rock in seven fathoms, sand and weeds. In the evening we landed on Seal Island, which we had much difficulty in effecting on account of the surf. Several seals were taken upon it, one of which we killed; and some penguins were also taken. On the summit of the island or rock, for it scarcely deserves the former appellation, the skeleton of a goat's head was found, and near it were the remains of a glass case bottle; both of which, we afterwards learnt, were left on the island by Lieutenant Forster, RN, who put into this harbour in 1815, on his passage from Port Jackson to Europe, in the Emu, a hired transport.[26] We searched in vain for the bottle which Captain Flinders left there, containing an account of the Investigator's visit; my intention, in looking for this document, was not of course to remove it, but to ascertain its existence, and to add a few lines to the memorandum it contained.*
>
> *Iguanas, geese, penguins, gulls, and seals of the hairy species were the sole inhabitants of this rock. After leaving Seal Island, we landed on the sandy beach abreast of the anchorage; in doing this the boat filled, and the instruments were so wetted, that they were left on the beach to dry during our absence. Our ascent, from the hill, being steep, and composed of a very loose drift sand, was difficult and fatiguing; but the beautiful flowers and plants, with which the surface of the hill was strewed, repaid us for our toil. These being all new to Mr [Alan] Cunningham fully occupied his attention, whilst I remained upon the summit, from whence a good view was obtained of the Eclipse Isles and Vancouver's breakers, both of which are well laid down by Captain Flinders, whose correctness I had already many occasions to admire.[27]*
>
> *An abundance of shells of the helic tribe [helix bulimus] was found on the top and sides of the hill; and a calcareous substance was observed protruding from the ground in every part, as noticed by both Vancouver and Flinders; the former also found it on the bare sandy summit of Bald Head, and supposed to be coral, a circumstance from which he inferred that the level of the ocean must have sunk. Similar substances have since been discovered by Dr Clark Abel, near Simon's Town, at the Cape of Good Hope, and are described by him to be vegetables impregnated with carbonate of line; but from the specimens we obtained, it would appear that it is neither coral, nor petrified vegetable substance, but merely sand agglutinated by calcareous matter.*
>
> *21st to 31st January 1818.*
> *During our stay in Oyster Harbour, many parts of the neighbourhood were visited by us; and on one occasion Mr Roe walked around its shores; in doing which he got into great danger. Upon leaving the vessel, his intention was only to go to a projecting head on the western side, for the purpose of taking a sketch; but being tempted to*

---

[24] Phillip Parker King. *Narrative of a Survey of the Intertropical and Western Coasts of Australia. Performed Between the Years 1818 and 1822.* Vol. 1, Chapter 1 and Vol 2. Chapter 3. 1827.
[25] Ibid
[25] Alan Cunningham (1791-1839) was a botanist and explorer.

extend his walk, he had half traversed the shore of the harbour before he thought of returning. He had already waded over the river that falls into the north-west corner of the port, which was not more than four feet deep; and to avoid crossing it again, he preferred returning to the tent, by making the circuit of the corner, about two miles to the eastward of the western river.

In attempting to ford this, finding the water deeper than he expected; but after preceding some distance further, he unexpectedly met with another river, deeper and wider than that which he had previously passed; this proved to be the Riviere de Francais [Kalgan River] of Captain Baudin; it falls into Oyster Harbour at its north-east, he was obliged to swim about two hundred yards, and, from being burdened with his clothes, narrowly escaped with his life…

No marks were left of the ship Elligood's Garden, which Captain Flinders found at the entrance of Oyster Harbour; but a lapse of 16 years will in this country create a complete revolution in vegetation; which is here so luxurious and rapid the whole woods may have been burnt down by the natives and growing again within that space of time, and it may be thus that the Elligood's Garden is now possessed by the less useful but more beautiful plants of the country.

Excepting the sea-fowl, which consisted of geese, wild ducks, teals, curlews, divers, sea-pies, gulls and terns, very few birds were seen and those chiefly of the parrot and cockatoo tribe; a species of the latter was noticed of a rich black plumage, and very like the black cockatoo of New South Wales. Kangaroos from their traces must be numerous, but only a very few were noticed; the only reptile that was found was a black snake, which Mr Cunningham saw for a moment as it glided past him. This gentleman made a large collection of seeds and dried specimens from the vast variety of beautiful plants and flowers with which nature has so lavishly clothed the hills and plains of this interesting country.

A small spot of ground near the tent was dug up and enclosed with the fence, in which Mr Cunningham sowed many culinary seeds and peach stones; and on the stump of the tree, which had been filled by a wooding party, the name of the vessel with the date of our visit was inscribed; but when we visited Oyster Harbour three years and a half afterwards, no signs remained of the garden and the inscription was scarcely perceptible, from the stump of the tree having been nearly destroyed by fire…

On 31 January… A boat was sent to Seal Island to deposit a bottle, in which was enclosed a memorandum informing future navigators of our visit, and intentions with respect to our further proceedings. When the boat returned she brought two seals, which had been killed on the island for the sake of the skins, to be used for the purpose of refitting the rigging.

The next day [February 1st] the cutter was warped out of Oyster Harbour; and, as the wind was from the eastward, we profited by it; after beating out of the Sound we steered along the coast, and at eight o'clock were abreast of West Cape Howe.[28]

---

[28] [28] Phillip Parker King. *Narrative of a Survey of the Intertropical and Western Coasts of Australia. Performed Between the Years 1818 and 1822.* Vol. 1, Chapter 1 and Vol 2. Chapter 3. 1827.

On 23rd December 1821 Captain King recorded his second visit to the area in the brig *Bathurst*, sighting of some Aborigines induced King to return to the Emu Point mooring. His reasoning is captured in the ship's log:

> *I found the brig could not anchor near enough to the shore to carry on our different operations without being impeded by the natives, even though they should be amicably disposed*[29].

Jules Sébastien César Dumont d'Urville - 1826

> *I decided to put into King George's Sound...it is perhaps the last point of New Holland worth colonizing; it suited us very well...*
> Jules Sebastein-Cesar d'Urville. October 1826.

Captain Jules Dumont d'Urville arrived in King George's Sound in *Astrolabe* in October 1826, two months before the arrival of *Amity*. His ship had been equipped to engage in exploration activities as well as undertake a detailed search for the explorer La Peruse. He established an observatory on the north bank of King George's Sound, on Point Possession

The first place visited by Captain d'Urville was King George's Sound and this is now believed to have been a deliberate action on his part. During their exploration of King George's Sound and its hinterland the French spent a considerable time collecting flora and fauna specimens. As to be expected they also made comprehensive surveys of three prominent anchorage points as well as noting potential future farming possibilities. The expedition established a well-equipped observatory near the entrance to The Princess Royal Harbour. It was this site that d'Urville later indicated in his reports that he considered the best location for a town and the banks of the Kalgan River he selected as being the most suitable for possible plantation type agricultural activity.

He was surprised that the British had not yet established a settlement at King George's Sound. Nevertheless, records indicate that the British were especially suspicious of any French, American or Spanish interests and intentions concerning land claims in or around Terra Australis. While part of Captain d'Urville's instructions emphasised the need to discover a safe anchorage for French vessels he was also tasked to search for a suitable place for a possible future penal settlement. However, the purpose of the voyage was officially presented as a voyage of scientific discovery.

Extracts from the reports from d'Urville provide an insightful and most valuable early record of the area around King George's Sound in 1826 before the arrival of Major Lockyer and the New South Wales Cantonment party.[30]

His general observations of King George's Sound as recorded in his report:
> *Sunday 15th October 1826.*
> *I have reserved a stay to visit the north of Oyster Harbour, the River of the French* [now the Kalgan River] *which was discovered by* [Thomas Nicholas] *Baudin's expedition (1803) extends four- and one-half miles from its mouth. Thereupon, at half-past five in the morning, I started off in the big dinghy accompanied by Messrs. Quoy, Lottin, Gimmard, Kmart, Sainson and (Pierre) Lesson (assistant surgeon). On our way we made a short stop on Green Island where our hunters vainly tried to surprise the pelicans. The birds are so vigilant it is impossible to get close enough to have a shot at them even when one hides.*
>
> *We went along the full length of the harbour and discovered nothing that appeared to indicate the mouth of the French River. I attempted then to push into one of the arms of the harbour and after having followed it for about a mile after which it forms a small river which I name the English River* [King River] *because it appeared to be indicated on Vancouver's map of 1791. But at the mouth of the English River, there was only 2 feet of water (over mudflats); after painfully dragging the dinghy for about a mile I gave up following it any further.*

---

[29] Ibid
[30] On the 8th May 1842 Admiral d'Urville, his wife and son were killed in a railway accident while travelling between Paris and Versailles.

We stopped on the edge of this river to have lunch and some hunting… the hunting would have been good except for the incessant rain and the ravenous mosquitoes that followed us everywhere… At about four o'clock we took ourselves to a spot near Swan Point under a beautiful clump of eucalyptus trees that had attracted our attention. Then, regretfully the rain redoubled its force and it poured, preventing us from doing a thing. We had to be satisfied to light a big fire and keep warm, we had some kind of repast. At eight in the evening, we pushed off, still soaking wet. As we passed close to Green Island our hunters jumped ashore hoping to surprise the pelicans. But they took off, besides the swallows and the oyster catchers made such a racket as we arrived, that it seemed as if they made it their job to announce our deceit to their friends. We steered towards the Astrolabe *and arrived back at ten o'clock, as tired as we were wet and cold. Mr Gilbert killed a five-to-six-foot snake on the trip judging by its teeth Mr Quoy reckoned it was a dangerous one.*

Monday 23rd, 1826.
…Later I left in the whaleboat with Messrs. Gilbert and Sainson to search anew for the river of the French… I steered directly to Green Island and then the place where I thought was a mouth of the river… Soon we recognised the true bed of the river in the centre of which was a regular channel that was five to six feet deep at low tide… It was not long before we were in the river itself, its course is well delineated, and its bed is quite clear and beautiful; from about one mile from its mouth the river is almost constantly eight to ten feet deep throughout its width.

We met along the way flocks of pelicans, geese, black swans, white herons, musk ducks and other types of ducks. We killed a black swan, a brown duck and two herons. The day was charming and the temperature delightful. We experienced a real delight to sail with full canvas on this beautiful river between two banks shadowed by immense eucalyptus, carpeted with the most beautiful thickets and adorned by the most elegant flowers.

We had travelled for about five miles without experience in the least obstacle when at two o'clock the boat was stopped by large granite rocks that blocked the river where its descent became more rapid. For a long duration, these waters were absolutely fresh. I ordered a stop and we settled on the left bank and under some magnificent eucalyptus.

Near this rocky bar, the natives availed themselves of the three islets that break the speed of the current and diverge its direction to establish their fairly stretched out fishery. These are stone dams that look like small pens rounded at the mouths and are faced seawards. Undoubtedly the tide rises up to that point and brings along the fish which are trapped with the small labyrinths. On the right bank of the river, there are many well-beaten small tracks, one of the sailors came across a hut…

I decided to retrace my steps. The part of the tidal river, although very often intercepted by little creeks flowing into it, is more pleasing than the other side and much more accessible. The soil appears excellent and I have no doubt that all kinds of crops could be successfully grown there.

Tuesday 24th, 1826.
Before leaving this anchorage, I must say the stay most certainly was one of the happiest of the campaign, we quickly recapitulated on the advantages it has afforded us and what we have got from it. The crew had perfectly recovered from the terrible crossing they had endured since Teneriffe. Water and wood have been completely replaced, rigging almost entirely checked and miscellaneous damage repaired. M. Jacquinot set the watches. The complete plans of the Sound and the two harbours, the numerous soundings as well as the topographical plans had been drawn up and ample zoological and plants collections gathered at the station. Sainson has been busy painting everything that caught his interest.

It is a very suitable place for anchorage, in spite of the frequent strong winds that prevail, vessels of any size have nothing to fear if they are well anchored, above all should they be able to place themselves at the very entrance of The Princess Royal Harbour. As we have previously said, water and wood are easy to obtain, the natives are peaceful, and the climate appears to do us very healthy.

According to the examination I have made of the River of the French and all the land around the port, I also concluded that should a colony be established at King George's Sound, no position for a town would be more convenient than that of our observatory… Initially, much clearing would have to take place for extensive cultivation and large plantations. It would be best along the River of the French, communications by waterways would be direct and easiest. Fishing which is singularly abundant would offer to the early settlers' great resources at the beginning of the establishments. Finally, there is no doubt that after a few years, the products of the soil, as well as grain and livestock, would be ample for their subsistence. [31]

Captain Dumont d'Urville's accounts of his time in and around King George's Sound also provide insight of the often-encountered tyranny of many the marauding bands of sealers and whalers in the area who were identified in later reports by Lockyer, as a posing not only a significant problem to the settlement but further, to the Aboriginal population as well. Two such reported incidents are presented here:

Sealers found Marooned on Breaksea Island
October, 12th

About 9 o'clock a small craft, apparently manned by Englishmen, came alongside: in reply to my questions one of them said he and his companions had been on the Governor Brisbane *engaged in seal fishery along the coast; their captain, after having abandoned six of them in Coffin Bay had left them on Middle Island and had departed, it was thought for Timor. They had settled on Breaksea Island where they had remained for 7 months, living on the fish they could catch and suffering great privations, hoping for the arrival of a ship to take them away.*

Dumont D'Urville took them all onboard and offered them passage to Port Jackson. As this offer was not enthusiastically received, he concluded that the majority of them were probably escaped, convicts. Three of them decided to join L'Astrolabe, the other 5 chose to remain.

Interactions with Whalers
October 17

At midday we sighted two strange whalers rowing between Observatory Island and Seal Island ... at three o'clock their boat came alongside ours. I was told that the second whaler was manned by five Americans and an Australian from Port Jackson, all belonging to the schooner Hunter. I authorised three men of the first boat to stay on board, from the other boat I only received a coloured American... I did not wish to allow them to sleep on board, these people being rather doubtful I did not trust them, I could not risk having a dozen audacious and determined individuals about who might dare to do serious mischief at night.

October 19.

Two English whaleboats returned with fish, petrels, oysters, a female seal, and some fairy penguins, - all these were obtained as food for the crew and for natural history in exchange for some gun powder and some rope yarn. The English had with them five Australian Aborigines (two young women from Van Dieman's Land a man and a woman from the mainland near Kangaroo Island and the little girl of eight or nine (from the mainland... all these individuals have for many years lived with these Englishmen.

I never wearied of considering the strange reunion of these miserable mortals - so different in origin and education brought together by chance to lead so pitiful, so precarious an existence... Their two boats, their whole fortune depended upon them for all their power, the loss of these wretched crafts would render the state of their unfortunate owners one hundred times worse than that of the natives of this country.[32]

Captain d'Urville's scientific expedition and general observations of the Sound made at that time were enhanced by the quality observations of some of the cohort of members of the French scientific community who accompanied him. In particular, Louis-Auguste de Sainson [draughtsman] and Midshipman Jean Rene Constant Quoy, both of whom contributed diary extracts to D'Urville's later published work.[33] Their observations and interaction with the Aboriginal people of King George's Sound were indeed insightful (see Chapter 1).

---

[31] Jules S-C Dumont d'Urville, *Voyage of the Corvette L'Astrolabe 1826-1829.*
A translation from the French by The Department of Lands, Perth (n.d) from an account in two volumes to The South Seas by Captain, later Rear Admiral Jules D-C Dumont d'Urville of the French Navy to Australia, New Zealand and Oceania. 1826-1829
[32] Ibid
[33] Jules Sébastien César Dumont d'Urville. *Two Voyages to the South Seas*. Volume 1. Astrolabe, 1826-1829.

Closing Remarks

The Eighteenth Century is often characterised as the age of science, with a ferment of scientific endeavour evident primarily among the activities of two rival nations, Great Britain and France. This renaissance in scientific thought and interest, particularly in the disciplines of botany, astronomy, archaeology, anthropology, physics and chemistry encouraged and, in many respects, underpinned many of the late eighteenth and early nineteenth-century voyages of discovery that eventually combined to have a significant impact on the history of Australia.

While it is recognised that there was also a strong imperialist undertow to these government-sponsored voyages, in no way does this fact diminish the degree to which human activity has impacted upon and affected the Australian continent. Albany was fortunate in many ways to be at the crossroad of some of these voyages and much of its subsequent history can be traced back to the endeavours of some of these extraordinary early explorers.

CHAPTER 3
FROM CANTONMENT TO SETTLEMENT

Finally, Sir, at a time when we have one French vessel of war in these seas… we hear of an American vessel of war being in this neighbourhood, seeking a place for settlement, it becomes important to prevent them from occupying a position of such value…

Captain James Stirling RN, to the Governor of New South Wales, 14th December 1826.

Overview

Born out of a distrust that had persisted about French and possibly the intentions of other nations concerning New Holland's West and South-West Coastal region the King George's Sound Cantonment was planned and implemented chiefly through the endeavours of Lieutenant-General Ralph Darling Governor of the New South Wales Colony in written communication with Lord Bathurst in London.[1] Major Edmund Lockyer of the 57th Regiment, a Senior British Army officer was subsequently charged with forming a Cantonment at King George's Sound, a task which began on Christmas evening, December 25th, 1826.[2] It is from this point onwards that the genesis of the Albany settlement begins to take shape.

Correction to The Historical Record

First, it would be remiss before commencing this section not to correct an issue with mis-information that has crept into The Historical Record concerning Major Lockyer's actions in respect to the Sound. Misconceptions about the early Cantonment at King George's Sound have, with time become evident in the record relating to this initial period of settlement. The first of these concerns Major Lockyer establishing a British presence in the area.

There is an important distinction and point of clarification that needs to be made about the terms, Possession and Settlement, as they have significant implications for the story of Major Lockyer and Captain Wakefield's arrival at King George's Sound and of their landing party on board *Amity*. The term 'possession' is the actual holding or occupancy of a territory, whereas settlement is the act of fixing in a secure and steady position the act of peopling or in colonising a new country or colony.

Both the New South Wales and British Governments were well aware that Vancouver and Broughton had made a claim for the area in 1791. Formal Possession of all the land he saw and explored '*north-westward to Cape Chatham, so far as we might explore to its coasts.*' took place initially in September 1791 by Captain George Vancouver and Lieutenant William Broughton both of the Royal Navy. At this time The Princess Royal Harbour was named by them to commemorate the birthday of the daughter of King George the Third. The Sound was named in honour of the King. No settlement was established by Vancouver and Broughton and furthermore, there is no evidence that a Proclamation relating to possession was indeed made by Lockyer in January 1827.

The first formal Possession by Proclamation was made by Captain Charles Fremantle on 28th April 1829 at Garden Island. On 2nd May 1829, he took possession of the West Coast of New Holland and the remaining area of the Territory of Western Australia that was not part of New South Wales Territory, in the name of His Britannic Majesty King George 1V.

Part of the log of *HMS Challenger* which is dated Saturday, May 2nd 1829 records the formal annexation of Western Australia on behalf of the British Crown. The log reads as follows:

---

[1] Lord Bathurst was Secretary of State for the Colonies at this time.
[2] Major Edmund Lockyer was at the time unattached from the 57th Regiment. Captain Joseph Wakefield was attached to the 39th Regiment of Foot.

Saturday, May 2 – a.m. Fresh breezes and cloudy. Sent parties on shore to dig wells and cut wood. Light breeze and fine. Captain Fremantle and Lieutenant Henry went with party to Swan River and took formal possession of the West Coast of New Holland in the name of his Britannic Majesty.[3]

Instructions had been given to the British Admiralty to take formal possession of the Western portion of the continent of New Holland and the Colonial Secretary then passed these instructions on to Captain Charles Fremantle RN, to undertake this role before the arrival of Captain James Stirling prior to his establishing the settlement at the Swan River.[4]

A Royal Proclamation is the official giving of public notice or posting up in public places or Government Gazette of important information. In Albany's case, it has been in respect to the issue of the word Proclamation through which certain myths, misunderstandings and misconceptions have been perpetrated. For example, "*History West*" April 2013 published by the Royal Western Australian Historical Society [on page 6 of that document] indicated in respect to Proclamation Day celebrations in Albany:
> *"The newsletter of the Albany Historical Society has just arrived and is full of the celebrations held to mark the day upon which Major Lockyer proclaimed the foundation of a British settlement at King George's Sound."*

In fact, Major Lockyer did not proclaim anything of the sort. He was instructed to go to King George's Sound in 1826 with the intention of making a report to Governor Darling in Sydney that would enable him to decide "*on the expediency of establishing a penal settlement*" in this location. No evidence has been found in the Historical Records of Australia, the Historical Records of New South Wales, the National Archives of Australia, the State Record Offices of New South Wales and Western Australia, the Historical Records of the British Army, the Lockyer papers in the Mitchell Library at Sydney nor the National Archives of the United Kingdom at Kew of any advice to the contrary.

There is, however, documentary evidence revealing that the Proclamation of Settlement was enacted by Captain James Stirling RN, Lieutenant-Governor of His Majesty's settlement in Western Australia on 18th June 1829 at Fremantle, as the official Proclamation document itself records. Only one Proclamation of Settlement was given on that 18th day of June 1829.

The official proclamation was read again at Garden Island on 18th June 1829 relating specifically as follows (spelling as per original documentation):
> *"Possession having been taken of the Territory aforesaid and the settlement here in having been actually effected."*

Proclamation

> *By His Excellency James Stirling Esquire Captain in the Royal Navy and Lieutenant Governor of His Majesty's Settlement in Western Australia. Whereas his Majesty having been pleased to Command that a Settlement should forthwith be formed within the Territory of "Western Australia" and whereas with a view of affecting that Object an Expedition having been prepared and sent forth and in accordance with His Majesty's Pleasure the Direction of the Expedition and the Government of the proposed Settlement having been confided to me, and whereas in pursuance of the Premises Pofefsion [sic] of the Territory having been taken, and the Settlement therein being now actually effected, I do hereby make the same Known to all Persons whom it may concern, willing, and requiring them duly to regulate their conduct with reference to his Majesty's Authority, represented in me, as good and Loyal Subjects may and ought to do and to obey all such Legal Commands, Regulations as I may from Time to Time see fit to enact as they shall answer the Contrary to their Peril.*
>
> *And whereas by the Establishment of His Majesty's Authority in the Territory aforesaid, the Laws of the United Kingdom as far as they are applicable to the Circumstances of the Case, do therein immediately prevail and become Security for the Rights, Privileges and Immunities of all His Majesty's Subjects found or residing in such Territory. I do hereby caution all to abstain from the Commifsion of Offences against the King's Peace or the Laws of the Realm upon pain of being arrested, prosecuted, convicted, and punished in the same manner*

---

[3] *The Western Mail*. Perth. 9th May 1908. A copy of the original document can be found in Clark, CMH. *Select Documents in Australian History, 1788-1850*. Angus and Robertson, Sydney. 1950.
[4] Clark, CMH. *Select Documents in Australian History, 1788-1850*. Angus and Robertson, Sydney. 1950.

and to all Intents and Purposes as is usual in similar offences committed in any other Part or Parts of His Majesty's Dominions subject to British Law. And whereas for the aids of Justice and the Preservation of Peace, I may hereafter see occasion to Nominate & Appoint a properly qualified Person to execute the Office of Sheriff of the Territory, having under his Direction responsible Individuals filling the Offices of High Constable, Constables, Bailiffs and Surveyors of HighWays. And whereas I may hereafter see occasion to issue a Commission to certain discreet Persons to proceed to the cognizance of Officers against the Laws; to hear and determine Complaints of Injury; to commit Offenders for Lieutenant-Governor Stirling's Proclamation of the Colony, 18th June 1829.

...I do hereby give Notice that the Conditions and existing Regulations under which Crown Lands will be granted, will be exhibited to Public Inspection at the Offices~ of the Secretary to Government, and of the Surveyor of the Territory, subject to such alterations and amendments as may from Time to Time be ordered, and all Persons desirous of obtaining Lands or of becoming Settlers for any other Purposes in this Territory, are as soon as may be practicable after their arrival in this Settlement to appear at the Office of the Secretary to Government and there to make application for Permission to reside in the Settlement, and all Persons found at large without having obtained such Permission will render Themselves liable to be committed to Custody and all Persons in like manner who may intend to quit the Colony are to give a week's Notice of their Intentions to Depart upon pain of being liable to be apprehended and detained and of rendering the Master of the Ship in which they may be about to Depart subject to a Fine as set forth by the Port Regulations.
God Save the King!!!
Given under my hand and Seal at Perth this 18th Day of June 1829
James Stirling
Lieutenant Governor
By His Excellency's Command
Peter Brown,
Secretary to the Government.[5]

Cantonment at King George's Sound

It being intended to establish a settlement at King George's Sound on the South-West Coast of New Holland, I am directed by His Excellency the Governor to signify to you His commands, to proceed thither on board of the Government Brig Amity now ready to receive you with the Detachment of Troops...the Convicts and Supplies intended for this Service ...
Alexander Macleay Colonial Secretary, Sydney to Major Edmund Lockyer
4th November 1826.

While some have questioned whether the French, Spanish or Americans had, at any time, a serious intention of establishing a colony or colonies on the continent of Australia, it is almost certain that about the year 1825, the French Government had enquired of their British counterparts what were the territorial limits that they were claiming for Australia. As the record has shown, there is no doubt that French ships were particularly active along the west and south coastal areas of Australia from the 1800s onwards. Given that the question of the formal occupation of the western portion of Australia in 1825 had been raised it was determined to correct the matter post-haste, particularly as it was strongly rumoured that the French had designs of establishing their own colony on areas not recognised as belonging to Britain.

Furthermore, Governor Darling was anxious that his commission as Governor did not give him command over the whole of New Holland. His awareness of the French activities in and around the Indian and Pacific oceans induced him to write to the Imperial Government in London voicing his concerns. He suggested to the Imperial Government before commencing his actions in respect to King George's Sound that it, adjust his commission, ante-dated, making him Governor of the whole of New Holland. This original proposal was not accepted, however, after some negotiations with Lord Bathurst in 1826 the initiative to establish a Cantonment at the Sound was fostered and then subsequently implemented.

---

[5] *Proclamation*: 18 June 1829 by James Stirling. Given under the Hand and Seal of Lieutenant Governor James Stirling, at Perth this 18th Day of June 1829 Registered in Register of Records. Page 4. No 33. Peter Brown Registrar.

Governor Darling writing from Sydney in October 1826 indicated:

> *It will not be easy to satisfy the French if they are desirous of establishing themselves here, but there is an objection to their doing so on the West Coast, and I, therefore, better suggest that the difficulty would be removed by commission describing the whole territory as within the government.*[6]

The *Sydney Gazette* also went on to state that:

> *"a curious Incident quick and the movements of the new undertaking. The French government having determined on forming settlements along the western coast of our vast island, sent a formal, notice of their intention to the British ministry who instantly dispatched orders to the Cape of Good Hope for the immediate departure of a man of war, with a suitable quantity of military, to Swan Port, and Captain Stirling himself was sent off with all possible speed. We would not by any means regret seeing a French colony established on part of New Holland. If it did no other good, it would have the effect of making the British government show some little liberality and consideration to the wants and wishes of these colonies; besides it is idle to suppose, that the immense continent of new Holland, containing nearly as much land as the whole of Europe, should remain (like the dog in the manger) forever uninhabited, waiting for the slow, means - the snail's pace method of colonisation adopted by Great Britain*[7]

The response was immediately forthcoming:

> *HMS Ariadne of 28 guns, which is at Plymouth, is said to be testing to proceed for an intended new settlement on the west side of New South Wales.*[8] *There was a rumour current that the French government have recently applied to the government of this country for permission to establish a colony on some part of that immense island, in which the latter have refused to acquiesce, and that upon such refusal being communicated, a confession made by the Ministry of France that the means to colonise had already left a French port, but in what part of Australia it was intended to establish the colony we have not learned.*[9]

It was this issue that prompted General Darling, Governor of NSW to despatch Major Lockyer and a party to raise the British Flag [for the second time] and establish a Cantonment at King George's Sound. Darling's correspondence with the Earl Bathurst was underpinned by his concerns about the arrival at Port Jackson of the French Captain d'Urville.[10] The d'Urville's ship *Astrolabe* had called at Sydney to refit and resupply in the course of a long exploratory voyage, the main object of which was said to be scientific research. Notwithstanding this assertion Governor Darling was not convinced and conveyed his concerns to Bathurst:

> *Captain D'Urville would lead me to believe that the object of his expedition is solely for the purpose of general science. It is perhaps a fortunate event that he has found His Majesty's Ships* Warspite, Success *and* Volage *lying here, knowing at the same time that the* Fly *has sailed with an Expedition to the Southward, as he may, in consequence, be more circumspect in his proceeding that he otherwise would have been.*[11]

In later correspondence Darling informed Bathurst of his subsequent actions:

> *Governor Darling to Earl Bathurst*
> *Government House, 24th November 1826.*
>
> My Lord,
> *I have the honour, in reference to your Lordship's private letter of 1 March last, and to my dispatch number 95, of this date, to transmit to your Lordship a copy of the "Secret Instructions" with which Major Lockyer and Captain Wright were furnished, the former proceeding as commandant of King Georges Sound, and the latter of Western Port.*
>
> *Your Lordship will observe the explanation, which I directed might be given, should any information be necessary with respect to the western boundary of this government; though, as the published maps are marked*

---

[6] *The Colonial Times*. 5th June 1829.
[7] Ibid.
[8] HMS *Ariadne* was a Hermes class ship built for the Royal Navy during the 1810s.
[9] *The Observer*, London. November 1828.
[10] The Earl Bathurst was at different times Lord of the Treasury, Lord of the Admiralty, President of the Board of Trade. He was Secretary of State for War and the Colonies from 1812 to 1827. From 1828 to 1830 he was president of the council in the Duke of Wellington's ministry and kept abreast of colonial matters in Australia.
[11] *The Historical Records of Australia*, Series I, Vol. XII.

through the centre from north to south, and my commission adopts that line as the western boundary, it would be difficult to contend or to satisfy any nation, desirous of making a settlement on the western coast, that we have an indisputable right to the sovereignty of the whole territory.

I, therefore, beg to repeat the suggestions, contained in my private letter to Mr Hay, dated 9 October, that I may receive a commission describing the whole territory, as within this government. If generally known that we had actually assumed the sovereignty, and we are proceeding to settle the western coast, it might possibly tend to prevent the interference of any foreign power and might set the matter at rest.
I have &c
R.A. Darling.[12]

This was the first claim made on behalf of the British crown to the entire continent of Australia. Prior to the commission given to Governor Darling, the territory of New South Wales had been defined as that portion of the island continent lying to the east of the $135^{th°}$ of East longitude.

Ralph Darling to Edmund Lockyer.
Government House
Sydney 4th November 1826
Secret Instructions.

Sir,
As the French discovery ships, which are understood to have been preparing for these seas, may possibly having in view of the establishment of a settlement on some part of the coast of this territory, which has not yet been colonised by us, I think it necessary to apprise you, confidentially, of what may possibly be their object; and I am to desire, in the event of their touching at King George's Sound, that you will be careful to regulate your language and communications with the offices, so as to avoid any expression of doubt of the whole of New Holland being considered within this government, any division of it, which may be supposed to exist under the designation of New South Wales, being merely ideal, and intended only with a view of distinguishing the more settled part of the country.

Should this explanation not prove satisfactory, it will be proper in that case to refer them to this government for any further information they may require. But should it also happen that the French have already arrived, you will, notwithstanding, land the troops agreeably to your instructions, and signify that it is considered the whole of New Holland is subject to his Britannic Majesties Government, and that orders have been given for the establishment of King George's Sound as a settlement for the reception of criminals accordingly.
I have, &c
Ralph Darling[13]

This direction was communicated in a despatch from the Colonial Secretary Macleay to Major Lockyer:
Colonial Secretary's Office,
Fourth November 1826.

Sir,
It being intended to establish a settlement at King George's Sound on the south-west coast of New Holland, I am directed by his Excellency the Governor to signify to you his commands to proceed there onboard the brig Amity *now ready to receive you and the detachment of troops placed and your command, and, in fulfilling the intentions of the government, you will be pleased to govern yourself by the following instructions: –*
Besides the troops, the convicts and supplies intended for this service are embarked on board the Amity, *which vessel will leave the port in company with His Majesty's ship* Fly *under the command of Captain Wetherall, as soon as the necessary arrangements are completed…*[14]

Consequently, Major Edmund Lockyer, Captain Joseph Wakefield and Lieutenant Colson Festing RN, were charged with the responsibility of selecting:
…such a site as may be most eligible for a Penal Settlement, having due regard to the safe anchorage and a good supply of freshwater, with fertile soil in the neighbourhood and such other conveniences as can be obtained.

---

[12] Ibid.
[13] Ibid
[14] *The Historical Records of Australia.* Vol. V1. Note: General Instructions to E. Lockyer.

When the site is determined upon, you will display the colours, with which you are furnished for this purpose, cause the troops to fire a 'Feu de Joie' and observe all other formalities which are usual on such and occasion.[15]

Senior British Army Officers Major Edmund Lockyer and Captain Joseph Wakefield Set Sail

The importance of King George's Sound as a place necessary to occupy must strike every person acquainted with this Country. Edmund Lockyer, 2nd April 1827.

The unfurling of the flag and the other requirements in Major Lockyer's instructions were fully discharged on 21st January 1827, at which time Major Lockyer established the desired British presence at King George's Sound.

Major Lockyer and Captain Wakefield were dispatched from Port Jackson, Sydney on November 9th, 1826, on board the brig *Amity* which was under the command of Lieutenant Colson Festing and two accompanying vessels at the beginning of the journey, *HMS. Fly* and the brig *Dragon*. These last two ships were designated to sail to Western Port (Southern Victoria) to establish a settlement there.

Major Lockyer's instructions were to establish an outpost settlement of New South Wales at King George's Sound and also to annex the remaining portion of the continent for the British Crown, hence forestalling any attempt at settlement by a foreign nation. Although he had fixed on a settlement site that served his needs, every endeavour was made by Lockyer to ensure that more eligible sites had not been overlooked. While Governor Darling in Sydney may have thought of King George's Sound as a temporary expedient, however, there can be no doubt Lockyer saw his work was forming the foundation of a possible permanent British colony in the west of New Holland.

The *Amity* anchored in The Princess Royal Harbour on the 25th December 1826. Major Lockyer and Captain Wakefield chose a site for the outpost (now Residency Point at the end of York Street) which he suggested be called 'Frederickstown' and formally re-claimed the territory on 21st January 1827.[16] However, Governor Darling did not support this naming of the outpost, and as the naming of the settlement was not authorised, the name 'Frederickstown' subsequently lapsed. A possible reason why Major Lockyer's choice of name for the new Cantonment was not confirmed by Governor Darling may have been because of his recollection that in Canada, India, South Africa and the West Indies there had already been towns named "Frederick's Town".[17]

Having accomplished his mission, Major Lockyer then returned to Sydney onboard *HMS Success* which was fortuitously under the command of Captain James Stirling. While Major Lockyer spent only 3 months in the settlement before his return to Sydney, his reports on King George's Sound and his interactions with soldiers, convicts, civilians in his party as well as natives were very detailed and informative. A selection of excerpts from his initial report are reproduced here:

November 8, 1826.
In compliance with my orders and instructions, embarked on board his Majesty's colonial brig Amity, *having a detachment of his Majesty's 39th Regiment consisting of one captain, one sergeant and 18 rank-and-file, with 23 prisoners to form a settlement at King George's Sound: and Mr Isaac Scott Nind, an assistant surgeon on the Colonial Medical Establishment…*

Monday, December 25.
Fine breeze; at twelve o'clock at noon made Bald Island, weather hazy; as we near the island, which is pretty high, observed it was all rock without any soil; we next saw Cape Manypeaks, Mount Gardner, the islands of

---

[15] Ibid. (Enclosures Nos. 1 and 2)

[16] It is worth noting that the Albany Centenary Celebrations were in fact held in 1927, not 1926.

[17] The settlement was in fact referred to as King George's Sound until officially named Albany by Lieutenant Governor Captain James Stirling in 1831. While Frederickstown was suggested by Major Lockyer to honour Prince Frederick, Duke of York and Albany, it was never gazetted and Governor Stirling preferred the name Albany, which still therefore, acknowledged the Prince.

the Sound and Bald Head; on Michaelmas Island as we passed, a great fire was made as if by persons requiring assistance; at half-past five in the afternoon anchored in Princess Royal Harbour about a mile off the north shore, it is a complete basin about nine miles in circumference with a narrow entrance from the east side opening into the Sound, and forms the most secure place for ships; no natives were seen on the shore or smoke to indicate there being near the harbour; being late did not land this evening but propose to go on shore early in the morning.

Tuesday 26th.

At daylight about four o'clock this morning went on shore with Lieutenant Festing; on landing, two natives met us with a little boy, and came up without the slightest hesitation; the youngest of the two men whom we have since called 'Jack', from a supposition that he is the 'Jack' of Captain King, whose native name is Mangril, he made signs to be allowed to go off to the vessel, which I assented to; the old man and boy going off in another direction from the one Lieutenant Festing and myself took, we proceeded in our walk, found plenty of freshwater though very high coloured from its running through' a peaty soil like bog; as it lays on a slope facing the anchorage, it might easily be drained and the water brought to as many reservoirs as might be required; and the ground would become excellent for gardens; and the scite [sic] between the two hills forming nearly an amphitheatre would be an extremely eligible situation for a town, though most of the ground in the neighbourhood is a loose sandy soil with a mixture of vegetable mould; with the exception of gardens, it will not answer for any other purpose of farming or agriculture; on reaching the summit of the highest hill under the which Captain Flinders had his tent.

We had a most extensive view of the country around with the two harbours and Sound ; from Bald Head as far as the eye could reach to the westward, presents nothing but a continuation of a ridge tolerably high hills of white sand and granite rocks, the sandy parts being lightly sprinkled with a course wiry grass and stunted Honeysuckle; in the hollows and ravines, the ground is peat or bog soil very black with decayed vegetable substance in it; on the west side of the harbour, a slope, reaching from the shore to the top of the hills narrowing gradually to the top, is nothing but a sheet of white sand on which when the sun is out causes a great glare; on the south side of the harbour, there is wood fit for firewood, but for no other purpose, nor is there any ground fit for cultivation or grazing on that side; from the hill we see the two lakes, which Captain Flinders visited when here, and the country in that quarter presented the same sandy appearance; at the back of the two hills, a large plain about four miles long and one and a half broad, which could be cultivated and cattle could graze on; a large freshwater lake about two miles long and a quarter broad is between the two harbours, with some sizeable timber on the rising ground this side of it.

Oyster Harbour with Green Island present a pleasing view from the hill, which at some future period, and a permanent establishment being fixed, would be the best place for a signal station, as it commands a sea view and both harbours; about thirty miles directly north inland [sic] is a ridge of moderately elevated hills covered with timber to the very summit, and, from the darker foliage and verdure about these hills, I should presume the soil there is very different from what it is in the immediate neighbourhood of the sea shore; shall therefore avail myself of the first leisure to examine that part. It being past eight o'clock, we descended the hill and returned on board…

After breakfast about ten o'clock, we again set out and proceeded along the shore towards the entrance of the harbour and crossed over the slope of the hill and descended to the lake, between which and the shore of the bay facing the Sound the ground undulates in ridges of sand, on which is some grass, stunted She Oaks and Honeysuckle; the wood of the latter when burnt produces a very agreeable smell quite aromatic; had the ground been good between the lake and the shore, it would have been a good place for settlement but decidedly it would not answer; whilst sitting down to rest at the head of the lake, a kangaroo of the largest sort came close to where I was sitting with Mr Nind, who fired at it and missed it though within ten yards; after walking nearly halfway to Oyster Harbour and not seeing any spot more favourable than the one we landed at, we directed our steps homeward to the brig…

I was extremely anxious to ascertain what persons were on Michaelmas Island as a fire was still kept burning and at night a light on the west end facing the harbour; I had requested Lieutenant Festing would cause a boat to be sent there the first thing in the morning.[18]

Thursday, 28th.
At six o'clock this morning set out with Lieutenant Festing for Oyster Harbour to examine its shores but could not discover a more eligible situation for the formation of the settlement than the spot described opposite to the anchorage in Princess Royal Harbour; on landing on Green Island, we found a dead body of a native; from its appearance, I should have considered it to have been dead about two months. It struck me there must have been some bad work going on there; the natives have no boats; they never venture above knee-deep in the water; near about four yards I think lay a miserable attempt at a raft from some dead wood tied together with grass; his head was pretty perfect, the hair still fresh, the skin on the breast bone is gone and his insides also, but his thighs and legs quite perfect and dry, but I dare say that, until put under ground, they will continue perfect and keep for a long time; not having a spade, we could not make a grave to put the body in; on my next visit I should not fail to do so…

Friday, 29th.
At eight o'clock we went on shore with Lieutenant Festing and Captain Wakefield, and fixed on the spot to erect huts and a store for the settlement; ordered the tents on shore with a guard also the sheep to graze; made arrangements to commence landing the detachment of the 39th Regiment and the prisoners tomorrow morning…

January 3, 1827.
The wind blew fresh all night from the south-east accompanied by heavy showers that did not penetrate the roof of the store hut, which is perfectly dry and will fully answer the purpose until it is determined where to erect a permanent building for a store. The harbour affords plenty of fish in great variety and excellent in its kind, particularly whiting, very fine oysters and sand cockles, periwinkles, etc; with little trouble, a meal can never be wanting here. Wild celery on the shore and samphire; the fish are so numerous, a large sort of cod, salmon as it is called, Sydney barracouta or sea pike, snipefish, whiting. small sorts of snappers, sharks or wrays [sic]; as soon as we have leisure to get baskets made, not the slightest doubt in the Sound we shall catch lobsters or crawfish…[19]

Sunday, 14th.
At eleven o'clock ordered the prisoners to be assembled for muster and inspection in general; found them very decent and clean; ordered the indulgence of tea, sugar and tobacco to be disallowed to John Ryan, one of the sawyers for the next week, for gross insolence and general misconduct; the natives have not been seen today; ordered the prisoners not to go further than half a mile from the camp, and on no pretence to go into the plain at the back of the hill without orders and the names to be called every four hours on Sunday…

Monday, 15th.
A party at work in the garden and others collecting wood, etc, for additional huts for the use of the offices, etc, of the settlement. Yesterday was counted twelve large smokes or fires at the back of the encampment about two miles apart, forming a complete semicircle; what the motive was for it cannot be known, but from so many fires they must be assembled a number of the natives. The wind has been very unpleasant blowing hard from the westward, covers everything in the tent with dust and sand…

Tuesday, 16th.
People employed as yesterday at the garden and collecting materials for huts and clearing ground, the stores being all landed, and having no further course for detaining the brig than will be necessary to make required reports for his Excellency's information of the progress made in the settlement etc., Lieutenant Festing proposed quitting this for Sydney calling at Western Port in about a week; it is but justice to this officer to say that I am under great obligations for his assistance and that he has exerted himself on all occasions to the upmost for the good of

---

[18] The unfortunate inhabitants of the island subsequently rescued by the longboat were four Aboriginals who had been marooned on the island by whalers or sealers that had been in the area prior to the arrival of *Amity*.
[19] Samphire is a name given to a number of succulent salt-tolerant plants that tend to be associated with water bodies.

the public service, and which I'm confident will be duly appreciated by his Excellency; on departure of the brig, I should be considerably at a loss for two experienced seaman as boat-keepers, and who would be able to act as pilots to bring vessels into the harbour from the Sound, as well as to visit Oyster Harbour occasionally, as also to enable us to draw the seine and to preserve it in good order; on the propriety of the above, Lieutenant Festing also agrees with me, as he has promised and undertaken to make them acquainted with the proper channel to take vessels in an out. It will also be necessary to have some local regulations regarding vessels actually visiting this place, which on the arrival should be made known to them.

Wednesday, 17th.
Had the two guns taken from the beach to the point over the landing place, where they are to be mounted and the flagstaff put up. From the lawless manner in which these sealers are ranging about requires some immediate measures to control them as, from what we know as also from what I have learnt from themselves, they are a complete set of pirates going from Island to Island along the southern coast from Rottenest Island to Bass's Strait in open whale boats, having the chief resort or den at Kangaroo Island, making occasional descents on the mainland and carry off by force native women, and when resisted make use of the firearms with which they are provided; amongst themselves they rob each other, the weak being obliged to give away to the stronger; at Kangaroo Island a great scene of villainy is going on, where to use their own words there are a great many graves, a number of desperate characters, runaway prisoners from Sydney and Van Diemen's land.

A government vessel or small man of war to be kept for the purpose of cruising on this would check a great deal of the lawless proceedings now going on, as also restrictions should be made respecting the seal fishery, which from their destroying the cubs as well as the old ones Will cause them to become scarce. I should think it would prove both beneficial to the government and the merchants and spectators if these islands were farmed out to those who offer a reasonable rent for them…

Sunday, 21st, 1827.
This day at sunrise the colours were displayed on the flagstaff; at twelve o'clock a Royal salute was fired from the battery and a Feu de Joie [French: "fire of joy"] *by the troops and an extra allowance of flour with raisins and suet was ordered on the occasion to be issued to the troops and convicts; a number of the natives having come to the settlement in the morning the seine was hauled on purpose to give them a feast; about three hundredweight was taken of capital fish. The day proved fine and the whole went off well. As the Amity is to sail on Tuesday, I have ordered that the little girl Fanny, who was taken off the mainland to the eastward of this and having no means of restoring her to the tribe to which she belongs, to be taken to Sydney for the disposal of his Excellency; not having been able to visit the interior for the present, I cannot, of course, give any opinion as to how far this part of the country will suit the views of settlers, though I have little doubt that there is good soil perfectly fit for cultivation, as I am informed by the sealers, some of them having been a considerable way up the Swan River, at 180 miles to the west-north-west of this, that there is plenty of fine Cedar on its banks and plenty of fine pine of a very large size. I propose leaving this to an expedition in about a week or 10 days.*[20]

At this point, it is important to once again clarify The Historical Record concerning Governor Darling's intention with respect to his instructions to Major Lockyer. Local historians writing about the settlement of Western Australia often confuse British expressions of interest in the outpost as resulting from concerns with the intentions of the French, and further, with official yet unstated French moves and motives. While the British were perhaps moved to action in establishing the King George's Sound outpost in part by their concern of French intentions and also the report of an armed American brig known to be patrolling near the Sound adding to this paranoia, there is no evidential basis for their suspicion.

Further clarification of this point is provided in French documentation of the time. Louis de Freycinet in the corvette *l'Uranie* was ordered to south-west Australia in 1818 to examine King George's Sound *'for scientific research'*. Instead, Freycinet headed northwards towards Shark Bay.

---

[20] *Despatches and Papers Relating to the Settlement of the States. Western Australia.* The Historical Records of Australia, Volume V1. Sydney. 1923.

In the mid-seventeenth century, Louis de Bougainville and then later in 1822 Louis Duperry (both French naval officers and explorers) were tasked to report on different colonial establishments in the East Indian Ocean and west Pacific area as an action by France to establish a colony for the possible transportation of convicts. Their main sphere of interest centred on New Zealand, New Guinea and the Polynesian islands and not New Holland.

As in England, by 1818, the rising cost of supporting convicts and overcrowding in prisons forced the French government to explore the possibility of establishing a convict colony abroad. Exploration was seen to be the prerequisite to the establishment of a colony. However, official French opinion shifted away from establishing a French colony in 'Leeuwin land' in the Indian Ocean, preferring to establish a colony in the more salubrious islands around New Zealand.

Interestingly, the French explorer Francois Alesne De Saint Allouarn had visited Western Australia and it is suggested that he claimed it for France on March 30th, 1772. [21] However, this point cannot be confirmed as no official documentation has been discovered relating to this matter, nevertheless, French officials at the time believed they had a legal right to establish a colony at some suitable place in Western Australia. However, Britain did not accept the principle of prescriptive right, instead of believing in the right to territory by effective occupation, consequently, viewing territories that were not occupied and garrisoned as vacant lands. Thereby in dispatching Major Lockyer and a detachment of troops to King George's Sound to establish an outpost there was an action designed to support this British position with power and if necessary, force.

Therefore, Major Lockyer and Captain Wakefield in coming to King George's Sound did not frustrate French endeavours because by then the French had relinquished any serious intentions to challenge the British there. So, while Major Lockyer was sent to the area to ensure a British presence there, the initial possession of all Western Australia was an act not legally carried out until 1829 at the mouth of the Swan River Settlement under the direction of Lieutenant-Governor Captain James Stirling, RN.

It must be remembered that the King George's Sound Cantonment was a very insulated outpost of the country, a distance of approximately three thousand five hundred kilometres from the then seat of government in Sydney. The site selected for the original settlement was on firmer ground in what is now known as Parade Street, north of Residency Point.

After receiving Major Lockyer's report on the establishment of the settlement, Governor Darling corresponded once again with Lord Bathurst on the developments:

Ralph Darling to Henry Bathurst.
Government House, Sydney
3rd May 1827.

My Lord
In reference to my Dispatch No. 77/1826, notifying that the Detachment of Troops and Prisoners to form The Settlement at King George's Sound had proceeded to their destination, I have now the honour to forward for Your Lordship's information a Copy of Major Lockyer's report, whom I employed to establish the Settlement.

It will be perceived that, as far as Major Lockyer proceeded into the interior, a distance of about five and thirty Miles, the Soil was very unpromising and held out no inducement to Settlers, though he appears to be of opinion from Certain Circumstances that the Land further from the Coast must be of a good description.

Major Lockyer states that water is abundant and of a good quality. That there is a variety of timber fit for every purpose, Limestone, Granite, and Iron Stone are common. Fish of a good quality and of various kinds

---

[21] The ship *Gros Ventre* under the command of Francois Alesne De Saint Allouran, sailing by the map of Mr De Mannevilette, sighted land on March 17, 1772, and according to the map it was Cape Leeuwin. Unable to find immediate anchorage he then headed north to Latitude 25 deg. 28'. His personal log states: "We sent a boat to take possession of the land in the name of France…" Translated from the *Voyage of Francois Alesne De Saint Allouran, 1771-72* by Kate Caldwell. The Western Australian Historical Society, August 1934.

may be had in any quantity, as likewise all the varieties of Water Fowl, Black Swans, Wild Geese, Ducks, etc.

The observations as to the importance of King George's Sound as a Naval Station during War appear deserving attention. If an Enemy were in possession of it, the Trade with this Colony and Van Diemen's Land might no doubt be easily intercepted. As to its establishment as a Penal Settlement, dependent on this Government, I beg to refer your Lordship to my public Letter by this opportunity to Mr Hay, dated the 14th Instant; and in reference to the difficulty of Communicating with King George's Sound, I do myself the honor to add the following Extract from that Letter in order the more immediately to place the subject before Your Lordship viz;

"King George's Sound is situated at the Western extremity of the South Coast. The direct Communication is open only from January to March and is even then attended with extreme difficulty and uncertainty. In proof of this, it is only necessary to mention that the Brig Amity, a Vessel much above the common Class, which was employed in conveying the Persons destined to form the Settlement, was obliged first to put into Port Dalrymple and afterwards to the Derwent, to repair at Hobart Town the damage she had sustained. Shortly after this a Second Vessel, a remarkably fine Schooner, was sent with Supplies for that Settlement in Company with His Majesty's Ship Success, when proceeding to Swan River, and, after being out nearly three months, returned to this in consequence of the loss of her Rudder without having reached her destination. Another Vessel will be immediately dispatched for that Settlement with Supplies through Torres Straits; and, as she must return to this South about, as it is termed, she cannot be expected here in a shorter period than three Months".

As to the Whale Fishery, to which Major Lockyer alludes, or the measures necessary for the preservation of the Seals, which abound on the southern coast, I have in fact given no attention to the Subject, being without means of carrying into effect any measures which it might be deemed expedient to adopt. I now beg to State to Your Lordship that I shall consider it my duty to continue the Settlement at King George's Sound until I am honoured with Your Lordship's Commands.

I have, &c.,
Ra. Darling.[22]

A New South Wales Report on the New Settlement - 1827

Newspapers in the colony of New South Wales were keen to keep their readers abreast of events as they unfolded over the years at King George's Sound with great regularity. They in turn relied on first-hand accounts and despatches from those officers and men returning from there. The first accounts based on Major Lockyer's reporting and his subsequent return to Sydney were communicated via *The Sydney Gazette and New South Wales Advertiser* newspapers in April 1827. An extract from that paper stated:

The brig, Amity, sailed from Sydney on the 9th of November last, with Major Lockyer, of the 57th regiment, as Commandant, a detachment of 20 of the 39th, twenty-three prisoners, and a surgeon, to form a settlement at this place. After experiencing much bad weather and contrary winds, during which, the brig touched at Georgetown, and having suffered severely in a gale at Storm Bay, came up to Hobart town to refit on the 1st December; the party arrived safe at King George's Sound, and anchored in Princess Royal Harbour, about a mile from the shore, on the 25th of the same month. The vessel was piloted into this noble basin by Lieutenant Festing of the Fly; it is nine miles in circumference, with a narrowing entrance from the east. On landing, they were met by two natives and a boy, who came up without the slightest hesitation. Major Lockyer immediately proceeded to explore the country, in order to find the most eligible situation for a town…

…On entering the harbour, Major Lockyer had observed a fire on Michaelmas Island, and as if from persons in distress. A boat was accordingly dispatched to the place and four natives were found upon the island in a miserable situation, having been left there sometime before, by a party of sealers. On the same day [December 27] a watering party from the brig [Amity] on the main were surprised by a number of natives lying in ambush, and one man, Dennis Dineen, had three spears stuck in him, inflicting very severe wounds so as to endanger his life. Fortunately, one of the party having gone to bathe, discovered the approach of the natives and gave the rest timely warning, else probably everyone would have been murdered. This attack was evidently made in

---

[22] Ibid.

consequence of the injuries the natives had received from the sealing gangs who visit these parts. By the very human and judicious measures of Major Lockyer, no other outrage has been committed, and it is probable that a good and amicable understanding will, by this means, be permanently established with the natives of the territory generally.

The formation of the settlement, if it were to be attended with no other good results than affording a check to the horrid barbarities committed by the unprincipled men infesting these coasts, both against the natives and against each other, as well as the destruction of the fishing itself, will be most desirable. All the enormities recorded in our columns, for so many months back, confirmed by Major Lockyer, and we remark, that the same means of removing them are recommended as by ourselves. He describes them as a regular set of pirates conversing from island to island in open boats, along the coast from Rottnest Island to Bass's Straits, having their chief resort or den at Kangaroo Island, making occasional descents on the mainland, and carrying off by force the native men. They rob and murder each other. At Kangaroo Island a dreadful scene of villainy is going on, where, to use their own words, 'there are a great many graves.' Their numbers consist to a great measure of runaway prisoners from Sydney and Van Diemen's Land. These melancholy truths were fully corroborated by the above attack of the natives, and other incidents which occurred during the time the Amity was at anchor in the harbour.[23]

Joseph Wakefield – 1826 to 1827

While Major Lockyer's three months stay in charge of establishing the first European outpost at King George's Sound is today perhaps the most celebrated and recognised in the history books, it is to Captain Joseph Wakefield Officer-in-Command of a Detachment the 39th Dorsetshire Regiment of Foot, his successor, that the town's Historical Record must attribute a significant accolade; that of having built and guided the outpost's development into a more stable and comfortable place for both the military and crown prisoners from that first landing. Governor Darling had selected this very competent and experienced officer to be the second in command at King George's Sound and, as arranged, he became the Military Commandant and Magistrate after Major Lockyer's hurried return to Sydney in April 1827.

While Lockyer's period of command of the settlement encompassed twelve weeks during the warmer months of December to April, it was left to Captain Wakefield to ensure that a more substantial building program was undertaken given the imminent onset of the winter period. It was after Lockyer's departure that the real task of building the King George's Sound outpost had truly begun.

The following extracts are drawn from a selection of letters and dispatches that Captain Wakefield reported in his roles as Military Commandant and Magistrate at King George's Sound. They were addressed to Alexander MacLeay, the New South Wales Government's Colonial Secretary in Sydney. The letter extracts from this correspondence to MacLeay gives an excellent insight into the early days of the Cantonment:

21st May 1827

Sir,
I have the honour to acquaint you that Major Lockyer set sail on 3rd April for Sydney in HMS Success, *leaving the charge of the settlement to me. Since taking this command my attention has been particularly directed towards erecting such buildings as were absolutely necessary for the health of those stationed here, and for the security of the stores, those at first put up were so extremely temporary that they are unfit to be occupied……*

The health of the people being of the first consequence, whatever is conducive to it should be most strictly attended to. We have had a few slight cases of scurvy. Of the numerous attacks of bowel complaints, all have terminated favourably excepting one (the soldier who died on 8 March). As the swampy ground immediately around the settlement is considered the chief cause of this last complaint being so exceedingly prevalent, I have lost no time in endeavouring to remedy that the evil by draining, a step also necessary to be taken before it can be bought into a state of cultivation. Thro' the centre of the marsh to the west of us, I have made a large drain about two hundred yards long and four feet deep, which, with the assistance of a few about eighteen inches deep, cut across to fall into the main one, will no doubt prove effectual. From the extreme sterility of the soil, we have completely

---

[23] *The Sydney Gazette and New South Wales Advertiser.* 20th April 1827.

failed in every endeavour to raise vegetables; this has induced me to select and clear a spot of tolerably good land for a garden on the south side of the harbour…on a part of which is a crop of turnips that at present looks remarkably well…

In order to obtain fresh provisions, I occasionally send to an island about four leagues to the eastward for Mutton birds; the boat generally returns with two days' supply for the whole settlement; they are exceeding numerous, easily caught in the holes in the ground, and average about a pound each. Having been so long on salt provisions, we find them very acceptable….

The brig Ann *(Grimes, master) with horses from Timor for Sydney, last from Melville Island, anchored here on Thursday; he reports the settlement to have been very short of provisions when the* Isabella *reached it. The Commandant there has employed that vessel to convey cattle from Timor, and she may be expected here on her return to Sydney in about two months. Mr Grimes has given us a few sickles, which were much wanted for cutting rushes for thatch, etc., and also several other things that will be very useful to the settlement. I have been able to get from the ship several boatloads of stable manure, which will ensure to us a few vegetables, and am gathering a quantity of seaweed for the same purpose; this is merely mentioned to assure you that no exertion of my part shall be wanting to establish a good garden. From the barrenness of the land here, I should conceive it absolutely necessary to form the farming establishment on the south side of the harbour, where the soil is much better. It is of a dark brown colour, and, at the depth of eighteen inches, limestone appears. The woods are small and not numerous, but the timber tolerably large. The plains are not very extensive, less swampy than that about the settlement, with but little herbage. It is very hilly and chiefly limestone. Horn cattle may thrive, goats and swine do remarkably well, but I fear sheep cannot succeed until grasses are introduced…*

In justice to the prisoners, I cannot close my letter without acquainting you that they are remarkably orderly and well behaved.

10th July 1827.

Sir,
… I am sorry to report the loss of prisoner John Brown, the Gardner, who died on 29 May. We were beginning to suffer much from scurvy; but by eating freely of the mallows which grew abundantly on some of the islands, all are now fast recovering. Our gardens are certainly improving, but we shall not at present derive much benefit from them. The stock thrives very well; a very great improvement has taken place in the sheep since they were removed to the south side of the harbour…

19th August 1827.

Sir,
I am happy in being able to make a more favourable report of this settlement that has hitherto been transmitted to you. Our sheep are thriving remarkably well, and the pigs are in excellent store condition. In addition to the 10 old pigs, I have been able to reserve some of the finest young ones, which I hope will soon add greatly to the increase of our stock. When the Amity *arrived, our flour and salt provisions had been exhausted some days, and we were upon half a pint of oatmeal per day, which, with mallows, Mutton birds and fish, we managed tolerably well. By the free use of the above vegetable, scurvy has almost entirely disappeared and thank God we are now all comfortable and in perfect health with the exception of a few who are triflingly indisposed. I am using every endeavour to raise vegetables for the settlement, and expect fully to succeed in about three months…*

Green Island, Oyster Harbour, has been planted with cabbages and lettuce seeds have been sown on it; the soil is shallow but very good, and they appear to grow tolerably well. There is no doubt melons, cucumbers and pumpkins will thrive there when the season for planting them arrives….

I beg to mention to you that the brig Amity *made the Sound on 22 July. I sent the pilot on board to assist in bringing her into the harbour, but the wind being contrary they let go of the anchor in the Sound. In consequence of the gross neglect of the chief mate, the cable was not secured to the vessel, so it ran completely out; a gale of wind came on, the ship was driven to sea, we saw no more of her for 17 days. It has proved of serious loss to us, for the whaleboat belonging to the settlement was carried away and a cow and several sheep died before her return.*

20th June 1828.

> *Sir,*
> *I have the honour to acquaint you that I have been on a short excursion into the interior; the object in view was to ascertain the course of the French River* [Kalgan] *and then proceed to mountains about 30 miles north by east of the settlement, running from east to west and called by the natives "Purrengorep", that I might be able to report on the nature of the country within that distance. On 17 March, Mr Tallemache, myself, one soldier, three natives and four prisoners, with five days provisions, sailed in the whaleboat from the settlement and proceeded up the French River... After landing we continued along the banks of it for about four miles, when we halted for the night... On the following morning about eleven o'clock, we reached the base of these mountains and halted for the day. Mr Tallemache, myself and one black immediately ascended them and observed a range* [later named Stirling Ranges] *beyond running near nearly parallel, and which I consider to be distant about ten miles. They and the valley between them and us appeared extremely barren. The country as far as the eye could reach to the eastward was one continued swamp, in which we could perceive four lakes, which our guide said were of saltwater; the most distant one was considered to be about fifteen miles off.*
>
> *On the 20th, we took a south-south-west direction, and, after a fatiguing march, halted for the night a mile north of a small mountain called by the natives "Woolyongup"* [Willyung] *and about nine miles from the settlement. The following day we reached home. The soil on Mount Purrengorep is very rich but thickly interspersed with blocks of granite; the timber is remarkably lofty and fine and consistent chiefly of gum, Apple tree, two kinds of box, and turpentine. The rest of the country over which we travelled is extremely barren, the soil very sandy similar to the neighbourhood of the settlement with small, stunted trees...*
>
> *The natives are represented to be numerous, but very friendly disposed towards us. We have never seen them, but they have heard of us and would not attempt to injure us. In the summertime when water becomes scarce, they retire to the banks of the river and lake. They also say that the rich land extends further than they have any knowledge of the country. I am inclined to give much credit to this statement and think is very probable that the good land they speak of extends to the Swan River.*[24]

The often-delayed re-provisioning of the Sound was a cause of much concern to Captain Wakefield during his tenure as Commandant. His exasperated correspondence outlining the problems is perhaps best summed up from this line of postscript to correspondence sent to Alexander MacLeay:

> *No clothing having arrived for the prisoners. I am fearful they will be in a state of perfect nudity before supply is received.*[25]

George Sleeman – 1828 to 1829

Lieutenant George Sleeman also of the 39th Regiment of Foot gained command over the settlement on the departure of Captain Wakefield on 6th December 1828. He retained the position until 3rd December 1829. Under his jurisdiction, King George's Sound continued as a penal settlement, with the settlement's building program continuing and in the twelve months he was commandant he was responsible for making the settlement more productive and self-sufficient. With a more stable settlement, Lieutenant Sleeman was able to devote some of the resources available to him to foster food collection (mutton birds, eggs, etc) and to disperse sealing expeditions to collect their oil and skins. It was on one of these hunting activities that a longboat was lost. Lieutenant Sleeman reports the incident:

> *I sent five men in her about two months ago to procure some soil for the use of the settlement and being tempted by success and a fair wind they went further than I intended and landed on an island called by the sealers, "Friendly Island" but as there was no water there two of the men were sent in the boat to the mainland to get some, endeavouring to do this the boat was wrecked by the surf. One of the three men left on the island swam to the mainland a distance of about a mile and a quarter and returned to the settlement before the two who had landed in the boat. I succeeded in getting the other men back to safety and also the materials of the old boat.*

---

[24] A selection of letters in dispatches from Captain Joseph Wakefield, 39th Dorsetshire Regiment on Foot, Second Military commandant and Magistrate at the King George's Sound Cantonment addressed to Alexander MacLeay, New South Wales Government Colonial Secretary in Sydney. *Despatches and Papers Relating to the Settlement of the States. Western Australia.* The Historical Records of Australia, Sydney.
[25] Ibid.

Except for the fur skins the others are of comparatively little value. There are twelve fur skins but only eleven of them perfect, one of which I gave to the Sergeant at this place [Sergeant Hoops] for his exertions in trying to get the men in from the island; another two major Harley and four with the defective one I have used myself. The remaining five are now in my possession which with those that I have used or given away I will replace.... In my accountantship, if his Excellency should be pleased to so direct.[26]

Lieutenant Sleeman was eventually replaced as Commandant of the settlement by Captain Collet Barker of the 39th Regiment of Foot in 1829. Travelling with Captain Barker to the Sound onboard the ship *Governor Phillip* was an exceptional surgeon, Dr Thomas Braidwood Wilson, who was passing through the fledgling settlement on his way to New South Wales. It was thanks to Dr Wilson's accounts of his observations and explorations that we are provided with the next instalment of the development of the settlement, and further a greater insight into the Aboriginal peoples and their culture as well as detailed descriptions of the area and its hinterland.

Thomas Braidwood Wilson - Surgeon, Superintendent and Keen Explorer - 1829

Between 1822-1829 Dr Thomas Braidwood Wilson was the Surgeon-Superintendent on British convict and immigrant ships travelling to Australia. It was during this time at sea that he became a member of the Royal Geographical Society. He was the author of a *Narrative of a Voyage Round the World* in which he recorded aspects of his visit to King George's Sound.[27] Dr Wilson extensively explored the settlement's hinterland, including the Plantagenet, Elleker and the Porongurup regions and provided one of the most informative records of the area in its early years of European occupation. Dr Wilson's journal of these explorations formed part of his work that was later published in London in 1835.

While Dr Wilson's extensive report on his excursions and explorations of the hinterland of the King George's Sound, as well as the Plantagenet and Denmark areas makes for excellent reading, nonetheless, only a couple of extracts from his lengthy report are presented here to give a flavour of his adventures and insight into the land surrounding the settlement during the settlement's infancy:

29th November 1829.
At noon on the 29th November 1829, we anchored in King George's Sound, within a mile of the entrance of Princess Royal Harbour. Shortly afterwards, we were boarded by a boat from the settlement, by which we learned that the Amity had sailed for Sydney, that the schooner Admiral Clifford had arrived a month ago, and that great fears had been entertained regarding our safety...

Captain Barker and I went on shore to breakfast with him [Commandant at the time Lieutenant Sleeman]. *The settlement was very healthy, not so short of provisions as we had imagined, and they had an abundance of vegetables.*

On our return, we walked to the summit of Mount Melville, whence we had a very extensive view of the surrounding country, which bore a decided resemblance to the land about Cape of Good Hope when viewed from the top of Table Mountain. A range of mountains extending from the north-west to the north-east, about the same distance from Mountain Melville as the Hottentot mountains are from Table Mountain. Another tier was observed to the westward, evidently the coast range; between these, there appeared to be level land, and thither I determined to make an excursion, during the time the brig remained in the harbour: as I had been informed by the Commander at eight or ten days would be required to caulk her and make the other repairs absolutely necessary before she proceeded on her voyage....

On making known my intention to take a little trip into the interior, Lieutenant Sleeman [who had not yet resigned command] *offered me the assistance of any crown prisoners I might wish, to carry provisions, etc, and also an intelligent native, Mokare who is now out shooting ducks for dinner: this I willingly excepted; and, on my reaching the camp, made arrangements for starting on Wednesday morning.*

---

[26] Ibid.
[27] Wilson, T.B. *Narrative of a Voyage Around the World.* London, 1885.

Mokare expressed much willingness to accompany me, and I was further gratified by Mr [John] Kent, the officer in charge of the commissariat, expressing a wish to join the party.[28] A soldier, of the 39th regiment, named [William] Gough [a veteran of the battle of Waterloo], who was esteemed a good bushman, volunteered, as did also two prisoners of the crown; one of whom had accompanied Mr [William] Baxter on all his botanical excursions and the other had attended the former expeditions made by Major Lockyer and Captain Wakefield...

On Wednesday morning, at daylight, we left the settlement, with the week's provisions. The only burden of Mokare was a fowling-piece, which he would not go without; and, as he was a good shot, we thought it might be of use, in procuring fresh provisions...

After having proceeded, by a native path, nearly seven miles we crossed a considerable stream, running easterly, which was supposed to be the principal branch of the King River; and about three miles further, we passed another, a smaller size, running in the same direction. We halted to the north-west of a detached hill; and, as the sun was powerful, we agreed to rest a little, and partake of some refreshment...

On Thursday, at daylight, we resumed our journey [towards Kendenup], all well; at nine o'clock we arrived at a large lagoon, where we halted, kindled a fire, and took breakfast; an empty preserved meat canister serving the double purpose of tea kettle and teapot. Being refreshed by a cup of strong tea and a cold bath in the lagoon, we renewed our journey, to the westward. In a short time, we perceived an extensive sheet of water, a few hundred yards on our right: from appearances, we judged that this was permanent, which supposition Mokare confirmed by informing us, that the natives came hither when, from long-continued drought, the smaller and shallow lagoons were dried up...

At eleven o'clock, we crossed a mountain stream, running to the southward, through a valley where the land assumed a more fertile appearance than that which we had hitherto passed over, which was either barren scrub or swampy ground. At six o'clock p.m. we arrived at another stream, running also to the south-westward, where we took up our quarters for the night...

Mr Kent and myself took a walk for some distance along the banks of this pleasant stream: we observed that its banks were covered with luxuriant grass, sprinkled with the yellow buttercup, which put us in mind of home.[29] The alluvial soil, however, extends no greater distance; but the gently swelling, lightly wooded adjacent hills are well adapted for sheep walks, and this is the more desirable, as, in all my excursions, in the vicinity of Swan River, I saw very little pasturable land.

On Friday morning... we turned to the eastward, to gain the summit of a hill perceived in that direction, for the purpose of getting a few bearings and obtaining a view of the surrounding landscape. Having left the situation, we altered our course and walked about 8 miles, over a tract of scrubby barren land. We then arrived at a swampy flat, where there being good water, we stopped, and dined. In the evening, we encamped near a stream through land bearing considerable resemblance, both in appearance and quality, to the cow pastures in the country of Camden, in New South Wales. We saw several flocks of kangaroos; and as Mokare had previously informed us, 'not one, - not two, -not three but many in a flock,'...[30]

Some days later Dr Wilson's report continued:

We were now nearly 70 miles, in a north-westerly direction, from the settlement, in the country well adapted either for pastoral or agricultural purposes; and I regretted, exceedingly, that want of time compelled me to make it the "ne plus ultra" of my excursion northward, where, I am convinced, the same kind of land exists, to a great extent.

On Sunday at daylight, we resumed our journey west, through the valley, which bought marks of being occasionally overflowed. We had not proceeded far when my eyes were saluted with the cry of the young man who was following close behind me, "Oh Dr! you are a gone man! A snake has hold of you!" I jumped

---

[28] John Kent was on route to assume command of the King George's Sound Commissariat, however, he proved inefficient and bothersome according to Captain Barker.
[29] Wilson, T.B. *Narrative of a Voyage Around the World*. London, 1885.

forward; and then, turning around beheld the ancient enemy of the human race, rearing its hateful form above the grass, and hissing defiance. It was soon dispatched, although I, having trod on it, was the aggressor. He caught me on the outside of the right knee, but my trousers being wide, fortunately, the bite did not reach my skin. This narrow escape caused some reflection; I thought it would have been a lamentable termination of my career – after having escaped the perils of shipwreck [Dr. Wilson had been shipwrecked twice] *– to perish by the bite of a black snake, in the wilds of New Holland....*

On Wednesday, at daylight, we proceeded in a southerly direction, through a country in general barren, but not altogether destitute of patches of very good land. About nine o'clock, perceiving a high, conical, insulated hill, we directed our course thither, passing through a rich valley, of considerable extent, where the dogs caught a kangaroo. About one pm, we halted close to a pebbly stream, which rushed, with impetuosity, through the bottom of a deep, narrow glen, where the trees were of enormous circumference and altitude. This being a delightful spot, it was agreed to pitch our encampment, and remain until morning, to allow such as required it, to take a little rest.

Being anxious to obtain a panoramic of the country, which could be advantageously seen from the top of the mountain, I determined to ascend it; and, accompanied by Mr Kent and Mokare, started from our encampment at four p.m., and reached its highest pinnacle by half-past six, when we enjoyed a prospect that more than repaid all our fatigue. The highest peak just north of Denmark is about thirty yards square, perfectly level, paved with minute particles of quartz and granite, and a huge block of the latter material adorns each angle. We observed the smoke from our encampment, hovering over the trees, far beneath us to the westward; and Mokare, who would much rather have been below, eating kangaroo, than admiring the sublime and beautiful from the top of the mountain, was very urgent in his entreaties for us to descend; and, at length, his wishes were complied with...

On Friday, at daybreak, we started; and Mokare, having gotten on known ground, now lead the way. After having travelled four hours, at a pretty brisk pace, we arrived at a river, upwards of 50 yards wide, and apparently deep, flowing slowly to the southward. We walked along its right bank, and, in a short time, reached its mouth, we observed that it poured its waters into the inlet [later named Wilson Inlet by Captain Stirling to honour Dr Wilson]. *Unfortunately, a bar of sand runs across it, – there were not more than eighteen inches or two feet of water, where we passed over; immediately inside, there is from three to seven feet water, and, at a little distance up, the river becomes deeper. I considered this termination of the mountain stream, where we encamped after the third day's journey. It was named the Hay, in compliment to the Under Secretary of State for the Colonies.*

We then walked along the shore, for about a mile and a half, when we arrived at another river emptying its waters also into the inlet; there is also a bar across its mouth, which was, at present, nearly dry... I considered this termination of the stream which we crossed on the afternoon of the second day, where the land began to improve. It was named the Sleeman compliment to the late, Commandant of King George's Sound ...

Having arrived within a few miles of home, we halted, for the purpose of shaving, and making ourselves as tidy as a means would admit, before we entered the camp. This being done, we continued our nearly finished journey at a pretty brisk pace, about noon we reach the southwest side of Princess Royal Harbour...

The natives crowded around Mokare, eager to hear the news from a far country; and the soldiers besieged Gough for the same purpose, but he wisely declined giving them the least information until they bought him something to eat; while Mr Kent and myself did justice to Dr Davis's proffered hospitality.[31]

And a parting comment in Dr Wilson's reflections on the area:
From the top of the most elevated Hill (Kandyup), we obtained an extensive view of the Sound, and its rugged islands; the Princess Royal, and Oyster Harbours, with the various windings of Kalgan and King Rivers, through an apparently fertile country, formed a landscape, not unworthy of the pencil of Claude Lorraine.
On Sunday, December 20th, we got under weigh, and at noon left Princess Royal Harbour [for Sydney].[32]

---

[31] Ibid.
[32] Ibid.

In all Doctor Wilson and his exploratory party had covered in excess of 320 kilometres, approximately 200 miles through country previously unknown to Europeans.

As a footnote to history, it is indeed sad that Dr Thomas Braidwood Wilson who had undertaken such an important exploration of King George's Sound and its hinterland areas was to later take his own life after a bout of depression at Braidwood on his farm that he had established in the Southern New South Wales district that today bears his name. He was only 51 years old.

Collet Barker - 1829 to 1831

On his way to King George's Sound Captain Barker of the 39th Regiment of Foot first visited the Swan River Settlement and had a meeting with Lieutenant-Governor James Stirling. It was there that it was likely that informed of the intention to incorporate the management of the King George's Sound settlement under the authority of the fledgling Swan River Colony. Stirling had voiced his disapproval of having a military post in Western Australia that was receiving its commands from the Governor of New South Wales. Consequently, he was able to remedy that situation by agitating for its removal and transfer of all decisions relating to King George's Sound to the new colony of Western Australia. The annexation of the King George's Sound settlement by the Swan River Colony was announced in the Government Notice of March 7, 1831:

Proclamation
It having been notified to the Lieutenant-Governor that His Majesties government has been pleased to direct the troops and convicts heretofore stationed at King George's Sound to be withdrawn and that settlement to be henceforth considered part of this colony, notice of the same to all whom it may concern is hereby given.

With the view of affording the settlers actually resident in the settlement and opportunity to exchange any grant they may at present hold in it for a similar extent of land in the southern districts annexed to this colony as aforesaid, the Lieutenant-Governor has directed the Surveyor General to receive until the last day of this month, and not after, all applications for permission to effect such changes, and the Surveyor-General has been further directed to afford to persons desirous of making application for that purpose full information as to the form of such applications and also as to the term upon which permissions will be granted.
James Stirling, Lieutenant-Governor
Perth, March 7, 1831.[33]

Accordingly, it could be assumed that Captain Barker on hearing this news did not anticipate that his stay in the Sound would be a lengthy one.[34]

Barker was accompanied to the settlement at King George's Sound by his friend Dr Thomas Wilson, whose explorations and reflections have previously been recounted. In correspondence, Barker conveyed to Wilson his own impressions of King George's Sound.

Dear Mr Wilson,
Anxious as I was when you left us, to set at rest the question of the western harbour, various circumstances prevented my setting out to examine it, till the third instant, when I proceeded with your old party, Mr Kent being very desirous of seeing out his adventure in that quarter. I had long since, however, learnt from Mokare, that the entrance to the inlet would only admit of boats, and the event is another confirmation of the general accuracy of the natives. I can only give you a hasty outline of our journey, as I found a government vessel here on my return, and have besides, been occupied by some tedious magisterial business.

On 3rd February, we started at six am, and avoiding your sandhills, by keeping to the right of the lagoons, stopped to breakfast at the end of eight or nine miles, on the banks of a river five yards broad, and nearly as many feet deep, which Mokare said divided above into three small streams, and came from no great distance. Five miles further, he pointed over some wooded hills on our left, to where you had slept the night before your return, soon after which we got on a plain, where for about a mile the soil (a reddish and black loam with clay

---
[33] *The Perth Gazette*. Perth. 7th March 1831.
[34] In March 1831 the military aspect of the Albany settlement was closed, and Captain Barker left onboard *Isabella*.

underneath), might perhaps be made something of; but except here, it was indifferent throughout the day; the rising grounds wooded and strewn with ironstone, the hollows and flats open and sandy. Mokare being unwell, and lagging much behind, we halted for the night, after going seventeen or eighteen miles, at a swamp where the water was very good...

Beyond the Hay, we found some very fine blue gum, though the soil was not apparently rich. The bay expands considerably, as you imagined, on the north shore, but not on the south. We followed its different windings, from the difficulty of getting over the points of land, where was often an almost impenetrable underwood, and about ten miles of not very straight course bought us from the Hay to the mouth of the 'Denmark', about forty yards wide, deep, with a muddy bottom, and little or no stream. We were obliged to make a considerable detour into the inlet to avoid deep water and passed where it did not exceed thirty inches. Those who preceded fell in with two native women, one of them perfectly naked, each carrying a child in a bag of kangaroo skin and leading another. They were a little startled till they saw Mokare, with whom they stopped to chat a few minutes, but would not wait for me. I was then a little up the river, swimming about for the three ducks that had been shot. We proceeded two or three miles further, quitting the inlet, and halted for the night at a water hole in the bed of a small mountain stream...

... The inlet, as you approach its mouth, for a mile or two becomes shallow all the way across. The communication between it and the sea is through a break in the coastline of hills (which appeared a calcareous sandstone, like those near us), of nearly 700 yards but it is only at very high tides did the water covers this... the surf outside, at a short distance from where I passed, was very heavy, and I think no boat would be able to come in, except in very fine weather, and with the wind off the land. I do not say but that a navigable passage might be made; but where is the equivalent for the expense, for one hundred years to come? A small stream of delicious water rises near the cliff, from in the west point of the entrance, and, running a few hundred yards, falls into the inlet... I have not leisure to calculate my distance but consider it about thirty-two English miles from the settlement in a direct line.

February 8 – Crossed several dry creek beds, over an indifferent country, and two branches of the Sleeman, one dry, the other inconsiderable. We eventually got into our old track near the plain, where the soil was tolerable, the first day. We afterwards turned to the left a little and slept on one of the small branches of our first day's river – reached home in the afternoon, having given the party a great part of the day, to enable them to carry some game into the settlement; but they met with no success.

The land during the whole of my excursion was generally bad, but it could hardly be expected otherwise in the route I took. I hear continued good accounts of that in the interior, but it is now in want of water, and I find that it is usually the case two or three months in the year; wells, however, might be dug. Mokare gives me the names of tribes he has heard of to a great distance northward and says he understands that their country to be very fine, but they have no rivers. All their water is procured from the lakes or wells...[35]

As a sad footnote to history, Captain Barker left the settlement now formally named Albany, to travel to Sydney but on that journey continued to explore the southern coast from Esperance to South Australia, in particular the area from around Cape Jervis and later Encounter Bay to the mouth of the Murray River. It was while exploring the Murray River region that he was speared and killed by local Indigenous tribesmen on 30th April 1831. It is believed that they had mistaken him for one of the infamous whalers and sealers who often tormented the local inhabitants of the area.

It would appear from his diaries that Captain Barker had earlier written his own epitaph in its last entry lines of a poem drawn from Alexander Pope's poem "Ode on Solitude" which reads:

Thus, let me live, unseen, unknown;
Thus, unlamented let me dye;
Steal I from the world, and not a stone,
tell where I lye.[36]

---

[35] T.B. Wilson, *Narrative of a Voyage Round the World*. London, 1835.
[36] *Captain Collet Barker*. Compiled by W.S. Lawson. University of the Third Age. Adelaide. 2001

Thomas Bannister – 1831

Captain Thomas Bannister a British Army Officer agreed to lead an expedition from Perth to King George's Sound through a country that was entirely unknown at that time. He was accompanied on this endeavour by an assistant surveyor and two other men. The party left Perth on 14th December 1830, but it took until the 4th of February 1831 for them to reach King George's Sound. The journey had been more hazardous than was expected owing partly to the fact that the assistant surveyor's measurements and instruments provided an inaccurate reference for their location and at times had them placed well short of where they thought they were. Consequently, they became lost and were fortunate to survive the journey.

Captain Bannister reported on his journey to King George's Sound, overland to Governor Stirling:
> Sir,
>
> …. *To Mr Smythe of the Surveyor General's Department was entrusted the direction of our route. I understood he had been furnished with all that was requisite from the office, to enable him to do so. I shall take as rapid as sketch as possible of our route, remarking merely what I consider main features on it, begging leave to refer his Excellency to my journal for details, and also to the plan which Mr Smythe will furnish. I have not attempted to give any details of the mineralogical or botanical productions of the country, as, even if I were capable, it would be impossible, except by accident, to come to any Sound opinion on the former, and the latter would have required more time than we had to bestow. I have confined myself simply to the nature of the land, the timber upon it, and the rivers, etc., flowing through it, together with the bearings of a few remarkable hills. As to the trees, I have used such terms as are generally known in the colony, with a view that the details in the journal, if thought worth reading, might be clearly understood by all… making the Canning, as I knew we should do so in several places, and also that we might cross the Darling Range quickly, we took a south-east course, and passed the range from the summit of Saint Anne's Hill in two days, travelling only about 20 miles. These hills are exceedingly rugged, but on them the finest timber, known in the colony by the name of mahogany; in some of the valleys some tolerably good soil, of a light hazel colour, with an abundance of herbage, fit for cattle on their way from a good interior country to the coast; on the uplands ironstone, with a little gravel and scrub.* [37]
>
> *Arriving on the eastern side of the range in the evening of the 18th, I was induced, seeing a hilly though lower country before us, to continue our route to the south-east, in the hope of entering on those extensive planes of which Mr [Richard] Dale and others have spoken so favourably, as being a few miles more to the northward; we, therefore, pursued the south-east course until 23 December…*
>
> *The character of the country through which we had passed, was generally not so good as I had hoped to have seen, but there were not wanting tracks of excellent land – that for upwards of six miles broad, for instance, as mentioned in the Journal of 19 December;- and as it is a country in which there is a great deal of food for stock, I would by no means condemn it; on the contrary, my impression was, on closer examination, there will be found available land to a considerable extent to the west and east, in both of which directions the watercourses tended generally, and in their courses, the soil was generally a very fair brown…*
>
> *From the 23rd to 5th January we pursued a south by east course for eighty or ninety miles of actual distance, though, in many tracks, a country which surpassed our most sanguine expectations; a very great proportion of this tract was land of the first description, fit for the plough, sheep, or cattle. The beauty of the scenery near to, and distant from, the rivers which we crossed, is equal to any I have seen in the most cultivated timbered country, in those parts of Europe which I have happened to pass through. The character of the country generally is undulating with here and there moderately high hills, some of them crowned with rocks of granite, pudding-stone rocks, and a bluestone; but there are broad flatlands and valleys, the former of which, as will be seen in the Journal, not infrequently extended several miles, even in some places far beyond our power to ascertain…*
>
> *As by Mr Smythe's observations we were to the east of King George's Sound, it was deemed necessary to proceed more westerly. By his observations we were quite near to our destination, but experience proved that his observations were erroneous and that our travelling had been greatly overrated… we were then, owing to the difficulty, it being mountainous and the underwood extremely thick, obliged to bear away to the south by west,*

---

[37] The Western Australian Jarrah has a rich reddish-brown colour like that of mahogany wood.

which course we pursued for a day and a half, making 16 miles and a half; thence coming to some granite rocks, and seeing from the high mountains, three of which, were conical and of considerable altitude, one of them had two bear heads, - and Mr Smyth being of opinion that this two-headed mountain was to the north of King George's Sound – we directed our steps towards it, halting for the night on the banks of a considerable river flowing to the south.

The following morning, 12th January on reaching it, left the men and ascended to the summit, from which nothing satisfactory could be seen; as far as the eye could reach, was one vast forest... The intermediate country presented occasional open valleys, winding between apparently moderately high hills to the eastward; in the distance, we saw high hills or mountains; behind the southern hills, we hope to come to the sea, a matter now of great importance to us, as our provisions were nearly expended; we, therefore, seeing as we imagined, through the smoke and haze, sandhills bearing south-west by west, directed our steps towards them, until the evening of the following day, making seventeen miles, when, not finding the hills we had hoped to have reached, returned due south, determined to pursue it, until I came to the sea, as, from whatever cause, I was almost certain that we were long a distance from King George's Sound, and that consequently, our provisions being all expended, with the exception of tea for twelve days, and a little tobacco, our very existence depended on procuring shellfish from the rocks. Shooting birds was very uncertain, and kangaroos more so.

On the 16th we made the coast, having for the last day, traversed as rough a country as can be imagined... Mr Smythe attributes the mistakes in his observations to his not having a watch, and partly to the instruments with which he was furnished from his office, being out of order. He will, I trust, be able to give a satisfactory explanation to his Excellency....

We had now been absent from Fremantle thirty-three days; we had halted, on account of our horses, six days, and had made, on some days, very little headway, on one occasion only three miles. We reached the coast, therefore, in twenty-seven days travelling; had we not turned off on the 5th January, I have not a doubt but that we should have reached our destination in 28 days including our six days halt, since we should soon have entered upon the country described by Dr Wilson, and we should have escaped a most difficult march to the coast, and also the disasters and sufferings to which we were exposed while on the coast for 19 days without provisions, and for several days before we reached it... I shall not trouble his Excellency with a long detail of our sufferings; I shall merely state; that we were on the coast for 19 days, depending entirely upon shellfish for subsistence; sometimes, where we found them and the surf was not too great, we fared pretty well. The delay this mode of procuring subsistence occasioned, together with the exceeding bad travelling of our horses [two of which, on arrival on the coast, we are very nearly exhausted, they had but little to carry], was very great, and the fatigue excessive, so that by the time we arrived at King George's Sound, we were all nearly exhausted, though we were able the last day, through the friendly aid of the natives, who showed us the path, to walk twelve miles...

On 4 February we arrived here. I have not words to convey to his Excellency the great kindness and friendship of which we stood in the greatest need with which we were received by Captain Colette Barker, the Commandant and officers of the settlement...

From what I have written, it will be concluded, and justly so, that there is a body of available land, with certain extensive tracts of the richest description, fit for the plough, sheep, or cattle or indeed any cultivation in the interior, commencing about twenty-five or thirty miles from King George's Sound, which, under a judicious system of colonization, the main roads being made in the first instance by forced labour, would, in the course of a few years, be inhabited by thousands of industrious men, sent out by the parishes of England, Scotland, or Ireland, or bought out by individuals bettering their condition as well as relieving their country. [38]

On his return to Perth Captain Bannister provided Lieutenant-Governor Stirling RN, with an updated and quite valuable report on the journey to King George's Sound. Stirling was indeed impressed by Banister's efforts and commended his efforts in a letter to the Colonial Office.

---

[38] Joseph Cross. *Journals of Several Expeditions Made in Western Australia...Under the sanction of the Governor, Sir James Stirling, Containing the Latest Authentic Information Relevant to that Country*. London, 1833.

James Stirling – 1831

Finally, Sir, at a time when we have one French Vessel of War in these seas...we hear of an American Vessel of War being in the neighbourhood, seeking a place for a Settlement, it has become important to prevent them from occupying a position of such value...

James Stirling R.N.,
To the Governor of New South Wales.
14th December 1826.

In 1827 after visiting King George's Sound, which did not impress him. Stirling reported to Governor Darling at great length that he believed that the Swan River was far better situated to accommodate a naval and military settlement on the west coast of Australia. To this end in May 1827, he applied to the Colonial Office seeking an appointment as Superintendent of the settlement at the Swan River. Stirling's initial application was subsequently rejected, Nonetheless, after applying again in November of the following year the commission he sought was granted to form a settlement at Swan River by the newly elected British Government.

Fortunately, one of the passengers on board *HMS Success* with Stirling during this first visit was Augustus H. Gilbert the ship's clerk, and he provided a further perspective of the visit of the *HMS Success* to King George's Sound in 1827:

We sailed from Sydney on Wednesday, 17th January, having on board as passengers Mr Fraser, Colonial Botanist, and Mr Garling, of Sydney, in company with a cutter attached to the Success by the Governor, for the purpose of being employed in surveying the coast and to carry provisions to King George's Sound, where an infant settlement has been formed, and which I shall speak of in the course of my letter...

We shaped a course for King George's Sound, and after having been beating for several days to windward off Cape Leeuwin we, on the 2nd of April, reached our destination, and came to an anchor off the entrance of The Princess Royal Harbour.

The settlement consists of about seventy persons...they have erected several little cottages, or rather huts, made of wood and plastered with mud, but even in the commandant's house the wind blows through in every part. The expectations formed of King George's Sound have by no means been realised; the soil is wretched, and with the utmost care and attention they have not hitherto been able to bring anything a few inches above the ground. The town is situated at the foot of an immense mountain. The harbour is excellent, and there is sufficient water for a three-decker up to the town. The people had only thirty days' provision at half allowance at the time we arrived, and it was thus fortunate that we touched there, for we found, to our surprise, that the cutter [the Success's tender] had not reached there. We had but a month's provisions remaining, and we had a voyage of upwards of two thousand miles to go before we could again be supplied. The captain, however, consented to give them all over a fortnight's provisions for the ship's company, and thus supplied them for two months at the same allowance.

...The natives are in other respects perfectly harmless; they have ingress and egress to any of the huts, and never attempted to take anything unless given to them. They appear to be very ill-used by the sealers, who frequent this part of the coast, by forcibly taking their women away, and shooting them for the slightest offences. Just before our arrival, the commandant had caused seven sealers to be apprehended for taking four natives to Michaelmas Island in the Sound, killing one, and leaving the others there with the evident intention of starving, and for violently taking two of their women away and landing them on some part of the mainland directly away from the tribe they belonged to. They are to be tried for murder the first opportunity that offers to bring them to Sydney. [39]

It was not surprising that in his first years of establishing the Swan River Settlement (June 1829) Lieutenant-Governor Captain Stirling initially was fully focussed on this endeavour. It kept both him, and his officers, fully occupied and therefore, unable to make an early journey to the Sound. However,

---

[39] Gilbert, A.H. *An Account of the Expedition of HMS Success* (Captain James Stirling, RN) *From Sydney to the Swan River, in 1827*. Perth, 1906.

this situation was remedied when Stirling eventually called into King George's Sound on HMS *Sulphur*, 12th November 1831.

The brig *Sulphur*'s stay at King George's Sound was short-lived as it was immediately sent to Van Diemen's Land and then Sydney to purchase additional supplies for the Swan River. Stirling was concerned about food stocks in that settlement and as a consequence, he had requested that *Sulphur* depart the next day (13th November) for Sydney to acquire the necessary provisions to remedy his concern while he remained for an additional six weeks in the King George's Sound settlement, now named Albany, after one of the many of the Duke of York's titles.[40] This extended stay was in part due to poor weather conditions in the Sound and a lack of a road to the Swan River settlement. Fortuitously, while in Albany Stirling was accompanied by the very accomplished surveyor John Septimus Roe, who used his time in the settlement to explore some of its hinterland.

During his stay, Stirling was resolved to set aside some lands for himself and subsequently, allotments were secured that included 1000 acres in the Plantagenet [Mount Barker area] area along with some areas extending towards Wilson's Inlet and Torbay to the west of the settlement totalling around 35 000 acres in total. As noted in her book "*James Stirling*", the author Pamela Statham Drew indicated that this land acquisition caused considerable consternation in the fledgling Swan River settlement, as it created the distinct impression among its settlers that Stirling was intending to make Albany the capital of Western Australia instead of the Swan River.[41] However, their fears were later allayed when he returned to Fremantle on the schooner *Ellen*.

On 7th March 1831 Albany was gazetted as part of the Swan River Colony. That same year the town was surveyed, and blocks of land were sold to free settlers. Convicts in the settlement were returned to New South Wales if they had at that point had not completed their sentences. In 1831 Governor Stirling officially named the settlement Albany, and that same year, Surveyor-General John Septimus Roe announced the first private land allocations, both town, semi-rural and rural land.

Alexander Collie R.N. - First Government Resident – 1831 to 1832

Dr Alexander Collie accompanied Lieutenant-Governor James Stirling, to Western Australia's Swan River Colony in 1829 aboard the *Sulphur*. In 1831, Collie was appointed as Justice of the Peace and became Albany's first Government Resident Magistrate.[42]

During his stay, he established what became a lifelong friendship with Mokare, the Menang Aboriginal leader who had already been of significant assistance as a guide to many of the early explorers of the King George's Sound. Dr Collie's 1831 explorations of the Albany hinterland were conducted with Mokare by his side. It was not surprising, therefore, that he was saddened by Mokare's death on 9th August 1831, having recorded that Mokare was:

> "*labouring under such organic disease and so much reduced in flesh and strength as to preclude him from recovery.*" [43]

Suffering from ill-health (tuberculosis) himself he returned to Perth from Albany to take up an appointment at the Swan River Colony as Colonial Surgeon which he did from 1833 to 1835. Due to worsening ill health however, he decided to return to England. He died before he left Western Australia and his body was returned to King George's Sound on 8th November 1835 with his specific request to be buried beside Mokare, his Aboriginal exploring companion and friend was initially complied with. Unfortunately, the

---

[40] Frederickstown had, as indicated, never gained traction as a name and suggestion was dismissed in 1827 by Governor Darling in NSW. The settlement was referred to as King George's Sound in most despatches written between 1827 and 1831.
[41] P.S. Drew. *James Stirling*. University of Western Australia Press. 2003.
[42] Cross, J. (Ed) *Journals of Several Expeditions made in Western Australia during the Years 1829, 1830, 1831 and 1832*. London.1833.
[43] *Letters with Respect to the Early History of The Swan River Settlement*. Presented to the Parliamentary Library of the Commonwealth. 1912.

graves of both Collie and Mokare were disturbed during the construction of the Albany Town Hall and surrounding area in 1887.[44]

Dr Collie's reports on his explorations were very detailed and extensive. Some pertinent extracts from them are presented here:

> *I departed, early on the 27th of April* [1831], *from the settlement, by boat, with three attendants, Mokare, and two privates of the 63d Regiment. On reaching the entrance of Oyster Harbour, the tide being very low, I spent some time in sounding the bar, which I found I could cross in not less than two fathoms; and I think I am quite safe in stating this to be the most water there is at the same height of the tide. Inside the bar, in the narrowest part of the entrance, I could not help remarking the facilities presented by nature, for repairing vessels, and for loading and unloading, by the great depth of water, for (three to five fathoms) to within five to seven fathoms of the sandy and rocky beach on the right-hand going in. It is at this spot that wells have been dug, and vessels watered. These wells are close to the beach, and although partly filled up at present, and much overshadowed by vegetation, they contain good water; not, however, in such abundance as to overflow.*
>
> *In directing my course to the French River, for which the natives have two names, Ya-mung-up, and Hal-gan-up, and the mouth of which lies on the northward part of Oyster Harbour, in a line with Mount Clarence and Bayonet Head, I was obliged to keep well to the north on account of the extensive and very shallow flats, which prevent a boat approaching it in anything like a direct course, from the middle of the harbour. By making a considerable detour, a channel can be followed of sufficient width for boats, and about eight feet deep, into the river, where the depth is also adequate to boat navigation.*
>
> *In ascending the river, the channel lies in a northerly direction, with moderate windings to the east and west, for about two miles and a half, its breadth varying from two hundred to fifty yards, and altogether narrowing, as the distance from the mouth increases. In three or four places, it is contracted still more by the rocky islets, either destitute of or covered with trees. The banks are generally shelving, with a few flats occasionally intervening, but they did not appear to have much to recommend them, and two or three small creeks, which I observed to run back, were, by Mokare's account, salt.*
>
> *The mahogany and red gum, of Perth, (the tyarreil and marré of the natives here) are predominant and clothe, but in little stateliness, the low and the rising banks. At the distance I have mentioned, (two miles and a half) a streamlet of freshwater joins from the S.W., flowing, as I afterwards ascertained, between two heights of unequal elevation. The lowest one, which is on the N.W. side, is of very excellent soil, (about fifty acres) covered with thick, but at present, dried up grass, and very slightly wooded with red gum. The most elevated on the S.E. side is of tolerable soil, (about 100 acres) a gravelly light brown loam, rather thinly wooded with the same species. The direction of the river, ascending from this place, is, on the whole, N.E., making considerable and rapid windings for about two miles and a quarter, although the direct distance cannot be more than one mile and a quarter, to the farthest part a boat can go. The breadth diminishes a little, and the channel is almost blocked up in several places, by small islands, and rocks underwater.*
>
> *The former aspect of the banks continues, except on the left, (the right hand going up) nearly half a mile beyond the fresh streamlet already mentioned, where there is a very pleasing and gentle declivity, thickly covered with dried kangaroo grass, some green wattle (the broomlike), and distant (by distant, I mean eight yards apart) trees of good size, of red gum. It is needless to tell those conversant with this colony, that the soil producing such vegetation, is of the best description. It extends 350 yards from the river and about 700 along with it. Fresh streamlets become more frequent, but the river itself continues, at present, brackish, to the stopping place.*
>
> *The stoppage is occasioned by the bed of the river being elevated by rocks, over which the water flows, in a small and rapid stream. A few yards farther on, the channel is again capacious,—the water deep,—and continues in this state, occasionally obstructed by fallen trees, for nearly a mile, when an impediment to the former presents itself; and, although it is of short space, and the river widens and deepens above it, I consider all hope of rendering*

---

[44] Collie's remains were subsequently interred at the Pioneer Cemetery in Albany.

the navigation farther up available, to be finally destroyed, by a third and longer similar stoppage to the two first, about half a mile beyond the second.

Leaving the boat, and also the river, at the first of these obstacles, I took a direction N.E., which led me on the eastern side of the river, and almost immediately within sight of its bed. At the distance of three-quarters of a mile, I crossed a tolerable sized stream running to my left, consequently, to join the French River; it seemed well adapted for driving mills.

After proceeding N.E. six miles and three quarters, the course was changed to N. ½ W. for a mile, then to N.W. by W. for half a mile farther, down a hollow, to obtain water and stop for the night. This hollow appeared to descend to the bed of French River, the outline of which could be traced at a short distance to the N.W. From an adjoining elevation, the eastern of two conspicuous hummocks of Porrangur-up, bore N.W. ½ W., and the eastern, apparently highest shoulder of the same mountain, N. W. ½ N. The surface walked over is slightly uneven; the elevated portions, which constitute five-sixths, are either sandy or stony, producing a tolerably close covering of low shrubs, and a rather thick wooding of mahogany and casuarina (possibly she-oak) *trees, the former of small size, and both much decayed and fallen; the depressed portions are a mixture of black sod and sand, in various proportions; swampy in the rainy season, producing no trees, a shrubby melalencat, a rushy vegetation, which will pasture cattle, but which is void of the soft succulency of good grass. The rock which protrudes, and, by its fragments, forms a general covering, in many places is of a clayey nature, of considerable hardness, produced by the exposure, and increased, perhaps, by the fires, with which the natives seem to have repeatedly consumed the vegetable productions. It seemed to penetrate the ground to a very small depth, and it never forms large blocks.*

Morning of the 28th

I followed a north course for a mile, then an N.N.E. one for one-fifth of a mile, when, being on a declivity, inclining downwards to the west, I could trace the bed of French River at its foot, a very short way off, following apparently a S.W. by W. direction, for three miles, and afterwards S. by W. one for a mile or farther. I continued N.E., E. and N.E., skirting the river, for a mile and a half, in the gently inclining slope, at first varied with sandy elevations, and rushy hollows, which appear to have been partly covered with water in the rainy season, and in some of which there are the dry channels of winter streamlets; then uniformly on a soil diversified with brownish gravel and good dark coloured earth, that has produced a very fine crop of grass now withered and beaten down. Granite, which is the prevailing rock, where the soil is good, is sometimes exposed, either in solid or bare blocks, or in fragments, so as to render the surface stony, but not to prevent a tolerable covering of grass. The extent of grassy land is about three quarters by half a mile wide, and the marri [red gum] *trees being distant from each other, and also tall, open an agreeable prospect to the view.*

After this, I went N.E. by N. half a mile, leaving the river, then N. by W. and N.W. by W. one mile over a sandy soil, with many stones of a hardened clayey nature already mentioned, producing some good-sized mahogany trees, several stunted shrubs, to a stream, either a branch or the main body of the French River, small where a current existed, but wide where none was perceptible. The place is called Kâl-um-up by Mokare. According to him, there is good ground to the N.E. three miles off, but without water in its vicinity, and his vague idea of distance decided my not going to look for it. My line of route now lay N. for one mile, and N. by E. for two more, the ground being slightly varied with ascents and descents, and showing very little good soil; afterwards a mile and three-quarters N.N.E. and half a mile N. to a river which Mokare called French River, but which could only be a branch of it, unless he was mistaken in what we afterwards followed, and what he called the main channel. Half a mile before coming to this branch, I emerged for the first time from a wooded country and enjoyed a view for several miles, W. N. and E. over slightly elevated plains, clear of trees; leaving this, and for the last quarter of a mile, I traversed a gentle acclivity, rising from the river on my right, unshaded by a tree, and bearing the remains of a most luxuriant crop of grass, and a few shrubs of green wattle. The soil is very good and only interrupted in a few spots by the protruding granite. The native name of the ground is Noor-ru-bup. As the party stopped here for the night, the examination in detail of this spot occupied me till dark.

Then later in his report, he indicated:

May 4th.

I crossed the moderate elevation that lies to the westward of our bivouac, at a short distance from the beach to the mouth of King River, and observed it to be rocky, and wooded in a great proportion with red gum. A swampy and boggy hollow separate it from the highest ground in the vicinity, on the west and north of the embouchure of the King. This hollow extends to some distance N.N.W., and contains fresh feed, even at this period of the year. After observing the considerable salt meadows on both sides of the lower part of the King, on which there is abundant produce of rushy and now dried vegetation, that might have made tolerable fodder, I proceeded up its northern or left bank in a westerly direction, without following its windings, for three miles, to a crossing place, by means of accidental tree bridges over two nearly equal streams, which, by joining a few yards below, form the main river. The ground thus passed over is chiefly sandy, with several portions of a gravelly light brown loam, intersected with several streamlets of freshwater. The trees are mostly mahogany, of slender girth, with shrubs, and the surface is free of grass.

We breakfasted on the south side of the south branch, and Mokare informed us that the ground was named Tan-num-bang-i-war. A hundred yards further up there were numerous channels leading to this branch, but all at about that; distance dry. The chief of them seems to come from Willyung-up through a slightly excavated valley, containing little shrub, and no trees larger than the Kingia Australis, similar to the grass tree, which very appropriately shades and adorns the head of its fraternal river.

In returning from the head of the King in a tolerably direct line to the settlement, I soon came to the same conspicuous granite rocks, in a watery hollow, leaving a grassy and open plain of about ten acres, and I should infer, good soil on our right I also passed a hollow of tolerable soil N. by E. two miles from Mount Melville, besides considerably rushy and green low grounds, adapted to pasturing cattle, more advantageously perhaps in the summer than winter, where they may be too swampy.

17th May

I had an opportunity of ascending the King River in a boat; towards its mouth it is shallow, and most so about three-quarters of a mile up, where the natives generally wade across. The least water we had was three feet at nearly high water, but the rise and fall seemed to be very little. Above this the depth is sufficient for boating; and the only obstructions are, scattered rocks in two or three places narrowing the channel and making it intricate (but leaving sufficient water), and fallen trees, which can easily be avoided, or might be removed with facility, until the boat reaches the point of division into twin branches, which I have mentioned to be close to where the accidental tree bridges afford a passage across. From the boat, I observed no decided indications of rich soil nor much pasture, except the salt meadows towards the mouth of the river. The first freshwater creek that I noticed is on the right bank, about two miles up (in a direct line), but freshwater abounds in the plain between this river and Mount Clarence, and a very short way farther up I found the river itself fresh.

The banks, a little way above the native's wading place, presents an inclination and height well suited to a horse-path for dragging boats; and for the purpose of landing and shipping goods, the head of King River, at the foot of Willyung-up, will afford the greatest convenience to the population of the interior...

June 15th

I went to the south side of Princess Royal Harbour and was much satisfied to find limestone in two, if not more, places, projecting in low cliffs on its shores, either close to or near, groves of trees, which will afford fuel for some years. Lime has hitherto been almost entirely procured from shells. The two large groves of trees adjoining the beach, one a little S.E. of the remarkable sandy patch, and the other about a mile and a half S.E. of this again (both denoted in the common chart), stand in good soil resting on granite, and are composed of large trees of red and blue gum, and a few mahoganies. A copious spring, formed into a convenient well, at the first affords a constant current of excellent freshwater; and a moderate-sized and rather rapid stream, at the second, not only presents the same advantage but would turn several mills. They are both to be approached by light boats, and even a deep one can go within some fathoms of the first.

The plain of considerable extent but varying in breadth between the south side of the harbour and the sea-coast range of hills, is, with little exception, destitute of large timber, but thickly covered with small shrubs, rushes, or rather scirpi, which make no despicable food for cattle, and possess the advantage of being verdant and good, throughout the protracted droughts of summer. The soil is very sandy, black loam and mould, similar to that in the hollows at the settlement, very retentive of water, and therefore, in the advanced months of winter, marshy, although at present still dry. The hills are shrubby with hollows of pasture.

The whole of this irregular tongue of land appears fitted by nature for pasturing flocks and herds of cattle, on their first importation, and one or two persons, at its western part or root, could readily prevent straying. A fresh-water lake, about four hundred yards from the S.E. extremity of the long sandy beach, that runs from the point where Mistaken Island nearly joins the mainland, round the western part of the Sound, may, at some future period, become highly advantageous as a watering place for large ships and numerous fleets. Wood for fuel is, however, here very thinly scattered.

The upper and northern part of the range of hills, looking to the plain before mentioned, often exposes, particularly on the slope, the peculiar calcareous formation of the S.W. coast, and seemed, from a superficial examination, to afford a limestone as well as the lower cliffs on the beach, freer from siliceous sand than those in the vicinity of Swan River. In the winter season, a marshy declivity, W.S.W. of Seal Island, sends streamlets of freshwater to the beach, where an American vessel once took in her water.[45]

The following year, 1832, Dr Collie continued his exploration of the hinterland around the King and Kalgan Rivers. Some further extracts of his report are presented:

February 10th

Our party set out, ascending the right bank of the Kalgan from our bivouac, which was on the elbow immediately above the upper boat stoppage, crossed the entrance of a small stream coming from our left, the same which was first passed when I had the pleasure of accompanying Mr Roe on a short exploring excursion a few weeks since; then traversed a small flat, encircled by an elevated terrace similar to the flat where we bivouacked, but distinguished from it at present by the remains of a native Hut in a good state of preservation; sometime after, and at a mile's computed distance from our bivouac, we passed the gorge of a deep gully with a dry channel in its middle, and in a few yards more the Kalgan, at a place where its waters flow over the projecting rocks of its bed. These rocks are an ironstone or flinty slate, but the banks, which rise above the river, are clay ironstone, or a ferruginous and reddish freestone. The soil passed over from the lower boat stoppage is very sandy but producing a good proportion of grasses and other herbage, and thickly wooded, for the most part with the marree [sic] or red gum. We ascended the left bank of the river, and after half a mile came to a valley and plain of fine soil and feed, having a small channel, partly dry, in which the water had flowed to the Kalgan.

We ascended a moderate elevation, and continued pursuing a N. by E. course for two miles, to a swampy valley then one mile and three-quarters N. by W., and one-quarter of a mile N.E. to a valley of tolerable soil, and a good deal of pasturage, where there was a moderate stream, and on its banks, at a common crossing place, a cheveaux-de-frise of wooden spikes, finely pointed, covered thinly with the resin of the grass-tree, and directed to each other and to the bank opposite to that in which they were fixed. They formed an angle with the plane of the horizon of about 50° or 55°, and no doubt were intended for staking kangaroo, which, being pursued on side of the stream, would select their accustomed crossing-place to evade their pursuers by gaining the other.[46]

Richard Spencer R.N. - Government Resident 1833 to 1839

Captain Sir Richard Spencer was a highly decorated and respected Naval Officer who had served under Admiral Horatio Nelson during the Anglo-French Napoleonic War and at which time he had exhibited considerable daring and acknowledged leadership skills. He was actively employed in a naval capacity until 1817. In March 1833 Spencer was pleased to accept an appointment as Government Resident of King George's Sound. His journey aboard the store ship *Buffalo* was a long journey and he arrived with his family in Albany on 3rd September 1833. Spencer had the foresight to bring with him on this venture a variety of livestock, seedlings and seeds to introduce fruits and vegetables into the settlement. He was applauded by subsequent visitors to the settlement for setting an example of enterprise accordingly.

---

[45] A. Collie, *An Account of an Excursion to the North of King George's Sound, between the 26th April, and the 4th of May, 1831.* London, 1835.

[46] Alexander Collie. *The Perth Gazette and Western Australian Journal.* Editions from 5th July 1834 to August 1834.

While his tenure in Albany lasted only six years, 1833 – 1839, it was under his somewhat autocratic leadership that Albany became a more stable settlement. Later many historians would in fact talk of his time in Albany in quite glowing terms.

Strawberry Hill, also referred to as the Government Farm in early despatches comprised some of the first lands to be cultivated in Western Australia. Major Lockyer indicated that it had excellent soil and was eminently suitable for pasture. Alexander Collie had a special interest in the strawberries grown on the farm. The original building on the site was constructed as per instruction from Governor Stirling as the Governor's summer retreat. When in March 1833 Sir Richard Spencer was appointed Government Resident, he was given the right to purchase Strawberry Hill Farm which he subsequently did.[47] In 1836 Sir Richard organised and had constructed a more substantial family dwelling at the farm. The area of the farm was originally cultivated in 1826 and become the Government Farm area supplying the early settlement on and off in its early years with much-needed vegetables.[48]

Sir Richard provided a very strong guiding hand in the town's development. He was very active on a number of issues during the town's early evolution as some excerpts from his correspondence held in the collection of Mrs Egerton Warburton, whose husband was his grandson indicated.
From a letter to a friend in the Ile of France (Mauritius):
> *You appear to be astonished that I should emigrate, what could a poor man in England do better to provide for 10 children? The best prospect I have for my eldest son was to get him the appointment of clerk in a public office, and to obtain that seemed almost impossible. I had some hopes, but the pain and annoyance of making application quite upset me, and I thought it better to make farmers of them all. The advantage of this place over the Swan is the climate. Without any exception, this is the finest in the world... I have one of the most beautiful fertile spots in the world, about 1 mile and a half from the town, and the same distance from Middleton Bay, which is in front of our windows and gives us a full view of all vessels entering the port. We have as fine a crop of wheat as ever was seen ready for reaping on New Year's Day, and we have eaten sea kale, asparagus, figs and almonds all of our growing. When you consider this was a wilderness when we arrived, and only 17 persons in the colony, you will see that we have not been idle, our sheep are now thriving wonderfully, they have only been a year and eight months at Hay, and they have trebled their number. Our inhabitants have not increased in numbers so fast as we might have hoped, and I'm sorry to say not one farmer has yet come out.[49]*

On September 13th, 1833, he indicated in correspondence to Alfred Hillman, Assistant Surveyor on the day he arrived in the settlement:
> *Having been appointed by Lord Goderich, Government Resident of this place, and having arrived with my family of nine children and 11 servants, under a promise from the Lieutenant-Governor, Sir James Stirling that I should be permitted to select a large grant of land in the immediate neighbourhood of Strawberry Hill, and having a letter from Sir James Stirling that I shall be allowed to purchase the Government Cottage and garden at a fair price, I have to request that you will be pleased to forward the necessary application to the Hon. The Surveyor-General for granting me the land specified in the form of application accompanying this letter. Having bought with me, at great expense a number of prize Merino sheep from Lord Weston's stock, with the choice breeds of cattle, etc., it is necessary that I should, as soon as possible, be put in possession of a proper place to secure and feed them.[50]*

Sir Richard Spencer's letter to The Right Reverend William Broughton, First Lord Bishop of Australia, May 25th 1837 in Sydney, concerned some interactions with some Aborigines in the settlement area. His first letter relates to the marooning of two young men by the sealer Anderson whose activities along the southern coast have already been mentioned:
> *Two years since (1835) two lads were shipwrecked about 240 miles to the east of Albany, in their long walk, for want of food, we are so reduced as to be unable to walk and could only speak in a whisper. Fortunately,*

---

[47] It was in late 1880's that it was purchased by Francis Bird. Bird, I. *The Story of Strawberry Hill, Middleton Road Albany, 1791 to 1891*. Albany, 2002.
[48] It later became known as the Old Farm.
[49] Old Time Memories. Captain Sir Richard Spencer, RN, "Founder of Albany" by D.C.C. *The Australasian*, Melbourne Saturday 5th February 1927.
[50] Richard Spencer, *Letter Book*, 13th September 1833.

they met some natives about 30 miles from the settlement, who not only gave them roasted kangaroo, fetched them water, and made them a hut, but occasionally supported them on their shoulders till they reached my house... [51]

In an article sent to the Editor of a Sydney newspaper, *The Colonist*, the writer included some concerned comments about Sir Richard Spencer's perceived ailing health:

Sir Richard Spencer is an old man, upwards, I should think, of 80 years of age. He is beginning now to betray a good deal of the various infirmities of age; and, indeed, considering the delicate and sickly state of health in which that worthy veteran has for some time been, we really think that it would be but gratitude in government to give him some comfortable retiring allowance, and put the management of that settlement into the hands of some active, liberal, and enterprising man. [52]

Sadly, the writer's observations soon became a reality and in July 1839 a local Swan River newspaper recorded:

The Government Resident, Sir Richard Spencer, Companion of the Bath, died after 48 hours of illness. With this gentleman's merits as a naval officer, we have already made our readers acquainted, it only remains for us to say a few words of his qualities as Government Resident at Albany. No one can doubt that he thoroughly identified himself with the place and its interests. He was no mere official deputed to administer and to collect. He set an example of enterprise, which was at first but faintly followed. He introduced (besides fruit and vegetables) livestock of every description and the best of breeds. At the cost of his experience, the pasture around Albany was proved unsuitable for sheep and he led the way discovering better sheep runs further inland...

There was also a ship on the stock at Torbay in course of being built. Sir Richard may therefore without any abuse of language, be called the founder of our settlement. Some who lived under his rule called him arbitrary, high-handed, and impatient. There is without a doubt something in autocratic sway which is exercised by the captain of a man-of-war that indisposes him to meet with much patience the petty opposition and radicalism of an infant settlement... [53]

While some early diarists wrote of Sir Richard that he was the real "founder of Albany" there can be little doubt that he brought both leadership and ongoing stability to the settlement at King George's Sound at a time when both qualities were needed.[54] As *The West Australian* reported:

But memories of bygone days, however interesting, must bow to the authority with which letters and diaries speak. [55]

Gwen Chessell in her book *Richard Spencer* sums up his contribution to Albany succinctly:

But for his decision to take the enormous step of emigrating, Richard Spencer's name would hardly be known and his story would remain hidden among Admiralty documents and long-forgotten accounts of naval actions written during the first half of the 19th century. By emigrating, and by resurrecting the moribund infant settlement of Albany, he became, in six years, Pioneer and one of the founders of Western Australian agriculture. He died...leaving behind him a thriving community... [56]

---

[51] *The West Australian*, Perth. 13th August; 24th September; 1st October 1932. *A Bundle of Old Letters* by Augusta Maude Bird.
[52] *The Colonist*. Sydney, 9th January 1838.
[53] *The Perth Gazette*. July 1839.
[54] C. E. Egerton-Warburton, '*Albany, past and present*' (newspaper clippings, State Records Office of Western Australia)
[55] *The West Australian*, Perth. 1st October 1932.
[56] Chessell, G. *Richard Spencer*. University of Western Australia Press. 2005.

George Grey - Government Resident 1839 to 1841

With the death of Sir Richard Spencer in July 1839, Captain George Grey was chosen to succeed him as Government Resident and Magistrate at King George's Sound. His links to the Spencer family were cemented when on 2nd November of that year when he married Sir Richard's daughter Eliza Lucy Spencer at the Strawberry Hill Cottage. During his time in Western Australia Captain Grey had developed a serious interest in native fauna and flora and also a particular interest in Aboriginal culture and language. While as Resident Magistrate he informed John Hutt, the then Governor of the colony of Western Australia:

> *I can only say that wherever I have been in the southern portions of the colony I could soon understand the natives.*[57]

In a few months of his residency at King George's Sound Captain Grey compiled a *Vocabulary of the Dialects Spoken by the Aboriginal Races or South-Western Australia.*[58] Interestingly, he was the first person of European descent to be able to speak the local Nyungar language. The preface to this work outlined his methodology in compiling the dictionary:

> *The words and phrases contained in this vocabulary, have been gathered amongst those tribes of Western Australia, whose location extend northward from King George's Sound to more than 100 miles beyond Perth. Throughout the whole of this extensive range of country, the language is radically the same, though the variations in dialect and the use of certain words by single tribes are very considerable; but certainly not more than, from the scattered and ignorant state of the population, the little intercourse existing between adjacent tribes, and the want of any fixed standard of speech, we might have been led to expect. No dialect spoken by a single tribe can therefore be considered as a fair specimen of the general tongue. Many words are altogether local, and, even in the same tribe. Individuals, that have recently mixed with another, will occasionally use different words from the rest to express the same idea, and I have not frequently found a word, used by one tribe in a particular sense, discontinued by an adjoining one, and again reappear amongst the tribe more remote…*[59]

His residency period was not noted for anything significant in terms of the expansion or development of the settlement and when leaving the post in 1841 he remarked on his stay:

> *The settlement at the Sound was quite small and I discharged all the duties of the state. I don't remember that I fined anybody!*

Perhaps it was this last comment that led Governor Weld to later call him, *"The artful dodger of Governors"*.

Unfortunately, Grey will be remembered for this snippet of gossip that was printed in the *Daily News* of Perth on Saturday, 26 November 1898 relating to his marriage:

> *Here is a starting little story of the late Sir George Grey, which will be new to most people, I fancy, says a London corresponded. Not many years after their marriage, the late Sir George Grey, when going out to the cape as its Governor designate, accompanied by his wife, was walking alone on the deck of the ship (HMS Forte). Seeing a letter on the deck, he picked it up and found it to be a note written to Lady Grey by the captain (later rear admiral Sir Harry Keppel; Still living and immensely popular Royal Navy officer, now of high rank. So, George's anger apparently got the better of his reason, for a violent scene with the captain, and presumably without his wife a chance of speaking for herself, he insisted on putting into port in South America and sending Lady Grey onshore. From that moment he separated himself from her, and never saw her again for 33 years. At the end of this period, by some means unknown, it was proved that Lady Grey knew nothing at all of the letter and was not even aware of the captain's feeling for her. The aged couple were at last reunited and spent about three years together before the death of Lady Grey, which took place only a few days before that of her husband.*[60]

Grey became a leading British Empire statesman and is buried in St Paul's Cathedral London with Arthur Wellesley, 1st Duke of Wellington and 1st Viscount Horatio Nelson. John Randall Phillips succeeded Grey as the Government Resident on 1st September 1840 and he remained in the role until July 1847. His

---

[57] Correspondence with Governor John Hutt. 1840. State Records Office of Western Australia.
[58] *A Vocabulary of the Dialects of Southern Western Australia.* By Captain George Grey, H.M.83rd Regiment. Published by W. Boone of London. 1 December 1840.
[59] Ibid
[60] *The Daily News.* Perth. 26th November 1898.

tenure in the role was acknowledged for having been a well-organised administration, and consequently, he was well respected by the community.

Patrick Taylor - Free Settler/Landowner 1834 to 1839

In terms of the general population of Albany at the time, Patrick Taylor was a quite wealthy man, although as it turned out not of sound physical health. In fact, there is some conjecture among historians as to the reason Taylor had migrated to Western Australia in the first place. Some writers indicating that it was due to underlying health concerns and the promise that a healthier Australian lifestyle may address them. On the other hand, others have indicated that perhaps he was following the tradition of the 'younger sons' from well-to-do families moving away to establish themselves in the world. Whatever the case, Patrick Taylor was 27 years old when he arrived at Albany in May 1834. Unfortunately, the occasion was marred by an accident to James Dunn who blew his arm off firing an unauthorised salute in welcome to Taylor.

It is worth noting that recollections and memoirs of people post the Dunn episode provides another example where The Historical Record can be inadvertently altered, albeit slightly, by taking as gospel the recollections and memories of someone post the event. An accurate Historical Record must be able to withstand the impact that both time and associated memory lapses can have on it. Recollections can be distorted with time resulting in the ongoing perpetration of inaccurate reporting and perhaps, later on, myth-making. A case in point is provided in the recollections of Mrs Elisa Chester. Mrs Chester indicated in her recollections later reported by the Albany Historical Society that she remembered an event at which time a cannon was fired and someone was injured:

> *Once we were sitting down to dinner, we heard one of the cannons go off. My father jumped up and ran out. He found two young men had tried to fire one of them, and the ramrod had been blown out, and one of the men had been badly injured. They had tried to fire the cannon to give a salute to the Champion, which was just entering the harbour, with one of their friends on board, bringing back a bride from Bunbury.*[61]

However, Sir Richard Spencer indicated in his report that:

> *One of the men, Dunn, who was contracted to build the pier, has blown his arm off in firing a salute the night of Taylor's return...*

Mrs Chester was born in 1841, seven years after the accident which occurred in 1834.[62] The event was obviously relayed to her when she was young and she had subsequently internalised it as part of her own experience. While her recollection was subtly different from the official report of the accident, the example highlights how The Historical Record can be distorted through hearsay or vicarious storytelling. This is a sobering point, just because something is written down in a book, it is not necessarily gospel as all sorts of inconsistencies, errors and omissions can cloud and distort the accurate recording of an event.

On the 22nd of December 1837, Taylor married Mary Bussell who had also migrated to Western Australia on the same ship, having arrived at the Swan River Colony in June 1834 onboard the *James Patterson*. Mary Bussell in a diary which she maintained on board the ship wrote of Patrick Taylor in 1834:

> *I had a long chat with Mr Taylor. The brother that was dearer to him than life itself is no more. It was that loss that gave him so serious a turn to his character. Mr Taylor must have inherited some spiritual adventure from his ancestors to have been tempted with a life in the Australian wilds.*[63]

Taylor purchased a property in Duke Street (now Patrick Taylor Cottage) in July 1837 from its original builder John Morley who had acquired the land while living in India working for the East India

---

[61] At the time of the Western Australian Centenary celebrations in 1929 memoirs of early settlers were published in various state newspapers. Several early settlers in Albany recalled participating in or having intimate knowledge of events in Albany, among them Chester 1924; McKail 1927 and Sale 1936.

[62] Elisa Chester was born on 20th August 1841 and was the third white child to be born in Albany. *Albany Advertiser*. 13th August 1931.

[63] *Letter to Frances Emily Cotton Bowker on the eve of the* James Pattison *sailing to Western Australia. 1834.* (3898A/9) State Library of western Australia

Company.[64] Later in 1837, he bought a parcel of land on the east bank of the lower Kalgan River which became known as '*Candyup*'.[65] The purchase of this land coincided with his marriage to Mary. The Taylor's subsequently called their Kalgan homestead '*Glenn Candy.*'[66]

It was not long before Taylor made his leadership qualities known within the settlement. In 1840 an acute case of food shortage inspired him to send to the editor of *The Inquirer* a missive explaining how the food shortage was impacting on both the colonists and the military:

To the Editor of The Inquirer.
Albany, King George's Sound,
August 13th 1840.

Sir,
I beg to call your attention to a fact of a very momentous nature, and I shall feel obliged by your affording an explanation if you know of any, of the reasons which induced the Colonial Government to adopt that measure, which undoubtedly has been the direct cause of the calamity to which I allude.

At present, there is neither Rice, nor Flour, nor Bread, to be purchased in Albany. The greater portion of the inhabitants are altogether destitute of any private store of the said necessaries; and so far, as I can learn, there is no reason for supposing that any supply will be thrown into the place before the end of September or the beginning of October. The Commissariat is also so short of flour, that so far from the inhabitants of Albany being able to procure any assistance from that quarter, I understand that the military will very shortly be on half rations. Such being the state of the case, the question arises, what has occasioned this scarcity? And to this, there can be but one reply.

The people of this district, depending on the many assurances of the Government, that a regular and frequent communication should be always kept up between the outports and headquarters, by means of the colonial vessel; made their calculation on this supposition, and consequently did not conceive that it was necessary for them to have more than three- or four-months provisions in reserve. Moreover, they knew that the actual condition of the place was known at Perth; because both private letters, and the official returns had been regularly transmitted to headquarters. However, we are now told that the Colonial Government in despite of their often-repeated assurances, and in the face of fact, of which they could not have been ignorant, has sent away the Colonial Schooner, as she is called, and are yachting to Madras.

Now, it is possible, that I may be in error in one or two points. Either it may not be true that the Champion *has been sent a yachting i.e., for the convenience and pleasure of His Excellency, and his Indian friend; but has been ordered to Madras because the most urgent reasons demanded that such an extraordinary measure should be adopted. Or, peradventure, the* Champion *is no longer a public vessel, kept by the Colonial Government, for the purpose of maintaining a regular communication between the outports and headquarters, and for the general benefit of the colony; but is a private yacht, allowed to his Excellency, for the amusement and convenience of himself and friends.*

If the latter of these two suppositions be correct, I shall only say, that it is rather an expensive toy to be allowed to a Governor of so poor a colony. And if the former supposition be the true one, why then, I shall be extremely

---

[64] Patrick Taylor Cottage was one of the first homes built for settlers in Albany. It is over 190 years old. It is noted that John Morley was the first private settler to acquire land in the township, but he later sold this holding to Patrick Taylor in 1834. Morley had imported several Indian workers to assist him with his building activities.

[65] It is suggested that '*Candyup*' was possibly an Aboriginal name for that area. There is reference to Candyup by Eyre in 1841. Initially, The Kalgan was renamed from the *Riviere de Francais [originally named by d'Urville in 1826]* by Alexander Collie in 1831, after Mokare his Aboriginal companion travelled with him expedition to the river's headwaters. However, while no official records can be found to substantiate any of the theories as to the origin of the name it is most reasonable to assume that Kalgan-up was of aboriginal origin. It is believed to mean either "place of many waters" or "place of first camp.".

[66] Candyup Homestead. Photograph courtesy of Albany Historical Society.

anxious to hear what were the reasons which rendered it so expedient to dispatch the schooner to India, at the very moment when her services were so much required in the colony. But if I have been at error on either of these two points; if the Champion *is not a private yacht, but a public vessel, intended to be employed for the general welfare of all parts of the colony; and if no good reasons can be assigned, why she should have been sent abroad at the time when urgent reasons demanded that she should be employed in the colony; then surely, it cannot be denied that the colonists in general, and especially the inhabitants of this district have great reason to complain; in as much as the public interest has been sacrificed, and the people left to starve, merely to suit private views and to gratify individual caprice.*

I have the honour to remain
Your obedient servant,
Patrick Taylor.[67]

The Editor of *The Inquirer* responded in the paper's September edition:

We are induced to publish Mr Taylor's letter, first because we are authorised to attach his name to it, and secondly because we think our friends at the Sound have just cause for complaint; at the same time, our sense of justice compels us to state that Mr Taylor has formed a very incorrect notion as to the object of the Champion's *voyage to Madras. We can confidently state that she was not sent a yachting, either for the convenience of the Governor, or for that of any other individual – the thing is out of all probability – the only question is whether the declared, as we believe the veritable, objects of the voyage were sufficiently important to justify the measure of sending her away at such a moment, and upon this question, we are inclined to accord with Mr Taylor's opinions.*

For the information of Mr Taylor, and our other friends at the Sound, we will state what were the objects of the voyage to India: firstly to bring back a number of domestic servants, labourers, and artisans; and secondly to convey an English mail, with despatches for this colony, which were supposed to be lying there; another object was, as we believe, to see what had been done with regard to certain negotiations for a communication between England and this colony, by the overland mail to India. The objects of the voyage have singularly failed, but it is not the less true that they were put forth with good intent, and in good faith, and we beg our friends at the Sound to believe that our local government of incapable of sanctioning any such idle caprice as that mentioned by Mr Taylor, even supposing for a moment that the head of that government would so far forget his duty as to wish it, which supposition we say again is "beyond all absurdity absurd". On the other hand, we confess that we think the voyage was ill-advised. It was undertaken as regards its principal object without due knowledge of the circumstances, and too ready an ear was lent to the representations of a certain "Visitor", who seems the only person likely to profit by the adventure. Again, the vessel should not have been sent away, unless for very cogent reasons, at a moment when the government knew that the settlers at the Sound were badly supplied with provisions.

We learn that information was received at headquarters, before the sailing of the Champion, *that supplies were by no means plentiful at the Sound, and yet in the face of it, the* Champion *was sent on a long and uncertain expedition, and thus the government was deprived of the only sure means of relieving the settlers in their extremity. Upon this point we entirely agree with Mr Taylor and think that the first duty of the Colonial Schooner is to keep up a constant communication with our outports – this being done she may be employed in such other way as may advance the general interests of the colony, but this first should not be neglected for any other purpose whatever.*

We consider that some explanation as to the causes which led to the failure of the expedition, is due to the public at large, and at all events, we trust that the Champion *will be dispatched with provisions to the Sound without delay. –*

The Editor.[68]

The Towns Improvement Act 1841 enabled local areas to assume some limited responsibility for decisions that pertained specifically to them and was the colony's first experiment in local government.[69] However,

---

[67] Patrick Taylor to the editor of *The Inquirer*. 13th August 1840.
[68] *The Inquirer and Commercial News*. Perth. 9th September 1840.
[69] *Towns Improvement Act 1841*, 4 & 5 Vic. No. 18.

Albany was slow on its uptake in accepting the responsibilities foreshadowed by the act, so it was not until 1843 that the first Town Trust was formed. Patrick Taylor became a member of the Town's Trust in 1845 two years later. In 1846 a rainfall event caused widespread flood damage across the town. Both York Street and Stirling Terrace were severely affected as were the various allotments along the east side of York Street.

While the local residents were able to temporarily deal with the damage, nevertheless a public meeting was convened by Patrick Taylor who was subsequently elected chairman. In this role Taylor wrote to Lieutenant-Colonel Andrew Clarke Phillips, the Governor at the Swan River Colony on the 1st September 1846 requesting help for the town to redress the storm damage issue:

> *We the undersigned inhabitants of Albany humbly beg to call the attention of your Excellency to the president ruinous state of this townsite, caused by a recent fall of rain of the most unprecedented character whether the respect is had to its suddenness or effects.*
>
> *Without attempting to estimate the precise amount of damage which has been done both to public and private property, it may suffice to furnish your Excellency with a slight sketch of the fearful traces which the storm has left behind it, too clearly the indicative of its character and course; and from which your Excellency will perceive not only the serious nature of the catastrophe, as a thing which is past, and the losses which private parties must have experienced, but may also be enabled to adopt the most judicious measures to prevent the future extension of the calamity.*
>
> *Commencing about the head of York Street the torrent has ploughed deep and long furrows along the road, for the distance of 200 yards undermining down the sides of the drain in various places. From this point, an immense ravine commences which is not less than 120 yards in length and varying from 10 to 15 yards in width and from 10 to 12 feet in depth. And throughout the entire length, it has broken in upon the allotments on the east side of the street, carrying away not only the front fences but also a portion of the allotment themselves. The trunks and masonry which were formally constructed for the purpose of carrying off the waters have also been utterly swept away…*
>
> *…In addition to the (four) great chasms which effectively destroy for the present the two principal streets of Albany (York Street and Stirling Terrace), there have been numerous watercourses cut at various places and a large quantity of sand deposited here and other parts of the town.*
>
> *Thus, the whole aspect of the place has been altered, the main lines of communication interrupted; the depth of the harbour diminished with a certain prospect (due to the sandy nature of the soil) of a continued enlargement of the chasms already formed, and a proportionate diminution of water in the harbour. So that is impossible to say to what extent the anchorage may be affected and unless some means are at once adopted, if not to repair the damage which has already been done, at all events, to stay the evil from farther.*
>
> *… we leave the matter in your hands, in the full confidence that your Excellency will lose no time in deciding on the measures which Emergency of the case may require…*[70]

Unfortunately, for the people of Albany, the problem was ignored until 1861 when Governor Kennedy allowed for tenders to be called for York Street's reconstruction.

One person who had a lot of social contact with Taylor initially was The Reverend John Ramsden Wollaston. On the 30th April 1843 he wrote in his Journal that:

> *He is a great favourite with me. I wish there were more in the colony of similar conscientious principles. We may differ slightly on one or two points in respect of church doctrine, but I really believe many mistakes and apprehensions arise from the church having been so long out of sight. I do not say this is the case with Mr Taylor, far from it; he is far more enlightened and candid than the generality of colonies, but I do not know many instances of the truth of these remarks.*[71]

However, five years later there appears to have been a falling out between the pair with Wollaston commenting in 1848 that Taylor was:

---

[70] Extract *The History of the Oldest Dwelling in Western Australia and Patrick Taylor*. Albany Historical Society. 2019. pp33-34.
[71] P.U. Henn (ed). *Wollaston's Albany Journals*. Perth. 1954.

a great hypochondriac – great pity for in other aspects he is a fine character for truth, integrity and piety with a well-formed mind cultivated by reading. Yet he fancies he is not well enough to come to church, although he goes about his garden, and works a great deal in the house having no servant. He has met with a great reversal, and I suspect this has something to do with his seclusion.[72]

On the other hand, others saw Taylor in a very different light. Wollaston's views were not supported in correspondence sent to the Editor of a Sydney newspaper, *The Colonist*:

As to Mr Taylor, the third magistrate of the settlement, we have only to say, that he esteemed as a worthy man and as a worthy man, a pattern for future colonists to imitate. Mr Taylor's farm is on the banks of the Calligan [sic], about 12 to 14 miles from Albany. He has erected a very comfortable house upon it, and from the attention, he has bestowed upon his farm, it has become a very pretty spot. Mr Taylor has five or six servants always at work; and though as yet he has not got a stock of sheep, he has some excellent milk cows, which are very valuable in such a settlement…[73]

Despite being recognised as a solitary man focussed on both his building program within the townsite and his farm at 'Glenn Candy', through his community service Patrick Taylor had made his mark on the town of Albany and its future. Patrick Taylor's health failed him, and he died at home on 30 December 1870 aged 70 years.[74]

Edward John Eyre and Wylie Explorers - 1841

In March 1841, Edward John Eyre, together with his Aboriginal companion Wylie, crossed the southern part of the Australian continent from east to west; from Adelaide to Albany by traversing the Nullarbor Plain and following at times along the Great Australian Bight. Previously Eyre had undertaken less extensive expeditions in both New South Wales and South Australia. As a farmer (sheep and cattle) he was hoping to discover good pasture lands for sheep husbandry. Before his Nullarbor adventure, Eyre had built a reputation in South Australia as an explorer and is credited with opening up much of that state's hinterland for settlement. In the previous year, Eyre and two companions had taken sheep and some cattle by sea to King George's Sound from Adelaide and then had driven them overland to the Swan River Settlement. It was during this journey that a friendship was established with Wylie, who would become an integral part of Eyre's later successful east-west venture.

The impetus for this expedition was two-fold. Firstly, to establish a route between South Australia and Western Australia to find good pastoral land and secondly, to establish an overland route for drovers to take cattle from Adelaide to Western Australia. Given his proven skills as a bushman and previous expedition successes, Eyre was appointed the expedition's leader.

Eyre travelled westward across what is now known as the Eyre Peninsula and along the south coast. The harsh conditions and lack of water forced him to send the majority of the members of his party back to Adelaide, except for John Baxter, Wylie and two other Aborigines. Eyre thought that a smaller party would have more chance of success. Water was always going to be an issue for this expedition, particularly as the Nullarbor Plain, as its name suggests is devoid of trees. Consequently, this lack of shade did not allow the explorers to rest and gain some respite from the sun's heat during this part of the journey. Even before reaching the West Australian border water had become scarce and fortuitously, at this time they were saved by local Aborigines who showed Eyre how to locate water by digging behind the sand dunes on the shoreline. During their travels, they were to experience considerable hardship. Water continued to be a scarce commodity; luckily, however, they came upon a series of wells that had been dug by Aborigines in and around the present site of Eucla on the border of South Australia and Western Australia.

It was during one night after about a month into the trek while Eyre was keeping watch, he heard a gun blast and found Wylie running towards him in alarm. Two of their Aborigine companions had murdered Baxter and then disappeared with most of the expedition's supplies and firearms. Wylie, however, refused

---
[72] D.S. Garden (1977) *Albany; Panorama of the Sound*. Nelson Press, p.99-100.
[73] *The Colonist*. Sydney, 9th January 1838.
[74] Ibid.

to go with them and stayed with Eyre. It was only through a chance encounter with the French whaling ship *Mississippi*, at Esperance, that both Eyre and Wylie were able to survive. The ship was under the command of Captain Thomas Rossiter (an Englishman), for whom Eyre named the location Rossiter Bay, reprovisioned them both which allowed them to regain their strength and then to proceed.

In July, they reached Albany, after travelling through heavy rains and generally inclement weather that had dogged them on the last leg of their epic journey. Their travels had lasted a total of four and a half months. Subsequently, Eyre was awarded a gold medal by the Royal Geographic Society for this incredible journey while his companion Wylie was rewarded with a pension. Wylie was obviously relieved to have successfully completed the journey and remained in Albany, satisfied to be among his own people once again. In 1845 Eyre returned to England and published a narrative of his travels.

Eyre's letter to the Colonial Secretary outlined the major events of the trip:
To the Hon. The Colonial Secretary, Perth.
Albany, July 7th, 1841.

Sir,
I have the honour to report to you, for the information of his Excellency the Governor, my arrival in the colony of Western Australia overland from Adelaide, and though I regret extremely that my labours have not been productive of any discovery likely to prove beneficial to either colony, I am induced to the hope that a slight outline of my route, and of the character of the country I have been traversing, may not prove uninteresting to his Excellency from a geographical point of view.

On 25th February, I left Fowler's Bay with a party consisting of an overseer and three native boys. I was provided with 10 horses, and provisions calculated for nine weeks. Upon entering within the limits of Western Australia, I found the country extending around the Great Australian Bight, for upwards of 500 miles, to consist entirely of fossil formation, with a considerable elevation above the level of the sea, varying, perhaps, from 200 to 300 feet, and forming the most part a country which presented the appearance of an elevated and almost level tableland. This extensive region is of the most desolate and barren character imaginable; almost entirely without grass, destitute of timber, and in many parts densely covered by an impenetrable scrub. There was no surface water, neither were there creeks or watercourses of any description.

The only supply of water procured by the party through this dreary waste was obtained by digging in the drift of pure white sand found along the coast at places where the great fossil bank receded a little from the immediate margin of the sea… In this fearful country our horses suffered most severely, and on two different occasions with seven days without any water, and almost without any food also. From this cause, we lost many valuable animals, and our progress was impeded by the frequent and long delays necessary to recruit those that were still left alive. Our journey thus became protracted to a period far beyond what had been calculated upon… in the midst of these difficulties, and then barely halfway through across the Great Bight, my very small party was broken up by an event as distressing as it was tragical, and I was left alone with a native of King George's Sound, Wiley. This melancholy occurrence, added to the weak and jaded condition of the few remaining horses, effectually prevented my examination of the country be on the line of my immediate route, in fact from the time of entering the colony of Western Australia, such was the dreadful nature of the country, that the whole party were obliged to walk; and it was not until our arrival at East Mount Barren that myself and the native boy could venture to ride…

… About 1-mile northeast of Cape Riche, we fell in with a considerable saltwater river from the west northwest which appeared to join the sea at a gap left by Flinders in the coastline, and marked as a' sandy bight, not perfectly seen'. We found several permanent pools of fresh water not very far distant, in deep narrow gullies, by which the country hereabouts is much intercepted. From the depths of the river and boggy nature of its bed, we were obliged to trace its course for about 10 miles from the sea before we could cross. Here the water-course was obstructed by a ledge of rocks, and its channel appear to become more contracted and rockier, whilst the soil, for the most part, is of an inferior description…

After crossing the river, we met for the first time, with stunted trees of the kind called mahogany, but it was not until we had passed some miles to the westward of Cape Riche that we saw any large trees or got into a country that could properly be called a timbered one. Here the mahogany, red gum, casuarinas, and other trees common at King George's Sound abounded and formed a tolerably dense forest nearly all the way to the settlement. From the head of Doubtful Island Bay, I have kept some distance from the coast, cutting off the various corners as circumstances admitted, and cannot, therefore, give an opinion of the country immediately upon the coastline. That portion of it, however, which lies between Cape Riche and King George's Sound, is, I believe, already too well known to require any further examination.

On 2nd June, we had met with a French whaler, the 'Mississippi', of Havre, commanded by Captain Rossiter. To this gentleman, I am much indebted for the very kind and hospitable reception I experienced during a residence of 12 days onboard whilst my horses were recruiting after their severe toils, and for the very liberal manner in which I was furnished with supplies for prosecuting what remained of my journey to King George's Sound.

At the latter place, I arrived on the 7th July instant, after having travelled over an extent of country which, from the sinuosities of the coastline and other obstructions, has exceeded upwards of 1241 miles in distance from Fowler's Bay; and for the last 691 miles of which I was only accompanied by any but a native of King George's Sound, known by the name of Wiley and to whom I would respectfully recommend to his Excellency the Governor as deserving of the favour of the government for services rendered under circumstances of a peculiarly trying nature…

I regret extremely that the very limited time of my stay at Albany has not permitted me to prepare a copy of the chart of my line of route, for the information of his Excellency the Governor.
I have the honour to be, Sir
Your most obedient servant,
Edward John Eyre.[75]

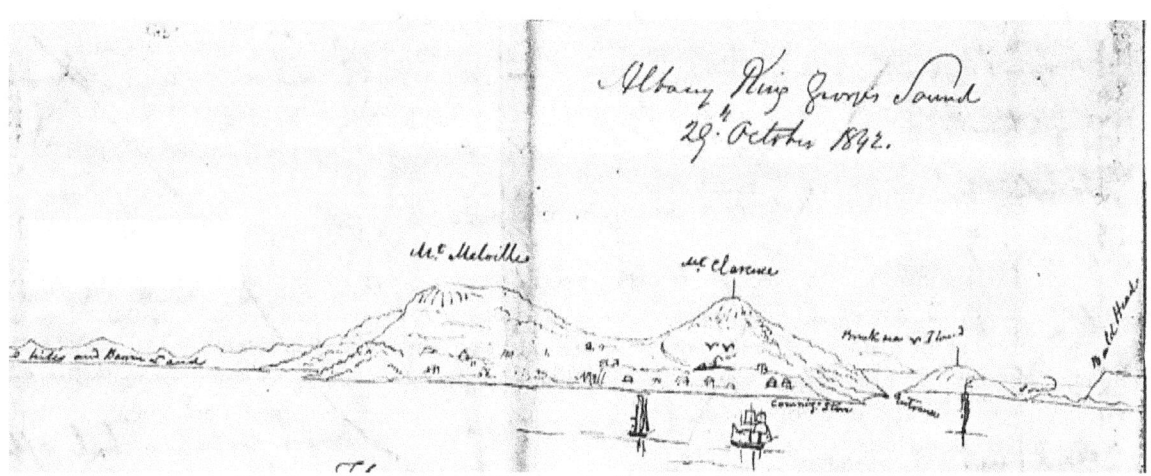

Drawing of Princess Royal Harbour by Robert Neill, 29 October 1842[76]

---

[75] A Correspondent, *The Australasian Chronicle*, Sydney. November 1841.
[76] *Correspondence to Sir George Grey by the artist Robert Neill.* GD18/3549/4

Albany in 1841
A Snapshot

An excellent overview of how the Albany settlement was progressing at the beginning of the 1840s was provided in *The Adelaide Chronicle and South Australian Record*, of 24 March 1841:

Albany, King George's Sound.

The great importance to which this town is rising is known to very few and has its advantages have never been properly placed before the public, we shall now endeavour, from an account from a person who lately visited it, to give a brief sketch of Albany. The seat of government being at Swan River, a distance of nearly 400 miles, places Albany in a similar position as Port Phillip; is placed with respect to Sydney but instead of a superintendent at Albany there is a Resident, who acts otherwise as a Justice of the Peace. The most prevalent complaint is the want of a regular communication with the seat of government; but this was likely to be obviated by the strenuous exertions of the Resident and the great influx of immigrants, and in all probability, there will soon be so much higher authority than the resident. The capabilities of Princess Royal Harbour as it is called, may not be known to many. It is said by many old navigators to be one of the finest in the world, and assimilating in almost every respect that of Port Jackson…

At present, there is only one wharf, which belongs to the government, but many vessels discharge on a sandy beach on the towns side. Wharves, it is said, could be erected at a trifling expense, and many persons were already commencing to build very expensive premises adjoining the waterside. So great was the demand for water frontages, that our informant says, he found it absolutely impossible to buy even the smallest portion, and when he left the town allotments were rising considerably. The contrast between the two harbours is immense, Swan River and Princess Royal, the natural advantages to be obtained in the latter compared with Swan River, being such as to induce many of the whalers that used to frequent Swan River, now to refit at Albany. An immense number of wrecks having taken place in Geographe Bay, particularly American whalers, some of which suffered considerably last year, has caused them now to take shelter in the Sound. About 60 whalers are expected this season to visit Albany, and, as the place becomes more knowing, the shipping will become more considerable…

Captains of vessels will find a good reception, and by presenting the natives with a little rice, they will render them every assistance in fetching wood and water. Are you ready market is always to be found there for produce of all kinds, ready money payments being always expected. A whaling company would do well if established in the port, as whales frequent even the Sound. This thriving little colony now presents every prospect of being one of the most promising of all the Australasian settlements.[77]

Closing Remarks

The period from Cantonment in December 1826 to settlement in 1841 established a foundation upon which the future development of King George's Sound and of the town of Albany would be built. It was not an easy period in the history of the settlement by any means and many hardships were encountered and eventually overcome by the early pioneers to the area. Their strength of character, foresight and endeavours are worthy of recognition and celebration. From this point on the town's development very much mirrored that of the colony as a whole.

---

[77] *The Adelaide Chronical and South Australian Record.* 24th March 1841.

CHAPTER 4
A SELECTION OF VISITOR IMPRESSIONS OF ALBANY

I visited Albany on my return journey. It struck me that in 'Sleepy Hollow' 90 per cent of the inhabitants were in bed the other 10 per cent were dozing on the seats on the parade. Harry Furness
(1859)

Now father, I think this is the promised land, but there are faults in it.
Letter in *The Bradford Observer*, 7 December 1848

Overview

There have been a number of people who visited Albany's shores during the nineteenth and early twentieth centuries. While it is not feasible to relate their full journal extracts, a selection has been made that gives both a positive and some perhaps less favourable insights into their stay in the town. It is also possible at this time to introduce some female voices into this narrative, because up to this point there have been but few journals or diaries that could be called upon to enhance the early perspectives that have been presented.

Reports and Travellers' Tales

A more accurate perspective of how the town had developed since *Amity's* arrival in 1826 can be sourced from visitor travelogues, personal diary entries, letters of correspondence that were prepared contiguously with an individual's visit and these were complemented by various newspaper and local Resident Magistrate dispatches. An excellent first snapshot of the Cantonment is provided by Captain Sir Richard Spencer upon his arrival in 1833.

> *By 1833 the King George's Sound settlement had been in operation for six years and at this stage it would appear from dispatches from the settlement that it was still struggling to establish a stable and firm presence in the area. At this time there were only six other settlers/individuals besides the detachment of troops, and three civic officers habiting the settlement. Furthermore, there were only three 'less than substantial' main buildings other than those used by earlier government and military personnel assigned to the Cantonment. One of these buildings was occupied by George Cheyne, a merchant entrepreneur and one of the others by Diggory Geake, publican. The third was not occupied.*[1]

However, by 1837, just four years later, there were in excess 180 inhabitants, among whom were identified three owners and masters of merchant vessels, which did a brisk Indian Ocean trade to places like the Isle of France [Mauritius] as well as with the neighbouring Eastern Colonies. At this time, it was reported that there were 43 more substantial houses in the town, many built of local stone and brick and covered with slate imported from England. It is recognised that the development which had occurred over the preceding years was perhaps largely due to the whaling and sealing ventures driven by both the American and French endeavours along the south coast of Australia.[2]

In respect to the whaling and sealing industries that were beginning to thrive in the area, Sir Richard Spencer wrote to Robert Hay, The Under-Secretary of State for the Colonies in 1834 indicating that two men:

> *Had returned today with 190 sealskins having left as many more on the coast for want of salt. In 1837 Spencer wrote, the Americans have made a fine harvest among the whales on this coast. The whales will, no doubt, be disturbed and destroyed in few years.*[3]

He continued this train of thought in 1837 when he indicated:

> *The Americans find plenty whales on the coast, and this year the French have commenced. A month since a French frigate was here to protect their whale ships. A large French frigate from the Havre remained in the harbour for a month to refresh the crew. She was then half full of oil and intends to remain on the coast till the*

---

[1] G. Chessell. *Richard Spencer*. University of Western Australia Press. 2005.
[2] *The Perth Gazette*. 28th February 1833.
[3]: *Richard Spencer Letter Book*, 25th May 1837.

winter to fill up. Here we are with only a sergeant and nine privates to protect this beautiful harbour and its inhabitants, where we are likely to have two or three hundred foreign seamen running about drunk. What a disgrace to old England to leave her subjects in such a helpless state. I suppose the English merchants find so much oil in the Greenland seas they are independent of what can be procured at so much less expense and risk, and leave this coast to poor foreigners... The Americans had six different boats fastened into six different whales in the same day. Will our government maintain this colony as a fishing ground for Jonathan? If they are quiet for a year or two longer, they will claim it as a right, and we shall want men of war to keep them out of the bays.[4]

Carl von Hügel 1833 to 1834

Baron Carl von Hügel was an explorer, amateur naturalist and officer in the Austrian Army. He had fought in various coalition armies of those European nations fighting against Napoleon Bonaparte. After these actions and having been spurned by his love interest at home, Hügel undertook a tour of the Indian subcontinent and Australasia, travels that resulted in a much acclaimed four-volume work published in the years following his return to Europe.

Of particular interest as far as Albany is concerned are his travels from November 1833 to October 1834, at which time Baron Hügel toured Australia, visiting the Swan River Colony and King George's Sound, as well as a number of Eastern Colonies venues including Van Diemen's Land and Sydney in New South Wales.

Besides making detailed observations during his tour he also collected native seeds for his garden in Austria. In addition to his acclaimed botanical observations, the rare anthropological insight into European's attitudes towards colonial Australia were well reported and received. Extracts from his extensive journals that pertain to Albany and his camping experiences along the Albany - Perth track is presented here:

Wednesday first of January 1834.
...At 2 o'clock we are approaching land and we are overjoyed to have a completely fresh view of the coast. Soon we could make out the two islands at the entrance to the outer harbour – Breaksea and Michaelmas islands - and then the tall rock, Bald Head, which forms the most westerly point of the bay... King George's Sound is the outer harbour or bay and very extensive. There are many good protected anchorages around the two smaller islands inside the bay, Seal Island and Mistaken Island, but the two main harbours, Princess Royal Harbour and Oyster Harbour, are separate but connected to the outer harbour only by a narrow entrance. The former is by far the best and we headed there.

The scenery at King George's Sound is majestic, but nature is not in a kindly mood there. It is surrounded by rocks, bare and rugged, menacing though shapely, or by long stretches of white sand. The above-mentioned two large islands at the entrance show no trace whatever of vegetation on the ocean side, likewise the aptly named Bald Head. The narrow entrance into Princess Royal Harbour lies between two mountains, Mount Possession and Mount Clarence. Mount Clarence is quite high, with some very picturesque spots near the harbour entrance. Just opposite, where the wind strikes it, there is a broad expanse of sea -sand covering the top of a mountain. Three miles from the entrance, at the other end of the bay and to the right, the huts and houses of Albany can be seen stretching over a mile. Albany lies on the slopes of Mount Melville, between this and Mount Clarence.

While still in the outer harbour we had fired a shot for the pilot, but firstly it seemed possible there was no pilot and secondly the entrance was so easy to find and we were so anxious to drop anchor, that we just sailed on. A brig which we had seen the Swan River, the **Brilliant** *and the schooner* **Ellen** *were lying at anchor. Mr Toby, master of the* **Ellen,** *had fixed marker buoys near the shallow north-eastern shore line, but it was difficult to know which side ships were to choose. He himself by now came up in a boat and made signs to us, but these were not clear either. And so, it came to pass that we ran aground and for a moment we were afraid we would be well and truly stranded, but the strong wind helped us to slide over the sand. And so, we succeeded in anchoring half a mile from the settlement, and all of us felt very snug in the still waters after all the hardships we had endured.*

---

[4] Ibid

It was seven o'clock when Captain George Lambert R.N, and I landed.[5] *On the shore we found a man called [George] Cheyne, who received us cordially and took us to his 'little house', to give it a grand name. Here we found Mrs Cheyne, his two nephews and the wife of one of these. She had a most interesting face and the loveliest eyes and hair in the world.*

Our destination was the home of the Resident, Sir Richard Spencer who lived over the mountain, about one and a half miles from the settlement…

Sir Richard received us most cordially and introduced us to Lady Spencer, once a famous beauty and still a very fine-looking woman. By degrees the numerous families of 8 [10] children then appeared, most of them are extremely handsome, particularly two girls of nine and ten years. We paid only a brief call, and as the light was fading when we arrived and it was dark when we left I was not able to judge much of the country around. On our return we took tea at Mr Cheyne's home and it was late when we reboarded the frigate.

Thursday 2nd January.
Sir Richard had invited us to breakfast next morning, and we set out at 7 o'clock to fulfil this engagement. The track leads over the lowest foothills of Mount Clarence and must be a most charming walk-in winter and spring. It runs beneath and alongside Banksias and past eucalyptus trees and is surrounded by the choicest flowers of New Holland. Most of these had faded by now and the soil was parched after the long dry spell, but the walk was not unpleasant and full of interest to me…

The Resident's house is beautifully situated with a splendid view over the bay and picturesque rock formations close by. It also has the beginnings of a farm – the only one in the settlement. A dozen acres have been turned into a garden and fields. The breeding stock consists of 20 to 30 sheep, one cow without a bull, three mules, seven rabbits, one gelding and a dozen ducks, fowls and geese. Sir Richard does not spare himself. With all my heart I wish and fully expect him to succeed here in spite of some of the rather mixed beginnings.

As I have heard, he came here not so much from personal choice as from a desire to acquire some property here for his numerous children, which was not open to him in his home country…

On that side of the mountain which I set out to climb today, enormous masses of granite have been deposited and poured on top of each other and have either been laid bare in many places by the passage of time, or, as it is perhaps more probable, have not yet been covered by vegetation. I climbed over these masses of granite to within a short distance of the summit until a fall into a cleft made me turn back. It was not that I was badly hurt, but I had fallen quite a long way down between sharp rocks and I reflected that, if I had been unlucky enough to break a leg, unaccompanied as I was, I might have perished there without anyone being able to come to my aid…

Friday 3rd January.
The length of our stay here was entirely dependent on whether or not it was possible to obtain a month's provisions for the ship. If not, we were to return to Swan River by the schooner Ellen *to get them there.*[6] *I was anxious to avoid the disappointment of leaving this place without exploring the country roundabout as much as I could, and so this morning I set out to walk a good distance inland, once again alone for some unknown reason. The further I went the worse the soil became, although the terrain sloped away more steeply in this direction, terminating in marshes which were dry just now, except for some water in the deepest hollows. There were only a few trees growing in these extensive marshes: Melaleuca, Beaufortia and Calistemon speciosum, none of them over 8 feet high. The ground was covered with Stylidium, a species of Epacris etc., and in many places with impenetrable Leptospermum and Persoonia thickets.*

I came upon a group of natives camped stark naked in the bushes. The men jumped up with their spears and set up a mighty shouting, which I reciprocated. They then approached me and displayed great pleasure,

---

[5] Captain George Lambert was Captain *HMS Alligator*.
[6] The early Government-owned vessels plying the Perth to Albany route were initially the *Ellen*, named after Stirling's wife and in 1836 the *Champion*.

particularly at my beard. They next carried out a kind of training exercise-not in my honour, but on their own behalf, for I was soon completely forgotten. The exercise consisted of throwing at each other the shaft of rushes about 6 to 8 feet long and thick as a thumb, as if they were spears. One man represented the enemy and all the others aimed at him while he had to take evasive action by jumping sideways. Both throwing and evasive action were executed with great skill. As soon as the enemy has been hit, he was replaced by another man...

Saturday 4th January.

The Alligator *obtained the necessary provisions partly from the local stores and partly from the brig* Brilliant *and so we were set to stay at Albany until the* Ellen *had been refitted. I calculated this would take a fortnight and made up my mind to explore the region systematically. I would begin with the remoter areas as far as the higher ranges, Mount Gardner and the rugged mountains* [perhaps Stirling Ranges], *and only then explore the better-known country near at hand.*

I began today with Mistaken Island, five or 6 miles away in the outer bay, which had been described to me as luxuriously covered with unique vegetation. Another reason for going there was to hunt pigeons and rabbits. The former were wild and the latter had been introduced by Mr Cheyne and multiplied prodigiously. The huntsman were motivated, not so much by a desire for sport as a longing for fresh meat. Captain Lambert had bought an adequate supply of fowls from Swan River, but in the first place the passage to King George's Sound, estimated at 3 to 4 days, had in fact taken a fortnight; secondly, several died due to the sea water invading the ship; and lastly, Mr Morley had painted an enticing picture of extra provisions we would find in the settlement. We found nothing at all and the salt meat was beginning to disagree with us all.

Our expedition had no luck in any respect and I found very little of botanical interest. Captain Lambert shot one pigeon, but the heat was so stifling in the airless shrub thickets that it was almost impossible to breathe. Just as we were about to leave I went once more into the thickets looking for plants and here I shot one miserable white rabbit. Incidentally, a breed of rabbits with dark eyes but snow-white fur has evolved here. Before we reached the ship, it started to blow hard and, even in the harbour, the waves we are so high that we were wet through when we boarded the ship. This is the most inconvenient feature of King George's Sound, in fact of this whole coast, scarcely a day passes without the wind becoming so violent that you can hardly cross from one side of the harbour to the other. Towards evening the wind became so strong that the master, Vanzetti, who was charting a spot on the coast less than half a mile from the ship, could not return on board but had to spend the night with the boat crew in the bushes. It is impossible to rely on the weather... A dead calm morning almost always ends up with a gale, often with rain.

Sunday 5th January.

Today I climbed Mount Clarence. Being the highest point for many miles around, it affords a very extensive panorama. The high mountains appear to be no more than a narrow range bordering the coastline. Inland as far as the eye can see, there are occasional small hills but no mountains, except for the above-mentioned rugged mountains, possibly 20 miles inland as the crow flies. From Mount Clarence, which is not more than 2000 feet, the interior looks like a grassy plain broken by hills and the occasional small lake. But, as I have said before, this is the typical New Holland configurations, where every plain has a marsh in which the water from the nearby mountains collects.

On my way home, I met Lindolf [An Aboriginal man travelling with the party], *who had renounced all his fine raiment and was wondering about in the woods stark naked, picking the fruits of the Banksia trees and sucking them. I asked him the name of the Banksia Dryandroides, long cones of which he had in his hand, and he replied: 'Manyat'. Banksia coccinea is 'Waddib' and Banksia occidentalis is 'Pia'. This shows that the natives of New Holland have a more highly developed language then has hitherto been acknowledged...*

Monday 6th January.

Captain Lambert, who did his upmost to comply with my wishes to explore any region, arranged an excursion to Oyster Harbour, 9 miles away. We set out from the ship at daybreak in his boat, taking with us provisions for two days, and were accompanied by Mr Cheyne... At 8 o'clock we reached the entrance to Oyster harbour, where there is a sandbar with a water depth of only 12 feet.

There is freshwater to be found here – a great rarity in New Holland – and we decided to breakfast here, on fish that were yet to be caught. All hands-on board took to fishing while I climbed around looking for plants. There are large numbers of Dryandra Formosa and Armata growing here and several species of Epacris. But it is ugly country, all stone or sand. When breakfast was ready I came back. There had been a good catch, including some very fine specimens of a kind of mackerel, to which we did full justice…

At 10 o'clock we set out from here to trace to its source the river called Kalgan by the Aborigines and Riviere des Francais by the French navigators. This rivulet rises in the rugged mountains and its banks have all the characteristics which I observed in those mountains. It is one of the two rivulets which have their outlet at the end of Oyster Harbour. The sand which they bring down from the mountains in the rainy season is responsible for the sandbank which makes the harbour entrance so shallow. Most of the harbour consists of shallow water, and for this reason, although it is better from every other point of view – picturesque scenery, timber, soil, water and the navigable rivulets – Princess Royal Harbour is preferred.

Tuesday 7th January.
…. I began to explore the surrounding country and went to the right bank of the Kings River, which flows into Oyster Harbour a mile from the house in which we spent the night. On the way I found much that was new and beautiful and, on the rivulet, quite close at hand, I saw three swans gliding along. Captain Lambert came up to within thirty paces of them from another direction and fired at them, without dropping one. By chance all the other huntsman turned up here, unbeknownst to each other. I was amused to see them, one after another, make their presence known by a shot aimed at these birds, but not one of them scored a hit. Every half hour on the dot there was a sharp shower, during which I had to shelter bent double under a bush – not that I wanted to avoid getting wet – I was already drenched to the skin – but to protect the plants and seeds I had collected. After wandering about for several hours, I turned back, when pushing my way through scrub and man high grass in this wet weather, became too much for me…

Saturday 11th January.
Today Captain Lambert planned to bring the ship out of the inner harbour and into the bay, and to anchor there waiting a favourable wind. Everyone on board had left something behind on shore, intending to fetch it that evening or the next day. But we had hardly reached the outer harbour when the wind turned and, as it is usual here, rose to such force within half an hour, that it was with great difficulty that we reached the anchorage… When we weighed anchor, it was 6 o'clock in the evening. The coastline receded quickly from view and, when darkness fell, it was not clear whether it was distance or the darkness of night that hid every trace of land.[7]

Charles Darwin 1836

On March 7th 1836, *HMS Beagle* arrived in King George's Sound, after a voyage across the Great Australian Bight from Hobart. At this stage in his round the world adventure the 26-year-old Darwin was exhibiting some degree of melancholy as his generally unflattering comments and naturalist observations on Australia would indicate.

Then, after a passage during which he suffered 'no little misery' from the 'strong westerly swell' the Beagle spent a week at King George's Sound (6th–14th March).[8]

While *Beagle* was anchored at King George's Sound, Darwin explored around the settlement and adjacent areas at which time he witnessed a native corroboree, undertook a geological survey around the Vancouver Peninsula and Bald Head, and visited Strawberry Hill Farm which, by then belonged to the Government Resident, Sir Richard Spencer.

Darwin saw King George's Sound as "*a neglected outpost, not 10 years old*". Furthermore, he indicated that it was in fact a 'penal colony' that he believed '*had gone to pot, eclipsed now by the Swan River Colony.*' His comments on the settlement and the features of the hinterland were less than flattering. Darwin saw the soil as being

---

[7] Excerpts *New Holland Journal: November 1833 – October 1834.* Translated and editor by Dymphna Clark, Melbourne University Press of the Miegunyah Press in Association with State Library of New South Wales, 1994.
[8] N. Barlow (ed), *Charles Darwin's Diary of the Voyage of HMS Beagle.* Cambridge. 1933.

sandy and of a very poor quality, the vegetation coarse and overall, the views uninteresting with the kangaroos scarce. However, while in and around the settlement, Darwin was able to add further specimens to his zoological and botanical collections including a native bush *rat (Rattus fuscipes) a* frog, at least 10 species of fish, several shellfish and 66 species of insects, 48 of which were new to him.

His disparaging comments on leaving Australian shores would not have won him many friends:

Diary 14th March 1836

And on departing: Since leaving England I do not think we have visited any one place so very dull & uninteresting as K. George's Sound. Farewell Australia, you are a rising infant & doubtless some-day will reign a great princess in the South; but you are too great and ambitious for affection, yet not enough for respect; I leave your shores without sorrow or regret.[9]

Nevertheless, his observations during this period from the nucleus from which he developed his theory of evolution by natural selection, which is set out in his books titled "*On the Origin of the Species by Means of Natural Selection*" London, 1859 and "*The Descent of Man*", London, 1871.

February 7th, 1836

The Beagle *sailed from Tasmania and on the sixth of the ensuing month, reach King George's Sound, situated close to the south-west corner of Australia. We staid [sic] there eight days; and we did not during our voyage pass a more dull and uninteresting time. The country, viewed from an eminence, appears a woody plain, with here and there rounded and partly bare hills of granite protruding. One day I went out with a party, in hopes of seeing a kangaroo hunt, and walked over a good many miles of country. Everywhere we found the soil sandy, and very poor; it supported either a course vegetation of thin, low brush wood and wiry grass, or a forest of stunted trees. The scenery resembled that of the high sandstone platform of the Blue Mountains; the Casuarina (a tree somewhat resembling a scotch fir) is, however, here in greater number, and the eucalyptus in rather less. In the open parts there are many grass trees, – a plant which, in appearance, has some affinity with the palm; but, instead of being surmounted by a crown of noble fronds, it can boast merely a tuft of very course [sic] grass like leaves.*

The general bright green colour of the brushwood and other plants, viewed from a distance, seemed to promise fertility. A single walk, however, was enough to dispel such an illusion; and he who thinks with me will never wish to walk again in so uninviting a country.

One day I accompanied Captain Fitzroy[10] *to Bald Head; the place mention by so many navigators, where some imagined that they saw corals, and others that they saw petrified trees, standing in the position in which they had grown. According to our view, the beds have been formed by the wind having heaped up fine sand, composed of minute rounded particles of shells and corals, during which process branches and roots of trees, together with many land shells, became enclosed. The whole then became consolidated by the percolation of calcareous matter; and cylindrical cavities left by the decaying of the wood, and thus also filled up with a hard-pseudo- stalactitical stone. The weather is now wearing away the softer parts, and in consequence the hard casts of the roots and branches of the trees project above the surface, and, in a singularly deceptive manner, resemble the stumps of a dead thicket.*

A large tribe of natives, called the White Cockatoo Men, happened to pay the settlement a visit while we were there. These men, as well as those of the tribe belonging to King George's Sound, being tempted by the offer of some tubs of rice and sugar, were persuaded to hold a 'corrobery' [sic], or great dancing-party. As soon as it grew dark, small fires were lighted, and the men commenced their toilet, which consisted in painting themselves white in spots in lines. As soon as all was ready, large fires were kept blazing, round which the women and children were collected as spectators; the Cockatoo and King Georges men formed two distinct parties, and generally danced in answer to each other. The dancing consisted in their running either sideways or in Indian file into an open space and stamping the ground with great force as they marched together. Their heavy footsteps were accompanied by a kind of grunt, by beating their clubs and spears together, and by various other gesticulations, such as extending their arms and wriggling their bodies. It was the most rude, barbarous scene, and, to our ideas, without any sort of meaning; but we observed that the black women and children watched it

---

[9] *Voyage of the Beagle*. Everyman's Edition, London. 1840.
[10] Captain Robert Fitzroy (1805–1865), hydrographer and meteorologist, in command of *HMS Beagle*.

with the greatest pleasure. Perhaps these dances originally represented actions, such as wars and victories; there was one called the emu dance, in which each man extended his arm in a bent manner, like the neck of that bird. In another dance, one man imitated the movements of a kangaroo grazing in the woods, whilst a second crawled up, and pretended to spear him. When both tribes mingled in the dance, the ground trembled with a heaviness of the steps, and the area resounded with their wild cries. Everyone appeared in high spirits, and the group of nearly naked figures, viewed by the light of the blazing fires, all moving in hideous harmony, formed a perfect display of a festival amongst the lowest barbarians. In Tierra del Fuego, we have beheld many curious scenes in savage life, but never, I think, one where the natives where in such high spirits, and so perfectly at ease. After the dancing was over, the whole party formed a great circle on the ground, and the boiled rice and sugar was distributed, to the delight of all.

After several tedious delays from clouded weather, on 14th March, we gladly stood out with King George's Sound on our course to Keeling Island. Farewell, Australia!!![11]

Anthony Trollope 1871 to 1872

The well-known author Anthony Trollope made two visits to Australia. The first was in 1871 through to 1872 and the second was in 1875. Trollope had made his name as a writer in Victorian Britain and had at the time of his journeys to Australia, developed an extensive oeuvre of works including novels, novelettes, and travelogues. He was 56 years of age when he made his first excursion to Australia during which time he wrote the bulk of is accounts of the Australian colonies, including a number of travel articles for *The Daily Telegraph* in London.

It was in 1875 that he made his second visit to Australia, however the purpose this time was to assist his son with the enterprise he was engaged in at Mortray, a farming property in New South Wales. It is from his recollections of time spent in King George's Sound and Albany that the following extract is drawn.

… I reached the colony of Western Australia from Melbourne at Albany, and I left the colony starting from the same town for Adelaide in South Australia. Albany is a very pretty little town on King George's Sound, –which is, I believe, by far the best harbour on the southern coast of the continent. It is, moreover, very picturesque, although not equally so with Port Jackson and the coves around Sydney. In Albany there are a few stores, as shops are always called, a brewery, a depot for coals belonging to the Peninsula and Oriental Company, a church, a clergyman, two or three inns, and two or three government offices. Among the latter I found an old school fellow of my own, who filled the office of resident magistrate, and in that capacity acted as judge in all matters not affecting life for a district about as big as Great Britain. His training for these legal duties he had gained by many years-service in the Prussian army, and, I was told, did his work uncommonly well. Albany itself was very pretty, with a free outlook on to a fine harbour, with bluff headlands and picturesque islands. The climate is delightful. The place is healthy. I was assured that the beer brewed there was good. The grapes were certainly good. For a few moments I thought that I also would like to be a resident judge at Albany, with unlimited magisterial power over perhaps a thousand people. It is pleasant, where everyone's lot is cast, to be, if not the biggest, at least among the biggest. But I was told that even at Albany there were squabbles, infections, and that the rose colour of the place did not prevail always. And then though the grapes grew there, and other fruits, and some flowers, I could not find anything else growing. The useless scrub covered the stony hilltops close up to the town. The capital was distant to 260 miles, and between it and the capital there is nothing. The mails come and went once a month. At each of my visits to Albany the mail excitement was existing. The Tichborne case was at its highest, and people had much to say.[12] *When I was departing, there were two bishops there. I fancy that I saw the best of Albany, and that it would be rather dull between the mails.*

I travelled to Perth with a friend, having made a bargain with the mail contractor to take us, – not with the mail, which goes through without stopping in 72 hours, – but by separate conveyance in four days, so that we might sleep during the night. This we did, taking our own provisions with us, and camping out in the bush under blankets. The camping out was, I think, rather pride on our part, to show the Australians that we Englishman,

---

[11] *Voyage of the Beagle*, London. Everyman's Edition. 1840.
[12] The Tichborne Case of the 1870s related to identity fraud which received widespread publicity in both England and Australia at the time.

—my friend, indeed, was a Scotchman [sic], could sleep on the ground, 'sub dio', and do without washing, and eat nastiness out of a box as well as they could…

… We lit fires for ourselves and boiled our tea in billies; and then regaled ourselves with bad brandy and water out of pannikins, cooked bacon and potatoes in a frying pan, and pretended to think that it was very jolly. My Scotch friend was a young man, and was perhaps, in earnest. For myself, I must acknowledge that when I got up at 5 o'clock on a dark wet morning, very damp, with the clothes and boots on which I was destined to wear for the day, with a necessity before me of packing up my wet blankets, and endeavoured, for some minutes in vain, to wake the snoring driver, who had been couched but a few feet from me, I did not feel any ardent desire to throw off forever the soft luxuries of an effeminate civilisation, in order that I might permanently enjoy the freedom of the bush. But I did it, and as well to be able to do it.

No man perhaps ever travelled two hundred and sixty miles with less to see. The road goes eternally through wood, – which in Australia is always called bush; and, possibly, sandy desert might be more tedious. But the bush in these parts never develops itself into scenery, never for a moment becomes interesting. There are no mountains, no hills that affect the eye, no vistas through the trees tempting the foot to wander. Once on the journey up, and once on the return, we saw kangaroos, but we saw no other animal; now and again a magpie was heard in the woods, but very rarely. The commonest noise is that of the bull-frog, which is very loud, and altogether unlike the Sound of frogs in Europe. It is said that the Dutch under Peter Nuyts, when landing somewhere on the east coast, probably near Albany, was so frightened by the frogs that they ran away. I can believe it, for I have heard frogs at Albany roaring in such a fashion as to make a stranger think that the hills were infested with legions of lions, tigers, bears, and rhinoceroses, and that every lion, tiger, bear, and rhinoceros in the country was just about to spring at him. I knew they were only frogs, and yet I did not like it. The bush in Australia generally it's singularly destitute of life. One hears much of the snakes, because the snakes are especially deadly; but one sees them seldom and no precaution in regard to them is taken. Of all the animals, the opossum is the commonest. He may be easily taken; as his habits are known, but he never shows himself. In perfect silence, the journey through the bush is made, fifteen miles to some waterhole, where breakfast is eaten; fifteen on to another waterhole, where brandy and water is consumed; fifteen again to more water, and dinner; and then again fifteen, till the place is reached in which the night fire is made and the blankets are stretched up on the ground. In such a journey, everything depends on one's companion, and in this I was more than ordinarily fortunate. [13]

Mary MacKillop 1873[14]

In 1866, Mary MacKillop, Sister of the Order of St Josephs, along with her sisters Annie and Lexie, had come to Penola in South Australia to open a Catholic school. MacKillop became the co-founder of the school that was subsequently opened there. After renovations were undertaken, the MacKillops started teaching an enrolment of more than 50 children in the school. It was at this time that MacKillop adopted the name of "Sister Mary of the Cross" and began wearing simple religious habits.[15]

Sister Mary travelled to Rome in 1873 to seek papal approval for the newly formed religious Order of Sisters of St Josephs of the Sacred Heart and was encouraged in her work by Pope Pius XI. Approval was given to this request 15 years later in 1888.

While in Europe, Sister Mary travelled widely to observe educational methods. She journeyed throughout Australasia to establish schools, convents and charitable institutions in the name of St Joseph. Her letter to her brethren pertains to a visit to King George's Sound on the 26th April 1873 as part of her travels.

S.S. Golconda
Arabian Sea
26th April 1873
May Jesus and Mary be praised.

---

[13] A. Trollope. *Australia*. Chapman and Hall, London. 1873.
[14] Now known as Saint Mary McKillop after her Canonization by Pope Benedict in 2010.
[15] A small group of nuns began to call themselves the Sisters of St Joseph of the Sacred Heart and moved to a new house in Adelaide where they founded a new school at the special behest of Bishop Lawrence Sheil.

My own dear sisters,

... As I wrote from King Georges Sound, you already know all up to that. You know I expected an uncle on board the mail at the Sound, when the Adelaide steamer [Rangatira] got in there, the mail had not yet arrived and was not expected till the next day. So, I was taken to a nice little cottage in quite a retired part of the town where, instead of having to go to the hotel, I was quietly attended to.

Whilst there I received an invitation from a Methodist preacher[16] to attend a 'meeting' that evening, which I politely declined saying I was a Catholic, after which he walked away, having first said that he hoped we should meet in heaven. I then made inquiries and found there was a Catholic church not far-off in which Rosary was said every evening. I found a Catholic child who took me there where I saw Father Delany[17] (but did not make myself known) ...

Then the steamer came in, and whilst I was wondering how I could ascertain whether uncle was on board or not and how I should find out the time to go on board, who should walk up past the cottage door but my uncle. Now see how the good God inspired him, the only one of the passengers who came that way, to take a walk just up to the very door of the house in which I was. He was surprised when I sent out for him, and I could not but see that he was struck with the peculiarity of having taken a stroll in that direction.

He then told me that his wife [Ellen Keogh] was also with him, that he had left her at the hotel, and that he would go and fetch her and we would return together. At the hotel, he introduced me to other old friends as 'Miss' – and as they were Protestants, I thought I had better tell the truth at once, and found them so nice. But they were puzzled what to call me, so I told them to address me as my uncle and his wife do – 'Mary' and thus ended that difficulty... We had a most prosperous voyage to Galle, the wind being favourable. ...

Once more, God bless you all – and don't forget to pray for
Your fond sister in J.M.J.
Mary of the Cross.[18]

The Prince George of Wales and The Prince Albert Victor of Wales.

An accident at sea during a gale off Cape Leeuwin in May 1881 caused the *HMS Bacchante*, with the two Royal Princes, both midshipmen on this ship, sons of The Prince of Wales, to seek harbour and assistance with a disabled rudder. The young princes and officers and crew of the ship were identified as being in good health after their ordeal. There were other vessels forming part of a naval squadron which continued to Cape Otway to await the return of *HMS Bacchante* after its repairs were completed. *The West Australian* newspaper printed the story:

From Resident Magistrate R.C. Loftie Esq.

The HMS Bacchante... anchored here at 3:30 pm yesterday [Sunday] with her rudder disabled. The accident occurred about 300 miles south of Albany. The Bacchante *parted company with the rest of the squadron on 11 May. The Rob Roy will tow in the* Bacchante *early this morning [Monday] from the anchorage, near Point Possession. Her commander [Lord Charles Scott] says he hopes to be able to effect the necessary repairs, with the assistance you can get here in the course for a few days. I shall do myself the honour of waiting upon the Royal Princes this morning.[19]*

The following extracts are taken from the diaries reprinted in *The English Illustrated Magazine*, March 1885, and '*The Cruise of H.M.S. Bacchante 1879 to 1882*, compiled from the private journals, letters, and notebooks of Prince Albert Victor and Prince George of Wales with additions by John N. Dalton, London 1886.[20]

---

[16] The Reverend Mr James B. Atkins, the Methodist Minister at Albany.
[17] The Reverend Bernard Delaney, the Roman Catholic Priest at Albany.
[18] Letter in the archives of the Sisters of the Josephite Order, North Sydney. Published in D. Sellick. *First Impressions*. West Australian Museum. 2000.
[19] *The West Australian*, Perth. 17 May 1881.
[20] Canon John N. Dalton, Priest-in-Ordinary to the Queen was the tutor to Their Royal Highnesses.

14th May, 1881

At 1 pm we passed under the west side of Breaksea Island, with the lighthouse on top of its red, rocky, precipitous sides, weatherworn from the westerlies that have beaten on it for ages... Bald Head, on our port and, seems covered with scrub, and here and there great patches of sand. After passing these two, the beautiful Sound opens out beyond. We steamed right on and up to the entrance of Princess Royal Harbour, away inside of which we can see the houses of Albany in the distance. Here we anchored about 3 pm for the night.

May 17th

... In the afternoon we went with Mr Loftie and Dr. Rogers and three ward room officers across to the opposite side of Princess Royal Harbour to the Quarantine Station to shoot quail. The low hills covered with dark trees, sloping down to the white sandy beach, with the blue water as calm as possible beneath the bright warm sun, reminded us very much in a general effect of Bermuda. We rowed across and landed at the small cottage which only a policeman and his family reside (as the place is very seldom used for quarantine), and there we lunched, and afterwards separated in parties to go over the hill for quail. There are a great many of them in the bush, but they are exceedingly shy, and require to be very silently and stealthily approached. There was too much chattering and laughing in our party, and so at first, we did not shoot anything. But afterwards the policeman took George and led him quietly aside in the bush when, whistling low, and so imitating the call of the quail, it was immediately answered by several of the birds, who thus were allured to come out from the very heather and shrubs along which we had been before walking without seeing a single one.

Standing on the top of the hill behind the Quarantine Station, we had a clear view of the whole of King George's Sound, and up into Oyster Harbour, which stretches away on the eastern opposite side is similar way to that in which Princess Royal Harbour does on the western. The hillside here abounds in Blackboys, curious black resinous stems, 3 feet high, and one in diameter with a small green tuft on top, and which makes a splendid fire in the bush when one is required. Of gum trees there also is no end, and we are told that so dry is the climate that if anyone catches a cold in the head here, he only has to take his blanket and sleep out in the open air, and he comes home cured; such effect have eucalyptus leaves.

Albany is said to have the finest climate in a continent of fine climates. Western Australia, close to India as it is, would make an excellent sanatorium for our English troops in southern India. At 4 p.m. we got into the boat again and rowed further up Princess Royal Harbour on the southern side, then again landed on a sandy beach; we walked up into the wood of gum trees behind the old cottage, once inhabited by a lime-burner of the name of McBride, but which is now deserted. The trees here were far larger and stood more thickly than any on the other side of the harbour; and the wood was full of parakeets who were shrieking and laughing, and from tree to tree were hanging all sorts of creepers and parasitic orchids, and the dry calm of the air was filled with an aromatic or resinous odour, while beside the path which was cut through the wood with several strangely shaped and brilliantly coloured flowers growing. Some of us wandered in one direction and some in the other, and as it was now time to get back to the boat, the wanderers were recalled by several 'cooeys'.

It was getting dusk when we shoved off from the beach to row back across the smooth surface of the harbour, in which we were reflected, as in a mirror, the rose, blue, green and golden hues of the sunset; a few streaky clouds alone were in the sky, in the water here and there were little scarcely perceptible catspaws made by puffs of wind. It was quite dark when we reached the ship, and the stars had all come out; there was no moon till two hours afterwards. So, ended our first day on Australian soil...

May 19th.

A cricket match between eleven of the ship, and in which George played, versus the Albany Union Club. We made 83 and they made 12 in the first innings; it was a good ground and the day was fine, with not too much sun, thermometer 65°. We then went in again and got 133; they made eighteen, but all their men were not out. The Bacchante's band came on shore, and played up at the cricket field, where there many of the colonists and a few Aborigines.

May 20th

Left the ship at 9 a.m. with two ward room and two-gun room messmates. Walked to the police barracks, there mounted our horses, and started with Mr Loftie for Marbellup and Wilsons Creek Inlet. Along the Perth Road for a mile out of the town, then turned off to the left through the scrub... We rode on to Marbellup, where we arrived about 4 p.m., 30 miles from Albany, at Mr Young's farm house and clearing. The mantlepieces, the tables, and the furniture are made of mahogany, or the darker jury [sic] wood and have a solid and handsome look. The broad large inglenook, with seats on either side, looks uncommonly snug with the iron dogs for the logs, a pile of which last are stacked on the veranda outside, so as to be conveniently handy for throwing on the fire all night through. Mr and Mrs Young, their two sons and two daughters, gave us a hearty welcome, and after taking a draft of warm, fresh milk of which there seems to be an inexhaustible supply all over the place, we walked up to a small shanty in which we are to stay. This consists of two rooms completely empty with bare floors. Each, however, has a large open fireplace, and plenty of jury wood stacked for use during the night. Two grand wood fires were already burning, bright and dry, such a contrast to what we have had for the last few weeks on board ship. A small two wheeled cart, that has brought our mattresses and rugs, and what few things we wanted for the night, had arrived before us, and we proceeded at once to make our toilet in the open air, for there is plenty of fresh water in the tank outside, and a small wooden trough does duty by turns for each of the party.

Bevis, a large kangaroo dog, sort of huge, brown, Scotch greyhound, looks on us as we make ourselves ready for Mrs Young's tea supper, for which we return to the farmhouse, and there everyone was very hearty and jolly, and did ample justice to the fowls, minced kangaroo, jam, cream, scones, and no end of the beautiful fresh milk and butter, such as which we have not tasted since we had left England... After tea, found our way up across the paddock to our night quarters, and there we slept as soundly as possible [nine in the two rooms] with the windows open and the fires burning. To iron bedsteads have been rigged up in one of the rooms, and the rest sleep on mattresses spread on the floor with their rugs wrapped around them. There are two pails of fresh milk, which some drink neat and others prefer to take mixed with a little whiskey before turning in. Some fall asleep at once, others not so soon... In the silent pauses between the tales, while they are collecting their wits, we can hear the croaking of the frogs away in the distance of the borders of the marsh, and with the sounds ultimately ringing out years we fell asleep.

May 24th

Sent birthday telegram to the Queen at Balmoral and received reply. Dressed ship rainbow fashion; then hang up the wash clothes in the rigging to dry... At noon fired a royal salute of 21 guns, and drank the Queen's health in the ward-room... The town council of Fremantle, the second town in the colony and chief port, telegraphed to us both their congratulations and expressions of loyalty, for which we thanked them, and said, 'We were glad to be spending the Queen's Birthday amid the loyalty of our fellow subjects on Australian soil'. The Queen's Birthday is the great gala day throughout the whole of Australasia; and each of the seven colonies vie with its neighbour in celebrating its loyalty. We had athletics sports for the ships company ashore on the cricket ground, which was great fun...

June 3rd

George's birthday. Raining hard nearly the whole day. Three bluejackets, who had gone ashore on leave, returned on board today, after having been lost for a night in the bush, which is very easily done when you want to get off the beaten track; after dark they had the sense, however, instead of wandering further about, to stop still where they were and lit a fire for the night. They had caught an opossum, which they roasted in its skin and shared amongst the three for supper; with the exception of that, the three quail which they managed to shoot, they had had nothing to eat for 36 hours, and therefore came on board at midday a bit hungry, and got a rubdown for their folly, which might have ended worse, except the good sense of one of the quartermasters, who was the senior of the party. We dined tonight with Mr and Mrs Loftie, and afterwards went to a ball given by Mr. Hassell at the court-house, or magistrates quarters, which was simply but effectively decorated, and which most of the officers of the Bacchante *and* Cleopatra *came...*[21]
The Bacchante's *band furnished the music.*

June 6th

... In the afternoon there was a riding party to King Point, from the high ground above which the best view is obtained all over the Sound and its twin offshoots, Princess Royal and Oyster Harbours, especially in the low light of the afternoon. From there we rode down over the hill to Middleton Beach, on the opposite slope, descending

---

[21] *HMS Cleopatra* arrived from Cape Otway where she had been detached from the squadron in order to see if *Bacchante* needed assistance.

> *to which, through the eucalyptus woods, another and quite different view opens inland over the scrub far away to the lagoons and high hills beyond... Mr Johnson, Rector of Albany, dined on board; as an Oxford man he is not more isolated here than he would be in many an English village, though he is 200 miles away from the nearest clergyman. For the telegraph gives him the latest European news every morning, and mail steamers which call in often bring him a passing colonial bishop on his flight homewards or outwards. The place is uncommonly healthy, and the people are hearty and kindly disposed.*
>
> *June 9th*
>
> *We were called at 1:30 am, as the mail was in. We went on board in the pinnace by the light of the moon and stars which, together with comet[22] and Saturn and Jupiter in conjunction, were all then brightly shining. We got two good cabins that happened to be vacant as far as forward as possible, and at 4 a.m. the* Cathay, *Captain Robbie, got underway... We steamed around the* Bacchante *and* Cleopatra, *whose lights, and those of the pilot's cottage, burning brightly at the top of the harbour, were the last sight we saw before we turned in and slept around till 8 a.m. the next morning.*[23]

As related in the diaries of Prince Albert Victor and Prince George it was Queen Victoria's birthday on the 24th May and, given the fact that at the time members of her royal household were present in the settlement, some exuberant celebrations took place among its citizenry. The *Albany Banner* newspaper reported on these celebrations:

> *24th May with Queen Victoria's birthday and a day the citizens of Albany won't forget in a hurry. The* HMS Bacchante *was anchored in the harbour and decorated with her bunting from stem to stern. Other ships had done likewise.*
>
> *The Albany Rifle Volunteers under Captain Finley, fell in for the parade about 11 am and after manual exercises had been gone through, and a march around town, the company drew up at the east end of Stirling Terrace opposite the Mount (belonging to Mr Clifton agent for the P&O company) and fired a 'feu de joie'. Punctually at 12 noon, a salute of 14 guns was fired from the* Bacchante.[24]

In July 1901 Prince George who would later become King George V made a further two visits to the town as the then Duke of York on his way to Melbourne. He was accompanied on these occasions by his wife the Duchess of Cornwall and York. The Royal couple arrived on the Royal Yacht *Ophir*. This visit was not a scheduled one on the Royal couple's agenda. This was because during the voyage from Adelaide to Perth, the *Ophir* had to stop at Albany due to stormy weather, and the Duke and Duchess subsequently continued their journey on to Perth by a special train. Originally Edward, the Prince of Wales and his wife Alexandra were scheduled to undertake a tour of the Empire, however, Queen Victoria's death on the 22nd January 1901 and with coronation duties to prepare for, Prince George and his wife Mary were assigned to undertake the voyage instead. The purpose of the visit was to officially open the first Federal Parliament in the Exhibition Buildings of Melbourne in 1901.

On the return homeward voyage to Melbourne, the Royal Yacht and its escort, which had been facing mountainous seas, took refuge in King George's Sound, arriving on Saturday 20th July, 1901. The Duke in his address to the people of Albany said:

> *It is an agreeable coincidence that for the third time in my life your port had proved to me a welcome harbour of refuge. I am glad that the Duchess thus unexpectedly has had an opportunity of visiting a place where, twenty years ago with my dear Brother, I spent three happy weeks, of which I have already preserved the pleasantest reminiscences.*[25]

---

[22] Tebbutt's Comet of 1881 or the Great Comment of 1881 (C/1881 K1) was discovered by the Australian amateur astronomer John Tebbutt. *Irish Astronomical Journal*, January, 1999. 26(1), 33
[23] The Royal Library, Windsor Castle, Berkshire. Reproduced with Gracious Permission of Her Majesty the Queen.
[24] *The Albany Banner*. 24th May 1881.
[25] D. Garden. *Albany: Panorama of the Sound*. Nelson. 1977..

Henry Archibald Lawson – 1889 to 1891

Among the many visitors to Albany during the Nineteenth Century was one Henry Archibald Lawson, best remembered today for his short story writing and poetic works and for being a contemporary of Andrew (Banjo) Patterson, also a celebrated writer and poet. Lawson wrote prolifically during the 1890s about life in the Australian bush. In fact, among his peers Lawson was well known for his laconic wit and prolific oeuvre of Australian colonial themed works.

Henry Lawson came to Western Australia on two occasions during the later years of the Nineteenth Century. Initially he travelled to the colony with his younger brother Peter. According to reports, apparently Henry was in some disgrace on the home front and had been exiled to Western Australia by his mother to stop him having an affair with a married woman. It is the five months of 1890 – 1891 that are of greatest interest in respect to the history of the Albany settlement, for while in Albany, Lawson worked for *The Observer* newspaper, writing a column titled *Straight Talk*. As he was only paid a penny a line by *The Observer* he needed to subsidise his writing income by working as a labourer during the day (as house painter among other occupations). Lawson said of Albany: *It will never change much - it is a pretty town but vague. I like it all the better for that.*[26]

Lawson was steadfastly a republican, and in his post Albany years regularly contributed to the Australian iconic magazine of the time called "*The Bulletin*". Unfortunately, Lawson struggled with alcoholism and was later diagnosed with a mental illness. Nonetheless, despite these health issues they did not diminish his contribution to the Australian culture that was evolving at that time in Australia.

The first extract reproduced from his writing on Albany is fittingly a poem titled: *On the Summit of Mount Clarence* (1890). On the top of Mount Clarence, Albany, W.A., stands a tall flagstaff, which was erected for signalling purposes before the telephone was laid from the town to Breaksea Island.

Wherefore the Muse:
On the summit of Mount Clarence rotting slowly in the air
Stands a tall and naked flagstaff, relic of the Russian scare,
Russian scare that scares no longer, for the cry is "All is well",
Yet the flagstaff still is standing like a lonely sentinel.
And it watches through the seasons, winter's cold and summer's heat,
Watches seaward, watches ever for the phantom Russian fleet.

In a cave among the ridges, where the scrub is tall and thick
With no human being near him dwells a wretched lunatic:
On Mount Clarence in the morning he will fix his burning eyes,
And he scans the sea and watches for the signal flag to rise;
In his ears the roar of cannon and the sound of battle drums
While he cleans his gun and watches for the foe that never comes.

And they say, at dreary nightfall, when the storms are howling round
Comes a phantom ship to anchor in the waters of the "Sound",
And the lunatic who sees it wakes the landscape with his whoops,
Loads his gun and marches seaward at the head of airy troops,
To the summit of Mount Clarence leads them on with martial tread,
Fires his gun and sends the Russians to the mustering of the dead.[27]

---

[26] Lawson, H. "*The Golden Nineties*", published in the Sydney based newspaper the *Australian Star*, Sydney. 1891.
[27] Ibid

Lawson's writing for *The Observer* was quite prolific, perhaps because he was being paid by the line. The following are extracts from a piece that he wrote titled *Albany Before the Boom*.

... Albany hasn't changed much since 1889 to 90, when the new town was built. There were one or two old families popularly supposed to exist there then, but they kept to themselves. It should be interesting to study the effects of nearly half a century of utter loneliness and isolation upon their temperaments. There were a few common white Aborigines [sic], who were supposed to have been, and doubtless were, more or less, the slaves of the one or two first families in the days before the advent of the first steam engine... The seeker after information, local, historical, genealogical, or otherwise, was met with growling monosyllables, ominous in tone, and warning frowns, which may have been intended for his good. For the rest, Albany was at camp of the T'othersiders and new-chums – tradesmen, labourers, and clerks; the train was running to Perth then, and things were going ahead in the building line in Albany.

Road makers, - and the Lord knows where those roads were made to, or why they were made, - went out into the wilderness, lived on Kangaroo when rations gave out before the contract was completed. Nice, soft, juicy new chums, poor devils. Went into the bush, fencing, clearing, running wire of contractors, and cooking for camps; and shed their skins, like snakes because of the heat and the mosquitoes; and broke their hearts-and went mad, some of them – because of the terrible loneliness in the past; and died, and were buried or not, as it happened. Or they fought out their own salvation, and got away East – never dreaming that, a year or so hence - as count of jumpers, clerks etc. in eastern cities – they might be scraping, and scheming, and stinting all the day, for the price of a steerage ticket to the Golden West, and lying awake, think, think, thinking over it till the small hours, to fall asleep and dream that they had got it in a lump sum. We were lonely T'othersiders then, and the first families didn't seem aware of our existence, and we clung together – never dreaming that in two or three years we would rush the country in thousands and swamp out the Sand Groper element as completely as if it had taken to the outer wilderness and committed suicide. But I mean to do the Sand Gropers justice later on...

Alleged Aboriginal names ending in up along the line from Albany; there are 'Marbellup", 'Kendenup', and there's a place called 'Chockerup'. The bush around there looks just the place for it. By the way, speaking of black means, the blacks around King George's Sound use the words 'boomerang', 'nulla', 'baal', 'budgeree', etc., and new chums-and most of the T'othersiders, I believe – think they are speaking from their own language; whereas those terms were bought by the whites from the East, and the blacks themselves, no doubt, take them as English words. They of course have a different dialect from that of the Aborigines of old Eastern Australia ...

Albany has long been the first and last corner of Australia as far as the world is concerned. It is the first spot of Australian ground seen and trodden by the majority of immigrants, tourists and professional wanderers; the last by most departing Australians. The first place from which we get to the gist of English mail news, the last whereat we post letters in Australia. Albany holds a unique position geographically and is unique in several other respects. It has the only harbour as far as West Australia is concerned; and I don't remember ever seeing it written about...

Albany is situated on the side of the ridge sloping to the shores of the inner Sound or harbour [apparently landlocked as viewed from the town], the ridge running in a concave curve between two rocky, rugged hills of considerable height – hills and ridge isolated: the whole something suggestive, from the steamer's deck, of a roofless grandstand, flanked by squat towers. Albany is something larger than Watsons Bay [a coastal feature in Sydney], built closer, would be. The parallel streets, from the water's edge to the top of the ridge are called 'terraces. The town has a good front, something quaint, yet because there is only a row of buildings facing you, and built close together, there is the suggestion of an imposing reality as retained by a model, on the smaller scale, of a great city... The Albany post and telegraph office (of more importance to eastern Australia than we realise) looks more imposing from the water than from the street front, on account of its deep basement. It is, if I remember, in situation about the first and last building in Albany – under the corner of Mount Clarence. The new, rounded wing, built in some quaint, old English style, is it a sighted improvement, being picturesque and refreshing to eyes grown weary of the square and oblong architecture of eastern Australian cities. The style of the new retaining wall, with its steps down to the water, is also original – pretty and pleasing...

Across the opposite shore from the town are sandhills, among which is situated many desirable town allotments, sold to innocent stay at home Sydney and Melbourne siders in the vague stir that preceded the gold boom. From the shallows at the head of the harbour (a great deal of which is barely covered by the tide) dark, dank, scrub and marshy ti-tree [sic] country running round to the coastal wastes of dry scrub. Outside are naked bluffs and headlands. And, from the back doors of Albany, on the top of the ridge, a brooding wilderness sweeping away and round to blazing sand wastes – to the great gulf and across South Australia into New South Wales and Queensland. Look at the map, and get some idea of the awful, hopeless immensity of it....[28]

Mark Twain (Samuel L. Clemens) - 1896

Samuel L. Clemens known perhaps more by his pen name Mark Twain, was an American humourist, novelist, writer, raconteur and lecturer. His career as a writer started with an array of articles for American newspapers, and it was not long thereafter that he began writing short stories to general acclaim. Initially however, Clemens had trained as a steamboat pilot and gained his licence after two years of study as an apprentice on the Mississippi River. The steamboat experiences would feature significantly in some of the plots in his stories.

Clemens's book *The Innocents Abroad*, published in 1869, contained anecdotes about his extensive travels around the world during which he would inspire audiences with his lectures and speeches in various 'stop over' locations. As a result of his many travels, he became a well-known and read global celebrity. Clemens was best known in America for the travel books he penned over a period of some forty years travelling the world, alone or with his family. In many of the countries he visited Clemens as Mark Twain was seen as "a self-appointed Ambassador for the United States of America", often functioning as both tour guide and tourist.

Clemens was in Australia from September of 1895 to January of 1896 and visited south-eastern territories: New South Wales, Victoria, South Australia and Tasmania. He showed great interest in Australia's economic history as a convict settlement; its treatment of its native peoples; and its unusual wildlife all of which became significant features which he made comment about during the Australian leg of his travels.

He saw the shoreline of Western Australia from his ship, *Oceania*, on its way to Ceylon. The ship anchored off-shore from Albany on January 4th, 1896 and remarked in his diary:

January 4, 1896.

Christmas in Melbourne, New Year's Day in Adelaide, and saw most of the friends again in both places... Lying here at anchor all day – Albany (King George's Sound), Western Australia. It's a perfectly landlocked harbour, or roadstead - spacious to look at, but not deep water. Desolate looking rocks and scarred hills. Plenty of ships arriving now, rushing to the new goldfields. The papers are full of wonderful tales of the sort always to be heard in connection with new gold diggings. Example: youth staked out a claim and tried to sell half of it for £5 (pounds); no takers; he stuck to it for 14 days starving, then struck it rich and sold out for £10,000...

About sunset, strong breeze blowing, got up the anchor. We were in a small deep puddle, with a narrow channel leading out of it, minutely buoyed, to the sea. I stayed on deck to see how we were going to manage it with such a big ship and such a strong wind. On the bridge our giant captain, in uniform; and by his side a little pilot in elaborately gold laced uniform; on the forecastle a white mate and quartermaster or two, and a brilliant crowd of lascars[29] standing by for business. Our stern was pointing straight at the head of the channel; so, we must turn entirely around in the puddle - and the wind blowing as described. It was done, and beautifully. It was done by the help of a jib. We stirred up much mud but did not touch the bottom. We turned right round in our tracks – a seeming impossibility... By the time we were entirely around and pointed, the first buoy was not more than 100 yards in front of us. Was a fine piece of work, and I was the only passenger that saw it. However, the others got their dinner; the P&O Company got mine...[30]

---

[28] Ibid
[29] A Lascar was a term used in the Nineteenth Century to refer to sailors from India and Asia.
[30] Samuel L. Clemens. *Following the Equator. A Journey Around the World*. Hartford. 1897.

Herbert Clark Hoover - 1897 to 1898

Herbert Clark Hoover was a mining engineer, humanitarian, and an American statesman; probably best known as the 31st President of the United States of America during the tumultuous depression years. After graduating in 1895 from Stanford University in California he worked for two years in various mining related jobs in the general south-west of the American continent. In 1897 an offer was made by the British mining engineering firm of Bewick and Moreing Company inviting him to undertake an examination and exploration of mines located in the West Australian goldfields. During his visit to the goldfields, he inspected mining activities in Coolgardie and Kalgoorlie and on an earlier trip, visited the remote but as yet to be developed goldmine the 'Sons of Gwalia' near Leanora. By the time he left Western Australia in 1898 he was one of the most respected mining engineers in the colony.

Hoover was known for his phenomenal memory and capacity for work. He was a co-founder of the Zinc Corporation that later became Rio Tinto Zinc Corporation at Broken Hill. Notwithstanding his mining prowess, Hoover is best remembered for his humanitarian relief efforts, particularly in Europe during and after World War I and further his tenure as President of United States from 1929 – 1933. Extracts from his three-volume book titled "*Memoirs*" relating to his visit to King George's Sound is reproduced here:

> *The firm had acquired a number of goldmines in the newly discovered fields of central Western Australia. American machinery and technical practice in gold mining were far ahead of those of the Australians and British My employment was for general engineering work among a group of some 10 mines and a number of prospecting ventures, and I was subordinate to a resident partner of the firm. With the journey to Western Australia came glimpses for me of further new worlds – in France, Italy, Egypt, and India. History became a reality and America a contrast.*
>
> *Arrival at the van port of Western Australia, Albany, was a rude shock, because smallpox had broken out on board, and I spent my first two weeks in a Quarantine Station. Finally arrived at the desert mining camp of Coolgardie, over the 300 miles of newly constructed narrow-gauge railway.*

Harry Furness - 1859

Harry Furness was a famous illustrator, caricaturist and writer. His most famous humorous drawings were published in *Punch*, a very popular British magazine. However, it is his two-volume autobiography, titled *The Confessions of a Caricaturist* published in 1902, that holds some interest in respect to Albany. As can be detected from the entry on the town in his book he was not enamoured with it, in fact he could not wait to leave.

> *"I thank my stars I am clean out of that one-horse town Albany! "*
> *Another traveller who had joined the ship at the same town and who lay huddled up in the corner more dead than alive after a severe attack of typhoid followed by pleurisy, remarked: "Well you must admit, sir, it is the healthiest place in Western Australia."*
> *"Co-rect [sic], stranger co-rect" replied to Yankee. "Correct! Guess that's why I have cleared out. This darned Albany is 90 per cent of climate and only 10 per cent of business."*
> *I visited Albany on my return journey. It struck me that in 'Sleepy Hollow' 90per cent of the inhabitants were in bed the other 10 per cent were dozing on the seats on the parade.*[31]

Eastern Colony Newspaper Reports on Traveller Reflections

Like Furness the Eastern Colonies were not impressed with the development of the town and in 1859 a strongly worded article appeared in *The Argus* Melbourne newspaper. Inter-colony rivalry was most evident in the following exchange in *The Argus* followed by a local 'Albanian' response to the criticisms it made about the town. Extracts from the article give a flavour to the opinion it expressed:

> *A Correspondent. The Argus of Melbourne. Tuesday, 22 March, 1859.*
> *The history of King George' Sound and the dreamy little township of Albany, appears to be wrapped up in considerable obscurity. But if any inquiring-minded traveller should expect to enubilate the historic fogginess of*

---

[31] Furniss, H. *The Confessions of a Caricaturist*. Unwin, *1901*.

the place by probing the intelligence of its inhabitants, let him at once prepare for the most utter discomfiture. The good people of Albany guard what stock of information they may possess with a heroism of reticence that sets at nought all attempts to get access to it. They treasure up the traditions of the settlement as jealously as the Peruvians guard their llama flocks and dole out their hoarded knowledge with a miserly reluctance that yields only to excessive importunity.

The brief account here following is therefore the result of such observation as was accessible in despite of these specified hindrances, and, in fact, the mere impression of a looker-on. King George's Sound is a safe, commodious and readily accessible harbour, with entrances marked by two precipitous granite rocks, equidistant from each other and the mainland. On one of these islands, the western and outermost, is a lighthouse, erected by convict labour, at a considerable elevation and visible far to the eastward, though not so available for ships in the opposite direction, owing to an intervening headland. A few miles from the entrance to the Sound is a narrow passage leading to the inner harbour, which is nearly circular and some three miles in diameter, with an ample depth of water.

On the shore of this harbour is the town of Albany, with its torpid population of two or three hundred souls, chiefly occupied in doing nothing. The great characteristic of the Albany people is thorough indolence and prodigious belief in any exertion, mental or bodily, that can possibly be avoided…

I go on board the Indiaman, a bluff-bowed, lubberly, strong timbered ship with nearly the mail steamer's beam but about half her length. I take my pocket-knife, cut through about 50 layers of white paint, and find the old John Company, teak-built of course.[32] She has been afloat some 80 years and one naturally pictures the original skipper in his nankeen, smalls and braided pigtail and perhaps a small sword and diamond shoe buckle, doing the stately and amiable to some gorgeous yellow-cheeked nabob tribe who had paid a small fortune to be bobbing about on the salt water for some eight months at a stretch and to be kept alive on tough poultry and claret. I go on shore, and the boatman bumps me clumsily on the beach, he falls back exhausted and extends his hand for the money.

I approached the nearest house, and a large dog stalks out solemnly, puts his head languidly on one side and with an evident effort, barks twice, producing a sort of sluggish double-knock effect suggestive of a worn-out postman. I pass several Albanians, who exhibit no sign of remark that strangers had come amongst them; but I intuitively feel that by the time they had passed by us some 20 yards a slight speculative emotion would appear in their countenances as to whether we might not have arrived by the mail steamer. A solitary windmill overlooks the town and has suddenly commenced turning tediously round, as though dreamily revolving in its great stupid head what such unwanted excitement might portend[33]. I make my way to the post-office, the position of which is providentially indicated by a flag, or the probability is that the Albanians might had a difficulty in directing strangers. I want stamps but the Postmaster General has gone off with the key to the desk and, being a clerk of Petty Sessions, he will have to look in at the Court, and then he will probably just step to his dwelling and give an eye to the dinner and so I have to while away the time by talking to the police. The police force numbers a total of three men – viz one inspector, one sergeant and one plain constable. The sergeant, a man of singular intelligence, took me over the Government office, and pointed out a curious old chart on which a strong dotted line marked the course of Captain Vancouver to King George the Third's Sound in 1791. On this chart the southern portion of Victoria is smoothly rounded off without any indentation in the coast line that can be construed into a recognition of either Port Phillip or Western Port.

A West Australian is fishing from the coal hulk, and the fish are squabbling in the clear water as to which shall bite first. The West Australian is smoking with both hands in his pocket and is evidently waiting for a fish to exhaust itself in vain struggling before he undergoes the fatigue of pulling him in. The West Australian has resided here for 17 years but has never heard of the greatest event associated with the colony – viz West Australia winning the Derby. I met with one old settler, who had been here for seven and twenty years. He told me, with a lachrymose air, that he had seen half-a-dozen whalers in the harbour at the same time, but the whales had most capriciously deserted the coast and the poor fellow seemed half inclined to blubber at the

---

[32] The Old John Company was a nickname for The East India Company.
[33] The windmill referred to here was built in 1858 on Albany lot S16, on the corner of Spencer and Frederick Streets by George Cheyne.

recollection. The population appear to subsist upon the mail steamers and the chance visits of whaling ships and traders, with whom they barter vegetables and native production for tea and sugar and manufactured goods. That the climate is healthy is beyond any question, it being the only point upon which the general testimony appeared to agree. An old woman, who declared that she was in her 70th year, and yet looked plump and mischievous, informed me that for five and twenty years she had never known one of her sex die at Albany and very few of the other sex excepting from accident. But said I, have they never any dangerous illnesses here?" "Oh yes" she replied sometimes they have serious ailments; but then they go to Perth for medical advice and die there. It appears to be not by any means colonial etiquette to die at Albany.

The soil for a long distance round King George's Sound is very sandy, and generally poor; but vegetables of every kind appear to grow well and we purchased some enormous onions that brought tears into the eyes of the gardener who parted from them. In fact, they weighed on an average 2lb each.

A poisonous herb infests the bush here, and is very destructive to cattle which, however, appear to in many instances acquire an instinctive avoidance of this pernicious food. The Aboriginal natives of West Australia have certainly a superior mental organisation to that of any other Australian tribe I have met with. Their physical conformation is also in more of a countenance with European ideas of propriety and comeliness. They have long, straight chestnut coloured hair and features by no means disagreeable or unintelligent and they have also a great philological talent and several I have met with possess lingual acquirements that are highly creditable to the supposed stunted intellect of the Australian savage. The natives are copper-coloured and uniformly wear a mantle of kangaroo skin looped at the right shoulder and classically draped around the body. Their feats with spear and boomerang are among the staple sources of amusement for strangers...

The booming echo of the recall gun for passengers rolls lazily around the harbour and this letter must be closed.
[34]

A local resident did, however, stand up for the town and its appellation as "Sleepy Hollow".

To the Editor of the Inquirer and Commercial Newspapers
King George's Sound, January 21 1863

Sir,
In your impression of 31st December, you reprinted from The Friend of India a paragraph to the effect that "there is nothing the inhabitants of the energetic portions of the colony more deprecate, than being identified in any way, as regards or action, with the apathetic denizens of that "Sleepy Hollow," King George's Sound, where love or money can scarcely procure fish, poultry, or vegetables, although the neighbouring bays abound with the first, and the others might be reared and cultivated to advantage, did the slightest modicum of energy pervade people."

It is not often that one single paragraph states so many truths, and yet arrives at such erroneous conclusions.

There can be little doubt that the dwellers on the "banks of the placid Swan" do not identify themselves with the so called "apathetic denizens" of Albany, but the question of the fitness of application of this term may be open to discussion when we know that the "energetic" inhabitants of our metropolis are content to permit the road to their mail port to be in such a state that letters take fully 5 days to travel 240 miles.

Nothing can be more true than that "fish, poultry, or vegetables can scarcely be procured," but a man labours at that which pays him best, and as people here are well to do, it is clear they find no lack of more remunerative employment than cultivating cabbages or rearing chickens. It is scarcely fair to stigmatize a people as being without "the slightest modicum of energy" when many of our fellow-townsmen began without a shilling, and, by application of ability, have amassed thousands, and while we daily read in your columns that any person purchasing the Government property, "formerly known as Daniel's Hotel, "must have made a fortune" while it is well known that Mr Daniel is an illustration of the truth of my remarks.

---

[34] The *Argus*. Melbourne. 22nd March 1859.

Albany is virtually cut off from the rest of this colony by want of roads; produce cannot be brought into the settlement from the cost of cartage, and consequently our money is thrown into the lap of South Australia instead of being scattered amongst our own population.

As West Australians we cannot but feel hurt that our very existence should be almost ignored by our fellow-colonists at Perth, and by our Government; that our splendid harbour should be neglected; that the Port of Fremantle, with its "modicum" of shipping, should possess a Water Police, a Harbour Master and his Staff; while our Port, with three times the tonnage, should have one solitary Pilot with a boat's crew of convicts.

Let it not be supposed that we complain of our want of prosperity; the shipping and the P&O Company circulate sovereigns enough to meet our wants, and to spare, but it is with sorrow we perceive this money diverted to another colony when our own only requires a good main road to retain the whole of it.
I am, Sir,
Your obedient servant,
An Apathetic Denizen of Sleepy Hollow,[35]

The Perth Gazette carried a similar piece from 'a visitor' refuting the 'sleepy hollow' tag that had be ascribed to the town claiming instead that government neglect of the towns needs was the underpinning issue that needed to be addressed:

To the editor of the Independent Journal.
Albany, November 1, 1853

Sir,
I have observed your remarks in several of the late numbers of the Gazette, endeavouring to stimulate and arouse energy in the settlers of Albany. Now from what I can see of the inhabitants generally of Albany, I should say they are quite as energetic as those of the 'metropolis' (if it can be so-called), were they not thwarted and opposed by some short-sighted old settlers and a revenue squandering government.

No roads are improved, bridges built, or anything done for the improvement of this part of the colony, which, were it properly attended to, would soon become of considerable importance from the advantages it will derive from at superior harbour situation, &c, but as the Albanian say what can I expect at such a distance when the whole, and more if it could be obtained, of the revenue money is required to build follies, government stables, steeples to school houses, and other absurdities in Perth.

If I ask a settler in the bush why he does not grow potatoes and other farm produce for the market, his answer directly is what is the good one such produce would cost more than that it's worth in carting to the town, through the most impossible state of the roads.
I have met several parties from the steamers who would have purchased and taken up land to a considerable amount but being so thoroughly disgusted with the shameful neglect in the public works and arrangements that they immediately gave up the idea of remaining and went onto other colonies, where, they felt convinced, the public welfare is better cared for.
I am, sir,
Yours respectfully,
A Visitor.[36]

During the latter years of the Nineteenth Century there were many tourists who visited Albany on their way either to or from the eastern colonies. Fortunately, there is therefore, a surfeit of diary entries to choose from that enrich The Historical Record of Nineteenth Century Albany. The extracts from the published diaries of Rosamond and Florence Hill who visited King George's Sound and the town in 1874, give a flavour to the general views expressed:

It was with a sense of exhilaration that, steaming up the narrow entrance to the inner harbour of King George's Sound, we felt we had happily accomplished so large a part of our voyage. In consequence of the delay in our arrival, we expected to find the branch mail boat, which was to convey us to Adelaide, with steam up, ready for starting. Indeed, the capture of these vessels were represented as being so impatient to carry off their mails, that

---

[35] The Inquirer and Commercial News. Perth. 18th February 1863.
[36] The Perth Gazette, and Independent Journal of Politics and News. 2nd December 1853.

cargo and even passengers might be easily left behind. The reason for this extraordinary haste, we were told, was the natural desire of the South Australians to obtain their English news as quickly as possible, and – softly be it whispered- before the Victorians could get theirs… By the telegraph, established between the capitals, the one which first received the news triumphantly flashed it to the other.

Before five o'clock on the morning of April 2nd, and consequently long before it was light, our bed-room-steward knocked at our cabin-door, telling us the Adelaide boat has arrived during the night, and would start at six precisely. There was no time to be lost, and we dressed as quickly as possible. Several of our fellow-passengers having heard we were departing, appeared in various forms of deshabille to wish us farewell. Ongoing on deck we found the captain's rig lowered and manned in readiness for us, and himself waiting to bid us good bye before he "turned in", to make up while he could for much sleep lost during our late rough weather. Under his chief officer's courteous escort, the six Chinamen rowed our one fellow-passenger for Adelaide and ourselves in a very few minutes to the Rangatira, but on reaching her deck we saw plainly she was not on the point of starting. She had not even finished discharging her cargo for the Sound and had yet to take in all we had brought her for Adelaide.

The sun, just risen, was lighting up the bay from point to point… over the water, now smooth as glass. But the morning aspect of the mouth are exceedingly fine in form – and beyond the ranges of the hills near the coast rises, some distance inland, a really noble peak; while the little township of Albany, close to the water's edge, with its English – looking church and one or two pretty country-houses on a slight eminence, has a nest and well-to-do air.

…Founded in 1827 on principle of colonization, the unsoundness of which were soon demonstrated, and constituting rather an out – station of Government police than a self-governing settlement, the colony never flourished, and in 1849 abandonment even was contemplated. This idea, however, was relinquished for a scheme which should furnish the place with labour in the shape of English convicts. The large sums which flowed into the colony from the imperial treasury for their support, until in 1867 were ceased "to take the scum of people and wicked condemned men" wherewith to argument the population of this new country, made money so abundant that the colonists could purchase all they needed.

West Australia is now awakening to a sense of the demoralizing process she has now undergone and rousing herself to honourable independence. She is beginning to boast of her vast resources, and to seek means for their development. Like each of her sisters, she says she will by-and-by be the leading nation of the southern world. But these at present are the aspirations only of her nobler spirits. No such patriotic ardour seems yet to have Albany, as this morning's experience taught us to our cost. After weary watching, the colonial postbag at length came lazily on board, but still we had to wait for the mails from England. Someone on shore had the contract for their transhipment, and that someone had not yet appeared. All Albany boats are moved by sail – because theirs crews are too indolent to row, say sarcastic critics – and there was no breeze. One rose at last, signs of activity showed themselves at a spot where a buoy marked our turning-place with the local mail-boat, and gladly did we draw up alongside.

From some West Australian ladies when after two or three days they ventured to emerge from their berths, and subsequently from other compatriots, we heard much which strengthened our intention of visiting their country on our homeward voyage; and it was and remains a source of much regret that, when occasion arrived, time did not permit us to do more than land for an hour at Albany.

What information we meantime gathered concerning this portion of Australia we may perhaps most appropriately relate when we describe that very short but interesting visit homeward bound...

We reached Albany about 11 p.m. February 4th, [1874], and as our ship would sail again at noon on the following day, we hastened on shore next morning, having but scant time for a glimpse'- all that was now possible - of West Australia. The little town is surrounded by scrub, or is rather actually built upon it, unreclaimed land intermingled with the houses and gardens. A closer inspection modified our previous conclusion as to its neatness, revealing indeed among its poorer houses a general untidiness invisible from the deck of the steamer.

Our first stopping place was the post office, both to enquire for letters from home and to despatch others to Adelaide. While we were transacting our business, which involved the purchase of stamps and some writing, a little boy approached with a letter he desired to post. Not wishing to detain the child, we made room for him to come up to the window; when, with a courtesy we shall always remember in association with West Australia, he drew back, saying "No, you are ladies, and must be served first".

Continuing our walk, we soon reached a plain but substantial school-house, and on entering found the master giving instruction to boys and girls together. Mixed schools prevail in West Australia. Out of sixty Government or public schools in the colony – to which "necessitous persons" are admitted free – there are but six in which the sexes are divided. The Albany schoolmaster told us that several of his pupils live as far as five miles off, at the same time pointing out quite a little lad who had come that distance. Some arrive in carts, others ride on horseback, "for", added he, "our children must learn to be independent". The scholars were healthy-looking and had an air of self-reliance pleasant to see.

...Here also were a few Aborigines, looking much more like savages than any we had seen elsewhere. Their shaggy straggling hair hung down on their shoulders, and their only garment was a blanket, leaving their legs and feet bare. Judging, however, from what was related to us of the natives of this part of Australia, they must be shrewd and quick-witted. They seem also to possess qualities which cause those taken into the houses of the colonists to be treated as petted children, and their most provoking misdeeds to be pardoned over and over again... Among the Aborigines at Albany some had boomerangs to sell, or to throw for the amusement of strangers. We had not seen them before in the hands of natives and should have been interested in witnessing the use of this curious weapon, and glad, also, to buy some to bring home; but the certainty that the money we should give would be spent on drink deterred us.[37].

Travellers' Remarks

The next insight into the colony's development is provided in 1854 by a P&O passenger on the steam ship *Chusan* and is garnered from his notebook containing observations of his journey from Sydney to England.

The Chusan is a beautiful new screw steamship of 750 tons... she is built remarkably strong, well found in everything and is, without exception, as fine a little vessel (considering her power) as ever floated the waters of the ocean. Her cabin accommodation is most superior, very lofty, and beautifully ventilated – a great desideratum in the warm climates she traverses. When clean, and in good condition, she can steam from eight and a half to nine knots; but with the addition of her sails and strong breezes, she can attain the speed of thirteen and fourteen knots with ease.

Captain Down is a thorough gentleman, and an able seaman; careful, but at the same time fears neither wind nor weather but has a peculiar weakness for dealing most liberally with canvas, studding; sails, booms &c, whenever an opportunity or half a chance offers. Rest assured of one thing, that if she misses the mail, or makes a long passage, it is not the fault of Captain Down, whatever other cause or circumstance may lay in the way. The purser and officers, including the engineers, are also gentlemen, thoroughly obliging in their manners, and seem evidently bent upon studying both the interests of passengers and owners.

...Saturday December 10.
At day light, land in sight, which turned out, as we approached further, to be Bald Head, about eight miles from the entrance to King George's Sound. The coast here presents a barren, broken appearance, very similar to that in the vicinity of Wilson's Promontory and the Islands in Bass's Straits; more prettily interspersed with low and lofty mountains, rising with tapered tops, but almost free from any symptom of vegetation whatsoever. As we continued our course, several other islands were in sight, two of which form the entrance of the harbour leading to the Sound, with Bald Head on the left, making three capital and safe passages for vessels of any tonnage; passing these, and about four miles of the harbour referred to, you enter the Sound, which forms a beautiful and extensive basin, and capable of containing any amount of shipping, and is certainly a most desirable place for just what it is, viz – a coal depot. There are here now nine vessels, principally foreigners, who have been chartered with coal for the Australian Royal Mail and P&O Companies; and another large vessel arrived this morning from Newcastle [England], out eighty-eight days, with about 1000 tons of coal.

---

[37] Rosamond & Florence Hill. *What We Saw in Australia*. London, 1875.

The town of Albany, situated on the northern side of the bay, is a small place with about fifty houses, which, with the district around, is supposed to contain a population of 500 people. There is a small church, a courthouse, public-house, and goal, with numerous other odd buildings, which have, at some time or other, had some connection with the Government, but are now in the occupation of nobody knows who. It seems a sort of place that was going to be something all in a hurry and then stopped; from the want of funds, or some other cause not originally anticipated. With the exception of a few idle seamen in the vicinity of the aforesaid public house, and a large number of men employed carrying coal on shore, you would almost fancy the place deserted, or given over to the possession of the Blacks, who seem the principal occupants of the city. There is, however, one large house being erected, and I should think, from the size of it, compared with the others, that it is intended for the Governor, if there is such an illustrious person, or if not, will be looked upon in the light of one, as soon as ever it is occupied.

Without any intention or desire of libeling the town or irritating the feelings of any of its inhabitants, I must say, in all my travels (which perhaps have not been great), I never saw a more cold, lifeless, petrifying place in all my life. The scenery from the hill, however, surrounding the town, of the Sound, Harbour, Ocean and country about, and islands, form a most beautiful and picturesque appearance. In many parts of the bush, Nature has planted her own garden with a great variety of native flowers, which flourish most luxuriantly, and far excel any in the neighbourhood of Sydney. The shipping lay about a quarter of a mile from the shore, which consists of a sandy beach with the town just at the back, the access to which is along a substantial jetty of 200 or 300 yards in length made for the purpose of ensuring coals to the above which, with the quantity afloat in the bay, is supposed to exceed 15,000 tons, belonging to the two companies. Having disposed of King George's Sound, and the town of Albany, we turn out attention on board the Chusan again, which we find busy taking in coals at all corners, and will continue all night, in order to get away tomorrow morning at 9 o'clock, for Point de Galle, Ceylon, where we hope yet to arrive in time for the mail.[38]

The Leader Magazine in Melbourne published an article by a 'Contributing Traveller" in 1873 which offered a snapshot of the colony 20 years after a passenger's 1854 remarks previously published in *The Sydney Morning Herald*:

After six days at sea, the ugliest and most dreary port in the most bleak and inhospitable country of the world would seem terrestrial paradise, a land flowing with milk and honey. No wonder, then, that Albany is regarded by passengers as a sort of oasis in a watery desert, and that the few hours' stay on shore amongst its flora and fauna, enjoying the aroma of its flower gardens and Aborigines – the esprit de corps I heard the latter styled by a Frenchman – is universally look forward to as an agreeable break in the monotony of the voyage.

…Convict labour has done a great deal for Albany; the roads are well formed, and the curbing and channeling would do credit to Collins Street. Full advantage has been taken of the physical formation of the ground, and the road from the jetty to the township is by a succession of terraces. But although many substantial improvements have been made within the last few years, Albany is still in a very primitive condition; the wants of the inhabitants seem to be very easily supplied, and commodities which in every Victorian village would be regarded as necessaries do not seem to form any portion of an Albanian storekeeper's stock-in-trade. The inns are execrable, and the largest does not rise above the level of a sailor's public house. The only decent buildings in the place are the Government offices, which are all under one roof, an arrangement which saves an immense amount of time and trouble to anyone who has business to transact, and the mansion of the P&O agent, who seems to be, and no doubt is, the great man of the place.

I had almost forgotten the church, a pretty ivy-clad structure, as elaborately decorated and ornamented as the funds of the congregation will admit, and in which a Church of England High-Church clergyman indulges in a number of eccentricities which would vex the heart of Bishop Perry, [The Lord Bishop of Melbourne]. *The walls of the building are covered with tablets commemorating the virtues of deceased parishioners, and one inscription in particular tells how a certain gentleman, who died in the full odor of sanctity, occupied while alive the distinguished position of vice-consul for the North German Confederation, and agent for the Australian Steam Navigation Company.*

---

[38] *The Sydney Morning Herald.* 30th January 1854.

The twenty-four hours during which the P&O Mooltan *remained in harbour, were made the most of by the passengers …Some few chartered horses, and indulged in a ride along the Perth Road, which is now cleared and a large portion formed and metaled; others made excursions to the top of Mount Clarence and enjoyed the thoroughly Australian character of the landscape, which for forty miles lay stretched at their feet… Of cultivated land there was little or none, although hugging from the abundance of fruit in the gardens, and the beauty of the flowers, both native and exotic, the soil, sandy though it be, would reward the labours of the horticulturist. Fishing was perhaps the most popular amusement, and some fine hauls of whiting, flathead, skipjack, and a special of mackerel were made by the Waltonians.*

…Nearly everyone at Albany was in a frightful state of disgust at the prospect of the mail steamers touching at Fremantle instead of at King George's Sound. The only exceptions were the officials, who seemed to look forward with great glee to being recalled from their temporary exile and relegated to the delights of that brilliant and festive capital, Perth. … The proposed change must, if practicable, be a decided boon to the greater portion of the colonists. Their only communication with the rest of the world is by way of Albany from which they are distant more than 300 miles, the only over land communication between the two districts being by a species of wagon which starts at irregular intervals and occupies some sixty or seventy hours on the journey.

At present the interests of Albany are diametrically opposite to those of the rest of West Australia. All the supplies are derived from South Australia and Victoria, notwithstanding the tariff, which is by far the heaviest of any colony in the whole group, and until very recently, in fact, up to the time that a line of electric telegraph was constructed between Perth and Albany, notes of the various Western Australian banks did not circulate in the latter township, except at a heavy discount… By inducing the mail steamer to touch somewhere in the neighbourhood of their centre of population, the Swan River people expect to draw more closely together the ties which bind the Cinderella of the Australian colonies to her richer neighbours in the south-east, to say nothing of Europe and India.

… The names of several habitual drunkards were posted outside the police court, and publicans were prohibited under a heavy penalty from serving them with fermented and spirituous liquors, or with liquors any portion of which is fermented or spirituous. Some ten or a dozen persons amongst the small community of Albany were thus picked out as victims to compulsory temperance. The police assured me that the system worked well, and that the justices never abused their power.

A visit to King George's Sound would not be considered complete without a corroboree, and an enterprising native, a sort of Aboriginal George Coppin, arranged to get up an entertainment, at which thirty or forty of his countrymen would assist, upon payment of a shilling a piece from each of the spectators.[39] *The performance took place after dark and was very good of its kind. The male and female black fellows, their naked bodies covered with all sorts of hideous colours, jumped, howled, and shrieked in the manner which is considered proper upon such occasions and seemed actuated by a conscientious desire to earn their fees. The imitation of a kangaroo hunt was especially clever. Two men, both excellent mimics, imitated the habits and actions of kangaroos, hopped about, ate grass, scratched themselves and gamboled in the ungainly fashion common to the foresters. Another black fellow, who played the part of a hunter, watched his opportunity, threw his spear, which the man-kangaroo caught under his arm and hopped into the scrub, whither he was followed by the hunter, who dispatched the marsupial with his waddy.*

Although perhaps not fit for horticulture and agriculture, the land in the neighbourhood of King George's Sound is not well adapted for sheep or cattle farming. A few stations are to be found between Albany and Perth, and settlement is steadily progressing along the sea coast between the Sound and Port Lincoln. The country over which Mr. Edward Eyre, of Jamaica notoriety, passed thirty years ago in his journey from the settled districts of South Australia towards Albany, is not so bad as he painted it.[40]

---

[39] George Coppin was an English comic and actor. He was the first importer of ice into Australia.
[40] The Travelling Contributor. *The Leader*, Melbourne. 31st May 1873.

Margaret Walpole's Diary

Perhaps one of the most detailed observations that gave a wonderful insight into the evolution of the town of Albany can be gleaned from the diary kept by Margaret Walpole, who accompanied her husband, a surgeon, to Australia. Originally sailing from London to Sydney, in *SS Pathan* in 1883, she returned to Albany later in 1883 with her husband to take up a doctor's practice in the town. Their voyage from Melbourne to Albany was undertaken on *SS Australia*. During her time in the colony Margaret Walpole kept very extensive notes in her diary of her life in Albany to January 1885. They offer a most valuable first-hand insight into life in the town during her two year stay (1883 – 1885):

With him on board we soon made more rapid headway and after a little while we found ourselves passing through a narrow rock clad channel which leads from the Sound into Princess Royal Harbour, one of the loveliest natural harbours in the world. Two little wooden piers made of native mahogany or jarrah wood, supposed to be the most durable wood in the world, project for some little distance into the water which is here so pure and clear that one can plainly see strange weeds and grasses growing on the pure white sand fifteen or twenty feet below the surface. Two dismasted vessels are used as coal hulks and ride peacefully at anchor and a few little fishing boats belonging to the inhabitants lie along the shore.

The little town of Albany itself consists of a handful of houses scattered between two richly wooded granite hills and at first sight it will almost seem that the sins and sorrows of our struggling world could not enter here. It looked bright and peaceful basking in the early morning sun light, too isolated to have anything in common with the busy, matter-of-fact life of cities. Hidden away among the trees, under the shadow of one of these hills, there stands a grim building of forbidding aspect with high walls around it and padlocked rooms and iron grated windows. Often through these pleasant sunny streets a gang of men march morning and evening in a white uniform decorated with a broad arrow.

After breakfast, ... I made up a party and first of all we went on an exploring expedition through the town. It is very small and oh, how small! No cabs or carriages or carts only, now and then, a butcher or baker's boy lazily cantering along on horseback, basket on arm, lead us to remember that even here the ordinary every-day business of life was carried on. During our excursion through the town, we found a little baker's shop and there were actually some penny tarts in the window; at once we went in and bought some and then we went off for our clamber up the hills.

September 23, 1883. Albany

We got into King George's Sound a little before midnight and Mr. Foules, the chemist who first told us of the new opening here, came in a little sea launch to meet us. He was so exceedingly kind. He had taken a room for us at the hotel and had done everything he could for us as well as put an advertisement in the paper, the usual thing in the colony when anyone is about to settle in a new place. ...The best of it all was that there was none up in the hotel. The door was wide open and a lamp was burning on the stairs so we marched up, parked our luggage in the hall, walked into the first bedroom we could find and took possession of it. Mr. Foules said the people knew we were coming and would not be surprised to find us there, but I must say the whole night's performance seemed perfectly absurd.

There is no gas here, in fact no street lamps at all so all the streets were dark and there were no policemen so we entered our new home without meeting anyone and took everything, as we evidently were expected to, in a most matter-of-fact, unconcerned way, but none knew how really thankful we were to have been spared all this extra expense that would have been demanded had we arrived in the middle of the day. Fancy such a thing being done in England, but most people here are half asleep. They are a hundred years behind the times, and, as long as I live, I shall never forget the cool way we marched about the hotel; we looked in all the cupboards to see if we could find anything to eat. We walked up and down the stairways. We piled all our boxes in the hall, but none seemed to mind in the last and finally, as I said before, we took a bedroom by storm and were soon asleep. At breakfast we made the acquaintance of Mr. Dimes, the Lawyer, who has also come here to settle. He has only been here a few days. He is a big stout man with plenty of assurance. Mr. Turpin was also there; he is the clerk at the bank and boards at the hotel. This pale, emaciated looking object has evidently been sent here for his health. ...

September 23rd, Sunday

To church in the morning for the second time. There is a little building with a square ivy-covered tower, the only old-looking church I have seen since I came to the colony. I am sadly disappointed in the service but, as it is the only church for two hundred and fifty miles, we have no choice in the matter but must go there or nowhere. The clergyman [The Reverend William Wardell-Johnson] *is not a good man and takes not the slightest interest in his parish. After he has conducted the service twice on Sundays, he practically disappears and is not seen again during the week. He considers himself a great musical authority and leads all the singing himself. The effect is most ridiculous. He seizes a hymn book when the number is given out and, shouting at the top of his voice, he beats time on the desk with his book and races away at full speed, never pausing until he gets to the Amen, the choir vainly trying to follow him and flounder along with best they can, coming breathless and panting one after the other, while the congregation patiently wait until they have all finished and then they resume their seats. This part of the service is a standing joke among the congregation, how different from the services at home. ...*

September 25, Tuesday

... Fancy, we have only one newspaper a week and the mail from home once a fortnight and from the colonies once a fortnight.

...All the leading citizens of the town are the old settlers who came out in the early days and have worked their way up. Some of them cannot read and write but that is not an accomplishment considered absolutely necessary here. One lady who called on me the other day with all the airs and graces imaginable, not many years ago used to drive the cow's home at night, minus a hat and without shoes and stockings. The one music master is a run-away sailor; he came here a prisoner, worked the balance of his sentence and is now professor; it is like this all over the colony.

October 30th

... A few nights ago, I again spent the night away from home. This time with some children who are ill with measles. George was attending them; and the mother and governess were tired out with nursing them, so he said he was sure I would not mind going. They accepted his offer very gladly. They are the children of one of the storekeepers here, about the wealthiest people in the place. They have a very nice house overlooking the whole township and harbour. ...When I arrived at the house about dusk, I was admitted by the Governess who greeted me kindly and after taking off my hat we went together to visit the patients. There are five girls ranging from four to fourteen, all in bed.

November 27th

...It is a great joke to see the mail arrive and quite the excitement of the week except perhaps, the P&O Boat itself is even more so. It is a huge wagon painted red and Royal Mail painted in black on the sides, which is covered over in canvas and there is a high seat for the driver in front. Any passengers have to sit on the mail bags inside and, as the road which they travel is very rough, and it takes two days and nights to perform the journey, you can imagine the condition in which the unfortunate travellers arrive.

December 2nd

... We have been to another party. Our hostess was formerly a kitchen maid and our host a cobbler. We start half an hour after the time mentioned on our notes of invitation and when we got there we saw no signs of anybody about. We were told that the young ladies had just gone up to dress, but they would not be long. We sat down patiently in the small sitting room for about ten minutes, then one of the bank managers and his wife arrived. They also are not long out from Home. How we laughed to ourselves at the peculiar customs prevalent here.

January 8th, 1884

There has actually been a wedding since I last wrote, a visit from the Governor [Sir Frederick Napier Broome] *and a birth in this out-of-the-way village. I arranged all the bride's maids' baskets and took rather an active part in the wedding. The bride was Miss Camfield, the adopted daughter of Mrs. Camfield, the widow of one of the Government residents here. She was the first here to start a school for the little black children, and I believe did a great deal for them. She has now returned to Perth as she is too feeble to carry it on now.*

There was great excitement in the town the day the Governor arrived. A large arch of boughs interspersed with flags was erected on the Perth Road and several people rode and drove out to meet him. They had a 'banquet' at one o'clock, and a ball in the Court House at eight. .... All the blacks were in the township today when blankets were distributed in honour of the Governor's visit. They are not a handsome race, at least none that I have seen could be called even passably good looking, and they have the thinnest legs imaginable. They often come around begging. ...

February 17th
We had been invited to go to Candyup any day we felt inclined ... We sailed out of our harbour in first rate style and across the Sound as there was a nice light breeze and ran down before the wind and reached a little landing place in Oyster Harbour in about two hours. We fastened up the boat and followed the little path which led up to the station, turning back many times to admire the exquisite bits of scenery. At last, in half an hour or so, we reached Candyup. A low rambling building standing on a cleared space, the dark hill rising behind and a glorious view across Oyster Harbour to the Sound beyond.

From the little garden in front of the house, we found Mrs. Campbell Taylor at home alone, everyone else was away on some expedition or other and, as she had not provided any midday meal for herself, the only thing she could offer us was some tea and bread and scalded cream. We were very hungry after our trip and thankfully took what was offered to us. After dinner we wandered all over the place and went down to see the shearing sheds and stock yards and then made our way down to the harbour again. We started about four o'clock and thought we should be home in good time before sunset, but alas for us, as soon as we got well away from the landing, about halfway across Oyster Harbour, a dead calm fell, and we were rocking helplessly in a sea of glass. Midnight found us still in the same predicament, cold, tired and hungry, unable to make any headway and not a ghost of a chance of getting home for several hours at least.[41]

Other Notable Visitors

By 1896 the cognomen of Albany as a place of little enterprise and action was highlighted once again by a visitor to the town who despaired at the lack of industriousness among its inhabitants:

Social life in the tiny township is naturally limited, considering its inhabitants scarcely number 3000. There are several charming families who seem to know how to make the best of life, spent though it may be in so remote a corner of the earth.

A short walk through the town soon, however, reveals the fact that energy is not one of the salient virtues of its inhabitants, for it would be difficult to imagine anything more inert than the aspect of the streets. This impression is well founded, four, from what I learnt, it appears that the people only rouse themselves into activity on the arrival of the different steamers which call-in here, and as soon as they have departed, they lapse again into the usual state of somnolence, which seems to thoroughly justify the cognomen of Sleepy Hollow, which was once given to this place. This condition of things certainly does not all go well for the rapid development of the town and strikes even the most casual of observers as a pity, for Albany ought to become a place of some importance in the colony.[42]

Other notable celebrities who visited Albany in the Nineteenth and early Twentieth Century included Rudyard Kipling, who arrived late one evening, sailed the next morning and did not disembark from his ship. He wrote in his autobiography *Something of Myself* that:

I found myself in a new land with new smells and among people who insisted a little too much that they also were new.[43]

---

[41] Extracts from a typescript in the National Library of Australia of the original diary of Margaret Walpole made in 1927.
[42] Price, J.M. *The Land of Gold. The Narrative of a Journey Through the West Australian Goldfields in the Autumn of 1895.* Marsden and Company. London. 1896
[43] Kipling began work on the autobiography *Something of Myself* on 1st August 1935. He died on 18th January 1936. The unfinished manuscript was edited and prepared for publication by his wife, Caroline Starr Balestier. The book was published by MacMillan, on 21st December 1937.

Madame Anna Pavlova known for her role as the principal artist of the Imperial Russian Ballet. Pavlova is most recognized for her creation of the role of *The Dying Swan* and, with her own company, became the first ballerina to tour around the world, including Australia:

Madame Anna Pavlova, the famous dancer, is due at Albany by the White Star Liner Ceramic *on March 3. She is bringing a company of 30 performers with her.*[44]

Dr W.G Grace (William Gilbert Grace) was a famous English cricketer who was instrumental in promoting the development of the sport during the Nineteenth Century. Grace visited Australia in 1873-74 as captain of *W. G. Grace's XI*.

[45]

Prior to the team's departure from Southampton, Grace said that his team "*had a duty to perform to maintain the honour of English cricket*".[46]

The local newspaper was keen to report:
It was on our cricket pitch the first English Eleven, captained by W.G. Grace, practiced in Australia. The team was on its way to the other states, and landed for the day, while the P&O steamer was coaling.[47]

Charles Yelverton O'Connor, CMG was an engineer who was best known for his extensive engineering works in Western Australia especially the construction of The Fremantle Harbour complex and the Goldfields to Perth Water Supply Pipeline.
C. Y. O'Connor, engineering chief, passed through Albany today on his way to the eastern colonies. He visited the sites for the proposed harbour improvements and made a recommendation to the government that he hoped that an early start will be made with the work.[48]

Closing Remarks

From their respective correspondence and diaries travellers and visitors to King George's Sound provided a texture to the character of Albany in the Nineteenth Century as the town gradually began to emerge from its 'sleepy hollow' attribution. These disparate travelogues and reminiscences provide a remarkable story of the development of the town from its Cantonment phase of some 45 persons to a town that until the turn of the century and the rise of Fremantle as Western Australia's main port of entry, was the most important centre for the colony.

---

[44] *The West Australian*, Tuesday 26th January 1926.
[45] Cricket match circa 1880 on Parade Street Oval courtesy of Mark Saxton and the Albany Historical Society.
[46] *Tour Itinerary* Cricket Archive. Archived 12th October 2008. Retrieved 28th November 2008.
[47] *The Albany Despatch*. Monday 29th October 1923.
[48] *The Western Mail*. 27th May 1898.

For some visitors to King George's Sound their travels were part of a personal odyssey, a grand tour of sorts, only instead of Europe it was 'down under' to the antipodes they came. Fortunately for history, they left a legacy in terms of their writing, providing a vital and relevant insight of Albany and its peoples. Together they exposed a palimpsest of historical Albany which has allowed future readers of their works to once again rediscover the unique character of the town's evolution.

Often histories are written from the narrow viewpoint of a single author and a single perspective, with the inevitable bias that it can entail. For example, if a reader was only to use writing offered by Charles Darwin in the summer of 1836 of Albany and King George's Sound as a guide, a very bleak and uninviting perspective of both the town and port would be conveyed to the reader. However, by accessing multiple viewpoints, a more thoughtful and perhaps engaging account and representative view of Albany in this period is provided.

By understanding which key events and influences shaped those perspectives and, to test the accuracy of the views of a foreign correspondent it becomes important therefore, to ensure a balance of material is presented to the reader. In this instance this has been achieved by casting a wider net to capture and distil the essence of the young settlement and way of life in and around King George's Sound during the Nineteenth Century. The immediacy of their reports, diary entries or correspondence together provide that rare insight and opportunity to witness through their eyes how the town was developing.

Unfortunately, the richness and sheer volume of available primary sources has meant that omissions have been, by necessity, inevitably made. However, every endeavour has been made to ensure variety of carefully considered writings that support the narrative has been presented.

CHAPTER 5
THE VEXATIOUS ISSUE OF CONVICT LABOUR

Overview

The unforgiving dense vegetation of the hinterland on the one hand that was bounded by a quite formidable ocean on the other reduced the need for a substantial walled prison to accommodate the prisoners at the Cantonment established at King George's Sound. There was indeed little prospect of escape from the camp, especially as little was known of the area and the nature of the local Indigenous population. Besides it was not the intention to allow the convicts selected for transportation to the Cantonment to sit idly in prison confines. Their labour was a commodity that was required for building public facilities, roads and houses in the settlement. The establishment of the convict depot through which the free settlers could access this cheap form of labour would also mitigate the need for substantial prison facilities.

It was important to recognise that the majority of convicts that were transported to Australia were most often drawn from the English lower classes and were indeed poorly equipped for the rugged life that awaited them in the early days of the Cantonment, particularly when agricultural skills would have been most useful.

In the first decades of settlement at King George's Sound, before the Government Farm and other attempts at producing its own food requirements were established, there was a heavy reliance on shipping for stores and provisions from the Eastern Colonies. In the first decade of the settlement's existence there were many times when the late arrival of an expected supply ship caused considerable consternation within the settlement with its European inhabitants forced to rely on catching mutton birds, skinks, fish and other wildlife for food in order to survive.

The arrival of Captain James Stirling RN, and others at King George's Sound in 1831 was significant for the town's development mainly because he was accompanied on this trip by several free settlers who were determined to make King George's Sound their home. They in turn would go on to encourage other people to do likewise. This was also the time when the administration of the settlement passed from military to civilian control. The settlement now was under the jurisdiction of the Swan River Colony Government.

The soon to be Surveyor-General of Western Australia, John Septimus Roe was one person who accompanied Stirling to King George's Sound and immediately began a three-month exercise in surveying the townsite and immediate adjacent areas. His work resulted in the creation of 28 privately owned town allotments that were subsequently offered for purchase.[1] His survey also included the town's first cemetery allotment.

While there were some positive outcomes from Stirling's visit it also had significant future implications for the town, especially concerning both his desire to remove the military aspect of the colony's leadership and further, the town's administration to the Swan River Colony. Both of these decisions had significant consequential implications for the future of town as a convict centre in Western Australia.

Global Update

It is worth taking time out at this point to set the scene for the period of Albany's development against the backdrop of contemporaneous global events. The period 1826-1850 was one characterised by continued European imperialism and expansion, juxta-positioned with periods of social upheaval and change.

---

[1] These allotments were sold at a price of £5 per acre in the town and £2 per acre in the out-of-town areas commensurate with the prices in Perth.

The Battle of Navorine (1827) had seen a short-lived alliance among some European nations engaging in a naval conflict with the Turkish and Egyptian navies that eventually resulted in the subsequent liberation of Greece from Ottoman control. Andrew Jackson was elected President of the United States of America (1828). He initiated a policy to relocate native American populations to reservations with long term consequences for that nation. The issue of slavery was to dominate American politics during this period, culminating in the American Civil War of 1861 to 1865 which resulted in a significant loss of life.

Once again France was embroiled in a revolution (1830), resulting in Louis Phillipe being crowned King. There was also significant social upheaval in other European nations, specifically, Poland, Belgium and Italy during this period. Robert Stephenson had developed the steam locomotive and in 1830 he completed a Liverpool to Manchester Railway service. On the Australian continent, South Australia was granted colony status in 1834 the same year that the slave trade was abolished in Britain.

In 1836, the same year that the battle of the Alamo took place in Texas, the Great Trek by Dutch settlers (Boers) to escape British rule in South Africa eventuated. They went on to found the Transvaal and Orange Free States. In 1899 the Boer conflict with Britain resulted in a war which was to have significant implications for both Australian involvement and Albany participation in particular.

In 1837 Queen Victoria ascended the throne to begin what was then to become the longest reign by a British monarch. Britain was engaged in the opium wars with China (1839-1842) resulting in the partial opening up of Chinese ports to European traders. The British Empire continued its Imperialist orientation by annexing New Zealand in 1840 through the Treaty of Waitangi and in 1843 Natal in South Africa also became one of its colonies. This was the same year that Samuel Morse transmitted his first telegraph message.

In 1849 the California Gold Rush had begun, eventually resulting in the annexing from Mexico of this landmass by the United States of America. In 1850 Victoria separated from New South Wales to become a colony in its own right. Together these events, among other social, scientific and political activities, contextualise the gradual developments that were to subsequently impact King George's Sound.

Convict Past

"There were instances in which our free settlers might take an example."
The *Albany Banner* in noting the good behaviour of convicts in the settlement.

The men sent out were to be selected as likely to develop into good settlers; the numbers were not to be excessive and, above all, for every convict sent out a free emigrant was also to be sent to the colony so that an undue preponderance of settlers within the criminal taint might not lower the moral tone of the community.
Earl Grey, Secretary of State for the Colonies. 1848.[2]

Governor Ralph Darling's instructions to Major Lockyer, whom he selected to command the expedition to King George's Sound, in part indicated that if contact was made with a foreign power ...
"Should it's so happened that the French have already arrived, you will notwithstanding, land the troops agreeable to your instructions... with orders have been given for the establishment of King George's Sound as a settlement for the reception of criminals accordingly".[3]

The last sentence of these instructions is in itself contentious, for whatever may have been the intention of Lord Bathurst there was no original intention or evidence of an attempt whatsoever made to establish a convict settlement in the locality of the Sound. The prime objective of the instructions of Lord Bathurst on behalf of the British Government admits of no qualification or misunderstanding. The evidence of this is conclusive and beyond question, as indicated in earlier reported correspondence from him in Chapter 3.

---

[2] *The Australian Dictionary of Biography*, Volume 1, 1966.
[3] *Correspondence from Governor Ralph Darling to Major Edmund Lockyer*. Sydney. 4th November 1826.

It was simply that occupation be affected on the western coast in an assertion of a claim to possession by the Crown of Great Britain to the whole continent of Australia.

While the number of convicts transported to the Sound was not excessive and given their overall productivity (sometimes under the encouragement of the lash) they nevertheless fulfilled an important role in helping to get the King George's Sound settlement established, whether they were assigned to building teams, food sourcing activities or supporting expeditions into the hinterland as for example, those reported in the despatches or journals of the likes of Major Lockyer, Dr Wilson and Dr Collie.

Initially on *Amity* in 1826 with Major Lockyer and Captain Wakefield was a detachment of the 39th Regiment of Foot and 23 convicts. This number of convicts transported to the Sound grew by four during Lieutenant Sleeman's command of the Cantonment in 1828 - 1829 bringing the convict population to only 27 in 1828 - 1829. Subsequent to this in 1831 Governor Stirling successfully petitioned for convict transportation to Albany to cease. Nevertheless, as the colony grew so did the demand for cheap labour and so in 1850 convict transportation to the colony of Western Australia once again commenced.

A permanent convict depot was built in 1852 as most of the convicts that were now sent to Albany were Ticket of Leave men and many were able to be hired by local free settlers accordingly. Nonetheless, this depot closed in 1855 only to reopen again later on when more convicts arrived in the settlement.

By 1850 the number of Imperial and Crown convicts had grown to 70 eventually reaching 165 in number by 1868 (most of whom were Ticket of Leave). It was during this 1860 period that increased resistance to the convict system arose within the local community from among the free settlers. The issue of convict transportation and subsequent continuance of the scheme at King George's Sound became quite contentious among the free settlers, particularly as the settlement developed a degree of stability and sustainability.

While by the beginning of the 1850s some issues had begun to ferment opposition to convicts being located in the settlement, the movement became manifest later on in the following decade. This change in perspective towards the transportation of convicts was in some instances inspired by matters relating to an increase in drunkenness and crime that were starting to become commonplace in the settlement. *The Inquirer* newspaper of Perth was very vocal at this time highlighting a number of convict-inspired misdemeanours:

Robbery at King George's Sound

It is to be hoped that the late robbery of the Government chest will suggest to the authorities here the necessity of taking some measures to make the hiring depot secure, for, notwithstanding the front door is, I believe, locked every night, and the names called over, it is well known, and was sworn to by an overseer of the depot at the late examinations of the prisoners before the magistrates, that the men have the means of getting in and out of the depot at all hours of the night through an opening made in the wall for a door, but to which a door has not yet been fixed, besides two unfastened windows, and that as there is no guard kept over the Establishment, and not a single policeman patrolling the town at night, it is a very easy matter for the men to commit any robbery, and get quietly back to their beds, without disturbing a single person on the premises. The confessions of the prisoners concerned in the later robbery prove that for many nights extending over a space of some months, in fact from their landing here, this and many other robberies had been devised by the same gang, which had met at all hours of the night for the purpose, and nearly every respectable person's house in the town had been watched and examined, and would undoubtedly have been robbed had not the temptation held out by the Government gold brought by the Eleanora *been too strong for them, and fortunately led to their capture. It is however a matter of surprise and reflects some credit on the men themselves, that, with all the facilities afforded them for the commission of a crime by the absence of a night force, the insecurity of the depot, the liberty allowed the men of being out at night till 10 o'clock, and a large amount of cash they weekly receive to spend at the grog shops, especially on Saturday and Sunday, when many come in "to church" they have allowed full four months to elapse without perpetrating a robbery on any of us; destitute as most of our houses of fire-arms, locks, and bolts, &c., which unfortunately are not to be had here. However, this great consideration on their part may in some measure be owing to our poverty, and the total absence of money and plate in our houses. But in sober earnest, ought these things so to be: It is to be hoped after this warning, for the peace and security of the town, that the Government will appoint constables or policemen to patrol the town at night, to enter all the public houses at 10 o'clock, visit the depot, and restore that feeling of security to the inhabitants which is at present lost, and which can only be revived by some such decisive measure.*[4]

Four months later the matter of convict behaviour was again raised in the colonial press, this time with the brazen escape of four convicts from the town's gaol facilities. The first detailed article that appeared in *The Perth Gazette* and not to be outdone was followed up in an article by the *Inquirer and Commercial News*:

Escaped Convicts
7th October 1852.

On Tuesday night last, great commotion was created in the town by the escape of 4 convicts from the gaol, and a ticket-of-leave man from the depot, it appears that these men had planned an escape two days previous. About 8 o'clock on Tuesday evening, Burrell, the gaoler, was writing in his room at the gaol, when these men called out to him to come and lock them up for the night, when he told them to wait until he (Burrell) was at leisure; when he went into the gaol yard where the men were, his son drew the bolt outside to prevent their escape whilst Burrell locked them up, the men seized him, and a struggle ensued, which was heard by the gaoler's family who hastened into his assistance, when the prisoners gained the upper hand and walked out, locking Burrell up instead of their being locked up. These were Haines, who had turned Queen's evidence in the case of the robbery of the chest, Tomlins and Brown, who were also under sentence for robbing the chest, and Thompson, a ticket-of-leave man, who was in for some misdemeanour; the 5th named Mansfield, was a ticket-of-leave man. Mrs Burrell, who was not locked in, released her husband, who immediately reported the circumstance to the Magistrates, who started the police off in all directions that night, but without success.

It appears that some understanding was entered into with them and the crew of a French whaler then at anchor in the harbour, to take them off that night at 7 o'clock. When they escaped they made for the jetty and secreted themselves until the boat came on shore, but fortunately, the mate of the ship came with the crew in the boat, and when these men asked to be taken on board he refused, they then returned to the gaol and equipped themselves with provisions, which they had previously got ready, and made off to the bush; they filed their irons two days previously and had nothing to do but slip them when ready to bolt.

Next day the policeman started off on foot and came upon their tracks about 5 miles from the settlement, and return at 10 o'clock, but owing to the want of hay and corn, the police horses are tethered out in the bush, and on this occasion when required, could not be got, otherwise, there is but little doubt the men would have been taken that day. An arrangement was entered into by the Magistrates with the Captain of the whaler to take the police down to Cape Riche, where it has been ascertained the men are gone, which vessel sailed this morning, but unfortunately on going out struck on the bank, and will have to remain there until the tide rises, which will be in the course of tomorrow. This disaster was occasioned by the death of Mr Hamilton, the government pilot, who died yesterday morning; and another man named Solomon Aspinall was appointed to take this vessel out and run her aground in the channel by accident. Last evening when L. Mooney, policeman, was tethering his horse at the back of the settlement, he discovered a red cap moving in some bushes near him, which he approached and found to be Haines, one of the prisoners, he immediately took him, and he is once more lodged in gaol; he states that he lost sight of the other men soon after they left the gaol, and lost his way in endeavouring to effect an escape.

8th October.

The George, French whaler, is still a-ground in the channel, and the police are on board. A ticket-of-leave man named Hawkins with another, who are living about 3 miles out of town, sawing timber, came in last night with a story that the convicts had been to his house the night before and had supper and were to be there again that night. The Magistrates placed some credence in Hawkins's story, send for the police out of the ship and despatched them to the spot, where they remained all night, but no tidings of any of them have been heard...

9th October – The police returned last night with the remaining three convicts, they took them at the hut of Hawkins, ticket-of-leave man, who I have already mentioned, on their way to Cape Riche; they apprehended them at 8 o'clock at night without any resistance whatever and lodged them once more in Burrell's hands. It appears not that they were under the impression that the police had started for Cape Riche, and their intention

---

[4] *The Inquirer and Commercial News*, Perth. 23rd June 1852.

was to rob the town that night, in the first place to get fire-arms, and then attack Mr Belches premises and the Commissariat Store.[5]

Reports from several correspondents to *The Inquirer* concerning escapes from the Albany Goal followed the theme of *The Perth Gazette* above. It is noted that a different twist is given to the report on how Burrell the gaoler was incarcerated. Furthermore, the first correspondent indicates that it was the Albany settlement they intended to rob and not Cape Riche:

Space would not permit us, in Thursday's supplement, to publish the interesting correspondence received from King George's Sound, and we now insert the communication of three correspondents, who address us from that quarter. We trust they will have the effect of inducing the Government to pay some attention to the requirements of the Albanians as regards a gaol and an efficient Water Police:

"About 3 weeks ago, all the native prisoners, 4 in number made their escape, with double irons on from one of the pensioners, of the name of Fitzgerald, who had charge of them at work, a short distance from the gaol; and none of them have been captured since. Also, four of the ticket-of-leave men made their escape from the gaol, and one from the depot: Haynes, Tomlins, Brown and Smith from the gaol, and Mansfield from the depot. On the 5th instant, about 7 o'clock in the evening, when Burrell, the gaoler, went into the gaol yard to lock the prisoners in their cells, and, when about to lock up the escaped convicts, they got hold of him, and tried to choke him. His eldest son, who was outside the hard door when he heard the scuffle, opened the door and went to his father's assistance; they took hold of him, and were serving him in the same way, when Mrs Burrell, the other boy, and the girl, went to their assistance; but they overpowered them all, and got out of the gaol-yard and bolted Burrell and all his family in."

They then went into the Gaoler's apartment, stole away bread, tea, sugar and three coats, and took to the bush. Burrell, with the assistance of the other prisoners, took the leg out of a stool, and with it wrenched out one of the bars of the door, got his hand through, and withdrew the bolt on the outside; when he got out, they were gone. He gave the alarm, but as the night was dark, they could not tell where they went. The next day, the Police followed their tracks as far as the King's River, and tracked them across the river, but found that they had returned towards the settlement.

The police came back and searched about the hills, and Lawrence Mooney came upon Haynes, where he had planted himself in sight of the town. Before he was alarmed, Mooney got close up to him with his pistol and told him if he did not walk before him into the town, he would blow his brains out. Haynes took the hint and walked before Mooney into the gaol, where he was put in irons. The next day, the three policemen, Golding, Chipper and Picket got on the tracks of the three prisoners on the Swan River Road. They came in the evening to a hut, belonging to two ticket-men who were sawing in the bush, about 6 miles from Albany; there was no one in the hut when they got to it, but they found a fresh supply of provisions, a bottle of rum, and the coats that were stolen from the gaoler, in it; they left everything as it was, and planted themselves and their horses at a convenient distance from the hut.

When the day was gone, and it was beginning to get dark, they saw the two ticket-of-leave sawyers coming to the hut, and commence cooking supper, and in a short time afterwards, the three prisoners came to the hut. When supper was ready, they all sat down to it in the hut; the police managed it so well, that they got up to the door before they were aware of their presence; they presented their firearms at them and told them their resistance would cost them their lives. They then allowed themselves to be secured and conveyed to gaol and put in irons. When they attacked Burrell, they shook all their irons off them, as they had the rivets of their irons filed off previously. They told the police that they went as far as the King River, to make them believe they were gone to Cheyne's Beach so that they might rob the settlement of arms and munition and take to the bush during their absence in search of them to the eastward. Mansfield has not been taken yet, and it is supposed he is gone in the French whaler."

From another correspondent to the same paper. In this report it is the child who unlocks the door letting the gaoler and his family out:

---

[5] *The Perth Gazette and Independent Journal of Politics and News*, 29th October 1852.

Outbreak in Albany gaol, and escape of four white prisoners, and their recapture, viz., Brown, Tomlin, Haynes and Smith. The three former were under sentence for the robbery of the Government chest at that place, and the latter was put in gaol for insubordination at the Hiring Depot, all awaiting the arrival of the Government schooner to proceed to Fremantle.

On the evening of the 5th October, as the gaoler was locking up the prisoners in their cells, after securing one cell door, and going to lock up the other, which contained the men referred to, one of them wanted a drink of water, which was in the yard. On returning to the cell, he seized the jailer, by what is called "hugging" and a struggle ensued when the other prisoners rushed upon him and tried to strangle him. When they had overpowered him, they succeeded in putting him in the cell, and when his family went to see what the matter was, they seized them also, and dragged his wife from her bedroom, with her child, and thrust her in the cell, leaving the child in the yard, and made their escape by bolting the outer door. They plundered the house, taking with them several coats belonging to the gaoler, and some provisions, but could not find the firearms. The child then opened the cell door and liberated the gaoler, but he was some time forcing the outer door. He then called for assistance from the barracks. After placing a sentry on the gaol, he went and informed the authorities of what had taken place. Every means at their disposal were immediately put in action for the recapture of the prisoners.

On the following evening, one of the police came upon a prisoner named Haynes, a short distance from the settlement, and brought him back to gaol. He was heavily ironed. Some clue as to their whereabouts was received, and the police being on the alert, succeeded in capturing the other three in a hut about five miles from the settlement where they worked, when on ticket-of-leave, for a settler. They were all brought back to gaol and placed in heavy irons. The circumstance which caused the outbreak was as follows: - A French whaler, which had been lying in the harbour for some time, was just about to sail, when some of the crew were put in gaol for drunkenness; and it appears that the prisoners arranged with the sailors to make their escape, when they were to be received on board at a given hour. After going to the jetty, the chief officer happening to come with the boat, he refused to take them, which overthrew the plans entirely. They afterwards took to the bush. A disturbance also took place at the hiring depot on the previous evening, when one of the ticket-of-leave men was sent to gaol for insubordination, and another made his escape and is supposed to be on board the French ship, although every search was made without success. It is supposed that the outbreak at the two places were to be made on the same night, but circumstances arose to delay the disturbance at the gaol until the following evening.[6]

Occasionally, some minor issues presented but were judiciously dealt with at the local level by either the Resident Magistrate or visiting Magistrates. By way of example, an issue concerning a strike by a group of Ticket of Leave men in 1853 over the quality of food they were supplied with was presented in *The Inquirer*. However, the newspaper did raise a concern that in giving in to the men a dangerous precedent may have been created:

A few days since a "strike" took place at the Convict Depot amongst the ticket-men, who persisted for successive days in refusing the rations of biscuit served out to them, and protesting that they could not eat it, as it was maggoty (sic), or, if they did eat it, could not work upon it. It would be naturally supposed that in this position of affairs the Assistant Superintendent would have requested the Visiting Magistrate to call a board of survey upon the bread, as is usual in such cases; but it appears that, either through timidity, or a conviction that he would be borne out at head-quarters, he permitted them to make, or rather made for them, an arrangement with a storekeeper to take their biscuit for bread, weight for weight, (a clear proof the biscuit was of good quality), and to sell their rice at 3d a lb; and upon this being settled, the men expressed themselves satisfied and returned to their duty. Now although there is no harm in allowing the men a little indulgence when their conduct deserves it, yet, surely it is a very dangerous precedent to yield to so unreasonable a demand; and where this will end it is hard to say, for it is not reasonable to support that the next batch of convicts will not do precisely the same, and not only in the article of bread, but of everything else with which they are supplied. Besides, it is only a temporary accommodation; for, as soon as the storekeepers have received enough Government biscuit and rice, they of course will decline taking more, and what will the convicts do then? - rebel of course, and refuse work, and give a great deal of trouble; and having by conspiracy succeeded in obtaining their demands, they are not the sort of people not to require more indulgences of a like nature.

---

[6] *The Inquirer and Commercial News*. Perth. 27th October 1852.

> *This very same biscuit came down in the* Louise, *a board of survey was held upon it, consisting of the visiting Magistrate, Medical Officer, and Assistant Superintendent of Convicts, and pronounced to be good and wholesome food; and I repeat that if objected to by the men, a special board should have been summoned, and if they decided that the bread was good and sufficient food, they should have been compelled either to eat it or go without; and if they could not work in consequence, mulct them of their pay, and keep them on biscuit and water as prisoners till they were brought to submission. It is really disgusting to witness such whims and fancies pampered and encouraged in this way, and by the very parties who had previously pronounced the bread of good quality. It can never do any good, and only renders the mess more clamorous, discontented, and independent, which, Heaven knows, they are enough already. The precedent is bad, and is only an earnest of the future, but we shall see.*[7]

Archdeacon John Ramsden Wollaston's Journal entry of 1854 provided a perspective from a more recent arrival at the King George's Sound settlement. He made comment on the part that convict labour had played in the development of the town and indicated that, from this point of view, the expenditure on the transportation scheme was indeed worthwhile:

> *The little settlement of Albany shows at the first glance the temporal advantages flowing from convict labour and convict expenditure. Seventy ticket-of-leave men are here located, employed on the roads, or hired out as farm servants. But all is not gold that glitters. Some do well, but a daring burglary was committed the other night on the Government Resident's Office and £200 taken from the chest. The thieves hope to have got possession of £1000 in sovereigns brought down for use of the commissariat. This, however, had been previously removed and so escaped. The parties concerned have been apprehended and sent to Fremantle; part of the plunder was discovered, but from the drinking which has latterly prevailed, it is believed that some £60, the remainder, has been spent in the purchase of spirits. It is obvious that a Superintendent and three constables cannot control some fifty or sixty "Exiles" who practically were at liberty to do pretty much as they please. One of the ringleaders was apparently a steady man, a tailor by trade, and actually earning £3 per week at the time. This event gives sad augury for the future and has unsettled the minds of other parties – a feeling of insecurity prevails and as meat has arisen in price from 3½d. To 8d. Per pound and flour is £26 per ton, the temporal advantages of the system are counterbalanced by the enhanced price of living to the free settlers. Such are the "sweets and sours" of a convict and penal colony.*[8]

The imbalance between the sexes of convicts transported to the colony began to be raised as an issue, particularly concerning the deleterious impact that it was having on the Aboriginal population and the subsequent increase in half-caste children requiring Government assistance.

> *The cry in the newspapers and throughout the colony is, and has been, the evil of the great disparity in the number of the sexes; and, to counteract it, the introduction of female convicts is advocated by many. Why not, before trying this hazardous experiment, perform an act of justice to the natives, by relieving them of the care and trouble of bringing up children that are half European. In many instances, they release themselves from the burden by killing them, and their mothers too. We deprive them of their land, their all, not as a noble and honourable people ought to do, but as tyrant boys at school act, who demand and seize upon whatever property of the younger ones they covet, regardless of the injury they do, because the owners are too helpless and weak to maintain their right.*[9]

Anti-Transportation Movement Gains Traction

As the settlement grew so did the arguments for more of a share of the colony's financial resources. While it had been the free settlers who originally had demanded the continuance of transportation of convicts into the town by 1861 public meetings were being conducted to bring to an end the practice which was now viewed as being degrading to the individuals involved. An escape by convicts in 1863 at which time they stole equipment from the harbour pilot added some weight to the call for greater assistance, particularly in the form of a greater maritime police presence in the Sound.

> *During the night of 16th March, four probation prisoners from the Albany Road party, absconded from their camp, stole one of the P&O Co.'s boats, with oars and gear from the Pilot station, and started off to the eastward.*

---

[7] Ibid. 21st September 1853.
[8] *Wollaston's Albany Journals. 1848*. Lamb Publications. Perth. 1954.
[9] *The Inquirer and Commercial News*. Perth. 18th August 1858.

Mr Pretious the pilot, missed his gear next morning and gave chase, followed by 2 of the company's boats, with police officers. The men surrendered at once to Mr Pretious, who landed them at the courthouse about noon. For the robbery, they were sentenced each to 7 years of penal servitude, and for the escapade, one to 3 years and three to 18 months' imprisonment. Considering the staff of officers at Fremantle, it is incomprehensible that this port, with twice the number of vessels, and three times the tonnage, should be left without a police boat or crew. Great praise is due to Mr Pretious and his coxswain for their courage, and to his convict crew for their willingness in effecting this capture.[10]

By 1864 the call to end transportation and convict labour in the Albany district was gathering steam with the issue seen in the wider context of concerns generally expressed in the colony by the free settlers. The following documentation not only alludes to the concern but specifically includes minutes taken at a meeting of Plantagenet and Albany district settlers called to discuss the issue:

The Western Australian
From our Correspondent.
King George's Sound, September 30 1864:

The often-reiterated statements that the people of this colony were willing to receive convicts are not true. Most of the inhabitants of this district and many in other parts of the colony have always been opposed to receiving them. The application to the Imperial Government to make this a penal settlement was the project of some interested people who had influence, and many of them after gaining their object took advantage of the temporary increased value of property caused by the Government expenditure occasioned by the introduction of convicts, and after availing themselves of that advantage left the colony.

The convict adult population now considerably outnumbers the free, and in a very short time, the latter will become a mere fracture of the community. If transportation is continued at the present rate, it must involve us in all the horrors incident to the disproportion of sexes, unless female convicts are sent out, for it is not likely female emigrants would select this colony, and no Englishman would perpetuate the injustice of forcing them to do so.

The uncontradicted statement in one of our newspapers, that upwards of 1,000 cases come before the Magistrates in a year, most of which are never reported leaves a fair inference of the amount of reformation effected, the Magistrates having the power to deal summarily with very grave offences when committed by ticket-of-leave men; and the number of reconvicted men now in the colony is sufficient cause for those who have not interfered in the transportation question to predict what will be the state of the colony in a few years.

A member of the Legislative Council stated in the debates that he did not feel insecure, but he was aware some others did: but he approved of the proposed measure for the cessation of conditional pardons, the increase of police, and suggested that a small vessel of war should be placed on the coast to prevent depredations and escapes and was glad a chain-gang was formed.

The last mail from Perth brought the news that six of the chain-gang had managed to cut their irons, and the warder in charge had barely time to procure assistance to prevent their proving to the advocates for transportation the class they had to deal with.

A preliminary meeting was held here on the 16th August, at which it was resolved to apply to the Resident Magistrate to call a general meeting of the whole district, and that gentleman having acceded to the request, a general meeting was called on the 29th September, and responded to by everyone who was able to attend: and those who could not attend, but who have since been made acquainted with the resolutions passed unanimously at the meeting have promised their signatures to a memorial, praying that transportation to this colony should be at once totally and finally abolished.

Subjoining is the memorial referred to above:

---

[10] Ibid. 15th April 1863.

> "To His Excellency John Stephen Hampton Esq.,
> Governor and Commander-in-Chief of the Colony of Western Australia &c., in Council.
> "The memorial of the undersigned farmers, graziers, merchants, tradesmen and free inhabitants of the district of Plantagenet and the town of Albany, humbly showeth -
> "That at a preliminary meeting held at Mr Moir's on the 16th day of August 1864, it was resolved to apply to the Resident Magistrate to call a general meeting of the whole district to allow the inhabitants an opportunity of expressing their views on the subject of transportation to the colony. That the annexed resolutions were passed and unanimously adopted at such general meeting held on the 29th September 1864, viz:
> That this meeting, composed of free residents of the District of Plantagenet and Town of Albany are opposed to the continuance of transportation to Western Australia, and desire to express their conviction that the influx of convicts tends materially to injure this colony."
>
> That the continuance of transportation by increasing the number of the class of men who are compelled to remain, will tend materially to damage the colony by rendering life and property unsafe, especially in this district, where the worse characters are certain to congregate, in the hope of effecting their escape by some of the vessels frequenting this port."
>
> That we avail ourselves of our privilege as British subjects to make our earnest protest against transportation in any shape, and had we followed the dictates of our own judgement we should have opposed their introduction as we never favoured the project. Many who are now prospering in the other colonies were discouraged at the prospects here, but we landed with the resolution of becoming settlers, and have not been driven from our purpose by want of energy or the difficulties that others shrank from, nor are we shamed, as honest men, to admit that we passively submitted to the introduction of convicts in deference to the opinions of the protectors, and to give them the opportunity of testing their scheme, which we are now convinced is a failure. The reasons assigned for sending prisoners here are not borne out. The system tends to drive free immigrants from the colony and is a bounty on crime, the prisoners being better provided for than immigrants. But even admitting the men sent here become industrious for a time, their incentive is to gain the means of leaving the colony, and the result if the worse class are left here to become a burden on the revenue after they obtain conditional pardons, thereby defeating the object proposed.
>
> Moreover, after struggling so many years against the privations and hardships incident to a poor colony, if any prosperity is gained (by the introduction of convicts), it has no weight to the demoralizing influence in this and the stigma of the other colonies on our children. We, therefore, submit that transportation to this colony ought to be at once completely and finally abolished." Carried unanimously.
>
> "We therefore humbly beg your Excellency, and your honourable Council will favourably consider our opinions as recorded in the foregoing resolutions and adopt such measures as you may deem most expedient to relieve us from a burden, we conceive injurious to our welfare and prosperity. And your memorialists, as in duty, bound will ever pray.:
> Here follow the signatures of every free inhabitant of this district of every rank or professions not connected with Government. [11]

Both *The Perth Gazette* and *The Inquirer* likewise picked up on this theme:
> Minutes of a public meeting of the free inhabitants of the district of Plantagenet and town of Albany held at the court-house at Albany on 29th September 1864, when the following resolutions were passed and unanimously adopted...That this meeting, composed of free residents in the district of Plantagenet and town of Albany, are opposed to the continuance of Transportation to West Australia and desire to express their conviction that the influx of convicts tends materially to demoralize the rising generation, and to discourage the immigration of free settlers... That the continuance of Transportation, by increasing the number of the class of men who will be compelled to remain here, will tend materially to damage the colony, by rendering life and property unsafe, and especially in this district, where the worse characters are certain to congregate, in the hope of effecting their escape by some of the vessels frequenting the port. That we avail ourselves of our privilege as British subjects to enter our earnest protest against Transportation in any shape so far as this colony is concerned, and had we followed the dictates of our judgement, we should have opposed their introduction, as we never favoured the project.

---

[11] *The Adelaide Observer*, 22nd October 1864.

> *Many who are now prospering in the other Colonies were discouraged at the prospect here, but we landed with the resolution of becoming settlers, and have not been driven from our purpose by want of energy, or the difficulties that others shrunk from; no we are ashamed, as honest men to admit that we passively submitted to the introduction of convicts, in deference to the arguments of the projectors, and to give them the opportunity of testing the scheme, which we are now convinced is a failure. The reasons assigned for sending prisoners to this colony are not borne out. The system tends to drive free emigrants from the colony and the result is, the worst class are left here, to become a burden to the revenue after they obtain conditional pardons, thereby defeating the object proposed. Moreover, after struggling so many years against the privations and hardships incident to a poor colony, if any prosperity is gained by the introduction of convicts, it has no weight to the demoralising influence in this and the stigma of the other colonies on our children. We, therefore, move that Transportation to this colony ought to be at once completely and finally abolished.[12]*

The initial introduction of convicts into the Albany settlement had originally been seen to have some positive benefits and was, therefore, a welcome commodity, particularly in terms of significant public works that were undertaken using this free labour as a source. Nevertheless, the presence in the town of convicts became increasingly controversial as the economy and employment opportunities expanded as the century progressed. An article from an 1864 *The Perth Gazette and West Australian Times* newspaper captured the essence of the complaints that were unfolding in Albany town at this time:

> *We learn from an Albany Correspondent that a numerously-signed anti-transportation memorial from the inhabitants of the district has been forwarded by this mail to head-quarters, in which there should be an immediate cessation of the present system. It is reported that the Governor is so anxious to relieve the memorialists from the evils they represent themselves as considering to arise from the presence of convicts among them, that he has given directions to withdraw all convicts from Albany, and that in future no passes to that town are to be granted by any Police or Resident Magistrate; it is to be hoped this concession to their opinions will be received with grateful appreciation by the dwellers of Albany.*
>
> *Since the above was in type, we have been favoured with a copy of the following letter addressed by the Government to the Chairman of the Meeting:*
>
> *Colonial Secretary's Office*
> *Perth, 16th November 1864*
>
> *Sir–*
> *I have had the honour to submit to His Excellency the Governor in Executive Council, the Memorial from certain Farmers, Graziers, Merchants, Tradesmen and free inhabitants in the town of Albany and the District of Plantagenet, praying that His Excellency the Governor in Council would adopt such measures as he may deem most expedient to give effect to certain resolutions passed at a public meeting held at Albany on the 29th September last.*
>
> *The resolutions passed at that meeting state that the free inhabitants of the Plantagenet District are opposed to the continuation of Transportation to Western Australia, and express opinions that the influx of Convicts tends materially to demoralise the rising generation, to discourage the immigration of free settlers; and that transportation ought to be at once finally and completely abolished.*
>
> *I am instructed to request you will be good enough to inform the memorialists that the Governor in Council has no power to prevent the continuance of transportation to Western Australia.*
>
> *In view, however, of the strong feeling expressed by the memorialists as to the evil resulting from the presence of Convicts in the Plantagenet District, His Excellency will issue the necessary instructions that arrangements be made for the immediate withdrawal from the District of all prisoners and ticket-of-leave men at present in it, with the exception of such prisoners as may be employed on the main line of road between Perth and Albany, where the work may be viewed as of general importance to the community at large, and in the Pilot's Boat at Albany, to which the same reason applies. The Comptroller General has been instructed not to permit from*

---

[12] *The Inquirer and Commercial News*, Perth. 16th November 1864.

> *this date the issue of any passes to men of the convict class to Albany, or the Plantagenet District, and some prisoners already on the road thither have been ordered to return to Head Quarters.*
>
> *I have &c.,*
> *Fred P. Barlee*[13]

An interesting perspective from an 1865 article prepared for *The Inquirer* from one Mr Stow provides an interesting aside to the discussions that were taking place at a district and whole of colony level on the issue of convicts in Albany where he made a facetious comment about what he termed Albany's open-air gaol.

> *Breakfasted at a convicts' fire. Most of the gang were young men. They had no guard over them, and could, of course, work or play as they liked; but the presence of an overseer would not make much difference in that respect. Here I witnessed an incident that made more impression on my mind than all the chains and broad arrows I had seen. We were some distance from the road, eating, or warming ourselves by the fire when a man passing quietly along was hailed with the enquiry "Who are you?" The reply was that he was looking for someone from whom he expected work. "Come and let us have a look at you," said the trooper. The Traveller obeyed, was questioned, and allowed to pass on. Western Australians would think this a trifle, but it would give strangers the uncomfortable feeling of being in an open-air gaol. We got into worthless country early in the morning. During the forenoon saw the hills about the Sound.*[14]

However, the remarks of Stow in his piece of correspondence were not mirrored in the travelogue prepared by Sir Charles Wentworth Dike in his 1866 entry on the town of Albany.

> *The contrast between the scenery and the people of West Australia is great indeed. The Aboriginal inhabitants of Albany were represented by a tribe of filthy natives – tall, half-starved, their heads bedaubed with red ochre, and their faces smeared with yellow clay' the "colonists" by a gang of fiend-faced convicts working in chains upon the esplanade, and a group of scowling expirees hunting a monkey with bull-dogs on the pier; while the native women, half-clothed in tattered kangaroo-skins, came slouching past with an aspect of defiant wretchedness. Work is never done in West Australia unless under the compulsion of the lash, for a similar degradation of labour is produced by the use of convicts as by that of slaves.*
>
> *Many of the "escaped" are made with no other view than to obtain a momentary change of scene. Two convicts once put to sea from Port Arthur in an empty oil cask. On the last return trip of the ship in which I sailed from Adelaide to King George's Sound, a convict coal-man was found built up in the coal-heap on deck; he and his mates at Albany had drawn lots to settle which of them should be thus packed off by the help of the others "for a change". Of ultimate escape there could be no chance; the coal on deck could not fail to be exhausted within a day or two after leaving port, and this they knew. When he emerged, black, half-smothered, and nearly started, from his hiding-place, he allowed himself to be quietly ironed, and so kept till the ship reached Adelaide, when he was given up to the authorities, and sent back to Albany for punishment. Acts of this class are common enough to have received a name. The offenders are called "bolters for a change".*[15]

Extracts from the diary of a recaptured escapee in *The Inquirer* in 1867 provides perhaps a different and yet, insightful perspective on life in a penal colony.

> *In our issue of last week, our Albany correspondent reported the capture of two probation prisoners, who, along with two others, made their escape in November last from the Warren Bridge party. We now give the statement made to the Convict authorities by one of the prisoners, which will be read with some interest:*
>
> *On Saturday, the 17th Nov., I absconded from the Warren convict camp, accompanied by Charles Ellis, John Smith, and Samuel Hooley; and the more effectually to evade the police, we started at dusk, all four of us plunging into the Warren River, down which we swam for about half a mile when we landed, and, crossing on some logs, obtained a quantity of flour and damper, which had originally been planted for the occasion; we then struck east, steering as well as we could by the moon, till about 1 a.m., when we came to a halt.*
>
> *18Th. Started at daylight, and after travelling in an easterly direction for about two hours came to a dense thicket, through which we had to make our way by pushing aside the brushwood, and, whenever opportunity offered,*

---

[13] *The Perth Gazette and West Australian Times.* 18th November 1864.
[14] *The Inquirer and Commercial News*, Perth. 8th November 1865.
[15] Dilke, C.W. *Greater Britain: A Record of Travel in English-Speaking Countries During 1866 and 1869.* London 1869.

mounting a log to peep through at the sun and ascertain how we were steering. We travelled but very slowly and camped at sundown, all of us feeling very tired and dispirited, but we resolved to push on through all obstacles to the eastward, hoping, in our ignorance, that after much privation and suffering, we should be rewarded by reaching South Australia.

Travelled toward the beach and sighted Albany from a high hill near the sea; we then held a consultation; I proposed to take Hooley where he would be found and cared for, and that Smith and Ellis should accompany me along the beach back to our own party; but this they would not hear of, and Smith started off for the Sound, which appeared to be only 6 miles off, leaving Hooley to the care of Ellis, until assistance could be procured; for my part I did not wish to give myself up in Albany, and therefore started back by the beach, having shaken hands with my companions, who tried their best to dissuade me from a course which they felt sure must result in my death.

I found myself travelling painfully through the valley of some sea-coast hills, when I became as a drunken man, reeling and falling down. I lay for some time isolated, weary, past all feeling of hunger and thinking that it mattered not how soon death released me when to my joy and astonishment I saw a white man approach; with some difficulty, I shouted to him, and as he came near I observed a double-barrelled gun in his hand; he told me that he knows I was one of the four convicts the police had visited his station in search of and asked for my three companions; I then gave him a most positive assurance that they were in Albany when he seemed satisfied, and kindly taking me by the arm, led me to his house, where I received every kindness; when somewhat refreshed he placed me on horseback and we arrived at the Warren Bridge party about dusk; as my old companions gathered round me I could plainly understand that I was to them as one they never expected to hear of again. To Mr Mottram, under Providence, I owe my life; and while that lasts, he will ever have the deep gratitude of a poor runaway convict, who had laid down to die in the wilds of Western Australia.[16]

In 1869 a traveller to King George's Sound, John Martineau wrote in a letter that formed part of his recollections and views of Australia that while he found the harbour to be of excellent quality, he saw the town itself as being quite backward and dull. Nevertheless, he did make mention of the convict labour force and his conviction that the Sound was, in fact, a suitable place for them as there was little opportunity afforded to them to escape:

As for Albany, the settlement, it is a pleasant, cosy little village of wooden houses, with three or four superior habitations for the Government officials and the Peninsular and Oriental Agent; and considering that it is on a splendid harbour and situated in the extreme corner of a great continent, it is about as quiet, dull, lifeless, and un-progressive a place as can well be conceived. For what is there to be done there? The climate is said to be particularly charming, but the soil is so poor and sandy that even the few hundred inhabitants can scarcely grow food for their own wants.

There is an establishment of convicts here, and they are to be seen doing such work as can be found for them; and in one respect it is a good place for them, for there is little chance of their escaping. From the tops of a hill, we could see to a great distance with the nearest station fifty miles off, and Perth, the only considerable town, two hundred and fifty. The road to it is plainly visible for miles and miles, stretching straight across the plain.[17]

Rumours of gold being found in and around Albany in 1870 caused little interest to *The Inquirer*'s correspondent in Albany, instead it was the 'mutiny' of a number of convicts outside of the settlement at Chorkerup that sparked the greater interest in the papers:

I have not much news to give you. Everything is very dull, notwithstanding the promising rumour of gold; but you know how long it takes to wake up an Albanian to anything beyond his own immediate interests.

All the convicts at the Chorkerup Camp, eleven men, were sentenced on the 23rd inst., to from 12 months to 2 years hard labour for mutiny; one of them, the ring-leader, to do some portion of his time on bread and water. This man was one John Holland, convicted at the last Quarter Sessions of perjury. He got 5 years penal

---

[16] *The Inquirer and Commercial News*, Perth. 23rd January 1867.
[17] John Martineau. *Letters from Australia*. London. 1869.

> *servitude, and was not satisfied, as he said he expected seven; so, this little game at Chorkerup enabled the Magistrates to give him fifteen months extra...*[18]

Through natural attrition and with no further transport occurring by 1876 only seven convicts remained in the settlement at this time completing what was left of their sentences:

> *During the past week, the only cases brought before the Albany Police Court were against two convicts, one a young man of only 23 years of age, and the other an old offender whose career in crime had kept place with his advance in years. The convict, Thomas Green, was charged with absconding from custody and pleaded that four men had to do the work of eight, as some of the prisoners were kept at work late in the Warder's garden. Upon inquiry, we find that the garden is cultivated for the benefit of the prisoners, in order to supply them with fresh vegetables, and the seeds are provided at Mr Passmore's own expense, and that their produce is shared by all the gang.*
>
> *We have further been informed that prisoners out on the works when they are kept a considerable time have always been allowed to cultivate a garden to grow vegetables for their own use, provided it is done after Government working hours. The prisoner Kelly seems to have been a notoriously bad character, and one who ought not to be allowed at large, as there are always to be found in every community men of careless business habits, who are easily gulled by any plausible story and induced to cash cheques, or advance goods without taking the trouble to investigate the circumstances. This prisoner is one of the few relics of the old convict days of the colony, which seldom come to light in this town, which is not invested by the "bond classes" in the same way as other places.*[19]

While there was general praise for the behaviour of those convicts sent to the King George's Sound, unfortunately, the town was not without its mischievous and anti-social element. *The Daily News* of January 1885 was damming of the behaviour of a few who bought some element unsavoury behaviour to the town:

> *Albany, or Sleepy Hollow, as it is (and not wrongly) facetiously called, has been lately the scene of much "larrikinism," or lawlessness, which is perhaps the more correct term. The depredations that have been committed a very serious indeed, entailing the loss of money on the sufferers. It is thought that the time has come when steps should be taken by the powers that be to put down such high-handed conduct on the part of mischievous scoundrels, whose conduct would hardly suit the bush, and therefore, totally out of place in the streets of a small and peaceful community like Albany.*
>
> *The resident magistrate and the inefficient police staff do not seem to take sufficient notice of the serious writings that have and are now taking place. Halyards of several flag-staffs have been stolen, a street lamp broken, the boat of a poor honest pensioner, that cost £13, although lashed to its moorings, cut and drifted away and afterwards stove in… Even the English church was not free from their sacrilegious hands, as you will see by the comments of the only paper, by no means an independent one, that is published here. Peaceable citizens, who are heavily taxed for police protection, cannot lay down peacefully in their beds with any sense of security in their properties, but have to sit up the greater part of the night to watch their belongings and to save their property from injury from the hands of herds of mischievous blackguards, mildly called larrikins…*
>
> *"Sleepy Hollow", it may well be called, when its law officers and all holding any authority whatever appears to be asleep…*[20]

So, issues with vandalism and social disobedience are not just a common problem of today, but also raised their head in yesteryear as well.

---

[18] *The Inquirer and Commercial News*, Perth. 7th September 1870.
[19] *The Albany Mail and King George's Sound Advertiser*. 2nd May 1883.
[20] *The Daily News*. Saturday, 17th January 1888

Closing Remarks

The issue of convict transportation and use of this indentured form of cheap labour was a vexatious and highly contentious issue for the young settlement. Initially the endeavours of convict labour proved very beneficial to the town as key public works were completed by them under supervision. However, as a settlement matured and the free settlers became more self-reliant the need for such labour significantly diminished. This led to the issue of transportation becoming the subject of much debate; locally, at the government level in the eastern colonies and internationally as well.

A number of issues presented with respect to these recalcitrant and involuntary pioneers to the settlement. The first related to the fact that most had committed crimes in large city centres like London and so their knowledge of simple agrarian techniques and bush craft skills was needless to say, severely limited. Such prior learning and awareness would have been extremely useful in the fledgling settlement very reliant on growing its own food supply at the time. The lack of women in the settlement, also had a significant impact on general social cohesiveness, particularly in respect to relationships with the traditional inhabitants of the sound. The number of half-caste children grew significantly with time as a consequence of the significant imbalance between the sexes.

By the 1860s many free settlers of Albany began to perceive that identified negative social ills such as crime and drunkenness in the community were a by-product of convict transportation and consequently it outweighed the economic benefits that were being derived from their labour.

CHAPTER 6
WHALING

The history of whaling at Albany dates right back to the early years of the last century, and much has been written at various times of the arrival in port, after strenuous cruises, of vessels of practically all nations seeking to replenish stores and water supplies.
The Western Mail, Perth. Thursday, 18th April 1946.

Foreign Whaling Around King Georges Sound

Whaling in Albany waters has had a very chequered past, with many early aborted local endeavours added into the mix. Records indicate that American whalers and sealers were known to have been operating in and around King George's Sound before the end of 1828. In fact, there is evidence of a stone structure commonly referred to as the 'Sealers Oven' (circa 1800), a man-made structure of mud and stone, located on Waychinicup Inlet, east of Albany, which gives some credence to this this claim.[1] Furthermore, there was evidence that a small freshwater lake supply at Frenchman Bay that was first charted by George Vancouver RN, and William Broughton RN, during their exploratory voyage along the coast in September 1791 was also used extensively by American whalers who operated off the south coast in the early part of the Nineteenth Century.

Comment has already been made in some of the earlier journal entries, particularly those of Major Lockyer, of the concerns that the unpoliced activities of some rogue sealer and whaler gangs were having on the Indigenous population and general safety of the inhabitants in the settlement. Some years later, this frustration with the behaviour and the intrusion of foreign whaling boats in Western Australian waters resulted in the then Governor Stirling being lobbied to restrict the activities of these vessels in local waters. There was a concern raised at the time about the sustainability of overfishing of whales and seals in the waters of the southwest of the continent and the impact that this activity could have on any future possible 'local' forays into the industry. The huge profits that the foreign whalers were making at the expense of the colony growing its own industry were cited as one reason to restrict fishing activities. It was estimated that in 1845 there were approximately 300 American, French, British and Australian whaling ships operating off the south coast of Australia. As a result of this lobbying, the government passed legislation in 1860 prohibiting unlicensed whalers from operating in Western Australian waters. However, without a means to enforce the legislation few foreign vessels heeded these legislative restrictions.[2]

An article in *The Perth Gazette and Journal* of 1836 indicated frustration that there had been very little local enterprise shown to capitalise on the whaling industry and potential profits to be made from it:

By the return of the colonial schooner Champion, *we have late intelligence from King George's Sound and Port Augusta, and we are happy to find, of a satisfactory nature, as relates to the capabilities of those places; but we hear, with concern, that there is not that energy and enterprise amongst the inhabitants, which must lead on to fortune. The whaling party established at the former place is on a small scale; the following fact, however, may offer sufficient encouragement to its extension: Fifteen whales were struck during the last season, and seven were taken, but whether from the insufficiency of means or the want of experience on the part of those employed,*

---

[1] The Sealers' Oven is believed to be a semi-permanent bread oven built by the early seal hunters around 1800, it predates European colonisation of Western Australia by over twenty years and is therefore one of the Western Australia's oldest non- Indigenous artefacts. It was classified by the National Trust in 1977 and has been part of the Waychinicup National Park since the park's establishment in 1990. *Heritage Council of Western Australia (1997).* "Sealers Oven" *(PDF). Register of Heritage Places – Assessment Documentation. Retrieved 13 May 2006.*}

[2] The Cheynes Beach Whaling Station started at Frenchman Bay in 1852. Initially the station was granted a quota of only 50 humpbacks, but this was increased and at its peak, the company took between 900 and 1100 sperm and humpback whales each year for processing. However, there was a ban on humpback whaling from 1963 which decreased the viability of the catch. Cheynes Beach struggled commercially for several years prior to its closure in 1978 because of increased fuel costs and the uncertainty of not being able to sell a product finally brought an end to the industry with the last whale, a female sperm whale, taken on 20th November 1978.

remains to be determined, not more than 15 tons of oil, and about 2 tons of whalebone, were obtained. We can scarcely credit the report that one boat was manned with two native women, two boys, and a headsman, the latter of whom it was necessary at times to lift into his station.[3]

Settler Forays in Whaling

Initially attempts to engage in whaling by an Albany based resident were through the efforts of a local merchant Thomas Booker Sherratt who began operating a whaling station at Doubtful Island Bay, east of Albany, in 1836.

However, the first actual whaling endeavour off the coast of Albany was from Middleton Beach, close to the settlement. While the letter of George Fletcher Moore detailed some optimism that such a venture would indeed be worthwhile, realistically, it was not a successful enterprise and ceased operations soon afterwards.

Whales frequent King George's Sound. Mr [Lionel] Lukin, who went with us to examine the Sound, in order to ascertain whether it be adapted to whale fishing, is considered highly eligible for that purpose and intends to attempt it immediately. I hope he will succeed; it would achieve a means of giving stability to the colony. I trust that we shall yet be able to avail ourselves of the advantages.[4]

The Perth Gazette of 1833 ran a series of articles on early whaling activities. Of particular interest was the article pertaining to King George's Sound:

We inadvertently omitted to notice a whaling establishment which is on the point of being formed at King George's Sound, Albany, Messrs. Lukin and Steele, of this port, are actively pursuing the projected plans, and no doubt is entertained of a prosperous result. Mr Lukin will take the management of the establishment, and from his known perseverance will, we fully anticipate, distinguish himself as the first to open to us extensive and valuable export. In consequence of Mr Lukin's craft which has been on stocks at Perth, for some considerable time, not being completed, an application was made a few days ago by the parties for the loan of the government schooner Ellen, *which, we are informed was declined.*

It is presumed that some arrangement we made with the captain of the Jolly Rambler, *who intends touching at King George's Sound, to convey the party down, but they not having a craft of any description will materially affect the extent of their enterprise for the season.*[5] *They will, however, establish the fact of the importance of this port as a whaling station and will lay the foundations of a plan on a more enlarged scale for the ensuing year. As a community, we are strongly interested in the success of these undertakings, and those that are the first to volunteer in so good a cause may find their labours amply rewarded is our most cordial wish.*[6]

Further insight into the whaling ventures at King George's Sound was provided by *The Hobart Gazette* of 28th February 1835:

The 'Jess' having passed King George's Sound in heavy weather, returned to that port with a passenger – Mr Lovett, of Hobart Town – who is furnished with the necessary equipment for an extensive whaling establishment at the Sound. Rumour states that this gentleman is about to join Mr Dring, who proceeded a short time ago to the neighbourhood of the Sound on a sealing trip, and Mr T.B. Sherratt, a gentleman already settled there (the latter is the grandfather of Mr Walter Sherratt, of Duke Street, Albany, who is born at the port). The experience of Mr Lovett who is one of the first headmen engaged in the whale fishery of Hobart Town augurs favourably for their undertaking, and as capital is not lacking to pursue the scheme to a favourable issue, we are disposed to prognosticate that this establishment will prove a valuable acquisition to the colony, as well as the source of wealth to the parties engaged in it.[7]

The Inquirer followed up on the whaling issue and the general sense of frustration that local enterprises had yet to reap a solid harvest of whale products when it reported on the success that French whalers had had in the Two Peoples Bay area:

---

[3] *The Perth Gazette and Western Australian Journal.* 24th December 1836.
[4] George Fletcher Moore extracts from his letters and journal. Perth 1835.
[5] The *Jolly Rambler* arrived at Albany from Fremantle on 18th April, 1833, but it is not recorded whether Lukin and Steele were passengers.
[6] *The Perth Gazette,* 1835-1840. From 15th February 1840-7 *The Perth Gazette* was not published due to the lack of a compositor. A small one-page sheet called *The Advertiser* was published instead.
[7] *The Hobart Gazette,* 28th February, 1835.

> *The last arrivals from King George's Sound report the presence of several French whalers in Princess Royal Harbour. A great many whales have been caught, and they are represented as plentiful, although the time of their entering the bays is stated to have been later than for many previous seasons. There are other whalers, both French and American at Two Peoples Bay, and also at Doubtful Island Bay, where several passed the winter. They have all been successful.[8]*

The Eastern Colonies newspapers were just as scathing of the lack of local enterprise with one correspondent writing:

> *Whales abound in their vicinity, yet they quietly submit year after year to see rich cargoes of oil carried off by the French and Americans without even evincing a desire to contest the spoils.[9]*

Many of the local shore-based operations could not compete against the well-equipped American whalers with their capacity for open sea whaling and processing capabilities. For example, stations existed at Torbay between 1844 and c.1864, Barker Bay 1849 to c.1873, Two Peoples Bay between 1842 and 1844 and c. the 1870s, Cheynes Beach 1846 to 1877, Cape Richie 1870 to c.1872, Doubtful Island Bay 1836 to 1838 and 1863 to 1870s and Barrier Anchorage c.1871.[10]

Newspaper articles on whaling were quite common in the latter part of the Nineteenth Century in Western Australia and expressed irritation with the lack of local enterprise and the perceived unfulfilled promise of such ventures was quite evident in their editorials. The ubiquitous premise was that the colony was missing out on a very real commercial opportunity by not demonstrating enough entrepreneurial acumen. *The Western Mail* summed up the issue for its readers:

> *It is now nearly 40 years ago since the French and American whalers plundered the "great leviathan" in the neighbourhood of King George's Sound, with a result rarely heard of on any whaling cruise. These enterprising fishers took on that occasion from before our very eyes some ten thousand barrels of oil, estimated, at that time, of the value of about £30,000. What is technically called deep-sea whaling was carried on largely in those years…*
>
> *Why is it that this legitimate source of large profits should be so much neglected by our own colonists? The great marine mammal has not been driven from his old haunts. Very few ships trading in our latitudes without entries in their logs relating to whales. We understand that the sperm whale is still to be captured within easy distance of our coastline… We are living near some of the best whaling grounds in the world, and, if we do not attempt to win from the deep its most valuable treasure, it is not because of want of encouragement to do so. Is it not a disgrace to us to look on quietly while other people are making, not a fortune, but a very good thing after an industry prosecuted in our own seas?*
>
> *Whales are now an unknown quantity. They are to be numbered by thousands. Never has sperm oil been more valued than it is in these days, and the unceasing and increasing demand for machinery of all kinds over the civilised world makes it most improbable that the value of this indispensable adjunct to smooth working will deteriorate…*
>
> *What would be more legitimate than a whaling company? When it is recollected that a whale, which will yield £1000 worth of oil is by no means considered a large one, and that a few vessels getting amongst a "school" could, in a day or two take £20,000 worth of oil, one would imagine that a whaling company is an enterprise that ought to find favour with any community eager to make money.[11]*

A year later *The Albany Mail* newspaper provided some insight into the whaling activities at King George's Sound in an article published in 1888 which stated:

> *……On Friday, April 27 about 5:30 am when the* Platina *was about 40 miles of land, south-south-east of Bald Head – two whales were raised [sighted], and at 8 o'clock two boats were lowered, which went in pursuit; the whales-one of which was large and the other small – running apart at some distance of seven or eight miles. The small while was soon killed, but the ship kept the run of the other one till 4 p.m., the boat being fast to*

---

[8] *The Inquirer and Commercial News,* Perth. 20th October 1841.
[9] *The Australasian Chronicle,* Sydney. November 1841.
[10] Sherratt, Lovett, Dring and Brooker operated an early whaling station from 1835. Cheyne was also involved in the local whaling industry, started in 1836-37 at Doubtful Island Bay.
[11] *The Western Mail.* 4th December 1886.

the whale, which was going to leeward. Night came on and Captain Slocum dispatched another boat to the assistance of the one is engaged in the chase, while he went with his ship in search of the dead whale, which she took alongside between 9 and 10 p.m. Before returning from the dead fish the captain signalled for the return of the first boat, which had eventually killed the whale near midnight and hung onto it but being out of sight of the ship and had not perceived the signal of recall. After securing the first whale, the Platina steered for where the missing boats had last been seen, but cruised about all night in vain, and accompanied by the Canton, which vessel had arrived on the scene between nine and ten o'clock and assisted in the endeavour to find the lost boats. Captain Slocum anxiously awaited daybreak in hope that the morning light would show the boats in sight, but no such luck.

About 9 a.m. Captain Howland, of the Canton, boarded the Platina, and offered to look for the missing boats while the Captain of the Platina cut into the whale he had alongside, and at 2 p.m. the same day [28th of April] the Canton sighted the two boats steering for Breaksea, and by 9 o'clock that evening took the cruise onboard. The Platina, which had taken the course for Breaksea after cutting up the whale, fell in with the Canton on the afternoon of April 29, about 3 o'clock, when the two boat's crews returned to their own ship, some the worse for their adventure, and only regretting that they had lost their whale, which they had abandoned about noon on the day after capture. It was a curious fact that the Canton and Platina, though cruising in company, had not cited one another for at least a fortnight previous to April 27. During her late cruise, Platina lost three large whales, the first being missed by the harpooner, the second fairly hit, but the iron came out, and the third was the occasion of the boat trouble, since when Captain Slocum secured for small ones, making about 80 barrels of oil.[12]

The Western Australian Government eventually did grant a licence to a Norwegian Whaling Company in 1912 to operate whaling stations out of Albany at Frenchman's Bay. Around 1911, Norwegian whaling interests were looking to the southern hemisphere for possible whaling grounds due to heavy competition in the northern hemisphere and Pacific Ocean area and further, as part of a planned expansion of their activities in the southern hemisphere. However, due to both a poor whaling season in 1916 which had understandably been impacted by The Great War and the rise of alternative fossil fuels on the market the company was forced to close. This closure was gazetted on 29th December 1918, but it was the 3rd March 1919 before an indenture legally surrendering the Company's licence occurred. Remnants of these operation can be seen at Whaling Cove in Frenchman's Bay.

Closing Remarks

It would be difficult to substantiate a claim that the shore-based whaling industry which operated from King George's Sound in the Nineteenth Century was in any way a commercial success. Those whaling companies established along the south coast in the late 1830s lasted for only a couple of seasons. During that period the industry provided limited financial returns to its investors and consequently after that time local direct participation and interest faded with just the occasional activity on the margins of the colony occurring, Cheyne's Beach and Doubtful Island endeavours for example. Even these operations were not a huge success, as again they only provided limited returns to investors.

Despite the poor returns to the local inhabitants directly participating in whaling, King George's Sound businesses continued to support the industry by servicing both international boats and their crews engaged in the activity. Consequently, it became an important part of Albany's seasonal economy with the earlier forays into this industry more often concerned with supporting those international whaling operations, chiefly American and French interests. There was ongoing concern expressed by more rogue elements of the industry that included sealers, runaway convicts and assorted others, pirates included, operating at the edge of King George's Sound settlement. *The Colonist* in Sydney remarked on the undesirable elements of the industry:

It appears, therefore, deserving of some consideration by what means their practices can be checked, as future settlers …will be made to expiate the crimes and outrages of these lawless assassins.[13]

---

[12] *The Inquirer and Commercial News*, Perth. 8th June 1888.
[13] *The Colonist*. Sydney. 10th January 1838.

CHAPTER 7
THE DEVELOPMENT OF EDUCATION FACILITIES

"Many families of respectability are deterred from emigrating in consequence of the reflecting that their children must of necessity run wild in the trackless woods of a new settlement." The Perth Gazette, 1833.

"Let us not hear any more of an education for the poor, fitted for the station of life in which they will be placed."
The Inquirer, 1855.

"...the fixing as a present limit on Education for Boys equal to that obtainable at a good English Grammar School, and, for girls, such a one as a respectable middle-class person would endeavour to secure for his daughter in England."
Governor Captain Charles Fitzgerald Kennedy.
Western Australian Government Gazette. 20th March 1855.

Overview

It could be said that Education in Albany did not have a history until the West Australian colony began taking the matter more seriously. There were of course attempts at schooling before the actions of the colonial government, but before then there were experiments at provision, but no real education policy as such until the Education Act of 1871, an initiative of the then Governor Frederick Aloysius Weld (1869-1875). It was under his leadership through the introduction of the Education Act of 1871 that a system for funding and administering schools was commenced. The Reverend John Burdett Wittenoom, Chairman of the colony's first Board of Education had directed attention to the need for the new colony to address the education of its young as far back as 1838.[1] However, it was not until a formalised Education Committee was established by the Western Australian Legislative Council in 1871 that substantial improvements started to crystallise to meet the demands of the colony, Albany included.[2]

The establishment of a school in King George's Sound took some time to achieve as understandably the available revenue of the colony had to be budgeted with meticulous care. Consequently, the funds available for the purpose of schooling the settlement's children was indeed meagre. This position can be understood given that the early settlers at King George's Sound were more focused on issues of survival and given the limited resources available to them, the education of their young was not initially seen as a high priority. Consequently, any early attempts at establishing a school were very reliant on both individual philanthropy and those who had some personal, even idealistic motivations to do so. It was not until the influence of the Roman Catholic Church and its general educational endeavours within the Western Australian Colony as a whole that government intervention and action was indeed forthcoming, chiefly as a means to counter the Catholic influence and to "defend" the Protestant faith. The development of education facilities at King George's Sound in many respects paralleled that of the colony as a whole. In most cases, schools in Albany took their lead from the Swan River Colony's efforts and policy initiatives.

The Need for a School

Much of Albany's early education history is concerned with the foundation of schools that could adequately accommodate the learning needs of the settlement's children, small but gradually increasing in number. The path to addressing the settlement's universal provision of educational opportunities for its young was not a smooth one. The capacity to satisfy the changing and expanding educational aspirations and needs of its people was indeed evident in the way schools evolved with time in the first four decades of the town's settlement. Although individual community-minded individuals, with philanthropy in mind, had made some forays into trying to organise and conduct schools in the early days of the settlement their efforts were generally hit and miss until the colony developed and implemented an education policy and philosophy about schools and schooling that bought some stability and equality into practices.

---

[1] John Burdett Wittenoom was the Imperial Chaplain and only the second Anglican priest to perform religious services in the fledgling Swan River Colony soon after its establishment in 1829.
[2] *Colonial Secretary's Office* (CSO) *Letter Book* 160, January – February 1838.

During these early years Church of England Schools also had acquired lasting significance along with the emergence of colonial Government Schools.[3] In one respect the Roman Catholic Church had a unique record entering the field early in the scheme of development of universal access to schools in Western Australia.

Mrs A.Y. Hassell contends in her pamphlet of 1910 that the first school to evolve in Albany was in 1835 and was started by Lady Spencer, wife of the Resident Magistrate Sir Richard Spencer:
> *This year Lady Spencer started a small school for native children, and a number of charitable ladies* [in London], *headed by the Duchess of Kent, sent a parcel of red flannel garments for the women and children.*[4]

However, no evidence can be found of Lady Spencer actually commencing a school for the Indigenous population in the town. There is notwithstanding evidence that she was concerned with the nakedness of the Aboriginal women and children and in 1834 wrote to friends in England seeking some cloth to make some appropriate clothing for them. In 1837 she was rewarded for her efforts with five bales of red flannel from England.[5] In fact, there had not been a stable school established in Albany during the whole of the 1830s. Notwithstanding that there was an unsuccessful attempt to establish a private school in 1836 by Thomas Booker Sherratt, but this venture was unsuccessful, and this school attempt soon closed.

In 1840 the government enquired whether Albany needed a school as some limited colony funding had become available to support the paying of the salary of the teacher. The community welcomed the initiative and accepted the offer. This was the first recognised school established in Albany and was a small private school, known as a 'Dame School.' It was established by Stephen Knight in 1840.[6] The Dame School was located in extant soldiers' quarters that were no longer required near what is now Lawley Park. The school opened on November 1, 1840 and was a joint effort, for while the Dame School was officially run by Stephen Knight, the teacher was in fact his wife Lucinda. It is noted that the school under their joint stewardship was a considerable success.

Governor Stirling had espoused the view that *'voluntary exertion was immensely admired and self-help was looked for it in all but the most abject'*, and although such attitudes were also evident enough amongst the early settlers in Western Australia, the absence of resources through individual philanthropy, characteristic of school provision in Great Britain and to an extent in the United States of America as well, led him to remedy the situation by endorsing an education position that would help to promote the establishment of some funded schools in the colony. Schools and the education they provided, although seen as a most valuable exercise, were also regarded by many at this time as more fitting for individual or group philanthropists to get involved with, especially as there were many other calls upon the limited available funds and resources of the colony at this time.

In Albany, the school sponsored by local philanthropists Mr and Mrs Knight highlighted the issues with regards to funding such a venture. The Dame School that they initially established was located in the old Commissariat store adjacent to Lawley Park. Knight wrote a letter to The Colonial Secretary seeking assistance with funds to keep their privately funded school operational:
> To the Honourable Peter Broun,
> Colonial Secretary
> August 23rd, 1834
>
> Sir,
> *I feel myself called on to take the earliest opportunity to lay before you for the information of Governor Sir James Stirling a Summary Report of the present state of the Perth School* [Albany], *urged by a sense of duty to bring this subject to His Excellency's Notice and to render an account of the progress of this Institution during the period it has been under my personal Direction. On Reference to the Accounts which I have by me of the proceedings of the school, it will be found that the Establishment commenced on the first of November 1832,*

---

[3] In 1834 an attempt was made to open Albany's first colonial school under the direction of Thomas Sherratt, a self-appointed lay preacher: £20 per annum was allotted to its teacher, but the school was short lived.
[4] *Early Memories of Albany* by Mrs AY Hassell, Pamphlet. *The Albany Advertiser.* (circa 1910)
[5] Chessell, G. *Richard Spencer.* University of Western Australia Press. 2005.
[6] *The Albany Advertiser.* 27th July 1924.

from which period until the 12th of July 1834 the subscriptions advanced by the Local Government and private Individuals, have been sufficient to meet the current expenses, as well a considerable sum required for the erection of a school room, and other incidental and unexpected outlays.

The Funds at my Disposal were exhausted on the latter day above mentioned, with little chance of being renewed; feeling, however, assured that His Excellency would regret the suspension of so useful an institution as this, and knowing also from the list forwarded from King George's Sound that a provision had been made for it, I felt it my duty to defray the schoolmaster's salary from my own means, which has (inclusive of this week pay) amounted of six guineas. ...

I beg to enclose the Information of his Excellency a list of the scholars at present under Mr Spencer's charge [a young schoolmaster not to be confused with Sir Richard Spencer, Resident Magistrate], *and I believe that a correct criterion may be thereby formed of the number of scholars usually in attendance. In reference to the appointment of a schoolmaster on the new regulations, I believe I need not solicit your Interest on behalf of Mr Spencer to ensure his continuance in the office, as his regular and attentive application to the duties of that situation are well known to yourself and others who have taken an interest in the welfare of the school: for my part, I have had favourable opportunities of judging his fitness, and it is with pleasure that I can recommend him as a- young man every way worthy of encouragement.*
I have the Honor to be Sir,
Your Obedient and Humble Servant,
William Knight Secretary and Treasurer. [7]

As a point of interest is that the attendance list that Knight included at the end of this letter to the governor as it is possibly one of the earliest examples of an attendance register of children to be found in Australia.

However, at this time a wider debate was unfolding in terms of educational provision in the colony. A strong advocate for the creation of schools was to be found in the Colonial Chaplain The Reverend John Wittenoom who in 1830 had established a grammar school in the Swan River Colony along British classical school lines. In part, this model of schooling was adopted because of the origins of the early settlers to the colony and the settlement at King George's Sound, who had grown up with a mindset of the English concept of schooling with its particular emphasis on social class distinctions. However, Wittenoom's advocacy went further than this as the following extract from correspondence to the Governor indicates:

John Wittenoom to Governor Stirling.
Perth, February 22nd, 1838

Sir,
The present state of the juvenile portion of the community and the great want of schools for the education of the same has lately induced several gentlemen to form themselves into a committee to take into consideration the best means of supplying the deficiency so much complained of. Having had considerable experience in the education of youth, I have been requested to furnish them with a place which might in any way conduce to the attainment of so desirable an object: I have done so, but as the accomplishment of it depends upon the continuance of support that they receive from your Excellency.

I need to not point out the importance of the measures now in contemplation but trusting they will receive from your Excellency every favourable consideration.
I have the honour, to remain
Your Excellency's
Faithful and obedient servant
J.B. Wittenoom Colonial Chaplain.[8]

Lack of educational opportunities and training was seen as a significant shortcoming of colonial life. Wittenoom's school experiment which had begun in 1830 relied on funding from Governor Stirling, but when Governor John Hutt later declined to renew the subsidy, the school collapsed in 1839. Hutt had

---

[7] *Colonial Secretaries Office Papers*, Vol. 33, Letter 150. 1834, in Battye Library, Perth.
[8] Ibid, Vol. 59, Letter 163. 1838, in the Battye Library.

withdrawn the education grants as he evidently disapproved of government expenditure being assigned to this endeavour. This action bought to an end Wittenoom's school experiment which had provided both an elementary education and one identified as being best suited to the children of middle-class settlers. Subsequently, the colonial press of the period reacted strongly against the Governor's policy, conveying to its readers this disapproval:

> *...if we would be consistent in our advocacy of the interests of the colony, we must do more than strive merely to promote the increase of its wealth. We must see that in its moral condition it for not in the wake of the parent country... Indeed, we believe it is... Imperative on those who are invested with the powers of government, to provide the means of proper instruction in this colony for the young of all classes, since here they are absolutely depended upon the government for aid, there being no private resources by which they can benefit. Without an efficient degree of mental culture, there is evidence that the next generation of colonies must be inferior to their parents and thus... a rapid deterioration must take place, and the white man would descend in the scale of humanity till there would be little to distinguish him from that debased on un-christianized (sic) denizen of the woods...*
>
> *Does the government think that in legislating for our country it has nothing more to do than to see that the revenue is properly collected and accounted for, and the citizens preserved from bloodshed and innovation (sic) of property and that it may then fold its hands in peace, and simper in the fullness of its self-complacency and virtuous contentment?*[9]

Nevertheless, in a nod to education and concern for the native inhabitants it is interesting to note the initiative of the Governor Hutt in respect to skills training of members of the Aboriginal population:

> *Colonial Secretary's Office,*
> *Perth, June 23, 1841*
>
> *It appears to His Excellency the Governor to be highly desirable to promote in every way the civilization and improvement of the Aborigines of this Territory, and to extend the measures already in operation for this purpose, His Excellency has directed it to be notified for public information*
>
> *1st. That a remission in the purchase of land to the extent of (£18) eighteen pounds will be allowed to any person who shall produce satisfactory evidence to the Government that a Native has been in his constant employment for the space of two full years, and that he has acquired a competent knowledge and skill in the usual operations of farming, threshing, reaping, mowing, &c.,*
>
> *2nd. That a remission in the purchase of land to the extent of (!36) pounds will be allowed to any person who shall produce satisfactory evidence to the Government that he has instructed a Native in a trade, calling or handicraft of such a nature as is usually brought under the system of apprenticeship; and that such Native has acquired such proficiency therein as would in the case of a European apprentice, entitle him to receive his indentures and be treated on the terms of a journeyman. The person applying for such remission will also be required to give the Native such a certificate as will entitle him to be treated as a journeyman.*
>
> *His Excellency conceives that the object contemplated in this notice will be materially facilitated by the present gradually improving the condition of the Aborigines, and by the kind disposition hitherto generally evinced towards them by the colonists...*[10]

Political Adversaries and the State Aid issue

The Roman Catholic school system in Western Australia evolved to a large extent through the efforts of Father John Brady.[11] Brady had been sent by Bishop Polding of Sydney to establish the Catholic Church in the Western Australian colony. In preparation for this venture, he undertook a visit to school systems in Europe before returning to the Swan River settlement on 7th January 1846. Brady was appointed the first Roman Catholic Bishop of Perth on his return. He had bought with him a cohort of 27 Catholic missionaries along with considerable funding that would allow him to establish a strong Catholic Church presence in the colony. Bishop Brady allocated to his missionaries certain district parishes in which to

---

[9] *The Inquirer*. 25th October 1843.

[10] *Western Australian Almanack*. 1842.

[11] Father Brady came first to Perth in December 1843 and then returned to Europe to seek financial assistance for the Roman Catholic Church. When he arrived back in the colony in 1846, he devoted himself to education - founding both a boys' and a girls' school in that year.

minister, with one of his cohort being sent to the Albany district with the stated objective *"to mission to the Aborigines and parish churches and establish schools as needed, especially for the European settlers."*

These endeavours of Bishop Brady were perceived to be a threat by some in the settlement and consequently, were opposed by many of the non-Catholic inhabitants. Between 1846 and 1848 the establishment and development of the beginnings of the Catholic school system in Western Australia ignited the colony's first State Aid to Schools controversy which in turn became the genesis for the formation of a state public school system. This period in the colony's history was not noted as being a time of religious tolerance between Catholics and Protestants.

Prominent in the thinking of colonialists was the belief that churches should be voluntary associations not subsidised by the state and this applied particularly to assisted schools. These arguments strengthened the case against support for a dual system of private and public schools funded from the government's purse. However, the final decision against it was primarily the outcome of local religious divisions and rivalries in the colony which found political expression among its electors. Taking up this argument was *The Inquirer* which advocated a Church of England response to the forays of the Roman Catholic Church in the education sphere:

> *The letter published by us this day from the Reverend. G. King*
> *to the Roman Catholic Bishop of Perth is of such a nature as required from us…*
>
> *If it be the intention of Dr Brady and his subordinates to establish schools in which our youth may be instructed without expense to their parents, we must do the same; so as to leave no shadow of an excuse to those who, under the mere plea of economy, might be induced to subject their children to the risk of inviting heretical notions, and freeing ourselves from the reproach of having left the young exposed to the allurements of what we are bound to consider as a most erroneous faith…*
>
> *In our opinion, the only proper and effectual remedy is the establishment of three schools in our turn, wherein our children may receive instruction in the usual branches of education, and we bought up in the religious tenants of the Church of England…*
>
> *We should take the opportunity now afforded of saying a few words to those who professed to see no danger in allowing other children to be educated under Romish influence… These persons express themselves satisfied with the promise that has been held forth there will be no interference with the religious belief of the pupils… If the promises be kept religion will form no part of the instruction received and education without religion is utterly worthless. But the promise will not be kept.*[12]

The *Inquirer* article along with other criticism percolating in some quarters of the colony was responded to by a writer under the heading; "*A Friend to Education*":

> *The opposition to the Roman Catholic Mission by the bigots in this colony has been exceedingly fierce and unmanly. Anathemas from the pulpit have been thundered against it, and at the prayer meetings and tea parties in the town the same system is kept up against that unoffending class of the Queen's subjects, and no engine is left untried, no foul accusation forgotten, to seduce scholars from their tuition. In this colony~ at least, Catholicism and liberality go hand in hand, and this is the true secret of the opposition of the Government and their retainers to the further progress of education…*
>
> *These zealots ostensible belong to the Church of England, and yet, strange inconsistency, they allow our children to be educated in sectarian principles, inimical to her establishment. The Catholics have a right to retort on all persons in authority like "A Protestant"…*[13]

This reply was quickly answered:
> *Sir,*
>
> *I trust that I shall be allowed to reply to some remarks made in last week's paper by the pseudo "Friend to Education". It is the duty of every Protestant to expose the insidious schemes of popery, but as I and the body*

---

[12] *The Inquirer.* 4th March 1846.
[13] Ibid. 11th November 1847.

with which I am connected, have been personally attacked, I publicly confront this snake in the grass in his vile assertions...

Your Obedient Servant.
W. Dacres Williams,
Master Colonial School[14]

The religious debate and the concern for the conduct of ostensibly non-sectarian, colonial schools as opposed to the issue of sectarian schools were gazetted on 17th June 1846. An abbreviated list that was published by the Colonial Secretary's Office, Perth, included the following rules and regulations (The number of each regulation is consistent with the original publication):

Rules and regulations for the schools established by the local government of Western Australia.
1. The schools are to be open to children of all classes and religious denominations, with a male or female.
2. The children whose parents cannot afford to contribute towards their education, will be admitted as free scholars, and those whose parents are in better circumstances, will be expected to pay a small sum to the teacher weekly in advance.
5. The schools will be open at all times of inspection of visitors, who comprise the members of both councils, the magistrates and clergy of the colony, and such others as his Excellency may from time to time appoint...
6. A book or register recording attendance, progress, and conduct of the children, is to be kept for the inspection of visitors, who are requested to make any remarks that may be necessary...
8. Parents who may feel themselves aggrieved by the improper treatment or for any neglect of their children's education, are requested to make an immediate complaint to any of the visitors, ...
9. The children will be required to come to the schools clean and decently are tired, and the parents to provide such books and stationery as may be necessary for their children's instruction...
10. Each schoolmaster will be required to furnish through the Colonial Secretary and Residents of the respective districts, for the approval of the Governor, the course of education each respectively may consider best adapted for their school.[15]

Brady formally applied to the colonial government for financial assistance for his Catholic schools in 1846 which was subsequently refused by the new Governor Lieutenant Colonel Andrew Clark (1846-1847). Governor Clark, and his successors Lieutenant Colonel Frederick Irwin (1847-1848) and Captain Charles Fitzgerald RN, (1848-1855), instead established a government-financed public-school system to counter the education initiatives and influences of Brady and the impact of the Sisters of Mercy whose influence in the colony was also growing. The Governor's actions re-established an emphasis on colonial schools, in part precipitated by the actions of The Sisters of Mercy who were establishing their Catholic schools in a predominantly Protestant leaning society.

In 1846 rules and regulations for establishing colonial schools were gazetted. Notably, these were the first education regulations for Western Australia. They were published by Peter Brown, the Colonial Secretary and directed all colonial schools to admit children of all classes and religious denominations, to charge fees according to the ability of parents to pay, and to allow free entry to the children of those who cannot:

Merits of public versus private education. Public education instils improvement, not only in the manners, but in the principles and tone of thought of the bulk of the population, and removal of that tendency to sorted selfishness and admiration for mere wealth.
General Board of Education Report 1847. [16]

The Board continued in its report to state:

The object of the colonial schools should... be to instruct the general public in such branches of learning as are required for the everyday business of life; and anything beyond this should be met... by private means... The committee does not consider that a finished education of the wealthy classes can properly be made the object of general taxation.[17]

---

[14]. Ibid. 7th December 1847.
[15] *The Government Gazette.* 60, 19th June 1846.
[16] *Colonial Secretaries Office.* 175; C.O.18/47, October 1847.
[17] Ibid

Governor Irwin had established a framework for the development of colonial schools in 1847 which included how the local district committee, Albany included, should operate. Some of the framework requirements included that:

> *7. The Resident Magistrate of the district is to be regarded ex officio chairman of the local committee…*
>
> *8. The appointment and dismissal of all salaried teachers rests with the governor…*
>
> *9. Every teacher at school is subject to the control of a local committee and wishing to communicate with the said committee must do so with the secretary of the local committee …*
>
> *10. Local committees are at Liberty to allow the use of school rooms for purposes calculated to afford general instruction, recreation, or legitimate amusement. But the general board reserves to itself the power to withhold this liberty if it be used in properly.*[18]

There were some influential members in the colony who believed that if Aboriginal children could be separated from their parents, then they may become more 'civilised' and consequently 'employable'. For example, there were initial plans promulgated around 1842 for such a venture in Albany nevertheless, it was not until 1843 that an early attempt was initiated to establish a school for these children, albeit without the separation aspect. A resident John McKail was appointed as the schoolmaster on certain other conditions being met (salary and Postmaster positions included in the incentive package). This school was not a success and later on the Annesfield School for Aboriginal Children grew out of this early Indigenous school endeavour.

Camfield House (also known as Annesfield) was opened in 1852 by the Church of England Imperial Chaplain Archdeacon John Ramsden Wollaston and Mrs Anne Camfield, and was regarded as the first school in the state that was recognised for its focus on educating Indigenous children.[19] The school operated in a room within the Resident Magistrate's residence. Archdeacon Wollaston and Anne Camfield believed that the participation of Aboriginal people in *"the comforts of civilisation"* depended upon their conversion to Christianity and education.[20]

The Inquirer and Commercial News newspaper reported on the *"useful domestic works"* being taught to the girls attending the school, sentiments that would appeal to colonists who viewed the Aboriginal way of life as somewhat aimless. The newspaper indicated that the curriculum on offer emphasised a work ethic and the acquisition of religious knowledge:

> *The asylum for the children of Aboriginal natives at Annesfield, King George's Sound, Western Australia, at present contains 18 children, 13 girls, and five boys. The ages of the six elder girls from 10 to 15 or 16; younger ones from eight years down to 18 months; the oldest boy is about eight years old, and the youngest is just for years and seven months. These children are under the special care of the government resident's wife, with or without an assistant, as the case may be. A mere hiring would be of little use in such a work, and if it is difficult to meet with those will undertake the situation from a simple love of God.*
>
> *Within the last year, a comfortable schoolhouse has been erected, containing a dry airy school room of 30' x 12, together with a kitchen and sleeping apartment accommodate six or eight children, and a snug little room for the assistant… The elder girls are taught all useful domestic works. They wash, iron or mangle, the clothes of the Institute. They bake and cook, and scrub. At present they have not learnt to milk, but they can make butter, and there is little housework they are not capable of doing… The school routine extends to be on reading and writing, and a little arithmetic. They read well, marking the stops, &c, and they spell very correctly. In writing on their slates from dictation, they seldom misspell a word, and if they do, they will immediately be corrected on it being pointed out to them…*
>
> *It has often been remarked to the writer: "no doubt the intention of the friends of this and such like institutions are very benevolent and kind, but to what end we all this expenditure of time, and labour, and money lead? Do what you will for the children as they grow up, they will run away to their own people in the bush." It may be so if only the small number at present in the institution are bought into training. The human heart, whether of white or black people, requires sympathy and mutual kindness, and if these children are not with these essentials*

---

[18] *Rules and regulations for the Colonial Schools of Western Australia* (n.d.), State Archives (South Australia)
[19] See Chapter 1
[20] *The Albany Journal of J. Wollaston*. Nedlands: University of Western Australia Press, 1975.

to happiness among the white population, and if the separation from the civilized portion of their own people in the Institute, when they leave it to earn their own living, deprives them of society and companionship, they may go back to seek congenial fellowship among those who are in their wild state. But even then, impressions made upon the minds of the young are too strong to be eradicated, and they will not be able to forget all that they have learnt here, and then going back may be the means which God may choose to use to extend the knowledge of himself among this portion of the heathen.[21]

A report in 1847 to the Governor Lieutenant-Colonel Andrew K. H. Clarke from the General Committee of Education that had been established under the chairmanship of The Reverend John Wittenoom, had indicated that the Board had been informed that a Government Free School had been established at Albany and among other locations; Guildford, Fremantle, York and Bunbury. While the Central Education Board's relationship with the government was not always a smooth one, it was interesting to note the committee's remarks in respect to the establishment of Government schools:

The committee feel inclined to recommend that the establishment of a school in a particular District should in some degree depend upon the exertions and sacrifices which the inhabitants are willing to make. At the same time, this rule must be moderated by the consideration that where religion or education are most needed, they are in general least valued or desired. However, although the outline of the institutions seems independent of private aid, get a large amount of such aid will unavoidably be required to give the system efficiency; as, for instance, to supply rewards and prizes; to furnish and even to build, school houses and teachers apartments. Much assistance may, however, be given by those who cannot afford to give money; but it will only be by the general mass of the public viewing the institutions as their property, and cherishing its interest, and labouring for its advancement, with such feelings, that the system can attain a proper efficiency.[22]

The Inquirer in an editorial included the following passages on education:
We lay down the following rules ...
That it is the duty of the state to provide the education of its citizens; that the education furnished by the state should be for the benefit of all classes; that is extent should only be limited by the means of obtaining competent instructors or the means of paying for them....
Let us not hear any more of an education for the poor, fitted for the station of life in which they will be placed.[23]

In some respects, the 1855 report of the Central Board of Education contradicted its earlier premise concerning class education, instead advocating for:
...an education for boys equal to that obtainable had a good English grammar school, and for girls, such a one as a responsible middle-class person would endeavour to secure a friend's daughter in England.[24]

The editor of *The Inquirer and Commercial News* supported this viewpoint by indicating as follows:
We despise class education and maintain that to hold that A should learn Latin because he is a gentleman son which B should not because he is a mechanic is a principal begot ignorant tried. The time must come when it will not be the station that will command respect but the intellect...[25]

And again, later on, *The Inquirer and Commercial News* contained the following pertinent comments:
There is not a man in the colony who may not hope to see his children occupying the highest offices in the colony and he has a right to insist that his children shall be so educated as to fit them for the duties they will have to perform.[26]

The Inquirer statement was further strongly supported in *The Commercial and Shipping Gazette* in Fremantle of March, 1855, under an article bannered by; "*We Ought to have No Class Education*":

---

[21] Ibid.
[22] *Colonial Secretaries Office* 175, 1848 pp 205–19, South Australia.
[23] *The Inquirer* 19th December, 1855.
[24] *The Government Gazette* 20th March 1855.
[25] *The Inquirer and Commercial News* 19th December 1855.
[26] Ibid. 2nd January 1856.

> *The perusal of the report of the board of education has caused us much pleasure, and we consider it as one of the most satisfactory official documents headed to published in the colony. The great evil of a new colony is the absence of proper education establishments, and that evil has been partially met by the government ...*
>
> *The smallness of our population is a great bar to our obtaining good educational institutions, the returns not being sufficient to encourage private enterprise in this direction. Under these circumstances, the people must either remain uneducated, or else the government must interfere, and find teachers capable of offering such instruction as will fit the recipients to become intelligent and useful members of society; and this interference is the more justifiable, as it clashes with no private interest, while its aim is the benefit of all...*
>
> *We cannot educate too highly. The day has gone for exclaiming against indiscriminate and excessive education. Knowledge can never be in excess, and we have no right to discriminate as to the parties to whom it is to be imparted. We ought to have no class education, but all should receive the benefit of a liberal course of instruction. As the report justly observes, the children of the middle, and some of the working classes, of this province, will, in all probability, become a part of its governing body, and they cannot be too highly accomplished, for the performance of their duties as citizens of this colony...*[27]

In 1857 Mr and Mrs Camfield had extended their dwelling to incorporate a purpose-built separate school room annex with a classroom, attached kitchen and accommodation for up to eight children. In 1858 a total of 23 children were attending the school; the number of attendees increased to 55 in 1868. However, after this period the school went into decline and closed in 1871 when the remaining Aboriginal and half-caste children were transferred to Bishop Hale's Institution for Native and 'Half-Caste' Children in Perth. Captain James Sales, who was given responsibility for helping to transfer these students to Perth remarked:

> *The Resident Magistrate prior to Sir Alexander Campbell was Mr Camfield. He was the principal of a school for the education of native children and turned out some fine handy boys and girls. In 1871 the natives were drafted to Perth under the care of Miss Trimmer who afterwards became Mrs Captain Thomas. I was selected to accompany Miss Trimmer and we took the native boys and girls to Perth in two large vans, one for the boys and one for the girls.*[28]

The matter of school funding was partly resolved with the introduction of the Elementary Education Act of 1871. The fundamental issue precipitating this act was state aid for sectarian schools. The schism which resulted between Protestants and Roman Catholics was complicated further by the newly arrived Governor Frederick Aloysius Weld, himself a Roman Catholic. He was, consequently, sympathetic to arguments for funding for assisted schools.[29] The period 1870 to 1896 in Western Australia saw quite profound changes in its social, economic and political fabric which was also evident in Albany.

The beginning of this period saw the introduction of a new system of education, the architect of whom was Governor Weld. Weld's strong advocacy for universal access to education was to have a long-lasting impact on the colony's approach to schooling. His approach to the provision of education facilities in the colony became manifest in the Elementary Education Act of 1871 which established a firm foundation for the organisation of schools, both government and private.

The resulting Education Act of 1871 was Western Australia's first education-specific legislation, which indeed was not repealed until 1928. The most notable effect of the act was to introduce a dual system of government and assisted (state-aided, church) schools which lasted until 1895. Under the act, the administration of schools was vested in a Central Board plus a number of district boards with local responsibility for the oversight of schooling left to local district committees. Interestingly sometimes it was necessary to recruit elementary school teachers from the lower strata of society because the curriculum was deemed less complicated.

---

[27] Source: *Commercial News and Shipping Gazette*. Fremantle. 29th March, 1855.
[28] Captain James Sale's 1936 remarks reported in *The West Australian*, Perth, 7th March 1936.
[29] Sir Frederick Weld was Governor of Western Australia from 1869-1875. He succeeded John Stephen Hampton (1862-1868) and was succeeded by Sir William Cleaver Francis Robinson (1875-77), and Sir Harry Ord (1877-80).

Government School Board Established

In light of the requirements of the 1871 Education Act in early November 1871 elections were held in the Albany district for representatives for the Local Education Committee. The election caused considerable interest and aroused significant debate as one of the major controversies was concerned with whether the clergy should be permitted to nominate for a position on the local education committee. This was not just an issue for Albany, but also in nine other districts that were conducting elections at this time. Consider the statement from *The Fremantle Herald* which indicated its views on the matter to its readers prior to the conduct of the election:

We... Hope that the forthcoming elections will not be made the arena for the renewal of party fights by bellicose secretaries, that no attempt will be made to excite ill-feeling of violent agitation, but that temperate moderation will prevail...

So far as it is possible to gauge public opinion there appears a very general desire that the district education board should, like the central board, consist entirely of lay members, and that the clerical, necessarily sectarian element, be excluded. It is argued that the clergy and the various denominational ministers and pastors are already, under the provision of the act, the absolute and virtually uncontrolled religious instructors of the schools, and their power, adroitly exercised, may be of immense influence. The selection appointment of schoolmaster rests with the district board - subject, it is true, to the confirmation of the central board which, however, it's not likely to interfere in such matters without strong reasons for doing so – and, here again, if the clergy were members their influence would come forcibly into play for, who would be more likely to undertake the whole management of the affair than the clergyman, who if imbued with severe sectarian principles would naturally select a teacher severely sectarian also.

What we want are candidates who will be prepared to sacrifice their own personal bias and feelings when convinced that regard for the public good requires them to do so. We want persons who also feel keenly the education requirements of the colony, and who, knowing what is wanted, will be actuated by the strongest mindset – an ardent desire – for providing it. What we require is sensible and laborious men, endowed with practical common sense, and unaddicted to chimerical theories or pet schemes; men who understand what is expected of them above all, is to extend and improve elementary learning among the people.[30]

By 1857, most of Albany's children of school age were attending the government-funded school housed in the old Commissariat Store that was then located near present-day Lawley Park. In 1871 after the passing of the Education Act by the Legislative Council the government subsidised a brick building to be constructed on a site that had been chosen in Stirling Terrace. where the present-day courthouse is located today. This school operated successfully until the 1890s when a significant increase in student numbers demanded the provision larger facilities. The increase is attributed by and large to the influx of people entering Albany encouraged by the gold mining boom in Coolgardie and Kalgoorlie. Albany was the main port of entry for prospectors seeking access to these fields.

Local boards were responsible for the enforcement of school attendance within the framework and by-laws that had been provided for them by the Colonial Office. From the beginning, this responsibility created difficulties in terms of workload for the board given that it was comprised of part-time members. The Plantagenet District School board was established and had responsibility for education in Albany and associated districts up until 1909. The Albany District Education Board area minutes of July 1876 illustrate the extent to which matters were occupying an inordinate amount of time of board members.

Minutes of meeting of the Albany District School Board, held at the schoolhouse, Albany Tuesday, July 11, 1876.

Present chairman, and Mr Hassel. The minutes of the previous meeting were read and confirmed Mrs Monaghan's report was then considered. The children under Mrs Pourcey's charge had since the notice served on her attended regularly.

Mrs Metcalf had not attended to the notice and was ordered to be summoned at the local court. Gorman, Norton and Brand to attend the next meeting of the board to answer for the irregularity in the children's attendance. It was decided that the children of J.N. Gray and C.D. Negus should be admitted at the sixpenny rate.

---

[30] *The Fremantle Herald*. 4th November 1871.

Mrs Monaghan drew the attention of the board to the character of the so-called afternoon school report by Mr Warne.
No other business was transacted, and the meeting adjourned to Monday the 24th inst.
T. Cockburn Campbell.[31]

Government School Albany in Stirling Terrace 1900 later demolished to make way for the new Courthouse. [32]

A visitor to the settlement in 1893 was not very impressed with the education standards of what he termed the lower classes. Mr Gilbert Parker was to write in his reflective memoir on his travels:

But I must speak frankly, though it may displease, and say that the average of intelligence among the lower classes, so far as I could see them, seemed very low. I talked with people in the carriages and at the railway station; I watched them, and if observation goes for anything, I should say that there is a type of citizen in Western Australia which give us one little hope, for nearly all the people will soon be voters. Isolation, belated progress, a narrow life, and no political or social teaching have done their work, and a torpid brain and low intelligence in the lower orders are the result...[33]

On perhaps a less pessimistic note Mrs A.Y. Hassell provided some of her recollections on what 'she had been told' about the development of education in the town during the Nineteenth Century. Mrs Hassell recollects that:

The first school in Albany was kept by Mrs Stephen Knight [Lucinda], a Devonshire clergyman's daughter, who held a small Dame School in her sitting room, in a cottage on the Terrace, on the site of Field's shop. That was in 1840.

Mr Thomas Palmer was the first State schoolmaster.[34] *He came in 1861 and taught boys and girls in a building (the old Commissariat store) close to the beach, below the tennis courts in Lawley Park.*

A school was later built on the site of the present Court House about 1873. With it, a school board was formed. Mrs Palmer was the first girls' school mistress, and she was appointed when the Terrace school was built. Mr W. G. Knight was on the Board.

There never was, however, much outside interest in school work. Gradually the elections were given up. Those on the Board nominated the members, finding out if they would serve before submitting their names to the Minister, who made the appointments. Then as the Board's powers were more and more curtailed it became very hard to get anyone to nominate.

---

[31] *Albany District Board of Education Minute Book.* 11th of July 1876. State Archives of Western Australia.
[32] Courtesy of The Albany History Collection, Albany Town Library.
[33] Parker, G. *Round the Compass in Australia.* London: Hutchinson and Company. 1893.
[34] Thomas Matheson Palmer was an English clerk who was transported in 1854 for having forged a money order.

> *The movement to start cooking classes originated with the Albany Board when Mr Cyril Jackson was Director of Education, but it was many years before anything was done. When Mrs Milne retired the infants' school was separate, from the senior school and had an independent mistress. That was done with the infants before the school was built. During the time Mr Jas. Gardiner was Minister, the schoolmaster's residence was bought.*
>
> *For many years the School Board had a paid secretary, who was a compulsory officer, but this arrangement was done away with sometime after free education was adopted. Before that, the children had to go to school, but the parents paid a small sum. The Board, as an alternative, had names submitted to it and inquired into the circumstances of the family; then decided if the children should be put on the free list. With the adoption of free education the police took over the duties of the compulsory officer.*[35]

However, by the time that the Government School in Stirling Terrace was operational a social divide in respect to education provision was occurring in the town with more affluent parents, holding perhaps greater educational aspirations for their children, preferring their children to attend one of the private schools that had begun operating in Albany. The fact that the Government School teacher was an ex-convict may also have influenced their decision accordingly. The issue of ex-convicts assuming teaching positions was in fact raised in the Legislative Council in 1870-1871.

> *There appears to be often a difficulty in obtaining efficient schoolmasters, with the means now disposable. The fact that many of them are drawn from the ex-convict class speaks for itself; and whilst I should be far from passing a hasty judgement upon individuals, and sympathise with those who are exerting themselves to regain the position they have forfeited, it must be admitted that the convict or ex-convict class are not, as a rule, fitted for the education of the young, either morally or intellectually, nor is there [sic] employment as schoolmasters calculated to raise the moral sense of the colony.*[36]

Albany Infants and Primary Schools

As the town expanded in the 1890s it became obvious that existing Government School facilities were inadequate. Consequently, in 1894 the government purchased land adjacent to the corner of Serpentine Road and Collie Street for the construction of new school facilities. The first section of the school began operations in 1895 with a completed building formally opened in 1896. The decision to construct a new school and relocate the students was fortuitous for the town as the previous now disused school site allowed for a courthouse facility to be constructed on the allotment. With a steady increase in enrolments, further accommodation was required at a new infant school that was constructed further down Serpentine Road adjacent to the existing school and opened in 1899.

Nevertheless, the school population in Albany continued to increase and once again a shortage of accommodation was noted. *The Albany Advertiser* reported:

> *New premises were badly wanted for the cooking school, while attention was directed to the need of extending the present school buildings and the school site and grounds. The question of acquiring a new site was one worthy of consideration in order that more up-to-date and commodious premises in keeping with the progress of the town might be provided.*[37]

This lack of necessary accommodation for students reached a point where the junior pupils enrolled had to be temporarily accommodated for a period in the Mechanics Instituted which was located on the site of the old Octagon meeting place.[38]

In late 1913 the Minister for Education, Mr Thomas Walker, who was also the Western Australian Attorney General at the time, agreed to the construction of a new infant school. The site chosen was on the Perth Road. The choice of site was not universally approved as it was not central to the main aspect of the town. While there were members of the community against the selected location there was just as vehemently many more who supported the decision, especially given the relative proximity of the new site to the existing

---

[35] *Early Memories of Albany* by Mrs AY Hassell, Pamphlet. Albany Advertiser. (circa 1910)
[36] Legislative Council. *Votes and Proceedings*, 1870-1871.
[37] *The Albany Advertiser* 12th February 1912.
[38] *School Journal Albany Infants School*, 1899 - 1912. PROOWA 45 Albany Acc. 1925, 1912.

school premises. The government pursued its original plan and on the 31st of January 1914, *The Albany Advertiser* reported that the site for the new Albany Infant School has been secured by the government on a Perth Road location.[39] This school opened in 1915.

Of particular note was that the new school design saw the innovation of an extremely wide veranda space (on the north face of the building) that enabled the school and all classrooms to take advantage of both sunlight and fresh air all year round which was a marked shift from earlier school designs of the period. The new school catered for students aged from 5 to 8 years of age and Standard 1 while the existing school continued to offer Standard 11 to V1 for students up to age 12.

Albany High School 1918

An agreement was reached to construct a High School in Albany in 1918 and in the interim period secondary level students were housed in the existing Serpentine Road senior primary school facility, thus creating what later became known as a District High School complex.

As of February 1900, the state system of education in Western Australia was confined basically to elementary school provision, with secondary education left entirely in the hands of private establishments at this time. Furthermore, Western Australia did not have a university to provide a high degree education or to facilitate teacher training. It would be some years later that both university and teacher training facilities would be established in Western Australia. However, provision was made to allow students to sit supervised examinations in Albany which would enable them to access Adelaide University in South Australia.

After the successful operation of state-funded high schools in Perth, the Eastern Goldfields, Northam, Geraldton and Albany it was recommended in the 1918 Education Department report to the government that:

Experience gained in the establishment of these schools makes it evident that there is a great demand for higher education in the country towns. There is little doubt that successful schools on the same lines could be established in at least four other country centres. The expense involved at the outset it's not great, the most costly items being the provision of laboratories. Special teachers of science and French would have to be added to the staff. In the absence of most of our young men at the war, the former are difficult to find…[40]

As Albany was one of the areas identified in the report it was not long before funding for Albany High School was provided under the State-funded system of education. The erection of a special building for the purpose gave reality to the existence of a High School in the town. The secondary school opened in 1918 initially sharing facilities with the existing Serpentine Road and York Street primary school facilities before moving to its current purpose-built site in 1924, the northern side of Mount Clarence. The Albany High School opened for student intake the following year.

The school's history reflects proud traditions, which include the well-known blazer with its distinctive green, brown and yellow stripes and the school crest. The school's crest contains the words "Keep Troth", reflecting the commitment to being true to oneself, the school and the greater community.

The recollections of schooling in Albany from Dennis Greeve an Albany resident who attended both the Infants school and then the upper primary school provides an insightful perspective of the time:
Albany's first purpose-built school was where the old Court House stands today in Stirling Terrace west.[41] *It was both State and Catholic and the headmaster was Mr Palmer, a Ticket of Leave man sent out to Western Australia for some minor offence.*
As youngsters, my father and mother attended this school.

---

[39] *The Albany Advertiser.* 31st January 1914.
[40] *The West Australian*, 26th August 1918.
[41] Situated in the old Commissariat store in Lawley Park was first the Government School, a white washed building, originally thatched, however, this roof material was replaced later on by shingles. In 1872 the school was moved to where the present courthouse now stands.

> *In the early 1900s, there was a private Boys Grammar School in Perth Road opposite the Infants School and a Girls private school in York Street, just above the Scotch Church. These two private schools had closed many years before I was born.*
>
> *Or the first three years we attended the Infants School on the Perth Road (now known as Albany Highway). Today the school building has been made into the Dome Coffee shop. Behind the Dome, the car park and Target store occupy what was our playground. There were three classrooms and a wide enclosed veranda over its full length. The girl's washroom at one end and the boy's washroom at the opposite end*
>
> *The Serpentine Road – Big School. On the first day of the fourth school year, my class was assembled at the Infants School and then the teacher marched us across Perth Road and up onto Serpentine Road and down the hill to the big school, where we became the first class at that school. This was referred to as Second Standard. There were 6 classrooms in the Serpentine Road school, first standard to sixth standard.*
>
> *When we were in Fourth Standard, we were permitted to spend every Thursday afternoon at the Albany High School; Boys learning woodwork, girls learning cooking. Thursday was the one-day worth going to school.*[42]

It is interesting to note that in February 1919 enrolments were taken for one of the first, if not the first, night school classes in Western Australia. Called the Albany Continuation Classes they were offered free of charge to interested community members. As The Albany Despatch indicated:

> *The continuation school commenced its year's work on February 17 with an enrolment of 158 students, divided among English, including business correspondence, 49; bookkeeping, 44; shorthand, 38; arithmetic, 15; woodwork, 12. The headmaster Mr Walker reports that it is still possible for students to enrol, and those intending to take any of the courses of study should make inquiries without delay. The English class has been divided, so that those students who require special work in business correspondence, may receive extra tuition in this branch.*
>
> *A special feature in the domestic subjects is invalid cookery and those who intend to take advantage of the opportunity to learn homemaking, such as upholstery and stencilling, and other domestic courses should enrol as soon as possible. The mathematics class, in which particular attention is given to office and work junior clerk's and apprentices and its shop arithmetic, is of great value. It is gratifying to note that quite a number of young people who realise the value of further practice in this essential branch of study have been rolled to date. The headmaster Mr Walker is in attendance at the high school daily and each evening from 7:15 pm to 9.15 o'clock. The work is entirely practical and offers a splendid opportunity for securing instruction free of all costs whatsoever, so parents should see that their children, starting out early in life, should avail themselves early of this opportunity.*[43]

After the Great War Governors of Western Australia resumed their practice of spending part of the summer at their Albany residence, The Government Cottage, the residence affectionately referred to as 'The Rocks' in Albany was built in 1913. Quite often during this summer sojourn, the Governor would take the opportunity to visit local schools. For example, Governor Sir William Campion and Lady Campion visited the Albany Infant School in 1924, 1925, 1928 and 1930, and on each occasion granted the students a customary day holiday.

It is also worth noting that the school's observance of Arbour Day each year classes would plant a commemorative tree. The species selected were generally of the pine tree variety. As with many such school celebrations the locations of where the trees were planted were not well recorded. Fortunately, the recollections of an early resident of the town can remember participating in one such Arbour Day tree planting and in so doing also remembers the importance of the tall Norfolk Island Pine that is located in the park adjacent to the Town Library in York Street in what are called the Allison Hartman Gardens. Dennis Greaves was a student who attended both the Infants and Senior School and he can clearly remember Arbour Days with great fondness.

---

[42] *Private correspondence.* Dennis Greeve, 2019.
[43] *The Albany Dispatch.* 24th February 1919.

Roman Catholic School Development

In 1853 the Albany Catholic Girls and Infants School opened in the cottage of Canadian whaler, Francis Legare. The teacher was Miss Elizabeth Mooney, aged 15 who later became Mrs Legare on her 16th birthday.

In May 1855 land was allocated to the Roman Catholic Church and it also acquired three other parcels of land centred around Aberdeen Street at this time. In terms of the growth and development of Roman Catholic education in Albany town, this was a significant event. Bishop Joseph Benedict Serra had previously visited Europe and returned with four sisters from the French Order of St Joseph of the Apparition, and it was sisters from this order that helped to significantly develop a Roman Catholic school as an alternative education presence in the town.

While government funding was withdrawn from the Roman Catholic School system in 1856 there were sufficient numbers of fee-paying students enrolled in their system of schools that enabled ongoing support to be provided for the continued expansion of its education system.

In 1869 Maria Rigney took charge as mistress of the Albany Catholic School for both sexes. At this time the 43 enrolled pupils attended class in the Stella Maris church building. By 1875 using lay teachers, Catholic schools had been established and were functioning at Albany and 11 other country locations. Community preference and church policy favoured separate boys' and girls' schools, which added to their appeal. Although the funding that eventuated from the 1871 Education Act and the dual system it encouraged ceased in 1895 with the introduction of the Assisted Schools Abolition Act, Catholic education provision throughout the state was at that time already on a sound financial footing.

The Education Act of 1871 stipulated the requirement for the local district elected board to monitor school attendance in both government and 'assisted schools', a nomenclature that was applied to denominational schools like those run by the Roman Catholic Church because of their receipt of state aid. However, the relationship between the Albany District Board and the local Catholic School was not a smooth one. A minute from the Albany Board's 1879 records demonstrate some of this angst:

> *Reverend Father Facundo Mateu held that the Compulsory Officer had no power to visit the school and that he was a very objectionable person, and then endeavoured to trump up a complaint of things that occurred about two years ago and had no reference to the subject and with reference to the weekly reports… There was nothing in the Act to justify the board and demanding them.*
>
> *The chairman then read the By-law on the subject of inspection viz. 'The board may delegate to such one or more persons as they may please any of their power under the act so far as it relates to the control, management or inspection of any school under their supervision and such personal persons should exercise those powers until withdrawn by the board…'*
>
> *Father Mateu said that he was not aware of these powers. Mrs Monaghan would in future be admitted but weekly reports would not be supplied. He was told that in that case the school returns would not be certified by the board. The chairman charged the Compulsory Officer as a delegate to inspect the school and compare the roll with the attendance and otherwise see that the Act was carried out.*[44]

Apparently, this was not the only point of friction between the Albany District Board of Education and Father Facundo Mateu, with the former requiring that the school displayed prominently both its timetable and what was termed a 'conscience clause', allowing parents to attend the local Government School as an alternative should they decide to do so.

In 1878 Mother Teresa and two Sisters of St Joseph of the Apparition, and a secular teacher arrived in Albany.[45] They assumed responsibility for the existing Catholic primary school and expanded provision to include the establishment of a secondary school, albeit initially in rented accommodation.

---

[44] *Albany District Board Education Minute-Book*, 10 January, 1879.
[45] There is some contention as to the actual date that the sisters arrived in the town. D.S. Garden (1977) indicates in his book, *Albany*, that it was in 1877 that the Sisters from the Order of St Joseph of the Apparition opened a

The construction of St Joseph's Convent in Aberdeen Street followed and the Sisters moved in on 21st June 1881. This was a notable development as the establishment of this school by the Sisters of Saint Joseph marked the fact that St Joseph's Convent school Albany was the first secondary school established in rural Western Australia. It was known as St Joseph's School for Young Ladies and offered a curriculum of 'higher learning' for boarders and day students which emphasised learning of such subjects  as foreign languages, music, art, rhetoric and needlework. In 1898 the Sisters extended the St Joseph's Convent building by adding a wing at each end of the building. Later a freestanding section was added behind the convent to accommodate growing class sizes and the increase in the numbers of students enrolled.[46]

The period 1871 to 1895 was also one of remarkable expansion for the Roman Catholic School System in Western Australia. In addition to the Sisters of Mercy and the Sisters of Saint Joseph of the Apparition three other religious orders came to the colony to establish and administer Catholic schools. They were the sisters of Saint Joseph of the Sacred Heart, who came from Sydney in 1887, the Presentation Sisters, from Ireland (1891) and the Irish Christian Brothers, from Melbourne.

Christian Brothers

In 1889 Anne Camfield sold her Serpentine Road property "Camfield" to Nathanial McKail who on-sold it to Father Facundo Mateu in 1896. On June 18th, 1896 Father Mateu wrote to his superior in Perth, Brother Thomas O'Brien seeking to establish a Christian Brothers school in the town for the specific task of providing: *"for the educational and religious training of our boys."*[47]

On 19th July, 1897 Brother Treacy of Perth wrote to the Superior General of Christian Brothers in Adelaide indicating:
> *I stopped almost two days in Albany… with Father Mateu and with Bishop Gibney to see if he could give me a site in Albany. I have decided that it may be more to our advantage to pay £1227 for a house and site…*[48]

The transfer of Camfield House from Father Mateu to Brother Treacy is recorded in the Western Australian Lands Office accordingly. The residence was in poor condition in terms of its cleanliness, with many domestic cats and other animals occupying the rooms. After being cleaned furniture was then secured from Sydney by Brother Treacy and the house was ready for occupation. Correspondence from one of the brothers indicated:
> *We opened school here last Monday, but numbers, I am sorry to say are not very cheering, only 49 turned in during the week, and 14 of these are non-Catholics! Albany is indeed a sweet spot but dreadfully quiet. In fact, there seems to be nothing doing except when the home steamers call. I am rather dubious whether we shall be able to live at all. We are in a sad way for the want of books, as we only have the lives of the Saints and a few works on Christian Doctrine.*[49]

The school opened with 28 boys which increased to 82 by Christmas. However, Brother Treacy wrote on 1st November, 1898 indicating his regretting the foundation of the school in Albany. With the population explosion on the Goldfield with the gold rush it was decided to move the school's operations to the more

---

convent school in the town, however, cross checking with the Heritage Council of W.A. indicates that the date of 1878 is more accurate.
[46] *Albany and Surrounds*: data relating to items of heritage significance. 1980. And *A Journey in Faith to Jubilee 2000*,". Parish of Albany, Bunbury Roman Catholic Diocese, 1999.
[47] Brown, J. (ed) *A History of the Christian Brothers in Albany*. 25th November, 1977. Christian Brothers, Perth.
[48] Ibid. pp. 5-6
[49] Ibid.p.8

lucrative town of Kalgoorlie and close the Albany Chapter of Christian Brothers. *The Albany Advertiser* covered the story:

Saturday, December 27, 1902
Exactly two years ago the Church of England Grammar School was closed owing to a lack of support. Now there is a danger of the Christian Brothers High School coming to a similar end. When the two institutions were running together there was a reason for both meeting with poor patronage. The educational requirements of Albany were then possibly exceeded. It must come as a reproach to many that at the present time not one establishment can be conducted as a financial success...

Such, however, was the statement that had to be made at the annual distribution of prizes ....
The announcement is of itself serious enough but made amid surroundings which evidenced the admirable work achieved by the institution, it was more regrettable. Fortunately, the evil time has not absolutely arrived. Another trial is to be made but if that fails, the Christian Brothers are to be withdrawn...
The school, cheaply as it is run, does not pay, and the Church authorities, who can only regard such matters from a business standpoint, deem it advisable to cease operations.[50]

After the school closed Camfield House was sold to Charles Newman in 1910 as a private residence.

Church and Private Grammar Schools

In the course of Albany's late nineteenth and early Twentieth Century history, there were several attempts at establishing Grammar schools in Albany, more often than not with the expressed purpose of offering an alternative to the state-run school system. Some of these were very short-lived and others only slightly more successful. The first mention of this form of school is the Albany Grammar school that operated out of the Masonic Hall from 1875. Unfortunately, there is a dearth of information available on this school, nevertheless, there is a brief mention of the school's closure in *The Albany Advertiser* in 1887, twelve years after it commenced[51]:

Albany Grammar School.
R. Warne offers his sincere thanks to those parents who have entrusted their children to his care during the past twelve years and begs to state that he is disposed of his school to Mr J. Phillimore in whom he has every confidence as a scholar and a gentleman.

What happens next is open to conjecture as four months later the following advertisement appeared in the local paper: [52]

Sale by Auction
Warne will sell by public auction at Annesfield on Thursday 29th instant the valuable household furniture and effects of J. Phillimore Esq., who is leaving the colony.[1]

A school modelled on an English Grammar School was opened on the Old Perth Road in 1890 by Richard Freeborn. In newspaper advertising, the school was presented as a high-class boys' school that would offer the public an alternative to the state school located on Collie Street.
The advertisement indicated that:
Mr Freeborn has arrived in Albany for the purpose of establishing if he is satisfied with his prospects here, a high-class school for boys. He has not yet obtained a suitable building for a beginning but hopes to do so shortly.[53]

Then three months later the paper indicated:
It will be observed from our advertising columns that Mr Freeborn has removed the school to commodious premises on the Perth Road. Albany is fortunate in having as the head of its chief private school a gentleman with such high qualifications as a teacher as Mr Freeborn processes. He has had experience in England as headmaster and also as a tutor to members of the Royal Family and to Lord Hopetown the present Governor

---

[50] *The Albany Advertiser.* 14th November 1902.
[51] *The Albany Mail and King George's Sound Advertiser.* 11th May 1887.
[52] Ibid. 21st September 1887.
[53] *The Australian Advertiser.* 5th March 1890.

of Victoria. He is a favourite with his scholars and not only attends to their mental but also their physical training, being himself an enthusiastic cricketer. We hope that Mr Freeborn will meet with every success in Albany and that he will eventually be able to establish a high school here on a large scale. There is no place in the colony better adapted for a collegiate school and Albany.[54]

The school operated until 1898 until it was amalgamated with the Church of England School that was being managed out of St John's Church Hall in York Street. The *Albany Advertiser* readers were informed:

The school, which was established some eight years ago by Mr Freeborn, and afterwards taken over by Mr Phillips, is to be transferred to the Church of England. Mr Phillips who has conducted the school successfully for some years is retiring and intends to return to England. The Reverend [David] Howell Griffith [Church of England Parish Priest], who is aware of the great need of such at school as that conducted by Mr Phillips has arranged to take over the school and carried it on in St John's schoolroom. This building is very well suited for the purpose, but the reverent how Griffith regards this is only the beginning and hopes to create a first-class day and boarding school. The school in its new quarters is to be known as the Albany Church of England Grammar School. The curriculum is to include English, mathematics, bookkeeping, shorthand, French, Latin, and Greek and boys will be prepared for university examinations and also for business pursuits. Mr Griffith was for four years headmaster of Scotland. The school opens on July 20.[55]

The amalgamated Church of England School was initially administered by the Rector The Reverend Howell Griffith and then subsequently, by The Reverend E.W. Taylor, the Curate at St John's. The amalgamated school was afterwards branded as the Church of England Grammar School and was relocated from the Old Perth Road site to St John's Church Hall. An advertisement in *The Albany Advertiser* of 14th June 1898 informed the readership of the paper that:[56]

Albany Church of England Grammar School.
The above school will open on Wednesday, 20th July in St John's schoolroom,
York Street, Albany.
Boys will be prepared either for university examinations or for business pursuits.
The curriculum will include English, Mathematics, Book-Keeping, Shorthand, French, Latin and Greek.
All communications to be addressed to Rev. D Howell Griffith,
The Rectory, Albany.

The next mention of the school is the following year when the advertisement in *The Albany Advertiser* stated:[57]

Albany Church of England Grammar School.
The class for younger boys is now in course of formation in the church of England Grammar School. An assistant master has been engaged and entered upon his duties on Tuesday morning. He comes to the grammar school with a record of five years of successful work in elementary education and will devote the whole time to this special class.
Parents intending to send their sons should make application at once to the principal,
D. Howell Griffith. Terms are most moderate.

Issues of student enrolments were always a concern for the school. While in 1900 the Church of England Bishop of Perth visited Albany to speak with Canon Thomas Louch, the Rector at St. John's Church to express his ongoing support for the continuation of the grammar school nevertheless, *The Albany Advertiser* conveyed its concern to its readers when it was announced that the Church of England Grammar School would close:

The Reverend Canon Louch presided, and the Bishop of Perth was present, in addition to the scholars and some 40 ladies. The chairman, after thanking the Bishop for his presence, referred to the work of the school in the past and intimated that the institution would no longer be carried on. He did not think that the Church of England Grammar School had been entirely a failure. He was certain the boys had been excellently taught. They could never get a more generous, patient, or kind-hearted instructor than they had in the Reverend E.W.

---

[54] Ibid. Friday 20th June, 1890
[55] Ibid. 11th June 1898.
[56] Ibid. 30th March 1899.
[57] Ibid. 30th March 1899.

Taylor. Mr Taylor loved the boys and he was sure he left his duties with great regret. There was, however, not sufficient demand to allow the school to carry on; the people were not sufficiently anxious to keep the school going, and now it had to close. Mr Taylor had been there 12 months. He had acted as the headmaster of the school and also an assistant clergyman of the parish.[58]

The school was temporarily closed in 1900 until it was reopened in 1904 under the direction of the principal Otto Berliner who moved the school to the location of the Scots Church.[59] An advertisement that appeared in the local paper indicated:[60]

Albany Grammar School.
The above school will be opened on January 14, 1904, at Scots Church schoolroom, York Street. Intending pupils may be in rolled any day at the above address. Mr Berliner will be in attendance during the hours of 9:30 am and 2:30 pm, Saturdays excepted.
Principal
Otto W. Berliner

Berliner moved the school from the Scots Church in 1910 back to the original premises that had been secured by Freeborn in 1890 on the Old Perth Road. The school remained in this position until 1915, at which time Berliner moved the school back to Scots Church in 1916 and placed the following advertisement:[61]

Church of England Grammar School. Perth Road.
Day and boarding school. Mr Otto W. Berliner, principal.
Pupils prepared for examinations Adelaide University primary, etc, Adelaide University music, Trinity College of music practical and theoretical, prospectus on application to the principal.

A follow-up notice in the newspaper indicated:[62]

The Church of England Grammar School
will reopen
Monday February 1, at Perth Road
Particulars on application

The Church of England Grammar School closed in 1918 coinciding with the opening of Albany Secondary School, which was at this time, co-located with the upper primary school in Collie and Serpentine Roads until the purpose-built Facility in Burt Street, its present site, was completed. A report in the advertisement section of the local newspaper from Mr Berliner, teacher in charge of the school relates to the closure of the grammar school. It indicated:[63]

Owing to the fact that I have been forced to close the Church of England Grammar School, I have decided to devote myself entirely to the practice of my profession viz., teaching of the pianoforte and singing. I have a limited number of vacancies in both branches. I should be glad to interview parents on any day except Saturdays, providing an appointment is arranged. I prepare pupils for all examinations from the Preparatory to the Licentiate of Music Diploma.
O. W. Berliner, Studio,
240 Rowley Street,
Albany.

In August 1891 an advertisement in *The Australian Advertiser* referenced Mr E H James' school that was to be operating out of Wesley Hall in Duke Street:[64]

Albany Collegiate School
The above school will be opened on September 7th 1891 in the Wesley Hall.

---

[58] Ibid. 18th December 1900.
[59] While Principal of the Church of England Grammar School Otto Berliner was also an accompanist on the piano three nights a week for Kings Pictures that operated out of the Town Hall from 1908.
[60] *The Albany Advertiser.* 14th November 1903
[61] Ibid.
[62] *The Albany Advertiser.* 30th January 1915.
[63] Ibid. *23rd March 1918.*
[64] *The Australian Advertiser.* 3rd August 1891.

> *Principal: E.H. James. – With competent staff assistance.*

The following year Mr James's school was advertising placements for the following term as well as letting the community know the bona fides of the teaching staff: [65]

> *Collegiate Albany School. Wesley Hall, Duke Street.*
> *The next term of the above School for boys and Girls will commence on April 1892*
> *Principal: Mr E. H. James - Trained Certificated Teacher from the South Australian Government Training College and having had eight years' experience in the public schools there; also holding Science Certificates from the Adelaide University and First-Class Certificate for Calisthenics and Drill.*
> *Assistants: Mrs E. H. James and Mrs Miles.*
> *The course of instruction will be similar to that of the First-class Public Schools of the Eastern Colonies.*
> *Teaching Strictly Undenominational*[sic]. *Kindergarten System Taught.*
> *Special Terms for Families. Prospectus upon application to the Head Master, Vancouver Street.*
> *Reference permitted to the Rev. T. A. James, Wesley Manse, Albany.*

And further in the same advertisement:

> *Evening Class.*
> *In response to several applications, I will open a Night School for Youths on April 4th, 1892, in the Wesley Hall, Duke Street, at 7.30 p.m. Terms and particulars upon application. E. H. James, Vancouver Street.*

Similar to other attempts at establishing a Grammar school in the town in 1899 readers were to find out that the school had closed and its furniture had been advertised for sale: [66]

> *For Sale:*
> *The Goodwill and Furniture of the Albany Collegiate School (Boys and Girls), established in 1891.*
> *Apply to E.H. James*

A private High School for Girls and Young Boys was opened in 1891 under the principalship of Mrs MacPherson. Unfortunately, only tantalising newspaper snippets of information can be gleaned from the advertisement sections of the town's papers of the late Nineteenth Century in respect to her school. There is a reference made to a Mrs MacPhersons School in 1890. It would appear that initially, the school operated out of St John's Church Hall.

> *The distribution of prizes to the successful scholars at Mrs MacPhersons School will take place on Monday next at 11 a.m. in the York Street Schoolroom. The school has an excellent staff and is making very good progress. Particulars of the terms will be found in an advertisement on our front page.*

However, there is some conjecture as to where this school actually operated. Some recollections place it in buildings opposite the St John's Church. Nevertheless, a year later the school has changed from Mrs MacPherson's School to the Albany High School for Girls and Young Boys: [67]

> *Albany High School for Girls and Young Boys – Including Kindergarten Class*
> *Principals Mrs MacPherson and Miss Allen.*
> *Mrs MacPherson, Kindergarten. Miss Allen holds a Certificate of Honour from the Cambridge University, Higher Local Examination.*
> *Terms on application at St. John's Rectory.*
> *Fees paid in advance. A Quarter's Notice necessary for removal of Pupil, or Quarter's Fees.*
> *Albany, July 23rd 1891.*

It would then appear that a year later the school re-opened in Pyrmont House in Serpentine Road opposite the state school: [68]

> *Albany High School for A Girls and Young Boys.*
> *Re-opened at Pyrmont House on Monday, February 1.*
> *Terms for the admission of Boarders and Day Pupils can be made with Mrs MacPherson and Miss Allen—Principals.*

---

[65] Ibid. 25th April 1892.
[66] *The Albany Advertiser.* 16th March 1899.
[67] Ibid
[68] *The Australian Advertiser.* Monday 25th April 1892.

Pyrmont House, Albany. April 25 1892.

This school was still operating from the Pyrmont building in 1897 as the reprinted public notice in the newspaper indicates: [69]

Albany High School Notice.
Classes will be resumed at Pyrmont after the midwinter holidays by Mrs MacPherson, Principal.
Terms and other particulars on application at Pyrmont.

However, there would appear to be a close relationship with this school and that which operated out of buildings on the Old Perth Road, Mr Freeborn's school venture as this 1898 advertisement indicated: [70] This was the last reference to be found of Mrs MacPherson or her school in the local press.

Scholastic Classes will Re-Open at Pyrmont on
Monday, January 31, 1898.
Mrs MacPherson, Principal
The School House,
Perth Road,
Albany.
The Easter Term begins on Monday, January 31st
Mr A.L. Phillips
Headmaster

By the end of the decade marking Albany's Centenary in 1927, there were four substantive schools in the town, three government schools; the Infant School located on the Old Perth Road, the State Primary School in Serpentine Road, the High School above Middleton Road and the Roman Catholic Church School in the centre of an open block of land opposite the Roman Catholic Church and Convent in Aberdeen Street. During the first hundred years there had been several attempts at establishing private schools in the town, some more successful than others. The number of parents willing to pay private school fees in the town were quite small and this in part made sustaining a private school very difficult.

Closing Remarks

A most significant issue in tracing the evolution of education provision in the town has related to historiographic difficulties involved in initially locating and collating material from quite disparate sources, including newspaper articles, personal correspondence and collections and historical archives, and then subsequently verifying the information gathered. What did become evident in sifting through the material was the fact that there was an ongoing distrust of the intentions of various religious influencers who were interested in establishing a school presence in the town. For example, while the Anglican Church's reaction to Roman Catholic Bishop Brady's positive progress in establishing a Roman Catholic supported education system may have been one based on admiration and envy for what he was able to achieve with limited resources, they also feared the possible undue influence that he would be able to exert through his schools. The effect was to galvanise a united Protestant coalition that would then challenge the influence that Bishop Brady had in the realm of education.

Governor Hutt's refusal to provide funding and aid to religious schools was a significant turning point in the development of education facilities and approaches in the colony. Hutt's argument was that if he gave colony resources to one religious denomination then he would be obliged to do the same for the other sects as well. Archdeacon Wollaston lamented:

...*and not one penny goes out of the colonial treasury towards the support of any of us.*[71]

However, an argument that had gained some currency among the colony's leaders in the mid-Nineteenth Century was that ignorance was a source of criminal behaviour and that education was the antidote that could minimise that ignorance. Therefore, it was implied, vis-à-vis, that education was the means through

---

[69] *The Albany Advertiser*. 15th June 1897.
[70] Ibid. 25th January 1898.
[71] *The Albany Journal of J. Wollaston*. Nedlands: University of Western Australia Press, 1975.

which criminal behaviours could be mitigated.[72] A similar proposition maintained that in educating the youth of the country, it was the country that would in turn benefit and be enriched.[73] It was this argument that eventually resulted in the creation of a dual system of assisted school funding by Governor Aloysius Weld.

In most respects what then eventuated in Albany mirrored the issues that were prevalent throughout the Nineteen Century in Western Australian and these were subsequently presenting in the Government policies relating to educational administration that evolved to accommodate the dual system of education that had come into existence, denominational schools subsidised by the colony and non-denominational schools administered by the Board of Education.

---

[72] Select Committee on Education 1852. Minutes of Victorian Legislative Council.
[73] Browne, F.H. *A Discourse on Education*. Windsor. 1865.

CHAPTER 8
CATERING FOR THE TOWN'S SPIRITUAL NEEDS

Nothing can be more melancholy and distressing to a clergyman who has been used to even the very imperfect order of things in England, to find here his countrymen and fellow churchmen running wild and lapsing into ignorance and greater darkness, for the want of any order at all or authoritative custom and requiring to be urged on to resume the religious habits of their native land.
The Journal of John Ramsden Wollaston.[1]

Overview

Albany's spiritual development was strongly influenced by the belief that through religion a moral compass would be provided that could guide the growth of the community. A social consciousness born out of the strong religious beliefs, initially with a predominantly Anglican orientation, that was fostered by both the town and colony's leadership was seen to significantly influence policy decisions that affected the town. Decisions in terms of education provision, law and order, the general relationship between the church and the state and the treatment of the Aboriginal inhabitants at King George's Sound all had fundamental religious overtones.

Early Protestant churchgoers living in Albany were able to occasionally use Sherratt's Octagonal building when the town was visited by a minister of that faith from the Swan River settlement.
> *Thomas Brooker Sherratt had erected at his own expense and upon his own property, an eight-sided building of wooden frame and plastered walls which he opened in 1836 as an undenominational church.*[2]

Unfortunately, the history in the evolution of the provision of significant places of worship in Albany is not generally well documented in The Historical Record.

The Church of England

Early Albany Link.
Interesting Gift to Church.
As a gesture to the commemoration of the Centenary of St John's Church in Albany, Mr Robert Stephens is making a gift to the historical old church of the prayer book and book of sermons used by Mr Thomas Brooker Sherratt at the opening of the Octagon Church in Albany on December 27 1835.[3]

It was not until 1848 with the arrival in the town of the Archdeacon John Ramsden Wollaston that an alternative form of worship was provided to the preaching of Thomas Brooker Sherratt who had constructed his own chapel, 'The Octagon building' from which he presented his own brand of religious fervour. Sherratt was known for his unorthodox and at times erratic preaching style and within a short period of time attendance at his church soon dwindled. A letter written by Seymour Spencer, eldest son of Sir Richard Spencer alludes to the Octagon building and further to the want of a priest for the settlement:
> *We are still without a priest, but a private individual has erected a small building in which he reads prayers and a printed sermon every Sunday, and I'm happy to say it is generally attended by all the settlement. A missionary priest has been sent to the Swan River by some religious society in England to endeavour to instruct the natives, as well as perform divine service in districts at a distance from the church.*[4]

---

[1] *The Albany Journal of J. Wollaston.* Nedlands: University of Western Australia Press, 1975.
[2] *The Albany Advertiser.* 16th November 1936.
[3] Ibid. 9th September 1948.
[4] The Church of England missionary priest referred to in the letter is Dr. Ginstiniani from the British Colonial Church Society.

It was a matter of record noted in Archdeacon Wollaston's Journals that there was significant animosity between Sir Richard Spencer and Thomas Brooker Sherratt. This disdain for each other was indeed well known within the settlement. It was noted and a matter of public record that Sherratt was a quite erratic and irritating person and Sir Richard Spencer was intolerant of people who questioned or opposed him or whom he believed to be fools. It was indeed a classic case of a clash of personalities.[5]

The Church of Saint John the Apostle and Evangelist

No mention of the octagonal building is found in Captain Sir Richard Spencer's correspondence to the Right Reverend Willian Grant Broughton, Lord Bishop of Australia in Sydney dated 25th May 1837, at which time he was seeking funding to build a substantial church in the settlement. While some argue that this may have been to strengthen his particular case for funding a church in the town, it is far more plausible that he saw Mr Sherratt's approach to worship as being less suited to the spiritual needs of the community at large and therefore, he was actively seeking an alternative to it. As Albany was at this stage part of the Diocese of Adelaide his request was sent to Bishop Augustus Short in Adelaide.[6] In this request for assistance Sir Richard lays out part of his case accordingly:

> *I take the liberty of acquainting you with a state of this beautiful settlement and request your lordship's assistance to procure the funds for erecting a church in Albany, and at the same time to increase the salary allotted by the government for a curate, sufficient for a gentleman to live. It's now only £100 per annum and if he will take charge of the school £50 per annum is added. We have now been four years without any clergyman residing among us. There are about 180 inhabitants. I think we can build a convenient church for £400.*[7]

This appeal by Sir Richard Spencer was indeed effective, and the Church of England Missionary Society agreed to contribute a sum of £200 towards the construction of an Anglican Church in the settlement. However, as Sir Richard Spencer died on 24th July 1839, the church project was subsequently delayed. The building of what would become the Church of Saint John the Apostle and Evangelist commenced in earnest on April 12th 1841, in time to be finally consecrated by The Right Reverend Augustus Short, Lord Bishop of Adelaide in October 1848.[8] The following day the Bishop consecrated the Albany Cemetery. In performing this ceremony, the Bishop ensured that the Church of Saint John the Evangelist in Albany was the first church to be consecrated in Western Australia, then part of the Diocese of Adelaide.

The Reverend John Ramsden Wollaston, Imperial Chaplain arrived from his parish in Bunbury to become the first resident Church of England Priest and Rector of St John's Parish. Wollaston continued the St. John's Church story in his journal:

> *Safely arrived, thank God, at the Haven, where we would be. They [the settlers] seem very glad indeed that I and come to reside among them. They have only had a few visits from clergymen at very long intervals during a period of almost 23 years. I was agreeably surprised to find the frame of an excellent stone church (begun a long time ago – seven years) which is now covering in, but it will far exceed the local resources of the place to complete it. I begin service tomorrow in a temporary building which have I have hired for a year, at the request of the inhabitants.*
>
> *On Sunday the morning congregation amounted to between 60 and 70, including children. The children are the best behaved of any I have seen in the colony, owing chiefly to the great pains which have been taken by Mr and Mrs Knight, who keep the school. I preached the first sermon on the text, 'A sower went forth to sow his seed'. In the evening the congregation was much less, but it rained hard...*
>
> *A great mistake has been made in place in the church the wrong way. The east window faces the west, the worst quarter for bad weather. Whereas if the tower had been built on the proper end it would have been a screen to the whole building. Amidst so much ignorance I only wonder how they managed to erect so good a fabric, it has*

---

[5] PROWA. CSO. Battye. AN 24 AAC49
[6] Interestingly, previously Albany was part of the Diocese of Calcutta, India.
[7] Richard Spencer, *Letter Book*, 25 May, 1837.
[8] The Apostle part of the title was later discontinued.

a nave 50 feet by 26 feet and 18 feet to wall-plate with a tower underneath which is the entrance. Called on the Roman Catholic Priest [Fremantle] yesterday, mild, humble and respectful, and a well-conducted man. He returned my call today. I believe he is in Italian. He goes away in a few days.

The contractor will soon begin to shingle the church. I tell the people they must hasten on its completion before the Bishop comes, that he may consecrate it. This has stirred them up... Obtained a little help towards our church from the officers of the H.M.S. Acheron. The commander himself brought it — would've been larger if they could have gotten bills cash. Mr Knight brought me some more money from some of the jurors who gave their allowances towards the organ. There was also a cask of wine in bond which is given to the church by the master of the Arpenteur.

For want of more shingles the contractor is obliged to go out and split them himself — they are made of sheoak and are very durable. Then the lime floor down the centre, flooring laid with lime after the West Indian method by a man luckily found here, well-trodden and rammed; then repeatedly worked, and smoothed with sugar water. It makes an excellent floor, if I may judge from some I have seen. The calico windows are made; altar floor and very neat rail of mahogany and temporary pulpit and desk. In short, if the Champion will keep away 10 days or a fortnight more, for the drying of the church, I think we should be ready.

At daybreak on Monday, October 23, the expected schooner was seen at anchor. I hasten to welcome them; the Bishop [the Lord Bishop of Adelaide, the Right Reverend Augustus Short] is a most kind, affable and pleasing man, and is 10 years younger than myself. The Archdeacon [Mathew Hale] is also an excellent person somewhat reserved, but very zealous...[9]

Bishop Short of Adelaide continued the recount of the next stage in the consecration of the Church of Saint John the Evangelist:

Fremantle, 17th November. 1848[10]

My Dear Hawkins,
I landed this day from the Champion, colonial schooner, at 2 o'clock, having embarked at Port Adelaide on Saturday, October 14th. We ran into King George's Sound after a quick and boisterous passage on Sunday night, October 22nd, about midnight...
The stone church stands about the centre, forming a striking object, and whenever the tower shall be finished will give additional beauty to the scene; but even as it is, the house of God is as it always should be, the principal building which meets the eye as you cast anchor in the Sound. Lonely and wild as are its shores, still its grey granite walls and pointed windows imparted a feeling of home even in this distant nook so sequestered from the other settled parts of Australasia.

The Reverent John Wollaston and the Government Resident Mr Camfield came on board early in the morning. The former having removed from Bunbury agreeably to the permission of the local government. By Great exertions, the church has been so far finished as to meet of concentration on Wednesday, 25th ...
It is calculated to hold 170 persons, about the number actually resident in the settlement.

More than half that number were present in the church, together with the captains of two American whalers then in the harbour. The collection amounts to £14.19.6 a considerable sum for this little place, the trade of which consists principally in supplying the whaling ships, a few bales of wool, and tons of oil. Notice of Confirmation was given for Friday and the Holy Communion on the Sunday following. On the former day 24 candidates presented themselves, 14 females and 10 males: among the latter a Sergeant and two soldiers of the 96th regiment. I doubt whether the rite was ever administered to a more devout and earnest body of persons. In the course of the morning prayer, I baptised three children, two half-castes who are brought up in the nurtures of the Lord by the interested kindness of persons and connected with them by the tie

---

[9] *The West Australian*, Perth. 8th July 1848.
[10] Ibid.

of Christian love. It is wonderful and consolatory to find in a place where for 18 years there has been no resident priest so earnest a desire for the ordinances of divine service…[11]

In the afternoon the burial ground, 1 mile from the town, was concentrated in the presence of the Resident and a few other friends. It is inconveniently distant, but the position was fixed agreeably to a local government ordinance. On Sunday, out of a congregation of 100, 33 remained to receive the Lord's supper, 23 of the 24 candidates for Confirmation being of the number. In the afternoon their worthy pastor most affectionately and powerfully addressed his flock and I believe all assembled felt that it was 'good for them to be there and that they had chosen the better part which should not be taken from them. We were to have embarked on Monday morning had the wind been favourable, but it blew a gale from the westward, which gave me another day off for visiting the inhabitants and an opportunity for them for testifying their satisfaction at the visit of their Bishop. An affectionate address signed I understand by everybody, young and old in the place, who could write, was presented to me at the Custom House; they followed me in fact with wives and children to the shore and I exhorted them to continue steadfast in the faith which worketh by love. On the following morning, we were summoned on board, the wind having become favourable, and soon after beat out of the harbour, leaving with regret the inhabitants of this sequestered place endeared to us by a thousand traits of Christian truth, simplicity, kindness, love and unfeigned and earnestness in the faith.
May the blessing of God rest on them forever.
Believe me, yours sincerely
Augustus Adelaide.

In respect to St John's Church, Mrs A.Y. Hassell in her pamphlet of memoirs of the town indicated that:
The church was built by voluntary labour, under the superintendence of Archdeacon Wollaston…

Mr P. Wollaston, the Archdeacon's grandson, told me when the church was completed there was not sufficient money left to put in glass windows, so canvas ones were nailed up. Several gentlemen decided to present the Archdeacon with a piece of plate (silver), in recognition of his untiring efforts towards the building of a church, but this coming to his ears, he asked them instead to put the altar window in, and this was done…
The church was the first consecrated Anglican Church in Western Australia. [12]

The Roman Catholic Church

There is a claim that the first Mass said in Albany was conducted in January 1833 by the chaplain of the French frigate *Heroine*.[13] It has been stated that the few Catholics in the settlement attended this open-air mass next to two large boulders located on Brunswick Road near Lawley Park. A commemorative plaque was installed at the location during Albany's sesquicentennial celebrations to mark the occasion. It reads:
Mass Rocks
At these rocks in January 1833 Holy Mass was celebrated for the first time in the settlement of Western Australia.
The chaplain of the French frigate 'Heroine'[14] *gathered the few Catholics of Frederickstown to this place and offered mass.*[15]

Unfortunately, there is no primary documentary evidence to support this claim. The matter has not been recorded in any report, letter, correspondence contiguous with the early Historical Record. It is one of those elements of Albany's past that has entered its history without a solid primary source foundation to support the claims made. Furthermore, as pointed out earlier, the town was never named Frederickstown and by 1831 two years before this event was supposed to have occurred it had already been gazetted as Albany.

---

[11] Photograph of St John's Church courtesy of Mark Saxton and The Albany Historical Society.
[12] A.Y. Hassell. *Early Memories of Albany*. Albany Advertiser. Circa 1910.
[13] Les Johnson writing on the topic as reported by the Heritage Council of Western Australia.
[14] The French frigate *Heroine* was sent to the Australian coast as an escort and to provide protection for six French whaling ships and was in Australian waters from March 1838. The date does not link to the "Mass Rock" statement. It is also highly unlikely that such a ship would have its own chaplain.
[15] Plaque mistakenly erected on 20th March, 1977 at Mass Rocks site, Bolt Terrace.

What has confused the situation even more is that near to what is commonly called Mass Rocks today is a large granite rock outcrop called Look-out Rock that was used as a lookout point to watch for the arrival of expected mail steamers in the early days of the settlement. According to the State Heritage Council there is an account which has led to this rock being called 'Pulpit Rock' by some, as it was supposed to commemorate the first mass held in Western Australia, this despite the common thought that Mass Rocks or Rocking Rocks being described by some as the possible site…[16] The State Heritage claim supports an earlier claim published in *The Albany Advertiser*:

> *Historic attention attaches to the strangely shaped "Pulpit Rock" … It was in the shadow of this rock that the first Roman Catholic service ever held in Albany was conducted by visiting priests. Pulpit Rock is off the Marine Drive, in private property close to the junction with Brunswick Road.*[17]

From the perspective of some questionable newspaper reporting in the Twentieth Century including some more recent documentation from the Roman Catholic Church it was Father John Brady who performed the first mass in Albany.[18] However, once again there is significant confusion in respect to the date that this open-air mass was supposed to have occurred and further, the place it was conducted as well. Some documentation indicates that Father Brady conducted the service in 1838, yet the Catholic Diocese of Bunbury Newsletter contradicts this view by indicating that it was on the 4th November 1843 that the open first open-air mass occurred before a substantial Roman Catholic Church facility was constructed.

With the lack of any substantial primary documentation relating to this event it will remain another of Albany's ecclesiastical mysteries.

A Roman Catholic priest by the name of Father Caubb arrived in Albany circa 1851. He immediately set about the construction of a small chapel beside a granite outcrop on a site opposite of the present St. Joseph's Church in Aberdeen Street. Father Caubb was able to reside in a small room that had been built at the back of the chapel where he also kept his medicines. Besides administering to the Catholic community in the town he also provided an apothecary service on the side. Father Caubb was well respected in the community for his endeavours as a chemist.[19]

Garden (1977) indicates that the first Roman Catholic Church building was commenced in 1853 but was never completed and ended up being abandoned.[20] Nevertheless, in 1861 the first substantial Roman Catholic Church was constructed by a Benedictine priest, Father Coll and appropriately for Albany it was dedicated to Saint Mary Star of the Sea.

Father Coll's successor Father Mateu became a significant representative for his church and a respected town elder statesman for many years up to his retirement in 1903. Father Mateu had taken up permanent residence in 1874, and built the present Roman Catholic Church, with its adjoining presbytery. In 1878, this new Church was opened on the eastern side of Aberdeen Street. It was consecrated the Church of St Joseph of the Apparition. Four years later he founded the Albany Convent which was completed in 1881. The convent proved a boon to the entire Catholic population of the Great Southern and became well respected for the quality of its musical and educational outcomes.

Scots Presbyterian Church

The Presbyterian congregation in Albany was the third to be established in Western Australia. In November 1888 the Victorian branch of the Presbyterian Church's General Assembly had instructed the Home Mission Committee to establish a congregation in Albany and invested the task to the Reverend Peter M. Camberwell. The first Presbyterian Church service was subsequently held in the Courthouse, which was at that time located as part of the Albany Post Office in Stirling Terrace. When Albany Town Hall had been completed in 1888 the Presbyterian Church accessed this building for its services. Grants of land from the government enabled a church of this faith to be constructed in the town with funds to finance the building

---

[16] *InHerit*. State Heritage of Western Australia. 10th March 2000
[17] *The Albany Advertiser*. 11th November 1935. Also repeated in the newspaper on 16th November 1936.
[18] See also *The Mount Barker and Denmark Record*. 29th June 1939.
[19] *The West Australian*. 12th April 1938.
[20] D.S. Garden. *Albany: A Panorama of the Sound*. Nelson. 1977.

collected from its congregation augmented by a grant from the Home Mission Committee in Scotland. There was no formal celebration for the laying of the foundation stone for this church, but a marble Stone was placed in position by Captain P.H. Nicholson at an informal ceremony held on 25 November 1891. The stone he laid made of marble and had the following inscription:

> *Nec Tamen Consumebatur.[21] Scots Church.*
> *This stone was laid by P. H. Nicholson esquire.*
> *25 November 1891.*
> *Come ye into his courts.*

The ceremony was fixed to take place at about 3 o'clock on this date and soon after that time there was a gathering of those interested in the event:

> *The Rev. T. A. James also spoke, referring to the needs of Presbyterian Church has said that the census returns show that there were 1000 Presbyterians in the colony and that there were churches of that order only at Fremantle, Perth and Albany. He wished the Presbyterian's success in the new church.*
>
> *The mayor-elect (CR. John McKenzie) here, in a few words, present to the silver trowel to Captain Nicholson and asked him to lay in the memorial stone of the new church. The stone within lowered into position and placed by Captain Nicholson who, with the trowel laid the cement for it to rest upon...[22]*

The church building was complete in 1892 and the opening service was conducted by the Reverend James of the Scots Church in Fremantle before a large Albany congregation. The opening was attended by the premier of Western Australia Sir John Forrest.

The Australian Advertiser of April 1892 indicated:

> *The new Presbyterian Church, which is situated on a commanding site in York Street, it's a handsome architectural addition to the churches of Albany. The building, which is of the Gothic order of architecture, it's built of stone and will cost altogether about £1400. Fronting the main entrance from York Street is a large and handsome cathedral stain glass window, which greatly enhances the appearance of your edifice... This window and others were supplied by Mrs Brookes and Robertson and company... There is the intention of the managers at the church when funds permit to complete an imposing tower, the base of which has already been constructed.[23]*

The church was open for public worship on Wednesday, March 30th 1892, and the first service was held on April 3 and was followed by a congregational meeting. From the report of the Reverend P.J. Murdoch:

> *Last night the first service of the Presbyterian Church in Albany was held at the courthouse. There was a crowded congregation. Many of the townspeople were present. The Reverend P. J. Murdoch who will spend a month here to promote the formation of a Presbyterian Church. The service which consisted of hymns, extempore prayers and discourse by the minister was, so far as the singing went enjoyed mostly heartily by the congregation. Before commencing his sermon, the reverend gentleman said: this is the opportunity for me to say a word or two about my appearance here tonight. In all our colonies a considerable portion of the population prefers the Presbyterian form of worship.*
>
> *It is also so doubtless in Albany and as the place increases there will be more and more Presbyterians. It is right that they should have the opportunity to worship in the way they prefer; a way that is consecrated to many of them by a long history full of holiness and heroism. Perhaps it belongs properly to the Scottish church to provide for Albany, but the Victorian church, seeing the need decided upon supplying it. They asked me to leave my congregation in Melbourne in order to perform a Presbyterian Church here. I can only be four Sundays here but as we shall arrange for another minister to follow me immediately there will be no cessation of service if we can help it. A Presbyterian congregation will be formed and will go on. I have only further to add that we sincerely hope to maintain perfect harmony with the existing churches in Albany...[24]*

The Wesley Methodist Church

In 1863 the first Methodist Church was erected in Albany after Mr and Mrs John Upglow, both keen members of the Methodist Church in England, in a philanthropic gesture resulting from their desire to see

---

[21] The Church's crest consisted of a shield with the words " Nec Tamen Consumebatur " (translated from Latin as " And yet it was not consumed) ...

[22] *The Robert Stephens Collection IRS/73M/3.* Local History Collection. The Albany Town Library.

[23] *The Australian Advertiser.*1st April, 1892.

[24] Local History Collection, Albany Town library. *The Robert Stephens Collection. IRS/73M/2*

a branch of the church established in Albany made a gift of a block of land to enable this to occur. Sunday school was conducted in the building.

Commenting on the opening of the Church *The Albany Mail* indicated:

> *Flags were flying from the building, the walls of which are in a forward state. The proceedings were opened by the singing of the 100th Psalm. The Reverend John Thompson pastor of the church read portions of the scripture appropriate to the occasion and the Rev. T. A. James Wesleyan Church engaged in prayer...*

Until 1871 the church relied on visiting ministers from the Swan River Colony, however, in that year the Reverent J. B. Atkins, of the Irish conference was sent out and took charge of the little church. With the death of his wife two months after taking up his appointment along with his concern at the state of Aboriginal spiritual development, he decided to concentrate his efforts on his perception of the latter's needs. The mission he established, however, met with no success and eventually had to be closed. By 1876 the congregation had increased in size to an extent that the small church provided insufficient accommodation for them and it, therefore, had to be extended. After the Reverend Atkins returned to Ireland in 1878, he was replaced for a short while by the Reverend John Higgins.[25]

A key founding member of the Methodist Church Society in Albany at this time was Herbert Robinson. In 1873 Robinson had immigrated to Melbourne in search of a better climate to address his health concerns. Before he immigrated to Australia he had worked in the Northern Bank of Ireland and later had become manager of the Ballybeg County Bank until ill-health again forced him to retire and seek a warmer climate. After a stint as a member of the staff at the National Bank in Victoria, he accepted a transfer as manager of the Albany Western Australia Branch in 1878. In 1883 he resigned to become a partner in the firm of McKail and Company. In 1888 he left that company to establish a similar business in partnership with Charles Drew. The establishment was known as Drew, Robinsons. When Drew retired in 1897 Robinson took over the whole enterprise. Robinson was very active in the Methodist Church and it was mainly through his endeavours and ongoing association with the church that his donation of funds enabled the Manse to be built.

Closing Remarks

The Anglican and Roman Catholic influence was extensive in the settlements early development and resulted in the construction of the towns first substantial churches, St Johns Church in York Street and later, the Roman Catholic Church in Aberdeen Street. An early census conducted in 1859 indicated that 67% of the population of the town registered themselves as Anglicans. During the 1880 to 1900 period, however, Methodist and other denominations, Presbyterian, Baptist etc., started to develop a stronger presence in the town, encouraged largely by the influx of immigrants that entered Western Australia through the Albany gateway attracted by the gold rush. In terms of religious affiliations, it was found that a large majority of people identified themselves with the faith of their ancestors in Europe.[26]

The 1870 census of the population of the colony remained the basis upon which the government's annual ecclesiastical grant was distributed. This was done on a per capita basis and allocated between the four dominant denominations: Anglican, Roman Catholic, Methodist and Presbyterian. However, the strong reciprocal relationship that existed between church and state began to decline with changes to funding arrangements as exemplified by the repeal of the State-Assisted Schools' Act and the Ecclesiastical Grant Abolition Act of 1895.

The authority of church and state had been mutually supportive and one adhered to by the colony's leadership elite and it remained the justification for church-state interaction during the Nineteenth Century. Religion was not only called upon to provide a moral compass for the settlement in its early years of development but it also supported the authority of those invested with the task of preserving social order inclusive of Albany's Resident Magistrates, Western Australian State Governors, etc.

---

[25] *Scots Church Albany Western Australia, 1889 to 1939 Jubilee celebrations*. March 26th 1939.
[26] A.L. McLeod. *The Pattern of Australian Culture*. Oxford University Press. 1963.

CHAPTER 9
SIGNIFICANT PUBLIC INFRASTRUCTURE

Overview

By the middle of the Nineteenth Century, most people in the settlement would be forgiven for believing that their world would go on as it seemed always to have done. The next half-century, from 1850 to 1900 saw many changes to almost every aspect of life in the town. Most of these changes were part of a consolidation of European hegemony and in essence, this was the major impetus behind many of the transformations that occurred in the settlement.

Increased contact with the outside world through improved shipping was one factor that underpinned some quite significant changes to Albany's infrastructure requirements. The construction of quarantine facilities, lighthouses, telegraph and postal facilities along with improved roadworks, and the construction of some significant harbour facilities alongside many commercial enterprises, accommodation and hotels among them, in many respects were accelerated due to the increased importance that the Albany port played in the overall expansion Western Australian society.

Global Update

As indicated earlier it is important to place developments in the Town of Albany through the lens of a more global perspective. The period 1850 -1890 was characterised by continued posturing between European powers resulting in several conflicts, and further continued imperialist annexations involving nearly every corner of the globe.

The year 1851 saw the Russian Empire engage with Turkey over Palestine, a conflict that would later evolve into the Crimean War. In London, the Great Exhibition of 1851 in the Crystal Palace in Hyde Park, initiated by The Prince Consort Albert, opened and Herman Melville published his novel, *Moby Dick*. Great Britain continued to annex various Indian provinces and the United States of America, not to be outdone, annexed parts of Mexico. Japan was forced to open its borders and become a trading nation and once again engage with international relationships.

The period 1853 to 1856 is chiefly remembered for the Crimean War, an alliance between Britain, France, Turkey and Sardinia against Russian imperialist intentions. This was the time of Florence Nightingale and the rise of professional nursing endeavours:
> *You gentleman of England... can have little idea from reading the newspapers of the horror and misery of operating on these dying and exhausted men.*[1]

Also, in 1853 the Treaty of Peshawar was finalised bringing the conflict between Britain and Afghanistan to an end. Closer to home, in 1856 Tasmania became a colony in its own right.

In 1857-1858 the Indian Mutiny took place that led to a general uprising on the Indian subcontinent. Once this was suppressed Great Britain assumed control of India from the East India Company. In 1858 France expanded its territorial acquisitions by first annexing Vietnam and then later in 1880 Cambodia and Tahiti.

The 1860's in Continental Europe there was a period of significant social and political upheaval exemplified by the emancipation of the serfs in Russia. In 1861 the American Civil War commences pitting the industrial north of the country against the more agrarian south. Also, at this time, there was a Maori revolt in New Zealand. In 1863 by constitutional amendment slavery was abolished in the United States and closer to home in 1864 convict transportation to Australia ended. That same year the United States of America purchased Alaska from Russia and within the British Empire the Dominion of Canada was established.

---

[1] From her letter to Dr. William Bowman of King's College Hospital London on 14th November 1854 that described in great detail the "appalling horror" of the war.

Importantly for trade between Europe, Australia and Asia in 1869, the Suez Canal was opened, coinciding with the completion of the transcontinental railway across the United States. Shortly after the declaration of the Third Republic in France, it entered into a war with Prussia with disastrous consequences with the loss of the Alsace Lorraine province to the growing Prussian Empire. The following year the German Republic was formed with Otto Von Bismarck as its Chancellor. Queen Victoria assumed the role of Empress of India in 1877, and in that same year the first cricket test was played in Melbourne between the English and Australian teams.

The Zulu wars involving both Britain and the Boers began in South Africa in 1879, and later on, this morphed into the first South African War between Britain and the Boers. The decade of the 1880's finished with the fall of Khartoum in Sudan after a long siege in 1885; and finally, the last battle between the American Indians and the United States occurred at Wounded Knee in 1890.

Quarantine Facilities

The quarantined people who have been isolated hitherto will be liberated on Monday next if all goes well. They are getting very dissatisfied with their confinement, and on that account have written to The Albany Mail finding fault with the quarantine officers for no supplying them with the necessaries of life, in the shape of food.
The West Australian, Perth. 14th February 1887.

One of the most contentious issues confronting the colony was associated with the transmission of infectious diseases, smallpox in particular, but also scarlet fever, cholera and typhoid. Albany with its port and coaling facilities, along with its role as the then gateway to Western Australia was especially vulnerable to the introduction of contagious disease especially given its exposure to the increasing frequency of steam ships arriving at the port to refuel.

The concern within the settlement of the spread of infectious diseases was recognised very early in its development. Lieutenant-Governor Frederick Irwin was initially sent to the colony as a Major in command of a detachment of the 63rd Regiment of Foot, whose mission was to protect and help establish the Swan River Colony. He arrived with his men on board *HMS Sulphur* in June 1829, six days after the arrival of the first settlers and Captain James Stirling on the *Parmelia*. Irwin's position as officer commanding the troops afforded him the further position of Vice Chairman of the Legislative Council that had been appointed by Stirling in January 1831. From September 1832 until September 1833, Irwin was temporarily appointed to act as Administrator of the Colony while Stirling was in England. It was under his command that a Quarantine Proclamation was issued in 1833:

Proclamation.
By His Honour Frederick Chidley Irwin,
Captain in His Majesty's 63rd Regiment of Foot, Lieutenant-Governor, Commander in Chief, and Vice-Admiral of the colony of Western Australia and its dependencies.
Whereas by an act of lieutenant-governor, with the advice of the Legislative Council, passed in the present year of His Majesties reign, intituled; "An act to enforce and regulate the performance of quarantine in certain cases in Western Australia."

It is amongst other things enacted that as often as the Governor or acting Governor of Western Australia, with the advice of the Executive Council, shall buy proclamation notify that any place or places beyond the seas is or are infected with any infectious disease and that it is probable such disease may be brought from such place or places to the said colony, then and immediately from and after such a notification all ships all vessels arriving from or having touched and any such place or places, and all vessels and boats receiving any person, goods, wares merchandise, packets, letters or any other article whatsoever, from or out of any vessels so coming from or having touched it such an infected place or places as aforesaid shall be, and be considered to be, liable to quarantine within the meaning of the said recited act...[2]

---

[2] *The Perth Gazette and Western Australian Journal.* 30th August 1833.

Despite the ship *Sir William Molesworth* in 1853 with close to twenty per cent of its passengers and crew on board suffering from scarlet fever, calls for a more permanent solution raised by the settlers fell on deaf ears in the Colonial Office. Resident Magistrate Henry Camfield took the necessary precaution of isolating both the ship and its company from the settlement. There was a further scare when the steamship *Salsette* in August 1860 arrived in Melbourne after a stop-over in Albany with several cases of scarlet fever on board. This was a significant issue as the ship had reported no illness at the time it reached King George's Sound. However, this was later seen as falsehood and for the first time, Albany suffered an outbreak of the disease within the settlement. This misadventure also had a devastating impact upon the Aboriginal population with little built up immunity to diseases of this nature.

It was not surprising, therefore, that these early cases and others resulted in the development of quarantine regulations for the port, with ships with known cases onboard isolated from the settlement. Unfortunately, sick passengers were denied the opportunity to disembark and there was little recourse to hospital or facilities in the town to deal with such illnesses. In 1865 the need for more permanent and suitable quarantine facilities was sought from the Colonial Administration but once again the request was denied. Consequently, no action was taken at the time even with reported cases of infectious diseases on the *Bombay* in 1865, and another suspected on the *Rangatira* in 1872. The arrival of the steamship *Baroda* on April 29, 1873, with a confirmed case of smallpox on board bought the matter of suitable quarantine facilities to a head. The poor handling of the issue locally raised the particular ire of the passengers on board as their letter to various government officials at the time testified:

To the Officer of Health,
King George's Sound
& His Excellency the Governor, Western Australia

Sir,
We, the undersigned passengers on the SS Baroda, *feel it our duty to yourself and the public to communicate to you officially the following facts:*

We arrived in the mail steamer Baroda at King George's Sound, from Galle, at 10 pm the 28th April. Upon the pilot's nearing the ship, he put the usual question - "Have you any infectious or contagious disease on board?" and he was informed by the captain that there was one case of smallpox among the Lascar crew. He directed us to anchor in the outer Sound, and then returned onshore.

About an hour and a half afterwards, the Health Officer came alongside, and having repeated these questions, forbade communication with the shore and placed the vessel in quarantine. He was asked whether the patient could be sent on shore and his reply was "No; we have no place for him." The purser of the ship then proposed to send some letters onshore and offered to place them on the foot of the ship's companion ladder. He refused this and said that they must be put in the coal lighter on the following day.[3] So, matters remained till the following morning. Between 8 and 9 am, the Australian Steam Navigation Co's SS Alexandra towed the coal barges down to us. On her captain being asked, he agreed to take the mails on board for Adelaide but refused all passengers and cargo. The Alexandra returned to us about 12.30 and lay off within hail. On enquiry, our captain was informed that the Health Officer was on board. He said he wished to give him a communication and was answered - "Put it on board the lighter with the mails." ...

Your Excellency will see that Captain Renoldson drew the Health Officer's serious attention to the memorial, requesting its return, and we proposed, in the event of the Health Officer not having sufficient authority, that we should transmit a message to your Excellency. We did not quit King George's Sound till 8 a.m. the following morning. In the interval, the P&O Company's store boarded and other communications reached us from the shore, but no reply was received, either to the memorial or the Captain's letter, nor did the Health Officer at any time come or send to us.
We therefore respectfully submit to your Excellency that the ship was hastily placed in quarantine without any personal inspection from the shore.

That no proper provision is made at King George's Sound for the reception of a patient or patients infected, and consequently, a crowded ship is made liable to a continuance of her passage in such company, with a further risk

---

[3] A coal lighter is a flat-bottomed barge used to transport cargo.

of danger to its more populous terminal parts. These risks, compared to the isolation that could be easily enforced at King George's Sound, present a most painful contrast.

That it was the duty of the Health Officer in the first place to have boarded the vessel, and, in any case, at least to have replied to the captain's letter, to our memorial, and to have returned the latter as requested. That we have no assurance that he complied with our just request that he should communicate with your Excellency's opinion, which he could readily have done by telegraph. We trust you will deem it no discourtesy if this statement is made public.

We have the honour to remain yours respectfully,
for Committee of passengers
Henry Alworth Merewether.[4]

Their concern was mirrored in part by a scathing follow-up article in the Fremantle press:

Great indignation has been manifested in Melbourne at the conduct of the Health Officer at Albany, in refusing to allow the infected Lascar to be landed at that port. The Argus of Melbourne referring to the subject says:

The Health Officer at King George's Sound must be a very curiously constituted individual and seems to have but a very poor idea either of the duties of his position or the manner in which they should be performed. The R.M.S.S. Baroda arrived at the Sound, on her voyage from Point de Galle to Melbourne and Sydney, with one case of smallpox on board. The patient was a Lascar in the employ of the P&O Company, and the Captain was desirous of landing him at the Sound, in order to prevent the disease spreading amongst the crew and passengers of a crowded ship, and also, to relieve the vessel from the necessity of undergoing an unnecessarily lengthened quarantine at the ports to which she was bound. This, however, the Health Officer refused to permit. He appears to have been seized with a violent fit of terror and to have utterly collapsed when for once he had a duty to perform. The excuse, that there was no place for the reception of the unhappy Lascar, was about the very lamest that could by any possibility have been alleged. The P&O Company would have had a comfortable tent erected for him in less than a couple of hours, would have provided proper medical and other attendance for him, and would have seen that everything was done for his subsequent comfort and restoration to health. The sapient Health Officer, however, was impervious to all representations, and through his stupidity, the passengers by the mail steamer were subjected to all the perils of the spread of a highly infectious and dangerous disease.

If there is anyone place in which a patient suffering from an infectious disease might be safely landed without the slightest danger of the disease spreading, it is at King George's Sound. The population only numbers a few hundred, and he might have been safely and comfortably located a mile or so away from the nearest habitation. All these considerations, however, had no effect upon the brilliant official who is charged with the care of the health of the inhabitants of the Sound. A grosser case of incompetency has seldom come under our notice. We observe that the matter has been submitted to the Governor of Western Australia, and we trust that steps will be taken to prevent a recurrence of a circumstance that might have proved most disastrous in its results. The following correspondence has been published and commented on pretty freely by most of the Victorian press.[5]

The Colonial Secretary Frederick Barlee initially responded to a further request after the *Baroda* incident by saying:

…tents will be provided… and every effort must be used to prevent persons landing…

The handling of the *Baroda* incident in 1873 caused considerable anger in Melbourne, the ship's next port of call. The claim was made that by inaction at King George's Sound in respect to effective quarantine processes the lives of eastern states people was put at risk.

In a remarkable twist of fate, it was not until the Colonial Secretary himself along with some other dignitaries were forced into quarantine in tents for a period of two weeks, and fortunately for the town during inclement weather, that the town's interest in having a permanent Quarantine Station close to the

---

[4] Lee, Sidney, ed. *Dictionary of National Biography*. London. 1894. Smith, Elder & Co.

[5] *The Fremantle Herald*. 7th June 1873.

port was realised. This was not the end of the matter for the colony, as there was disagreement between various factions in the town and government as to the most suitable location for the proposed quarantine facility. The local townspeople desired Mistaken Island while the Government wanted it placed on Geake's Island.[6] The locals were overruled and tenders for its construction were called with construction commencing in 1873. The facility became operational in 1875.[7]

However, again in 1876 the issue of quarantine for infection diseases was heralded, this time by the local colony's press. It emanated from identified logistical issues in respect to procedures at the quarantine facility:

> *We have at present smallpox and scarlatina amongst us, and we shall not be surprised to get yellow fever by the next mail steamer. Our quarantine regulations are perfect. Eight passengers were landed at the Quarantine Station from the* Sumatra *– a steamer from Galle, with smallpox on board, at mid-day, and they were not supplied with anything to eat until half-past seven in the evening. On the arrival of the steamer from Melbourne, she also is placed in quarantine, although she brings on purpose to meet the case, a special bill of health from Melbourne and endorsed at the Adelaide port. Nine passengers are landed from her and put into two empty tents on the quarantine ground; they have nothing to eat or drink, and it is found that the lantern given them for a light has no oil in it, and none is to be got at the station. The small-pox passengers kindly come and chat with them and help to carrying their luggage up to the smoking house. The process of fumigation over, at about midnight they are brought across to the main, having mixed the whole time with the men in quarantine from the small-pox vessel, and are turned loose amongst us here, while the eight men they have been mixing with are kept over at the Quarantine Station fourteen days. Surely this is a farce ...*
>
> *What we really do want at the Quarantine Station is a home capable of accommodating all the convalescents likely to be placed there, and a hospital for the sick some distance away – and these places should always be kept supplied with provisions and other necessaries. Until this is done, the quarantine rules cannot be carried out. We have only one medical man here, and if he goes over to attend a small-pox case, he has no right to come and mix with us all again, as would have to do if the patient received the attention they expect and require.[8]*

On the 6th April 1883, Charles K. Mackellar, MD, Health Officer and Medical Adviser to the Government of New South Wales, in Sydney raised the alarm once more about the nation's preparedness for an infectious disease epidemic. He argued that the existing system of hit and miss where each colony went its own way in addressing the issues of quarantine would be better served if there was a more substantial universal federal approach to intervention adopted:

> *Not only would I advise the maintenance and strict administration of our quarantine law, but I would go a step further, and urge upon the Government the desirability of seeking the cooperation of the other colonies in establishing stations at various parts of the continent distant from the great centres of population, for instance at Thursday Island to the north, and King George's Sound on the west, so that vessels approaching the continent with an infectious disease on board might land the sick persons at as early a period as possible, and then proceed to their destination. These stations might form a sort of federal quarantine and be maintained by a contribution from each colony in proportion to the number of its population.*
>
> *I think I need hardly pursue this matter further. We recently had bitter experience in our own city of the difficulty and expense which inevitably attend the eradication of an infectious sickness once established in a community, and we can hardly flatter ourselves that our attempts to stamp out disease will always meet with the success which crowned the efforts of the Government in the late epidemic of smallpox in this colony.[9]*

In 1884 a meeting of Australian Colony representatives in Melbourne with the interesting nomenclature of 'The Intercolonial Sanitary Conference' was convened. The impetus for the conference was in part a

---

[6] Named after Digory Sargent Geake who as the story goes was collecting supplies of rum from a ship in the harbour and, while inebriated himself, was blown off course at what is now known as Geake island, the south side of the entrance into The Princess Royal Harbour.
[7] "*An insight into Albany's history*" (PDF). Archived from the original (PDF) on 28 February 2015. Retrieved 24th August 2015.
[8] *The Inquirer and Commercial News*, Perth. 21st March 1876.
[9] *The Sydney Morning Herald.* 12th May 1883.

response to a significant cholera epidemic that was raging in various parts of Europe at the time. The agenda for the conference focussed on the best and most effective method of preventing the introduction of infectious disease to Australia especially pertinent given that smallpox had found its way into Victoria and spread from that colony to New South Wales and South Australia. Subsequently, there was a concern was raised that Australia's present cumbersome and disparate system of quarantine may prove to be altogether ineffectual to prevent contagious disease obtaining a footing on the continent:

> *There is indeed a safeguard against the ravages of smallpox, which may be effectually guarded against by vaccination. But a greater danger now threatens, and if the cholera germ is once introduced in the colonies there are no such means by which our population can secure an immunity from its attacks. The possibility of the contagion being transmitted long distances by sea admits of no doubt. The introduction to France by a troop-ship from Tonquin, and it rapidly spread through Italy and Spain, show what may possibly happen in Australia unless strict and efficient quarantine regulations are provided and enforced. There are indeed several circumstances that would render the introduction of the cholera germ in Australia especially disastrous and dreadful. The hygienic state of most of our large cities, as well as a number of our country towns, is anything but satisfactory, and the prevalence of typhoid and enteric diseases is a sad proof of the very general neglect of sanitary precautions…*
>
> *…an Intercolonial Sanitary Conference has met and is now sitting at Melbourne, where various regulations for the better exclusion of infectious disease from the continent are being discussed. It was at first proposed that vessels bearing a clean bill of health should not be allowed to land passengers or receive pratique at any port without a "thorough sanitary inspection" being first made…*
>
> *To avoid extremes on either side, the Conference finally resolved that provision should be made for sanitary inspection at all ports and that the fact of a vessel bearing a clean bill of health should not necessarily exempt her from a more searching and thorough one. It is highly undesirable that our commercial intercourse with other countries should be restricted or interfered with in any way not absolutely necessary for public safety; and as under these arrangements, a vessel which calls at the chief Australian ports would be liable to ten days; loss of time through quarantine precautions between King George's Sound, in Western Australia, and Sydney, the establishment of a federal Quarantine Station is highly desirable…*
>
> *The site of the station admits of no question. The first port of call is Albany, on King George's Sound, a port that has an excellent harbour, and is, moreover, in a very isolated position. The people of Western Australia are not, of course, very eager to have their colony made a depot for infectious diseases; but they have sufficient Australian spirit to waive their objections to a scheme that is for the benefit of the colonies as a whole. The expense of maintaining a federal Quarantine Station either at Albany or elsewhere, could not, of course, be thrown upon the colony in which it was established. As it would be maintained for the benefit of all, it should be supported by all, and in proportion to the benefits derivable from it; and the subsidies, therefore, should be based upon the ratio of populations…*
>
> *The proceedings of the representatives so far, have been marked by great unanimity of feeling and purpose; the decisions which have been arrived at are such as will be generally commended and endorsed by the public; and the only fear is, that all the deliberations and resolutions through legislative inaction and delay; but this fear it is to be hoped will prove unfounded.*[10]

The concerns that were raised on 16th December 1884 concerning the possible spread of contagion were again bought to the fore by an outbreak of smallpox on board *Preussen* which had docked at King George's Sound. Fortunately for the settlement, the impact of the disease was subsequently limited.

> *The recent outbreak of smallpox on board the* Preussen. *which ship is at present in quarantine is assuming a much more serious aspect than was anticipated. The passengers are all onshore now and the ship has been thoroughly fumigated. Vaccination has been resorted to and every possible precaution taken against the spread of the disease. In spite of this, there are now three cases fully developed of smallpox and nine other patients exhibiting symptoms which it is feared will prove to be the same disease.*[11]

---

[10] *The Port Augusta Dispatch and Flinders' Advertiser*. Adelaide. 22nd September 1884.
[11] *The West Australian*. Perth. 31st December 1886.

On a lighter side, when two sailors absconded from *Elderslie* that was in quarantine due to the identification of scarlet fever on board, it caused quite a stir among the local Albany populace:

Two sailors gave the police and townspeople a little gentle excitement on Friday last. The vessel was quarantined on account of having scarlet fever on board. It appears that the two then contrived to conceal themselves on a lighter alongside the ship. When the cargo, which had been transferred from the Elderslie to the lighter was fumigated, they suffered considerably, but managed to survive the fumigation, and made themselves comfortable with some whisky which they had broached. When the lightermen returned on board the following morning and removed the hatches, the two stowaways were discovered by Mr J. Moir, the ship's agent, who reported the matter to the police.

The two men got into a boat and came towards the jetty but were warned off by the police and ordered to return to the Quarantine Station, which they refused to do, and made for the beach below Mr Sherratt's store, where they were interviewed by the police again, and invited to retire and make a home with their shipmates, but they would not listen and went again towards the jetty. Here a constable was put on board the fugitive's boat and two of the water police in the police dingy proceeded to tow them away to the Quarantine Station. But they had not proceeded far on their return when one man jumped overboard and swam to the other police boat, which was at anchor and began to joist the job and make sail. Hayman and Simmons, of the water police, had then to defy contagion and secure the sailor, who was violent and kicked, so they tied him hands and feet, and stowed him away comfortably in the bottom of the boat...[12]

The episode was captured again in *The Daily News*, Perth:

An amusing incident occurred on the 7th instant about 10 a.m. It appears two of the crew of Elderslie had managed to stow themselves away in a lighter and subsequently got on board a gig belonging to Mr Moir, which they pulled close to the beach and there lay on their oars, refusing either to go to the Quarantine Station or on board their vessel, notwithstanding the threats made by various officials. They then made their way to the jetty and were chaffing the crowd who were looking at them, when one of the police boarded the boat with the intention of having them towed back to the vessel, but one of the intruders sprang overboard and made for the police sailing boar, on which he commenced hoisting sails. This he would have succeeded in doing but for the water police, who, after securing one man made all haste to secure the other, who had to be handcuffed and tied to the mast of the boat.[13]

The following month *The Albany Mail and King George's Sound Advertiser* ran two more articles on the fate of the *Elderslie* crew and passengers who were to spend in excess of six weeks in quarantine at King George's Sound. The first in its 12th February 1887, edition:

The unfortunate passengers by the Elderslie *are still in quarantine and as far as we can judge likely to continue so for some time to come – much to their annoyance. What their feelings must be when they hear that fellow passengers who went on to Tasmania rather than endure quarantine have now returned to Albany and are already on their way to Perth, can be better imagined than described.*[14]

The following week the paper reported in its 19th February 1887 edition:

After six weeks of detention in quarantine the passengers of the SS Elderslie, to the number of 150, were landed in Albany on Wednesday afternoon. They were brought over in Mr Douglas' two steam launches and a lighter, shortly after four o'clock. Mr J.F.T. Hassell's store sheltered most of them for the night, and yesterday the larger number left for their camps. There are still amount forty emigrants at the Quarantine Station, principally members of three or four families, not yet free from suspicion of infection, and three runaway sailors.[15]

Five months later, on 28th July a public meeting was enjoined in the town to seek a Federal intervention and acceptance of responsibility for the Albany quarantine facility and its further expansion. [16] In many respects, this intervention was sought in order to expand the facilities and defray some of the costs that had been borne by the local townspeople in addressing extant services. A letter to the local press by a prominent

---

[12] *The Albany Mail and King George's Sound Advertiser*. 12th January 1887 and 12th February 1887.
[13] *The Daily News*. Perth, 7th February, 1887.
[14] *The Albany Mail and King George's Sound Advertiser*. 12th February 1887.
[15] Ibid. 19th February 1887.
[16] The Federation of Australian Colonies was now being discussed.

citizen, Lancel de Hamel effectively outlined the issues confronting the town in respect to the dilemma associated with quarantine facilities:

Letters to The Editor
The Recent Public Meeting and Federal Quarantine 28th July 1887.

Sir,
I heard today for the first time of the meeting held last evening, for the purpose of ascertaining the views of the public on the question of making Albany a Federal Quarantine Station. Had I known of the meeting I would have attended it, but not having done so, I venture to trespass on your space for a few remarks, on which I deem to be a question of great importance with regard to the future prosperity of Albany. I understand the meeting decided against Albany being made a Quarantine Station, and I judge from this decision that the question could not have been considered in all its bearings, and I would like to put a few plain facts before your readers. Albany has no natural resources – the land is too poor to make agriculture a paying pursuit – there are no manufacturers and no mineral wealth. Albany must therefore depend for her prosperity on the outside world, by obtaining popularity as a health resort, or by the encouragement of commercial intercourse.

A Federal Quarantine Station here might (I do not say it would, but simply that it might) prejudice the former alternative, but what have we to count on in support of Albany as a health resort? The coming of perhaps half a dozen families from Perth for a couple of months in the summer! Some people may say that we shall obtain visitors from the other colonies. I doubt this. Visitors require something beyond a fine climate and flowers, however lovely – they require amusements – here there are none, and the beauties of Albany can be seen in a week. There are therefore no attractions for the wealthy classes from the other colonies, whose wealth puts the world at their command; and from the middle classes, we can expect nothing. A man who can take but a month's holiday in the year will not incur the expense and discomfort of bringing his family over a thousand miles by sea for three weeks at Albany. Hence Albany cannot flourish as a health resort until this colony numbers at least four hundred, instead of forty thousand inhabitants, which will not happen in our day.

Now for the other alternative. If Albany be made the Federal Quarantine Station, the following things must happen:

The erection of a suitable hospital, at the joint expense of all the colonies.
The maintenance of a skilled medical and nursing staff at the same expense.
The stopping of many vessels at this port which now never approach it.
The formation (for this must follow) of a Federal coaling depot here.
The establishment of Federal fortifications and the stationing of a man-of-war here to protect both the Quarantine Station and the coaling depot, and the formation of a naval dockyard.

Are all these advantages to be tossed aside for the fanciful idea that a Quarantine Station might frighten half a dozen families from Perth spending a month or two in the year here? Surely not - especially as it must be borne in mind that whereas now, persons passing through Albany are often detained here a week or ten days, waiting for means of prosecuting their journey, their stay will be limited to a single day as soon as the Southern Railway is opened for traffic.

The question is surely too serious to be considered as settled by the resolution of last night, but the meeting has ventilated it, and I think that now people have had time to give it more consideration than they could possibly bestow upon it in the hurry of a meeting, at which I am told one side was alone discussed, it would be desirable to hold another meeting when the matter might be further considered, and the resolution comes to thereafter be taken as final.

I am, sir, your, etc.,
Lancel de Hamel[17]

Lady Anna Brassey was a respected authoress and a person who travelled quite extensively around the globe on her yacht *Sunbeam*. She visited Albany in May 1887 and wrote of her experience when visiting the town. This was in fact to be her last voyage as she died at sea of malaria in September of 1887. Her diary of the voyage was subsequently published posthumously in 1889 and extracts from it were indeed insightful as to life in the townsite and mention an outbreak of typhoid in Albany:

---

[17] *The Albany Mail and King George's Sound Advertiser.* 30th July 1887.

> *Tuesday, May 10th*
> *... Dogs are not allowed to land in any part of Australia until they have performed six months' quarantine, but I was able to take mine ashore at Quarantine Island, which we found without much difficulty with the aid of a chart. A little before one o'clock we landed at the pier, where Mr Loftie met us and drove us to the Residency to lunch. It was a great treat to taste fresh bread and butter and cream once more, especially to me, for these are among the few things I am able to eat. After lunch, several ladies and gentlemen came to call on us.*
>
> *I was sorry to hear that a terrible epidemic of typhoid fever seems to be ravaging this little town. Built as it is on the side of a hill overlooking the sea, and with a deliciously invigorating air always blowing, Albany ought to be the most perfect sanatorium in the world. Later in the afternoon, I went for a drive with Mrs Loftie all-round the place, seeing the church, schools, and new Town Hall as well as the best and worst parts of town. It was no longer a mystery why the place should be unhealthy, for the water supply seems very bad, although the hills above abound with pure springs. The drainage from stables, farm-buildings, poultry yards, and various detached houses has been so arranged as to fall into the wells which supply each house. The effect of this fatal mistake can easily be imagined, and it is sad to hear of the valuable young lives that have been cut off in their prime by this terrible illness...*[18]

The increasing incidents of sickness onboard ships arriving in Albany led to the development over time of the Quarantine Station. The quarantine facilities were located on Geake Island. Later improved vaccination processes along with stricter quarantine measures eventually led to fewer contagious diseases being encountered and a safer community overall.

An interesting aside is that there were no cases of the Spanish Influenza (1918-1921) recorded in Albany.[19] At this time Fremantle was the main gateway for shipping to the colony and the travel between Albany and Perth was still a lengthy process, therefore, isolating the town from this epidemic.

Lighthouses

By the mid-Nineteenth Century, King George's Sound had evolved into a significant port of call on the Australasian to Europe sea route. For those travelling from the eastern colonies, it was the last port of call before a voyage across the Indian Ocean. For those travelling to Australia Albany was usually the first port of call. The increase in coastal traffic raised issues relating to improved navigation of the waterways into the harbour. Consequently, the issue was identified as needing to be urgently addressed.

Given the concerns relating to available funding in the fledgling settlement, in 1857 the British Government offered to erect two lighthouses in King George's Sound to assist with navigation. One lighthouse was earmarked for erection on Breaksea Island and the other on Point King on the mainland approach into the harbour. The caveat attached to the offer, however, was that the local government needed to agree to meet their ongoing running costs. The offer was accepted, and the decision was warmly received from the P&O Company and other shipping companies that plied their trade along the southern coastal waters.

Building started later that year with the majority of work undertaken by convict labour. The Breaksea Lighthouse comprised an octagonal base made of stone that also was designed to provide accommodation

---

[18] *The Last Voyage, To India and Australia, in the Sunbeam*. Published posthumously by Cambridge Press in London 1889.
[19] Private correspondence with members of Albany's Medical Profession.

for a keeper's cottage. However, in 1889 two purpose-built keeper's cottages were later constructed on the island. The Point King lighthouse, now only the ruins of which remain, was the first navigational light for King George's Sound and only the second lighthouse to be built on the West Australian coastline. In May 1857 Captain Wray and Sergeant Nelson from the British Army's Royal Engineers along with a party of men were sent to Albany to select a suitable site and commence construction of a lighthouse for King George's Sound. They chose an area at Point King as being an ideal location for the purpose even though several extant site issues had to be addressed by the engineers in constructing both the lighthouse and the accompanying keeper's cottage. With convict assistance, the task was completed by mid-1857. [20]

The lights were operated for the first time at Point King on 1st January 1858 with a Mr William Hill appointed the lighthouse keeper. The original light was oil-fired. Subsequently, Samuel Mitchell was appointed to the position 1867 and held that position until 1903 when he was replaced by a Mr John Reading.[21] The lighthouse was replaced in 1901 with a more substantial facility. With the advent of automation, the Point King lighthouse was made redundant in June 1911. Unfortunately, the building remained unused for many years with the subsequent loss of its roof and tower and has remained derelict for some time.

Even with the lighthouses in operation there were still boating mishaps, the first major issue was that of the P &O Steamship *Northumberland*. Captain Humphreys writing on the loss of the ship *Northumberland* reported:

The ship Northumberland, *...consigned to the P&O Company was totally wrecked off Bald Head, King George's Sound, on the morning of the 20th June 1868. The crew were completely worn out as they were kept continually pumping, the water gaining on the ship very fast; the first mate suffered so much from exhaustion that he is not expected to recover.*

...we kept along the land for King George's Sound; found that the water was rapidly gaining on the pumps, and at 8 o'clock she had 15 feet in her; kept close inshore, with the view of saving a life if she went down; at 10 o'clock saw the land just ahead and tried to haul her off, but such was her sluggish motion that she only just fetched it and struck on the reef off Bald Head; she did not stop, but the rudder was broken, and she canted with her head to seaward; directly afterwards we happened on the light on Breaksea Island, which previously had been masked by Bald Head; now gave up all hope of saving the ship, stopped working at the pumps, and got the boats out; we then got into them, saving only a few articles, and with what clothes we could get hold of, the water at the time being over the lower deck beams; sailed under the lee of the ship till the morning of the 20th, when we left her in the hope of getting some assistance; at 8 a.m. Landed at Breaksea Island, when the lighthouse keeper hoisted a signal of distress, which brought off the harbour master, but too late to be of any avail, for about 9 a.m. The ship foundered in a line between Cape Vancouver and Breaksea Island, distant from the latter about eight or nine miles, and as nothing further could be done started for Albany...[22]

There were many occasions when travellers to the Sound wrote pleasingly in correspondence or despatches about seeing the lights as they approached the harbour. For example, John Martineau who was a traveller to King George's Sound wrote:

... At sunset, about five days after leaving Melbourne the land is in sight again, and soon after the distant glimmer of the lighthouse which stands on a little rocky island at the mouth of King George's Sound. In a few hours we enter the Sound, a large harbour or bay, land-locked except to the south and south-east, embraced by a confusion of long irregular promontories and islands between which the eye cannot distinguish, and bare of tree or house to disturb their undulating outline.

---

[20] A Sketch of the Point King Lighthouse made by Captain Wray to Colonial secretary, May 23rd, 1859 in The Albany History Collection, Albany Town Library.
[21] Photograph of Point King Lighthouse in 1903 courtesy Mark Saxton and Albany Historical Society.
[22] *The Sydney Morning Herald.* 10th July 1868.

So white, the look in the moonlight, that they might be bare chalk hills, and even by daylight it is difficult to make out that it is only pure white sand which covers them. A few lights on the shore ahead of us are the only sign of life. Even the pilot seems to be asleep, for we have to burn blue lights and rockets to summon him as we steam on at half-speed. At least he comes on board, looking very sleepy; we enter the inner harbour, the anchor drops, and the twelve hours' work of coaling is at once begun, and goes on continuously throughout the night.

It is hard to understand how the settlement contrived to exist at all before the days when the Peninsular and Oriental steamers made it a coaling-station, and a place for meeting the Adelaide steamer…[23]

The cruise of HMS Bacchante in 1885 of which a previous report was referenced was fortunate to have serving as a Midshipman on board Prince Albert Victor and Prince George of Wales who were both also keen diarists. They also make mention of the lighthouses and in their notations:

May 14th

The wind is still falling, though the swell is heavy. At 9 a.m. sighed Mount Gardner, a peak in Western Australia, and afterwards Bald Head, at the entrance of King George's Sound, and then Breaksea Island… At 1 p.m. we passed under the west side of Breaksea Island, with a lighthouse on top of its red rocky, precipitous sides, weather-worn from the westerlies that have beaten on them for ages. The only way of landing is by means of a rope ladder on the east or lee side. Bald Head, on our port hand, seems covered with scrub, with here and there great patches of sand. After passing these two heads, the beautiful Sound opens out beyond. We steamed right on and up to the entrance of Princess Royal Harbour, away inside which we can see the houses of Albany in the distance.

May 22nd

So high was the wind and sea… even if they should have succeeded in turning the boat, it seemed exceedingly improbable that even if they fetched Breaksea they would be able to effect a landing there in the darkness of the night, and when the rope ladder, by means of which alone anyone can get on to the island, had been hauled up; and if they did not fetch Breaksea, the only other alternative was that they had been swept out to sea past the island by the wind and tide. As it providentially happened, however, they had succeeded in turning the boat round before the worst of the storm broke upon them, and when they neared the island, by firing off their guns they had attracted the attention of the lighthouse-keeper, who lowered the ladder, which they were thankful to scramble up and find themselves once more on terra firma. There they were most hospitably received by the lighthouse-keeper and his wife, found everything most beautiful, clean and comfortable, and were warmly housed for the night. But their friends who had made the shore were not aware of their good fortune, and the utmost anxiety prevailed for them, until at dawn the next morning the harbour-master made a signal to the lighthouse-keeper to inquire if he knew anything about them, and received the welcome reply, "Party safe". …

May 28th

At 2.30 p.m. we went up to the lighthouse to lunch, where Mr And Mrs Turner received us very kindly; they are the only people who live on the island. After lunch, we went on shooting again, and our bag at the end of the day was two wallabies, three quail, and twenty-two rabbits; there are plenty of these last on the island, and we might have got more if we had had dogs to put them up.[24]

The key role that the lighthouses at Breaksea Island and King Point played in directing coastal shipping into the Sound was understandable, so when a boat captain complained that the light on Breaksea Island was not on at a specified time the Resident Magistrate, Sir Alexander Cockburn-Campbell sought an investigation from the Harbourmaster George Butcher who occupied that role. He subsequently reported his findings concerning the complaint to the Magistrate accordingly:

To the Resident Magistrate, Albany
From Harbour Master Station, King George's Sound 20/6/1868.

---

[23] John Martineau. *Letters from Australia*. London, 1869.
[24] Extracts from The Cruise of HMS Bacchante reprinted in *The English Illustrated Magazine*, March 1885 by Canon John Neale Dalton a Priest-in-Ordinary to Queen Victoria and from The Private Journals, Letters, and Note-Books of TRH's Prince Albert Victor and Prince George of Wales with additions by Canon John Neale Dalton in the Royal Archives, Windsor Castle, Berkshire.

Sir,

In reference to a report made by Capt. Farquhar of the R.M. S.S. Avoca *respecting the light not being light at Breaksea at 5.30 a.m. June 3. I have the honour to report that I have strictly investigated the affair, which is as follows. Mr Pretious, acting Harbour Master states that he saw the light quite clear a few moments after 6 a.m. on the date mentioned. The Head Light Keeper informs me (which corresponds with his daily report) that he entered the light tower at 5 a.m. and did not leave it until he sighted the vessel at daylight. The light was burning brilliant all the time. He walked from the light room and hoisted the signals which were seen and answered from the Pilot Station. The weather upon that being very squally, one of the squally passing over the high land at Bald Head must have hidden the light from Captain Farquhar. Looking at the position of the ship and the direction of the wind on that date, I am of opinion that such was the case.*

I have the honour to be ...
George T. Butcher.

There were, however, issues with the lights at times as this correspondence from the Harbourmaster indicated:

To: Resident Magistrate, Albany.
From Harbour Master
June 29, 1869.

Sir,
I have the honour to report for your information that on Sunday 28 instant at 4.15 a.m. a steamer was sighted. When rowing out to meet the vessel, I observed that Point King Light was all but out. When one and a half or two miles from it, no light could be seen. When boarding the "S.S. Alexandra" Captain Paddle called my attention to the fact.

G.T. Butcher, Harbour Master.

The strategic importance of the Breaksea lighthouse and the weak light that it emitted was a cause of concern, particularly when discussed in relation to the defence of the harbour.

An 1886 report summarised the issue:

The inadequacy of the light on Breaksea Island has been constantly a source of complaint, and attention has been drawn to it in these columns on several occasions. Last year on the return of his Excellency the Governor Sir Frederick Napier Broome from England, a deputation of townspeople waited upon him and asked for a sum to be placed on the estimates for a light of the first-class order. His Excellency, though he received the deputation most courteously, considered that the present light was quite sufficient for the requirements of this port for some time to come, especially as the Commander of the P&O steamer, Rome *(in which vessel the Governor arrived from London,) had informed him that he saw the light on one occasion at a distance of 28 miles.*

Now we are quite prepared to grant that the Breaksea Island light may be seen at that distance at very exceptional times, and when the weather is particularly favourable, but in ordinary weather, it is not visible for more than 20 miles and then it appears very dim and might be mistaken for a ship's light, a bush fire, or a star rising. Captain Calder of the steamer South Australian, *who arrives at this port twice a month, if not oftener, has constantly complained that the light is too dim. Now Captain Mann of the ship* Thomasina Maclellan, *which arrived here last Tuesday, reports that on Monday night he was within six miles of the light and it went out on two occasions, once for over an hour, and again for twenty minutes. The danger to a large vessel like this ship, if the weather had been stormy or if a strong breeze had been blowing, and she had been working up to King George's Sound, can be very well imagined.*

... What is wanted is a revolving light of the first order, that will be visible at a distance of over thirty miles. A flash or occulting light would be equally good. But the present one is totally inadequate for the requirements of the shipping which constantly passes our shores, and in order that the Breaksea Island telephone cable may be utilised to the fullest extent, it is absolutely necessary that a first-class distinguishable light should be placed on the island in order that it cannot be mistaken for any other light.

In the opinion, however, of the most competent navigators who trade on the coast, and of the officers of Her Majesty's Navy now in the Australian squadron, the proper point for a lighthouse for this port is Eclipse Island. Now Eclipse Island is the most southerly point in South Western Australia. It is some 55 miles farther south than Cape Leeuwin and consequently right in the ocean track of vessels coming round the Cape of Good Hope, or through the Suez Canal, or from Mauritius. It is also an excellent guide for vessels to keep clear of the dangers at the south of King George's Sound, the Maude Reef and Vancouver Ledge. If therefore the Government would go to the expense of erecting a lighthouse of first-class power on Eclipse Island, the present light on Breaksea Island would be sufficient. They might very well go to this expense, considering the monthly profits they have made out of this port for many years past, which in the aggregate would more than pay the cost of erecting a lighthouse on Eclipse Island as well as on Cape Leeuwin. We consider that the former would be quite as advantageous as the latter, as ships from the west always give the Leeuwin a wide berth, while they approach the coast just at this point, and Eclipse Island lying so far to the south, a light there would be one of the finest beacons ever erected on the Australian coast. It is indispensably necessary that either on Eclipse Island or on Breaksea a light of the first order should be erected, and unless the necessary funds are placed on the estimates this session of the Legislative Council those interested in the welfare of this port will have to make their complaints heard, and if no redress is granted, they must appeal to the highest authorities...[25]

This position was supported further by the Swan River Colony's newspapers when it reported that Breaksea Island would in fact be an ideal Signaling Station:

The value of Breaksea Island, writes The Australasian, King George's Sound, as a signalling station will henceforward be considerable. It is the first land made by inward-bound mail steamers after passing Cape Leeuwin. There has long been a lighthouse on the island, but until it was connected with the mainland by cable, the signals exhibited by vessels as they went by were only useful to enter in the Lighthouse Keeper's book and could not be transmitted to the eastern ports of Australia. All P& O steamers are telegraphed from the Sound because they turn aside to land mails at Albany; but Orient Line steamers until lately were not heard of, though spoken with by the Breaksea signalman, until they arrived within sight of Cape Borda, Kangaroo Island, where they bear up for Adelaide.

The steamer **Orient** *was signalled off Breaksea Island on Saturday, and thus persons expecting friends or letters of cargo had time to prepare for the landing of mails and passengers in Adelaide on Monday. ... The cable across the Indian Ocean keeps us in daily communication with London, so we are not so dependent as we used to be on the mail steamers for important news. But in time of war, the sea and landlines of telegraph may be interfered with, and Breaksea Island is the first point at which news coming by water can be dropped by steamers which desire to avoid turning out of their course to call at Albany. Hostile men-of-war may be seen off the Australian coast by mail steamers, and they will be able to hoist signals, putting us all on our guard, as they pass the lighthouse. Breaksea Island will besides be an excellent station in itself for detecting the approach of ships of war. The enemy will either have to give King George's Sound a wide berth, or risk being observed and reported. The first requirement of men-of-war on entering Australian waters will be coal; and the only outlying ports at which it will be obtainable, provided they are strong enough to seize it, are Albany, where supplies are stored, and the Bay of Island, New Zealand, which is the site of working mines. Without coal, a powerfully armed fleet would soon become helpless from its inability to move about; and herein lies one of our safeguards against attack.*[26]

Discussion in the Federal Council[27] on the Defence of Albany in 1886 added its voice for some action on developing the existing lighthouse facilities:

Moved by Mr Lee Steere.
That this Council, considering that the undefended position of the important strategical point of King George's Sound would be a source of great weakness in the general defence of Australasia in time of war and that the protection of the Sound and Princess Royal Harbour, is of vital importance for the general security of the Australasian colonies, is of opinion that some united action should be taken by the Imperial Government, and the various colonies, with a view to their arriving at a decision which will enable the question to be dealt with at the next session of the Federal Council; and that the advisability of the erection and maintenance of a lighthouse and signalling station at Cape Leeuwin, to be united by telegraph with the Sound, should be considered in conjunction with the fortification of that place,"[28]

---

[25] *The Albany Mail and King George's Sound Advertiser.* 3rd July 1886.
[26] *The Western Mail,* Perth. 23rd October 1886.
[27] The early precursor to what would be after Federation a Commonwealth Government response.
[28] *The Albany Mail and King George's Sound Advertiser.* 9th March 1886. Note that this was Sir James George Lee-Steere.

In 1888 the adequacy of the equipment of King George's Sound lighthouse was again raised:

Mr Henry K. Toll of King George's Sound, West Australia …. proceeds to describe the state and condition of Breaksea Island Lighthouse which was as follows:

No chart of the locality, no reliable day and night glass, no stand-by lamp, no foghorn, no life-saving apparatus, no boat at the island, blue lights, a few, but not replenished, coal oil used instead of mineral oil, no national flag, no furniture, library, nor fitting service books. This was the state of affairs when he joined as head light-keeper in August last year. Since then, by requisition and by letters, there had been provided a chart (old survey) which is obsolete, as several rocks and dangers are not in it. He contends that the lighthouse-keeper should be provided with a chart of the latest survey, so as to sign ships when they are running into danger. A large coal ship came into the Sound without a chart, and miraculously escaped being wrecked on account of bearing in through a channel with rocks in the centre. A telescope had been since supplied and an apology for a stand-by lamp, he had also been furnished with a lifebuoy. This is the only item in the shape of a life-saving apparatus, and consequently should a vessel, either in a fog, or crippled from disabled machinery, drift on to the rocky gorges of Breaksea Island, every soul on board would be lost before assistance could be had from Albany.

Coal oil is used at Breaksea Island lighthouse, although he had pointed out to the authorities over and over again that mineral was a preferable illuminant to vegetable oil, giving light in the proportion of about 10 to 8, and being cheaper in the ratio of about 3 to 1. Mineral oil had for the last sixteen years been in use in the South Australian lighthouses and found to answer admirably. There is no library at Breaksea Island lighthouse. Meteorological books are provided by the Board of Trade, but neither a logbook nor fitting service books, nor is there a correct watch-book, although he sent a pro forma leaf to the authorities which he had procured from the colonies. There were only two men to keep a strict watch day and night and in all weathers. They had to attend to the light, which required sighting every fifteen minutes, to signal passing vessels, work the telephone and perform all the duties connected with the transport of the stores daily from the landing-place three-quarters of a mile up a hill." [29]

For the latter part of the nineteenth and early Twentieth Century the lighthouses on Breaksea Island and Point King joined later, by Eclipse Island provided a reassuring beacon of light across the often, foreboding seas along the Albany coast:

The Eclipse Lighthouse.

The work of erection of the new Commonwealth Lighthouse on Eclipse Island is being pushed on with a pace, considering the difficulties under which the construction is being carried out, and it is expected that before many weeks pass the light will be in position. The concrete tower which is to carry the light is now over 20 feet high. [30]

At a time when Albany was experiencing frenetic activity associated with its port facilities, these structures offered a safe passage into King George's Sound. Today with the age of automation and new navigation technology their role of never-ceasing watchfulness has almost become obsolete.

Telegraph

On 21st June 1869, the first telegraph message was transmitted between Perth and Fremantle. The private line was erected by Mr Edmond Spencer and Mr Cumming. Within 12 months the services had proven to be very successful consequently, the Western Australian Legislative Council acceded to a request to construct a telegraph line linking Perth with Albany as well as other southwest towns in the colony. These were operational by 1872. While an agreement was reached in principle in 1873 between Western Australia and South Australia to construct a telephone link it was not until 1877 that the first message was transmitted from Perth via Albany through Bremer Bay, Esperance, Israelite Bay relay stations to Eucla where each of the colonies had officers who would pass on the communication for further transmission to their respective capital city or point of destination.

---

[29] *The Daily News*, Perth. 21st February 1888.
[30] *The Albany Dispatch*. 22nd April 1926.

When Edward John Eyre and his Aboriginal companion Wylie entered the settlement at King George's Sound on 7th July 1841, the groundwork for a plausible scheme to establish a land-based as opposed to a coastal communication link between the east and west coast had been laid. Nevertheless, after years of procrastination it was left up to the various colonies to agitate for action:

> ..., *two things are urgently wanted; first, a line of telegraph from Adelaide to Albany, thence to Perth and the north; and secondly a line of steamboats from King George's Sound to Fremantle and the northern ports, thus bringing all the principal stations along the coast in direct communication by sea. Neither of these projects would put the colony to any considerable outlay at the start, and after a few years both of them are likely to be self-supporting; in any case, the benefits they would confer on the community are obvious, and in the interests of trade and progress their usefulness can hardly be over-estimated.*
>
> *A telegraph connecting Adelaide with King George's Sound would be a work of some magnitude, and one which would be probably beyond the limited means of Western Australia; but this would be a project in which the Eastern colonies and South Australia would be jointly benefited, and a reasonable aid granted by her rich neighbours would enable this colony to carry out the work. Telegraphic communication with King George's Sound would give you the English news in Melbourne four or five days earlier than at present; all the Eastern colonies would reap the benefit, which is one of no small importance in itself.*[31]

This call to action had previously been argued in *The Inquirer* which had this to say on the matter:

Telegraph to King George's Sound

> *The Melbourne Examiner contains a long and interesting letter advocating an extension of the Australian Telegraph system to King Georges Sound. The readers of Mr Todd's annual reports will be aware that this is no new idea. That gentleman long since expressed his opinion that the colonies should look forward to a line around the continent, so as to touch at Western Australia, and at any new settlements that might be formed on the coast in preference to a line across the uninhabited interior. The great advantage which he has pointed out from the adoption of this course is that the colonies would be at once, on the completion of the line to King George's Sound, brought several days nearer to England, as the mail could be anticipated on its arrival and supplemented on its departure.*
>
> *The letter which we now refer to dwells largely on this point and enters into particulars as to the cost of the line and the best mode of paying for it. The writer states that a proposition to take the adventures of the several colonies at the market value in payment of plant for telegraphic communication to the Sound, is it this moment under the consideration of one of the most responsible mercantile electro-telegraph manufacturers in England and it is by no means impossible...*
>
> *A line to King George's Sound would be undoubtedly an advantage to all the Australian colonies, and any schemes submitted to the several governments would, no doubt, be fully considered.*[32]

The concept of telegraph linking various locations both internally for the colony and expanded to encompass the rest of Australia was openly discussed in the local press, even postulating the possible route it could follow. *The Inquirer* continued:

> *Preliminary, however, to anything that could be effected for the purpose of extending our telegraph to King George's Sound, some exploration would have to be undertaken for the purpose of ascertaining the character of the country to the west of Fowler's Bay. Nothing has been done yet towards examining from an inland point, the three degrees of territory lately added to South Australia by the Home Government. It is possible that suitable timber for telegraph poles and an easily accessible track for the erection of a line might be found in this direction, and these are matters that would greatly affect the question of telegraph extension to King George's Sound.*[33]

Two years later the issue of a linked telegraph service for the colony and also for contact with the eastern seaboard was again highlighted. *The Perth Inquirer* newspaper of October 1864 railed against the apparent apathy in respect to a lack of decision on the matter:

---

[31] *The Express*. Fremantle. 16th February 1870.
[32] *The Inquirer and Commercial News*. Perth. 21st May 1862.
[33] Ibid. 21st May 1862.

> *The feasibility of establishing telegraphic communication in the colony has of late been discussed and inquiries made respecting the probable cost. It is thought that the expense of constructing a telegraphic line between Perth and Fremantle will not exceed £10 per mile but the expenses of the establishment, which will be heavy, are not taken into account. A line between Albany and Perth would be of great service and enable us to obtain the latest news from all quarters immediately on the arrival of the mail.[34]*

Finally, the agitation bore fruit and a line from Perth to Fremantle was completed on 21st June 1869. However, it was more than eighteen months later that the concept garnered enough traction to warrant action to extend the line from Perth to Albany, and then it was only with strong support from Governor Frederick Aloysius Weld. The Western Australian Legislative Council passed a resolution in May 1870, authorising the Albany to Perth line to be constructed and subsequently the line was opened on 26th December 1872.

As an interesting aside is that in its early years of operation the line was maintained by men using bicycle transport.

In 1870 an overland expedition was planned to further open the way for an expansion of the telegraph line from King George's Sound to Adelaide in South Australia. The press outlined some of the detailed thinking underpinning the planning of this venture:

> *Telegraph Line from Albany to Eucla.*
>
> *Mr Fleming, Superintendent of Telegraphs, originally recommended a direct survey of the line, with a view to set forth the real capabilities of the several landing places hereinafter mentioned; and he suggested the chartering a vessel and the formation of a party for this purpose. He advised the adoption of the coastline because materials may be landed at convenient distances, and because this line runs through immense patches of the country set down by Mr H. Y. L. Brown, the Government Geologist, as of Silurian and metamorphic formations.*
>
> *Mr John Forrest, of the Survey Department, who has traversed the whole country, and had a perfect knowledge of it, expressed his concurrence as to the adoption of the coastline but considered that the chartering a vessel to convey persons to examine the country would be a waste of time and money. He gave reliable opinions from his own observations and other sources, of the various harbours along the coast. He does not hesitate to affirm that freshwater can be obtained in abundance at the several places indicated for telegraph stations and that the subjoined particulars in sections as arranged by the Superintendent of Telegraphs, are correct.*
>
> *In regard to this Mr Fleming proposes, if practicable, to run the line between Forrest's track and the coast because he believes there are several places on the low sandy shore where materials may be landed in favourable weather, and he knows of nothing to be gained by following the track, which runs about fifty miles inland. Water is shewn (sic) in rock holes, but no doubt water will also be found in gorges and pulleys on lower lands near the coast, the maximum cartage over the section is estimated at' fifty miles. It is very clear and grassy under the range, which is never more than about twelve miles from the sea and gets closer till at Eucla it is only one mile, there are also many rocks water holes along the cliffs. The line would be much more substantial, also, than if constructed along the sand-hills near the seashore. The entire distance is seven hundred and ninety-four miles, but deviations may increase this length at the rate of one in sixty.[35]*

So, it was that on 1st January 1875 the first Telegraph post for an extension of the line to Eucla was erected in Albany with Governor Weld officiating at the event. The line was completed two years later, as a memorial outside the old Post Office building on Stirling Terrace commemorates. This made telegraphic communication possible with Adelaide in South Australia and then from there on to the eastern seaboard.

> *Their only communication with the rest of the world is by way of Albany from which they are distant more than 300 miles, the only overland communication between the two districts being by a species of wagon which starts at irregular intervals and occupies some sixty or seventy hours on the journey. At present the interests of Albany are diametrically opposite to those of the rest of West Australia. All the supplies are derived from South Australia and Victoria, notwithstanding the tariff, which is by far the heaviest of any colony in the whole group,*

---

[34] *The Perth Inquirer*, 26th October 1864.
[35] *The Western Australian Times*. 9th October, 1874.

and until very recently, in fact, up to the time that a line of electric telegraph was constructed between Perth and Albany.

The reason for this extraordinary haste, we were told, was the natural desire of the South Australians to obtain their English news as quickly as possible, and – softly be it whispered- before the Victorians could get theirs. Adelaide is about 200 miles nearer to King George's Sound than Melbourne; but as the P&O Company's large steamers surpass the local boats in speed, a good start was of importance to the latter. By the telegraph, established between the capitals, the one which first received the news triumphantly flashed it to the other.[36]

A benefit of the telegraph link with the eastern colonies was not lost on local situated colonial newspaper correspondents. As there was not a cable service from Europe at this time the colonies newspapers depended on the mail for their foreign news. As Albany was the first port of call with the Royal Mail, passengers and European newspapers, eager journalists would telegraph to their respective newspaper offices significant news items in an attempt to get a 'scoop' on their competitor papers. It was often a race from the jetty to the telegraph office as this traveller insight indicates:

The anchor had hardly been dropped when the steamer was invaded by three or four excited individuals inquiring wildly for the Purser". (These were the representatives of the big papers of the Eastern States, and their object was to grab the telegrams and summaries of mail news sent from Ceylon and put them on the newly opened overland telegraph line from Albany to Adelaide.) "There was quite an exciting race among these gentlemen in getting to shore, each trying to reach the telegraph office first." said the traveller. "The man in the winning boat told me afterwards with a smile of triumph that he had won by 20 seconds and had thus secured the exclusive use of the telegraph line for a period of two hours.".[37]

The completion of the telegraph link with the eastern states was acknowledged in an address by Governor Ord at the time and carried on the telegraph to various papers in the colonies:

His Excellency (Governor Ord) …. congratulates the colony on the completion of the Eucla telegraph line – a feeling which I am sure will be reciprocated by this House. The colony has already derived considerable benefits from the opening of this line, and I have no doubt that, in time, its utility will increase. His Excellency does not seem to think that the colony will immediately derive such substantial benefits from this work as to reward us for the foresight and energy which promoted the undertaking, but I understand that the line is already largely availed of by the neighbouring colonies. No less than six newspapers published in the sister provinces have already established agencies at Albany for the transmission by telegraph of monthly budgets of news received by the English mail, and I am informed that the wiring of one of these budgets the month before last involved an expenditure of no less than £65. This colony will no doubt derive no inconsiderable revenue from this source alone.[38]

In reflecting on the pre-Fremantle port days, the Perth newspapers reflected adversely on this state of affairs for as with the eastern state's press, they also relied on their local correspondent telegraphing key items of interest garnered from the news obtained from the mail steamers when they arrived in the port:

Those were the bright days of newspaper work when a world champion in sport might justifiably have been engaged as a journalist because of his physical prowess. Without the necessity of teaching him to spell, he could have earned his newspaper salary by pulling a dinghy from the mailboat to the shore at Albany.[39]

The fact that local correspondents would race from the jetty to the telegraph office and monopolise the service was a cause of irritation for some locals and visitors, nonetheless, the revenue it generated was quite significant as this extract from the report of the superintendent overseeing its operations explained:

The General Superintendent of Telegraphs says that the newspaper despatches forwarded by telegraph from Albany to the neighbouring colonies, on the arrival of the English mail, are steadily increasing in length. The other day, one newspaper had eight columns of news communicated in this manner, at a cost of about £100.

---

[36] Rosamond & Florence Hill. *What We Saw in Australia*. London 1875.
[37] A reflection piece in *The West Australian*. Perth. 17th April 1936.
[38] *The Western Australian Times*, Perth. 7th June 1878.
[39] *The West Australian*. Perth. 17th April 1936.

> *We noticed by the telegraph board yesterday that there was an interruption on the line beyond Israelite Bay, but communication was restored in the course of the afternoon.*[40]

During the uncertain global positioning of major European powers in the latter part of the Nineteenth Century, and in particular the perceived threat from possible Russian naval activity and the identified vulnerability of King George's Sound defences, accordingly, telegraphic communication was given an even greater prominence:

> *…During the Russian Scare expected as our Government thought it only prudent to keep the telegraph line open to Eucla both day and night, in order to receive immediate news if such an untoward event occurred;*[41]…

Not all visitors to the town were happy with the quality of service that was offered by the telegraph office as this disgruntled traveller communicated to the local newspaper:

> *We went to the Post Office at 4 o'clock in the afternoon but to our great surprise it was closed as it regularly closes about that hour, but our surprise was not yet complete – we would hardly believe that it was not a practical joke, - when we read a notice in the window, to the effect that letters and papers would not be delivered from the window to persons residing within a mile of the office. The whole workings of the Post and Telegraph Office are very inconvenient for the public, and the sooner the Government makes laws and regulations for carrying on this most important business of the colony, in accordance with those of other parts of the civilized world, the better it will be for Albany and the rest of the colony.*[42]

It did not take long for the benefits of the telegraph to be felt in the colony. In 1877 the overland telegraph was linked between Western Australia and South Australia through the Eucla relay station. In 1886 Albany was able to communicate with Breaksea Island lighthouse by a submarine cable.

Towards the end of the Nineteenth Century, there was a general awakening of self-consciousness among the colonies and a growing desire to move towards a more unified national Australian identity. The development across the country of the telegraph that had linked all the disparate colonies facilitated the demand for Federation and on 1st January 1901, this was achieved.

The Telephone Exchange

Interestingly, there was a government requirement that at least 50 subscribers were necessary before a locality could obtain a telephone exchange. In Albany, while this number could not immediately be secured, nevertheless, a petition was sent to Premier John Forrest seeking his consideration to provide the town with this facility,

> *Telephone Exchange for Albany.*
>
> *Fifty subscribers are, we believe, necessary to induce the Government to establish a telephone exchange in Albany and yesterday a petition promoted by the Hon, J. A. Wright was signed by about 35 intending subscribers. There are several other firms in the town who intend to sign. Below we give a copy of the petition:*
>
> > *To the Honourable Sir John Forrest, Knight Commander of the Most Distinguished Order of St. Michael and St. George, K.C., &c., Premier of the Colony of Western Australia.*
> >
> > *The humble petition of the undersigned inhabitants of the town of Albany sheweth (sic)*
> >
> > *1. That your petitioners are desirous that telephone exchange be established in Albany by your Government.*
> >
> > *2. The erection of posts and wires would not be very expensive, as the main body of intending subscribers have their offices and places of business within a limited area.*
> >
> > *3. The expense of upkeep and interest on the expenditure would be more than covered by the subscriptions, and thus the undertaking would at once be a profitable one for your Government.*
> >
> > *4. Your Petitioners would suggest that the Exchange be placed under the management of the official in charge of the Telegraph Office in Albany, with the assistance of the telegraph repairers, and thus save considerable expenses and that the rest of the working be carried on as in Perth.*

---

[40] *The West Australian Times*, Perth. 16th August 1878.
[41] *The Inquirer and Commercial News*, Perth. March 17th 1886.
[42] *The Albany Mail and King George's Sound Advertiser*. 8th August 1888.

5. Your petitioners hereby severally agree to become subscribers to a telephone system if established here and guarantee to pay the rent and abide by all the conditions at present levied and imposed on the subscribers to the Perth system.

Your petitioners therefore humbly pray that your Government may be pleased to authorise the expenditure of the monies for the erection of and carrying on of a telephone exchange in Albany. And your petitioners will ever pray, etc. Here follow the signatures of the leading business people in Albany.[43]

The Albany telephone exchange was established in 1895 and initially was operated by Louise Parish and Charlotte Prideaux. By the end of that year, many of Western Australia's main country towns were connected by telephone.

The Albany to Perth Road

Initially what passed as the road from Perth to Albany was established by 1835 with the average journey taking between 10 and 14 days by horse and as expected many weeks when travelling on foot. The history of the Albany to Perth Road begins with the trek of Captain Thomas Bannister in 1831:

... when Captain Bannister set out from York to mark a route to King George's Sound. Five years later surveyor Hillman marked a track from Albany to Mount Barker. In February 1837, Dr Harris, accompanied by Hillman, Lieutenant Armstrong and a detachment of troops, left Albany for Williams, a journey taking 12 days. Previously, Hillman had marked a track from Kelmscott to Williams, so the accomplishment of the southern portion of the journey actually completed the marking of a direct track from King George's Sound to the Swan River settlement...

It was in 1841 that the more direct route from Williams to Perth was opened up, and a military post was established at Banister. The volume of traffic between Albany and Perth was now fast increasing and the packhorse mail service was discontinued in favour of a monthly mail, conveyed in a spring cart...

[In 1848] ...the survey of the Perth-Albany Road was completed, but the actual clearing of the line was not commenced until 1850-the year that the first convicts arrived in the Swan River settlement. Their labour was extensively used for road construction and other tasks.[44]

The agitation for better access to facilitate coach, wagon and other traffic movements between Albany and Perth came from many quarters, but primarily from visitors to the state and Albany in particular. Correspondence sent by this traveller to the local press gave a very full account of how the settlement as of 1867 had so far developed while raising the issue of overland transport:

...To these colonies, however, and to all business communities elsewhere, the advantages of easy and direct communication are of the highest importance, and it is among the greatest drawbacks to this country that so many obstructions exist in the way of traffic.

The visitor to these parts has only two ways of getting to Perth; he must either take his chance in some trading craft – mostly small sailing vessels, and the prospects of such a cruise are not enlivening – or else he must take the Peninsular and Oriental Company's steamer, or go via Adelaide to King George's Sound, and then make his way across 260 miles of sand and bush by means concerning which he is unable to gather the slightest information. This latter route, which I should think will be mostly preferred, is by no means such a terrible thing as it is made out to be.

The aspect of the coast on approaching King George's Sound is rough and arid in the extreme; mountains of granite and plans of sand appear alone to compose these bleak and barren shores, and hardly a speck of vegetation can be seen to brighten the dreary prospect. The Sound is a good harbour, formed by an inlet of the sea, deeply indented, and bordered on all sides by mountainous rocks of granite. On the northern shore, at the upper end, lies the little township of Albany, a mere sprinkling of houses in a hollow of the hills, with a few straggling trees intermingled.

---

[43] *The Albany Advertiser*, 21st August, 1891.
[44] Ibid. 31st May 1930.

> *The main street runs parallel to the water's edge and is lined on the upper side by a row of houses, comprising two hotels, and some stores. Another wide street, running at right angles to the first, crosses the saddle of the hills at the back of the town and forms the commencement of the main road to Perth. This street is got up in a most elaborate style, with gravelled sidewalks, gutters, and curbstones; all it requires to make it a really handsome street is a row of houses on each side, and that, I am told, will come in time. Albany is a very small place, nor does it show many prospects of rapid advancement. Its only resources lie in the harbour, which is the coaling depot for the P&O mail steamers and is occasionally visited by whalers. The total number of inhabitants in the town and neighbourhood is, I believe, about 1,000.*[45]

The matter of road access was also raised in the Western Australian Legislative Council in July 1867, and reported in the colony's press directly:

> *Sir,*
> *I was much pleased on perusing the Report of the opening of the Legislative Council, which appeared in the last issues of the Inquirer, to find that His Excellency the Governor was at last enabled to give so satisfactory a statement with reference to the Albany Road, which has appeared to many of us so long neglected. His Excellency stated in his Address on that occasion that there were, I rejoice to be able to say so, as many as 123 men, with the necessary superintendence, and assistant in the shape of horses and carts, employed on the line, which must surely be considered by all as indicative of a determination on the part of the government to make a thoroughly practicable road from the City to the Sound – while convict labour is at its disposal – necessary, not only as being the means by which our mails are conveyed across but to meet the demands of the increasing amount of traffic between Perth and the outlying Southern districts; at any rate as far up the road as Narrogin, where numerous tracks concentrate.*
>
> *I had occasion, a short time since to travel along the road, when I observed that the late rains had made sad havoc in some of the unsound parts, laying open enormous ruts which ought at once to be looked to, or traffic upon the road must entirely cease; indeed, it was them rumoured that two or three teams had been passed in the neighbourhood had been hopelessly bogged. Surely a few of the men employed on the clearing nearer town might be detached for a week or so to temporarily repair the broke parts and render the road in some measure fit for traffic.*
>
> *This line of road, which is perhaps the most important in the colony, and necessarily requires the most attention, is remarkably suggestive of the necessity of all the districts in the colony seeing about and thinking seriously upon forming Road Boards, similar in constitution to those existing in South Australia. They might for the present be made subservient to the government, but there would be one thing gained – the appointment of a Road Surveyor or two. In conclusion, I would ask you, Sir, what the settlers expect the government will be inclined or able to do for them in making or keeping their roads in repair when transportation to the colony shall have died out? It may be our colonists are ready to give you a reasonable answer, but it is very obscure to me.*[46]

Perhaps two of the most interesting perspectives of travelling from Perth to Albany was one provided by an adventurist soul who completed the ride by bicycle in 1899 and the other by the writer Anthony Trollope:

> *Perth to Albany on the wheel. A four-day journey. (by pedal).*
> *It is difficult to realise that but a few years ago, comparatively speaking, a journey to Albany from Perth with the undertaking of some magnitude. Moreover, with one which was only possible under ordinary circumstances once every fortnight. Too many of the older residents of the colony, the old coaching days and experiences are still fresh in their memories. This I learned during the recent ride on the wheel on the old coach road which connects the capital with the southern port...*
> *These several travellers gave such an account of the almost impassableness of the roads and the difficulties to be overcome that it was with a considerable amount of trepidation that I set decided to undertake the ride.*[47]

Anthony Trollope who travelled to Perth along the Albany Road was obviously not enamoured with the journey as he wrote:

---

[45] *The Fremantle Express.* 3rd March 1870.
[46] *The Inquirer and Commercial News*, Perth. 3rd July 1867.
[47] *The West Australian*, 2nd October 1899.

> *We lit fires for ourselves, boiled our tea in billies and cooked bacon and potatoes in a frying pan and pretended to think that it was jolly…*
> *No man perhaps ever travelled two hundred and sixty miles with less to see.*[48]

An item of humour appeared in *The Inquirer* concerning travelling along the Perth Road and the offer of a government incentive to encourage a faster mail transit from Albany to the Capital:

> *We learn that the Government has offered £5 per trip additional to the contractor if he conveys the mail from Albany in six days. This new arrangement comes into force this trip. We fear the state of the roads will not permit the mail carrier to derive any benefit from the new arrangement.*[49]

By the time of Albany's Centenary in 1927 only four roads in the townsite had been sealed. These were York Street, Stirling Terrace and the beginning sections of some of the adjoining roads, Duke Street and Grey Street West.[50] The area of York Street and its immediate surroundings were at one time extremely swampy. Convict labour had been used to excavate rocks and gravel from Mount Clarence to retain the area and to drain the land. Large drain structures were constructed along York Street as gutters to divert the flow of water into the harbour. This had the impact of affecting the ecology of Hanover Bay by slowly filling it with sediment.

Administration of Albany

In 1831 the jurisdiction of the town had passed to the Swan River Colony and the Governor of Western Australia. However, the day-to-day administration of the affairs of general administration in the settlement resided in the position of Government Resident who was appointed in turn by the State's Governor. This scenario of settlement administration remained in place for 12 years until 1843 when the Act for The Improvement of Towns was applied to the Albany District and enabled a delegated body of appointed citizens to provide advice to the Government Resident, primarily for issues relating to the provision of rural road infrastructure.

In 1848 a Towns Trust was appointed to undertake more of a role in community and town decision making. Members of the 1848 Towns Trust included the Government Resident John Randall Phillips, Patrick Taylor and Edmund Spencer, son of Sir Richard Spencer. There was considerable responsibility assigned to the Towns Trust and its membership as the day-to-day activities of the town was in their purview.[51] However, the small population size of the settlement frustrated attempts to make the Trust a viable entity and as a consequence, its functions were relinquished back to the State's Governor.

Albany was Incorporated as a Municipal Town in 1851. While there are various references to Albany and the 'town of Albany' in the Government Gazettes even before 1851, nevertheless, the first reference to "Town of Albany" (with a capital T) is in the Gazette for 22nd July 1851, where reference is made to the appointment of "Mr. S. Knight to be Supervisor of the Town of Albany, to carry out provisions of Ordinance 14 Vict. No. 26". This Ordinance was titled "An Ordinance for The Further Improvement of Towns, and the Greater Security of Life and Property Therein." In this Ordinance, Perth, Fremantle and Albany are explicitly called out as 'towns'.[52] The 1871 Municipal Institutions Act and Roads District's Act resulted in the broader municipality of Albany being created. At this time the Municipality of Albany was gazetted to incorporate the Plantagenet region as well. The Act also created the City of Perth along with other municipalities including Fremantle, Guildford, Bunbury, Busselton, York and Geraldton. The Roads Board Act of 1888 further facilitated the formation of the

---

[48] A. Trollope. *Australia.* Chapman and Hall, London. 1873.
[49] *The Inquirer and Commercial News.* 8th July 1857.
[50] The Albany to Ellen Cove, Middleton Beach Road was completed in 1837.
[51] Other districts enabled at this time included Vasse, Canning, Pinjarra, York and Swan.
[52] *State Library of Western Australia.* Reference YES125920.

Albany Roads Board. *The West Australian Government Gazette* announced the creation of the Albany Roads Board:

Albany Roads Board District.
Department of Lands and Surveys, Perth,
1st April 1896.
It is hereby notified for general information that under the provision of the Roads Act 1888, His Excellency the Governor in Executive Council has been pleased to designate and define the Albany District as a Roads Board District…
A.R. Richardson
Commissioner of Crown Lands[53]

It was only in 1896 that a separation of the Albany and Plantagenet Districts was initiated and at the time Albany was designated a town in its own right.

Closing Remarks

The second half of the Nineteenth Century saw significant changes made to the infrastructure of the town with Albany's infrastructure expansion mirroring step by step developments in transport and communication.

Much of the town's early infrastructure was created as a response to changing world events, increased population and the introduction of innovations like steam shipping, the telephone and telegraph. This period in Albany's historical evolution was also one of greater economic prosperity among the polity as a whole, particularly as the hinterland became more settled and productive. The intake of free settlers due to the gold rush proved to be a boon for the town. Immigration during this time was the single most important determinant of population growth in Albany, far outweighing local births.

The port facilities were a significant factor in the town's sustained economic growth and the main catalyst for infrastructure development, funnelling much needed overseas capital into the settlement.

---

[53] *The Western Australian Gazette.* 10th April 1896.

CHAPTER 10
THE GREAT SOUTHERN RAILWAY NETWORK UNFOLDS

Development, the exploitation of resources to achieve economic growth and population-building, acquired heightened meaning in the second half of the nineteenth century as new colonial governments became responsible for ensuring the economic and social progress of the colonies and the prosperity of colonists.
The Oxford Companion to Australian History.[1]

Settlement Comes to Life

The construction of the Albany to Beverley leg of the Great Southern Railway commenced on October 20th 1886, and the line was in operation by the 31st of May 1889. Once operational the provision of the rail link saw several towns gaining a more prominent status along its route through the Great Southern; from Albany to Beverley. Towns like Mount Barker, Cranbrook, Broomhill, Katanning, Wagin, Narrogin and Pingelly owed their new-found prominence and prosperity to the railway which linked them together. In many respects, the railway allowed for the opening up of the Great Southern District heralding a significant movement of new settlement into the area.

Initially in the first decades of the town's evolution there was among the early colonists some who had argued that Lieutenant-Governor Captain James Stirling RN, was in error in choosing the Swan River as the site for the primary settlement for Western Australia, especially given they maintained that Albany with its outstanding natural harbour facilities would have been a much better choice. Unfortunately, Albany's agricultural potential did not show early promise given that its hinterland was mostly characterised by poor soil condition and a prevalence of poisonous vegetation that inhibited the development of cattle and sheep stocks. Furthermore, Albany's economic activity was clearly focussed on its harbour and occasionally suffered from the uncertainty of continued service by shipping companies. It was the advent of The Great Southern Railway that was to play a significant role in the development of the town.

The story of the Albany to Perth railway is one of two parts. The first centred on the vision and entrepreneurship of Sydney man, Anthony Hordern. The second part relates to the era post-Hordern's unfortunate demise.

As Robert Kennedy famously said; "*Some men see things as they are and say why. I dream of things that never were and say why not.*"[2] In the case of Hordern, the latter adage definitely applied.

Anthony Hordern - the Albany to Perth Railway

The Western Australian Government had perceived that the way to growth and development of the colony was going to be through agriculture, particularly through the expansion of agricultural land settlements. Railways that linked agricultural areas to ports and towns were seen as a way to overcome any barriers that may inhibit this agricultural growth. Given that colonial revenue was not sufficient to engage in railway building schemes at the time, the Colonial Government offered land as an incentive to encourage private investment in railways.

The Legislative Council adopted a resolution supporting the proposed land-grant scheme in March 1881, to which the Governor added his support and forwarded it to the Secretary of State, Lord Kimberley, in June. On the 27th July 1881, Kimberley's replied as follows:

---

[1] Davison, G., Hirst, J. B. and Macintyre, S. *The Oxford Companion to Australian History*, Rev. ed. Melbourne. Oxford University Press, 2001.
[2] *RFK, His Words for Our Times*. William Morrow Publishers. 2018.

> *I have the honour to acknowledge the receipt of your Despatch No. 106 of the 9th of June, with its enclosures, respecting the proposed opening up of the South-western part of Western Australia by the construction of Railway accommodation between the Eastern Districts and King George's Sound on the Land Grant System.*[3]

When negotiations between Anthony Hordern and the Crown Agents in London reached a stalemate in 1884, the matter was referred to the Western Australian Legislative Council for a decision. The Legislative Council reached an agreement with Hordern and Governor Sir Frederick Napier Broome then signed the contract.[4]

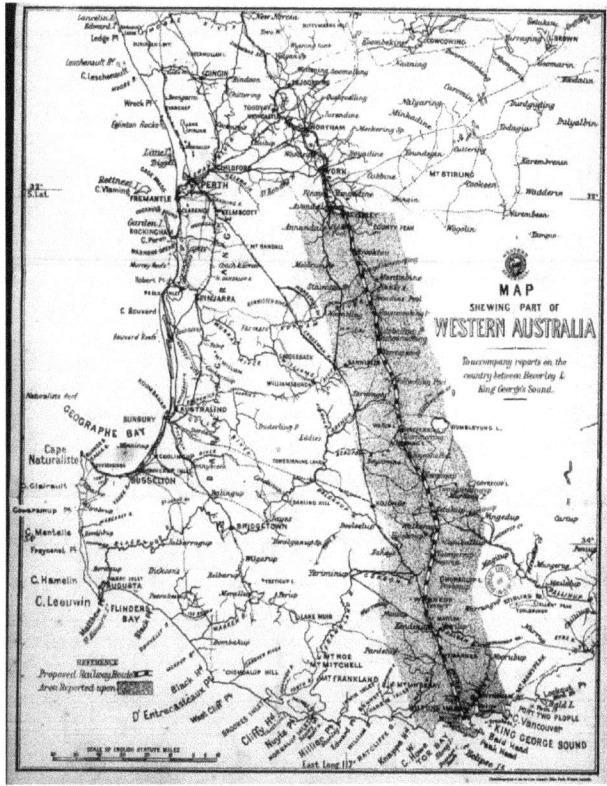

The map outlines the land grant allocation for the railway Albany to Beverley as was considered and approved by the Legislative Council in 1882.[5]

Initially Hordern's idea was to construct a railway link from Albany to Wyndham in the Kimberley via York, Geraldton, Roebourne, and Broome. However, the concession given to him was to build a railway from Albany to Beverley and in so doing one of Albany's and the colony's most pressing transport problem was solved. Furthermore, the construction of the railway had been funded by private capital on the inducement of land grants without using any of its own capital reserves.

In many respects Hordern's involvement in the Great Southern Railway scheme was at two levels, the first igniting the public's interest, the second was establishing a syndicate to raise the necessary capital to progress the venture. His first task was securing the Western Australian Government's support for the proposal and this he did in negotiations with Governor Sir Frederick Napier Broome and the Legislative Council. Broome signed the contract of intent on October 25th 1884. The eventual contract agreement offered Hordern and his syndicate two million acres of land between Albany and Perth with an addition to the agreement that he would facilitate the settlement of 5000 migrants into the colony. This contract was modified at a later date to increase the land grant to three million acres and a ten-pound bounty for each new settler he encouraged to migrate. *The Albany Mail and King George's Sound Advertiser* related the details of the scheme:

> *A public banquet was given to Mr Anthony Hordern on his arrival from the capital by the overland mail on Saturday, September 6, in recognition of the advantages that his railway scheme, now finally settled, will confer upon the colony at large and on Albany in particular. A sumptuous spread was prepared at the London Hotel, by the caterer, Mr J. Norrish. The tables were tastefully laid and the viands*[6] *provided would do credit to a Lord Mayor of London's dinner. Nearly sixty sat down, including nearly all the leading residents in the town… At half-past eight o'clock the company arrived and before sitting down, the Chairman introduced Mr Hordern to those present. Full justice was done to the good things provided, after which the usual loyal toasts were proposed and heartily responded to…*

---

[3] *Correspondence on the Subject of the Construction of Railways on the Land Grant System.* Votes and Proceedings of the Legislative Council during the session, Legislative Council, Parliament of Western Australia Perth: Government Printer, 1881.
[4] *Papers relating to the Construction by Mr A. Hordern of a Land Grant Railway between Beverley and Albany.* A33, Perth, WA: Legislative Council, 1884.
[5] *Votes and Proceedings, Legislative Council of Western Australia, Perth, 1882.*
[6] A viand is an item of food.

Mr Hordern, who was greeted with cheers then stood up and thanked the gentlemen present for their kind reception and said he was highly honoured to be presented at such a social gathering. …He believed the railway would benefit this portion of the colony more than any other, and he hoped shortly to see all the lines of steamers calling here, the Orient, the French line and the German line. The town wants advertising, the beauty of the climate made know and attractions for visitors initiated. A park ought to be laid out and amusements provided. These would make Albany the most attractive city in Australia. He had much pleasure in proposing the toast of this Town and District…

With regard to the Albany-Beverley railway, I believe it will be one of the chief means of commencing the important work of opening up the country and the development of its resources. From its first settlement, W.A. Has been insufficiently known or unfavourably reported of, with the consequence that the tide of immigration is diverted to other channels, and the manifold advantages presented by this vast country are overlooked. But when it begins to be opened up so that its products can be brought down speedily and cheaply to the seaboard for export, then we may hope to find its name mentioned in the great markets of Europe and the advantages of its beautiful climate appreciated. The railway passing through the most populated parts and connecting them on the one side with the capital and on the other with this splendid port will, I believe be the beginning of a new era, (cheers), and I cannot be too delighted at the way in which my proposals have been received and taken up generally throughout the colony. Especially has this been the case in Albany. (Hear, hear.)

I do not remember having heard of a single opponent to my proposals in this city. On the other hand, I know I have many warm supporters and if I may be permitted to use the term, staunch friends, and amongst these I must not omit to mention one who has used his influence most energetically on my behalf, I need hardly say I allude to the editor of The Albany Mail, Mr C.J. Ashwell. I have regularly read that paper and have often felt gladdened on seeing myself and my project mentioned so kindly by him, and yet more so by the reflection that his words were but the expression of the general feeling of the inhabitants of Albany. I am duly grateful, gentlemen, for the support you have generously given me, and can assure you that in the worry and harass of tiring negotiations, the thought of your sympathy and support has often spurred my flagging energies and inspired me with fresh zeal…

Again, I beg leave to thank you for the kindness with which you have received me and to hope that this may be by no means the last of many happy occasions of our meeting together.[7]

The fact that Hordern had selected such a large swathe of land along the foreshore of The Princess Royal Harbour raised the ire of many in the town. These criticisms had reached a point where Hordern was forced to personally defend the proposal in the local newspaper:

The Editor of The Albany Mail,
London, July, 10th 1885.

Sir,
I am only sorry that the length of time required for the transmission of mails may cause my letter to have an air of inopportuneness. Under the circumstances, however, I think I shall better do my duty towards my Syndicate and the good people of Albany by writing than remaining silent.

I have just seen the letter of Sir Thomas Cockburn-Campbell, in your issue of 26th May last, which presents the case in a nutshell. It is precisely because we are looking to the future of the town and port of Albany that we are advised here that it is necessary to take so large a water frontage. It must be remembered that in order for Albany to hold her own in face of the contemplated harbour works at Fremantle, it is of the greatest importance that there shall be every convenience for the loading and unloading both of passengers and merchandise. As you have seen, I am contemplating the introduction of a large number of settlers into the colony and, when the system of placing immigrants on the lands of my Railway Syndicate shall have begun to operate, I shall be able to show more clearly by practice what I contemplate for the great development of the industries of the colony, necessitating plenty of accommodation for wharves, warehouses, stations and other such appliances.

---

[7] *The Albany Mail and King George's Sound Advertiser.* 16th September 1884.

> *...I, like Sir Thomas, have a 'dream of the future and I can promise him that if I have health and strength to carry out my plans, he shall not be disappointed. I hope to see not merely a promenade, the finest in all the 'Australias', but a beautiful watering place overlooking the port, yet removed from the disagreeables which are the concomitants of a large shipping trade, having its parks, squares and magnificent avenues, so that when the present memorialists see the results of their deprivation they will be more than satisfied by the return which my Company have made for their sacrifice. I hope to see King George's Sound doing a vast trade in the southern and south-western districts of the colony, while above it shall rise the fair city of Albany with its large hotels and mansions, the sanitorium of the Southern hemisphere, popular as a resort for our invalid population from all parts of the world...*
>
> *Yours faithfully,*
> *Anthony Hordern[8]*

City of New Albany

However, the route of the railway line along the foreshore continued to cause some considerable agitation among many of the town's inhabitants and there was ongoing debate in the local newspapers about the way land had been excised that had in effect cut the town off from its waterfront along The Princess Royal Harbour:

> *...The locomotive engine generally imparts such an impetus, and so it need not occasion surprise when we say that Mr Anthony Hordern hopes, by means of the great railway he has projected, to give to Western Australia the City of New Albany. The object of building a new city at King George's Sound is to induce an expansion of the present Albany. The country wherein lies the route the railway will take from Albany has already been surveyed. The terminus will be on a site in the present town of Albany and will be bounded on one side by the sea and on another by Stirling Terrace. Starting from this point, Mr Cheesewright (the surveyor) has surveyed along the route of the line for a distance of ten and a half miles from Albany. The site he has chosen for the new city is situated at a distance of six and a quarter mile from the terminus in Albany. It consists of a plain two miles wide by four miles long, surrounded by picturesquely wooded hills...*
>
> *The survey for the new town is complete, and the plans are being prepared, with a view to the blocks being put up for sale at auction on an early date. Capitalists in other colonies have, we are informed, sent in applications for good sites, and some of the leading Melbourne firms have intimated that they intend to open stores at New Albany when it is established...*
>
> *The survey party is now traversing the two rivers that empty into the lake in order to discover their sources. Their labours in this direction being concluded, they start for Beverley for the purpose of selecting the land that Mr Hordern is to receive in return for his railway. An important feature in the preliminary arrangements for the new railway is the fact that Mr Hordern's syndicate have acquired the whole of the property in Albany from Steamer Point to the present jetty, including the P&O Company's jetty. Should the port of Albany develop in the way it is expected to do when the railway is opened out, this property that the syndicate has acquired will prove highly valuable; and New Albany will become more than a name, for it will naturally receive that part of the population that could not find quarters within the present town...[9]*

Hordern returned to London where he established the West Australian Land Company. Unfortunately, after succeeding with this part of the venture while returning to Albany to personally oversee the work on the railway's construction he passed away in transit on 16th September 1886 (of sunstroke). He was buried in Albany:

> *Mr Anthony Hordern never took an active interest in politics but devoted his energies to business and to various large enterprises. The first great scheme on which he embarked was the Beverley-Albany Railway, which, in the face of great difficulties, he had before leaving England placed on a safe basis, having transferred the project, except his interest as a shareholder, to a limited liability company. Similarly, he floated a large company in England for the reclamation of a vast extent of the portion of land in this colony. Both of these schemes, will, we understand, not be affected by the death of him on whose energy their success depended prior to the floating of the companies. He was the holder of a large quantity of land and of house property in this colony, and it is*

---

[8] *The Albany Mail and King George's Sound Advertiser.* 18th August 1885.
[9] *The Western Mail.* 26th December 1885.

estimated that he has expended fully £30,000 in Western Australia. He had many schemes in view for the advancement of the colony, and his intention was, in the course of time, to settle here. By Mr Anthony Hordern's death, the country has lost a genuine friend and one whose energy and capital would have made him a most valued settler.[10]

The funeral for Anthony Hordern was well attended and his contribution in terms of vision and enterprise on behalf of Albany were appreciated when the town honoured him at his funeral:

Funeral of the Late Mr Anthony Hordern

The funeral of the late Mr Anthony Hordern took place on Wednesday last at 4p.m. The cortege left the residence of Mr E.G.S. Hare, where the coffin had been placed on being brought ashore from the mail-steamer, Carthage, and proceeded to St John's Church, where the Rev. W. Wardell-Johnson, M.A., read the first part of the funeral service in a most impressive manner. The building was crowded with all classes of the community, and when the procession left the Church on its way to the Cemetery it reached half the length of York Street. There much have been 300 persons present, including the volunteers. The road at the Grave-yard was lined with women and children, and nearly all of the townspeople turned out to pay respect to the memory of the deceased as his remains were conveyed to their resting place…[11]

Fittingly for a man of some vision, his endeavours were appreciated by a grateful community and in 1890 a monument was erected at the top of York Street in his honour:

The ceremony of unveiling the monument erected at Albany to the memory of Mr Anthony Hordern, the promoter of the Great Southern Railway scheme, was performed yesterday. The monument is a very handsome one, having a blue granite base, while the column of red granite on which it is standing is twenty-seven feet six inches high. It was designed and cut by Messrs. Heslop, Wilson & Co., of Millband, near Peterhead, Scotland … The arrangements for the unveiling ceremony were made by the Hordern Memorial Committee, the Mayor and Town Clerk, and were of a most complete character. The site selected for the monument was the top of York Street where the four chief arteries of the town meet. This point will undoubtedly be the centre of Albany when the town has undergone further development. The Town Council put on the necessary labour to form the road around the Monument, and this was completed yesterday…

The monument, which was draped in black, was then unveiled. The band played, and the spectators cheered. The inscription is as follows:

"*This monument was erected by the people of Western Australia to perpetuate the memory of the late Anthony Hordern, who, by his energy and enterprise, obtained from the West Australian Government sanction to construct the Great Southern Railway, the first in the colony constructed on the Land Grant System, and who died on board the* RMS Carthage, *on his way from England to Australia, on the 16th day of September 1886".*[12]

Anthony Hordern had always entertained grand ideas of the future of Western Australia.[13] Another less reported aspect of his vision for his railway venture was the creation near Torbay Inlet some 29 kilometres west of Albany of the City of New Albany. Garden (1977) also makes mention of his idea for another new town which Hordern had conceptualised in the region of the now suburb of Spencer Park to cater for the expanded growth of the town as a consequence of his railway vision.[14] Neither of these eventuated although today Spencer Park is the home to the Great Southern Regional Hospital, St Joseph's School and a significant number of private dwellings and commercial enterprises.

It is interesting to note that as with some other proposed initiatives in Albany that the site for the Hordern Monument was also hotly debated in the local press. It was eventually decided to place the monument at

---

[10] Ibid. 25th September 1886.
[11] *The Albany Mail and King George's Sound Advertiser*. 25th September 1886.
[12] *The Daily News*, Perth. 4th July 1890.
[13] Photograph of the Albany railway station courtesy of Mark Saxton and Albany Historical Society.
[14] D. Garden. *Albany: Panorama of the Sound*. Nelson. 1977.

the 'top-end 'of York Street as this was perceived to be 'out of town'. From the period 1890 till the start of the Second World War Stirling Terrace was seen as the business centre of Albany and land in this precinct of the town was indeed a scarce commodity.

Hordern's Vision Unfolds

The Albany Mail and King George's Sound Advertiser was able to succinctly capture both the importance of the Great Southern Railway to the town and the vision of the men behind its creation while at the same time summarising for its readers the controversies that accompanied the decision regarding routing the tracks along the foreshore:

> *Western Australia is the largest of all the Australian Colonies with the smallest population…All agreed that railways would improve the country much. How to get them was the question. The Government built some but had not the money to build all that were required, and instead of taxing the necessaries of life and the hard earnings of the few poor labourers, as they do at present to raise the revenue if they had put a tax on the land and built the railways and kept the land to draw a population the country would now have probably been in a better situation than it is. Clever and wealthy men in the United Kingdom, the Colonies and elsewhere saw the situation and took advantage of it by forming a company agreeing to build a railway to connect Albany with the Government Railway which runs to Perth, on condition that the Government gave them 10,000 acres of land for every mile of railway built. Everything was agreed to. A bill passed through the Legislative Council, the railway started and nearly completed as we all know it is at present. The Government were so anxious to get this line of railway built that they allowed the company to form rules and regulations and frame the Act almost as they liked. The company could probably have got greater concessions if they had demanded it…*
>
> *This was the railway we referred to at the beginning of this article running along the water's edge, and it should not have been run between the town and the harbour, but it is too late to complain about that now. Another great mistake made in the railway is the narrow gauge. Apart from the danger and low speed of such a gauge, there will yet be the difficulty of meeting South Australia, as there is between New South Wales meeting Queensland and Victoria. The gauge here should have been the same as in South Australia.*
>
> *… Both parties agree that it was a mistake to have allowed the Railway line to run between the Town and the Harbour and that the two crossings now in existence are sufficient for the present requirements of the town. Both agree that the townspeople should have a right of access to the harbour at every street if required, and at all times; they must and will, have it no matter at whose expense as the Government would be compelled to do it. All reliable legal opinions agree that the local Land Company had the power to keep these streets closed and compensating the Company for taking that right from them when it is required is the proper course to pursue. Both the parties are like the two children quarrelling about who will pump water from an empty well.*[15]

At an event celebrating the opening of another significant Albany landmark, the Albany Town Hall, acknowledgement was made of the contribution that the Great Southern Railway had made to the town:

> *…The next toast – that of "Success to the Great Southern Railway" - was proposed by the Mayor, who said he did not require to go into details to show what had been done by the railway since October 1886, when he believed, the first portion of the plant arrived. If they considered what had been done since that time, he thought they would agree that when the railway was finished the colony would make as rapid strides as Albany had done during the last fifteen months. The railway must improve the colony, and, to a particular degree, Albany…The toast was drunk with musical honours……*
>
> *Major Young, in reply, said it was quite refreshing, and he was not at all sure that it did not make him feel a few years younger, to find himself hailed a "jolly good fellow" in Albany, where hitherto it had been usual to think he could not do anything that was not bad. He was sorry to say that he had to give a small lecture, as much misapprehension existed regarding the railway, and he would take this opportunity to try and remove some of the misconceptions. All present knew that he came to Albany to discharge a great work, requiring personal energy and the assistance and encouragement of all, which he did not receive; but he thought it was beginning to be understood that they were not as black as they had been painted. He would state a few facts. The railway was conceived by the late Mr Anthony Hordern, who came here and in conjunction with the people*

---

[15] *The Albany Mail and King George's Sound Advertiser.* 19th December 1888.

of Albany, formed certain schemes of which the speaker knew nothing, being at the time unconscious of the existence even of Mr Hordern, and knowing Albany only as a dot on a map. Mr Hordern, having become possessor of the railway contract and plans, he went to London to raise the capital for a company, and on these plans and details a company was formed, considerable difficulty being found in raising the necessary capital. At this stage, the company and the people of Albany came face to face...

If the railway proves a success Albany would be a town of great magnitude. Nature had given her what Fremantle could not secure by the expenditure of £1,000,000, namely a natural harbour, and there is every prospect of the town becoming a military and a coaling station. It must not, however, be forgotten that Fremantle and Perth are stronger and larger towns, so if Albany and the company study their own interests their policy is to take a "long pull, a strong pull, and a pull all together." He hoped that the time was not far distant when trains would be running daily to Perth, and returning with passengers, bringing prosperity to the town and its inhabitants.
At the conclusion of his speech, Major Young sat down amid prolonged applause... [16]

In 1896 after six and a half years of operation, the Great Southern Railway was purchased by the State Government and was incorporated into the West Australian Government Railway System. The purchase price paid at that time was £ 1 100 000 (approximately £146 000 000 today or $260 000 000)

The railway was a boon for travellers to Albany as this excited response indicates:
The circle of pleasure and invigoration at Albany being exhausted, the tourist can take a ticket for £2 15s 3d. and travel to Perth, 340 miles distant, by the newly constructed Beverley - Albany railway line, which is a continuation of the Government Railway.
New scenes are opened to view, new vistas of forest, of park-like lands, of sandy downs covered with short shrubs that in their seasons bear flower of every hue, and anon in summer, a glimpse of a dried-up sale lake is obtained gleaming through the foliage like the driven snow.

The first day's journey ends at Beverley; - stop-over privileges can be had, and the tourist can rusticate for a day at this little town. Here he may botanize, and gaze in wonder on trees that shed their bark annually instead of their leaves, whose smooth trunks tower upwards, and are crowned with small, thick, shining leaves arranged in parasol like groups....
Yours faithfully,
William Traylen,
Perth, W. A.[17]

Gilbert Parker, a visitor already mentioned was not shy in expressing his views about the town and some of the interesting activities he encountered in his travels. First on the Great Southern Railway:
I fancy I should not have visited Western Australia just now, had it not been that a railway was opened up between Albany and the capital. I had but a limited time to spare, and when I found that there was no longer the long coach ride of 350 miles to take, or the old coasting journey to undergo, I determined to attempt what, under other circumstances, might have been put off till a more convenient season. Western Australia is isolated now. What that isolation was before there was a railway, can only be understood properly by those who have been in the colony. Even now the place has a faraway feeling; an antique loneliness that ranges from the quay at King George's Sound to the Cambridge Gulf. It is but a step from the hotel to the railway station at Albany, and at 8 o'clock in the morning, I am off to Perth by a land grant railway...

As to the advantages which this West Australian railway company has gained, I cannot speak. I only know that it is a very excellent service and that the line is better constructed than the government line from Beverly to Fremantle, with which it connects, thus completing the communication between Albany and Perth. The carriages on the Company's line are excellently kept, and the guards and conductors are attentive and good-natured...[18]

---

[16] *The Albany Mail and King George's Sound Advertiser.* 6th June 1888.
[17] *The Daily News, Perth.* 6th March 1890.
[18] Parker, G. *Round the Compass in Australia.* London. 1893.

His further observations of the activities and living conditions of the sandal-wood cutters along the path of the track into the hinterland also make interesting reading:

The first thing that struck me was the number of tents erected along the line and a few houses that one saw. But I answered the question to myself immediately, for in my nostrils was a well-known perfume; one that I had inhaled in other lands, the "faint, sweet smell of the sandal tree." These tents were the homes of the sandalwood cutters. And here were the piles of sandalwood, hundreds of tons here, thousands of tons altogether, ready to be shipped to China for incense and for making into boxes. Thus, it is, that this new Southern civilisation provides the old orient with a means for preserving its heathenism...[19]

At one stage there was a significant controversy regarding the Great Southern Railway within the town precincts. A controversy that divided the town and was never fully resolved to everyone's satisfaction. The railway location had the effect of separating the town from The Princess Royal Harbour and thereby contributing to reduced recreational activity on the foreshore. *The West Australian* of Monday, 20th January 1890 outlined the issue:

District News. Albany.
From our Correspondent.
The York Street Crossing.
I am horribly afraid we have not heard the last of the York Street question. What better subject of contention that sit ½ of Albany against the other half. We had fondly hoped that the action taken in the matter by his Excellency the governor just before his departure for England, has successfully laid the dispute at rest forever. So much was this the case that it was reported that Mr Otto, the local photographer, had received instructions to photograph a group of the town champions in the street controversy, posed near the obstructive rails. And another group of the same heroes on the site of the of the objectionable railings, after their removal. However, though the first group may have taken for all I know it does not mean at all certain the time has yet arrived for taking the second. It's now just a month since Sir Napier Broome's order regarding the opening of York and Spencer Street, and Mr Wright interview with the local Municipal Council seemed to have happily decided the difficulty. But the obstructions are still standing, and very considerable dissatisfaction is felt in consequence, and there are signs that if the obnoxious barriers are not soon removed, there will be a renewal of the old strife.[20]

The issue still rankled some sections of the community and a follow-up article in *The West Australian*, Saturday 5th July captured the feelings.

From our correspondent. (By Telegraph.)
The Hon. C.T. Mason met the Municipal Council last night, with respect to the "crossings question". He gave the council distinctly to understand that he had no power to order any alterations, now that the Railways Amendment Act had been disallowed. He also said that he considered the crossings at York and Spencer Streets, all that was necessary, and as 'good and safe' as any crossings in the colony. The council was disgusted at being defeated and wanted to know what was the use of meeting Mr Mason if he could do nothing for them. They suggested that an appeal should be made to the secretary of state.[21]

About two miles from Albany, on the west side of the town, the railway foundry and workshops were situated. They occupied 10 acres of land and contained among the workshops large wagon and blacksmith establishments with premises for machine and foundry operations. All the engines and wagons engaged on the Great Southern Railway were overhauled there, and all necessary repairs to them effected. The foundry and workshop areas created work opportunities for a large number of mechanical engineers and labourers in the town further adding to its prosperity. It was indeed a boon to the town at the time and its future looked indeed very bright. That was until the Premier John Forrest decided to move the railway workshops out of Albany to Midland on the outskirts of Perth in 1904 while also consolidating these facilities by moving the smaller Fremantle workshop to the same site.

---

[19] Ibid. p.371.
[20] *The West Australian.* 20th January 1890.
[21] *The West Australian.* 5th July 1890.

Closing Remarks

There was an expectation that the various Australian State Governments would continue to operate the railways that were built by their Colonial Governments predecessors in the Nineteenth Century. This was most definitely the case in Western Australia when initially it was the Colonial Government that secured the purchase of the Great Southern Railway from the West Australian Lands Company that had been established by Anthony Hordern.

While the original Great Southern Railway and associated infrastructure was constructed and operated by a private enterprise consortium that was registered as the Western Australian Lands Company, the railway was subsequently purchased by the Colonial Government and then responsibility was assumed by the State Government when Western Australia received Responsible Government status in 1890.

The advent of an effective rail network between Albany and Beverley and then between Albany and Denmark enabled much of the Great Southern hinterland to be opened up for settlement and agriculture particularly grain and sheep grazing adding further to the town's importance and economic prosperity, as much of this produce was exported through the town's port facilities. It also fostered the creation of a number of towns along its route including Katanning, Broomehill, Tambellup and consolidated the settlement of Mount Barker.

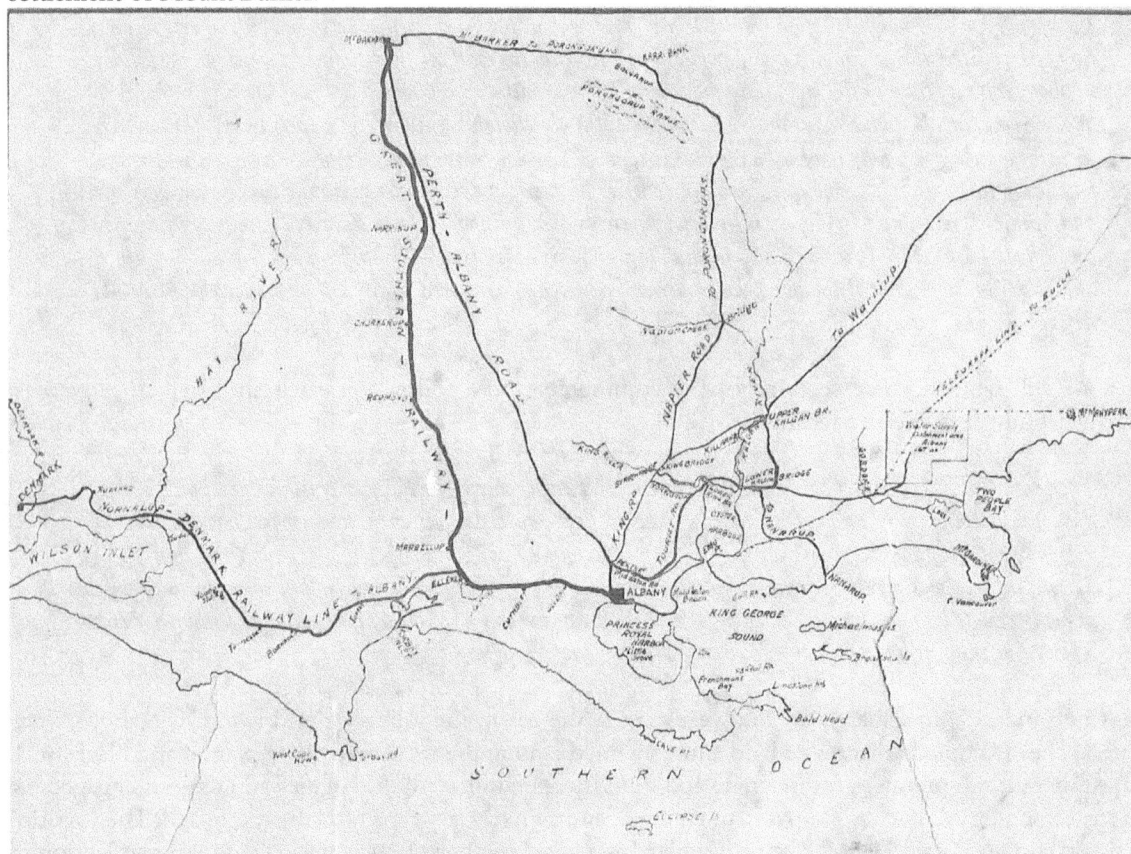

Map of the Railway Routes to Mt Barker and Denmark

CHAPTER 11
THE ROYAL MAIL AND THE POST OFFICE

Overview

Albany was not well served with public buildings in the mid-Nineteenth Century with Government concerns like the Post Office, HM Customs facilities, Bond Store and Courthouse being located in rented accommodation throughout the town. For example, the first Postal Officer in Albany was Mrs Sarah Lyttleton the town doctor's wife, who held the honorary position of postmistress from October 14th 1834 until July of the following year when she resigned from the position. She had operated the Post Office, as it was then, from her own home as a service for the town's people. It was not until 1837 that the position of Postmaster became a paid position in Albany. The first paid Postmaster was Edward Spencer, son of the Resident Magistrate, Sir Richard Spencer. As there was not a purpose-built government-owned Post Office building at this time and until the building of a permanent mail facility was constructed in the town, it was the Postmaster's store or shop or, in one case, his private house, that doubled as the local Post Office.

Mail from Perth delivered to the port of Albany was carried between Bunbury and Albany a journey that normally took five days by horse, with the driver then resting to 3 days before completing the return journey. The task of delivering the mail over such a large distance was exacerbated by the need to cross many rivers and creeks during the journey. The degree of difficulty undertaking the journey was as a consequence very dependent on seasonal weather factors. As was reported that:

> *In the dry season, the water rarely came above the saddle girth; however, in winter, swimming the rivers was a hazardous venture, and on one occasion reported the mail bags were lost and one of the drivers nearly drowned.*[1]

There were times of apprehension within the community when the expected mail delivery from Albany did not arrive at its terminus in Bunbury within an anticipated period of time. For example, *The Inquirer* reported of one such occasion when in 1847 after a particularly wet winter there was a concern for the safety of the post's contractor who was long overdue and had not been seen. A search party was organised to look for him and it was subsequently reported that:

> *Serious apprehensions having been entertained at Bunbury for Mr Watson, who was more than three weeks over-due on his return with the Sound mail, Mr Eliot, on the 16th instant, sent out a party, under Mr Hester, to proceed to Kojenup [sic] in search of him. Happily, they met Mr Watson on the following night about 20 miles from Bunbury, and he arrived there on the 18th, much exhausted by the difficulties he had encountered. It appears that he was 17 days on his journey to the Sound, having been detained 5 days at the Gordon before he could cross that river, and had been 21 days in reaching Bunbury on his return. He describes the country as being much inundated, and the rivers running with almost resistless force.*[2]

Delays in the transport of the mails from King George's Sound caused by inclement weather were a continued threat to its timely delivery. As reported in *The Inquirer* from August 1849 Royal Mail bags being transported from Albany had been lost on two occasions within a couple of months. In one instance the regular delivery contractor was too ill to undertake the task and had therefore employed a replacement driver from the settlement. During the return trip from Albany, this driver placed the mail bags too close to his campfire at night which resulted in the loss of the mail. A further mishap reported occurred when the delivery contractor, in attempting a passage across the Blackwood River, had the misfortune of seeing the girth straps on his horse break with the subsequent loss of not only his saddle but the mail bags as well.[3]

Prior to the completion of the Albany to Perth Road the post was taken to Bunbury via Kojonup as a more suitable track existed between these settlements than between Albany and Perth. However, once the Perth Road was completed with the assistance of convict labour, a more direct route for the mail service was possible.

---

[1] *Stanley Gibbons Monthly Journal*. December 1923.
[2] *The Inquirer*. Perth, 25th August 1847.
[3] *The Inquirer*. Perth, 22nd August 1849.

When the colony once again became a convict station in 1852 a police escort was occasionally employed to provide for the long-haul Albany to Perth mail conveyance by horse and coach. Initially, the mail journey took between 16 and 17 days but familiarity with the route eventually enabled a mail run to be concluded in six days:

> *The road was not good, and it was estimated at the time that constructing a road between Perth and King George's Sound, suitable to allow the four-horse mail coach to travel at 10 miles an hour, would take eight years and be prohibitively expensive*[4]

The remuneration offered to Postmasters was quite meagre and consequently few residents cared to accept the responsibility associated with the role. On March 22nd 1848 Governor Fitzgerald had suggested to the Legislative Council the propriety of establishing a fee structure similar to South Australia with a low rate of postage for short distances increasing with the extent to which each letter was to be conveyed. Instead of adopting this plan, the Legislative Council decided to increase the rate on those letters carried by shipping services.

Governor Fitzgerald tried as an experiment the use of local Aboriginals as postmen. He noted that:

> *"When they were not on duty they went back to being 'puris naturalibus'".*[5]

Fitzgerald expressed his opinion on the 10th February 1849, that:

> *It was perfectly hopeless to give the Aborigines book learning, but they might be taught industrial habits and with that possibility, he had sent 5 to serve in the industrial schooner, two to the pilot boat, and two with the harbourmaster, and no less than 5 to take colonies postal communications which they performed with the utmost punctuality.*
>
> *It was noted ... that the expenditure was considerably reduced by the internal mails being principally conveyed by native carriers.*[6]

Governor Fitzgerald then attempted to get around the difficulty and cost of improving the Albany to Perth overland route by dispatching the Royal Mail by sea from Albany to Perth, but the Government vessel proved unequal to performing this task. In another move born out of frustration Fitzgerald decided in an endeavour to make the mail coach become a cost-neutral service to allow it to take one passenger on each both its inwards and outwards journeys:

> *On November 6, 1848, the Overland Mail started by taking one passenger from Perth via Mandurah, Australind, and Bunbury then on to Albany at a cost of 5 pounds, with the return journey costing 8 pounds.*[7]

Finally, after much procrastination it was determined that given the denseness of vegetation separating Albany from Perth and that transport by sea although more convenient was still a hazardous option, the colonial administration decided that the time had come to improve the road:

> *"I have,"* writes the Governor, *"employed two parties, one of Ticket of Leave men and the other of colonial prisoners, in June 1853, to the very arduous job of bridging all the rivers and opening and making a good line of road, 300 miles in extent."*
>
> *In a year, in spite of great difficulties, especially in keeping parties supplied with provisions and reconciling them to salt rations, which had to be conveyed on several occasions more than 120 miles, the road was opened and the six bridges bridged above the influence of flood except for the Gordon, which is now in hand. Wills are sunk at convenient distances, so at the height of the dry summers, the mail carrier goes monthly in his tandem cart without any other inconvenience in the absence of inhabitants along the line, and, consequently, no places of refreshment or shelter.*[8]

In a report received by the Legislative Council in 1854, it was noted that the rivers between Perth and Albany had been bridged and a road had been marked out by Francis Thomas Gregory, Government Surveyor, and cleared through as far as the Gordon River. A *Perth Gazette* article outlined for its readers the

---

[4] Ibid
[5] Ibid
[6] Ibid.
[7] Ibid.
[8] *Minutes of Western Australia Proceedings of the Legislative Council*. 4th May 1854.

difficulties that had been faced in provisioning both the men and horse teams involved. The paper also praised their efforts in constructing the track within a short period:

This road was commenced in June last by two parties, not averaging together more than 70 working men; the ticket-of-leave party was under Mr Henry Gregory, and the Colonial prisoners (generally sailors and Natives) under Mr Vincent, yet with such questionable instruments in comparison with the magnitude of the work, the road was opened in the month of October, 14 months after its commencement, to the mail carrier, who now says he can travel the whole distance from Kojenup [sic] to Perth, a distance of 150 miles, in three and a half days without injury to his horses.[9]

The new road from Perth to Albany along what was termed the 'Gregory Line' opened in 1853. During that year bridges were commenced over the King and Kalgan Rivers under the supervision of Lieutenant William Crossman.[10] Six bridges were constructed in a year on the Perth Road due to a massive joint effort by ticket-of-leave men and colonial prisoners and except for the Gordon River, it was reported that all were above the annual flood levels.

The route to Albany via this 'track' was still not without its difficulties, especially in the winter months, when large tracts of land became flooded. Over the following years, there were varying reports of the quality and reliability of the mail service between Perth and Albany. An article published in 1856, entitled 'Twins Born in the Bush', reveals the difficulties facing passengers, especially the women:

One of the female passengers by the mail cart from Albany was suddenly taken ill during the journey, and it was discovered that she was in labour. She was removed from the cart and left with her husband in the bush, the mail cart proceeding on its journey. In due time the patient was safely delivered of twins. Luckily a house was distant only 14 miles from the place, and the mail carrier having informed the occupants of what had occurred, a cart was sent down to convey the husband, wife, and the two little strangers thus far on their journey. They all safely arrived at the Canning, and mother and children are doing well.[11]

Royal Mail and the Advent of Steam Ships

From 1852 until the end of the century Albany enjoyed the prestige of being the colony's first port of call for overseas passengers, freight and Royal Mails bought by steamship. This pre-eminent position was only superseded when Fremantle port began its operations and assumed responsibility for the mail deliveries in 1900.

In 1852 the first Royal Mail delivery originating from England was landed at the Albany port facilities from the Royal Mail Steam Navigation Company's vessel *Australian*. After unloading the mail, it was then repackaged and loaded on to pack horses for its long journey to Perth. This initial steamship mail delivery was then followed a month later by the first P&O steamer to visit Australia, *Chusan* which collected its Royal Mail, passengers and cargo from Singapore.

In 1861 the Stirling Terrace roadworks were deemed to have been completed to an acceptable standard. York Street was finally completed to the same standard in 1870. As Stirling Terrace offered the best location for postal and HM Customs services due to its proximity to the harbour and port facilities, including the then town jetty, it was identified as the most suitable location to construct desired government office facilities. The Government had purchased a house and inn in Stirling Terrace as temporary accommodation for these offices, formerly known as Daniel's Hotel, but as the location was an inconvenient distance from the then town jetty could only be used as a stop-gap measure. Consequently, it became evident that a new office complex building was required in the town to meet the growing demand for particularly postal and customs facilities. Sir Alexander Thomas Cockburn Campbell Bt, was the Government Resident at the time and he initiated a proposal for more substantive facilities and recommended the creation of a Post Office, Customs Office and Court House complex.

---

[9] *The Perth Gazette*, 5th May 1854.
[10] Sir William Crossman was in charge of various public works in Australia from 1852 to 1856 and became a Magistrate at Albany.
[11] *The Inquirer*. Perth, 20th February 1856.

Dr John Stephen Hampton, the Western Australian Governor in 1862 was particularly supportive of the plan.

In 1863 the decision was made to construct a building that would meet the town's growing requirements for these services. A site was subsequently chosen on the south side of Stirling Terrace. Nonetheless, it was not until l866 that the concept gained enough traction for the purpose-built facility to go ahead, Tenders were called in 1867 and the building of a three-story complex commenced in 1868 using convict labour sent from Fremantle for the purpose. The building was opened and occupied in 1869.[12] The original plans entailed a HM Customs store located on a lower level adjacent to The Princess Royal Harbour, nearest the jetty and with the second story to be entered from Spencer Street housing the Post Office, mail-sorting room, general customs house and a caretaker's quarters. The third level was entered from Stirling Terrace and was to be occupied by the courthouse, Magistrate's office, prisoners' room and jury room. This original building complex was extended in 1895-96.[13]

Initially, it was the police who were given the responsibility for the transportation of the Royal and general mail to Perth via a specially constructed wagon for the purpose. A question was subsequently posed to the editor of the local paper which asked whether it was or should be, the police officers' duty to carry the mail from the point of delivery at the lower level of the building to the top floor on Stirling Terrace. The replay was very straightforward:

> *A correspondent writes asking if the police are supposed to do the work of the post office officials, in carrying the mail bags up the hill to the mail van? It appears that the coach used to be driven down the hill below the post office and the mails lowered to it from the Veranda. Inspector Hare considering that it was not a good thing for the horses in starting away to have to make a rush and a jerk to get the cumbrous coach up the hill, ordered them to be drawn up in Stirling Terrace and the mail bags carried from the post office to it. This we understand was done merely in the interest of the horses, so that they should not have to make the hardest pool in the whole journey at the start. The police have always assisted the postal officials to load the van and it may be a little heavy at work to carry up the bags, but if the police feel aggrieved, they complain to the superintendent, and we think they are quite able to take care of themselves without any outsider construing himself as their champion.*[14]

In May 1841 the Royal Mail bags from King George's Sound were dispatched by way of a cart, on the first day of each month and the journey took approximately 12 days to complete. By 1867 the coaches travelling the direct route to Perth were able to reduce this travelling time to three and a half days each way. In 1875 the Police Department had taken over the conveyance of mails with a twice-weekly delivery in a van drawn by four horses.[15] In April 1880 two coaches of the Cobb and Company style were delivered from the Eastern States for the commencement of the police mail service run Albany to Perth. The Albany to Perth route required 36 horses with the service now running fortnightly instead of monthly. Local police stations along the route became changeover locations for fresh teams and prisoners were tasked with grooming and feeding the horses.[16]

On the 23rd June 1884, the first mail delivery service started in Albany with the first pillar box installed at the corner of York Street and Albany Highway. The last mail coach left in June 1889 and after that mails

---

[12] D. Garden in *Albany: Panorama of the Sound* indicates that the building was occupied in 1870 whereas Robert Stephens from the Albany Historical Society maintained that it was occupied in 1869.
[13] State Library of Western Australia document. *The Albany Post Office Complex.* Reference b2399141-5.
[14] *The Albany Mail and King Georges Sound Advertiser.* 22nd May 1886.
[15] Photograph courtesy of Mark Saxton coordinator Albany Historical Society photographic collection.
[16] *Inquirer and Commercial News.* Perth, 13th February 1889.

were dispatched by train; the journey taking only 18 hours. A specially modified wagon on the Great Southern Railway was fitted up for the sorting of mail on route to Perth. 1895 saw the opening of the telephone exchange in the building.[17]

A Purpose-Built Post Office

In 1867, after six years urging by the Government Resident, Sir Alexander Cockburn-Campbell, the Clerk of Works, Mr John Manning, was instructed to draw plans to house a post office, courthouse, municipal and road board meeting rooms, and customs house; and in 1868 the building was commenced. It was from this building that the Intercontinental Telegraph Line was started on January 1, 1875, when Governor Weld planted the first post which is to be seen outside this building today. The building was completed in December 1869.

Before 1877 one officer served as Postmaster and sub-collector of HM Customs at Albany, but on 1st January of that year, the two roles became separate identities and occupied by different personnel.[18] In June 1921 *The Albany Advertiser* carried an article celebrating the career of John Norman, who had just retired from the role of Postmaster after 44 years of service. The paper interviewed him, and some extracts of that interview are included here:

Mails were received from England and from the Eastern States once a month by the P&O mail steamer, while from Perth there was a monthly mail by coach to meet the steamer from England and also a monthly service by the steamer Georgette, *to connect with the mail steamer from the Eastern States. There was also mail for letters only to Perth and towns en route once every four weeks, carried by mounted police. After the* Georgette *was wrecked near Busselton the coastal service was carried on by the* Rob Roy *and* Lubra *the last name vestal meeting with exceptionally heavy weather on one trip, taking five days to do the voyage and missing the mail steamer here… later a monthly steam service was established between Fremantle and the Eastern States, the steamers* Otway *and* Macedon *being used. This meant, of course, more frequent mails.*

The mails from England were always made up in separate bags for Perth and Albany and the coach had to be dispatched with the Perth portion within two hours of the steamer's arrival. The whole of the mails from the Eastern States had to be sorted here and the coastal steamer despatched not later than six hours after their receipt, and usually, an extra hand had to be employed to help with the sorting.[19]

It was not until 1895 that construction of an eighty-foot clocktower and arched doorways to the western portion of the building was added with the assistance of the famous architect George Temple Poole.[20] The original Post Office which faced Spencer Street occupied only one story of the three-storied building, with the HM Customs House occupying the lowest level, the Post Office on the second floor and the Courtroom the top story. It was from this site that the mails were collected and despatched.

For Want of Service

This letter to the editor of *The Western Australian* in 1889 expresses a gripe about the quality of the service then being offered by the Albany Post Office:

---

[17] *Albany. Western Australia The First Hundred Years. 1791-1891*. D.A.P. West. *The Albany Advertiser* 1932.
[18] Sketch of the Early Post Office by E. Bracey, The Albany History Collection, Albany Town Library.
[19] *The Albany Advertiser*. 1st June 1921.
[20] George Temple Poole was a British architect who worked in Western Australia from 1885. He was the colony's principal architect during its gold boom. Poole assisted in the formation of the Western Australian Institute of Architects. He designed aspects of the Albany Post Office and Courthouse as well as the Albany Cottage Hospital.

> *Sir,*
> *I think it would be a considerable advantage… If the Post Office Department would return to the old system of bringing the mail from Albany by the mail van instead of the railway. Through the delay at Beverly, in any case, it takes two days to carry a mail from Albany to Perth: but when we add to this the delay at Albany, and the constant blundering of the Post Office Department, we are now very much worse served then we had the mails conveyed by horses.*
>
> *Within the past few weeks, we had frequent instances of the mail being in Albany four days before they reach Perth, a length of time much in excess of the time occupied by the mail cart. And on two occasions we have had our mails for the colonies delayed more than a week in Albany, having been too late for the steamer. We are, in many respects, a very long-suffering people, but surely there is a limit; and if the colonists are willing to enjoy the present state of things, all I say is, they deserve it. It is to be hoped that some member of the Legislative Council will call attention to our mail service between Perth and Albany: I am sure a parallel will not be found in any other part of Her Majesties dominions.*
>
> *Yours,*
> *Long-suffering.*[21]

And another comment with a similar highly critical perspective of the service that was being offered in the town:

> *We went to the Post Office at 4 o'clock in the afternoon but to our great surprise it was closed as it regularly closes about that hour but our surprise was not yet complete – we would hardly believe that it was not a practical joke, - when we read a notice in the window, to the effect that letters and papers would not be delivered from the window to persons residing within a mile of the office.*
>
> *The whole workings of the Post and Telegraph Office are very inconvenient for the public, and the sooner the Government makes laws and regulations for carrying on this most important business of the colony, in accordance with those of other parts of the civilised world, the better it will be for Albany and the rest of the colony. We leave the Post Office for the present, as we shall have more to say about this matter when we come to the description of the people and their mode of carrying on business, so will first have another look at the scenery around the town.*[22]

In 1879 an article was published in the *South Australian Chronicle* by a correspondent who offered an unflattering description of his travels in the West by mail coach:

> *The coach carrying the English Mails between Perth and Albany is what you would scarcely expect to see in a civilized neighbourhood. It resembles a very dilapidated vegetable cart and does the distance of 200 miles in the remarkably short time of 72 hours.*[23]

The Last Mail Coach

The year 1888 ushered in a whole new era when in August the mail was first carried by train, on a private railway line constructed between Albany and Beverley. Up until that time the Albany to Perth mail service had had an interesting history, undertaken variously by private contractors, Aboriginals, the Police Department and later by Government employees. Many anecdotes have been related through the colonial newspapers of the dangers and discomforts faced by the drivers and their passengers, who took up the challenge of travelling in the early days before the completion of the Albany to Perth Road, along narrow unformed roads. Such a memoir is provided in an article published in an 1888 edition of *The Albany Mail and King George's Sound Advertiser*:

> *The overland mail coach left on its last journey to Perth from Albany on Saturday afternoon. Up to 1879, the mails had been carried by private contract but in December of that year Sir Harry Ord, the then Governor of West Australia, instituted the system of the Government mail coach service horsed by the police. Mr John Chipper drove the first mail coach and was afterwards joined on the box by his brother Mr Harry Chipper,*

---

[21] *The West Australian*, October 30, 1889.
[22] A Visitors Views of Albany as reported by a Correspondent for *The Albany Mail*, 1888.
[23] *West Australian Times*, 26th August 1879.

and these two well-known and expert drivers have handled the ribbons ever since in "tooling" Her Majesty's Royal Mail van over the road from the capital to the shores of Princess Royal Harbour. In the old days before 1879 Messrs., Chipper and Horton had carried on the mail contract for nearly 28 years, one partner being the father of the afterwards noted Jehus.

It is said that at first starting the mails the horses always gave trouble and were "itchy" in getting to work, but since the brother's Chipper appeared on the scene the fortnightly mail service has been carried on with remarkable easiness and in good time.

The old service was a monthly one only, and the coach lumbered on at a very slow rate, so that when the new arrangements were made nine years ago it was quite felt that marvellous progress was being made, and he would have been a bold man who would at that time have prophecied that the iron horse would run the one of flesh and blood off the track within a decade.

A curious coincidence is attached to the first and last trip of the overland mail. Mr Howard, an Inspector of Police, was the first passenger carried by the coach from Perth to Albany, and his brother Mr Ernest Howard was the only passenger carried on the last trip the whole distance, whilst we believe Sergt. Cunningham assisted in loading at Perth the first bag of mails that were carried and also helped to hoist in the last one that left Albany. There were not many spectators to attend the last despatch of the old coach, but the Commissioner of police and Mrs Smith assisted at the ceremony; being present in a waggonette, and Mr Otto took a photograph of the conveyance before its departure. And so, another era passeth away, viz that of the coaching days.[24]

Mysterious 'Alcove' Under the Old Post Office

As an aside, in researching eyewitness accounts of Albany's chequered mail service history there was an interesting note made of an article that appeared in *The Albany Advertiser* in 1936 that concerned an examination of the construction processes employed in building the Albany Post Office. The article was headed "Albany Catacombs Under the Old Post Office".

It needs to be explained that the editor was perhaps using the word 'catacombs' as a metaphor as it gives a quite misleading impression. The term catacomb refers to an underground cemetery consisting of a subterranean gallery with recesses for tombs, as constructed for example by the ancient Romans. The alcove under the Old Post Office does not resemble such a structure in any way.

The Albany Catacombs Under the Old Post Office
The cables a few days ago announced the discovery of a new catacomb under Rome. Not many Albany people know of the catacombs under the local post office. We only heard of them a few days ago, and we are fortunate enough to be allowed to explore them, under the proper supervision. We mention the supervision because to get into the dungeons, it's necessary to pass through the Bonds Store of the Customs Department, where there is usually a quantity of material stored, set material being in barrels and bottles. Some of it, it is rumoured, has been there for many, many years, and must buy now have acquired a Bouquet that would make a can connoisseurs nose wrinkle with pressure. But that is a mere digression.

Possibly, among the older of the old residence Albany, there may be some who remember the construction of the Post Office and Customs House. Probably they could tell a quite interesting story about it. Legend has it that the bottom portion, now used as a Bond Sore, was at one time a prison, either for civil or military prisoners. Long, narrow windows, guarded with massive iron bars give point to that belief… It never really occurred to us to worry about the point before, but has anyone ever decided which is the back and which is the front of the Post Office building? Anyway, there is the cloister, some 20 to 30 feet below the main entrance of the Post Office, a man-made cave into which the light of day never penetrates. On the one side is it 3 feet foundation wall of the main building, with its long, narrow, heavily barred slits of windows, and on the other a massive wall, set at a slight slope, which apparently acts as a retaining wall for the portion of Stirling Terrace opposite Spencer Street.

A good deal of mystery attaches to this place, but the indications are rather that one time the now dark and noisome cloister was open to the sky. If not, why trouble to pierce those massive walls with windows, they would

---

[24] *Albany Mail and King George's Sound Advertiser.* 1st August 1888.

certainly admit no light, and they would be little use for ventilation? Another thing. Although the walls are hidden completely, they are finished as for the outside walls, with squared stones at the corners and all joints elaborately tuck-pointed, just as in the wall facing to the Lower Terrace. The theory is held at one time what is now the Customs House and Post Office may have been a gaol or barracks one story in height and with that sunken alleyway on the northern side, used as a sentry walk, or as an exercise yard for the inmates. Behind the massive retaining wall is now solid earth which underlies Stirling Terrace, but that it may not always have been so suggested by several archways in the wall, now walled up, but apparently at some time having served as doorways. One noticeable feature of all this buried masonry is its high standard of craftsmanship. Walls of this type are not often built nowadays; the cost would be far too high. Along the gloomy cloister runs the gurgling stream of water, welling up from the ground in little springs, and running along a rough drain in the middle of the passageway, to find an exit at the eastern end of the building. The drain is a comparatively modern innovation, but the water has evidently been flowing through the building for a long time, for the floor of the Bond Store has several openings, filled with broken stone. At one time, he said the water used to get away through these, but in exceptionally wet times, it would overflow, and run out over the floor. Although that portion of the old building still holds its communion with the days of long ago, another portion of the basement floor has been put to use that its builders never envisaged. It serves as a garage for the brand-new utility motor truck...[25]

Closing Remarks

Albany's association with HM Customs, the Colonial and Royal Mail service played an important part in the town's history. Next to the later development of the Great Southern Railway the management and responsibility for the Colonial and Royal Mail operating through the port was one of Albany's most important public utilities at the time. As the collection point for the delivery and despatch of both Royal and Colonial Mails from shipping that was in transit from Europe to the Eastern States and vice versa, the town had a significant role in both the sorting and transporting of the mail to Perth and the hinterland as well as preparing the colony's return mail for similar despatch. As the frequency of Royal Mail ships into the port increased so did the town's responsibility and importance as Western Australia's link in this service grew. It was only when Fremantle became the colony's designated port for HM Customs and Royal Mail deliveries that Albany's importance with respect to this role was significantly diminished.

---

[25] *The Albany Advertiser.* 20th August 1938.

CHAPTER 12
HEALTH FACILITIES AND DEVELOPMENT OF THE ALBANY HOSPITAL

A Need for Improved Hospital Facilities Identified

Without the provision of private hospital facilities, by default, it fell to the administration of the settlement to provide for the rudiments of healthcare. There was the initial claim that King George's Sound's mild climate would be a boon to those with some identified health conditions or weakness. As indicated previously one theory is that Patrick Taylor immigrated to King George's Sound to remedy a weak health disposition.

A makeshift hospital facility was constructed in 1829 at Residency Point in the new settlement to accommodate the sick and further, to isolate them from the rest of the population. It was a one-room building attached to the Albany gaol constructed of wattle and daub with provision limited to quite primitive facilities by today's standards. Records indicate that it contained a surgeon's house, infirmary and 'a few bunks'.

Medical care had been devolved to the colonial surgeons who were poorly reimbursed for the work that they undertook within the settlement. As can be expected the responsibility that accompanied this role took a significant toll on the health and well-being of the doctors. For example, in 1867 a concern was raised by the Resident Magistrate, Sir Alexander Cockburn Campbell Bt, with the Colonial Secretary concerning the mental health of the then Albany surgeon, Dr Baesjou.

Resident's Office
Albany, 20th September 1867.

Sir,
The friends and relatives of Doctor Baesjou have requested me to submit his present mental and bodily state of health, and the apparent hopelessness of such amendment as might enable him again to undertake his medical duties, to the favourable consideration of his Excellency the Governor.
…Dr Baesjou's State of health and will only say that he himself believes he will never be able to resume his profession and is consequently greatly distressed in thinking of the unprovided state, in which he, and his family of wife and five children, must soon find themselves.

This is the case in which nothing but pecuniary assistance can be of any avail, the loss of the use of one side of his body from paralysis rendering any other occupation as impractical as his own. Dr Baesjou's anxiety renders amelioration of his state more difficult that his mind was addressed; and I, therefore, trust his Excellency the governor may be able to hold out some hope of at least an absence of destitution should no amendment take place.[1]

I have the honour to be Sir
Your Very Obedient Servant,
A. Cockburn Campbell

After a series of communications between the Resident Magistrate and Perth, the Surgeon General of the Swan River Colony, after examining the case, responded on the 4th October that:

I concur in believing with Dr Rosa Lottie but there is a serious and organic disease of the nervous centres, that it is very unlikely that Dr Baesjou's life will be prolonged over a few, perhaps a very few, months…

In all probability, therefore, a pension to Dr Baesjou would only be paid once, and a gratuity according to the length of service would best meet the requirements of the case and be to his family the safest mood of receiving any recompense for his services…

Brinsley Nicholson, M. D.
Surgeon General.[2]

---

[1] Aveling, M. *Westralian Voices*. University of Western Australia Press, 1979.
[2] Ibid.

Unfortunately, correspondence from the Resident Magistrate's Office of the 3rd October 1867 informed the Colonial Secretary that:

> *Honourable Colonial Secretary*
> *Perth*
>
> *Sir,*
> *I have the honour to inform you that I was the night before last called by Reverend Mr McSorley as stated, that Dr Baesjou had cut his throat. An inquest was held the following morning when it appeared, that ever since Mr Rossellotty's arrival at Albany, if not previously, Dr Baesjou has been quite insane. He had made two previous attempts at self-destruction, one with opium, the other with the lancet. His surgery door was then locked, razors, knives, etc. taken out of his way, but the lancet seems to have been unfortunately overlooked...*[3]
> *I have the honour to be Sir*
> *Your Very Obedient Servant,*
> *A. Cockburn Campbell.*

Tuberculosis was also a major concern in the Nineteenth Century. The promise of relief of this ailment in the mild climate of King George Sound did much to influence many to immigrate.

Agitation for Better Facilities

At a public meeting in 1886, there was a call for the Resident Magistrate Rowley Crozier Loftie to seek from the Colonial Government the necessary funding to establish a more appropriate hospital facility for the town. A growth in population through increased ship traffic through the port due to the gold rush highlighted the need for improved hospital facilities to replace the makeshift 'eyesore' that was seen as a blight on the town. Local townspeople were adamant that the gaol annexe hospital was not a fitting facility for Albany. The long process of petitioning the Governor and Legislative Council for funding was gathering momentum:

> *The following petition is being sent around for signatures.*
> *The increasing importance of the town of Albany and the continual stream of passengers en route in the various steamers calling at our port, the coming influx of the immigrants that are about to be introduced to settle the land of railways syndicate, and the number of hands that will shortly be employed on the railway works, necessitates the establishment of a suitable hospital in Albany.*
>
> *We, your humble petitioners, therefore, pray that you will cause to be placed on the estimates, to be submitted to your honourable legislative council, a sufficient some just afraid the cost of erecting and maintaining a hospital in Albany.*
>
> *We beg to point out to your Excellency that the present place used as a hospital is in the precinct of the gaol, and is merely a single room with a few bunks, at which it can hardly be expected that patients would recover very rapidly...*
>
> *We believe, therefore, that the hospital in Albany would be largely supported by paying patients, who would take the opportunity afforded to obtain skilled nursing, and medical attendance on the spot, especially taking advantage of our salubrious climate, which would attract those whose health requires recruiting, if they could do so without incurring any great expense. We, therefore, consider that the cost of maintenance of the hospital we are now asking your Excellency to have money set apart for, would not be great, and in course of time would be almost a reproductive institution, burdening the government with a very small proportion of the cost of its upkeep.*[4]

The proceedings of the Legislative Council were keenly followed by the local press which reported:

> *The session of the Legislative Council being now close at hand the people of the district are exercising themselves as to what works out to be undertaken by the government. For many years Albany has not received a fair share of the money spent by the government, in proportion to the revenue collected from the district, from customs duties, land rents and sales and all other sources...*

---

[3] Ibid.
[4] *The Albany Mail and King Georges Sound Advertiser.* 22nd of May 1886.

> *The inhabitants of this town are asking for Hospital to be erected, to afford sufficient accommodation compatible with the increasing importance of Albany. The want of a proper hospital has been long Felt, and if Geraldton is to have one, Albany is entitled to a like advantage.*
>
> *There are in fact more arguments in favour of Albany as a site for a hospital than Geraldton. Albany is the port of call for the mail steamers and recently two patients have been brought ashore to die and had to be taken to a hotel. Now if Albany had a local hospital, worthy of the name, invalid passengers would constantly break their journey here and take advantage of such an institution, to recruit their health, at the same time paying for their residence and attendance.[5]*

As a response to the petitioners on their submission for improved hospital facilities an offer was made by the Legislative Council of a 'cottage system' to replace the existing facilities at Residency Point:

> *To the Chairman Local Progress Committee Albany*
>
> *Dear Sir,*
> *I've just received your letter of 28 June…*
> *I should be kept recapitulate the subject brought under my notice with the steps, if any, taken in regard to them. One. Hospital accommodation for Albany. Provision will be made for immediate requirements on the 'cottage system', admitting of indefinite expansion. The Geraldton hospital to which reference has been made is utterly condemned and the 'cottage system' advocated as infinitely preferable in principle.*
> *Sir Thomas Cockburn-Campbell.[6]*

In the local news section of the newspaper the following snippet of information was printed:

> *Local Intelligence.*
> *The site that was chosen for the erection of the proposed new hospital turns out to be private ground, and the new site will have to be selected.[7]*

As a consequence, the planned for improvements to Albany's hospital development were delayed:

> *… If the W.A. Land company are the proprietors of all the grounds suitable for custom goods sheds they do not own all the building sites in about the town appropriately situated for the direction of a hospital, and yet we appear as far from being supplied with the one need as the other. The authorities evidently credit Albany with enjoying a remarkably healthy climate, or they would highly consider that the Hospital requirements of the town were efficiently met by the accommodation at present available of one little room containing for little beds; and whilst taking our hats off to the implied compliment paid to the sanitation of the town by this arrangement for the sick, we would remind the heads of the medical and public works department that the town has lately suffered severely from an epidemic of enteric fever, which, if there had been hospital provision sufficient to accommodate those who were first attacked, might prove less fatal than has been the case.*
>
> *… yet this particular fever, which is at present prevalent, does appear to be contagious in a degree and it is possible that a patient taken to the hospital, and predisposed by weakness and ill-health to catch an infection, would suffer from being cooped up with the fever patients in the wretched little apology for Hospital that Albany possesses…[8]*

A further update with some 'local intelligence' supplied by the newspaper followed up on the hospital matter:

> *Local Intelligence.*
> *The readers will be pleased to hear that there is a prospect of the hospital; direction of which we have so constantly urged, being commenced at once.[9]*

---

[5] Ibid.
[6] Ibid. 10th July 1886.
[7] Ibid. 29th January 1887.
[8] *The Albany Mail and King George Sound Advertiser.* 30th April 1887.
[9] Ibid. 4th June 1887.

Of interest is a memorandum distributed to health practitioners by Governor Napier Broome at the time of Queen Victoria's Jubilee in 1887 that provided a Government perspective on the categorisation of patients. It indicated that those accessing a public hospital facility, whether convicts or those of 'paupers' status were treated with basic rudimentary cover, whereas those community members with means, termed "respectable", were treated in their own home. His memorandum indicated that:

I think that arrangements should be made, by the departments concerned, to render 21 June, the day of her majesties Jubilee, a day, as far as possible, of relaxation, and even within proper limits of pleasure, in every public institution in which men or women are domiciled and maintained at the public expense. This will include hospitals, poor houses, and prisons. Every inmate should be provided with a really exceptionally good dinner. Tobacco should be given to those who smoke...

F. Napier Broome, Governor.[10]

The new Albany 'Cottage' Hospital was designed by the Colonial Architect George Temple Poole. He was given a government brief to design an appropriate hospital complex to meet the needs of the town. While his new hospital facility was operational in 1888 it was perceived still to be inadequate to meet the town's needs. Another wing that was to complete the complex was eventually added in 1896.[11]

Intertown rivalry resulted in a claim that Albany was not a healthy place as it was made out to be. *The Albany Mail and King George Sound Advertiser* newspaper was quick to respond to these allegations and provided for the public record the cause of those deaths recorded in the town:

The alleged unhealthy state of Albany.
In consequence of some misleading reports having been published regarding the death rate in Albany, by which it is apparently demonstrated that the town Bears the enviable distinction of an abnormally heavy death rate, due, it is suggested, to its unhealthy state, we have taken some pains to ascertain whether this was the case or not, and, we leave it to our readers to judge from the results of our inquiries as given below, whether the charge port against the town was a just one or not...
18 Chinaman was killed by an accident; three deaths were due to senile decay, rather creditable to Albany that then otherwise (we allude to the senility, not the decay); 2 to heart disease: one from apoplexy one from asthma and bronchitis, an old man of 73...
...A child of two years died from croup; two from tubercula meningitis, one debility from birth, one infantile diarrhoea, one apnoea or asphyxia, one natural causes (decision at the inquest), two of improper feeding, one dysentery, one premature birth, and one dentition...

Neither does an analysis of the courses to which the cases are due to show that anything but a small proportion are due to the sanitary state of the town. On the contrary, considering the manner in which human beings have been crowded together, and the numerous dwellers in tents that we have scattered about within the town precinct, we have come to the conclusion that Albany came out in a very creditable manner from the scrutiny of a bill of mortality.[12]

However, it was a year later that the paper was able to report to its readers:

That melancholy relic of a bygone age, the old Albany Hospital, has it last ceased to Cumber the ground and cast discredit on the town by assistance. Its demolition commenced on Monday morning, and we are glad that it has disappeared. [13]

The creation of a morgue facility in 1889 attached to the new hospital was reported briefly in the local press:

---

[10] *The Jubilee Government Gazette*. June 1887.
[11] Artist Impression of Cottage Hospital 1906 by C.J. Batelier, Mark Saxton, Albany Historical Society.
[12] *The Albany Mail and King George Sound Advertiser*. 2nd June 1888.
[13] Ibid. 18th July 1888.

> *An Albany Contract.*
> *(By Telegraph.)*
> *Perth, October 11. The tender of Messrs Parry and Company to erect a dead house at Albany Hospital for £109 has been accepted by the government.*[14]

While plans were developed for the new hospital in 1887 it was not until 1896 that its construction was finalised and the new hospital located between Vancouver and Festing Streets opened. It served the community of Albany until it was replaced in the 1960s.

The 1922 Royal Commission

In 1922 a Royal Commission was established by the Legislative Council to investigate hospital provision in rural areas of Western Australia. It was also charged with examining the quality of the service that they provided. The Matron of Albany Hospital made a submission to the Royal Commission in May 1922. Matron May Miller provided the following insight into hospital services in the Albany District:

> *... I have had experience in other hospitals for about 20 years. In this hospital, I also carry out secretarial work. The institution is maintained entirely by government aid; no contributions are made locally, though fees are sometimes received from patients... The doctors in the town send their patients to the hospital and attend to them here. I have found that the system works satisfactorily. Indigent patients are also treated here. If they come to the hospital without having seen a medical man, I asked them whether they have a preference for any particular doctor, and if they have not, I request one to look after the particular case...*[15]

She then described the facilities at the Albany Hospital

> *I am not satisfied with the appointments at this hospital; in some ways that they are inconvenient on account of the age of the building. The drainage and the closets are not satisfactory because we have no system of sewage. The kitchen and scullery are in shocking condition, and on that account is very difficult for me to keep cooks... I have made representations to the medical department and requested that this state of affairs be altered. The public works department inspector went through the hospital and all of the series of defects were pointed out to him. Nothing, however, has been done... The roof of the building is in a defective state, and whenever it rains heavily water comes*
> *through to the floors...*[16]

Closing Remarks

Initial health provision and conditions in the town were quite primitive. As those who could afford to do so were treated in their own homes by the local doctor a general advocacy for a more substantial hospital facility was not seen as a great priority, especially given the limited resources that were available to the settlement at the time. Furthermore, as a hospital service relied on accessing the public purse for funding patient attendance it was perceived by the population at large that accessing the facilities provided was akin to being of poor or lower social status. It was only when the social position of the patients that were being admitted had improved and secondly, the concern for introduced pathogens from increased shipping visitations became a very real threat that the community demand for better facilities eventuated. While the climate of Albany had been advertised as being advantageous to one's health, it should be noted that the impact of the introduced pathogens on the Aboriginal population of King George's Sound was most significant.

---

[14] *The Australian Advertiser.* 11th October 1889.
[15] Royal Commission into Hospitals: Rural Conditions. May 1922 in *Westralian Voices*. UWA Press, 1979.
[16] Ibid.

CHAPTER 13
THE PROVISION OF AMENITIES IN THE TOWN

Albany has long been the first and last corner of Australia as far as the world is concerned. It is a spot of Australian ground seen and trodden by the majority of immigrants, tourist, and professional wanderers, the last by most departing Australians Henry Lawson, 1899.

Overview

One of the main preoccupations of the Albany Municipal Council in the latter part of the 1880s onwards was the question of securing an adequate water supply for the town. This concern exercised the minds of both the Town's Counsellors and the community in general for some time. Attempts were initially made to seek permission for the Municipal Council to connect with the water supply that had been established for railway and shipping use. The Government had sanctioned the use of the abandoned Fish Ponds catchment on Mount Melville as a reservoir for these industries to use. Initial rejection of this request forced the Municipal Council to explore other avenues to supply the town's water supply needs. Eventually a scheme that involved piping freshwater from the Angove River in the Two Peoples Bay catchment area was settled upon.

Underpinning this issue for the Municipal Council was predicting the probable increase in population for the future years. The sudden increase in population brought about by the influx of people coming to Western Australia in search of gold and transiting and then remaining in the town brought the matter to a head as it helped to highlight the point that the existing water supply was quite inadequate for the town. Even though the town's water supply was supplemented by a series of wells, unfortunately, many of these were contaminated by the unsanitary conditions prevailing at the time. Disease was not a stranger to the town, and it was not until well after the turn of the century that Albany was able to obtain a satisfactory water supply that met the continuing needs of the town.

The sanitary conditions of the town were another significant concern that initially resulted in the appointment by the Municipal Council of the 'Office of Inspector of Nuisances'. The local newspaper would often print the monthly reports of the Inspector, including the names of people who were seen to be acting against the public good in terms of their living habits. Public ignorance of the underlying safety hazard caused by poor sanitary practices were not an easy obstacle to overcome.

By the beginning of 1900, the sanitary conditions within the town were still of a most primitive kind. Human excreta along with household rubbish were often tipped into open cesspits, which were infrequently cleaned out to be disposed of further out from the town's centre. Unfortunately, many of these cesspits were in close proximity to the open wells from which the inhabitants of Albany obtained their drinking water. Consequently, it was not surprising that frequent cases of typhoid and other sickness plagued the town during this time. A partial solution was seen in the appointment of contractors who were charged with removing night-soil from the dwelling houses in the town.

The Municipal Council appointed a committee to enquire into the relative merits of electric light and gas lighting. The recommendation was to accept gas and a contract was subsequently led to the Council accepting the offer by Coates and Company to provide gas lighting to the main streets of Albany. Although not all the streets were illuminated this way, as kerosene lamps still existed in many sections of the town. In 1910 it was suggested to the Council that electric lighting should be introduced; however, it was not until an initiative by the Drew, Robinson Company in 1919 that electric lighting began to be taken seriously by the Municipal Council.

Water Supply

It was no longer a mystery why the place should be unhealthy, for the water supply seems very bad, although the hills above abound with pure springs. The drainage from stables, farm-buildings, poultry yards, and various detached houses has been so arranged as to fall into the wells which supply each house.
Lady Anna Brassey[1]

---

[1] *The Last Voyage, To India and Australia, in the Sunbeam."* London 1889.

Lady Anna Brassey's diary comments summarised well the unsavoury and unsanitary nature that sewage and general animal effluent was having on the townsite by the time of her visit in 1878. One of the attractions of King Georges Sound had always been the fact that it was well served by natural fresh-water supplies. However, with the steady increase in population the number of contaminants, particularly sewage, entering the groundwater in and around the settlement area eventually became a cause of significant concern to its inhabitants. Increased shipping to the Sound mid-Nineteenth Century along with the town's growth in population necessitated the need to locate alternative clean water sources for domestic and industry consumption.

The issue started coming to a head in the 1880's as exemplified by a local newspaper article contributed by a concerned member of the community:

To the Editor of the Mail

Sir,

Don't you think that we want for Albany an Inspector of Nuisances who will fearlessly perform his duty… An Inspector of Nuisances is greatly needed for Albany for if this town was anything like as hot as any of the other parts of the colony, we would be eaten up by all manner of diseases caused by the nauseous odours which are inhaled in certain quarters from slaughter houses or sheds and filthy pigsties etc., even in the heart of the town. Nightmen and chimney sweeps we certainly have, but the closets in certain quarters are something abominable, the nightman is seldom if ever called in to cleanse them…

Such things would not be tolerated in Perth or Fremantle and why should they be allowed here… Surely something could be done in these matters… or we will become before long like natives wallowing in dirt.[2]

The following year another article appeared that was highly critical of the Municipal Council's procrastination on Sanitary Reform in the town:

Sanitary reform is a matter that should engage the attention of the local civic authorities. As a town grows the necessity becomes more and more pressing for some measures being adopted to provide for proper drainage, and depositing refuse, which if allowed to accumulate would poison not only atmosphere, but water wells in the vicinity, and engender fever and disease… it is the duty of every community, no matter how small, to provide for such matters…

Though loud complaints have been made through the columns of this paper and otherwise of bad smells and unhealthy drains the Municipal Council seem utterly to ignore them.[3]

The need to cater for horse watering as well as making provision of an accessible well for general domestic use was raised by the Mayor William Grills Knight at a Municipal Council meeting in 1886:

The Mayor brought forward a proposal for constructing a well and horse trough and erecting a pump for public use in Frederick, York and Grey Streets. After some discussion it was resolved that these additions should be made to Frederick and York Streets as an experiment.[4]

However, while the proposal was bought forward by the Municipal Council it was still necessary to resolve an issue with respect to where the well would actually be located and the form it would take:

Regarding the proposed well in York Street, some difference of opinion arose as to its location. During the discussion Counsellor Hare stated that the public generally had expressed much approbation with the well scheme. It was resolved that the wells in future shall not be raised, but be flush with the ground level, and supplied with a pump and trough.[5]

While the Albany Municipal Council took a very keen interest in the existing Fish Ponds area on Mount Melville as a potential reservoir for the town, its petition to the Government in October 1888 was not to eventuate as a counter proposal for the use of this water supply had been received from the Western Australian Land Company to use for the railway and shipping interests and these took precedence. The response from the Government to the Municipal Council request from the Colony's Attorney General Sir Thomas Cockburn Campbell was unequivocal:

---

[2] *The Albany Mail and King George Sound Advertiser.* 25th April 1883.
[3] Ibid. 15th January 1884.
[4] Ibid. 15th December 1886.
[5] *The Albany Mail and King George Sound Advertiser.* 16th March 1887.

I am directed by his Excellency the governor to inform you that the Ponds, in question, which would not, the Government is advised, have been of use as a source of town water supply, have been leased to the West Australian Land Company, for 21 years at a nominal rate, as it was necessary for the public interest, that the water should be secured for the use of the railway.[6]

The issue of water supply for domestic and local commerce was to drag on for several years despite ongoing letters of complaint to the editors of the local papers and Municipal Council:

Water Cure

And utterly careless, a happy-go-lucky system of sinking wells and erecting objectionable little sentry boxes in close proximity to them, which has been the fashion in Albany, time out of mind, has at length brought its natural punishment, and people who recklessly took no head of repeated warnings, are now terrified with the effect caused entirely by their own action. Sufficient care is not taken by the townspeople of their drinking water, one of the most important matters in everyday life, but in the colonies, this fact is very generally overlooked. As an example of the importance of this matter, we would instance a well-known case near London, with some 500 persons were attacked with typhoid symptoms... on further investigation, it was elicited that the pans in which the milk and cream stood, and the other dairy utensils, were washed in water that came from a well situated close to one of these abominable little sentry boxes to which we have before alluded...[7]

Continued community agitation for a clean water supply ensured that the issue regularly appeared on the agenda of the Municipal Council. Some progress was foreshadowed in late 1888 discussions unfortunately, with little effective outcome noted:

A Water Supply for Albany.

Attention has been lately turned to the question of a water supply for this town, and we are glad to see that the Municipal Council have commenced to move in the matter, and at the last meeting on the 28th ultimo, unanimously resolved that the Government be asked to place a sum of money on the estimates for the purpose.

It may be thought that this resolution, though excellent in its way, is not a very prodigious step towards the desired end; but it is the first formal expression of the public feeling that the time is arrived when Albany finds, like other towns in the colony, that her health, and comfort depend on plenty of fresh water, and as such, the day of small beginnings it's not to be despised... Now that the necessity for a supply of water has become acknowledged by the entire community, we may hope that the matter will not be allowed to rest till the need is met...

Excellent water is to be found in abundance on the higher ground throughout the town as vide Grey Street, York Street, and last, but not least, on the west at the Fish Ponds, which could be utilised as the nuclei of a large reservoir.[8] There is here a proved and never-failing supply of fresh water, and it is stated on professional authority that the side of the fishpond is it least on a level with the top of York Street, a sufficiently exalted position to enable nearly the whole of the town to be supplied from...[9]

The issue of supplying shipping with its water requirements was highlighted by *The Albany Mail and King George's Sound Advertiser* which took up the issue in August of 1888:

Water Supply for Shipping.

If it were not for the endeavours of Messrs Baillie, Davis and Wishart's water cartage endeavours ships would have had to make longer transit stays at the King George's Sound Port to take on sufficient water supplies from existing sources to continue their journey.

---

[6] *The Albany Mail in King George's Sound Advertiser.* 21st November 1888.
[7] Ibid. 19th March 1887.
[8] The Fish Ponds referred to in this article relate to an experiment that was undertaken in Albany in 1874 to a acclimatize imported trout ova for breeding purposes on a commercial basis. The experiment was placed under the direction of Gustavus Hare and was not successful, consequently the venture was soon abandoned. The reservoir that had been created to breed the fish later became a chief water source for industry and later domestic and commercial use.
[9] *The Albany Mail and King George's Sound Advertiser.* 4th April 1888.

> *The arrival of* HMS Orlando *in the harbour has again showed how wretchedly inadequate are the arrangements for vessels requiring water at this important shipping port. A miserable little 2-inch pipe, which runs alongside the town jetty, and dribbles a scanty stream, filling the water tanks at the rate of about 100 gallons an hour, is all that the town possesses to meet the requirements of vessels wanting water…*[10]

Community frustration was noted at many levels and the need to water animals created obvious problems in the town. A disgruntled person wrote to the paper expressing his frustration accordingly:

> *An Albany Nuisance.*
> *To the editor.*
>
> *Sir,*
> *Can you please permit me through your valuable paper to draw the attention of our civic fathers to the great nuisance in Spencer Street caused by carters and others watering their horses at the well in front of the Post Office. A trough has been placed on the street and the pipe leading to the jetty is constantly being stuffed up. The consequence being that the will overflows, and the street has become almost impossible. Great inconvenience is also caused to ships and steam launches who depend on the well for their supply of water. Trusting the nuisance will be abated.*[11]

As with many issues requiring a Municipal Council response in the 1880-1900 period the town's inhabitants had to wait sometime before action on this important issue was noted. Reporting on a Council meeting in 1897 the following extract about the water supply issue was noted by the local newspaper:

> *The question of a town water supply still engages the attention of the Town Council, and recently a report has been furnished to the Council by the Government in which Limeburner's Creek is spoken of as the purist and nearest supply, but as a doubt exists as to the sufficiency of the supply from this source for the growing needs of the town, the Government has been asked to take further gauging with this summer.*[12]

The pressure continued to mount not only on the Municipal Council but also the government to find a solution to the town's water issue which was being exacerbated by a significant increase in the local population and the number of ships visiting King George's Sound. A Government report in 1897 again highlighted the need to rectify the water supply issue, for shipping, the railways and then for domestic use. With Fremantle Port becoming operational in the near future there was a great reluctance on the part of the Government of the day to allocate funds to address the Albany water supply issue. Nevertheless, two years later an article in *The Inquirer* in 1899 reported that:

> *A new cast iron 25,000-gallon tank has been erected near the Post Office. There is a fall of about 35 feet from the tank to the main jetty, which is now several sources of supply, namely the fishponds, the Brunswick Road Stoke, and the Frederick Street Stoke, as well as the old 10,000-gallon cement tank close to the new tank. Shipping is now well supplied with water.*[13]

The drama associated with the provision of a sustainable water supply for Albany was a point of contention for local residents. The Editor of *The Albany Advertiser* captured these sentiments in an article in 1901:

> *After the heavy rains that have fallen recently, it is astounding fact that shipping should be hung up in Albany Harbour for want of water. Unless vessels can have their wants supplied it will not pay them to call, and as water is an important consideration, the welfare of the calling industry, a material element in the prosperity of the town, must be affected by the existing deficiency… the water for shipping is mainly derive from the fishpond, too small and primitive reservoirs served by excellent catchment and a series of springs…Under ordinary circumstances, and especially at the present time, the source of water supply with adequate conservation should be equal to meet the wants of the shipping and railway as well. Just now, it*

---

[10] Ibid. 18th August 1888.
[11] Ibid. April 27th 1889.
[12] *The Albany Advertiser.* 11th November 1897.
[13] *The Inquirer and Commercial News.* Perth, 12th May 1899.

> *doubtless would be but for the very defective condition in which the pipeline has been allowed to lapse... No time should be lost in arriving at a decision so that the shipping trade of the port may be saved...*[14]

A ratepayer meeting was called to consider using water from Limeburner Creek in Frenchman's Bay for local use:

> *A special meeting of the ratepayers was subsequently called during the half year to take into consideration the advisableness of a comprehensive water supply scheme for the town and shipping, with a result that it was the term decided to accept the West Australian government's proposal and offer of a scheme to supply the shipping only, and that a ballot of the ratepayers was to be taken to decide whether the Limeburner's Creek scheme should be carried out for the reticulation of the town, which, as you were aware, was eventually taken in due course...*[15]

Throughout 1907 the capacity of the reservoir area known as the Fish Ponds catchment was increasingly expanded to meet the town's domestic and commercial needs. An announcement by Premier John Scadden that his Government would commit to building an appropriate and adequate water supply by 1912 was well received in the town. The solution agreed to was to pump water into a reservoir on Mount Melville from an area of the Angove River that flows into Two Peoples Bay. The scheme was operational by the time of the outbreak of The Great War in 1914. From the account of the Albany Town Directory for the 1928-29 Season the matter of freshwater supply to the town had been well resolved:

> *Analysis Makes it One of the Best in the Commonwealth.*
>
> *Founded in 1913, the water scheme which supplies the needs of Albany has its source in the natural spring of unsurpassed purity at Two People's Bay, a beautiful spot situated on the coast to the east of Albany. The storage reservoir at Two People's Bay has a capacity of 300,000 gallons and the mains to the town is 18 miles in length. The town reservoir is situated on the western slopes of Mount Clarence and can carry 250,000 gallons. The Water Department of the state controlled the scheme from its inception in 1913 until it was handed it over to the Municipality some four years later in 1917.*
>
> *The service enjoyed extensive patronage from shipping in the early years of its existence and throughout the Great War, with many transports well supplied... The main runs as far as Middleton Beach, and it is proposed to increase the capacity of the pipes running northerly there and recirculating to service the golf links.*[16]

It is of interest that the first four to five miles of pipeline that supplied the townsite with its freshwater from the Two peoples Bay area was made of Oregon wood from America. Local Historian Dennis Greeve relayed the following observations relating to the use of wooden pipes:

> *The pipeline from Two Peoples Bay to Mount Melville was a significant feat of engineering for its day. The beginning of the pipeline was made of American Oregon. The wood was cut to lengths of about three metres. A number of curved pieces were wired together and bitumised to form one length of pipe. These pipe lengths were then joined together by a tongue and groove feature. Once placed together the join was then bitumised as well. Close to 2500 pipes made of Oregon were required for this fresh water project.*
>
> *The Oregon was transported to Albany from America and was then hauled by a cart to the location required. The haulage contractor happened to be my mother's brother, William 'Billy' Bishop.*
>
> *The route followed the more substantial pipeline of today from Two Peoples Bay, over the Kalgan and King Rivers into town and then up to the reservoir on Mt Melville. A steam pump was used to get the water into the town reservoir. It was then gravity fed the town and those allotments who were in a location that was not able to receive their water by gravity feed missed out on the service and had to make other arrangements.*[17]

These observations were confirmed in a series of articles in *The Albany Advertiser* relating to the construction of the freshwater pipeline into the town:

---

[14] *The Albany Advertiser.* 31st December 1901.
[15] Ibid. 20th May 1902.
[16] *Western Australian Gem in a Granite Setting.* Official Albany Directory. Season 1929.
[17] Personal Correspondence with Dennis Greeve.

On the advice of experts and in the interests of sound economy this proposal was amended in favour of using patent wooden pipes for the first 5 miles out from the pumping station. Apart from being much less in price, these wooden pipes, it was found, can we carted to the place where they will be use at a great saving of money as compared with cast iron pipes…[18]

Three months later the newspaper reported:

The Water Scheme.
Work to be Completed by Christmas.
All that remains to be done, as a matter of fact, is the reticulation of the town. The weir at the catchment area was all but completed some weeks ago and the finishing touches are at present being put to the pumping station. The boiler has been bricked in and the pump erected. The plant is now being housed in and the building should be completed by the end of the month. Very little remains to be done to link up the source of supply with the service reservoir on Mount Clarence. All the 8-inch iron pipes are laid and of the 4 miles of wooden pipes required to complete the length, upwards of two have been placed in the ground…[19]

A very positive perspective on the purity of the Albany fresh water supply was indeed echoed by the local paper which reported that:

Albany's Water Supply.
It is a proud and justifiable assertion that Albany possesses a water supply unequal for purity in the state, and even the Commonwealth. This is a desirable quality indeed, especially in a town so famed as Albany has a health resort. Nevertheless, at the moment the extension of the scheme presents a perplexing problem to the authorities in whom its control is vested. Demands upon it are growing each year, and such is the call for extra and augmentation of services that ere long the board will be forced to take steps to remedy the position.

Counsellor Maslin approached the subject on broad lines, his vision carrying him past our immediate needs to those of future generations. He deplored the fact that the scheme as it stands today failed to cope, in the summer months, with the calls made upon it. On a couple of occasions last year and early this year the desperate expedient of direct pumping to the town reservoir had had to be resorted to. There was a certain element of risk in such, owing to the faulty condition of the wooden section of the pipe track. Counsellor Maslin said it was not his desire to pose as an alarmist, but the question could not be deferred to long.[20]

The Town's Sanitary Issues

Expansion of the town necessarily created issues relating to basic services including sewerage and water provision. There was a heavy reliance on both individual water tanks to supply needs which were replenished in winter but reduced somewhat in the summer months, resulting in extensive use of available wells in around the town. Given the issues of sanitation and rubbish disposal the quality of the water collected from the wells was at times questioned:

Albany is at present a small place and hence its rubbish is of small amount, but in many parts of the town, the sanitary precautions are so little regarded, that cesspools and wells in close proximity, within a few yards of one another, are common neighbours, and an epidemic once breaking out would have a good chance of a lively run. In this case would it be possible for one medical man, however active, to attend to the wants of the public?[21]

The issue was still of concern eighteen months later when the local newspaper's editorial indicated:

The hygienic state of most of our large cities, as well as a number of our country towns, is anything but satisfactory, and the prevalence of typhoid and enteric diseases is a sad pro That laws sanitary and hygienic should be amongst the first to demand attention from all reasonable men goes without saying, and experience teaches us that such places as are noted for their immunity from zymotic disease are those most eagerly sought after both by visitors and intending settlers. Everything, therefore, done to lower the death-rate and advance the claim of a town to salubrity is a distinct net gain. For this reason, we hailed with satisfaction the appointment of a Board of Health; but while the body

---

[18] *The Albany Advertiser.* 16th July 1913.
[19] Ibid. 22nd October 1913.
[20] *The Albany Advertiser.* 25th July 1929
[21] Ibid. 15th January 1887.

exercises its functions, it is necessary that no arbitrary rules should be introduced. of the very general neglect of sanitary precautions.

The result, from a sanitary point of view, is far from satisfactory. Neither water nor drainage have been dealt with by concerted action. In its isolated position, with no settle country behind it, Albany had remained a small but no unprosperous town of less than 2,000 inhabitants.[22]

Adding the complexity of the sanitary concerns of the town was the issue of penned livestock that were being maintained within the residential areas of the central business district. The issue was raised in a letter to the local press and the subsequent resolution of Council:

A letter was read from Mr H Cowden, complaining of Mr Muir's pigsties etc. Counsellor Hare pointed out that there any objections as to nuisances must be brought to the Council's notice through the Inspector of Nuisances.[23]

The issue of Mr Muir's pigs then resulted in the Municipal Council listing the following motion to be placed on notice:

That a special meeting be called to make the following by-laws.
That no person or persons carrying on the trade of butchers be allowed to kill any pig or animal of any description on any premises in the town of Albany, other than those specifically set aside for the purpose.
That no person be allowed to keep more than two pigs at one time, within a radius of 1 mile from the corner of Stirling Terrace in York Street.
That all pigsties be floored with either brick or stone, and that they be cleaned out at least once a week.[24]

During the 1890 period, the Albany Municipal Council was increasingly confronted with the issue of provision of an appropriate sanitary collection and disposal process for the town. At each Municipal Council Meeting, the Inspector of Nuisances would provide a report on his findings. These reports constantly raised sanitary disposal as a key issue:

Monthly report.
Inspector of Nuisances Report.

Gentlemen,
I have the honour to report that in accordance with instructions received from the board, I visited the tents erected both on public and private grounds in Albany. On a block of land in Brunswick Road, seven or eight people are living in tents, and at the time of my inspection had no privy accommodation whatever, and at the surveyor's camp, also in Brunswick Road, the night-soil was being deposited in a large hole and was intended eventually to be covered and left there. I served notices to the occupiers of the tents to have privies erected within the week. These orders have been carried out; each Privy has a bucket, and the Night-man attends to them. At the surveyor's camp, satisfactory arrangements were also made for the removal of the night-soil by the board's contractor. At the Fish Ponds there are but two tents, one close by the water, and the other far off. I was informed that the owner of the tent situated near the Ponds had received orders to, and was about to shift from his present quarters, and the other tent is too far away for the night- soil buried to it any way affect the water.

Night Soil Pans.
At present kerosene, biscuit, and other tins are being used, as receptacles for night soil. These tins are too flimsy and altogether unsuitable for the purpose used. I would advise the board to enforce the adoption of a uniform galvanised iron bucket with a handle attached I'll say 4 gallons for private houses and 8 gallons for hotels and boarding houses. It should also be made compulsory for the owners, and not the tenants to provide the buckets. Occupiers come and go, and if they have substantial buckets remove them, and others will not supply suitable buckets on the pretence that they may be shifting into other houses at any time or are about to leave the town. This difficulty would be overcome if the owners were made responsible for providing of regulation buckets.

---

[22] The *Albany Mail and King George's Sound Advertiser*. 11th July 1888.
[23] Ibid. 16th March 1887.
[24] Ibid. 16th March 1887.

Bedroom Slops.
It is in the interest of the public health that the board should make an order that all bedroom slopes be carted away by the night man. The bedroom urine in most cases at present is mix with water and thrown on the ground, and even sometimes into the drains. This practice naturally causes the stench to arise and renders the air impure.[25]

Drainage was also an ongoing issue, particularly in the York Street and Stirling Terrace areas of the town during heavy rains. A suggestion was placed before the Municipal Council at its January 1891 meeting to address part of the problem:

Mr C. R. Fenwick wrote suggesting a remedy for the complaints made of the Stirling Terrace drain. He had used, he said, with very satisfactory results upon sewage works a highly efficient system of flashing by means of Field's self-acting syphon. The syphon was placed in a specially constructed chamber in such a manner that when a sufficient quantity of water had accumulated the syphon came into action and sent down the whole of the water at once into the drain. This caused a rush of water strong enough to scour the drain. The water again accumulated in the chamber until it again brought the syphon into action when another flush took place and so it went on continually night and day so long as water was supplied to the tank. A very small stream was sufficient for the purpose… After some further discussion it was resolved to write to Mr Fenwick thanking him for his letter, inviting him to forward any information bearing upon the subject of this letter.[26]

The appointment of an Inspector of Nuisances by the Municipal Council was designed to give the local inhabitants a point of contact for complaints. At each Municipal Council meeting the Inspector would provide a detailed report on his activities. The report was then published in the local newspaper. The issue of household waste and sewage continued to dominate Albany's Inspector of Nuisances reports during the 1890s through to the early 1900s. A member of the public wrote expressing concern at the Council's priorities at this time:

Public Nuisance
The frequency of bad smells in the town so early in the summer shows clearly that unless prompt steps are taken by the Council Albany will soon get into a bad sanitary position. For typhoid cases to arise locally would be disastrous for the town and no sacrifice should be too great if it will prevent such a state of affairs. The Town Council are not justified in spending money on street making or other works until they have dealt efficiently with the sanitation of the town. The town would not suffer one-hundredth part as much from a bad piece of road as it would from the loss of its reputation as a health resort. Perth dallied in the same way with sanitation and spent its revenue upon other works and the consequence has been the loss of hundreds of lives.[27]

Part of the Inspector of Nuisances responsibilities were associated with inspecting properties throughout the town and then reporting to the monthly Council meeting on his findings:

I have completed the house-by-house inspection and finding a whole the back yards of the town are cleanly kept. Inflammable rubbish is usually burnt; but bottles, tins, etc, to be found in almost every yard. The rubbish bin system should be adopted at once; all rubbish could then be removed; and the yards thus kept in a clean and sanitary state; and offensive fumes from the burning of objectionable matter done away with. With one exception the town is entirely free from soak wells. As a result of the inspection a number of nuisances were detected and were abated by the responsible person in being ordered to do so. Private drains should be construct it in different parts of the town, but owing to the want of street trains it is not advisable to order their construction…
I think we'll has been made at the hospital for the reception of household waste waters. I would advise the board to make it order for the same to be cleaned out and filled in at once.[28]

In November 1898 the Inspector of Nuisances again reported as follows:

---

[25] *The Albany Advertiser.* 23rd March 1897.
[26] *The Australian Advertiser.* 7th January 1891.
[27] *The Albany Advertiser.* 25th November 1897.
[28] Ibid. 19th February 1898.

> *I have to advise you in accordance with the provision of Clause 180, 62 Victoria, Number 24 to order Mr J.F.T. Hassell, owner of Albany Town Lot 40 to erect a privy thereon to serve the house occupied by some Chinamen. At present, the house is without privy accommodation of any kind...*
>
> *According to the plans of the new Government School, provision has only been made for two urinals of two buckets each to serve the boys' and infants' schools. So far as the boys' school is concerned, this will be insufficient accommodation. I have to advise the board, therefore, to make an order calling upon the government to provide for buckets to serve the boys school and two to serve the infants' school.[29]*

At a 1906 Board of Health meeting, it was decided to take affirmative action concerning the problem. A Select Committee was appointed to devise means for the introduction of a sealed pan system for the removal of night-soil and the recommendations were duly accepted, and an appropriate sanitary system of night-pans and a collection roster was then established for the town.[30]

However, into the 1920s the issue of night-soil collection was still occasionally raised in the local paper:
> *Albany is a holiday resort, and it would be very unpleasant for business and ourselves to see the carts going about the streets in the daytime. Under the contract system, the contractor can be made to do the work properly at night. Under the council, we would have no one to listen to any complaints, as we know under the present administration there is little or no control of the workmen and a few of employed by the council the better would be for the ratepayers...[31]*

The issue of night-soil removal was still raised an issue in 1931:

A Public Nuisance.
To the editor.

Sir,
May I be permitted a small space in your valuable columns to draw attention to one unpleasant subject... I refer to the unnecessary parking of particularly obnoxious sanitary carts, sometimes four or five, at the junction of Perth Road and York Street, opposite the Hordern Memorial for any time up to an hour almost every night of the week. As a visitor to the town, I would like to suggest that this hardly does credit to the controlling authorities...

It strikes me as being a pity that the town that has come to be regarded as the southern city of the state should be made by poorly arranged sanitary for service. I am etc.,[32]

Street Lighting

As with many other decisions affecting Albany the development of public and private lighting facilities caused considerable debate within the Municipal Council and public arena. An early commitment to gas offered by Messrs Coates and Company was eventually selected after considerable discussion followed by some more years of Council procrastination. The gas lighting initiative was finally achieved with the completion of gasworks on the shore of The Princess Royal Harbour and the laying of gas mains in the townsite. Before this arrangement lighting of some aspects of Stirling Terrace from the jetty along York Street was achieved using either kerosene or oil lamps. There was a belief, that Albany street lighting was initially fuelled by oil but as *The Albany Observer* and *The Albany Mail and King George Sound Advertiser* reporting of the time suggest kerosene was the fuel of choice that was employed.[33]

Resolving the issue requires drawing some parallels with what was happening in Nineteenth-Century London and in Great Britain generally before the use of gas and electricity for street and shop lighting. The Argand oil lamps that were initially used in London between 1780 and 1850 used as the source of

---

[29] *The Albany Advertiser.* 19th November 1898.
[30] Ibid. 18th August 1906.
[31] Ibid. 28th July 1923.
[32] Ibid. 28th January 1931.
[33] D. Garden. *Albany: Panorama of the Sound.* Nelson, reported that - "In 1884 the first streetlights, 10 oil lamps were erected..." 1977, p.196

fuel oil a variety of plant-based (olive, sesame, castor, flax and nuts etc.) and animal fats (fish oil, whale or seal blubber etc.). From the 1850s onwards, kerosene or paraffin lamps were employed.[34] Termed 'parish lamps' they consisted of glazed glass (sometimes semi-opaque), that encapsulated a small tin vessel half-filled with kerosene or oil with a piece of cotton twist to form a wick which had to be lighted by a lamplighter.[35] The glow from the lamp was reported as being relatively dim.

Providing street lighting to Albany's main thoroughfares characteristically began with long and protracted community discussions and debate, followed by periods of considerable procrastination on the part of the Municipal Council. In 1884 the first street lighting was initiated, 10 kerosene lamps from the jetty area, along a section of Stirling Terrace and then into York Street. It becomes clear from the evidence that these lights were fuelled by kerosene. A good description of the effect of this lighting on the area is provided by a letter written to *The Albany Mail and King George Sound Advertiser* in 1885:

To the Editor of the Mail.
Sir,
On Saturday night I was asked by strangers the question, how it was the town lamps were not lighted. As I could not answer I thought I would refer the question to you.
The same thing occurred on Sunday night, and I should like to know why this is thus. Whatever excuse there may be for one night (not that I admit any excuse for neglect of public limbs) there cannot be any for the second, and it shows apathy, and neglect, on the part of the officials that reflects on the whole council.

Possibly it may be the funds have run out. In that case, some person should go-round with the hat and I for one would put in my mite and no doubt the sinews would be raised, for no-one would run the risk of breaking their limbs in the many man-traps that the council seem necessary, at the intersection of many of the streets when a shilling or two would lighten our darkness.

If on the other hand, it is pure neglect, the Council must recollect that they are the guardians of the public welfare and should not take the honours and dignities of office and neglect the duties or allow any officer in their employ to neglect theirs.

O eave the town nights in succession without a light shows something more than neglect, and the Council should see those public duties, as far as they are concerned, should be carried out without excuse, fear or favour...[36]

The nature of the fuel for lamps required the very necessary employment of a Lamp-Lighter.
The issue of costs associated with lighting the town's streets was raised in the Municipal Council by Councillor O'Keefe:

Counsellor O'Keefe asked whether the government had refunded the amount charged to counsel for Mr Chipper's services in lighting the jetty lamps, as she objected to the payment of this account. The Clerk stated that when the lamps were erected, the mayor had told Mr Chipper to light them till the government made some other arrangement, and now the government refused to pay the amount. It was determined to allow settlement to stand over for the present, though counsellor O'Keefe said he supposed the council would eventually have to pay for lighting the lamps, but he considered the charge of 3 pounds and excessive one for the work performed.[37]

Replacing the existing kerosene lighting required that the Municipal Council make a choice between either gas or electricity as the source. Various companies and individuals representing both perspectives were asked to present a 'pitch' to the Council. As the choice made would have significant implications for the town it is not surprising that the local papers were eager to report on the debates that were taking place:

---

[34] Abraham Gesner distilled coal to produce a clear fluid in 1846 that burned with a much brighter light than oil. He named this new liquid kerosene after the Greek word for wax oil.
[35] P. Ackroyd. *London: The Biography*. Vintage Press. London. 2001.
[36] *The Albany Mail and King George Sound Advertiser.* 8th December 1885.
[37] Ibid. 11th February 1888.

The Electric Light.
On Tuesday evening last Mr Thomson was he representing the firm of Messrs Harrison and Whiffin gave a very interesting lecture on the subject, of electric lighting, in the courthouse. Mr S.S. Young took the chair, and the lecturer said that he hoped that the present Bijou exhibition will result in the town of Albany being lighted with the electric light, and so do away with the miserable attempts by kerosene. He called the attention of the audience to the

steady and brilliant light in the courthouse, and also to the strong and effective light of the art lamp on the flagstaff outside, which threw its light along the street in all directions…

Mr Thomson continued with his presentation:
Gas lamps cost 6 pounds per jet, and if a company were formed to light Albany by electricity, they would be able to give the inhabitants a better light than gas at about half the cost, and cheaper than kerosene lamps. As regards the streets, they would be brilliantly lighted by arc lamps such as the one on the flagstaff outside. Mr Thompson drew the attention of the audience to the fact that this exhibition was held under difficulties. All the fittings had been only put up temporarily and the plant had not been landed from the steamer till late in the afternoon of Monday. In a permanent installation, the wires would all be covered up, but even as they were in the courthouse, there was no possible danger of anyone receiving a shot from touching them. Also, each light will be supplied with the safety fused to prevent any extent. One great advantage of having the electric light one's premises was that the insurance premium on buildings lighted by it is very much less than when the light is obtained from gas or kerosene; and also, there are no fumes or smoke arising from the Compton lamps to spoil furniture, picture frames, etc…[38]

The importance of the following article *The Albany Observer* of 1890 is the clear reference that is made to the historical use of kerosene as the source of fuel for the town's street lighting:
Albany has now a place of importance and required and improvement in its lighting. Kerosene had done very well in the past, but its day has gone and was now necessary for the ratepayers to make a decision as to whether they would improve the lighting, and in so doing adopt gas or electricity…

Mr Swinburn, on rising said: five years have elapsed since correspondence had commenced between Messrs Coates and Company and the municipal council on the subject of lighting the town with gas, but he had been unable before to make a personal visit. He had now come at considerable expense, and was prepared to give all the information in his power…

They required no guarantee as to the amount of gas to be consumed, I only wish to be allowed to supply such of the ratepayers as desired to use gas. Those present would agree with him that the time has arrived for Albany to look for some improvement in her lighting. There was no likelihood of Gas being extinguished by other and your methods of lighting. Electricity was supposed by some people to be preferable…[39]

The paper was explicit in naming kerosene as the lighting source in this excerpt discussing the presentation made by a representative of the gas interests, Mr Swinburn in his address stated that:
One light did not exclude another. Kerosene had not superseded candles, and if electric comes forward later on, as good light, by all means, use it, but we should always have gas. In the days when Robert Stevenson was constructing his railway, the farmers thought it would do away with the use of horses, but horses are used more than ever. So, it would be with electricity, more candles, Walker is seen, and more gas would also be used.

The advantage of gas was that it could be utilised for cooking and other purposes, and was available at all times, night and day, where is electricity could only be supplied while the engines were at work from sunset to sunrise…[40]

---

[38] Ibid. 27th July 1889.
[39] *The Albany Observer.* 27th November 1890.
[40] Ibid. 5th March 1891.

There was a belated representation for the Crampton Electric Light Company when Mr Ottley made an appearance at a Municipal Council meeting. He addressed the Council just before the vote was taken that resulted in the acceptance of the offer for a gas supplied lighting proposal by the firm of Coates and Company. *The Albany Observer* had taken a keen interest in the discussion and reported that:

A proposal from the representative of a well-known firm engaged in the business of supplying electric light plants came before the Municipal Council on Tuesday night. The proposal made by Mr Ottley was to the effect that he should be granted permission to erect the poles necessary to carry the wires and to light the town.

Several speakers appear to think that it would be premature to wed the town to a system of lighting by gas to have been ascertained with electricity would not prove, the better light producer. However, after considerable discussion Mr Swinburn stated that he was not so infatuated with the excellencies of gas as to desire its acceptance without question, but made it clear it was simply a commercial matter that caused his advocacy of gas in preference to the lighting by electricity, declaring also that if he thought the latter would've proved the best for purpose, he would gladly have offered to utilise it in the place of gas.

It was almost unanimously agreed to accept Messrs Coates and the Companies offer, which was generally agreed on all hands to be a most liberal one and bound the ratepayers to nothing beyond allowing the firm placing the mains under the streets. ... The land on which the firm is to erect its gasworks has been purchased, and the ratepayers look forward with satisfaction and pleasure to being supplied with gas in a very few months...

It is perhaps well, for the town that the Crampton Electric Light Company did not send their agent here at an earlier date, for he had appeared simultaneously with Mr Swinburn and made his application at that time, public opinion regarding the two methods of lighting was so divided, that it is more than probable that nothing would have been settled, and we should have continued to grope along the streets in the semi-obscurity of primitive kerosene.[41]

Arthur Symons writing in London in the 1840's described a typical gas lit street scene as:
A dim wet pavement lit irregularly with shimmering streaks of gaslight, faint and frayed.
It is not too difficult to extrapolate the street scene he describes as being not too dissimilar to the York Street and Stirling Terrace setting on a wet evening in the late Nineteenth Century.

A Move to Electrifying Albany

The development of Albany's Street Lighting and the Municipal Power Station were fully summarized in *The Albany Advertiser* article that was published in 1932.

Albany Street Lighting
Prior to 1887 the inhabitants of Albany depended on kerosene and candles as an illuminant for lighting purposes, but by Queen Victoria's Jubilee year, the town had grown to be a place of importance, so much so that the citizens decided to advance with the times...
...At this juncture the Colonial Gas Association sent their representative to open up negotiations with the Town Council with a view to getting a concession to supply the town with gas. An agreement was finally reached, and so the citizens were blessed with a good lighting service...This system of lighting the town continued for many years. Early in 1910 the Town Council discussed the matter of establishing an electric light and power service, but the concession to the Colonial Gas Association, in the matter of street lighting did not terminate until the end of 1922.

A few months after [1910] the late Mr H. Robinson approached the council with a request to use the streets for electric cables with a view of supplying private consumers with electricity... At the end of six years nothing further was done in the matter... but in 1919 Mr Robinson approached the Council and asked for a concession of 21 years.[42]

---

[41] Ibid.
[42] *The Albany Advertiser*. 5th December 1932.

After a number of teething issues and after "many mistakes were made" a steady electricity supply eventuated for the town through Drew, Robinson and Company until the generating source was eventually purchased by the Municipal Council. *The Albany Advertiser* concluded its summary:

> *Electricity had become a great utility in the town and the continuity of service could not be broken. Dozens of places were using the current, such as factories, hotels, boarding houses, churches, etc., and to cut them off would have been little short of a calamity.*[43]

From the mention and actions associated with the lighting of Albany's streets back in 1884 it took a further 35 years before electrification of the town commenced. Initially the power supply was generated privately through the Drew, Robinson Company however, in 1926 the Drew, Robinson power plant system was purchased and then expanded upon by the Municipal Council.

Closing Remarks

During the latter part of the Nineteenth Century, the earlier perspective of Albany as a 'Sleepy Hollow' was surpassed by a range of significant developments in the town in terms of its infrastructure, political and social growth making it comparable to other major Australian towns of the period. In by 1927 there were still some outstanding issues that needed resolution, such as sewage, rubbish disposal, drainage across the town, road sealing, etc. nonetheless, the extensive port infrastructure, general town and railway developments as well as simple lifestyle improvements such as street lighting and fresh water access were areas in which the town could take considerable pride.

---

[43] Ibid.

CHAPTER 14
THE GOLDEN ERA OF STEAM SHIPS 1851-1900

"King Georges Sound is one of the most important waterways in the world."
Lord Randolph Churchill. *The Times*, London, June 4th, 1887.

Overview

The first steamship to arrive King George's Sound was *HMS Acheron* in 1848 and with its arrival, the genesis of a future steam Royal Mail route between Europe, India, Asia and Australia now became a reality. The steamer mail service to King George's Sound would continue for the remainder of the Nineteenth Century using Albany as the initial port of call. It was not until the port facilities in Fremantle had become operational that the mail, cargo and passenger steamship service to Albany service discontinued. Until 1900, Albany was Western Australia's port of call for the Royal Mail and passenger steamers of the Peninsular and Oriental Steam Navigation Company (P&O), White Star, Aberdeen, the French Messageries Maritimes Group and North German Lloyd Companies. Their services to the town were curtailed when Fremantle was substituted as their first and last port of call in Western Australia.

Arrival of Steam

It was on the 22nd July 1848 that *HMS Acheron* visited Albany. It was the first steam ship to arrive at King George's Sound after a voyage of seven months from England on route to New Zealand to conduct a marine survey of that county's islands. *Acheron* was a Royal Navy Hermes-class wooden paddle sloop. Archdeacon John Wollaston noted the arrival of the ship in his Albany Journals:

> *Last night, to the great surprise of everyone, and the consternation of the natives the* Acheron *came steaming into our harbour, seven months from England. This is the first steamer ever seen here. I wish her mail had bought me more letters, but I am very thankful for one from Tullie giving me a better account of my dear sister…*
>
> *The* Acheron *must have been detained somewhere. She touched at Rio, and the Cape. She will be here some days, and then proceeds to New Zealand. Thus, already have more vessels been here than we used to see at Bunbury in a twelve month. I was at tea at Mr Taylor's on the beach, and when I returned home this great black thing, close inshore, loomed in the obscurity, like some phantom visitor. Her motions without sailing perfectly bewildered the aborigines, and such a gaggle arose about what she could be as must have kept them awake in their wigwams after night, for they encamp about the town.*[1]

P&O Working the Sound

P&O had originally won the contract for a service to deliver the Royal Mail, passengers and cargo between the United Kingdom, Spain, Egypt, India and the far east of Australia. However, in the 1850s the company also would have a most significant impact on the development of Albany where its flag could be seen on the foreshore of The Princess Royal Harbour for many years. It would not be unfair to state that for much of the latter half of the Nineteenth Century Albany had become a P&O Company town. This was because in the fledgling days of steam these services by necessity required large ships and the establishment of coaling stations, docks, storage facilities and a repair capacity at strategic points along the route that the ships took. Such an undertaking, therefore, required considerable capital investment.

On the 31st December 1840 The Peninsular and Oriental Steam Navigation Company of London had become a limited liability company that was incorporated by Royal Charter and was soon known by its famous acronym P&O.

Commercial steam communication with Australia was inaugurated in 1852 by means of an extension of the line from Singapore and in 1854 the Bombay mail service passed from the hands of the East India

---

[1] Reverend John Wollaston. *Wollaston's Albany Journals.* 1848 – 1856 Volume 2. Perth. 1954.

Company into the much safer and more reliable hands of P&O. With this move, P&O had become the chief trustee of British steam shipping services to the Asiatic region, providing the only regular and reliable Royal Mail, passenger and cargo service between Europe and Australia.

Excitement in the Town

The arrival of the Royal Mail steamers would elicit significant excitement in the port among the local residents, most particularly when the mail and passenger steamer service began operating a more regular fortnightly service to the town in the 1860s. The advent of steam ships and their regular visits to the port had given Albany a 'raisons d'être' outside of it being simply a coaling depot. Besides providing the locals with the first news from abroad by way of its shipment of newspapers and correspondence from Europe, the return service from Sydney also provided an update on the Eastern States colonies activities:

> *All is bustle and excitement in Albany, and we noticed the great activity at the pilot station. The crew go down to the shed, launch the boat and wait for the pilot. The boat sails are hoisted, the pilot jumps onboard and a start is made for the outer harbour. We watch the boat, but cannot yet see the steamer, as Point Possession obstructs our view. In a few minutes, the boat sails are lowered, the oars are manned, and the steamer's nose begins to peep around the corner and almost immediately the rest of the hull. The boat is pulled alongside. After a slight delay, while the usual questions are asked as to the health of the crew and passengers, the pilot boards her, and a course is shaped for the harbour.*[2]

Coaling Depot

With the advent of coal-fired steam ships, Albany became a bunkering port of call for ships en route to the Eastern Colonies from England and westwards to Africa and Europe. With the decline of sailing ships, many of these old vessels were then on-sold as coaling hulks to ports like Albany. The coaling hulks were manned by local crews providing an important source of employment in the town. Consequently, the presence of the coal bunkering operation for steam ships contributed significantly to the economy of Albany in the mid-Nineteenth Century. The Albany Coaling Depot for the Royal Mail run to and from the Eastern Colonies was operated by P&O which commenced its operations in the town in 1853.

The benefits of King George's Sound as a coaling port had been recognised in an article entitled "Scattered Notions" garnered from a traveller's notebook that recorded his journey from Sydney to England. Extracts of the article were reproduced in *The Sydney Morning Herald*:

> *…the harbour referred to, you enter the sound, which forms a beautiful and extensive basin and capable of containing any amount of shipping, and is certainly a most desirable place for just what it is, viz. A coal depot. There are here now nine vessels, principally foreigners, who have been chartered with coals for the A.R.M. and P&O companies; and another large vessel arrived from Newcastle (England), out eighty-eight days, with about 1000 tons of coal…*
>
> *…It seems the sort of place that was going to be a something all in a hurry, and then stopped, from the want of funds, or some other cause not originally anticipated. With the exception of a few idle seamen in the vicinity of the aforesaid public-house, and a large number of men carrying coals onshore, you would almost fancy the place deserted…*[3]

The *Larkins* was the first sailing ship to be converted in 1857 into a coal hulk to service Albany.[4] With the advent of steam, *Larkins* was transferred to The Princess Royal Harbour where it was followed in turn by the coal hulks *Kingfisher* in 1859 and finally by the last hulk to grace the port, the *Sierra Colonna*. In 1875 *Larkins* was declared unfit for service and the remains of the hulk are believed to have been used

---

[2] *The Western Mail*. Perth. 3rd February 1927.
[3] *Sydney Morning Herald*. 30th January 1854.
[4] The *Larkins* was built in Calcutta in 1807/8. Initially named *Louisa*, it was the last and largest of the vessels built by Hudson and Bacon. The ship was renamed *Larkins* after it was transferred to John Pascal Larkins, a member of a well-known East India Company family. The *Larkins* was used for the transport of convicts and freight on the Australian and India runs, during which time it passed through the hands of several owners.

as landfill. The figurehead of the hulk had been removed and now resides in the Museum of the Great Southern in Albany.

The advent of the Crimean War in 1854 along with contractual issues and poor management involving the Australian Royal Mail Steam Navigation Company that had previously been assigned the mail run resulted in mail services to Albany becoming intermittent and therefore, not reliable. A passenger on the P&O *Chusan* in 1854 provides a glimpse of their personal travel experience from Sydney to England:

> The Chusan *is a beautiful new screw[5] steamship of 750 tons, about 100 horsepower, and is under the command of Captain Henry Down, who so greatly celebrated himself and ship in having been the first to introduce the great boon of steam communication between England and Australia, in the month of August 1852; she was originally built by Miller, Ravenhill, Salkeld and Co, of London, for the cattle trade, in March 1852, to run between Hamburg and London, but afterwards purchased by the above company, to continue the line of postal communication from Singapore to Sydney...*
>
> *Captain Down is a thorough gentleman, and an able seaman; careful, but at the same time fears neither wind nor weather but has a peculiar weakness for dealing most liberally with canvas, studying; sails, booms &c, whenever an opportunity or half a chance offers. Rest assured of one thing, that if she misses the mail, or makes a long passage, it is not the fault of Captain Down, whatever other cause or circumstance may lay in the way ...*
>
> *Monday, December 5.*
> *Morning fine, the wind still strong ahead, not doing much. Kangaroo Island in sight, terrible heavy sea all day; vessel pitching much. Passengers exhibiting strong indications of misery.*
>
> *Wednesday, December 7.*
> *... light winds, smooth seas. Passengers looking and feeling more sociable as they improve in health; all sails set; at noon, 200 miles from King George's Sound; afternoon and evening fair wind, but increasing, ship going 9 and 10 knots.*
>
> *Saturday, December 10.*
> *At daylight, land in sight, which turned out, as we approached further, to be Bald Head, about eight miles from the entrance to King George's Sound. The coast here presents a barren, broken appearance, very similar to that in the vicinity of Wilson's Promontory and the Islands in Bass's Straits; more prettily interspersed with low and lofty mountains, rising with tapered tops, but almost free from any symptom of vegetation whatsoever. As we continued our course, several other islands were in sight, two of which form the entrance of the harbour leading to the Sound, with Bald Head on the left, making three capital and safe passages for vessels of any tonnage; passing these, and about four miles of the harbour referred to, you enter the Sound, which forms a beautiful and extensive basis, and capable of containing any amount of shipping, and is certainly a most desirable place for just what it is, viz – a coal depot. There are here now nine vessels, principally foreigners, who have been chartered with coals for the Australian Royal Mail and P&O Companies; and another large vessel arrived this morning from Newcastle (England), out eighty-eight days, with about 1000 tons of coals.*
>
> *The town of Albany, situated on the northern side of the bay, is a small place with about fifty houses, which, with the district around, is supposed to contain a population of 500 people. There is a small church, a courthouse, public-house, and gaol, with numerous other odd buildings, which have, at some time or other, had some connection with the Government, but are now in the occupation of nobody knows who. It seems a sort of place that was going to be something all in a hurry and then stopped; from the want of funds, or some other cause not originally anticipated. With the exception of a few idle seamen in the vicinity of the aforesaid public house, and a large number of men employed carrying coals onshore, you would almost fancy the place deserted, or given over to the possession of the Blacks, who seem the principal occupants of the city. There is, however, one large house being erected, and I should think, from the size of it, compared with the others, that it is intended for the Governor, if there is such an illustrious person, or if not, will be looked upon in the light of one, as soon as ever it is occupied.*

---

[5] The screw propeller was patented by Francis Pettit Smith in the United Kingdom in 1836. The first screw propelled ship to arrive in Albany was the aptly named *Great Britain* in 1852.

> *Without any intention or desire of libelling the town or irritating the feelings of any of its inhabitants, I must say, in all my travels (which perhaps have not been great), I never saw a more cold, lifeless, petrifying place in all my life. The scenery from the hill, however, surrounding the town, of the Sound, Harbour, Ocean and country about, and islands, form a most beautiful and picturesque appearance. In many parts of the bush, Nature has planted her own garden with a great variety of native flowers, which flourish most luxuriantly, and far excel any in the neighbourhood of Sydney. The shipping lay about a quarter of a mile from the shore, which consists of a sandy beach with the town just at the back, the access to which is along a substantial jetty of 200 or 300 yards in length made for the purpose of ensuring coals to the above which, with the quantity afloat in the bay, is supposed to exceed 15,000 tons, belonging to the two companies. Having disposed of King George's Sound, and the town of Albany, we turn out attention on board the Chusan again, which we find busy taking in coals at all corners and will continue all night, in order to get away tomorrow morning at 9 o'clock, for Point de Galle, Ceylon, where we hope yet to arrive in time for the mail.[6]*

The impact of the loss of a reliable passenger and mail service due to the Crimean War had a devastating immediate impact on Albany's economy. When the Crimean War had finally reached its conclusion in 1856 discussions were held to address the issue of a regular mail service to Australia which resulted in the formation of the European and Australian Royal Mail Company. However, there was no provision in the service contract of this new mail service for the inclusion of ports of call in Western Australia. Fortuitously, the need for the company to access coal necessitated the need to use the King George's Sound facilities and the P&O assisted the venture by making its facilities available. Unfortunately, this venture suffered the same fate as the Australian Royal Mail Steam Navigation Company through bad management, break downs and the occasional accident and consequently the mail service once again became intermittent. In 1859 P&O had regained the tender for the carrying of Royal Mail and as result a more predictable and regular service re-commenced.

It is prudent to turn to Captain James Sale an Albany resident who in his written accounts of shipping in the period 1850 to 1860 observed and recorded that the ships visiting the town at this time had begun to transition from sail to steam power:

> *… In its mail boat days, the P&O company had a big establishment at Albany, employing about 300 men in their coaling depot. The company paid their men weekly and that money in circulation made trade brisk…*
> *… two lighters, Jonathan and the John Bull, were being launched for the P&O company. One was christened by Miss Kate McKenzie. She said, "Long live Jonathan!" The John Bull was christened by Miss Keating, and she said Long live "John Bullock!" A few years later for other lighters were built, these later being used as water tanks by Armstrong and Waters, tug owners. The first P&O steamer I saw at Albany, and I think she was the first to visit here, was the Chusan; the next was the Oneida. These vessels were paddle steamers, and were barque-rigged…*
>
> *… The names of other P&O boats were Malta, Rangoon, and Hindustan. …These vessels traded with the Indian coast and to Singapore before they came down to Australia. We got mail at Albany from London every three months. Later these paddle steamers we converted to screw. The first was Malta. Insufficient ballast was put in her, and when she arrived at Albany, she was on her beam ends…*
>
> *The only light at that time was one on Point King, a small stationary beacon. The Breaksea light was not erected until sometime in the 1860s…[7]*

Sale referenced in his recollections the inter-colonial shipping trade, specifically between New South Wales, Adelaide and Albany:

> *There were several small brigs engaged in the interstate trade if you could call it that before there were any states. One was a small brig, the Emily Smith, of about 250 tons. Owned by Captain Davidson, she traded out of Albany bringing a full load of supplies such as flour and merchandise about once every two months. Our sugar came from Mauritius, and we got our tea from any passing ship. The sugar was like brown mud and was in*

---

[6] *The Sydney Morning Herald*. 30th January 1854.
[7] *The West Australian*. 7th March 1936.

> *big lumps. We were often short of tea, but there was a native tree growing at Albany that made a very good substitute…*
>
> *… the circumstances of the loss of the* Emily Smith *on Kangaroo Island were tragic. The owner had decided to retire and to give up the command to his son, John Davidson. The son stayed in Port in Adelaide to pass examinations, but the ship was wrecked on Kangaroo Island, the only survivor being a Chinese cook.*
>
> *There was another small brig that used to trade from Adelaide to Albany called the* Kestrel; *she would often go to Fremantle also. She brought general cargo. This was in the 1860s when Albany was growing rapidly, and the* Emily Smith *could not keep the place supplied…*
>
> Verlum, *a barque of 800 tons, commanded by Captain Angel. She came to Albany every year and cleared the season's wool clip. There were no means of dumping in those days and the wool had to be screwed into the ships hold with large screws.*
>
> *All the ships in these early days and up to about 1878 had to sail in and out of harbour through a narrow passage between Point King and Point Possession- some of these ships through as much as 25 feet- and I do not remember a single accident during all the years… The pilots were very skilful. The first pilot I remember was Captain Precious. After his retirement came Captain Butcher…[8]*

Henry Lawson in his laconic style reported on the excitement in the town with the arrival of a new ship into the harbour and the events that subsequently unfolded on the town's jetty:

> *There was no regular intercolonial line of steamers to Albany in '89. The town depended, first, on the fact that it had the only harbour handy in the colony, and (for existence) on the ocean liners that called there. Way back of that there were the jarrah and sandalwood industries, and kangaroo skins, and the whalers, and, I think, a few sealers. Then the railway syndicate, the Navy army, and the line to York, and so to Perth… There were several coal-hulks in Albany old sailing ships with histories, and 'Albanian' labourers got fairly regular spells of lumping and wharf labouring…*
>
> *The mail boats often arrived at King George sound on Saturday night; the Post Office was not opened on Sunday morning. When the boat was signalled, a red flag by daylight, or Red Lantern at night, was run up on the P&O flagstaff. That lantern was a dull red beacon of hope, which set many a longingly heart, that was breaking for home, beating quickly. If not too late, Albany will drift down to the jetty, but there were always a few going out with the tender into the moonlit Sound, where, rising above the horizon, or out of the faint, and certain haze of the water in the nearer distance, like the evening star, was seen the headlight of the liner…*
>
> *Presently, suddenly, it seemed, in the moonlight haze, when distances and movements are so uncertain, the whole line of the ships electrics which swing to us and blaze out. Presently, the great anchor jolted down, the tender ran alongside. A row of cloaked figures and curious faces at the rail. We can imagine the emotions of new chums at their first glimpse of Australia – the land of their hopes and dreams…*
>
> *A hurry comparison of notes between the agent and the post official, and the corresponding satellites on board; a trotting up and down the gangway with mailbags and luggage…[9]*

The coastal steamers were the main carriers of passengers and cargo between Western Australian ports before the advent of the Great Southern Railway. Captain Reynolds was a whaling steamship captain and had an interest in the local coastal and Royal Mail steamers which made port calls to King George's Sound. During his stay in the town, he made note of some of the names of steam ships which visited Albany:

> *Otway.* (Captain J. Clark) A popular West Australian Coastal steamer of 271 tons serving ports and landings on the South and West Coast.
> *Malwa.* (Captain G.W. Atkinson) Peninsular & Oriental Steam Navigation Company Royal Mail steamer of 2850 tons.

---

[8] Ibid
[9] "The Golden Nineties", *The Australian Star*, Sydney 1889.

Macedon. (Captain Craig) a local coastal steamer of 532 tons owned by James Lilly & Company of Fremantle. *Macedon* was wrecked off Rottnest Island in March 1883.
Ravenna. (Captain A. Stewart) P&O Royal Mail steamer of 3572 tons.
Sutlej. (Captain A.N. Johnson) P&O Royal Mail steamer of 4194 tons.[10]

Through a succession of articles that reported on the proceedings at King George's Sound the community was kept apprised of waterfront events. For example, a Correspondent of *The Albany Mail and King George's Sound Advertiser* wrote:

> *One of the P&O steamers, from Melbourne, having dropped anchor at 5 am. in Princess Royal Harbour, King George's Sound, a short time ago, a number of the passengers were soon on deck admiring the harbour, but remarking what a barren appearance the surrounding hills presented. In about a north-easterly direction from them stood Mount Clarence, the highest visible point, and about a mile distant in a westerly direction, stood Mount Melville, not quite so high; both standing on the edge of the water.*
>
> *From the shore running up over the gap which separates these two hills, the town of Albany is situated with a population of 1,500. Between the vessels and Mount Clarence was to be seen The West Australian Land Company's wharf. A little farther to its left was another shorter pier known as the coal wharf, and nearly a mile farther along, close to the busiest part of the town, was the Government wharf at which we were landed from a steamer in a steam launch. Our luggage was put on a truck and pushed up to the Custom House and examined as is usual at such places. The only kind of conveyances to be seen were two ramshackle looking spring carts: one of them was built of such a shape that it resembled a cart turned upside down, with the bottom knocked out. Five of us chose this curiosity to get our luggage to a hotel: it was very convenient to load as the bottom of it was only about a foot or eighteen inches from the ground.*
>
> *Not being very strong after the effects of a rough sea voyage, some of us felt inclined to wish that we were trunks or carpet bags and go in the cart with our luggage instead of having to ride Shank's Pony. In front of us stood a three-storied building known as The Government Buildings; the upper story, at the opposite side, is level with the street. This building consists of the Post and Telegraph Offices, HM Customs and Court House.*
>
> *The entrance to the harbour is through a short narrow straight passage about a quarter of a mile in width from the sheltered waters of the Sound. All the P&O Company's boats come into the harbour and allow passengers to come ashore, but the Orient Line Company's boats lie outside, and the steam tugs and lighters bring and take passengers and luggage to and from the vessels. Looking in a southerly direction across the entrance we see a sheet of water running in from the left hand toward the Quarantine Station. This sheet of water is known as Frenchman's Bay and separated from the entrance to the harbour by a low round bald hill of granite rock running round separating it from the harbour and meeting a high mount, which we see on the other side. This mount has an abrupt termination on the land hand but runs along to the right separating the main ocean from Frenchman's Bay.*
>
> *Looking a little farther to the right, across the Quarantine Station and harbour to the right of it, we see hilly country with here and there a hut or house, which we are informed are lime burners residences, that it is a limestone country: we were also informed that there is plenty of galena, showing on the surface at the Quarantine Station, but it has never been tested to show the amount of silver or gold that it may contain.*
>
> *There are about the harbour a number of small boats or various kinds, and some old wooden vessels without topmasts which contain* coal to *supply passing steamers.*[11]

A dichotomy of views is expressed in the correspondence and available remarks from the early steamship passengers. Some viewed Albany as a miserable place: although sill recognising its importance and noting its dependence upon the P&O coaling facility and recognising the wonderful natural setting of the harbour. Other writers saw it in a different light. A passenger onboard the P&O steamship *Malta* visiting King George's Sound remarked:

> *It was late at night before the lighthouse on Breaksea Island, at the entrance of the Sound, heaved in sight and, notwithstanding that we had shipped about 1,000 tons of coal at Galle, there now remained so little in the*

---

[10] Our Own Correspondent. *The West Australian*, Perth. 31st July 1882.
[11] *The Albany Mail and King George's Sound Advertiser.* 19th December 1888.

Malta that she had shifted over on her side to by no means a pleasant angle in the eyes of landsmen. It was doubtful whether we should be able to enter the Sound that night, especially with so large a steamer in so bad a trim, and the majority of the passengers remained on deck till a late hour, notwithstanding a cool breeze which was quite biting after the heat of the day...

To make the Sound in safety, Captain Gaby had taken a round of ten miles, entering by a larger channel than usual, and one gun-signal for a pilot was duly responded to; but we were doomed to disappointment, for after passing into the outer harbour, the steamer could not be got to answer her helm satisfactorily, and we cast anchor for the night, sending away for some barges of coal, to effect a sufficient trimming to enable the Malta to run in next morning. On the 12th, daybreak came to find the temporary coaling began, the steamer for Adelaide alongside, and the mails being rapidly transferred. Formerly the P&O steamer called in at Kangaroo Island, opposite Port Adelaide, and delivered the mails en-passant; but this service was attended with so much delay and danger, that a boat of the Australian M.N. Co meets the mail-steamer at King George Sound and runs down with mails and passengers in a little more than four days. The Benares *lost the other day in China was always deemed one of the most unsafe of the P&O boats, on one occasion ran ashore on her way to Kangaroo Island, but after wobbling about with her foremast high and dry, and her stern in deep water, quite long enough for the passengers' tastes, the prompt action of the commander and the reversal of the engines brought her off without any serious damages.*

King George's Sound is, in many respects, a curious and interesting place. The usual place of anchorage in the inner harbour is several miles distant from any of the entrances at the heads, and the passage winds its way amidst huge masses of rock (evidently of primary formation), formed into islands or prolonged ridges, covered with dense low scrub, and connected with the mainland. The course is intricate and circuitous, but the inner harbour, after passing the second light, presents a sheet of smooth, clear water, of considerable extent, and almost entirely land-locked. The depth, however, is not great, and the main channel only – 500 yards wide – can be depended upon for vessels of any size, which are obliged to anchor a considerable distance from the wooden jetties constructed on the beach. The shelter afforded from the storms, which completely blow around this coast, is complete; but sailing vessels are often prevented from taking their departure for long periods, owing to adverse winds at the heads. As the Malta *steamed in, we passed a whaler which had been lying wind-bound for three weeks. The harbour does not present a very lively appearance, there being little business at this port of call at any time. Two colliers, the many huge, heavy coal-barges of the P&O Company, with a floating dock constructed for their repair; a small coasting schooner, a yacht or two, and the passenger-boats, made up the scene on the water...*

The P&O Agent's handsome residence, surmounted by the company's flag, seemed the most prominent building in the place; but all the houses had a fresh, clean appearance, from the admirable stone employed in building, and the neatly cut shingles with which they were roofed. Of course, every passenger gladly escaped from the Malta *during coaling operation, anxious besides to stretch one's limbs and enjoy a change onshore...*

The convicts did not present a very interesting sight at work on the roads, some in chain-gangs, and all alike displaying the broad-arrow on their trousers, which marked them as the Queen's Own. Every diversity of countenance was presented amongst them, but perhaps the best example of this was to be found in the crew of the pilot's boat – some half-dozen ticket-of-leave men – of whose history I got a few particulars. The main in charge, a thin, short, sharp-faced, high cheek-boned Scotsman, had, it seems, scuttled a vessel in his charge as mate for some reason or other, and so had to cross the ocean at his country's expense...... Not much is ever heard of King George's Sound, and if it were given up as a coaling station for the P&O Company, its existence would be very probably forgotten out of Australia... A miserable night on board the Malta *followed with the coaling, which was not finished was far advanced, at 2 p.m. On which day we started, expecting a fair wind in our easterly course...*[12]

Diary entries from the many travellers to the port in the latter part of the Nineteenth Century offer a further glimpse of the town during the latter part of the Nineteenth Century. For example, an extract from a from William Traylen in 1890:

The SS Orient, *Feb 2nd 1890.*

---

[12] *The Inquirer and Commercial News*. Perth. 23rd June 1869.

The magnificent steam ships of the Orient Line and of the P&O Company being Albany within 10 days of Colombo. The ocean to be traversed offers less danger to the traveller than that between Ceylon and England. There is not even the Australian Bight to be crossed. Some time can be pleasantly spent in the picturesque and prosperous town of Albany. The ever-changing scene on the jetty; the come and go of those "floating palaces," the mail steamers, twice a week; excursions on and around the Bay; drives to the uncleared bush and to the virgin forest; all offer charms to the languid European-Ceylonese.[13]

P&O Shareholders Meeting Dissenting Opinions

As with all privately-owned companies the need to maintain profitability for owners and shareholders was always a concern. The minutes from a P&O shareholders meeting give testimony to the issues that needed to be addressed by the company:

At the half-yearly meeting of the P&O Company, held in London on 2 December last, statements were made that I scarcely correct. The chairman said, the service continued to be efficiently performed, and their friends in Australia, who were not usually favourable critics were at length constraints [sic] quick knowledge that they received their letters regularly and that the service was carried out in a manner with no room for complaint.

The chairman in making this statement was exaggerating, and to some extent misrepresenting the opinions held in these colonies in reference to the operations of the P&O company. It is true, male [sic] communication has been well-maintained, though even in this matter the delays which have occurred have been far more frequent than the remarks of the chairman would leave the public to suppose. But in all other matters, the people of Australia I know are more satisfied with the P&O company now than they have ever been. There is still plenty of room for complaint, as far as the passenger traffic of the company is concerned; and the disagreeable character for incivility which the servants of the company have acquired appears to be every day becoming worse instead of better…

… Instance of the arbitrary conflict of the officers and agents connected with the P&O company occurred on the arrival of the last English mail at King George's Sound, when, from mere caprice, the South Australian mails were detained until all the boxes for Western Australia had been sent ashore. This caused the branch steamer to be kept three hours beyond the necessary time; a detention which occasioned much inconvenience to persons throughout the colonies, for the news brought by the mail, instead of being distributed by electric Telegraph early on Thursday night, was not received in Adelaide until Friday morning. But this is only one instance out of money in respect of which the people of these colonies have room for complaint. In fact, the P&O Service in Australia is administered in a spirit which plainly shows that the company would not be bothered with the colonies if its other interests could be secured without the aid.[14]

Facilities to Service the Ships

It was in 1837 that a jetty structure was constructed to serve The Princess Royal Harbour. Until that time ships arriving in the port relied on the services of small boats coming alongside to transport cargo and passengers to the shore, usually at either Middleton Beach or Ellen Cove. As expected, such a process was most difficult when conveying stock to the settlement. To overcome the issue of landing stock, particularly horses and cattle, the solution was simply to swim them onshore.

Jetty Structures

In 1835 Governor James Stirling selected the site for a jetty at the foot of Bridge Street, which is half a mile east from the town centre. While the jetty he proposed was planned to be 130 yards long the potential cost was so great that only 70 yards of it were eventually able to be built. It was in 1837 that this, Albany's first jetty project was completed.

---

[13] *The Daily News*, Perth. 6th March 1890.
[14] *The Inquirer and Commercial News*. 6th May 1863.

There had been some controversy over the site, as Major Lockyer and Captain Wakefield, had by necessity initially constructed a small landing platform at the foot of Parade Street. Unfortunately, the water at this site was very shallow, consequently, it was decided to replace it with one at the foot of York Street, which later on evolved into the main street of the town.

> *The structure that Captain Wakefield had built there and which was wrongly called the York Street jetty, consisted of only a few piles worked into the sand; It was a small landing stage for small boats. There were several of these along the waterfront. All cargo had to be landed in boats along the beach at Parade Street until the town jetty was built and connected with that road access." The only access to the Terrace in those days was by Parade and York Streets. On each side of Parade Street, there was a hotel. The one on the west was run by Captain McKenzie.[15] This was called the 'Ship Inn'. The hotel on the opposite side was the 'Sailor's Rest' and was kept by Mr Humphries. York Street was just a watercourse and had a bridge to connect the west and the east side of town.[16]*

The colonial government decided to extend the town's jetty structure in 1849. The popular choice among the townspeople was to have a new jetty constructed at the foot of York Street. Work started on this in 1850 but again unfortunately, later that year a storm covered the pylons that had already been partially erected with silt and sand to the extent that work on the project had to be abandoned. As Captain Sales indicated: *Well, some people talk of the York Street jetty, however, no formal jetty was ever built there.[17]*

In the interim, it was decided that the existing jetty had to service the town's needs. The first substantial jetty built at Albany was the P&O jetty. This was built for the landing of steamer coal supplies and was constructed about 1852. Subsequently, it was determined that a jetty complex on a site below the present Lawley Park was required. This was, however, found to be very inconvenient, as everything had to be handled and transported along the shoreline of the harbour, and further, the depth of water in which the structure stood was only 12 feet in depth. In 1859 the new town jetty was commenced at the foot of Spencer Street. This structure was not completed until 1864, however, and even then, it was found to be too short. It was subsequently extended in 1868 and then again in 1870:

> *The Albany town jetty was built by Mr Covert, about 1859. A great deal of responsibility devolved to the contractor for any job because all the timber had to be cut by hand. At first Mr Covert thought that he could bore and, by placing the pile in the case, the pile would then slip down as the bore went down. He found that this would not work because of the clay underneath the topcoat of sand… he made a monkey, and every pile was driven with the wooden monkey. All the piles and planking had to be boated from the King and Kalgan rivers. The jetty was called Covert jetty for many years. Notwithstanding the fact that the town jetty was built in 12 feet of water, all cargo had to be lighted into small boats and lifted onto the jetty by cranes. Previous to that it had to be carried onshore and drays from the stores would come alongside the boat wherever she grounded. In the early days, supplies were obtained from the American whalers. Things such as salt pork, beet, biscuits, molasses and clothing were bought by the whalers for trading. I have seen as many as 10 or 12 whalers in the inner and outer harbour at the one time. They came in for water and to give the men liberty. Firewood was also taken to be used as fuel for the boiling down of the oil.[18]*

During the latter half of the Nineteenth Century, Albany clearly had earned the cognomen as a P&O Company town. P&O made significant investment in the town both in terms of infrastructure development and as the town's most significant labour employer. William C. Clifton, the P&O Branch Manager at Mauritius, was appointed to Albany in 1860 and arrived at the port to take charge of company business as of February 1861. The activities of the P&O company continued to be regularly reported in the local newspaper:

> *An agency house, The Mount, was erected by the company in Brunswick Road, in 1867, and there the Clifton family resided until 1882 when Mr and Mrs Clifton and a portion of the family returned to England. The*

---

[15] In the early 1860s Mr J. McKenzie was whaling at Doubtful Island Bay, Cape Riche and Cape Arid, and the Sherrett brothers were out around Rabbit Island and in King George's Sound. One season Mr McKenzie had a bad mishap at Doubtful Island Bay and had two men killed by a small whale. McKenzie was knocked overboard, but scramble back into the boat. This event occurred in 1868.
[16] *The West Australian*, Perth, 7th March 1936.
[17] Ibid.
[18] Ibid.

first chief clerk of the company at Albany was Mr W.G. Knight who later was a partner in the firm of John McKail and Company and his father, Stephen Knight was the one-time Postmaster at Albany.

In 1868 a Co-operative store was started by Mr Clifton and in which the employees' held shares. Goods were sold at the margin over cost, sufficient to pay expenses. Operations commenced at Dunn's cottage, vacated by Mr Clifton (upon the completion of The Mount) and subsequently, a building was erected at the corner of Spencer and Frederick Street. The Co-operative property later passed into the hands of the late Edward C Barnett, founder of the well-known firm Edward Barnett and Company Limited.[19]

P&O Floating Dock 1886

A local correspondent for *The Perth Gazette* provided readers with the following account of the construction and launching in the town of a large floating dock for the P&O Company's service:

> *As I have occasionally seen references in your Albany Correspondent's letter to the floating dock, building for the P&O Company. I think you may possibly be glad to learn some particulars of what I believe to be the largest craft yet built in the Colony.*
>
> *At the recommendation of Mr W.C. Clifton, the P&O Company's Agent at King George's Sound, in the year 1862, four iron lighters (of 120 tons burthen) were sent out in sections, and built there, the last of which was launched in April 1864; and it was clear some provision must be made for cleaning and repairing these lighters as well as the hulk* Kingfisher, *Mr Clifton pointed out to the Company that either a patent slip or a floating dock would be necessary.*
>
> *The peculiar nature of the shore of the harbour and the remarkably small rise and fall of the tide, seldom exceeding 24 inches, and often not reaching 18, rendered a slip very undesirable if not altogether impracticable; he consequently strongly recommended the construction of a floating dock according to the plans he then sent home, and which were drawn by Captain Van Zuileom whom some of the old Colonists may remember when in command of the* Hindoo. *The Directors having approved of the recommendations and given Mr Clifton authority to make the best arrangements in his power issued notices for Tenders for timber on 14th April 1864, and early in July commenced the dock, which was launched on 14th April 1866.*
>
> *The work has been entirely carried out under the personal inspection of Captain Van Zuileom and reflects great credit upon him and those under his orders. From the nature of the ground where the dock was built, it was necessary to be constructed broadside to the sea, consequently, it was obliged to be launched in that unusual and difficult position; to effect this, five ways were constructed, and so admirably were they made by Mr Daniels the P&O Co.'s shipwright at Albany, that at the order being given the dog-shores*[20] *were knocked away and the immense fabric glided with the utmost ease into the water, amidst the continued cheers of the great majority of the population, many of whom could not bring themselves to believe it was possible for the dock to be launched.*
>
> *For the occasion, three temporary masts were erected on board, at the heads of which floated the Union Jack, the British Ensign, and the P&O Company's well-known Flag. The Company's office and the* Larkins *were dressed, and the day being remarkably fine a prettier sight has perhaps never been seen in Albany.*
>
> *The Lord Bishop of Perth has taken a great interest in the floating dock since he arrived a month ago and has been several times on board while she was on the stocks and was also present at the launch.*
>
> *As the process of docking may not be generally known, I will describe it: - The dock is moored in a suitable situation and being fitted with 3 valves on each side, which are opened and shut by rods from the dock (which runs all round except aft), the water is gradually let in and the dock grounded; the vessel is then floated in and the gates which are most carefully made watertight, are closed and firmly secured to a strong beam by contrivances for the purpose. After the vessel has been shored up, the dock is pumped dry by five powerful pumps, and as in this case only manual labour can at present be employed, it is calculated that it will take about four hours to get*

---

[19] *The Albany Advertiser.* 27th October 1928.
[20] Dog-shores are the pieces of timber that are used to shore up a vessel, to keep it from falling or from starting during the preparations for launching, knocked aside when the ship is ready to be launched.

rid of the water. The vessel will then be left quite dry for the purpose of undergoing any repairs. The un-docking is simply the reverse of the above, the water being let into the dock to float the vessel out.[21]

In the 1890's significant work was undertaken to fortify the port facilities given the perceived threats from foreign shipping, the 'Russian Scare' by way of example. Therefore, it was again determined to undertake further development of the port's infrastructure. As *The Esperance Times* was to report:

> *The Government surveyors have started surveying the harbour' in the neighbourhood of the town jetty at Albany, with a view to improvements.*[22]

Eventually two jetties were constructed that extended into deeper water, one near the entrance of Princes Royal Harbour, having a depth of 30 feet at low tide and the other closer to the town end. The jetties were constructed by the West Australian Lands Company. The new Deepwater Jetty was constructed in 1888 to service shipping at King George's Sound:

> *The New Jetty at Albany,*
> *Western Australia.*
>
> *We give elsewhere a very accurate view of the new jetty or pier, which has lately been constructed by the West Australian Land Company, for the use of the Great Southern Railway, at the important seaport town of Albany, Western Australia. Our readers will, no doubt, be interested in learning a few particulars concerning this massive structure. It is unnecessary to dwell upon the excellence of the natural harbour known as Princess Royal Harbour, as that is a matter of worldwide notoriety. The erection of a deep-water pier or wharf was an addition without which the natural qualities of the harbour were only partially turned to utility.*
>
> *The terminus of the Great Southern Railway will be at Albany, and the line has been continued along the foreshore, for about a mile to the eastward of the Post Office, to a spot nearly under the harbour master's house…*
>
> *The whole of this, in the end, consists of 65 tiers of three piles each, with timber walling and bracings to form a rigid structure. Both sides of the south end of the narrow portion is a platform with steps for the convenience of boats, and from this broad step ladders leading up into the deck of the main jetty…*
>
> *The jetty was designed in the first instance by the late Mr William Rogers, and since his death, Mr Frederick Stafford, who succeeded to the post of Chief Engineer, has worked out all the remaining details… Mr John Wishart senior, started the work, and in April 1887 Mr Adolf Nehneemiah took charge as general foreman and he remained until completion…*
>
> *Experts and others who have visited the jetty both during construction and near completion, have pronounced it to be a most magnificent job and say that both workmanship and materials of the highest and most finished quality.*[23]

The later structure had a depth of 22 feet. It was at the 'Deep Water Jetty' as it became known that the largest steamers from the North German Lloyd Company, the *Frederick der Grosse* for instance, and the ships of the White Star Line could readily be brought alongside in relative safety; leaving the town jetty to accommodate the inter-colonial steamers traffic.

Reporting the commencement of the Western Australian Land Companies Jetty *The Albany Mail and King George's Sound Advertiser* paid particular attention to the ceremony associated with the installation of the first pylon:

> *Driving of the First Pile.*
>
> *At 3:30 on Tuesday last, the following guests met on the jetty by invitation of Mr Wishart, of the firm of Messrs. Davies, Bailey and Wishart, of Adelaide to witness the driving of the first pile of the new jetty to be erected for the West Australian Land Company… (guest list…*
>
> *Armstrong's steam launch was waiting to convey the party to the scene of the ceremony. The afternoon was fine, and after an enjoyable little run over, the passengers disembarked on a platform erected about 400 feet from the shore in front of Captain Butcher's house and connected by a planked footway with the land. Mr Martin, Captain*

---

[21] *The Perth Gazette and West Australian Times.* 4th May 1866.
[22] *The Esperance Times.* 9th December 1896.

[23] *The Pictorial Australian.* December 1888 Edition with the information attributed to *The Albany Advertiser.*

Thompson and Mr Young, Junior, met the party on the platform, and after a short interval, during which the monkey was raised by a winch which drove the pile about 6 inches further down.

After this, those present adjourned to Captain Butcher's house, where refreshments for the inner man were provided by Mr Wishart, and the wherewithal to toast access to the undertaking.

On assembling for this later laudable purpose, Mr Young said that before partaking of Mr Wishart's hospitality he thought it would be well to say a few words regarding the important work, for though the railway which was being constructed would help largely into the future development of the country, yet it would be of a small value without a means of ingress and egress for the goods to be conveyed by the railway, which wants this jetty would Supply. The work had been placed in the hands of well-known contractors, and he hoped that before 12 months relapse the firm represented by Mr Wishart would establish a construction, second to none in the colonies... Mr Young then said that when the work with accomplished the largest ships float will be able to come alongside the jetty, and the accommodation will be sufficient for two P. & O. steamers and four other large vessels to be unloading cargo simultaneously, and he hoped the happy would arrive when such a sight might be witnessed. In conclusion, he proposed success to the undertaking, coupled with the name of Mr Wishart.

Mr Wishart, in replying, thanked all present for their attendance, and said that the people had heard for so long a period that the work was going to commence, that they had begun to think it never was going to take place, so he had commenced matters on the principle of "better late than never."[24]

Closing Remarks

Albany's fortunes in the Nineteenth Century were clearly linked to the sea through shipping, whaling and sealing activities. It was not surprising therefore, that when in the mid-century the town through its strong links to steam powered shipping had become very reliant on the economic benefits derived from its support of the dominant P&O company's endeavours particularly in its role as an important coaling port.

The Albany Advertiser would often carry several advertisements from various shipping companies competing for the now quite lucrative passenger and cargo trade entering and exiting the port as this representative sample demonstrates:

French Mail Steamers.

(Compagnie des Messageries Maritimes.)

The Fleet consists of the finest and fastest vessels trading to Australia.

Accelerated and rapid services between Albany, Marseilles and London, calling at Mahé (Seychelles Islands), Aden, Suez and Port Said. The Steamers for Marseilles leave Albany on or about the 3rd of each month.

Rates of Passage Money to Marseilles, £20 to £65, including Wines or Ales at Meals and Bedding requisites in all classes. Cuisine Recherché. Electric Light throughout. Return Tickets issued at reduced rates.

SALOON PASSENGERS booked through to London via Paris.

Best Railway Accommodation, luggage conveyed free and a fortnight allowed from Marseilles en route.

ENGLISH STEWARD AND STEWARDESS CARRIED.

Upon arrival at Marseilles an interpreter meets the steamer and gives passengers every assistance in disembarking, passing their luggage through the Customs, etc. He also accompanies them in the train to Paris and Calais.

The steamers for Adelaide, Melbourne, Sydney and Noumea, leave Albany on or about the 30th of each month.

Passengers and Cargo booked to Mauritius and the African Coast, via Seychelles. Full information given respecting rates, etc., to the South African Goldfields.

For Freight, Passage and further particulars, apply to the

AGENTS:
JOHN McKAIL & CO., ALBANY.
DALGETY & CO., LIMITED, PERTH.
JAMES LILLY, FREMANTLE.

THE Peninsular and Oriental STEAM NAVIGATION COMPANY.

Head Office:—122 LEADENHALL STREET, LONDON.

Chief Office in Australia:—147 COLLINS STREET, MELBOURNE.

THE P. & O. S. N. Co. under contract with the Imperial, Victorian, New South Wales and South Australian Governments, despatch their Mail Steamers Homeward fortnightly. Booking Passengers and Cargo to London, America, India and China. Outwards—fortnightly, to all ports in Australia.

PASSAGES. Single and Return Tickets issued First and Second Saloon at very moderate rates.

PASSAGES can be prepaid HERE from London or any of the Company's Agencies in India, China or Australia. Liberal concessions made to Families.

Passengers at Albany are landed and embarked in a Steam Launch at the Company's expense.

For all information, apply at the Office, Lower Stirling Terrace.

JNO. F. T. HASSELL,
AGENT,
ALBANY, KING GEORGE'S SOUND.

---

[24] *The Albany Mail and King George's Sound Advertiser.* 2nd April 1887.

Albany had reached the zenith of its prosperity as a port in the period between 1880 and 1900. At that time there was six companies operating mail, passenger and cargo steamers using the port and refuelling facilities. This seaborne traffic was further complimented by passengers disembarking for the Coolgardie and Kalgoorlie goldfields with Albany the main gateway to them. In this, its heyday as a centre for shipping in Western Australia and many visitors from all parts of the world who came to King George's Sound tended to agree on the fact that Albany was entitled to rank as one of the finest natural anchorages in existence.

The Princess Royal Harbour was in commission until 1900 as the coaling port for the mail and cargo ships of those many nations trading with Australia. When in 1899 the then Premier of the state, Sir John Forrest, made the official announcement that he would make Fremantle the regular port of call for mail steamers Albany lost its connection with many of the overseas companies that had for many years plied their trade and refuelled using the port and its facilities. Some companies, however, did retain their allegiance to the town notably the White Star, Aberdeen and Blue Funnel lines.

When the port of Fremantle eventually assumed the mantle of the chief port of Western Australia at the turn of the century the impact on the local economy and employment was devastating. This situation was exacerbated further with the relocation of the Great Southern Railway workshops from the town to Midland then on the outskirts of Perth. Unfortunately, at this time there was not sufficient hinterland agricultural development to mitigate the loss of these industries to the local economy. As a consequence, there followed a corresponding depletion in the number of skilled and unskilled labourers in the town as many families preferred to follow the work and seek opportunities in the capital, Perth.

The ill feeling generated by the Western Australian Government's decision in respect to making Fremantle the chief port of the colony was a source of much aggravation among Albany towns people:

Albany, October 26.

'The Advertiser' today says "it is reported that Mr Brooklyn has abandoned his intention of building a large hotel in Albany on account of rumours as to the mail steamers leaving Albany for Fremantle. This is only another instance of the great harm that has been done to this town and port by the constant reiteration on the part of ministers of the statement that the mail steamers are shortly going to Fremantle, when ministers know very well that is not so.

A vast amount of work has to be done at Fremantle before the mail companies could think of such a thing, and neither Ministers nor the companies can say whether when all the work is done the steamers can call at Fremantle. The Government owe a great deal of reparation to Albany for the damage that they have done to the town by the wild talk as for the mail steamer is going to Fremantle." [25]

Even though the move was inevitable the frustration was already being felt in the town. This animosity felt towards the Government, and Premier John Forrest in particular, was significant and *The Albany Advertiser* captured some of this sentiment in its editorials as this 1897 article indicates:

Sir John Forrest and his Creed
Extracts from his remarks to the Fremantle Chamber of Commerce

He had been glad to hear the Mayor [of Fremantle] *speak so hopefully of the prospects of East Fremantle. Those were the observations that he liked to hear… For his own part, he believed they were yet only on the threshold of what was in store for the colony (Applause)…*

He hoped that the fear that seemed to have come over some people [Albany and Esperance] *that because he was committed to Fremantle harbour works and the Coolgardie water scheme, they must not raise another sixpence, on loan until those works were completed, would be dispelled. He was not going to subscribe to any such doctrine as that. (Applause)…*

It had been charged against him that he centralised everything in Perth and Fremantle. These same critics, however, did not mind centralising everything in New South Wales under Federation. (Laughter)…What had been the object of the centralisation with which he had been charged? It was to make Fremantle the principal port of the colony and put Fremantle on the high road of trade and commerce with the old country

---

[25] *The West Australian.* Perth. 27th October 1897.

and Australia (Cheers). It had been his desire to, as far as possible, make all the railway systems converge at the seat of government and the port of Fremantle. (Applause)

He did not wish to injure any other place in doing so if he could avoid it. Through this policy, which he had tried to follow out (Applause)…The Albany paper had a leading article every week accusing him of wishing to kill the town, and Esperance said he had already destroyed that port. (Laughter).[26]

Unfortunately, for the town there was little warning provided when shipping actually stopped using the port in favour of the Fremantle harbour facilities. The impact was immediately felt among the inhabitants of Albany with a subsequent downturn in economic conditions felt in almost every sector of the community:

The Fate of Albany Decided.
The telegram which appeared in The Advertiser on Saturday last to the effect that the mail steamers had decided to call almost immediately at Fremantle instead of Albany, feel like a bombshell in the town. Although the people had been kept in a state of suspense for the last two or three years the news came with great suddenness, for it was understood the conference of the Postmaster Generals of the Eastern Colonies would have some bearing on the subject, or that it would be dealt with by the Federal Parliament. No one expected to hear that the mail steamer calling at Albany the following day would be the last that would arrive here from the Eastern Colonies.

Knots of people gather together principally on the Terrace and in York Street discussing the situation, and it continues to be the all absorbing topic of conversation. Its effect on the people was discussed and it was generally agreed that while it meant ruination to some it would affect directly or indirectly every person in the town… Of course, no notification of these reductions as yet been received by the heads of the departments [including Customs, Railways and Post Office] but it may be expected very shortly.

When seen by our representative on Saturday Mr J.F.T. Hassell, agent for the P&O Company, stated that until he saw the news in The Advertiser, he was unaware that his company intended to change their port of call. Immediately he telegraphed to the Superintendent in Sydney asking for confirmation of the news and received the reply that the first P&O steamer to call at Fremantle would be the India *leaving Sydney on August 11…[27]*

---

[26] *The Albany Advertiser.* 28th October 1899.
[27] Ibid. 7th August 1900.

CHAPTER 15
THE DEFENCE OF KING GEORGE'S SOUND

"...if Her Majesty's Government thought it necessary to establish what has been termed a Gibraltar there, the eastern colonies would object; certainly not Western Australia."
Sir William C.F. Robinson. A past Governor giving evidence to the House of Commons Select Committee. London, May 1890.

Setting the Scene

The Nineteenth Century was seen as the Age of Imperialism, with the rapid expansion of European empires and interests spreading across the globe. This is also the Age of Victorian Great Britain. The British Empire on which 'the sun never sets' had already grown to incorporate Canada, Australia, New Zealand and India along with many islands around the world. By the end of the century, South Africa would also come under British influence. Not to be outdone, the French Empire, Belgium, Portugal and Germany were also spreading their tentacles across most of the north and west of Africa and into Southeast Asia.

The Crimean War of 1854 was the first action that began to herald a change in the geopolitical state of global, and significantly European conflicts in the latter years of the Nineteenth Century. France, knowing that it had the support of Great Britain, engaged with the Russians under Tsar Nicholas 1, who it had been argued was attempting to annex the Balkan states under the guise of protecting Greek Orthodox Christians in Turkey. Eventually, the European alliance was successful, however, an ongoing distrust of Russian intentions on a global sphere remained which had some later implications for Albany.

The continent of Africa in the late Nineteenth Century became an area of increased European rivalry. Exploration of Central Africa by Livingston, Speke, Stanley, Burton, Fraser and others had begun to open up the continent to European interests. For example, King Leopold of Belgian annexed a great swathe of land known at that time as the Congo. Further, a system of alliances between continental empires originally negotiated to prevent intra-European conflict after the Napoleonic wars began to break down towards the end of the Nineteenth Century and a residual ongoing distrust among nations who had been previous allies would eventually end with the First World War. Prussia had initially flexed its muscles in defeating the Second French Republic under the presidency of Napoleon III, nephew of Napoleon Bonaparte. The French were defeated by the Prussians at Sedan and Gravelotte and in 1870, eventually leading to the fall of Paris and the Second Republic. Also, at this time in world history, the rise of Germany as a global power became evident with Otto von Bismarck appointed as the new German Chancellor.

Both Albany residents and the colony at large were acutely aware of the impact that the Crimean War involving European powers was having on global power struggles. Consequently, when a Russian cruiser entered King George's Sound townspeople became convinced that an attempt would be made to take the port, which at the time was identified as being vulnerable to attack.

It was not surprising therefore, that the town's sentiments were reported in the local newspaper which was keen to elicit support for the fortification of the harbour and its defences.

> *The imminence of a war between England and Russia has awakened our people to a sense of the extreme insecurity of this harbour. Our distance from the headquarters of the Australian Squadron creates the possibility of a foreign cruiser seizing upon so important a point, which could be held as the basis of offensive operations. The necessity for the fortification of Albany was recognised years ago. But day after day, week after week and month after month have been allowed to go by and no single act has been taken for our protection and preservation in case of war. The people of Albany, who are most concerned in the matter, having the security of the property and the safety of their lives at stake, have at last forwarded a memorial to His Excellency the Administrator requesting immediate steps to be taken to fortify the harbour, and in the meantime asking him to communicate with the Admiral commanding the Australian Station with a view of having a British man-of-war stationed here till the defence works are completed or the present imbroglio is*

settled. Suggestions have also been made for the appointment of an Intercolonial Defence Conference, to consider what arrangements should be made for the defence of the colonies generally.

Such being the case, Russia is not a power likely to let such a proceeding pass without some resentment. Of course, she could not spare a large expeditionary force necessary to chastise the colonies, but such an important point as Albany, if unprotected, offers her an opportunity to damage British and colonial commerce at the expense of very little trouble. One large cruiser holding the harbour would cause great annoyance to the shipping passing our shores daily, and if once the port was blockaded, it would be extremely difficult to retake. On the other hand, if Albany was efficiently fortified, it would make an impregnable harbour of refuge, in which merchant vessels, which might otherwise be the prey of the enemy, could find a haven of security.

The precise nature of the fortifications necessary for the harbour have already been recommended by Major-General Scratchley[1], Sir W.F.D. Jervois and Commodore Erskine, and from such eminent military engineers we may very well be satisfied with what is proposed. The principal question now to decide is the cost and who is to bear it. This can only be settled by a conference of all the colonies concerned, and we hope to hear shortly that the necessary steps have been taken to convene it, and that the same liberality and unanimity will be displayed in taking measures for our own defence, as that exhibited in sending assistance to the British Forces in Egypt.[2]

The Colonial Secretary of Western Australia wrote to the United Kingdom's Colonial Secretary of State in London, Lord Derby dated Perth, May 1885 on this very question:

As you may be aware, Albany has become of late a somewhat large coaling station for steamers and has been found a great convenience to those passing to and from the ports of the Eastern colonies.

King George's Sound, being absolutely undefended, the coal stored there afloat and onshore would in time of war be likely to fall an easy prey to an enemy, and if once seized it would enable him to strike a very heavy blow at the commerce of all the Eastern colonies.[3]

The reply from Lord Derby to Sir Frederick Napier Broome, Governor of Western Australia and the other colonies dated the 12th June 1885 responded to this initial correspondence:

The Secretary of State for the Colonies
To the Governor of Western Australia

You have recently drawn the attention of Her Majesty's Government to the defenceless condition of King George's Sound.
This question has already, on more than one occasion, been brought into notice, and it was alluded to at the Intercolonial Conference held at Sydney in January 1881.
At that conference, a resolution giving expression to the colonial view was adopted in the following terms…[4]

The despatch from Lord Derby continued:

Although this resolution would apparently contemplate that each colony should have the cost of fortifying its own ports, yet there are some ports the cost of defending which it is hardly reasonable to expect that a single colony should bear, and with regard to which the Australian Governments might well, in the opinion of Her Majesty's Government, consider the expediency of providing her defence in common. King George's Sound is a strong case in point, for as Colonel Scratchley, after a most careful investigation on the spot, reported:
'The protection of the Sound and of Princess Royal Harbour is of vital importance for the general security of the Australian colonies in time of war. If left undefended, the Sound becomes the weak spot in the Australian system of defence.

---

[1] Major General Sir Peter Henry Scratchley was a military engineer and colonial administrator. Scratchley returned to Australia on 8th March 1877 in the ship *Tutor* to join Sir William Jervois to provide advice the colonies on their defences.
[2] *The Albany Mail and King George's Sound Advertiser.* 17th April 1885.
[3] Ibid. 9th March 1886.
[4] Lord Derby. *Correspondence from the Secretary of State for the Colonies to the Governor of Western Australia and the other colonies*, dated the 12th June 1885.

It is, however, obviously unreasonable to expect the Colony of Western Australia to provide and maintain the defences of this port at her sole expense, even if her means permitted her undertaking such a charge.
I have, &c.
Derby.
Lord Derby.[5]

Albany Defence Rifles.

In July 1878 local volunteers formed a local military force that in 1885 was re-organised as the Albany Defence Rifles in response to the perceived threat of war between Britain and Russia. The Albany Defence Rifles were an early version of an Australian 'Dad's Army' Defence Corps. *The Western Australian Times* correspondent in Albany wrote of the occasion:

Our usually quiet little town has been lately enlivened with the bustle attendant upon two special parades of the military under the direction of Colonel Harvest. Bristling bayonets and helmet spikes have been glistening ever and anon in our streets, giving the town quite a military and warlike appearance. Last Wednesday afternoon, a parade was held in front of the Customs House, when a special inspection was called by Colonel Harvest who I may observe came here for the purpose of inspecting the pensioners in the district and the Albany Volunteer Rifle Corps. The various evolutions were gone through in a highly credible manner, and the gallant Colonel expressed his satisfaction therewith and said he was quite surprised at so recently a form company proving themselves so efficient.

We were very much pleased to observe the great interest the Colonel seemed to manifest in the corps, pointing out the proper position to hold the musket, how to form squares, etc.; but the leading feature of the day was a 'charge', in which the Colonel took the command. The 'charge' being quite a novel movement to the corps, caused it to be very irregular, but probably the volunteers were carried away by enthusiasm, imagining it was the Russian canon ahead instead of a blank wall. Conspicuous in the front ranks I noticed private vines and Bugler Ashton. Regarding the former, I cannot but acknowledge that the spectators were much struck with his soldiery appearance, especially whilst the corps were in that position known as 'company in line', and we regret that it was not the private who was individually singled out of the ranks and publicly complimented. According to the report, however, his merits have not been overlooked, for I hear he has been appointed medical officer to the corps; though perhaps his services would be appreciated more by the Albany rifles if he held the same position in the enemy's lines. Touching private Ashton, we can say he blows the bugle nicely and loud.

Before the dismissal of the company, the Colonel congratulated the members on their soldierlike bearing and promised to make a favourable report to his Excellency, as he said, he would justly do; and give every possible assistance that laid in his power. He also spoke in complimentary terms of the drill instructor, Sergeant Furlong, and of Lieutenant Finley. I quite concur with his sentiments and can show that both deserve all the credit they get, as they have spent no end of time and trouble to drill the colonel received 'three times three', followed by equally hearty cheers for Lieutenant Finley and Sergeant Furlong. The company then dispersed…[6]

A Letter to the Editor of *The Fremantle Herald* newspaper of May 1885, indicated the extent to which the town was approaching a level of preparedness for a possible threat from either Russia or another country. The Albany Rifles were reconstituted in 1885 as the 'Albany Defence Rifles' Corps with the looming Russian scare. *The Fremantle Herald* outlined the recruitment and re-organisation processes that was being employed in the town:

When it became necessary for various reasons, to disband the Albany Rifle Volunteers, it was known that the company would be re-organised, but it was not supposed that the movement would have been so rapid. The Russian war scare, however, precipitated matters, and His Excellency the Administrator having to visit Albany, to consult with the naval officers belonging to HMS Opal and Diamond, occasion was taken to resuscitate the corps, and a public meeting was called on the 6th inst. and held in the Court House, for the

---

[5] Ibid.
[6] *The Western Australian Times*, Perth, 14th March 1879.

purpose of enrolling members in the Albany Defence Rifles. The chair was occupied by the Government Resident, (Mr R.C. Loftie,) and upon the platform were His Excellency the Administrator, Colonel Angelo, and Mr G.V. Phillips, the Assistant Colonial Secretary. On that evening 40 members enrolled themselves, among whom were Mr Finlay, the late Captain.

On the following evening, 25 additional members joined the ranks, and on Saturday night the roll had reached 81 members, of which, however, only 60 were able-bodied men. Colonel Angelo recommended the appointment of Dr Rogers to the temporary command, which his Excellency has sanctioned. His Excellency in the course of an eloquent address referred to the fright the inhabitants of Fremantle and Perth had received, and the possible danger to Albany, the key to Australia. Albany people, he thought, had gone to sleep, and he had come to give them a nudge and wake them up again. Under their late commander, they had gone to sleep, and they might drop off again, he, therefore, would ask them to introduce fresh blood and, in naming a gentleman who was likely to command the Corps in the event of war, he was one who was a born soldier, he meant Captain Phillips. [7]

The Russian Scare

The Imperial Russian 'scare' as it was called, was at the front of the town's thinking when in May 1886 a Russian warship *Vestnick* was moored in the port for close to a month to initiate and complete repairs to its engines.

Whatever might be thought by some of the objects of the visit of the Russian corvette **Vestnick** *to Albany the other day a paragraph which appears in the local paper shows plainly enough that, for some reason or other, the movements of her officers were not all aboveboard, and were well calculated to excite suspicion. Our contemporary says: The Russians of the* **Vestnick**, *which left on Friday last, during the week were out several nights surveying the harbour. We believe it is usual for any foreign man of war on arrival at a British port and as it is for a British man-of-war on arrival at a foreign port not before visited to take soundings and bearings, but it does not look quite the thing to do this at night. Considering the courtesy with which foreign warships are treated on entering a British port by exemption from the port's dues and by the attention afforded offices by the local authority to take advantage of the night-time to make their observations seems mean and underhanded. Nevertheless, we know of no international or local ordinance to prevent them, but it is well to be on our guard and hurry up the fortifications, and there is no knowing how soon fresh complication may arise and result in hostilities. The Russian officers of the* **Vestnick** *made particular inquiries as to everything in connection with this port, the number of sovereigns in the banks, the exports, imports, and the quality of coals stored here. They expected to find only a few tons of this last in stock but were quite surprised to find that there were over 5000 tons available.* [8]

The desire to have King George's Sound fortified continued to fester within the colony. *The Inquirer and Commercial News* carried a feature article addressing the issue. In part it explained:

In the opinion of all competent naval authorities who express their views upon the matter, Albany is at once the weakest and yet the strongest naval strategic position in this "Land of the Golden Fleece." The strongest-inasmuch as if the hostile power once ceased possession of it, the port could be easily retained despite every effort made to dislodge the enemy from it; thus, our foes would obtain not only a point d'appui as a base for the further hostile operations, but they would also effect a lodgement from which they could be induced to retire only at the cost of an enormous amount of tribute.

At the same time, Albany is and is at present in a defenceless state, the weakest strategic position on the coast of this continent-island. Although we had two British man-of-war in the harbour during the last crisis, yet the captain of the Diamond *stated that if a Russian ironclad had gone there with hostile war purposes, it could simply blow the two English warships out of the water with the utmost ease. "of course, we should have shown and fight", Captain Brooke remarked 'but we would have been like a couple of lambs before a ravenous beast of prey; the Russian bear would have destroyed us without getting a scratch in return".*

---

[7] *The Fremantle Herald*. 23rd May 1885.
[8] *The Daily News*. Perth. 26th March 1886.

> *That experience of what might possibly occur in the event of war breaking out between our mother country and holy Russia was not without a practical result, when, in January last, the first Australasian Federal Council met at Hobart, the delegate of our Governor, Mr J.G. Lee -Steer boldly ventured to go beyond the limits of the programme of business drawn up for the consideration of the council, by insisting upon the paramount necessity that existed for all the Australian colonies uniting in defraying the expense of rendering Albany impregnable to capture by any hostile neighbour force whatever.[9]*

At a meeting of the Federal Council[10] on the Defence of Albany 1886, James George Lee Steere[11] a Western Australian representative in moving a motion relating to the issue again argued:

> *Mr President, in rising to draw attention to the resolution which stands in my name, as to the undefended position of King George's Sound, I think the importance of the subject must recommend it to Hon. Members of the Council, as sufficient reason why we should deliberate upon it. None of us can have forgotten how, a few months ago, all the Australian colonies, felt themselves in a state of great insecurity in consequence of certain complications between England and a foreign power (Russia). We felt then that many portions of our coast were in an undefended position; that both the towns on the coast and the commerce of the various colonies might be very much harassed by vessels belonging to a power at war with England making depredations on the coast of Australia. Nothing, sir, can lend more to allay that feeling of want of confidence in our security which was then felt for some action being taken by the Australian colonies to place, at any rate, the most strategical points in such a position, that they may be able to defend themselves. It appears to me that the only thing that now remains for the consideration of the various Australian colonies, and the Imperial Government is in what manner, and by whom these positions should be fortified.*
>
> *The question of the fortifications of King George's Sound has been under the consideration of Her Majesty's Government, and that of the various Australian colonies, for some years past. Some few years ago, in consequence of correspondence that took place between the Australian colonies and Her Majesty's Government, the late Major-General Scratchley was sent to King George's Sound to make a report upon the fortifications that were required to be undertaken there for the purpose of rendering that port safe from attack.[12]*

At this first session of the Federal Council of Australasia in 1886, a resolution was passed that advocated for the creation of an armed strategic harbour at King George's Sound. The Colonial Conference of 1887 in London led to two important results affecting Australian defence, viz., the increase of the Australian Squadron under an agreement concluding in the following year, and the progression of defences at Thursday Island and King George's Sound at the cost of the contributing colonies, the armament being provided by the Imperial Government.

In 1887 Sir Thomas Brassey, later Lord Brassey, visited Albany and among his many observations of the settlement made particular mention of the vulnerability of the port and its facilities to a hostile takeover.[13] Brassey maintained the need for the 'proper fortification' of this important maritime port, in a letter which appeared in *The Times* of July 28 Brassey, reporting from Melbourne after his sojourn in Albany wrote:

> *The observations which follow have been suggested by a recent visit to King George's Sound. It is scarcely necessary to insist upon the importance of the position. Port Darwin, the nearest harbour on the west coast of Australia available for large vessels, is distant 2,100 miles. On the south coast of the continent, a distance*

---

[9] *The Inquirer and Commercial News*, Perth. 17th March 1886.
[10] The purpose of the Federal Council was primarily convened to discuss the concept of Federation of the nation's colonies.
[11] James George Lee Steere was a pastoralist and politician who had an extensive career in Western Australian politics, initially as an elected member of the Legislative Council and then in 1886 as Speaker. In 1890, he was elected a member of the Western Australian Legislative Assembly when responsible government was introduced and was unanimously elected its Speaker.
[12] *The Albany Mail and King George's Sound Advertiser*. Tuesday 2nd March 1886.
[13] Sir Thomas Brassey had an acknowledged reputation as an authority on naval matters. He was a strong proponent of further strengthening the case for Australian colonies in their demand for assistance in the fortification of King George's Sound.

> *of more than 1,000 miles divides King George's Sound from Adelaide. The nearest route from the great ports of Australia to the Suez Canal passes within a few miles from the entrance to the harbour. Protection against first-class ironclads is needed. In a time of war, such ships as* Peter the Great *or the* Admiral Duperre *will be retained in European waters. The attack on our commerce in distant seas will be made by swift and lightly-armed steamers, unprotected by armour. It is essential, and it should not involve a large expenditure, to place ourselves in a position to deny King George's Sound to vessels of this class.*
>
> *The necessity has long been recognised but nothing has been done. The cost cannot in fairness be laid on Western Australia. It should be distributed in due proportion between the mother country and the Australian colonies. I regret to learn that no decision was taken on this point at the recent conference.*
>
> *During the last Russian scare, a corvette and a sloop were detained at King George's Sound for the defence. Their united crews could not have numbered less than 400 men. Fighting from a battery 40 men would have given greater security against the attack of a cruiser making a rush for the harbour to fill up empty bunkers.*
>
> *If no defences are provided, King George's Sound can be barred in by sinking coal-hulks in the narrow entrance. It would be a miserable alternative.*[14]

The sense of frustration caused by the Australian colonies' procrastination in coming to an acceptable solution to King George's Sound's defence at the specially convened Intercolonial Committee of Officers on the Defence of Albany conference in Melbourne was of continual concern to the town. By 1890 the issue of Albany's defence had still not been resolved. The local press, somewhat frustrated by the inaction once again brought the issue before its readers with some suggestions as to what these fortifications could entail:

> *The recommendation of Sir Peter Scratchley that Albany should be fortified, will, in some form or other be carried out; but we consider that all the necessary protection for Albany could be secured by a chain or torpedoes laid down at the mouth of the Princess's Harbour, enfiladed by a small battery of howitzers or machine guns to prevent boats from removing the obstacles and clearing a passage…*
> *We regard King George's Sound as a point of extreme strategical importance to the whole of the colonies. The station at King Georg's Sound is so situated that if possessed by an enemy's cruiser, it would influence very nearly the whole trade of the Australian colonies.*[15]

Nevertheless, intra-colonial vested interests resulted in not everyone supporting the views expressed by Major General Sir Peter Scratchley and others with respect to the importance of King George's Sound as a defensive installation. A call to instead fortify Bunbury was also being made at the same time:

> *The effectual fortification of Albany would cost a very large sum of money, as it would be found to include extensive entrenchments on the land-sea as well as on the seaboard, and even then, could never be artificially made so strong for defence as Bunbury is by nature. Enemy's ships could easily, with the long-range guns now in use, fire over the obstructing spit of land into the town of Albany from the Sound itself, while any guns on the heights could be turned by an enemy effecting a landing in Frenchman's Bay or in Oyster Harbour. There would seem to nothing either, to prevent a landing at Torbay to the south-west of Princess's Harbour, and an attack made upon the town from that quarter. The Albany heights are stone, those at the mouth of Princess's Harbour being sheer blocks of barren granite, and most unfavourable for the construction of batteries; this was pointed out to General Scratchley, who admitted the difficulty and the consequent heavy cost of construction…*
>
> *To hold Albany, an enemy in possession of the town and harbour would have to throw up very extensive entrenchments to repel any attack from those quarters, and should a superior British naval force appear in King George's Sound, the enemy would be caught in a regular cul-de-sac. Such a trap no naval or military strategist would be likely to incur the risk of running into. Breaksea Island, in King George's Sound, is considered by many to offer advantages as an outpost for the defence of Albany. Outposts, especially when detached, are dangerous things and far better dispensed with whenever they can be avoided; but the very fact that an island in the Sound could not be safely disregarded constitutes it rather an element of weakness and*

---

[14] *The West Australian.* Perth. 26th September 1887.
[15] *The Albany Mail and King George's Sound Advertiser.* 9th March 1886.

danger than of strength and safety. Were it not included in the defence it would become an excellent base for hostile offensive operations, and if it were included, as of necessity it would have to be, experience tells us that such outworks invariably succumb to an enterprising enemy and vigorous attack, proving far more prejudicial than beneficial to the defence of the main position...

Such being the case, it would seem that the best possible scheme for the defence of Western Australia generally, and of the large population its shores, would be to render Albany practically secure against all but the most powerful attacks, and to form a really strong fortress and harbour at Bunbury. It must not be forgotten, either in this connection that, if Bunbury is not made secure, and if it were to fall into the hands of an enemy, it would give him an enormous advantage. Before coming to a final decision, we trust that the Australian Governments and their advisers will carefully consider the present strategical value of Bunbury and its probable commercial importance in the near future.[16]

The costs to defend the Albany port and its facilities were also questioned in editorials in Eastern Colonies newspapers which offered some novel solutions to the problem at the same time:

Some military experts have given it as their opinion that the only attraction for an enemy at King George's Sound would be the stock of coal kept there during wartime, which might become an invaluable factor in furthering larger operations in more important parts of the continent. It is not thought likely that a large ship would be detailed for the task of reducing such a position, but that the work would be detailed to a second-class vessel with a force of perhaps 300 or 400 men. Replies have not yet been received from the other colonies as to whether the dates proposed will suit the military commandants of each, but in view of the time and expense saved in meeting Captain Moore[17] *at Albany, it is not considered that any serious objections will be made to the proposal, even in cases where the dates proposed for visiting Western Australia may not be altogether convenient.*[18]

Fortress Albany.

King George's Sound...a place of strategic Imperial importance.
Captain Sir John Colomb, Royal Marines; March 16th 1885.

An Australian Colonial select committee was established to review the issues of defending King George's Sound and charged with the responsibility of making recommendations on how to proceed. The Committee arrived at Albany on the 23rd November 1890 and spent the first two days examining all possible sites for gun emplacements and subsidiary necessary infrastructure requirements. The general description of The Princess Royal Harbour and its surroundings is fully outlined in Sir Peter Scratchley's Report of 1890:

1st December 1890
Report of the Committee of Officers on the Defence of Albany,
Western Australia.

Two of these guns should be mounted on the high ground above Point King, marked "378" on the chart. This is a splendid site and the only one which admits of fire on both Sound and Harbour. The fire of these guns will extend over an arc of nearly 300 degrees from Middleton Beach on the left to the head of the railway pier, inside the Harbour, on the right. The third gun to be mounted on Point King, below and well clear of the large boulders on that point – elevation 115 feet... Owing to the commanding sites and the good backgrounds obtainable they will be little exposed, and rapidity of fire combined with the simplicity of construction and economy are of great importance...

There should be the simplest possible form of submarine mining defence across the narrow entrance to the harbour. This defence to consist only of four lines of 250-lb ground mines, fired from the pilot station by means of a short-range depression position-finger.

---

[16] *The Daily News*, Perth. 2nd October 1890. Copied from *The United Service Gazette*, London.
[17] Captain George Hateley Moore of the Royal Artillery.
[18] *The Melbourne Argus*. 17th October 1890.

Signal stations, in telegraphic communication, are important adjuncts to coast defence. The movement of vessels can then be watched, and timely notice given of the approach of hostile cruisers. The signal station on Breaksea Island can report vessels coming from the eastward, but those from the westward, especially if they take the inside passage, cannot be seen until they are within half an hour of the Harbour. The Committee, therefore, recommend that a signal station be placed on Grove Hill, in telegraphic or telephonic communication with the battery on Point King, and through it into the town of Albany. They further strongly recommend that a similar station be placed on Cape Leeuwin, or its vicinity, and, above all, a first-class light.

The southern end of Middleton Beach can easily be protected against a landing. Lake Seppings, and the marshy ground which runs parallel to the sea, almost cut off the narrow line of sandhills which extends the whole length of the beach. It would be comparatively easy to excavate a ditch, making this ground impassable almost up to the base of the hill on which it is proposed to place the battery. Within 300 yards of this battery, there is also a position from which a quick-firing gun can command the whole of Middleton Beach...

The Committee recommend that, until other intercolonial arrangements can be made for a Federal Regiment of Australian Artillery, the permanent garrison for King George's Sound be furnished by South Australia, whose permanent force should be increased accordingly.

The cost of this Permanent Garrison with the necessary reliefs, to be divided between the colonies, as suggested in a circular from Downing Street dated 11th January 1890... As the total population of Albany is only 2000, it will be necessary to look to Perth and Fremantle, with a population of 20,000 to provide the Infantry Force. In the event of hostilities, actual or apprehended, the troops may be called out for a lengthened period, and as they cannot afford to be taken away from their trades for more than two or three weeks at a time, it will be necessary to allow a certain number to return periodically to their avocations.
Alex B. Tulloch
Major-General, Commandant, Victoria, President.
Francis Downes,
Major-General, Commanding the Forces, South Australia.[19]

In 1891 the residents of the town began to see some action at last on the town's fortifications with the arrival of John Blackbourn, the government-appointed engineer. The local press was keen to convey the news to its readers accordingly:

The people of Albany have an assurance of an early start being made with the constructions of fortifications in the arrival by the Oruba from Melbourne of Mr Blackbourn, the engineer appointed to carry out the scheme settled by the Defence Commission. Mr Blackbourn is an engineer of high standing in the Victoria Defence Department. He was an assistant to General Sir Peter Scratchley, and it is under his supervision that all the defence works at Port Phillip have been constructed. All the guns there have been mounted by him with only one exception. His appointment as an engineer for the Albany defences may be accepted, therefore, as a proof that the work will be well done and that the Colonies consider them of some importance.[20]

A reporter from *The Albany Advertiser* was given a tour of the facilities by Blackbourn six months after work had commenced. He was able to report on the progress at that time:

...Having marked and inwardly approved what I beheld at Mount Adelaide, I proceeded to the lower battery situated above the lighthouse. This is reached by a steep path straight down the side of Mount Adelaide, a veritable Jacob's Ladder – and here let me advise those who are desirous of visiting the fortifications to make their way first to the upper battery and so down to the lower one for if they follow the other plan and visit the lighthouse battery first, those of them, not members of an Alpine Club excepted, will assuredly on beholding Jacob's ladder elect to remain below and so miss the most interesting part of the defence works and the loveliest view in or about Albany...

Mr Blackbourn was kind enough to pilot me into the bowels of the lower magazine, a work of some difficulty, owing to the complicated nature of the wooden stays and barricades that shaped and held the concrete in

---

[19] 1st December 1890. *Report of the Committee of Officers on the Defence of Albany.*
[20] A Correspondent. *The Australian Advertiser.* Albany. 25th May 1891.

place, and getting through and over which, was like negotiating the hindrances put up for an obstacle race, as another visitor who accompanied us remarked. The darkness of the magazine chambers was Egyptian in density and was hardly made light by the candle held by our guide.[21] The cement lining of the walls and roof was hard and smooth, showing careful finish, and the interior only required rendering, or in other words, a final polishing up to complete it.[22]

Twelve months after Blackbourn's arrival to undertake the formidable building challenges associated with the defences of King George's Sound the works were all but completed. Again, the local press was eager to share this update with its readers:

The fortifications now being erected for the defence of this port are rapidly approaching completion, and a few weeks will see the whole of the works ready for the reception of the military force which is to be stationed here.

On Thursday afternoon a representative of the Advertiser visited the site of the defence works and through the kindness and courtesy of Mr Blackbourn, the engineer in charge was shown over the whole of the buildings in connection with the upper and lower forts. From these forts, perhaps some of the finest marine views of the world are to be seen.

The barracks for the troops is expected to be finished in a few weeks' time. The building is quite close to the upper fortifications and it has been laid out in two detached portions with an eight feet wide veranda running along both the front and back portions of the structure…

One of the guns on the upper fort has a complete sweep of Middleton Beach, the Sound and the entrance to Princess Royal Harbour; the other gun sweeps from Herald Point round and will cover the whole of the inner harbour. These guns will throw shot and shell a distance of 4000 yards, which at that range will pierce four-inch armour, a thickness of plate not yet carried by swift armed cruisers of the type that would be used in actual warfare away from an enemy's base of operations… The lower fort at Point King is to be fitted with one gun of the same calibre as those in the upper fort. There is also a magazine at the lower fort similarly constructed to the one above but on a smaller scale. Mr Blackbourn has here taken advantage of the splendid covering of rocks and has constructed the magazine immediately behind this natural protection, all-round which he has covered over with earth to a depth of ten feet, which is also sown with grass…
It will thus be seen that the guns to be mounted on both forts will have a complete sweep of alike, King George's Sound, Middleton Beach, the entrance to the inner anchorage and the whole of Princess Royal Harbour.[23]

Almost prophetic, many schemes were developed and proposed concerning the strategic importance of Albany and in particular its harbour and facilities, in readiness for any future conflict involving extant world powers in the vicinity of King George's Sound. *The Daily News* in Perth commented on one such proposal:

The victory of Japan over China shifted the central political gravity of the world, and the Eastern Sea almost takes the place of the Mediterranean in strategic importance… The re-distribution of the balance of power makes it absolutely necessary for England to have some new strategic base in these seas, a great naval arsenal and military depot where a fleet, after a great fight, say in Japanese waters, might refit…

Mr A. Silva-White writes …in Australia as a strategic base in which he contends that Albany is in a unique strategic position and would serve as an effective base for warlike operations in the far east. "It is an ideal spot, he, says for supplementing the naval and military resources of the Empire." Mr White elaborates with much force all the arguments for making Albany a naval and military depot second only in importance to those of the motherland; or a rival in strength and resource, say to Gibraltar for Aden. If Mr White's counsel prevails, we shall in a word see Albany become the Malta of the Indian Ocean- a mighty fortress, keeping watch over the eastern seas…[24]

---

[21] It is important to clarify at this point that there are no tunnels in The Forts area, there are however, Artillery Storage Chambers.
[22] Our Special Reporter, *The Albany Advertiser*. 11th December 1891.
[23] A Correspondent. *The Australian Advertiser*. Albany. 13th June 1892.
[24] *The Daily News*, Perth. 23rd June 1896.

However, others were quick to assuage the angst of the local population in respect to a possible attack from a foreign power. General John Nicholson pointed out this fact by indicating:

> *Just remember what these ships have got to do: they have to come out to Australia, they have to carry large quantities of coal; there are no stores of coal anywhere near that they could get coal at, none within a reasonable distance. It appears to me improbable in the extreme that anything like a very serious attack could ever be made upon a place like King George's Sound as long as it has any defence at all to fall back upon. As I said before, if it is not defended, then I think the probability is that the temptation will be too great, and that an expedition will be fitted out, and that they would make use of King George's Sound as a point d'appui.*[25]

A Historic Engineering Marker installed in 1988 in The Forts area of Mount Adelaide to celebrate the Australian Bicentennial that was dedicated by The Institute of Engineers Australia acknowledged the engineering feats of John Blackburn, Defence Engineer of the State of Victoria, in constructing The Princess Royal Battery and Magazine. It's stated in part that:

> *…the battery, built to guard Princess Royal Harbour and King George's Sound, never saw hostile action, but its design and durability are good examples of the military engineering techniques of the period.*[26]

The Boer War. 1899

> *"… on the outbreak of war in South Africa…evoked throughout Australia a feeling of military ardour and enthusiasm which surprised the whole world…"*
> Twentieth Century Impressions of Western Australia. Perth, 1902.

> *"…flag poles in the town were hung with bunting, the British ensign being predominate…the Royal George Hotel, was to the fore in the display of flags, but unfortunately hoisted amongst others, the Dutch tricolour…"*
> The Albany Advertiser, 2nd November 1899.

The Declaration of War.

On Monday 16th October, Great Britain informed other European nations, Germany in particular, that a state of war had existed between Transvaal and the Free State settlers since October 11th 1899. Not surprising, in response the German newspapers took the position that the Boers (Afrikaners) were indeed not rebels. Britain warned Germany that it had to stay strictly neutral in the conflict, with Germany's support for the Boers attributed to a perceived desire to promote their own growing military strength on the global stage.

Although the Boers were originally given partial independence from Great Britain when the South African Republic was created, towards the end of the Nineteenth Century with the discovery of gold in the area, an attempt was immediately made to protect the goldfields from British exploitation. The war, essentially a result of grievances held by foreign gold miners (mainly British) against the Boer Government inevitably led to war in 1899.

The call to arms in support of the 'Mother Country' was immediately answered at the local level as it was across the Australian colonies generally.

> *The Albany Volunteers.*
> *Albany, Tuesday, 17th October. 1899.*
> *Thirteen local residents signed their names to the list of volunteers for the West Australian Contingent for the Transvaal. Only three of that number passed the medical examination of Captain Frederick Ingoldby. They were F. Brown and C. Lloyd of Albany and F. Brown of King River. These three volunteers left for the Karrakatta encampment by train yesterday morning. Charles Lloyd, one of the successful candidates, who had been employed at Messrs. Drew, Robinson & Co's store was made a presentation by the employees*

---

[25] Paper delivered by General John Nicholson at 1907 Imperial Conference.
[26] State Library of Western Australia.

on Saturday evening last. If any volunteers are required from the Garrison at The Forts to make up the West Australian unit of 125 men, it is probable that a maxim gun and squad will be sent.[27]

King George's Sound began to be fortified in 1893, and from their placement positions on the crown of Mount Adelaide the guns were well placed to guard the entrance to the Sound and the inner anchorage of The Princess Royal Harbour. The Forts compound was initially garrisoned by forty men of the Permanent Artillery, a force which was initiated in March 1893.[28] This garrison was maintained at the joint cost of all the Australian colonies:

Undoubtedly by far, the most striking feature in the relations between Western Australia and the outside world was manifested in the latter part of the year 1899, on the outbreak of the war in South Africa. The early reverses sustained by the British army in the campaign against the Boers, coupled with the extraordinary malignity exhibited towards the British race by almost the entire Press of Continental Europe, evoked throughout Australia a feeling of military ardour and enthusiasm which surprised the whole world. This was the more remarkable, as the general feeling had hitherto been freely expressed, not merely in England, but in Australia, that the sentiments of the Australian people, as a whole, were opposed to taking any active part in military operations outside of such as might, at some unfortunate period, be forced upon them in connection with the defence of their own shores against a foreign foe…

In common with the rest of the colonial sections of the British Empire, Western Australia offered a unit of 125 men and five officers, and these men, who formed the first Western Australian contingent, were dispatched from Perth on November 4, 1899, to join the transport Medic *at Albany, en route for South Africa. Major Hateley G. Moor an Imperial officer (at that time in charge of the garrison at Albany), was placed in command. With him were associated Lieutenants Parker, Darling and Campbell, and Surgeon-Major McWilliams. Those who were entrusted with the duty of selecting the contingent had no easy task, owing to the large number of splendid men who presented themselves as candidates. Out of the whole number finally chosen, only twenty-six had seen previous service. A scene of extraordinary enthusiasm was witnessed both in Perth and Albany when the men took their departure, and the subsequent behaviour of these fine troops at Slingersfontein and other fields of battle fully justified the confidence bestowed by the colonists of Western Australia in their military representatives.*

The outbreak of war was the signal for enthusiastic volunteering throughout the continent. In every district members of the various defence units, as well as civilians, offered their services to the Empire, and in the first year and a half of the war, the following quotas of men and horses were sent from the several colonies.

The total number of troops sent from Australia between October 1899 and the end of the war in June 1902 was 16,632.[29]

The New Zealand Shipping Company's steamer *Waiwera* arrived with the New Zealand contingent for the Transvaal on board on Monday, 2nd November. The contingent comprised 214 officers and men. The members of the contingent belonged to the Mounted Rifles of New Zealand and were to serve in the Transvaal as mounted infantry. Among their ranks were several officers who resigned their commissions in the New Zealand Army so that they might accompany the contingent. On the arrival of

---

[27] *The Albany Advertiser*, 16th – 17th October 1899.
[28] A Boer War Contingent. Photograph courtesy of Albany Historical Society
[29] *Twentieth Century Impressions of Western Australia*, Perth, W.A. 1902. Hesperian Press, Perth, 2000.

the steamer at King George's Sound the flag poles and verandahs in the Albany town were hung with bright bunting and flags:

> *The officers then came ashore and were invited to the Albany Club where they were received by the Government Resident, the Hon. John Arthur Wright. In the afternoon the members of the Club provided vehicles and conveyed the officers to The Forts and round the Marine Drive. They then returned to the Club and were given a parting send-off. The men were also allowed ashore in two divisions. They appeared to be a fine body of men and presented a splendid military appearance…*
>
> *The members of the West Australian Contingent will arrive [in Albany] by special train on Sunday. A church parade of the Contingent will take place on the Recreation Ground at which the Lord Bishop of Perth [Right Reverend Charles E.L. Riley] will officiate. The Medic will be sometime in port as she will require 1,000 tons of coal and 200 tons of water.*[30]

Again, *The Albany Advertiser* indicated that:

> *Great interest was centred in the arrival of the troop ship Medic with the Victorian, Tasmanian and South Australian contingents on board, and there was considerable disappointment when the vessel did not put in an appearance on Saturday afternoon in time for the men to come ashore. The Medic was sighted at 5.30 p.m. and anchored in the Sound two hours later…*
>
> *There were 200 horses on board principally belonging to the Victorian Mounted Rifles. The South Australian Contingent had six mules… The men were all in the best of health and spirits and had quite recovered from the dreaded seasickness. That was, he said, the only sickness there had been on board. The men had been drilled daily, in the morning having to do physical drill and, in the afternoon, marching drill.*[31]

An Enthusiastic Send-Off.

The troops were dispatched from the town to the port then out to sea amid great fanfare and enthusiasm. The event was fully covered with some ebullient reporting in *The Albany Advertiser*:

> *Sunday and Monday last are days that will long be remembered in the annals of the town and of the whole colony. Sunday was the day that marked the arrival of the West Australian contingent for the Transvaal at the port of embarkation. An event such as this has never before been recorded in the history of the colony, and young colonists have previously had but a hazy idea of what it is to have friends and relatives of theirs taking part in actual warfare and risking their lives in order to prove their loyalty to the Queen and to assist in upholding the honour of the Empire. The arrival of the troops from the various colonies during the past few days has led to a good deal of enthusiasm on the part of the residents of Albany, but that was nothing to the enthusiasm displayed on Sunday when the unit provided by our own colony arrived at Albany for the purpose of embarking on the troop ship Medic. The town was decorated in the same manner as on the preceding day. The inclemency of the weather, however, completely upset the arrangements that had been made for the reception of both the West Australian contingent and those onboard the Medic…*
>
> *The town was crowded with people, for not only residents partook of the scene, but farmers from the country districts, city folk from the metropolis and millhands from Denmark who arrived by special trains. The morning mail train had on board 80 passengers, the special from Perth at 3.00 p.m., and the Denmark special. On the arrival of each train, the station platform was thronged with people and cheering appeared to be the order of the day. The Headquarters' Band arrived by the first special in order to greet the troops two hours later. By 10 o'clock the Terrace was crowded and lots of people gathered together discussing the situation, and the part the Australian volunteers would play in the campaign. The marching of the Headquarters' Band to the bandstand playing "Soldiers of the Queen" and other patriotic airs was the signal for an outburst of cheering. Nothing further was done until the whistle of the special was heard as she rounded the bend from the 2-mile when a rush was made down the embankment for the railway gates…*
>
> *The band poured forth the stirring strains of "The Soldiers of the Queen". Hearty were the handshakes extended to the members of the contingent by their friends as they left their compartments and drew up into*

---

[30] *The Albany Advertiser*. 2nd November 1899.
[31] Ibid.

line on the platform. Colonel Hoad, the senior officer of the other colonial contingents then called for three cheers for the Western Australian contingent. There was no lack of response to the call and the building almost shook beneath the volume of sound. Major Campbell, chief staff officer of the W.A. Permanent force, called for cheers for the other contingents and needless to say he was heartily supported. The men were joined by the six Albany garrison artillery men and then marched two deep off the platform and formed in marching order in front of the building, where the cheering recommenced. The band then headed the procession and the contingent marched from the station along Lower Spencer Street, Stirling Terrace and York Street to the Town Hall. The Terrace was lined with sightseers, while a great crowd followed besides, and in the trail of the contingent. All Albany, so to speak, was "out" and the gathering in the streets must have numbered over 2,000. As the men passed along, they were greeted with tremendous cheering. The comments passed upon their appearance was altogether favourable and the opinion was freely expressed that they will do credit to the colony they represent. Considering the fact that until a week or two ago a number of the men had had no military training whatever it speaks volumes for the ability of the drill instructors and the smartness of the men that they have gained such a splendid military bearing in such a short time.

The object of proceeding to the Town Hall was for the purpose of giving the men luncheon. The opportunity was also taken to extend to the contingent a welcome to the town. On the platform were seated the Mayor (Mr C. McKenzie), the Premier and Lady Forrest, Colonel Hoad, Major Campbell, Bishop Riley, the Hon. A. P. Matheson and Mrs Matheson, Messrs. A. E. Morgans, G. Leake, B. C. Wood, G., Hubble and J. J. Higham, M's L. A., the Revd. D. H Griffith and Mrs Morgans. Mr Castledine was brought forward by Surgeon-Captain Ingoldby and at the invitation of the Premier took a seat on the platform amid loud cheering. The portion of the hall not set apart for the contingent was occupied by the public.

The Mayor said he had to welcome the members of the contingent on behalf of the townspeople. He trusted that when they got to the Transvaal they would fight together shoulder to shoulder and uphold the honour of themselves and their country which he was sure they do. (Cheers).

The Premier, on rising, was greeted with applause. He said he expected the members of the contingent would be glad when all the leave-taking was over and they were safely conveyed on board the troop ship. He was proud of them (cheers), proud to see his fellow colonists volunteering to serve their country, not in their own land of Australia, but to serve Her Majesty in a distant part of the Empire. (Cheers). The feeling had spread throughout the colonies that Australia should be represented in the difficulties and troubles that had arisen in South Africa and the departure of the contingents was a source of gratification to all the British people and especially to Her Majesty the Queen. He had received a telegram from the Governor giving the substance of a telegram from the Secretary of State for the Colonies in which he stated that Her Majesty's Government were most gratified at the action of the West Australian people, and Her Majesty herself had expressed her high appreciation of the loyalty displayed by her subjects in this part of the world. (Cheers). All that now remained to be done was to see them on board ship and wish them "God speed and a safe return". They had to overcome great difficulties and would endure many hardships, but by their great pluck – so noted in the British race – they would come through all their troubles and would surmount all their difficulties (Cheers). He wished them God-speed and hoped to welcome them back having done their duty and won distinction.
Loud cheering followed and then under the leadership of the Rev. D. H. Griffith [Rector of Albany] *all present united in singing "God Save the Queen".*

…Shortly after 2 o'clock, the men formed into marching order and amidst cheering from the large crowds assembled en route proceeded to the foot of the jetty where they were dressed into line and allowed to stand easy while preparations were being made for their embarkation. Friends and relations then crowded around them. A sad heartbeat within the heart of the mother, sister, or sweetheart at the parting, but most of the faces of the men wore a joyful expression. When the body of troops was given the order to "march" the jetty was soon one mass of people and a great rush took place for the vantage points. The crowd remained most orderly and interfered as little as possible with the movements of the troops. First, the officers and then the men embarked on the transport Yaralla, *while the spectators gave each man an encouraging cheer as he passed along the gangway. … Cheer upon cheer was given by those on the jetty and the contingent replied from the steamer. The waving of handkerchiefs and hats was then made a token of farewell, and the scene was made more impressive by the band playing spiritedly "Soldiers of the Queen". "Auld Lang Syne", and*

"The Girl I Left Behind Me". It was not until the Yaralla had passed through the channel that the last of the public had streamed off the jetty.

...The scene throughout the day was one grand display of patriotism. Even far into the night, the sounds of patriotic airs could be heard in all parts of the town. Fortunately, the day passed away without a mishap of any kind.[32]

Andrew Barton "Banjo" Paterson, a special war correspondent for *The Sydney Morning Herald & The Argus* in Melbourne, 9th November wrote:[33]

Leaving Albany, the pilot took the Kent through the harbour channel very slowly, while the troops bound for the seat of war all stood on the bridge deck watching...and at last, we dropped the pilot and were away at full speed to the open sea. Leaving the lights of Albany blazing behind us..."

The *Albany Advertiser* noted the final farewell scene with respect to the departing troops:

The departure of the West Australian contingent was an inspiring sight. Nothing has so stirred the blood of the people of Albany as the departure of the soldiers of their colony to the war. Although the weather on Sunday was very rough nearly the whole population turned out and marched with the troops to the Town Hall and then again to the jetty. The people were enthusiastic, and, on all hands, one heard the greatest satisfaction with the appearance of Western Australia's representatives at the seat of war.

...Whether it be wise or not for Western Australia to send a contingent to the war, there is no question that with all classes it is popular, and if it teaches the public the importance of defence matters, the money spent upon the adventure will not have been lost. We have previously urged that Western Australia had no right to send a contingent until she had taken proper measures for providing for her own defence, but perhaps the sending of the contingent was just the one thing needed to strike the popular mind with the necessity for military preparation.

...When Federation has been accomplished there will be raised an Australian army which will certainly compare for fighting purposes with the troops of any country in the world. Behind that army, there will be a nation and a national spirit, whereas today the contingents are representing only their particular colonies. The one matter for regret is that the West Australian contingent could not be selected from the defence forces of the colony. It was found necessary to take in men who had never served in the volunteers and in some cases men who had seen no service at all. Many men who were eager to go were debarred because they had not joined the local forces, and we trust that the effect upon them will be to induce them to become volunteers. The school children should all be drilled, and every young man should be obliged to put in so many evenings in each year at military training, for that is the only way in which so large a country as Australia could be made ready to meet invasion. The sending of the contingent should be of great service to those who are charged with the duty of preparing defence forces, and we may look forward to considerable military development in the years to come throughout the continent.[34]

Notwithstanding the celebratory events seen in the town with the departure of some Albany volunteers for the South African Boer 'adventure' the cost of the war was soon driven home when the death notices of some residents appeared in the obituary and news columns of the local papers:

The Death of Major Hateley George Moor, Royal Artillery.
The late Commandant, the Princess Royal Fortress, Albany, while leading the first detachment of the West Australian contingent under his command on Thursday 19th of July 1900.

News of the death of Major Moor in South Africa evoked a general feeling of grief today. The deceased officer was at one time in command of The Forts here when holding the rank of Captain. He was highly respected

---

[32] *The Albany Advertiser.* 7th November 1899.
[33] Andrew Barton 'Banjo' Paterson (1864-1941) trained for the Law and at an early age he combined his legal work with writing establishing a following through *The Bulletin* magazine. He was War Correspondent for *The Sydney Morning Herald* and the Melbourne *Argus* during the Boer War. Later he became the Editor of *The* Sydney *Evening News* and *Town & Country Journal*. In the Great War, he was appointed Special War Correspondent to *The Argus* of Melbourne.
[34] *The Albany Advertiser.* 9th November 1899.

and very popular with all classes in the community. As soon as the sad news was made public all flags in the town were at half-mast, also at the Residency and on the Town Hall.[35]

It is interesting to note that the Boer War was the first and last occasion that Western Australia took part in a military campaign in its own right. In 1901 the Federal Government assumed control of its military forces and those of the Australian Colonies.

No one was to know that the scenes and feeling of adventure supported yet cautioned in the abovementioned article in *The Albany Advertiser* just two days after the contingent of Western Australians had left for the South African conflict, would be repeated fourteen years later when the colonies troops were once again called upon to support 'the mother country'.

As an aside, on the 22nd January 1901, the guns at The Albany Forts were fired in five-minute intervals to announce the death of Queen Victoria.

Hail Columbia!
15 White United States Battleships Welcomed

In my own judgement, the most important service that I rendered to peace was the voyage of the battle fleet around the world…
Theodore Roosevelt, 26th President of United States of America. 1916.

… Crowds flopped into Albany… Did not matter if the wind was as cold as it came off icebergs, or if the rain should soak their clothes, neither disturbing element could dampen their enthusiasm…
The Albany Advertiser. 17th September 1908.

The Great White Fleet as it had become known many years after 1908, was the United States Navy's Atlantic Fleet that comprised 16 battleships painted white for Peace, two store ships, a repair ship and a hospital ship.[36] The fleet put to sea on a circumnavigation of the world from 16th December 1907 to 22nd February 1909 by the order of President Theodore Roosevelt, one-time Secretary of the Navy. He wished to demonstrate to the world that the United States Navy was capable of operating worldwide, and in particular, in the Pacific where a United States presence was small and the tension between the Empire of Japan and the United States was just beginning to be noticed.

The Fleet, which was manned by 14 000 sailors visited twenty ports on six continents and consisted of four divisions of marines from San Francisco to Manila. The fleet was under the command of Rear Admiral Charles S. Sperry in the Flagship *Connecticut*.

A number of interesting facts have been discovered relevant to the voyage and also the voyagers who took part in this adventure. At the time of the fleet's sailing, there were four senior officers who had previously served during the American Civil War of 1861-1865 and who were eligible to have retired before the end of the voyage.

Furthermore, a new wireless telephone was installed to be employed on the battleships for communication purposes, specifically between the ships and shore stations. However, by the time the fleet reached Albany it had been hardly ever used and was subsequently scrapped by the time the ships returned to base.

As a point of historical interest, among the junior officers who visited Albany were four men who would go on to significant United States naval leadership roles in later years. Ensign Stark became an Admiral and Chief of Naval Operations just before Second World War and later became the Commander of United States Forces in Europe. He helped coordinate the United States Forces at the Normandy landings in 1945. Midshipman Halsey became Admiral of the Third Fleet at the time of the Japanese

---

[35] *Ibid*. 26th July 1900.
[36] Only 15 ships of the fleet arrived at the Albany, the 16th *Kansas* had remained in Melbourne.

Empire attack on Pearl Harbour, and later carried out a number of naval sorties in the Philippines and South Pacific from the Battleship *New Jersey* (the second battleship named *New Jersey* to visit Albany). Admiral Halsey retired in 1945. Midshipman Spruance became A Task Force Commander at the Battle of Midway, Chief-of-Staff to Admiral Chester Nimitz and in June 1944 Commander of United States Fifth Fleet in the Pacific which helped defeat the Imperial Japanese Fleet in the Battle of the Philippine Sea. Finally, Midshipman Coontz became Admiral Robert E. Coontz who was later to become the Chief of Naval Operations for the United States.

37

The world voyage was an extraordinary complex operation and Albany was chosen as one of the major coal and bunkering ports which, under the circumstances it coped with to great effect, receiving comprehensive coverage in news articles from around the world. *The Albany Advertiser* ran in all its September editions in 1908 aspects pertaining to the visit of the 15 Battleships to King George's Sound and the reaction of the local and visitor populace to the exciting event:

> *It was not originally my intention that the fleet should visit Australia, but the Australian Government sent a most cordial invitation, which I gladly accepted; for I have, as every American ought to have, a hearty admiration for, and fellow feeling with, Australia, and I believe that America should be ready to stand back of Australia in any serious emergency. The reception accorded the fleet in Australia was wonderful, and it showed the fundamental community of feeling between ourselves and the great commonwealth of the South Seas. The considerate, generous, and open-handed hospitality with which the entire Australian people treated our officers and men could not have been surpassed had they been our own countrymen...*
> Theodore Roosevelt, President United States of America.[38]

However, prior to the fleet's arrival in Albany there was significant background lobbying and agitation from both the Fremantle Town Council and its Chamber of Commerce and associated business interests as well as some Government ministers attempting to have the fleet call at Fremantle.

> *The American fleet is due here* [Albany] *for coal in October. That is unalterable. The agitation in favour of a visit to Fremantle nevertheless proceeds with unabated fury.*

Metropolitan papers record many happenings:

> *The Prime Minister informs me that he has official information is to the effect that the American fleet will not visit Western Australia for ceremonial purposes but may visit Albany for coal.*

> *The telegram was made available to the various governing bodies at the port, with the result that during the morning a deputation from the Citizens League and the Traders Association waited upon the Mayor of Fremantle in order to urge him to take some steps in the matter with a view to securing a visit of the fleet to Fremantle... it was also urged that the State Government should spend no effort to secure a visit from the fleet...*

> *A series of urgency telegrams was sent between various government offices inducing them to accede to bringing the fleet to Fremantle including one to the local parliamentarians of Western Australia:*

---

[37] Great White Fleet in The Princess Royal Harbour. Far right *HMS Gibraltar*. *Courtesy Albany Historical Society*.
[38] Theodore Roosevelt, *An Autobiography*, New York City. 1916.

> *Please arrange with Sir John Forrest and Western Australian senators for a deputation to the Prime Minister or American Consul, with such a request, as we understand a portion of the fleet will be passing by Fremantle...[39]*

A letter to the Editor of *The Albany Advertiser* captured the emotion of the moment:

> *Sir,*
> *I think by the tone of the Acting - Premier and the Mayor of Fremantle they are almost at their wits end to try and convince the fleet to visit the capital's port, but without affect. Now let me, as a resident of a placed called Albany, with such a beautiful natural harbour, one that will accommodate all the ships of the fleet, let me throw out a suggestion; as they cannot get their own way the next best thing for the Mayor of Fremantle, Mr Gregory to do is to give a substantial sum towards entertaining the fleet and get the Acting-Commissioner of Railways to run excursion fares. Then they can take a run down to the much-despised town of Albany and see how nobly the fleet will ride to their anchors in this beautiful harbour.[40]*

The American fleet of 15 Battleships entered into King George's Sound at daybreak on Sunday 12th December 1908 and from all newspaper accounts was an imposing spectacle.

> *Albany, Saturday, 12th September.*
> *Seen but by a few, although thousands of people in town had looked forward for months to witnessing the spectacle, many of them having travelled a thousand miles for the express purpose of doing so, the American Battleship Fleet, which is now making a peace tour of the world, entered King George's Sound at daybreak yesterday. The weather, which had been gloriously fine during the preceding week, had become unsettled in the night and rain was falling intermittently as day dawned. Looking to seaward a heavy mist restricted the range of vision, and the vessels must have approached within 12 miles of the shore before they became visible. As they came nearer, however, the light proved to be less unfavourable than might have been expected and every movement of the ships could be clearly discerned from the points of vantage overlooking the Sound. Six o'clock had just passed and the light of day had hardly become established when the first battleship emerged from the misty barrier which approached so near to the land as to almost obscure Breaksea Island. One by one the magnificent engines of war came into view until 15 could be counted, and it was then remembered that the fleet, for the time being, was complete for the* Kansas, *a sister to the flagship had remained behind at Melbourne for special duty. Under easy steam, the vessels advanced into the Sound and at a quarter past 7, the* Connecticut *dropped anchor within 2000 yards of The Forts. Two others took up positions in line with the flagship and then, in rows of four, the remainder settled down into places nearer Middleton Beach. At a quarter to 8 the last anchor was run out and the 15 ships, which, after all, only occupied a very small section of the protected waters of King George's Sound, presented a spectacle that will long live in the memories of those who witnessed it.*
>
> *The arrival of the fleet was attended by no little disappointment; not that it fell short of popular expectation in appearance, but because so many missed witnessing it. One unfortunate weakness of the arrangements was the absence of definite information as to what hour the battleships were to be expected. It was known that the Reception Committee had communicated with Admiral Sperry expressing the hope that he would find it convenient to make his appearance about noon. No reply had, however, been received and the public assumed that the entry might be looked for somewhere about 11 o'clock. All marine excursions were timed on that calculation. Thanks to the courtesy of the commander of* HMS Gibraltar, *the Premier on Thursday night was, it transpires, notified that the fleet would arrive at 7 a.m. Owing to Mr Moore's many engagements it was late before the communication reached him and it was not then possible to make the information generally available. Townspeople and visitors alike thus slumbered while the White Armada made the Sound, and the majority awoke only to find the battleships at anchor.*
>
> *...Close under Point King a strange steamer, painted white, rode at anchor and this was ascertained to be one of the store ships attached to the fleet.[41] Well, out in the Sound was a second vessel that proved to be one of the expected colliers. While yet the day was sufficiently young as to make the light uncertain, the first battleship emerged from the misty background as a black shadow. Gradually she assumed a definite shape*

---

[39] *The Albany Advertiser*. 23rd May 1908.
[40] Ibid.
[41] This was the fleet's hospital ship.

and as her lines became clearer another appeared. Yet another followed in due course and by degrees, all the ships came into view. It was observed as they came nearer that they were steaming at some speed, as white foam marked their progress through the water. The vessels approached from the south and shaped in the direction of Bald Head, an interval of several lengths appearing between them. Before the last of the 15 had become visible the Connecticut, *which of course led the way, had reached a point inside Bald Head, and she then abruptly put about and took a course across the Sound. As each of the vessels reached the same spot, they followed suit and the effect was remarkable. To the turning point, they appeared bow on, with crested waves thrown on either side. They seemed to linger then for a space and were next seen broadside on and moving under easy steam. The flagship continued in a north-easterly direction until getting inside Michaelmas Island, and she then once more put about and came to a position just outside of the fairway for the Harbour and about 3,000 yards from The Forts. The fleet is divided into two squadrons and the squadrons are again halved into divisions.*

…As before indicated the ships in the squadrons must have been about 800 yards apart. In the course of the manœuvre the fleet assumed a formation resembling the letter Z. The order of the procession was thus: Connecticut, *(16,000 tons) 24 guns;* Minnesota *(16,000 tons) 24;* Vermont *(16,000) 24;* Georgia *(14,948) 24;* Nebraska *(14,918) 24;* New Jersey *(14,948) 24;* Rhode Island *(14,948) 24;* Louisiana *(16,000) 24;* Virginia *(14,948) 24;* Missouri *(12,3500) 20;* Ohio *(12,500) 20;* Wisconsin *(11,552) 18;* Illinois *(11,552) 18;* Kearsarge *(11,520) 22; &* Kentucky *(11,520) 22.*

The Minnesota *and* Vermont *anchored to the eastward in a line with the* Connecticut. *The* Georgia *then led the second division in parallel line nearer the shore, the* Louisiana *similarly leading up the* Virginia, Missouri *and* Ohio *on the land side again and the* Wisconsin *heading the* Illinois, Kearsarge *and* Kentucky *in a fourth line. It was a quarter to 8 before the last anchor was dropped. Immediately anchors were lowered in each division, launches were seen to leave the sides of the different vessels, and towards the end, the water fairly swarmed with small craft. When all had been made fast the* Connecticut, Georgia, Louisiana *and* Wisconsin *ran up a series of signals. Eight bells rang out on all hands and within a minute or two the flagship fired a salute of 21 guns. This was replied to by The Forts. HMS* Gibraltar *then saluted, and the* Connecticut *having responded, the* [an unconnected visiting] *Chilean warship followed suit to have the compliment similarly acknowledged.*

The Connecticut *remained outside until about 11 o'clock when she entered the harbour and was anchored just off the end of the Deepwater Jetty… Then, in turn, during the day the* Louisiana, Georgia, Nebraska, Rhode Island *and* New Jersey *steamed into the harbour and anchored. The three colliers –* Teviotdale, Tottenham *and* Kildane *– the only ones that have yet arrived, were immediately attached and coaling started. It was anticipated that by this morning three of the battleships will have finished bunkering, and they will, as completed, proceed outside, the intention being to bring in four of the others to take their places. During the day the United States Navy store ships,* Panther *and* Glasier *were also brought inside. The flagship was among the first vessels to start coaling, and when finished she will retain her present position in the harbour.*

At night the battleships were brilliantly illuminated, but the unsettled condition of the weather marred the effect and kept many people from witnessing the display.[42]

Decorations and Illuminations in Albany

The decoration of the town was complete by Thursday night, and the streets presented a gay appearance. Flags of all colours were festooned on Venetian poles from the landing stage of the Town Jetty along the eastern side to Spencer street, whence they continued along Stirling Terrace, from Lawley Park to the Courthouse, on the southern side of the street. Then they continued up York Street on both sides to the Monument. Electric lights were hung at close intervals on cables between the poles along the Jetty and Stirling Terrace to the Courthouse, and the display, together with the illuminations of the business houses on the other side of the road, added to the effect at night. At the foot of the Jetty a single span arch bearing the motto, We Greet You: and "Welcome" first called for attention. The mottoes, "Welcome from Albany", "Hail Columbia", "Hands Across the Sea",

---

[42] The *Albany Advertiser*. All editions for September 1908.

and "Welcome from Perth" were artistically displayed on the Post and Custom House Offices. Another arch was thrown across the Terrace and bore the simple words "Welcome". In York Street, in front of St. John's Church, a three-span arch was erected with the mottoes, "Hail Columbia" on the south side and "Greetings to Our Kinsmen" on the other. The arches were decorated with velvet bush, peppermint, and wattle, and surmounted by flags. All the business houses were dressed with bunting, as also were the steamers Penguin, Burrumbeet, Zephyr, Una and Vigilant, lying alongside the Jetty.[43]

Police Protection

In view of the great influx of people expected in connection with the visit of the American Fleet, the local police force has been considerably augmented. Inspector Sellenger arrived on Wednesday with ten extra foot policemen and four mounted troopers, thus bringing the local strength up to two officers, two non-commissioned officers and 30 men.[44]

The Streets and Crowds

Albany, 17th September.
Albany on Saturday night presented an appearance which it is safe to say will never be witnessed again in this generation. The little imperfections in the electric illuminations on the previous night had been rectified, and the result was that Stirling Terrace for the time being was more like fairyland than the normal appearance it generally presents on a busy Saturday night. It would be an exaggeration to say that the streets were packed, but they were "comfortably crowded". One could get along by the exercise of a little patience, and plenty of good temper... But it was an orderly crowd on pleasure bent and nobody need have found trouble unless he was seeking it. Patrol parties were ashore from HMS. Gibraltar and the American fleet, but up to midnight they had very little do in the way of escorting the liberty men to the jetty to be conveyed to their respective ships. The British and American bluejackets were fraternising in the most cordial manner and giving practical illustration of the old adage "that blood is thicker than water". In every way, it was a pleasing crowd to be sauntering amongst. As one stood on the Rotunda watched the soldiers and sailors passing along and saw the happy faces of the people in the glare of the brilliant illuminations, even the cynic could not help admitting that it was worth travelling a long way to see Albany on this particular Saturday night. The police on beat duty, by the exercise of considerable tact, kept the crowd moving, and by making a liberal allowance for properly celebrating the visit of the 'White Armada', did not trouble any but the very drunk and disorderly and they were few and far between...

...The Gibraltar and visiting warships in the Sound were brilliantly illuminated, while a long line of electric lights extended along the Town Jetty, presenting a charming effect. The steamers conveying visitors round the warships were largely patronised, notwithstanding the cold breeze that was blowing across the water. But "Fleet Week" is not like "Albany Week". It does not happen once a year, and the crowds that flocked into Albany recognised this fact, so what did it matter then if the wind was as cold as if it came off an iceberg, or if the rain squalls soaked their clothes, neither disturbing element could damp their enthusiasm. They had come to see the 'White Armada', and neither wind nor weather would stop them.[45]

The Albany Advertiser Editorial

Wednesday, 23rd September.
The visit of the United States Battleship Fleet to Albany has left many agreeable recollections. Chief among them is the knowledge that the mighty squadron accomplished its purpose in coming here under circumstances that allowed those on board to go away thoroughly satisfied with the asylum afforded them. The Fleet only called as a matter of necessity. From a local point of view that is the most gratifying feature of the association. It was not desired that ceremonial should attend the visit outside Sydney and Melbourne. That was where the hospitality of the Commonwealth was to begin and end. But once in Australian waters, the White Armada of America had to provide for the journey hence to Manila. The route via Torres Strait was considered hazardous for such

---

[43] Ibid.
[44] Ibid.
[45] *The Albany Advertiser.* 17th September 1908.

a huge array of shipping, and the journey round the south-west of the continent being the only alternative it followed as a matter of course that King George's Sound should be selected as the rendezvous for coaling operations prior to entering upon the long run through the Indian Ocean.

The fact that the Fleet was ordered here was at once proof of the value of the port's geographical position and a recognition of the unrivalled advantages it offered for the object in view. Had political considerations been allowed to weigh at all the battleships would have assuredly passed on. As a tribute to the utility of the port, therefore, their presence here was doubly welcome. A deeper gratification still is to be found in the fact that even when deciding to come to Albany those in authority were not fully seized of the conveniences to be found here. Admiral Sperry was, indeed, altogether unaware that he could make use of Princess Royal Harbour. On arriving he anchored his ships in King George's Sound and straight away announced his intention of coaling there. A little practical experience, ensuing on representations that had been made to him, however, conduced to an alteration in this plan and the work was conducted inside.

In the course of an interview subsequently, the Admiral referred to the harbour as a grand one and regretted that the result of the money wisely expended on it was not shown on the Admiralty chart. There can be no doubt that the Harbours and Rivers Department of Western Australia supplied him with the latest information regarding the accommodation available, but he was evidently prepared to accept nothing that did not bear the stamp of the British Admiralty. The chart is understood to be 20 years old, and it would, at first sight, appear as if someone must be at fault for not having had it revised. The dredging of the harbour has, however, been trifled with. It was claimed that the scheme laid down was finished four years ago, but it is still incomplete. There has always been the prospect of its early completion and on that account, the final survey has been delayed. That is why the Admiralty chart has not been revised, but in view of what has occurred the town should be given some encouragement to hope that the dredging will be finished at an early date and an up-to-date chart issued.

Notwithstanding Admiral Sperry's conservative preference for the Admiralty chart on the way over, he accepted a statement of the position when it was made verbally, and he placed himself entirely in the hands of the Harbour Master.

No greater compliment could be paid any man than that, and happily for the reputation of Albany Captain Winzar, justified to the full the confidence reposed in him. The Connecticut *and* Minnesota, *as flagships of the two squadrons forming the fleet, were given anchorages in the harbour for the whole of the visit. The others were, however, brought in to coal and taken out when finished. As the colliers were limited more than three or four vessels could not coal simultaneously, and consequently, the number of battleships in the harbour at one time did not exceed six. At least four more could have been found places had the situation required it, and that in addition to the other shipping in port, which on one occasion comprised,* HMS Gibraltar, *a White Star liner, three colliers, and the two store ships. …It is true the fleet remained longer than was intended. That, however, was due to defects in their own arrangements. Two colliers arrived late, one too late to be utilised. One effect of this was to almost double the work and responsibility of the Harbour Master, yet nevertheless, he kept nobody waiting. Little wonder Admiral Sperry and his officers expressed appreciation of the treatment meted out to them. The American Commander-in-Chief, in his farewell message to the Commonwealth, asked:*
"Who shall compute the national importance of Australia".
In the same vein we may locally ponder over the question:
"Who shall compute the importance to Albany of the visit of the United States Fleet".[46]

The New York Times in a lead article indicated that the American battleship fleet was supposed to leave the port of Albany on the 16th of September, however, its departure was delayed a day. Admiral Sperry who was in command of the fleet received a telegram of salutation from the Australian Prime Minister of the Commonwealth, Alfred Deakin. It read:

Tomorrow you leave Australia after experiences, I trust, that has been as pleasurable to you as to the people of the Commonwealth. The officers and men of your fleet have been welcomed everywhere warmly and sincerely. We have learned to know you, and we are under obligation to President Roosevelt and the American government for the honour of this visit. Although your stay with us has been short, we rejoice in this fortunate opportunity to refresh the

---

[46] *The Albany Advertiser.* 23rd September 1908.

cordial relations existing between progressive and related peoples. We cherish the same traditions and ideals as do you. It is the ardent hope of our citizens that the friendship between the British Empire and the American Republic be strengthened, and with us, in Australia, many new personal ties have been established, which, we trust will endure and flourish. Your flag, your fleet, your sailors and yourself carry the good wishes of all Australia.[47]

Charles S. Sperry had been a wonderful Ambassador for the United States of America during this venture into the Sound and won many accolades from the people of Albany for his statesmanship. The local Harbour Master was also praised for his work and *The Albany Advertiser* was very complimentary on his endeavours in particular with the fleet:

Admiral Sperry…placed himself in the hands of the Harbour Master…he handled the battleships with as much freedom as if they had been dinghies…[48]

Extracts from *Ode of Welcome* by Louis Esson reproduced here as an extract from *Punch* in Melbourne was distributed as part of a Souvenir for the USA Fleet visit to the Australian colonies. While its language, that of its time, would today be seen as very politically incorrect, it does capture some of the prevalent attitude exhibited in early publications of this type and the warmth exhibited to the American show of strength in the Southern Ocean:

Ode of Welcome

The Eagles sweep great wings and soar
Above the dragon haunted sea,
And past the dragon guarded shore.
Southward the Eagles Sweep, and we
Rejoice that kinsman reunite
To keep the Southland ever white.

For brothers of the blood are they
With those who left their fiord and dun
In rough-hewn ships to Cleave their way
And sale beneath the setting sun,
The track of blood and phantom gold
Like Sigurd strong, like Drake the bold….

War clouds may streak the southern sky
And Asian arrogance deep stain
The scarlet scroll of history:
But through the murk one thing is plain
Though seas divide, to each lone land
Kinsmen will rally, hand-in-hand….

Hail to the Eagles! With strong beat
Their wings Sweep over threatened seas.
Australia hails a kinsmen fleet
That guards the future centuries.
The white man's grip must never fail
Sea Eagles of Columbia, hail![49]

Apparently, some people enjoyed the visit of the American seamen perhaps somewhat more than others, as this extract from a letter of a participating youth clearly indicates:

---

[47] *The New York Times*, New York City. 1908.
[48] The Editor, *The Albany Advertiser*. 23rd September 1908.
[49] Ode of Welcome by Louis Esson. 'Punch's' *Souvenir for the USA Fleet Visit, 1908*. National Library of Australia.

I saw Admiral Sperry, U.S.A. fleet in 1908, made a great speech from that Rotunda much big brother uncle Sam, bonds and cheers. A barmaid in the White Hart (now Star) had a U. S. Sailor under her skirt behind the bar but the S.P (shore patrol) saw his feet and dragged him out from beneath the lady's pants.[50]

The Arrival of Imperial Japanese Warships

A little known or celebrated event was the arrival of a Japanese squadron of warships in April 1910. The squadron was on a goodwill mission to Australia and had started with visits to the country's eastern seaports before making its way to the port of Albany.

The Japanese squadron.
Arrival at Albany.
Three days visit.

The Japanese Squadron now visiting the Commonwealth arrived at Albany at 7:30 yesterday morning. The announced intention of the Admiral was to arrive here at noon on Thursday, but heavy weather crossing the Bight upset all arrangements. The ships dropped anchor in the outer harbour in the same spot as United States fleet anchored on the arrival here. Salutes were exchange between the ships and The Forts.

At 10 o'clock the SS Dunskey *left the town's jetty with the Mayor, Mr Armstrong, [and party] … On arrival alongside the flagship the Albany visitors were received by Captain T Sato, of the* HIJMS Aso, *Captain K. Suzuhi, of* HIJMS Soyo, *and Flag Lieutenant C. Shimmomura. The visitors were conducted to the Admiral's state room and introduced to the Admiral commanding, His Excellency Rear-Admiral H. Ijichi…*

A return visit to the Mayor and military offices was paid by the Admiral and staff at 3 o'clock in the afternoon. A reception will be tended the visiting offices by the Mayor and counsellors this morning. The ships will be thrown open to visitors after 1 o'clock this afternoon and tomorrow.[51]

Closing Remarks

Even though the importance of King George's Sound port facilities had been somewhat diminished with the development of the Fremantle anchorage and infrastructure which had assumed the mantle of the main portal for shipping into Western Australia, Albany, nevertheless, as a defensive port retained its relevance. The town had proved to be most effective in its handling of the Boer War contingents, The Royal Navy, The Great White Fleet, The Imperial Japanese and the British Squadron visits. Unknowingly together these events had proved to be an excellent apprenticeship for Albany's later role in the Great War that was only a few years distant. The town responded admirably by ensuring that these events were skilfully handled and well supported.

It was in 1914 that the Albany port facilities and the towns inhabitants were called upon once again to provide significant support for the Great War. Support that was seen to be manifest in the way the townspeople responded to the call to arms, with virtually every family contributing in some way to the war, whether it be through the enlistment of family members or work on the home front that supported the country's overseas endeavours the town responded with great patriotic enthusiasm.

---

[50] *Robert Stephens Historical Collection.* The Albany History Collection, Albany Town Library.
[51] *The Albany Advertiser.* 30th April 1910.

CHAPTER 16
ALBANY AT WAR AND ITS ANZAC CONNECTIONS

The Great War 1914 - 1918

… My whole empire at home and overseas have moved with one mind…
His Majesty King George V
8th September 1914.

"… tomorrow we put to sea, and the greatest national undertaking yet attempted by Australia will have commenced in earnest…"
Andrew Barton Paterson. 31st October 1914.

1914 Departure for War

It was from *The Albany Advertiser* that Albanians were told of the grave happenings in Europe and around the Empire and then informed that troop mobilisation in Western Australia had begun. In the meantime, Western Australian military personnel had arrived in town via a special sleeper mail train from Perth. They were met at the Albany Railway Station by local civic and military officials who were impressed by the fact *"the response and mobilisation were completed with remarkable despatch"*.

Upon arrival, the infantry and naval personnel were directed to The Forts on Mount Adelaide. However, at this time townspeople had not been informed that King George's Sound had been selected as the principal assembly point for a convoy of merchant ships that would transport troops and horses from both Australia and New Zealand to the war zone. King George's Sound was but one of the muster points for the troops, the other was Fremantle. The rendezvous for all His Majesty's troop ships and their escorts was to be 31 deg. 30 min. South and 114 deg. 28 min. East in the Indian Ocean.

Still at this point, many in Albany were quite unaware that the Albany port had been selected for the vanguard of naval and merchant ships on their way to war. Altogether, thirty-six troop ships departed from Albany and not the 38 often reported by some local historians who failed to acknowledge that two troop ships also sailed from Fremantle.

By 1914 Albany had been identified strategically as one of the important bunkering ports to and from Europe, Africa, the Indian Empire and Asia. Not surprising, therefore, that its importance throughout the war was considerable because of the town's strategic military fortifications and its position on the south-eastern extremity of the Indian Ocean.

Interestingly, a little-reported fact is that in less than two months after the first Australian Imperial Force convoy left Albany's shores with troops on board, the second convoy of ANZACs weighed anchor and left the same harbour on December 31st, 1914. Such was the success of the troop recruitment, there were a further 11,000 troops on board the second convoy of 17 troop ships bound for the Middle East. Their journey would take them via Colombo, in Ceylon (now Sri Lanka); Aden, the Suez Canal and Port Said, in Egypt, before they reached Alexandria in Egypt on 3rd February and completed their disembarkation four days later. Dr David Stevens, Director of Strategic and Historical Studies at the Royal Australian Navy's Sea Power Centre, said the second convoy of Australian and New Zealand troop ships was notable in part because it was one of the last to leave Australian shores until 1917.[1]

In an article from the November 1936 edition of *The Albany Wizbang* a soldiers' recollections on board one of the troop ships relating to the sinking of *Emden*, which was seen as a particular threat to the convoys leaving Albany, highlights the relief felt within the convoy when news of this filtered down to the troops:[2]

---

[1] Correspondence from Mr William Gaynor, OAM. Ex-President of the Western Australian R.S.L.
[2] *'The Albany Wizbang'* was the official publication of the Albany Branch of the RSL and was issued monthly to its members. It was designed to keep its membership in touch with the organisation's activities.

The Emden.

It was well-known on the troop ships that the Emden *was in southern waters and all sorts of precautions were taken from the time we left Australia. On the morning of ninth November there appeared to be unusual activity amongst the escorting ships and the* Sydney, *with volumes of smoke issuing from funnels and foam pouring over her bowels, dashed across our front and disappeared over the horizon. There was much conjecture amongst the troops and some of our "know-alls" who claim to be able to read the signals passing between our flagship and the battleship said the* Sydney *was after the* Emden…

Later in the day and official message was received by all troop ships from the flagship that the Sydney *had engaged the* Emden *and sunk her. When the message was received the troops were all on the troop decks having their midday meal and the orderly offices – down to their respective units and announced the news. The cheers and pandemonium can be imagined and very little attention was given to training for the rest of the day.*

Later, orders were issued that the Sydney *would be passing through our lines on her way to Colombo with the wounded and prisoners on board and that there was to be no demonstration, or cheering, which might disturb the wounded. However, when the* Sydney *did pass the order was forgotten and she was cheered from one end of the convoy to the other.*[3]

Furthermore, because the German cruiser *Emden* had been sunk and consequently Germany's presence in the Indian Ocean was regarded as a negligible risk, convoys were no longer a necessity and this resulted in many independent troop ships sailing from both Albany and Fremantle. [4]

Over the course of the next six years, single troop and hospital ships would routinely call at ports at either Albany or Fremantle. The point needs to be reinforced here that there were 2 convoys and 45 single voyages to the Middle East and Europe from these ports in the course of the war.

A message from His Majesty The King was received in all Dominions of the British Empire from London pertaining to the conflict and the expectations held for member states to support the endeavour:

Buckingham Palace
London, SW1.
Tuesday, September 8th, 1914.

'To the Governments and Peoples of my Self-Governing Dominions.

During the past few weeks, the Peoples of my whole Empire at home and overseas have moved with one mind and purpose to confront and overthrow an unparalleled assault upon the continuity of civilization and the peace of mankind. The calamitous conflict is not of my seeking. My voice has been cast throughout on the side of peace. My Ministers earnestly strove to allay the causes of strife and to appease differences with which my Empire was not concerned. Had I stood aside when in defiance of pledges to which my Kingdom was a party when the soil of Belgium was violated and her cities laid desolate when the very life of the French Nation was threatened with extinction, I should have sacrificed my honour and given to the destruction of the liberties of my Empire and of mankind. I rejoice that every part of the Empire is with me in this decision.

Paramount regard for a treaty, faith and the pledged word of rulers and peoples is the common heritage of Great Britain and of the Empire.

My Peoples in the Self-Governing Dominions have shown beyond all doubt that they wholeheartedly endorse the grave decision which it was necessary to take.

---

[3] Ibid. 30th November 1936.

[4] The German cruiser, *SMS Emden*, was attacking the British cable and wireless station on Direction Island (Cocos (Keeling) Islands) when the commanding officer, became aware of the enemy approaching. The staff at the station had been able to make a distress call, which was received by the allies before the station was attacked.
The cruiser *HMAS Sydney*, under the command of Captain John Glossop RAN, was ordered to attack the German cruiser. *Sydney* had the advantage over *Emden*, it was faster and had greater fire range. *Sydney* caused significant damage to *Emden* and the commander ordered his men to run *Emden* aground. *Sydney's* defeat of *Emden* in the Battle of Cocos was the Royal Australian Navy's first naval victory and the end to *Emden's* dominance in the waters around the Cocos (Keeling) Islands in the Indian Ocean.

My personal knowledge of the loyalty and devotion of my overseas Dominions has led me to expect that they would cheerfully make the great efforts and bear the great sacrifices which the present conflict entails. The full measure in which they have placed their services and resources at my disposal fills me with gratitude, and I am proud to be able to show to the world that my Peoples overseas are as determined as the people of the United Kingdom to prosecute a just cause to a successful end.

'The Dominion of Canada, the Commonwealth of Australia, and the Dominion of New Zealand have placed at my disposal their naval forces, which have already rendered good service for the Empire. Strong expeditionary forces are being prepared in Canada, in Australia, and New Zealand for service at the front, and the Union of South Africa has released all British troops and has undertaken important military responsibilities, the discharge of which will be of the utmost value to the Empire. Newfoundland has doubled the numbers of its branch of the Royal Naval Reserve and is sending a body of men to take part in the operations at the front. From the Dominion and Provincial Governments of Canada large and welcome gifts of supplies are on their way for the use of both of my naval and military forces and for the relief of the distress in the United Kingdom, which must inevitably follow in the wake of war. All parts of my overseas Dominions have thus demonstrated in the most unmistakable manner the fundamental unity of the Empire amidst all its diversity of situation and circumstance. [5]

George R.I.

The King's telegram message was followed by one from General Lord Herbert Kitchener, who was now The Secretary of State of War in the Imperial Parliament. It had been addressed to the British Expeditionary Force on its way to France. The message was also telegraphed to Australia by special permission of The King who knew that most of his troops in the Australian Imperial Force were then at King George's Sound and Fremantle, places he knew well. The message from the War Office in London was printed in *The Times Documentary History of the War* published between 1917-1920 as follows:

You are ordered abroad as a soldier of the King to help our French comrades against the invasion of a common enemy. You have to perform a task that will need your courage, your energy, your patience. Remember that the honour of the British Army depends on your individual conduct. It will be your duty not only to set an example of discipline and perfect steadiness under fire but also to maintain the most friendly relations with those whom you are helping in this struggle. The operations in which you are engaged will be, for the most part, in a friendly country and you can do your country no better service than showing your shelves in France and Belgium as the true character of a British soldier, by being invariably courteous, considerate and kind. Never do anything likely to injure or destroy property, and always look upon looting as a disgraceful act. You are sure to meet with a welcome and to be trusted. Your conduct must justify that welcome and trust. Your trust cannot be done unless your health is sound, so keep constantly on guard against any excesses in this new experience. You may find temptations both in wine and women. You must entirely resist both temptations, and while treating all women with perfect courtesy you should avoid any intimacy.

Do your duty bravely, Fear God, Honour the King.

Kitchener. [6]

Of special note, Lord Kitchener had visited Western Australia for 4 days in January 1910. He had travelled by train from Perth to Albany, where he inspected The Princess Royal Battery at The Forts on Mt. Adelaide and observed some firing practice. Kitchener then departed from Albany on his way to Adelaide on 28th January onboard *HMS Osterley*.

Lord Kitchener's message was addressed to the Australian and New Zealand troops, while the Commanding Officer of the A.I.F. Major-General (Sir) William Bridges' message was one of farewell and addressed the people of Australia from King George's Sound on board his Flagship *HMAT Orvieto*, which had just sailed into the Sound from Melbourne. Kitchener's telegram which appeared in Australian newspapers the next morning read:

I hope from time to time to be able to report to the Minister of Defence that the conduct of the Australian troops, both in camp and in the field, is all that it should be, and worthy of the trust reposed by the people of the

---

[5] *The Times Documentary History of the War- Overseas*. Volume V1. London, 1918.
[6] Lord Kitchener, the 1st Earl of Khartoum and of Broome is perhaps best known for defeating the Dervishes at the Atbara in April 1898 and by the final victory at Omdurman on the 2nd October 1898, at which time he won back the Sudan for Egypt.

> *Commonwealth. The men are a fine lot, soldierly, and patriotic. I am grateful to the soldiers and citizens for the help given me in organising and preparing the force, which is now about to do its part for the good of the Empire. In saying goodbye, I would like to express the hope that no matter how great the demands upon their patience, the Australian people will see to it that there is no diminution of their determination to face their responsibility. This spirit cannot fail than to pervade the troops.*
>
> *Kitchener of Khartoum*

With respect to the logistical effort and the departure of His Majesty's troops the Melbourne newspapers indicated under the banner of "*The Secret Departure*" that:

> *The embarkation of the Commonwealth fighting men and horses, with baggage and wagons, occupied altogether five days, during which the weather was always particularly favourable. As the transports were loaded, they shaped their course for King George's Sound, in West Australia. The naval authorities had arranged their dates of departure in each case, so that all steamers should arrive at the rendezvous at King George's Sound on October 25 or 26.*
>
> *The ten steamers carrying the New Zealand force linked up with the Australian naval division, and the fleet of transports moved off across the Indian Ocean without delay from King George's Sound and Fremantle. The journey will be slow enough. The rate of progress for a fleet is governed by its least speedy vessel, and the* Pera, Southern, Soldbara, *and* Katuna, *amongst other transports, steam only at 10 knots per hour.*[7]

It was at King George's Sound that the Australia troops had met their New Zealand counterparts for the first time. The New Zealand troop ships had arrived in secrecy and were greeted positively by the citizens of Albany as news of their arrival at the port became known.

The great armada of merchant ships was escorted by the cruiser, *HMS Minotaur* along with a light cruiser *HMS Psyche* of the New Zealand squadron, and an Imperial Japanese battle cruiser *HIJMS Ibuki* together with the cruisers *HMAS Sydney* and *HMAS Melbourne*. The Royal Australian Navy had been in existence only a few years when the war broke out as previously naval operations came under the jurisdiction of the individual states.

Captain Arthur Gordon Smith R.N., the convoy's commanding officer, vividly recalls his experience with the arrival and mustering of the fleet in King George's Sound:

> *Of many thrilling scenes, it needs no great effort of memory to recall that King George's Sound and The Princess Royal Harbour as those on the flagship saw it first through the thick grey mists of the early morning of 26th October, I could see ships gradually resolving themselves into definite shape, much in the way a conjurer brings from the gloom of a darkened chamber, strange realities. The troops were astir and crowded to the ships' sides. They stood to attention as the liner glided down the lines of anchored transports, for the mass of shipping was anchored in ordered lines. The bugles rang out sharp and clear the assembly notes, flags dipped in salute to the General's flag at the masthead. It was calm now inside this refuge, A large warship the Japanese cruiser, the Ibuki remained there a few days and then steamed out for Fremantle, … in her place came the two Australian cruisers,* HMAS Melbourne *and* HMAS Sydney. *Each night the troops watched one or others of these scouts put to sea, stealing at dusk to patrol, …, the entrance to the harbour wherein lay the precious Convoy.*
>
> *On the morning of the 28th the New Zealand Convoy, consisting of ten ships, arrived and anchored just inside the entrance of the Sound. From shore, the sight was truly wonderful… What signs of habitation there were on shore were limited to a whaling station on the west and a few pretty red-roofed bungalows on the east; while the entrance to an inner harbour, the selected spot for a possible destroyer base of the Australian Navy, suggested as snug a little cove as one might wish. Opposite the main entrance behind the anchored Convoy was the narrow, channel leading to the port where the warships anchored, protected from outer view behind high cliffs from which frowned the guns of the Princess Royal Fortress. It was, from this fortress that I looked down on to the ships – that was after nearly being arrested as a spy by a suspicious vigilant guard… All was in readiness. It only needed the signal from the Admiralty to the Convoy and its escort and the army of 30,000 would move finally from Australian shores. This was the mustering of a complete Division for the first time in the history of the young Dominion.*

---

[7] A feature in *The Argus* of Melbourne followed under the heading the "Secret" Departure.

We entered King George's Sound early one cold and misty morning. The Australian cruiser Melbourne *(Captain Mortimer L'Estrange Silver, RN) was doing watchdog at the entrance, and about a dozen transports rode at anchor in their berths. King George's Sound is something like Plymouth Sound, only much bigger. There is a small inner anchorage at The Princess Royal Harbour, in which is the little town of Albany. The Sound itself is well sheltered, except that it is open to the south-east – a couple of islets are situated at its entrance…*

By the evening of the 31st, we were all ready… Our departure was rather impressive. Almost on the horizon, protecting the movement were the cruisers. The day was breaking, and the sombre blue hills and islands enclosing the Sound were tipped with a rosy glow. Over the Sound hung a canopy of funnel smoke. We filed out in single line; Orvieto *leading, followed by the first division of transports. The morning was calm, and there was a strange stillness, broken only by the long-drawn surges at our bows as we began to plunge into the ocean swell.*

By 8 o'clock the whole convoy was formed up as a fleet in cruising order, and we increased speed and set forth into the Indian Ocean on our adventures.[8]

A more succinct perspective from Claude Farrere a French correspondent who was a witness to the fleet's arrival and departure:

What a mob!! They are all much more afraid of running into each other than of being attacked by an enemy; each keeps well away from his neighbours; … By morning the convoy, which should have covered about five miles, stretches away for fifteen or sixteen….[9]

Major Fred Waite from a New Zealand Army detachment provided yet another perspective of the departure event:

Thirteen days after leaving Wellington the New Zealand ships crept into the spacious King George's Sound of Albany on the south coast of Western Australia. Here were gathered innumerable vessels of every line trading in the Southern oceans. Not painted uniformly grey like our ships, but taken in all their glory of greens, blues and yellows, they rode on the calm water of King George's Sound packed with the adventurous spirits of the First Australian Division. The cheering and counter-cheering, the Maori war cries, and answering Coo-ees would have moved a stoic. Young Australia was welcoming Young New Zealand in no uncertain manner in the first meeting of those brothers-in-arms soon to be known by a glorious name as yet undreamed of.[10]

"Banjo" Paterson was the Special War Correspondent for *The Argus* of Melbourne, sailed with the first convoy onboard the His Majesty's troop ship *Euripides*. His first article in *The Argus* was headed "*An Army on The Sea*" *and* was telegraphed from Albany to the editor of his newspaper in Melbourne:

Tomorrow we put to sea, and the greatest national undertaking yet attempted by Australia will have commenced in earnest… It is not a subject written off lightly. Rather let us pray that the success may attend our venture and that we may manfully do our share towards bringing about victory, followed by an honourable lasting peace…[11]

An often-overlooked aspect of The Great War histories is the heroic efforts of the female nursing staff who worked on the front and behind the lines to address the large numbers of wounded and sick among the troops. There is, in fact, a dearth of original documentation available on this area and further, more recent commentaries and analyses particularly as they apply to this conflict are few and far between in the acknowledgement of Australian women who worked in war zones. Fortunately, we have the diaries of Sister Alice Elizabeth Kitchen to fall back on to give a feminine aspect to the events as they unfolded in the town.

Alice Kitchen enlisted in the Australian Army Nursing Services in August 1914 at the age of 40. She sailed to Egypt with the first detachment of soldiers from the Australian Imperial Force. Kitchen spent the following five years tending the sick and wounded during the war. She was working at a hospital in Cairo when the first group of casualties from Gallipoli arrived. She later saw service on a hospital ship stationed in ANZAC Cove and after serving for the duration returned to Australia in August 1919. Alice Kitchen

---

[8] Smith, A.G. *The First Australian Convoy. The Blue Peter,* Volume 5, London, 1926.
[9] Farrere, C. & Chack, P. *Comats et Batailles sur Mer*. Paris, 1914.
[10] Major Fred Waite, DSC NZE, *The New Zealanders at Gallipoli*. Auckland, 1915.
[11] A.B. *Banjo* Paterson. Special Correspondent, *The Argus*, Melbourne. 20th November 1914.

was both a nurse and writer/diarist who was able to provide valuable insights into the behaviours and emotions of the time.

At Albany... the men went for a route march, some not returning and the pickets were sent out after them. All were found but one... all the rest were rounded up the next day and sent back to the boat... Col. Mcphee took us out for a short drive to King River where we had morning tea at a little refreshment place with lots of flowers...[12]

Extracts from her diary of October 1914 talk of preparing for departure:

October 24.
Albany this morning early. A good many troop ships already in. We were given permission to go ashore but owing to some delay with the launch we could not go as it was too late and no boats must approach the troop ship after dark. It was nice to be able to post letters and send telegrams to relieve their anxiety at home. I wish we could send a wireless daily but that cannot be. It is nice to see our own land once more. Sorry to hear the Emden has been busy again. We are looking forward to having a week off duty, the work has been so constant. So many things to see to. A concert on the well deck.

October 30.
The wildflowers are beautiful so many varieties, of all colours and kinds, one lovely blue one thick in the grass, like thick forget-me-nots being particularly lovely. Big patches of bottle brush, red and a very pretty blue shrub also thick with flowers. We had dinner with the party, Capt. Jackson and S.W. White, at the Freemason's Hotel and then did shopping for the ship and ourselves; found it slow work as the employees were constantly running out to look at the various bands of soldiers and bands as Afric *was also at the pier.*

November 1, Sunday, All Saints Day.
At 8 a.m. we began to move out in single file to the sea: it was a fine sight to see the long line of ships, going out one by one and moving into 3 long lines, the cruisers leading and the N.Z. convoy last. We travel about 800 yds behind each other and a mile between the 3 rows. It seems a little difficult to get the correct speed and they occasionally have to drop out of line if they get too close, but seem to have all sorts of arrangements made for contingencies; we are 5th in the starboard line, the Afric *before us and the* Rangatira *behind; if too close we move in and the* Rangatira *moves out, and so on right down the lines, till they cool down and then fall into line again. It is an anxious time for all those in charge. We hear the Captain never leaves the bridge at night. If attacked by enemy cruisers, we are to go 8 miles out of our course till the cruisers do their work. A cruiser leads the way then the* Orvieto, *then 3 lines of ships 3 abreast, a cruiser on each side and one far away in the rear. They say there are scouts as well beyond these.*

...I often look out at them at night and think of all it means too many at home and wish Australia could get the wireless daily to tell of our safety. If the Emden *comes in amongst us in the dark what a commotion there would be. Most of them would be horribly mixed up in a collision. We all realise our danger but are in God's hands. At night all portholes are covered when the light is on and as few as possible used, partly to minimise the difficulty of steering by the boat behind each other.*

November 2nd 'All Souls' Day.
Very rough and rolly. Hospital full, so many sore throats. Very busy. I am fortunate in being able to keep to my feet and not be too seasick. Nursing at sea is not what it is cracked up to be. Dishes of water roll everywhere, and it is necessary to leg-rope the hot-water cans to the posts to avoid scaled feet. No floating rubbish to be thrown overboard.[13]

---

[12] Alice Kitchen was one of 24 Nursing Sisters in the Australian Army Nursing Service. She is recognised for her service in the Australian War Memorial. Unit -Australian Army Nursing Service. Conflict -First World War, 1914-1918.

[13] *Alice Elizabeth Kitchen Diary.* Manuscript Collection, State Library of Victoria, Melbourne. 1916.

The War at Home.

In aid of the war effort an amusing extract from *The Albany Advertiser* alludes to the efforts of the Albany 'Sandbags committee' endeavours:

> *On Friday last the annual working bee met at the Lower Town Hall and 600 bags were completed. This makes 3,124 up to date. The organisers wish to make 1,000 per week and would be glad to see more workers. No response has yet been made to the appeal for beeswax, which is urgently needed.*
>
> *At the Town Jetty baths, and in ideal weather, the Sandbag swimming carnival and exhibition of Mr G. Pazakos and life-saving of Mr Clark passed off on Saturday afternoon most successfully. Over 400 people passed through the gates and the result was the return of over £17 to the local sandbag fund, which is very gratifying to the promoters. In the greasy pole item, it was impossible to decide the winner, so Mayor Robinson kindly donated an additional prize. After a long run of high tides, it was unfortunate that a very low tide prevented Mr Pazakos from giving a full display of his powers underwater. Mr Cuthbert McKenzie M.L.C. and Mr Mutton kindly acted as judges. Afternoon teas and sweets were dispensed by Mrs Pitt and a committee of ladies. The committee desire to express their thanks to Mr Pazakos for the free use of the baths and to Messrs. Clark and Davidson for making the carnival the success it was.*[14]

The town's war effort in administering to the troops and addressing their medical needs was also acknowledged during the visit of Sir Roland Crawford Munro-Ferguson, The Governor-General of Australia in June 1916:

> *Albany, June 28.*
>
> *The Governor-General and Lady Helen Munro Ferguson, who landed last night in cold and unpleasant weather conditions after a trying trip from the Eastern States, were today able to enjoy their first day in Western Australia under ideal conditions after days of rain. The surrounding hills and the town itself looked at their best in the sunshine of a glorious day, and the harbour, with its picturesque surroundings, presented a charming appearance. The present visit of the Governor-General is, it is understood, regarded as official only in an initiatory sense, and according to reference at the civic reception tendered to Sir Ronald Munro Ferguson this morning, it is his intention to pay a longer visit to Western Australia in his official capacity as Governor-General at a later date.*
>
> *The Vice-Regal party were early astir this morning. The town wore an animated appearance, flags being flown from many of the principal buildings, while in some places bunting was suspended over the verandas and balconies. The first act of their Excellencies was to pay a kindly tribute of respect and consideration to the sick and wounded soldiers who are at present located at No. 4 Auxiliary Military Hospital. The premises, known as The Rocks were purchased by the Government as a summer residence for the State Governor, and the deal was completed just before the war broke out. Its suitability as a hospital for wounded soldiers was immediately recognised, and as a result, the building was speedily converted into a comfortable home for the returned heroes. …*
>
> *There are at the present time about 30 men, representing various Australian units, at the hospital, and with each one of them, both the Governor-General and Lady Helen Munro Ferguson spent some time chatting over their experiences and inquiring as to the nature of their injuries or ailments. Their Excellencies were particularly appreciative of the beauty of the view obtained from the hospital grounds and complimented the staff, including the nursing sisters and Warrant Officer Robinson, on the manner in which the premises were conducted.*
>
> *Visit to the Schools.*
>
> *During the time the Governor-General was occupied at the civic reception, Lady Helen Munro Ferguson, accompanied by the Mayoress, Mrs Scadden, and other ladies, paid a visit to the several schools in the township and was shown over the premises by those in charge. At each school, after the children had assembled and had sung to Her Excellency, who congratulated them upon their fine, healthy appearance. At her request, the children were granted a half-holiday in honour of the occasion.*[15]

---

[14] Ibid. 12th January 1916.
[15] *The West Australian*, Perth. 29th June 1916.

A Wartime Military Wedding.

In order to maintain community morale, some traditions needed to be maintained, if for no other reason than to convey a sense of normalcy in times of collective uncertainty and stress:

The Hamlin-Louch Marriage.

A military wedding of profound interest to the residents of Albany, as evidenced by the crowded congregation that assembled on the occasion, was celebrated in St. John's Church on Thursday morning, when Mary Grace, the only daughter of the Venerable Archdeacon and Mrs Louch, [Archdeacon Louch was the Rector of Albany] was married to Herbert Bowen Hamlin, son of the late John Preston Herbert Hamlin and Mrs Hamlin, of Panmure (N.Z.) and a lieutenant in the 10th Light Horse, who is home on furlough after months of service in the trenches at the Gallipoli Peninsula. The event was marked by an exceptional display of public concern due to the popularity of the bride, who has spent her girlhood in the town. The picturesque old church was beautifully decorated by the girlfriends of the bride. A very handsome wedding bell, with the happy couple's initials, and made by the Misses Warren, was hung from the chancel and created a very pretty effect. The service was fully choral. The choir, of which Miss Louch was a member, met her at the church door and preceded her to the altar, singing "The Voice that Breathed o'er Eden". Mr O. W. Berliner officiated at the organ.

The bride, who was given away by her father, looked exceedingly well in a dainty creation of lacy net over satin charmeuse, the short skirt of modern fashion giving her a very girlish appearance. Her veil was prettily caught up with orange blossoms, and in her hair was arranged her mother's wedding wreath. She carried a sheaf of the white California poppy, tied with her husband's regimental colours, Blue and gold, which lent a charming touch of colour to her costume. ... Lieutenant Louch attended Lieutenant Hamlin as best man. Bishop Goldsmith performed the ceremony and was assisted by the Rev. Arthur White, B.S.B. [Brotherhood of St. Boniface] As the bride left the church she was met by the Girl Guides, who, dressed in khaki, lined the pathway to the Rectory and presented her with a floral horseshoe tied with blue and gold ribbon.

After the ceremony, the Archdeacon and Mrs Louch held a reception at the Rectory. Mrs Louch was gowned in a very becoming grey satin charmeuse, hat en suite, and carried a lovely bouquet of crimson and yellow roses. Lieut. And Mrs Hamlin received the congratulations of their friends in the drawing-room surrounded by a handsome lot of presents, many of which were substantial cheques. After some wedding photographs had been taken, an adjournment was made to the dining room, where light refreshments were served and the health of the happy couple drunk. A beautiful three-tier wedding cake occupied pride of place on the table and was eventually cut by the bride with her husband's sword. The first toast, "The King", was proposed by the Archdeacon. His Lordship the Bishop proposed "The Bride and Bridegroom". The bridegroom responded in a happy speech and asked the guests to drink the health of the bridesmaids. Lieutenant Louch responded. ... The bride's going-away costume was a navy-blue satin charmeuse coatee and skirt, with a picture hat of blue silk, trimmed with white silk cactus dahlias. Lieut. And Mrs Hamlin left by motor for the country.[16]

Arrival of Hospital Ships and the Wounded

While such celebrations as noted above gave those in the town a sense of normalcy reality once again soon returned when the wounded from Europe and the Middle East return to Albany in 1916:

Another New Zealand hospital ship, with wounded soldiers on board, is due at Albany towards the end of this week, and the Mayoress (Mrs E. G. McKenzie) invites the co-operation of the ladies of the town in order that provision may be made for the entertainment of the men ashore or the delivery of the usual comforts on board. An attempt made yesterday to entertain the soldiers passing through to the front failed in face of the poor response of the public. Some scones and cakes were sent to the Town Hall, but as these were altogether inadequate for the purpose the scones and ready perishables were sent to The Rocks, while the cakes were kept for the hospital ship expected. The Mayoress says the Red Cross Society are making a special effort to collect eatable luxuries for the wounded men on their way here and she invites the townspeople generally to assist. Cooked dainties, eggs, milk and such like gifts are requested for delivery at the Town Hall on Thursday so that the men who have already earned our sympathy and care may be fittingly provided for. The approach of the hospital ship will be signalled from the flagstaff at the Town Hall as usual.[17]

---

[16] *The Albany Advertiser.* 15th January 1916.
[17] Ibid. 19th January 1916.

Two perspectives of the impact of the war on the town of Albany are contrasted in separate articles presented initially in The Western Mail in January of 1916 and The Albany Advertiser of September and of that year:

War Time Holidays in Albany.

The holidays we are responsible for the infusion of a lot of life in the town, and the business houses are unanimous in declaring that the period was the best commercially ever experienced. All trains since a week before Christmas have brought large numbers of visitors, and the hotel and private accommodation has been and still is, taxed to the utmost extent. The weather has stood well for the town. Not a single day as the mercury surmounted 80°. For Albany, they have been warm days, but not once has the breeze failed. Indeed, on occasions visitors have complained of the cold, a condition of affairs, however, all welcome it at night time. There have been no organised attractions, but the usual picnicking resorts have all been generously patronised. Indeed, 2000 persons spent the time at Middleton Beach.

On New Year's Day, the wounded soldiers at The Rocks held a picnic at Little Grove with funds provided by the Leanora miners and the public naturally made holiday with them, the result being the muster of as many as could get across the harbour.

A further batch of 16 wounded soldiers arrived to spend a period convalescing at The Rocks. This brings the number there now to 55. The townspeople provided means for Christmas dinner for them...[18]

A more sombre perspective was conveyed through the 'In Memoriam' Notices in the local paper:

Among the fallen: The Archdeacon (The Venerable Thomas Louch, Rector of Albany) yesterday received a telegram from the Chaplain-General of the Forces stating that Corporal William Brown died of wounds on July 24. He was the son of Mrs Edward Brown, of Duke Street, a much-respected resident of Albany. Corporal Brown was one of the first to enlist and in the 11th Battalion went away with the first contingent. He was in the memorable 'land' of April 25th, 1915, and later on, was wounded at Gallipoli, and in hospital for many weeks. He was again at the front and last wrote was "somewhere in France", his younger brother being still in the ranks, presumably in Egypt.

And another:

Albany has been robbed of another young man in the person of private Ben Roberts, the sad news of his being killed in action between August 12 and 16th having been conveyed to the deceased's relatives by the Venerable Archdeacon Louch on Wednesday. Private Roberts was, prior to the war, one of the best footballers in the town, and in addition, he was an all-around athlete, being successful in running, swimming and cricket, and the news of his death will be learnt by a large circle of friends. The greatest sympathy is extended to his young wife, who is left with a child of tender years.[19]

And another this time acknowledging and paying tribute to the tireless efforts of the nursing corps. Ms Lily Ethwynne Saw, Charge-Nurse Saw, died of exhaustion on active service after a long illness in Albany on Monday 31st March 1919. She and was buried with full military honours in the Albany Cemetery. Her letter home outlines the enormous application of the nursing corps in administering to the troops on the battlefield:

"Somewhere in France"
1916.

Well, we have started on the third year of this great war... The tales the boys tell us of the fighting since the great advance. Oh! It is dreadful. We are getting our own back again the last few days.

... There is really a joy in our work, which helps to keep one up and seems to give one extra strength to go on. It's just the living in each moment and doing our very best for these dear boys who bear their pain so bravely and are so grateful for the little we do for them... Well, there is no more news of interest, except the sad, exciting, but a monotonous rush of work... which at present make up our existence...

---

[18] *The Western Mail.* 7th January 1916.
[19] *The Albany Advertiser.* 30th September 1916.

I am starting my night duty tonight, at least it is now morning, and I am feeling very tired, as I had only one hour's sleep after I came off day duty at 2 p.m. it is very nice to have patients to look after again after being in the operating theatre for the last seven months. Last Month was one of the worst I think that we have had. We were going all day and night; sometimes from 20 to 30 operations a day, often working up to 12 midnight and sometimes until 2 a.m. Most of them were very bad cases, so you can see we have been fairly busy. Thanks for the "Western Mails". I have read them and handed them on to patients. Papers are eagerly read in the wards"[20]

The following message, issued by His Majesty The King, was received by the Governor-General of the Commonwealth Sir Ronald Munro Ferguson:

Another Christmas finds all the resources of the Empire still engaged in war, and I desire to convey on my own behalf, and also on behalf of the Queen, a heart-felt Christmas greeting and our good wishes for the New Year to all who, on land and sea, are upholding the honour of the British name.

In the officers and men of my navy, on which the security of the Empire depends, I repose, in common with all my subjects, a trust that is absolute.

In the officers and men of the armies, whether now in France, in the East, or in other fields, I rely with an equal faith, confident that their devotion, their valour, and their sacrifice will under God's guidance, lead to victory and an honourable peace.

There are many of their comrades also in hospital, and to these brave men also, I desire, with the Queen, to express our deepest gratitude and our earnest prayers for their recovery.

Officers and men of the navy and army! Another year is drawing to a close as it began with toil, bloodshed and suffering. But we rejoice to know that the goal to which you are striving draws into sight. May God bless you and all your undertakings.[21]

George R.I

Anti-German Feelings

As was to be expected at the time anti-German feelings were running quite high among the colony's residents. Albany was not immune to this sentiment. Those with names that sounded Germanic were often the target of malicious gossip within the town. One resident Mr C.E. Kohler, who ran a local boarding house in Clifton Street, was forced to access the local press to clear up any misunderstandings about his origin:

A public notice.
To whom it may concern.

Interested and mischievous people having circulated false reports as to my nationality, I hereby give notice that it is my intention to invoke the aid of the law, such a course being rendered necessary to safeguard the interests of my business. It seems that I am under suspicion because of my name, but I have in my possession documentary evidence of the fact that both my father and mother were born in London in the early 40s. I myself was born in Sydney. Neither my parents nor myself ever lived anywhere but in the British Empire. I have my birth certificate to prove these assertions.

C.E. Kohler,
Clifton Boarding House
Albany, May 24, 1916.[22]

The Returned Soldiers and Sailors Imperial League of Australia and TocH.

The Returned Soldiers and Sailors Imperial League of Australia was formed in the Eastern States in 1916. The aim of the organisation was to offer support to returning troops and further to aid in their repatriation. The Western Australian Branch of the Returned Sailors and Soldiers Imperial League of Australia was officially charted on April 25th 1917. A meeting had been held in the Albany Town Hall in February of that year to ascertain local interest in forming an Albany branch of the association:

Returned Soldiers Association.

---

[20] Ibid. 15th November 1919.
[21] *The Albany Advertiser.* 1st January 1916.
[22] Ibid. 27th May 1916.

The Men Seek to Help Themselves.
March has been heard of Government and public movements for the benefit of return soldiers, but a real development arising out of the present situation is the formation of a Returned Soldiers Association among the men themselves to watch over their own interests. The organisation is reaching important dimensions in the East and when it is stated that in Western Australia 7000 of the 15,000 men who have returned have become members of it will be realised that some progress has been made in this state. With a view to extending the work, a meeting of return soldiers will be held in the lower Town Hall tomorrow (Thursday) afternoon, when Lieutenant Collins and Sergeant Jaggs, officers of the association, will be present to explain things...[23]

With interest shown among the veterans an Albany chapter of the Returned Soldiers and Veterans League was established:

Albany Notes.
Returned Soldiers Association.
Albany, October 13.
The first meeting of the recently formed branch of the Returned Soldiers and Veterans Association was held at the London hotel on Friday night. Private J. Lake was voted to the chair, and there was a fair attendance of members. Letters were read from the general secretary dealing with matters affecting the branch, including notification that the formation of a branch at Albany has been approved by the executive.[24]

The official journal of the Albany branch of the league was called *The Albany Wizbang*. It was published regularly between 1936 through to 1941 and contained several Albany returned service member recollections concerning World War I activities with particular relevance to the town and district's returned soldiers.

There was considerable support for the Returned Soldiers and Sailors Imperial League in Albany and also for its very active associate organisation, The Women's Auxiliary. In 1937 *The Albany Wizbang* reported on a significant busy bee activity by its membership was aimed at acknowledging the role that women played in supporting the troops through the creation of a special memorial garden:

Rose Garden Memorial.
The suggestion of forming a Rose Garden [Memorial] was eagerly taken up by members and working bees converted the waste into land [below the Rotunda] suitable for planting. Enthusiastic gardeners then took the matter of the making of an ornamental garden in hand. Now that there was a garden in embryo the question of naming it was unanimously decided that the gardens should commemorate the service in the World War of that gallant band of women, the war nurses, who served so nobody to alleviate the suffering of men on him warhead taken its toll. That's the name Memorial Gardens.[25]

Fittingly it was Mrs Carla Elsie White, a former nursing sister and one of the first Australian women to join Queen Alexandria's Imperial Military Nursing Service reserve who performed the opening in 1937 of the Rose Garden Memorial. She was the wife of The Reverend Arthur Ernest White, Rector of Albany, whom she married in 1918.[26]

Unveiling the Plaque.
Our president Mr E. Y. Butler ...called upon Mrs A. E. White to unveil the plaque on behalf of the nursing sisterhood. This Mrs White did after a happy little speech of thanks for the honour of being chosen to be the representative of the nurses to perform so pleasing a duty. The Mayor proposed a vote of thanks to Mrs White, which was carried with great at acclaim.[27]

The Returned Sailors and Soldiers Imperial League [RSSIL] had strong links with the Talbot House movement [TocH] which grew out of The Prince of Wales's experiences in France during the early stages

---

[23] *The Albany Advertiser.* 21st February 1917.
[24] *The Daily News.* 15th October 1917.
[25] *The Albany Wizbang.* Journal of the Albany Branch of the Returned Soldiers Association. 27th February 1937.
[26] Her maiden name was Wellman when she joined the nursing service. Sister Wellman travelled to England on 3rd March 1915 to join the Queens Imperial Military Nursing Service and served from the 15th May 1915 to the 16th November 1917.
[27] *The Albany Wizbang.* March – April 1937.

of the Great War.[28] It was named after one of his Oxford friends killed in July of 1915 and was started in December of that year by his friend's brother as a soldiers' rest and recreation retreat where all soldiers were welcome, regardless of their armed forces rank. Ex-Servicemen were able to join the movement and the Albany Branch had strong links to it through the Edward Barnett and Company of Stirling Terrace. Len Barnett was the editor of the RSL Albany newsletter *The Albany Wizbang*.

> *The Talbot House Movement, reborn after the war, arrived in Australia in 1927. In Western Australia, one of the most enthusiastic sponsors of the movement was the then Governor Sir William Campion but the actual seed was sown by Padre Pat Leonard who had come out from England, as the organisation's representative. Sir William Campion and his son, Simon were responsible for the formation of the Albany unit, which was later to become the Albany Branch of TocH...* [29]

Talbot House was a Christian based organisation that became primarily United Kingdom based but had houses throughout the Commonwealth and in some other parts of the world. An Australian branch was formed in Victoria in 1925 and in Adelaide the same year. The Talbot House Charter asked its members to:

> *"Seek to ease the burdens of others through acts of service. To also promote reconciliation and work to bring disparate sections of society together."*[30]

This endeavour included such activities as organised local hospital visits, entertainment for the residents of care homes and organised residential holidays for special groups.[31]

Albany War Memorials

As to be expected the post war peace presented an opportunity for friends and family of the fallen to acknowledge their ultimate sacrifice. A most cathartic way for family members and friends to honour and acknowledge those killed in the Great War was through the construction of large public war memorials. Other memorials comprised simple small plaques of white marble or bronze inserted on the walls of the local church, with greater community awareness of the importance of their ultimate sacrifice a more substantial edifice was constructed through public subscription.

> *St John's Church of England.*
> *Memorials to Fallen Soldiers.*
> *On Sunday in St John's Church, in the presence of very large congregation, including many return men, two private memorial tablets to fallen soldiers were unveiled by Major P.H Meeks, VD. The Venerable Archdeacon Louch officiated...*
>
> *The first tablet unveiled was erected by friends of the officer and bore the following inscription:" in loving memory of Lieutenant James Coombe Birt, M.C., 28th Battalion, A. I.F., who fell in action near Beaurevoir, France, October 3, 1918. He is risen".*
>
> *The second memorial, erected by public subscription, for the inscription: "In dutiful remembrance of residents of this parish who laid down their lives in the Great War, 1914 to 1918".*[32]

A further Parish memorial was installed in St Johns Church in the form of an iron rood screen. The screen was dedicated by the Archbishop of Perth the Most Reverend C.O.L. Riley at a service conducted on the 9th May 1920. The rood screen located between the Nave and the chancel of the church was "A memorial to the fallen men and women -1914-1918 in the Great War."

---

[28] The Talbot house code TocH was a result of the cipher for TH, and then, in the radio signallers' phonetic alphabet of the day as Toc Aitch.
[29] *The Albany Advertiser*. 28th September 1939.
[30] Letter to the *Adelaide Advertiser*, 28th July 1931.
[31] The Founder-Padre of TocH The Reverend P.B. 'Tubby' Clayton, who was a Priest-in-Ordinary to King George V1 and spent a short period in Albany on 22nd September 1952 mainly to meet members of the local branch.
[32] *The Albany Advertiser*. 1st December 1920.

A Dedication Service was held where a reference to the rood screen was made:

At the entrance to the chancel, where the screen is erected, two returned soldiers in uniform were stationed, one and either side, and in the chancel proper, were three returned nursing sisters. The screen was draped with flags.

The Archbishop, Archdeacon and everyone who took part in the procession stood in the aisle as the screen was dedicated and the prayers were said.

The Archbishop explained the peculiar function of the chancel in olden times; and its modern use and related the difference between a communion rail and a chancel screen. He emphasised the memorial character of the screen and urged that a role of the names of all who have given service in the war from this church should be placed somewhere in it.[33]

The construction of the Albany War Memorial was a significant occasion and *The Albany Advertiser* followed its construction and later on its subsequent erection:

The Mason at work.

The contractor for the work of eruption of the memorial to fall and soldiers of Albany district, Mr J.A. Hartman, is making rapid progress with his task and anticipates but little trouble in having everything in readiness for the unveiling ceremony on August 21st. A representative of this paper was afforded the opportunity yesterday of viewing the work in progress. The final touches we've just been given to the massive block of Albany pearl grey granite which constitutes the die upon which the names of the fallen heroes will be inscribed.[34]

In respect to this memorial a follow-up article was published in *The Albany Advertiser* on 24th August 1921 to commemorate its public unveiling.

Unveiling the monument.
Impressive ceremony.
His Excellency the Governor officiates.

The memorial erected by the residents of Albany districts to perpetuate the memory of the men from this centre who fell in the World War was unveiled on Sunday afternoon by his Excellency the Governor Sir Francis Newdegate, who made a special journey from Perth to perform the solemn ceremony. The weather was fine but bitterly cold. Nevertheless, a crowd, which may with safety the estimated at 1500 assembled to pay homage to the fallen heroes. The site chosen for the memorial is the triangle alongside the Church of England, at the intersection of York in Duke Streets. The monument, which is undoubtedly a beautiful piece of work, reflects the greatest credit on the contractor Mr J A Hartman, is comprised of locally quarried pearl grey granite and stands 20 feet in height.[35]

Notable Post War Visitors

Albany was to see a number of highly esteemed visitors in the aftermath of the Great War. One of the first in 1920 to visit was the well-respected British Army General William Riddell Birdwood who was Commander of the Australian and New Zealand Army Corps during the Gallipoli Campaign in 1915. Birdwood was later appointed Aide-de-Camp General to King George V in 1917 and was raised to the peerage in 1938.

General Birdwood.
Visit to Albany

General Sir William Birdwood and party arrived at Albany by special train last night…

At the station, although the train arrived a quarter of an hour ahead of time, a tremendous crowd of the townspeople congregated to greet the distinguished soldier…

Never before has such a crowd of people congregated together in Albany. The guard of return soldiers formed up outside under the command of Captain Metcalf. General Birdwood inspected the guard, and chatted freely with each member… When passing from the street to the hall, a well-known local resident shook hands with the general, then kissed him on both cheeks to the delight of the onlookers…

---

[33] Ibid. 10th May 1920.
[34] Ibid. 6th August 1921.
[35] Ibid. 24th August 1921.

> *Referring to the part Australia played in the war, he said while not boosting one state against another, the West Australian soldiers was good as any troops which fought in the Great War…*
> *An enormous crowd attended at Lawley Park on the occasion of reception tended the general of the members of the RSA…[36]*

His schedule for his Albany visit was a very full one and he made every attempt to interact with those who not only supported the troops while overseas, but also those who had been so unselfish and assisted with their later repatriation and rehabilitation.

> *In the afternoon the general spent a couple of hours at Lawley Park, as a guest of the local branch of the R.S.A.[37] Welcomes were attended to him on behalf of the RSA, the mothers, wives, fathers, and dependents of return or fallen soldiers and on behalf of the Repatriation Committee and the Patriotic Fund workers…*
> *He referred with gratification to the opportunity afforded him of meeting personally and speaking to so many of the parents, wives, and sisters of men who had fought with him in Gallipoli and France… The object of his visit he said was primarily to see again his old comrades who had fought with him in the Great War, and he was glad to meet those who have assisted the men while in the fighting line by supplying them with comforts in necessities.[38]*

A Royal Visit

The visit of Prince Edward, The Prince of Wales, later King Edward V111, on the battleship *Renown* again exposed the rivalry between Albany and Fremantle. It was revealed that the Mayor of Fremantle had been in communication with the Eastern States to attempt to ensure that the program for the *Renown* could be altered to permit a visit of the ship and His Royal Highness to the port of Fremantle. Several representations were made to both the Government and the Admiralty and a number of arguments were advanced to support the idea. However, the Admiralty determined that the ship would not have its itinerary changed to include Fremantle. The local paper had got wind of these attempts and was pleased to report in its issue of the 21st April 1920:

> *It is clear that the suspicions all along expressed in the columns of The Albany Advertiser were well-founded. The committee appointed to arrange the program delayed making any announcement until all efforts to get the renowned from Albany to Fremantle had failed.[39]*

> *Local arrangements*
> *Hail to the Prince.*
> *It is indeed quite in the fitness of things that the Prince of Wales should first set foot on the soil of Western Australia at Albany, as he will today, for it was here that his illustrious father, King George V, then Duke of York, twice landed some years ago* [on one of these occasions to Australia he made two visits to Albany in 1901]. *On the first occasion, in 1881, he and his elder brother, the late Duke of Clarence, both of whom were serving as midshipman on* HMS Bacchante *paid an enforced visit owing to an accident to the vessel's rudder. The second time was in 1901 when, accompanied by his wife, the present Queen, a triumphal tour of the Commonwealth was being made. The original programme provided for the landing to be made at Fremantle* [on the return voyage] *but owing to stress of bad weather it was decided that Albany with its safeguards was preferable as a haven to the dangerous waterway leading into the northern port.*

> *He liked the 'digger' he said and would like to see the digger at home. While his visit in a sense is the fulfilment of that promise, one can be certain that in the mind of the Prince it is associated with the gratification of inherent love of adventure. What healthy minded normal young man no matter how eminent in his station in life would be thrilled at the thought of a world tour in a battleship, embracing strange new lands and wonderful people.[40]*

---

[36] *The Daily News.* 9th January 1920.
[37] The Return Service Association [RSA] was a forerunner to the Return Services League [RSL]
[38] *The Western Mail.* 15th January 1920.
[39] *The Albany Advertiser.* 21st April 1920.
[40] Ibid. 30th June 1920.

The visit to Albany by The Prince of Wales on *HMS Renown* in 1920 received some mixed newspaper coverage when a less than flattering account of this visit in the form of an aide's diary became public knowledge.[41]

Who Is Sneers at His Host?
Renown's *Visit to Albany Officially Described.*
We have received a copy of well-bound and elaborately be printed and illustrated book entitled "With the Renown in Australia. A magazine of HMS Renown *December 1919 to October 1920... What we want to direct attention to is the hoggishness and execrable taste of the person, whoever he was, who wrote up the section dealing with the Albany visit. Let us give a few extracts.*

Albany is a Quiet Place.
A One-Horse Spot...
The golf links, the best in Australia, were dreadful.... Nearly all the holes were blind, and a pull or a slice more than the yard out of the straight brought endless and undeserved trouble with the Australian bush... Only one of our team won his match. Which by the way, probably accounts for the boor's criticism of the links. Anyhow they conclude in off handed manner. We got plenty of fresh air and amusement."

The Duties of a Guest.
It is an essential factor of civilisation that no guest with any manners will reflect on his host. The person who wrote this patronising paragraph concerning the visit to Albany must go down self-condemned as one of the worst social offenders we have ever entertained... His outpourings stamp him as possessing as much an idea of common courtesy as an untamed baboon... We believe that the majority of them [visitors] were gentleman. But one at least; the man who wrote the description of the visit to Albany, to wit, was evidently an insufferable prig, a bounder and a snob of the worst type.

A matter of protest.
Isn't it about time Australians protested against being made butts by blow-ins who consider that a trace of ancestry, pretention to rank, or professional prominence entitles them to be common cads? And as a common cad we name the writer under discussion[42]

On a more positive note, *The Albany Advertiser* outlined the planned attractions that would accompany the Prince of Wales visit on *Renown*:

From 10 a.m. HMS Renown will be thrown open for public inspection. The Awhina [tugboat] will leave the town jetty at intervals.

The Rifle Club, Golf Club and Tennis Club have also received grants from the general fund for entertainment and prizes and each of these bodies will arrange programmes [sic]in accord with their respective branches of sport.[43]

The Arrival of the British Squadron Navy Including *HMS Hood*

The post war arrival of a contingent of British warships caused tremendous excitement in the town. The Special Service Squadron was comprised seven vessels: The Battle Cruisers *Hood* and *Repulse* and the Light Cruisers *Delhi, Danae, Dauntless Dragon* and *Dunedin*.[44] At the time of its arrival in Albany *HMS Hood* was the world's largest Battle Cruiser. The Albany Advertiser gave significant coverage to the fleet's arrival:

British Squadron.
In King George's Sound.
Magnificent picture.

---

[41] This visit was part of The Prince of Wales' "Thank You Australia "Tour. On this occasion his aide-de-camp was Lieutenant Louis Mountbatten RN, later Lord Mountbatten of Burma.
[42] *The Call.* 25th February 1921.
[43] *The Albany Advertiser.* 30th June 1920.
[44] HMS *Hood* was laid down during the Great War and completed in 1923 and was in her time the largest warship in the world. The ship was sunk in action May 1941.

Impressions on HMS Hood.
From our special reporter.

Albany, W.A. Monday: Lying in harbour at Albany the vessels of the visiting British Squadron have a much more picturesque setting than at Fremantle. Albany is 'round the corner' from Fremantle, the corner being the south western extremity of the continent.
King George's Sound, at the head of which Albany is situated, is a magnificent stretch of water; the inner portion is known as Princess Royal Harbour. At the mouth of the Sound lies the small Breaksea Island. Its bold shape stands out clearly in view from the town. The south side of the harbour presents a contrast to the eye, for its natural beauty has not been touched by the march of settlement. Skirting the sound is a gleaming stretch of white beach, and to the east of the town to rivers the King and the Kalgan, empty into the harbour.[45]

The local newspaper ran several articles relating the importance of the fleet's visit and stay in King George's Sound as well as capturing the town's excitement at seeing and visiting the ships:

Naval Importance of Albany
Special correspondent on the HMS Hood reports:
The importance of the visit of the squadron to Albany will be very considerable. King Georges sound was, of course, the rendezvous for the transports of the AIF during the war, and it provides one of the finest sheltering places on the Australian coast. It may be assumed that advantage will be taken of the squadrons visit to make a very thorough examination of the Sound's potentialities as a naval base in Australia. Indeed, it may be said on the authority of very high Australian political quarters that the visit of the two Admirals will have an important relation to any decision that may be arrived at with regards to a base in Australia.[47]

Local reporters waxed lyrical about the fleet's approach and anchorage in the Sound.:
More favourable weather conditions could not have been imagined than that in which the thousands of people who assembled around the Marine Drive, and the hill above it, were privileged to witness the arrival of the Special Service Naval Squadron ... Over the vast expanse of water embraced in King George's Sound not a breaking wave was to be seen, and when the Warships were first picked up the visibility was so good they seemed to tumble over the horizon...

Thousands had arrived in the preceding day or two, and the hills from point King to Middleton beach were well lined by people in unprecedented numbers long before the fleet appeared...

The Hood and Repulse were seen as imposing shadows away back in the gap between the coastal hills. Several miles separated the battleships from the cruisers, and as the latter steadily advanced in line towards the onlookers the big ships came more clearly in view... It is doubtful if such A spectacle would be possible anywhere else in the world. Many of the spectators gazed from an altitude that gave them a range of vision of fully 30 miles... The cruisers advance together until well inside Breaksea. Then the Delhi, Danae and Dunedin came on, while the Dauntless and Dragon remained stationary. The three leaders made straight for

---
[45] *The Argus*. Melbourne. 4th March 1924.
[46] Photograph of *HMS Hood* Courtesy of the Albany Historical Society and Mark Saxton Coordinator.
[47] Ibid. 5th March 1924.

the harbour and passed in with bands playing. Crowds were assembled on the rocks about Point King, and a biscuit could have been thrown onto the decks of the cruisers as they went by…

By 5 o'clock all the cruisers were inside, and the Hood and Repulse had dropped anchor in King George's Sound, just off Middleton beach…

Inspection of the Vessels.
Despite the fact that the ships are undergoing painting and overhaul while at anchor, Vice-Admiral Field has placed every facility in the way of visitors for the inspection of the vessels. Daily the launches of Armstrong and Waters have conveyed many parties to the boats, most attention naturally censoring on the Hood.[48]

Church of England ANZAC Day Dawn Requiem
The True Story of 1930, 1931, 1937 and 1938.

Given that a significant part of the early Twentieth Century Historical Record of Albany is entwined with the two ANZAC convoys and the ANZAC Dawn Service story it is therefore an important one to convey. Misconceptions, inaccuracies and of several myths have infiltrated The Historical Record and therefore, need to be dispelled. Unfortunately, a great deal of this misinformation and myth making has emanated from the history recorded in many tourist publications and on the plinth at the entrance to the Albany Anglican Parish Church St John's [now removed] concerning its parish priest and the various civic commemorations that occurred on between 1914 and 1938 is a classic example of local mis-information.[49]

The main part of the incorrect text on the plinth reads:
… On the morning of 24th February 1918, a very special service was held at St John's Church that would shape future ANZAC Day commemorations. A Mass for the war dead of World War I was offered by visiting reverent and army chaplain, Arthur Earnest White. Reverend White – or Padre White as he was known – followed the service with a pilgrimage to Mt. Clarence looking across King George's Sound, memories were conjured of the great fleet which had departed only a few years earlier. To pay tribute to the troops, "the flower of Australian manhood", Padre White arranged for a boatman to cast a wreath into its waters.

On the same theme, *The Albany Advertiser* of 26th April 2019 reported incorrectly that:
The Easter dawns with tradition. Worshippers packed into St John's Anglican Church in Albany for the 9:30 am Easter Eucharist. The service followed the traditional Easter Sunday dawn service honouring padre Ernest White, who held Albany's first ANZAC Day dawn service in 1930 at the top of Mount Clarence…[50]

Both of these examples illustrate the way that the story of the Albany ANZAC Dawn Service has been distorted. Consequently, it is important to correct The Historical Record and to address some of the myth masking that has evolved with time. What follows is information that has been drawn from detailed research using primary source material not hearsay, or second-hand or popularised versions of events in the years 1914, 1916, 1918, 1923, 1930, 1931, 1937 and 1938.

The Albany ANZAC Day story must start with the 1912 arrival in Albany of the Reverend Arthur White, a London born and English trained Anglo-Catholic [High Church] priest member of the Bush Brotherhood of Saint Boniface in Western Australia whose clergy house was located in the town of Williams to the north of Albany on the Perth Road.

Father White BSB, visited Albany often in the pre-war days and made a considerable number of acquaintances in the town. He delivered his first Albany sermon at Evensong in St John's Church on Sunday 27th of October 1912 and celebrated Holy Communion for the first time in Albany at the 8 am in St John's Church of England on Christmas Day in 1913. On 17th March 1916, Father White was given leave and permitted by his Bishop to join The Army as a Church of England Chaplain. He received a commission to

---

[48] Ibid.

[49] A requiem is a formal church ceremony of worship and does not apply to informal RSL silent gatherings or parades of service men and women.

[50] *Ibid.* 26th April 2019.

join the 44th Battalion of the Australian Imperial Forces (AIF) which was then en-route to Europe. He departed from Fremantle and not Albany.

On his return from the war in 1918 he resigned from the Bush Brotherhood of Saint Boniface and The Army and accepted various parish roles in the Eastern States. In 1929 after fulfilling duties in Melbourne and Riverina parish positions, he became Rector of St John's Church in Albany, then one of the many High Church Parishes in the Church of England Diocese of Bunbury. Father White first celebrated a Requiem Eucharist at dawn in St John's Church on 25th April 1930, and not as some reporting has indicated in 1914, 1918 or 1923!

While Archdeacon Thomas Louch was away from the parish on the Sunday, 24th February 1918, Padre White officiated in services conducted in the church on this occasion. Unfortunately, there have been some historians and myth makers who have claimed that this was the date of the first Dawn Service at St John's and that it was celebrated by him on this occasion. The Church's Service Register clearly indicates that Father White only conducted the 8 am Holy Communion, a 10 am Litany and an 11 am Matins service on Sunday 24th February 1918. There is no record in the St John's Churches Service Register of any other service or private mass celebrated during any of his recorded visits to Albany prior to 1929.

One example of a much-repeated false-hood is that Father White returned to Albany in 1923 for a holiday and celebrated a requiem Mass on ANZAC Day. However, for that full year Anglican Church records indicate that he was working at that time in Broken Hill and the Riverina and only left that area to spend a few weeks on Kangaroo Island. Unfortunately, typical of this form erroneous reporting can indeed be found on the Father White's gravestone at Herberton in Queensland, which states in part:

On 25 April 1923 at Albany, Western Australia Reverend White led a party of friends in what was the first ever observance of the dawn parade on ANZAC Day, a tradition that is endured Australia wide, ever since.

The First Albany public ANZAC Day commemoration of the district's war dead was held in St John's during Matins at 11 am in 1916. This event was subsequently followed by a civic ceremony conducted in the Albany Town Hall which was organised by the Returned Soldiers and Sailors Imperial League of Australia, the Women's Auxiliary and the Sons of Soldiers League.

The Albany Anglican Dawn Service in 1930 was simply following traditional Church of England liturgical custom of an early celebration of the Eucharist. Immediately after this Dawn Requiem Mass Father White, using a steel nib and black ink, filled in his Service Register as required by Canon Law and the Bishop. No other person is permitted to make an entry in this register other than the parish priest. Unfortunately, alongside the main entry of this day in a blue ink inscription someone, a person or persons unknown, bracketed the words 'First Dawn Service held in Australia.' This mysterious inscription was certainly not made by Father White as the celebrant of that mass and forensic analysis of the handwriting confirms this point. Furthermore, if written on this particular day at that point in time how was the writer to know it was Australia's first dawn service that had just been celebrated. It is far more feasible that an ever helpful and enthusiastic parishioner or local interested historian has at a later date alongside the principal service entry of the day perpetuated misinformation concerning this event, and in so doing has helped to facilitate the myth. It will indeed remain one of Albany's ecclesiastical mysteries

Albany was just one of the many places to hold a Dawn Requiem on 25th April in the year 1930, not as some have suggested 1914, 1916 or 1923. Father White was aware of the Anglican Church's custom of celebrating Holy Communion on special religious days throughout the year and, on his own initiative, thought it appropriate to conduct a Requiem Eucharist for the fallen on the 15th anniversary of the Gallipoli landing in 1930. A member of the congregation who attended that particular service takes up the story:

Destined to become one of the most impressive ceremonies enacted by ex-servicemen, the dawn service had its humble origin in Albany, eight years ago. The Rector of St John's held a service for ex-servicemen in the ivy girt church at 6 am on ANZAC Day. Immediately following the church service those present, preceded by the choir, proceeded to the Soldiers Memorial where in silence, a wreath was laid. As one of the ex-servicemen present on that occasion,

> *I have vivid recollections of my reactions to that simple ceremony. Although I have attended all the dawn services since none has affected me nearly so much as did that first one…*[51]

It is also important to realise that the present day Returned Services League dawn civic parade bears no resemblance to or has any historical or heritage connection with the Dawn Service held in St John's Church on the 25th April 1930. However, many Anglicans in the RSL attended the service for many years.

It was the following year in 1931 after the ANZAC Day Dawn Requiem that a small group of his congregation made the pilgrimage to the summit of Mount Clarence.

1931 Parish Pilgrimage

This Anglican parish Pilgrimage of 1931 began after the second dawn service had been concluded by Father White. He and some of the congregation climbed to the rocky summit of Mount Clarence at around 8 a.m., well after dawn had long since passed and there they gathered in silence to remember those whose names were not recorded on either parish or district war memorials but nonetheless had passed by Albany throughout the war and did not return.

The Albany Advertiser on Monday 27th April 1931 under its "Church News": reported:
> *following the dawn service at St John's a small party climbed Mount Clarence to overlook the Anchorage wherein 1914 the first convoy of transports assembled to carry the ANZACs to war.*[52]

It is important to recognise that the remembrance on the summit of Mount Clarence was not an organised service as such, and that Father White in fact wore his street attire and not his vestments on the walk. Also, it must be noted that this was not a pilgrimage held at dawn.

In the years following, this simple pilgrimage to the summit of Mount Clarence, initiated by Father White, became part of the Anglican Parish ANZAC Commemoration that was considered by him to be his *'personal pilgrimage.'*[53] Father White's pilgrimage ended with him quoting the fourth verse of the now famous ode *"for the fallen"* by the British poet Lawrence Binyon:

> *They shall grow not old, as we that are left grow old,*
> *Age shall not weary them, nor the years condemn.*
> *At the going down of the sun and in the morning,*
> *We will remember them.*

The custom declined shortly after the start of the Second World War.

It is important to acknowledge that this pilgrimage site and custom is not be confused with the present day RSL civic dawn remembrance and parade recently established and held at the site of the Desert Mounted Corps Memorial which is a short distance down from the summit of Mount Clarence. This RSL gathering originated shortly after the relocation from Egypt of the famous Desert Mounted Corps Memorial. This memorial, incorrectly called locally the ANZAC memorial, was originally situated on the banks of the Suez Canal and was relocated and dedicated at Albany on Sunday 11th of October 1964.

1937 ANZAC Day Harbour Wreath Laying

In 1937 Father White as Chaplain to the local RSL and TocH suggested to members that they might like to arrange for a boatman to drop a wreath into the narrow entrance of The Princess Royal Harbour. He thought the wreath would float out into King George Sound on the early tide. The first occasion the custom was successfully carried out by a member of the Harbour Master's staff, standing on the end of the Harbour Master jetty was on ANZAC Day, Sunday 25th of April 1937. It was decided on that day that the boat was not necessary to be used for this purpose. This event lasted only a few years and declined shortly after the start of the Second World War.

---

[51] *The Albany Wizbang.* 1938. An account by 'Asco' an ex-serviceman who was in attendance at the event.
[52] *The Albany Advertiser.* 27th April 1931.
[53] As relayed to one of the Anglican Sisters of Sacred Advent at Saint Mary's school in Herberton Queensland.

The 1938 Famous Summit Photograph

A frequently reproduced black-and-white photograph of Father White on the summit of Mount Clarence was taken in 1938 by a young girl, who later became Mrs Patricia Davies, the widow of an Anglican priest and a close friend of the Rector. Her photograph depicts Father White standing on a large rock in silhouette in his street clothes looking out to sea. Unfortunately, this photograph has like many other aspects of the Albany ANZAC story become the focus of some mischief and subsequent myth creation. The photograph has been reproduced in various printed works with the caption reading:

Arthur Ernest White, at Mount Clarence, ANZAC Day service, 25 April 1930.

This incorrect caption has been frequently used also in local and tourist publications and by amateur historians.

The actual story behind this photograph was that when the photograph was taken Father White was enjoying his last visit to the summit of Mount Clarence on that very day with his family. After the photograph was taken on that day, he and his family sailed from Albany; Father White to become the Anglican Parish Priest at Forbes in New South Wales. The date that the photograph was indeed taken was in fact Friday 20th May 1938.[54]

The photographer, Mrs Davies confirmed the circumstances of the when and why the photograph was taken, and it was her opinion that it had fallen into the hands of an unknown amateur parish historian who must have misunderstood its real significance. Again, the person who is unknown has obviously mistakenly captioned the photograph with made up details. Unfortunately, this photograph has been used incorrectly in many exhibitions and publications and later including the exhibition and guidebook for the National ANZAC Centre which reads:

Arthur Ernest White, at Mount Clarence, ANZAC Day Dawn Service, 25th of April 1930. Courtesy of St John's Anglican church Albany.

Commemoration of ANZAC Day 1916

The first overseas ANZAC Day Service and parade was held in 1916 in the ANZAC Hostel Auditorium in Cairo. The Anglican Bishop in Jerusalem, The Right Reverend Rennie MacInnes presided and the Principal Middle East Force Army Chaplain in Cairo, an Anglican priest, the Reverend Arthur Hordern addressed the gathering. The Albany civic parade of 1916 followed the Order of Service used at that service that became the proto-type for the RSL parade services in later years.[55] After the Cairo service a convoy of army ambulances and trucks filled with floral tributes left for the cemetery where the wreaths were placed on the recent graves of the ANZACS.[56]

Given the fact that much of Albany's recent history has revolved around the part it played in the ANZAC troop ship's departures throughout the Great War it is important that we recognise the origins and purpose of ANZAC Day in order to be fully aware of the genesis of the commemoration. Research into this topic has been hampered by the competing claims made by various local history organisations and state bodies as to its origin.

The first ANZAC Day Commemoration Committee was established in January 1916 in Brisbane, Queensland. To understand why this event was to have its origins in this state it must be understood that in Queensland and the Brisbane region in particular there was a particular awareness of the losses inflicted on Australian troops during the landing at Gallipoli at dawn on 25th April 1915. The first troops ashore were from the 9th Battalion of the 3rd Australian Infantry Brigade which was raised in Queensland. Consequently, the casualty lists published in the Australian press at the time were at first particularly prominent in the Brisbane papers.

---

[54] Personal contact with Mrs Patricia Davies with Mr Douglas Sellick.
[55] Referenced in the Mitchell Library in Sydney
[56] Bean, C.E.W. *The Story of ANZAC. The Official History of Australia in the War of 1914-1918*. Volume 1: The First Phase. Sydney, 1941.

The extent of the fallen that was published was indeed a shock to the state and subsequently on Thursday, 10th June, 1915 a Requiem Eucharist for the Fallen was conducted by the Lord Archbishop of Brisbane The Most Reverend St Clair Donaldson and held at 10 a.m. in St John's Anglican Cathedral, Brisbane at 10.00 am. The explanation for this, the very first recorded memorial service for the losses at the Gallipoli campaign was in essence because the numbers of the fallen were so disproportionately high from Queensland that a need for the Church both to commemorate the fallen and to minister to the bereaved was acute. A Requiem Eucharist was employed as it was based on the traditional public services of the Church in a time of national crisis. It was to Canon John Garland to whom is attributed this initiative. Incidentally, Canon Garland was a frequent visitor to Albany in the years before the Great War.[57]

Understanding this initiative in Brisbane enables us to better comprehend the rise of the ANZAC tradition. By December 1915 the Dardanelles campaign was recognised as a failure and the bulk of the remaining Australian and New Zealand infantry forces were sent to France to fight on the Western Front while most of the Light Horse and the New Zealand Mounted Infantry returned to Egypt and Palestine to resist the Turkish southward advance towards the Suez Canal.

The commemoration of those men who had paid the ultimate sacrifice and the continued recruitment of new troops to replace them, and to keep faith with the Gallipoli fallen who had fought and died required remembrance as they had acquitted themselves valiantly. It was Canon Garland who worked tirelessly in establishing ANZAC Day throughout the entire Commonwealth, as his care for the welfare of soldiers, defending their reputation and evangelising them had long been his self-nominated special vocation. Canon Garland was, indeed, the architect of ANZAC Day. From that first service on the 10th January 1916 that established Australia's first ANZAC Day Commemoration Committee, he then successfully agitated for the maintenance of ANZAC Day as "Australia's All Soul's Day":

The documentary evidence is overwhelming that the establishment of ANZAC Day observance, in the way it emerged, was largely due to the efforts of Canon Garland. His intrepid lobbying in the corridors of power, his assiduity and attention to detail in the preparation of each ANZAC Day celebration since 1916, with exception of the years 1918 and 1919 when he was doing chaplaincy work in Egypt and Palestine, in fact made it work. [58]

Message from King George V

"Tell my people of Australia that today I am joining them in their solemn tribute to the memory of their heroes who died at Gallipoli.
They gave their lives for a supreme cause in gallant comradeship with the rest of my sailors and soldiers who fought and died with them. Their valour and fortitude have shed fresh lustre on the British Arms.
May those who mourn their loss find comfort in the conviction that they did not die in vain. But that their sacrifice has drawn our peoples more closely together and added strength and glory to the Empire.
George R.I.

The first ANZAC Day services were held in Cairo, London, Albany and on ships at sea on Tuesday 25th April 1916 to mark the first anniversary of the landing at Gallipoli. The Cairo service that followed the pattern that Canon Garland had recommended in Brisbane was described in a report by Lieutenant John L. Treloar. The Senior Chaplain who conducted the service was the Reverend Arthur Venables Caverley Horden CMG.

---

[57] Details from St John's Parish Service Register, Albany.
[58] This information is drawn from the following sources:
The Reverend Dr John A. Moses. "Anglicanism and ANZAC Observance: The Essential Royal Historical Society of Queensland Journal, Volume 17th May 1999. "The Struggle for ANZAC Day 1916-1930 and The Role of the Brisbane ANZAC Day Commemoration Committee", Journal of the Royal Australian Historical Society, Volume 88, June 2002. "Was There an ANZAC Theology?", Colloquium Volume 35, 2003.
Contribution of Canon David John Garland". Pacifica 19th February 2006, and relevant extracts from "Canon David John Garland and the ANZAC Tradition in Brisbane, 1916-1939", Reviving Australia, Centre for the Study of Australian Christianity, 1994. "Canon David Garland as Architect of ANZAC Day",
[58] The Reverend Dr. John A. Moses. "Anglicanism and ANZAC Observance: The Essential Royal Historical Society of Queensland Journal, Volume 17th May 1999

In Cairo, many of the first ANZACS who had sailed away from King George's Sound at Albany are buried in the Commonwealth War Graves Cemetery just outside the city. To mark the first anniversary of the landing at Gallipoli, commemoration services were held around Australia in various forms and in many overseas locations as well.

In London, the Collegiate Church of S. Peter, better known as Westminster Abbey, was packed with Australians, New Zealanders and Britons and for a formal service conducted by the Priests-in-Ordinary to the King. The service was attended by the King George V and Queen Mary, the Prime Minister of Australia and representatives of allied nations. The day before the King had sent a telegram from Buckingham Palace to his Governor-General in Melbourne, then the temporary seat of the Commonwealth Government of Australia, requesting it be transmitted to the Governors and Administrators of all Australian States and Territories. The message was read out at many of the first ANZAC Day memorial services across Australia.

The form of observance that had evolved had to be acceptable to all denominations as well as to the political leaders. What resulted was the product of a unique act of ecclesiastical diplomacy. There are two types of public commemoration that must be distinguished at this point. The first is the one conducted at war memorials that were increasingly being erected throughout Australia in the 1920's and 1930's and which were ecumenical in form. The second public service was usually held in the evening in a Town Hall or cinema. These services were most emphatically secular.

In 1930 Albany was just one location in Australia where Anglican Dawn Services were conducted. Others were also held at that time around Australia including a number of Western Australian country towns including Collie, Northam and Roebourne. The service of the 25th April was a Dawn Requiem Mass which also commemorated Saint Mark's Day in the Anglican Church Calendar and was following the then Church of England liturgical custom of the daily early morning celebration of the Eucharist. The Albany tradition lasted at St John's Church for about 50 years and was never revived, being replaced on ANZAC Day by the present day Returned Services League (RSL) type service and parade.

Visit by Sir Henry Rider Haggard

A British Empire Mission Visit by Sir Henry Rider Haggard involved both Mount Barker and Albany in his itinerary:
> *Sir Henry Rider Haggard, the novelist and author of "King Solomon's Mines", "She" and many other stories was also an authority on Empire migration, agriculture and social conditions. He travelled around the world as a member Dominions Royal Commission in 1912-1914 and again in 1916 as a member of the After the War Empire Settlement Committee of the Royal Colonial Institute. He was a great friend of Rudyard Kipling who shared his interest in all matters concerning the British Empire.*[59]

Sir Rider Haggard travelled extensively throughout the Empire as it was at this time. After some engagements in Perth, he headed south to Mount Barker and then on to Albany by train. His observations of that journey are outlined in his diary entries:

> *Saturday, 13th May.*
> *On Friday night we bade farewell to Perth & came aboard this special saloon* [The Governor's State Carriage] *where we slept - starting early in the morning with Mr Johnson and Mr Sutton the Wheat expert. ... After dinner, we walked to the station & entered our carriage which was attached to the Albany train & started on a 200-mile journey to Mount Barker...It was very cold in the night & is so still. Now I am off to see fruit lands.*

> *Sunday, 14th May.*
> *...our carriage had been attached to a Luggage* [Goods] *Train which was waiting, then hauled us off to Albany about 35 miles away. There we dined on the train & then proceeded to the Freemason's Hotel, a nice place, where we slept.*
> *This morning (Sunday) we were taken by the Mayor, Town Clerk for a motor drive & saw the neighbourhood. It is the prettiest place, on the whole, I've seen in Australia with its splendid harbours, its hills, & its surrounding woods. Most of the land & neighbourhood is wild & under bush & to be obtained from the Government cheaply.*

---

[59] *The West Australian*, Perth. 3rd February 1916.

A feature is the outcropping granite which lies about in huge boulders. I am much impressed with the possibility of Albany, which as yet is a village, with its harbours it must go ahead. It is the most interesting of any place I've seen in Australia.

On our return, I stepped into the Church [St. John's] where a service was about to be held. A neat little square-towered building similar to any English parish church. I also visited the army hospital which is the Governor's country residence [The Government Cottage - The Rocks] an ordinary house with a lovely view over the harbour. Then we came on to our ship, the Katoomba, which we boarded in a tender. She is a splendid boat with every modern comfort, glass-enclosed decks etc. The Company has kindly given us a beautiful deck suite, large bed and sitting room oak-panelled with bath-room attached, so we are in luxury.[60]

Haggard was very concerned that even with hostilities of The Great War coming to an end, that the world could look forward to more conflicts between the warring nations in the future. Extracts from his personal diary about his visit to Albany and the comments he is reported as saying during his official engagements are captured by the local newspaper accordingly:

It is very likely that the Empire will want her sons and daughters, too, more than ever after the war. They will be wanted to protect the Empire against possible trouble in the future. It is only foolish people who think that after this war is over our troubles will be ended. On the contrary, our troubles will more likely only be beginning, not only from an industrial or social point of view but from the standpoint that we will never know, after this experience when an armed nation will be up against us. Germany is not likely to remain inactive after the cessation of hostilities so, I for one, do not believe that this is going to be the last war.[61]

His journey around the Empire was featured in leading newspapers of the day. He died on 22nd January 1926.

Origin of the Word ANZAC

Fortuitously, Lieutenant-General William Birdwood leaves little doubt to how he sees the word ANZAC having evolved:

It may be of interest to readers to hear the origin of the word "ANZAC" When I took over the command of the Australian and New Zealand Army Corps in Egypt a year ago, I was asked to select a telegraphic code address for my Army Corps, and then adopted the word "ANZAC" Later on, when we had effected our landing here in April last, I was asked by General Headquarters to suggest a name for the beach where we had made good our first precarious footing, and then asked that this might be recorded as "ANZAC Cove" - a name which the bravery of our men has now made historical, while it will remain a geographical landmark for all time.
W.R. Birdwood. Lieutenant-General,
Commanding Australian and New Zealand Army Corps, Gallipoli, December 1915.[62]

However, Charles Bean the Great Way historian gives a slightly different perspective on exactly how the name originated.

General Sir William Birdwood's headquarters in Cairo were in the southern corridor of Shepherds Hotel. Some of the clerks were detached from the division to work with the Army Corps; others were brought from England. The ground floor corridor outside the clerk's rooms became boarded with cases containing stationary addressed in large black stencilled letters to the "A. and N.Z. Army Corps. The name was far too cumbrous for constant use, especially in telegrams, and a telegraphic address was needed. One day early in 1915 Major C.M. Wagstaff, an officer of the Indian Regular Army and a junior member of the operations section of General Birdwood's staff, walked into the general staff office and mentioned to the clerks that a convenient word was wanted as a codename for the corps. The clerks had noticed the big initials on the cases outside their room A. & N. Z. A. C, And a rubber stamp for registering correspondence had also been cut with the same initials. When Major Wagstaff mention the need for a code word, one of the clerks, according to most accounts Lieutenant A.T. White, a British Army Service Corp officer who for a time was a superintending clerk at the corps headquarters, suggested; "How about

---

[60] *H. Rider Haggard Pape*rs. Norfolk Record Office, Norwich, England.
[61] *The Albany Advertiser.* 17th May 1916.
[62] *Field-Marshall Lord Birdwell of ANZAC & Totnes. GCB., GCSI., GCMG., CIE., DSO., LL.D., DCL., D.Litt. Khaki and Gown. An Autobiography.* London, 1941 *& The ANZAC Book.* Written & illustrated in Gallipoli by The Men of ANZAC, for the Benefit of Patriotic Funds connected with the A.&N.Z.A.C. London and Melbourne, 1916.

> *ANZAC?" Major Wagstaff proposed the word to Sir William, who approved of it, and ANZAC thereon became the code name of the Australian and New Zealand Army Corps.*[63]

The benefit of rank is highlighted in this case given that General Birdwood then claimed that he was the originator of the word.

Closing Remarks

The Great War has been termed the war without a decision. The history of the period from the armistice in November 1918 until the conclusion of various peace treaties was one of calm but with some uncertainty. The Great War had global repercussions and resulted in a redefining of many national boundaries and the significant weakening of European empires. Fortunately, throughout the conflict, Albany remained in the war's shadow and the guns of fortress Albany were never fired in anger.

In the aftermath of The Great War the focus of European nations was clearly on reconstruction which had precedence, relegating their various colonial interests to a low priority. This had the impact in Australia of a greater more independent and self-reliant approach to domestic matters.

The events leading up to and during the Gallipoli campaign in Turkey occupy a most significant chapter in Albany's Historical Record. Interestingly, in 1985 the links between the town and Turkey were fostered by an Australian Government initiative which saw the entrance into The Princess Royal Harbour named Ataturk Straight (after the 'father' of modern Turkey Mustafa Kemal) in a reciprocal agreement with the Turkish Government which named the beach at Gallipoli where the ANZAC troops landed "ANZAC Cove. A statue of Mustafa Kemal Atatürk was erected overlooking the straight in 2002 and included his compassionate message to Australia acknowledging the men who had lost their lives in the Gallipoli campaign:

> *Those heroes that shed their blood and lost their lives ... You are now lying in the soil of a friendly country. Therefore, rest in peace. There is no difference between the Johnnies and the Mehmets to us where they lie side by side here in this country of ours ... You, the mothers who sent their sons from faraway countries, wipe away your tears; your sons are now lying in our bosom and are in peace. After having lost their lives on this land they have become our sons as well.*[64]

It is not surprising that throughout the eighteenth and nineteenth centuries, a time of Imperialism and Empire, much of what was subsequently been written about Albany during this period displays a strong bias towards 'Mother England' and the British Empire. However, this was also the time when an Australian identity was forged.

The subsequent impact of the Great War with its global economic repercussions and reconstruction endeavours were most strongly felt by European societies. New alliances were formed, and a slew of peace treaties negotiated. With time many of the legacies of the Great War diminished. However, for Albany it was not long before post war visitors arrived to acknowledge the town's significant role in supporting the British Empire in its time of need, for example, General Sir William Birdwood (January, 1920), Prince Edward (April, 1920) and the British Squadron (March, 1924).

---

[63] Bean, C.E.W. *The Story of ANZAC. The Official History of Australia in the War of 1914-1918*. Volume 1: The First Phase. Sydney, 1941.
[64] Information available through the Albany ANZAC Centre. www.nationalanzaccentre.com.au.

CHAPTER 17
THE DEVELOPMENT OF NOTABLE PRIVATE COMMERCIAL INTERESTS

Overview

It is appropriate once again to place Albany's Historical Record of the period 1890 to 1900 within the context of those events occurring contemporaneously on the world stage.

In New Zealand, Universal Suffrage was introduced in 1893, the first country to do this. Meanwhile, in the United States of America, the first automatic telephone exchange was opened in La Porte, Indiana in 1892. European imperialist activities continued with France gaining the Ivory Coast in Africa and also adding Laos to create French Indochina. Great Britain annexed Zimbabwe (then Southern Rhodesia) to add to its African interests. The Sino-Japanese war over the Korea Peninsular began in 1894. This conflict was a portend of what was to be a significant power shift in the Asian Pacific Region in the early Twentieth Century. The Kuomintang Chinese Nationalist Party created by Sun Yat-Sen seized power from the Qing dynasty during what was called the Xinhai Revolution. As the leader of the Kuomintang Sun became the first President of the Republic of China and was affectionately called the "Father of the Nation".

Meanwhile, the Dreyfus Case involving a Jewish Captain in the French Army, falsely accused of treason was playing out in French courts. The case inspired the work titled *J'accuse* by Emile Zola. In 1896 the first Olympic Games of the modern era were staged in Athens, and then in the following year, Greece and Turkey were at war over ownership of the island of Crete.

1898 saw Great Britain gain a 99-year lease over Hong Kong and the United States of America's annexation of Hawaii. The United States of America was then subsequently drawn into a conflict with Spain resulting in the Spanish American War. The conflict resulted in Spain ceding the Philippines, Cuba and Puerto Rico to the United States.

1899-1902 a war erupted between Great Britain and the South African Boers, a conflict that would ultimately involve Australian troops. Interestingly the Australian contingent of troops departed amid great fanfare from King George's Sound. Sadly, it was unknowingly at the time a precursor to The Great War convoy and troop-ship's departure. Subsequently, Great Britain annexed the Orange Free State and the Transvaal regions of South Africa. Meanwhile in China, the Boxer Rebellion against European and Chinese Christians had erupted and was violently quelled by an interim European - Asian alliance.

1901 was an important year for Australia as it marked the creation of the Commonwealth of Australia through the federation of its colonies. It also marked the end of the reign of Queen Victoria who died then to be succeeded by King Edward V11.

In 1904 the Russo-Japanese War that again saw the continued rise of Japan as a significant power in the region resulted in the destruction of the Russian Baltic Fleet in the Battle of Tsushima Strait.

Reporting the News

Until the creation of *The Albany Mail* in 1883, the inhabitants of King George's Sound initially gained their news from Eastern States Colonial newspapers, predominantly from New South Wales through the agency of *The Sydney Gazette and New South Wales Advertiser, The Colonial Times, The Colonist, The Sydney Morning Herald* and *The Australasian Chronicle*. Nevertheless, other newspapers were also a source of important news and information at this time including from Victoria, *The Argus* of Melbourne, *The Port Phillip Patriot and The Melbourne Advertiser* and *The Adelaide Chronicle and South Australian Record* and *The Adelaide Observer* from South Australia. Later, when regular mails arrived at King George's Sound from Great Britain and the far east through the steamship contracts European news could be read by local editors from *The Observer* in London.

Typical of the type of tactics employed by Eastern States newspapers in their approach to news collection was well documented in an article in *The Argus* of Melbourne:

A branch steamer met the mail steamer at Albany and came on Independently to Glenelg with the Adelaide mails, cargo, and passengers. The method of the Argus was to send a member of the staff to Albany on the branch steamer. He obtained the latest European newspaper files, and then on the way to Glenelg, on the branch steamer, extracted, condensed, and prepared the news for publication in the Argus. At Glenelg, a fast-rowing boat met the steamer, and the Argus man went onshore and Telegraphed his news to Melbourne. Often it happened, however, that the branch steamer was delayed by heavy weather in the bight, and then the mail steamer reached Melbourne before the prepared news arrived from Adelaide. Elaborate precautions had been taken, however. At Queenscliff, the Argus correspondence had a fast whaleboat, and he met the incoming steamer outside the heads, obtained a set of the newspaper files, and raced back to the Queenscliff pier. There his buggy was waiting and it was driven at breakneck speed to the Telegraph office.

There was keen competition in this work, for other papers we are equally anxious to obtain news, and often the race went to those who could first put the news on the wire. The corresponded of the Argus, in order to hold the wire until he could return from the mail steamer with his buggy, frequently adopted the plan of handing in the Bible before he left, with orders to Telegraph it to the Argus Melbourne and by this means nobody could use a Telegraph wire until he had finished with it and that was not until his News had been sent through. It was well known in the Argus office when the book of Genesis began to arrive that the European mail was not far behind it.[1]

Newspapers were the most significant conduit for information, discussion and debate in the colony and were highly respected mediums of communication. While only one copy now survives there is mention that the first paper printed in Western Australia was circulated during Lieutenant-Governor Stirling's time in 1829.[2] Newspapers have always played an important part in giving voice to the concerns and aspirations of the citizens of Albany and the Western Australian colony as a whole. Fortunately, it is through the immediacy of the reporting of correspondents throughout the Nineteenth and Twentieth Century that much of the town's history has been successfully captured.

A discussion of the various colony's newspapers is a pertinent matter to raise at this point because they contained a significant amount of primary source information that has contributed significantly over the years to The Historical Record of Albany and King George's Sound. Both the Eastern Colonies and Swan River Colony's newspapers were well placed to have 'local' correspondents in situ in the town who managed to capture in the course of their reporting many of the major events in the settlement as they were unfolding. Correspondents of the calibre of both Henry Lawson and Andrew (Banjo) Paterson by way of example both posted reports at one point from Albany to their respective Eastern Colonies newspaper outlets.

The earliest 'regular' newspaper in the Swan River Colony, which was written in longhand and sold for 3 shillings a copy, was *The Western Australian Gazette*. It was first published in March of 1831 and was printed in Fremantle at a press owned by William Kernot Shenton. *The Western Australian Gazette and General Advertiser* often carried official notices issued by the colony's government and has been a source of many references linked to articles in this Historical Record, including for example the appointment of Dr Collie as Government Resident in Albany. Several publication titles emanated from this Fremantle establishment including *The Fremantle Observer*, and *Perth Gazette and Western Australian Journal*, all quoted extensively in this work. These newspapers were reliant on their local correspondents for information as well as overseas stories to compliment general advertising and social aspects pertaining to the colony. For example, besides the news they also carried local items of interest including information on births, deaths, marriages, etc.

Two other newspapers that appeared early on in the colony were *The West Australian Colonial News* and *The Inquisitor* both of which began publication in 1833. While some of these papers had a very short lifespan, the material that they contained has been a time capsule of sorts for the historian.

---

[1] *The Argus*, Melbourne. 16th October 1934.
[2] *The Fremantle Journal and General Advertiser* was the first newspaper published in Western Australia. It was edited and published by James A. Gardner, with the first issue appearing in 1829. As there was not a printing press in the colony, each issue was handwritten.

Acknowledged as the most conservative newspaper in the colony *The West Australian* and its subsidiary, *The Western Mail* were both owned by Mr John Winthrop Hackett and had significant influence within the Western Australian colony.

> *The West Australian, loaded and fired daily by Hackett, is a little less moss-grown than The Melbourne Argus and little more squint-visioned than The Sydney Daily Telegraph. Hackett… Is the supreme rajah of the production, and an interesting substance to contemplate… Ascribe made a certain proposition to him once which, at a reasonable weekly cost, would have much enhanced the attractiveness of his paper. "Pooh", he said, "Why should I? As far as ink goes, I own the state.*[3]

The Western Mail commenced circulation in 1885 and operated until 1955; to be superseded by *The Countryman* in that year.

As the Western Australian colony grew, particularly in the Perth region the inter-colonial papers took on a lesser role in providing Albany with its news. Papers like *The Perth Gazette and Western Australian Journal* (1833-1847), *The Inquirer* (1840-1855), *The Perth Gazette and Independent Journal of Politics and News* (1848-1864), *The Inquirer and Commercial News* (1855), *Perth Gazette and Western Australian Times* (1864-1874), *The Western Mail* (1885), *The Daily News* (1882) *and The West Australian (1879)* each at one time or another influenced local discussions and municipal debates and town policy decisions.

One of the most significant features of all the newspapers produced in the Nineteenth Century was the outstanding high standard of English and grammar evident as editors of these papers were indeed recognised as excellent wordsmiths in their own right.

Newspaper Development at King George's Sound

The first local newspaper ever published in Albany was *The King Georges Sound Observer*. Number one of volume one of this newspaper was issued on Thursday, 27th of August 1868, and was printed in Albany on a small hand press, at premises located in Stirling Terrace. The name of the printer and publisher was given as Charles George Allen. However, it is noted that the publication was discontinued after the first few issues.[4] This publication was followed in 1881 by *The Albany Banner*, which was printed in Perth in the early 1870s and circulated in the town by post. It belonged to Edmund Stirling who was also the founder of *The Perth Inquirer*. *The Albany Banner* was not a success financially and soon disappeared from the scene.

The *Albany Despatch* was founded in 1914 and survived until 1927 when it was purchased by the newly formed company which acquired *The Australian Advertiser*. Interestingly, the amalgamation of these two papers eventually led to a major newspaper strike in the town. *The Australian Advertiser's* owners had planned to retain employees of both papers but found this was not an economic proposition to do so and therefore decided to retrench surplus employees. A worker's strike was called on the issue claiming victimisation, but the paper continued to be produced, although it did encounter some serious difficulties in doing so, at least until the industrial trouble was finally settled.

With the town's growth and increased prosperity, some newspaper broadsheets emerged that had an emphasis on more parochial interest items. The earlier newspaper endeavours included *The Albany Banner*, *The Albany Despatch* and *The Albany Mail and King George's Sound Advertiser*. There is a dearth of information relating to the first two newspapers mentioned, and not many copies of these papers were deposited in state archives.

---

[3] Bennett, B. (Ed). *The Literature of Western Australia*. University of Western Australia Press. 1979.
[4] *Albany's Yesteryears*. 28th November 1938.

The Albany Mail and King George's Sound Advertiser was started by a group of local Albany businessmen in 1883, with Christopher James Ashwell as the printer and publisher. Ashwell was originally from New Zealand.

The lead article from the first edition of *The Albany Mail* January 1st 1883 was very prophetic and saw the future of the town in quite glowing terms:

> *Before our mind's eye there arises in its splendour an Albany overshadowing in extent and beauty the Albany of this year or grace. We see a city stretching miles along the shores of a beautiful bay, rising in gentle terraces up the acclivities or hills and spreading far and wide upon the plain. We see lines of lofty and spacious warehouses, and course after course of stately, well paved and well-lighted streets. We see quite avenues and squares of finished dwelling houses from which traffic is banished and where noise is hushed, and the clustering walls of grimy factory reverberating with the clatter of machinery and the clamour of bury artisans.*
>
> *The city has spread its wings across the placid waters of the charming bay and the hills once bleak and silent, are instinct with life. Piers and wharves running in an unbroken vista along the shore grown beneath piles of merchandise which, despite the efforts of creaking crane and rolling trolley, still choke the ways.*[5]

Nevertheless, competition with *The Australian Advertiser* was more than *The Albany Mail* could stand and records indicate that it appears to have been absorbed by the former although neither paper seems to have referred to the amalgamation in its various editions. As far as history records *The Albany Mail* simply ceased publication and there was no indication in the final issue of the last edition of the paper printed under this banner on 28th August 1889 that it was indeed ceasing publication. A notice in *The Australian Advertiser* of 25 Sept 1889 stated:

> *'The proprietors of this paper have purchased the Albany Mail with its plant, stock etc, and henceforth it will be incorporated with the Advertiser.'*[6]

The name *The Albany Advertiser* first appeared on 20th February 1897 and was previously known by its banner *The Australian Advertiser*. There is considerable information available on the creation of *The Australian Advertiser* that was started in 1888 through a partnership between Lancel Victor de Hamel and William Forster.

Lancel Victor de Hamel arrived in Albany in 1886 and soon after announced his intention to run for mayor. While the construction of the railway from Perth to Albany was enthusiastically awaited in some quarters of the town there were nonetheless others, Lancel de Hamel included who were vehemently opposed to aspects of its planned route that would take it along the foreshore of The Princess Royal Harbour. Subsequently, he engaged in a campaign against the Western Australian Land Company over its choice of route, and, found himself denied little support from the only paper in town, *The Albany Mail and King George's Sound Advertiser*, which was a more conservative paper in its editorial leanings. As a consequence of being rebuffed by the only newspaper in town, de Hamel set up a second publication with his then partner Forster, called *The Australian Advertiser*. This newspaper was first published on 14th May 1888. The newspaper was very pro-de Hamel and it was not a surprise to many that shortly afterward its creation that he was elected as Mayor of Albany.

As indicated previously *The Albany Mail* could not survive against the newly formed competition in the town and was absorbed by *The Australian Advertiser* in September 1889. It was then that *The Australian Advertiser* changed its name to *The Albany Advertiser* without making any fuss of the matter and so the issue of Saturday, February 20th 1897 carried the new banner name. Hamel continued to use *The Australian Advertiser* as a platform to further launch his political aspirations and in 1889 he defeated Sir Thomas Cockburn-Campbell for the seat of Albany in the Legislative Council. He won the seat again the following year in the newly formed Legislative Assembly.

Underpinning the success of this newspaper enterprise was that the Great Southern Railway had fostered greater settler access to a large extent of good country, which in turn helped to significantly increase the

---

[5] *The Albany Mail.* 1st January 1883.
[6] *The Australian Advertiser.* Albany. 25th September 1889.

population of Albany and circulation of the paper. *The Albany Advertiser* was able to capitalise on this market by giving special attention to local questions of perceived significant importance to the town. After the retirement of Foster from the editorship he was succeeded by Arthur Catling. For many years *The Albany Advertiser* continued to print a wide coverage of international, British Empire, local news and special features.

While in February 1897 *The Australian Advertiser* became *The Albany Advertiser* from January 9th 1924 until the 24th December 1927, it was also known as *The Albany Advertiser and Plantagenet and Denmark Post*.

The Albany Despatch Newspaper

In an attempt to break the newspaper monopoly in the town a competitor paper was launched under the banner of *The Albany Despatch*. *The Daily News* in Perth reported on the publication of its first edition:

A copy of the first issue of the Albany Despatch has been received. And explaining the purpose and policy of the new publication, the editor and proprietor (Mr P.W. Smart) says: Albany is a town long enough established to have defined and permanent features. It has, in the course of its development, evolved different phases in its public interests. Such phrases may or may not be of vital importance, but without dissemination and consideration, the value cannot be ascertained. Everywhere in our day, public prints are the means of that dissemination and consideration being given. But one public print left to itself in a mature town ostensibly becomes a medium for organised interests, either great or small enough and it will lose sight of the interest of others within its area and become cribbed, cabined and confined, without really being aware that it is so. It is because of this, as a town grows in commercial significance, and increases in population, but two newspaper propositions are recognised to be of service in its public affairs. No town is likely to lapse into a lethargic state where the divided instincts of sentiment and definiteness of opinions are represented through more than one newspaper, nor is the expansion of resources in a district liable to be neglected where they are worthy of attention or inquiry.... with a desire to make the dispatch a factor in this and be representative of the great democratic principle involved in the phrase the voice of the people it is now poised to launch forth on its career...and it is on these grounds it hopes to win the favour of the residents of the town and district.[7]

Unfortunately for the paper its survival was very much linked to the endeavours of its owner Patrick Wood Smart. He was the driving force behind the creation of this paper and his demise would impact the longevity of the paper. His obituary stated:

Mr P. W. Smart passes.
By the death of Mr Patrick Wood Smart late proprietor of the Albany Despatch which sad event took place in St John of God Hospital Subiaco after a brief illness... He came to Albany in 1919 and founded the Albany Despatch, which he ran solely for the benefit of the town and district of Albany, and while he did not see eye to eye with other residents on many points, still as far as he was concerned the town and port came first. He took a keen interest in public matters and was one of the foundation members of the Albany Land Development Committee, which was responsible for the clearing of the bottlebrush land on the plain. In his writings, he put forward many suggestions for the improvement of the town's progress, but was on many occasions misunderstood... The news of his demise was received with expressions of regret on all sides.[8]

It is therefore not surprising that this newspaper folded shortly after Mr Smart's death with the last edition of *The Albany Despatch* issued on December 22nd 1927.

The Booming Hotel industry

The history of Albany hotels makes for a very interesting reading. There appears to have always been a surfeit of hotels and inns servicing the town and the challenge of unravelling the history of their development required some detective work. What has complicated matters is the fact that a number of the hotels went by different names during their lifespan, some as can be expected referred to by a local colloquial reference. All early hotel and inn license applications had to be endorsed by the Resident

---

[7] *The Daily News*. 16th January 1919.
[8] *The Albany Despatch*. 17th October 1927.

Magistrate which provided some limited insight into the area as paperwork relating these applications is available.

With many short-lived and home-based inn enterprises with varied nomenclatures it is not an easy task to follow the development of the hotel industry in Albany. With names like 'The Old Stone Jug', 'The Bucket Inn' and 'The Hen and Chicken' alongside the development of more substantial enterprises Albany can certainly lay claim to a very varied and evolving hotel industry.[9] Coupled with this issue there are many associated stories of smugglers plying their trade in an attempt to avoid customs duties and taxes.

First Liquor License - 1835.

The first public and general license granted in Albany was issued at a special session and licensing meeting of Justices of the Peace on June 29th 1835, to James Elphe who afterwards conducted the Waterman's Arms Inn operating out of a house on the shore of The Princess Royal Harbour. The license was signed by Sir Richard Spencer, the then Resident Magistrate that gave the permission with the caveat:
> *"from the date hereof, until the first day of January next"*.[10]

This license permitted:
> *…all such spirituous and fermented liquors as the said James Elphe shall be licensed and empowered to sell under the authority of any retail license issued by the collector of colonial revenue, to be drunk or consumed in his said house, or premises thereunto belonging, provided he do fraudulently dilute adulterated, any liquor by him sold, or sell the same knowing them to have been fraudulently diluted or adulterated, and shall not use in the selling their of any measures that are not of the legal standard.*[11]

The licensee was also reminded that he was not to permit drunkenness or disorderliness in his place nor to permit notoriously bad characters to assemble there, nor to:
> *knowingly suffer any unlawful games or any other gaming whatsoever therein.*

The license issued stated that:
> *…the licensee was duly licensed to sell, exchange or otherwise dispose of by retail any rum, brandy, arrack, whiskey, gin, or other spirituous liquor, and any ale, beer, wine, cider, perry, or other fermented liquors in his house called the Waterman's Arms situated at Albany on the shore of Princess Royal Harbour, but not elsewhere…*[12]

Unfortunately, other than this licence application there is subsequently very little information available on the Waterman's Arms Inn and it is very likely that it had a very short lifespan.

The Albany Inn/ Commercial Tavern or Inn/ Ship Inn/ Hen and Chicken Inn

The first hotel established in Albany was Diggory Geake's Commercial Hotel located on a block of land adjacent to what is now the Old Goal Museum. It comprised a two-story brick building and initially included 10 rooms for visitor accommodation. Geake had arrived at Fremantle on January 9th 1830 onboard *Nancy*. After 15 months in The Swan River Colony, he moved with his family to Albany arriving on *Sulphur*, 1st April 1831. Geake immediately secured an allotment of land in the town which today is partly occupied by the Old Gaol. He built what was to become the first licenced hotel in the townsite which he named the Albany Inn. In more common parlance it was referred to as the Commercial Inn. Besides operating the hotel Geake was also able to secure a further allotment in Big Grove where he operated a lime kiln.[13]

---

[9] The Old Stone Jug was demolished in August 1909 by its purchaser who had acquired it earlier that year. In its time it was recognised as one of the landmarks of the town. It was built in 1840 by Mr E.H. Barker for use as a dwelling house.
[10] *The Register* (Adelaide). National library of Australia. 24th November 1923.
[11] *The West Australian*. 10th April 1935.
[12] Ibid. Also note that perry is an alcoholic drink made from the fermented juice of pears.
[13] Lime burning for the manufacture of cement was an extensive industry on the southern shore of The Princess Royal Harbour.

After a mild stroke, Geake had some reduced physical capacity and interestingly tried to use this disability to seek from Sir Richard relief from paying licence fees on his imported spirits, mainly rum at this time. Spencer would have none of this request commenting in correspondence to the Colonial Secretary Mr Brown that:

> *Mr George Cheyne and Mr Diggory Geake are making large profits by buying rum at five shillings a gallon and selling it for 25 shillings a gallon and so Mr Geake can well afford the licence fee.*

Further, Spencer reported:

> *His claim regarding lack of customs is belied by the fact that large numbers of intoxicated persons are to be seen leaving his premises.*[14]

George Cheyne also had a relationship with Sir Richard that was indeed very acrimonious. Often their overt dislike of one another created factions within the town, either pro Sir Richard or pro George Cheyne. Cheyne was a prominent well-connected businessman and quite often his many commercial interests would necessitate engaging with the Office of the Resident Magistrate. Whenever the opportunity arose, he would try to undermine the authority of Sir Richard.[15]

The Commercial Hotel (originally referred to as the Commercial Tavern) traded under this name until it was leased as a residence to Hugh McKenzie in 1840. Later McKenzie travelled to the Eastern colonies and New Zealand before returning to Albany in 1843 to establish the Ship Inn.

Given the Ship Inn's location near to the approach to the then existing town jetty on lower Stirling Terrace it was recognised as perhaps one of the first commercial buildings erected in Albany during the early 1830 settlement period. The location of the inn made it well-placed to cater for those transiting through the port and also for local officials working in the area:

> *The Ship Inn was the favourite resort for customs offices, members of the police force, shipping people and town proprietors while awaiting the arrival of mail boats, for which Albany was then the regular port to and from the Eastern States. Their approach was signalled by flags during the day and coloured lights at night, these being hoisted onto poles at the Post Office. The display of a red light at the office was a prelude too much excitement and bustle. The little launch* Loch Lomond, *later lost at sea, set up such noise, barges were got ready and moved into midstream: Male passengers at the various hotels were called, and the port medical officer was called so that he might check the vessel early as possible…*

> *Like other old buildings, the ship in was lavishly supplied with fireplaces, almost every room having had one. The building had remained in surprisingly good condition until recently, although it was a long time since any maintenance had been done on it, but over the years the sand bricks of which it was built had become exposed to the weather and had fretted seriously, it was getting into dangerous condition…*[16]

In May of 1843 McKenzie's licence application transferred the name of the Ship Inn to the Hen and Chicken Inn. It has been strongly implied that McKenzie was a known smuggler, of not only spirituous and fermented goods but also other merchandise as well.

The de-licensed and then vacant old Ship Inn building was originally used by the Albany Branch of TocH for its regular meetings and the building was renovated by its membership at the time. However, the later poor state of repair of the Ship Inn building resulted in its demolition in the 1950s. The local paper reported on its demise:

> *Ship Inn Demolished*
>
> *One of Albany's oldest buildings and possibly one of its first licensed hotels, the Ship Inn, was demolished by railway department workmen last week. The Ship Inn which stood in the lower end of Spencer Street, behind the Post Office, was built by John McKenzie probably in the late 1830s. The building just demolished was possibly not the original structure but is known to have stood on its present site since before the Great Southern Railway was built. It had not been licensed for many years, probably more than half a century.*

---

[14] *Richard Spencer Letter Book*, 20th December 1833. State Library of Western Australia: Annotated and Typescript copies of Letters by Richard Spencer.
[15] West, D.A.P. *Early Government Residents of Albany*. Albany Technical College Lecture. 1985.
[16] *IRS/141M/3*. The Albany History Collection, Albany Town Library.

When the Ship Inn was first built, shipping was served by a short jetty which later was extended to form the town jetty which was in active use up to the end of World War II, though by then it was used mainly for small ships of the Navy and occasionally by small freighters. When it was decided to construct the new wharves, the town jetty was officially closed and has been used since only by small craft such as the whale chasers.

How much of the town jetty existed when the Ship Inn was built is not known definitely but there is probably perhaps a clue in the fact that a few bays of the present jetty, at the shoreward end, are built of hand squared piles, whereas the rest was rounded piles…

Until 10 years or so ago when foreshore reclamation covered them over, piles of stones could be seen along the shoreline, where ballast from sailing ships had been dumped. The original shoreline was only a few yards from the walls of the Ship Inn, and it can be imagined with what joy passengers from the small sailing ships would welcome its solid floors and hospitality. It can be imagined to, that there must have been some fairly riotous gatherings. The Ship Inn was later used for the storage of goods and other commercial purposes. Part of it was used for some years as a meeting place.[17]

The Sherratt Family Inn

The Sherratt Family Inn was also located in Lower Stirling Terrace at the bottom of York Street on a property now occupied by an Auction House and liquor outlet. The fact that the local Family Hotel (Sherratt Family licensees) was owned and operated by the self-proclaimed local preacher did not escape the ire of a local visiting seafarer to Albany, Joseph Gatchell. In a quite scathing piece published in the local newspaper he highlighted this contradiction:

I remained at Swan River nearly 3 weeks; when the schooner Elizabeth, calling to take in cargo, I got a passage on board her to King George's Sound. Here is a thriving little settlement; and here I saw hypocrisy with a vengeance. There were many a company of soldiers stationed in the place: and they, with the crews that were ashore from the whale ships putting in to recruit, were most excellent customers to the rum store, which was kept by Londoner. This man not only exercised the calling of a rum seller, but he also officiated as a parson. He would remain in his store till late on Saturday night, charging most exorbitant prices for the poison he dealt out, and listening to the oaths and curses of the drunkards himself was making; and on Sunday, with the greatest himself was making; and on Sunday, with the greatest Pharisiacal [sic] devotedness, he would mount the pulpit, and expound to the people the word of God, which declared, "wo to him that putteth [sic] the bottle to his neighbours' lips, and making him drunken." How strange it is that people can trifle with, or pervert to their own purposes the pure, the holy religion of our God.[18]

The original licence application for the Family Inn in 1841 was refused to Sherratt as he held the joint Government Posts of official Albany Postmaster and Government Auctioneer at that time. A licence was subsequently granted to him in 1842 for the Family Inn owned and operated by Thomas Brooker Sherratt which he kept until 1843 when due to mental health issues the license was taken on by his son-in-law Hugh McDonald.

Thomas Brooker Sherratt had arrived in the Swan River Colony with Sir James Stirling on board *James Pattison* in 1834. He was accompanied by his wife Amelia (1800-1842) and a large family. Sherratt was a highly religious man and had considerable capital to invest in the new settlement. He acquired several blocks of land at King George's Sound including three at the corner of York Street and Stirling Terrace and a further block adjacent to Duke and Parade Streets and Stirling Terrace. This is where he established his family and business interests. He constructed a two-storey house on the southwest corner of Stirling Terrace and York Street. This building later doubled as his hotel.

After the death of his wife in 1842, Sherratt broke down emotionally and mentally, and in 1843 he was locked away in his room in Perth for about two years. In 1843 the licence was taken over by his son in law,

---

[17] *The Albany Advertiser.* 7th April 1959.
[18] Joseph Gatchell. *Disenthralled: Being Reminiscences in the Life of the Author; His Fall from Respectability by Intemperance – and Rescue by the Washington Society: Containing also his Life as a Sailor, Shipwreck and Residence among the Savage Tribes in New Holland.* Troy, New York. 1844.

Hugh McDonald upon Sherratt's confinement due to his deteriorating mental state. McDonald took over the management of all of his affairs which included completing the partially-built brig *Emma Sherratt* with another business entrepreneur in the town, John Hassell. McDonald subsequently acquired Sherratt's share of the *Emma Sherratt*. By 1846 Sherratt had partially recovered from his breakdown and then began what became a long and acrimonious campaign against McDonald, whom he believed had robbed him. After 1846 the hotel came under the management of his daughter Emma and her husband.

Freemason's Hotel/'Stricklands'

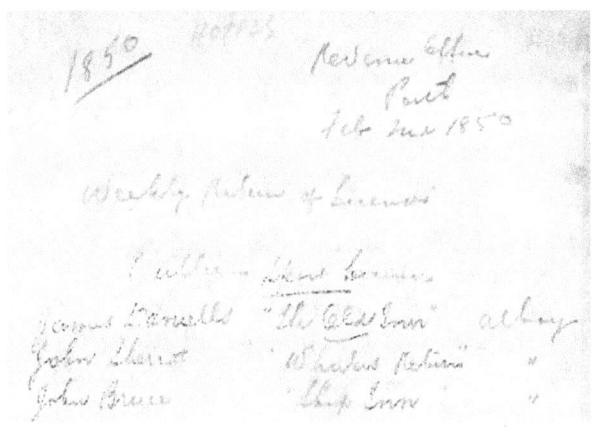

Originally the Freemason's Hotel was a private house with an inn facility run by James Daniells called "The Old Inn".[19] In 1861 the Government made an offer for the property with the intention of using the building for office accommodation. It was renovated in 1863 for this purpose. However, the facility ended up not meeting the government's requirements and it was subsequently leased to Mr. Hugh McKenzie in 1868 to begin its life as a hotel. The building was later purchased by McKenzie outright in 1870. The original licensee of the hotel was a William Strickland and colloquially the hotel was often referred to as 'Stricklands".

In 1903 a British born architect Joseph Herbert Eales was commissioned by John McKenzie to develop and remodel the Freemason's Hotel. It is at this time that a third story was added to the existing hotel structure.[20] From the many historical descriptions and comments made about the Freemason's Hotel it was for its time a wonderful building. In 1912 the booklet *Alluring Albany* indicated that:

"Although always a leading local house of public entertainment, the Freemason's Hotel was not always the fine establishment it is today. It is of historic interest to remember, however, that it was one of the first two-storied house to be built in Albany, as it is, at the present time, the larger of the two buildings of three stories in the southern portion of Western Australia.[21]

The Freemason's Hotel was indeed a well-regarded establishment in the town. *The Albany Advertiser* was quite effusive in its description of the hotel after recent renovation work that had been undertaken which included the addition of a third story to the existing structure:

Old residents of Albany would find it difficult to recognise in the palatial structure recently completed in Stirling Terrace any trace of the sombre-hued, shambling and old-fashioned, but nevertheless, cosy-cornered and comfortable, if homely, hostelry which for over half a century has borne the name of the Freemason's' Hotel and boldly faced all the winds that blew. The former building has been entirely metamorphosed, the old order giving place to the very newest.

It is a most striking and splendid addition to the architectural features of the town, the very greatest credit is due to the proprietor of the building, Mr John McKenzie, an ex-Mayor and one of its most energetic and enterprising citizens.

---

[19] Letter from the Robert Stephens Collection *IRS/196/15* that relates to hotel licensee returns. The Albany History Collection, Albany Town Library.
[20] Joseph Herbert Eales has been associated with Albany, both professionally and as a regular visitor, since 1887 when he arrived in the Eastern States and as a man of 23 just starting his professional career, he passed through the town on the P&O liner *Ormuz*. He arrived in in Western Australia in 1897. Eales had specialised in church architecture in England before emigrating to Western Australia. After completing an architectural commission for the Freemason's Hotel and the Albany Masonic Hall he accepted one from F. R. Dymes to undertake planning for the Weld Arms Hotel as well as one for the London Hotel for the W.A. Trustees Company. Later he was also won a commission to remodel the White Star. He was responsible for developing plans for the proposed Esplanade Hotel for its future proprietor Matson. He was instrumental in creating plans for many of Western Australia's prominent houses and buildings.
[21] Ibid.

> *In raising this fine building, he has manifested a public spirit and a belief in the future of Albany which are exactly the qualities that make for the accomplishment of what is desirable. A community happy enough to possess members of this sterling and progressive stamp are bound to prosper if prosperity be anywhere within the range of human effort. The outside alterations to the old structure, endeared by many cheery associations with the town but now grown old and out-of-date for these go-ahead times, consist mainly of the addition of a storey-making three in all-and an entire renovation of front in accordance with the latest modern designs in hotel architecture, and these changes have been carried out with complete success and most agreeable effect under the direction of Mr J. Herbert Eales, of Fremantle, the architect.*
>
> *When the design of the new building was first submitted, some doubt was expressed as to the wisdom of adding a third storey, the question being raised whether an edifice thus heightened would withstand the force of the fierce gales that rush upon this sea-front front at certain seasons and sweep the town with raging fury. But the plan of solid construction adopted in increasing the duration of the building completely disposes of any such misgivings, and the new structure faces the wind and the weather as stoutly as the old one did for so many years.*
>
> *As it now stands, the building presents a pleasing example of the Italian Renaissance style, the general contour and appearance suggesting memories of the prevailing architecture of Monte Carlo, the suggestion being emphasised -by the rich, warm Italian tone, resembling that of – English bath stone, of the exterior. "The interior has also been entirely re-modelled and renovated, and the hotel now contains: from 56 to 60 apartments, many of a very spacious character, including the usual saloon bars, with dining, drawing, smoking, billiard and bedrooms, kitchen and other offices. A most happy effect is produced throughout the house by the stained glass liberally employed in the windows and doors. It is necessary to point out that all the enterprise of Mr McKenzie and the architectural skill of Mr Eales would have been lost had not the contractor for the new work, Mr Chas. F. Layton performed his part of the undertaking with the most conscientious faithfulness. All, however, who were concerned in the work seemed to have been imbued with the spirit which emanated from the enterprising proprietor of the1 building, and with his desire to make the new Freemason's Hotel a model of its kind, with every modern equipment, and an ornament to the town. The extensive plumbing work on the premises rendered necessary by alterations which practically amounted to entire re-building was executed by Mr Reeve, of Albany while the lead glazing, which forms a conspicuous feature of the new state of things, was carried out by Mr D'Estcourt, of Perth.*
>
> *… the excellent system of electric bells was installed by Mr Arthur Wright, electrician, of Fremantle. The hotel trims enlarged and improved out of all recognition, is leased to Mr J. S. Deykiu, who holds the license. No excuse has been spared in furnishing the new apartments, and under his capable management, the good old house in its new and handsome form is assured of the continued and enhanced prosperity which the enterprise is shown in its renovation on such an extensive and artistic scale so thoroughly deserves.*[22]

Twenty-five years later the newspaper was again full of praise for this Albany building icon:
> *Freemason's Hotel House with Historical Associations.*
> *Although the mail steamers have now eliminated Albany the very high reputation enjoyed in those palmy trading days by the Freemason's hotel remains, and successive proprietors have ever sought to maintain its hospitable traditions in this respect the present licensee, Mr J. Horswills, is well to the fore, and the large measure of success attending his efforts testifies to his qualifications as a host. The saloon and public bars are noted for the best attention and the highest quality refreshments, while the dining and residential sections of the house find general favour with all classes of the travelling public. Mr Horswill's motto is "Service."*[23]

Unfortunately, with time, the Freemason's Hotel was demolished to make way for alternative commercial interests in 1972. Both the Freemason's Hotel (1868-1910) and Devonshire House (1908) were demolished by Sir Thomas Wardle owner and proprietor the "Tom the Cheap Grocer" Company in order to build a

---

[22] The *Albany Advertiser*. 21st Jan 1905.
[23] Ibid. 14th June 1930.

shopping complex. Nonetheless, the proposed redevelopment never happened, and the area that it occupied in Stirling Terrace remains vacant to this day.[24]

Albany Hotel/White Swan/Horse and Groom Inn

One of the oldest hotel establishments in the town is the Albany Hotel situated in York Street. Records indicate that it was initially known as the White Swan. An application for license dated 23rd December 1842 was submitted by George Swift, who sought permission to sell spirituous and fermented liquors from his house and continue operating it as an inn or public house. His establishment was then known as the White Swan Inn. Unfortunately, Swift was caught stealing and was subsequently sentenced to 10 years transportation to the Van Diemen's Land penal colony in 1843. In that year John Craigie successfully applied for a license for the same location and traded under the name Albany Hotel. Interestingly, the land on which the hotel stands was originally property granted to Patrick Taylor in December 1840 at a peppercorn rent.[25]

On the 16th July 1889 the hotel and property were transferred to John Norrish who also happened to be the owner of the Weld Tavern on the Old Perth Road. It was Norrish who opened the hotel in October 1889 as the Horse and Groom Inn. During 1890 Norrish applied unsuccessfully for a general publican's license for his hotel, however, as it was felt that the town was already well served with hotels and consequently his application was denied. The property was then leased in October 1891 to Frederick Johann Schruth, who was a general store keeper and plumber. In 1892 Schruth successfully applied for publican's general license and then changed the name of the premises back to Albany Hotel.[26]

Esplanade Hotel

The original Esplanade hotel was built on a prime location adjacent to Middleton Beach in 1898 by a French national John Galle. This was the first of four iterations of the hotel as it was originally built of a weatherboard construction that in 1908 burned to the ground. An inquest into the cause of the fire was held, however, no evidence could be found on how the fire originated.

Fire at Albany.
Esplanade Hotel Destroyed.
Albany. April 3rd.
The Esplanade Hotel at Middleton Beach was completely destroyed by fire at an early hour this morning. The building, which was entirely of weather-board was consumed before assistance from The Forts could be made effective, with very little of the furniture and the stock of liquor being saved. Only two persons slept in the house overnight, the licensee (Mr A. H. Vicklers) and another man named Julius Quitman. At daybreak, the licensee observed a smell of fire. He got up and found that a fire had started in one of the back rooms. Mr Vickers immediately called Mr Quitman, notifying him of what had happened. The fire had obtained such a hold, however. that all efforts to save the building were fruitless.
The building. which was owned by Mr Charles Patterson, was insured…
An inquiry into the cause of the fire was opened today and adjourned for a week.[27]

A new hotel was built and opened in April 1911, replete with modern conveniences such as hot water, electric bells and telephones. The local press provided an insight into the new establishment:
The New Establishment.
Phoenix-like, from the ashes of the old wooden hotel at Middleton Beach, has arisen the present handsome Esplanade Hotel in brick. The magician of the wondrous change is Mr Isaac Matson, one of the best-known mining men of this State, and it speaks volumes for his enterprise and faith in the growing popularity of Albany as a tourist resort that he has sunk in the venture, in bricks and mortar, fittings, etc., … With the

---

[24] When 'Tom the Cheap' was placed in administration the liquidators for the company attempted to demolish another period building in the terrace in 1978, the Albany Light Opera Company Building, but fortunately in this case the Albany Town Council prevented it and today that building is 'Dylan's on the Terrace'.
[25] Rent Book Information. The Albany History Collection, Albany Town Library.
[26] Battye, J.S. *The Cyclopedia of Western Australia in Two Volumes*. 1912. (Reprint) Hesperian Press, Perth, 1985.
[27] *The West Australian*, Perth. 4th April 1908.

further development and prosperity of Western Australia, it is very unlikely that that faith will be shattered, and ere long the Middleton Beach Hotel should become one of the best known of tourist hotels.

Middleton Beach is reached after a two-and-a-half miles' drive along a road that becomes prettier as the hotel is reached. Within a stone's throw of the gently lapping waves stands he handsome building, and from its balcony a magnificent view of the bay and the bold headlands and islands is obtainable. Almost at one's feet extends, crescent-shaped, one of the finest sandy beaches in Australia-a veritable children's delight. Here mothers may allow their little ones to scamper or splash in the -wavelets to their hearts' content with a minimum of risk.

Further, along where the rollers sweep in unfettered, those who enjoy surf bathing may have it as perhaps it is to be had nowhere else along the coast-fine steady rollers that curl, and, breaking, spread themselves over the shallows and gently sloping beach without leaving a deadly back-wash. But, to return to the hotel. Altogether there are 100 rooms, 75 of which are bedrooms. On inspection, the visitor is at once impressed with the warmth and colour tones of the various rooms-welcome change from the dead-white plaster walls of many hotels.[28]

White Star/White Hart

Both the White Star and Royal George Hotels were originally built as merchant stores, the White Star by John McKail and the Royal George by the Moir family. The decision to refurbish McKail's existing merchandising store into a hotel was announced in the local newspaper in December 1909:

White Hart Hotel.

A start was made last week with the reconstruction of the White Hart Hotel in Stirling Terrace. Practically new premises are to be erected and the plans, prepared by Mr J.H. Eales, provide for a building that will be a distinct gain to the architecture of the main thoroughfare of the town. The new house will have a 70-foot frontage and it will measure 45 feet from the ground to the top of the pediment… In the new building there will be parlours to both bars, 14 bedrooms, a billiard room, baths with hot and cold service and sanitary arrangements of the most complete character.[29]

The White Star Hotel was rebuilt and superseded the previous White Hart Inn in Stirling Terrace that had operated out of the building. Its significant remodelling and renovations were completed in 1910. The licensee, Charles Reddin had applied to the Albany Town Council on September 12th 1910 for a reduction in his rates due to the rebuilding of the hotel and this application was subsequently granted.[30] Reddin was identified as a very forward-thinking and ambitious businessman and entrepreneur.[31]

The name White Star it was implied was named as such for marketing purposes recognising the importance of the White Star Shipping Line that was one of the more significant and influential passenger and freight shipping companies that operated out of the Albany port complex towards the latter decades of the Nineteenth Century.

Royal George/Railway

The Royal George Hotel was built in 1885 during the halcyon days of the Western Australian goldrush in the 1880s and 1890s. Unfortunately, there is some ambiguity concerning the history of the site on which the original Royal George Hotel is now situated.

---

[28] *The Albany Advertiser.* 2nd August 1911.
[29] Ibid. 25
[30] Albany Town Council Monthly meeting notes. *The Albany Advertiser.* 17th September 1910.
[31] J.S. Battye, *The Cyclopedia of Western Australia*, Cyclopedia Co., Perth 1912.

One source maintains that the site on which the hotel was co-located was a then an occupied store and house complex called Aberdeen House in Stirling Terrace. This source maintained that the original Aberdeen House was constructed prior to 1867 and was the home of Alexander and Catherine Moir and that some of this dwelling's structure was later incorporated into the rear of the new Railway Hotel complex. However, another source produced as part of an Albany promotion during the Australian Bicentennial rightfully claimed that Aberdeen House was originally the Oddfellows Hall that was built in 1891. This claim maintains that the building on the site was a one roomed house and inn known as The Bucket Inn. The conclusion drawn is that the latter building which still exists on Aberdeen Street, and which now houses the Albany Club was indeed built in 1891 and was also named Aberdeen House as the original building had now become the Railway Hotel.

"BAILYE'S RAILWAY HOTEL,"

Stirling Terrace, Albany,

WESTERN AUSTRALIA.

THIS HOTEL having been extensively enlarged and renovated, will now be found replete with all the comforts and appointments of a First-class Hotel, and possesses the further facility of being the nearest Hotel to the Railway Station, Jetties and Post and Telegraph Offices.

CHARGES MODERATE.

FINEST BRANDS OF WINES, ALES AND SPIRITS ALWAYS IN STOCK.

ENGLISH DRAFT ALE, A SPECIALTY.

HOT AND COLD BATHS.

READING & WRITING ROOMS. PRIVATE SITTING ROOMS.

ALCOCK'S "MATCH" BILLIARD TABLE.

Special Stabling Accommodation complete with Horses and Traps always for Hire.

C. H. BAILYE, PROPRIETOR.

Nevertheless, what is not dispute is that the Moir's leased the Stirling Terrace building to Frederick Watts in the mid-1880s and he was the person responsible for converting the extant building into a hotel. Initially it was named the Railway Hotel as it occupied an aspect opposite the Great Southern Railway depot building that had been built just below it. In 1892 Moir leased the hotel to Charles Bailye, who then changed the name to the Royal George Hotel.[32]

In 1910 began to extend the hotel adding a second storey and balcony to the existing structure.

Royal George.
Loitering on the footpath.
…. The magistrate said he was glad the case has been brought forward as a test case. The loitering of a number of men under the veranda of the Royal George hotel was a scandal and a nuisance. Ladies had also been frequently insulted when passing by.
In this particular case as it was the first of its nature, he would dismiss it on payment by defendants of the cost of the summons. He would ask the Sergeant to keep watch on the movement of the lawyers in that facility and to put a stop to it. He warned them the next time a similar case report for the culprits would be dealt with severely.[33]

Premier Hotel

The original Premier Hotel was built in 1891 and was and still is located on the corner of Grey and York Streets. It was the third substantial hotel built in Albany during the Western Australian gold rush era. Only the Premier and the Albany Hotel still retain their original names as the Chusan was renamed the London, the White Hart to the White Star and the Railway Hotel renamed the Royal George. The first meeting of the Albany Roads Board was held in the hotel dining room of the Premier Hotel in 1896.[34]

Richard Burridge purchased the hotel in 1912 and the then licensee was Marcus O'Grady. In 1929 after Burridge's passing the hotel was acquired by William Harper who was also the licensee of the Freemason's Hotel located on Stirling Terrace at that time.[35]

Like many of its counterparts the hotel has evolved with the times and in 1913 underwent a significant renovation as *The Albany Advertiser* noted:

---

[32] *Royal George Hotel*. Heritage Council of Western Australia. Western Australian Government. 2016.
[33] *The Albany Advertiser*. 28th of October 1899.
[34] *The Premier Hotel*. Heritage Council of Western Australia. Western Australian Government. 2015.
[35] *The Albany Advertiser*. 11th December 1912.

And Up-To Date-Establishment.
Albany has a reputation to maintain as a health and holiday resort, and consequently the hotel accommodation is a matter of importance to the town. Of recent years there have been many changes in this respect. There is not a hotel in the place that has not been remodelled or rebuilt. A high standard of excellence has thus been attained all-round. Nevertheless, still further enterprise has been brought to bear on the Premier Hotel, in York Street, with the result that the premises have been enlarged and brought thoroughly up-to-date…
The house has been doubled in size, doors and passages have been widened, windows enlarged and replaced by casements, windows and doors have been closed and new ones substitute for them, and, indeed such alterations have been made as to justify the statement that the building as it stands is a new one. And being new, it meets all modern requirements in the interests of health, comfort and convenience.[36]

London Hotel/Chusan

The Heritage Council of Western Australia indicates that the London Hotel was built on the site of the Chusan Hotel which had stood on the site since 1849 and further, that it was rebuilt in 1871. Unfortunately, this date contradicts Garden (1977) who indicated that the Chusan Hotel, later renamed the London Hotel began life in 1855.[37] Garden's date for the building of the hotel is supported by an article from *The Inquirer newspaper* which stated:

King George's Sound
The Antilla *brought a large hotel in frame, which was much required at Albany. It is the property of Mr McDonnell and is to be put up for the accommodation of passengers visiting the port.*[38]

Nevertheless, both sources agree that the London Hotel was initially called the Chusan and that it began **operating out of an imported prefabricated wooden structure that was** constructed by John McDonnell.[39]

Due to the nature of the hotel's initial construction, there were concerns that it was a possible fire risk and that it also exceeded local building regulations. To overcome the problem, it was agreed by McDonnell that he would brick the bottom storey of the building. Unfortunately, a downturn in the local economy during the Crimean War period coupled with a reduction of shipping to the port meant that he could not afford the cost of bricking the building. The hotel was renamed the London Hotel in 1861.

Over time the London Hotel has changed ownership on several occasions. With each passing decade different aspects were added to the building's layout and façade.

Big Property Deal.
London Hotel Sold.
An important property deal took place during the week when the London hotel chain stands for price stated to be in the facility of £5000. The new owner of the property is Mrs Ruse of Perth, who is expected to enter into possession on the expiration of the present lease, at the end of October.
The London hotel, which was built in 1909, was that originally by the late Mr McKail. In 1929 the property was sold by auction to the late Mr J.F. Cowin, and since his death it has been held in trust for the estate.
One of the most popular residential hotels in Albany, the London Hotel has been conducted for some years by Mr W A Schurer.[40]

---

[36] Ibid. 8th October 1913.
[37] D. Garden. *Albany: Panorama of the Sound.* Nelson. 1977.
[38] *The Inquirer.* Perth. 21st February 1855.
[39] *London Hotel.* The Heritage Council of Western Australia. Western Australian Government. 8th February 2015.
[40] Ibid. 7th October 1935.

Spencer Inn

The Spencer Inn was initially a private house that was constructed circa 1850s. It was originally an accommodation boarding house. Later in 1865 it was purchased by Richard Nesbitt. In 1874 Richard Nesbitt sought and was successful in obtaining a wine and beer licence to enable him to operate the house as both an inn and boarding house. In the 1890s it was renamed the Earl of Spencer Inn. However, in 1920 it was de-licensed and was then subsequently used as a grocery store until the building was abandoned and became a dilapidated relic. A consortium of Albany businessmen restored the building in 1987 and it once again came to life once again as the Earl of Spencer Inn. The name Spencer Inn was taken from the street of that name on which it is located, and it has no association with any British Earldom.

Weld Arms

Once situated on the Old Perth Road the Weld Arms, later the Weld Hotel, was a recognised establishment in the town and was well respected for the quality of the accommodation it provided for travellers.

Like other Albany hotels the Weld also had an interesting history, as originally it was a just a small building that was later incorporated at the side of the later remodelled hotel. The first owner of the Weld Arms was W.J. Cooper. Although he built it and was the original owner, he was not granted the publican's license. This was held by John Norrish. Later a publican's general license was granted to James Flanagan for the Weld Arms in December 1892.[41]

In 1886 a cricket and sportsground existed immediately behind the hotel, and it was on this ground that a cricket match was played in that year between a local team and a combination team from the cruisers HMS *Opal* and HMS *Diamond*. The warships were then in port of Albany having been sent here in connection with the Russian scare of that year.[42]

> *The Weld Hotel, on Albany Highway, is one of Albany's smaller hotels, but has always held a good reputation for comfort and cleanliness. It was conducted for many years by the late William Peel, and after his death by his daughters, Christina and Nellie. In 1938 the Peels purchased a hotel from the estate of the late Miss Annie Dymes...*[43]
>
> *The Weld Hotel.*
> *Miss E Peel.*
> *A very popular figure in Albany is Miss E Peel, the proprietress of the Weld Hotel, on the Perth Road. Possessed of the vitality of disposition so necessary to a successful hotel manager, she has proved during the course of her management that she knows the art of making her hotel a place of welcome and rest to all....*[44]

Summary of the Albany Hotel Industry

It is apparent that several of the early inns commenced their life as domestic abodes with a specific area designated as a bar with perhaps some limited accommodation for the traveller as well. As the town developed the hotels became more sophisticated in both appearance and construction. However, not all visitors accessing the accommodation provided by these hotels were enthusiastic about the quality on offer:

---

[41] State Records Office of Western Australia. *Weld Arms*. Publicans Licence 1892.
[42] *Robert Stephens Collection*. Royal Western Australian Historical Society.
[43] *The Albany Advertiser*. 25th January 1951.
[44] Ibid. 24th February 1941.

> *Hotel accommodation is not one of the strong features of Albany when one considers it is, so to speak, the front door of the colony. I was, however, given to understand that I should look back even upon this as a little paradise compares to what I should have to put up with up-country.*[45]

Records indicate that by 1913 there were 7 hotels operating in the town of Albany: The Albany; London; Premier; York; Freemason's; Royal George and Weld Arms. A point of interest is that the town at this time now also accommodated 2 breweries, three banks, two baker's shops, a chemist and three bootmakers.

With the increase in steamship arrivals in the port in the latter decades of the 1800s, the need for extra hotel accommodation for overseas and local visitors had often been highlighted. An Albany correspondent for *The Daily News* wrote in 1889:

> *Want of House Accommodation at Albany*
> *There is a great cry here for house accommodation, and premiums are being paid to holders of cottages in order to rent them. A number of well-paid artisans, with their families, have been compelled to take to tent living, and considerable consternation is evinced as to what will be done in order to obtain shelter for our surplus population during the coming winter. We sadly want a hotel here on the lines of the Federal at Fremantle, in order to induce passengers by the great ocean steam ships to break their voyage at this port and catch the following boat, in order to permit strangers visiting Perth to leave us with good an impression of the colony's resources. Under present circumstances there is nothing here to induce passengers to leave their floating palaces, consequently, a great injustice is done to the colony in many ways, while a large amount of outside money is taken away by tourists and others which would be left with us if we were in a position to afford the luxuries that travellers can now obtain on a large number of steamers at present calling here.*
>
> *The Albanians are a self-satisfied race of people, and unless help comes in this direction from the centres of the population it will be impossible to permit the colony, and strangers thereto, to enjoy the full advantages of the Great Southern Railway. As an instance of the present state of our hotel accommodation, let me mention that a few weeks ago the steamship* Albany *arrived here from the colonies, and about twenty of her passengers desired a night onshore. They each tried to obtain a bed, and although the* Albany *was the only steamer in port that night, not a single passenger could be accommodated in any shape or form. How must this state of affairs affect the colony in the minds of the passengers by the large ocean steamers, some of which have onboard as many as five hundred travellers?*[46]

By 1913 the hotel landscape had changed to an even further degree with some of the earlier premises giving way to more substantial hotel building complexes. The booklet *'Alluring Albany'* printed in 1912 mentions only 6 hotels, with the addition of the London Hotel (1909) and the Weld Hotel situated on the old Perth Road. The year after the publication of this book the Premier Hotel (1913) was opened.[47]

In 1920 with a decline in Albany's population growth rate subsequent to The Great War a state-wide referendum was conducted to determine an optimum number of licensed premises in the state. The Albany electors voted to de-license two hotels, and those selected to be de- licensed were the York Hotel and the Earl of Spencer or Spencer Inn.[48]

---

[45] Price, J.M. *The Land of Gold. The Narrative of a Journey Through the West Australian Goldfields in the Autumn of 1895.* London. Marsden and Company. 1896.
[46] *The Daily News*, Perth. 21st February 1889.
[47] *Alluring Albany.* (1912). A Town of Albany Publication.
[48] "The Licensing Poll. York and Spencer Inn abolished." *The Albany Advertiser.* 30th July 1921.

June 1898 the Albany Advertiser.
De-Licence
At the courthouse on Wednesday morning, the Albany licensing branch… delivered its reserved decision in respect of the cancellation of two hotel licenses in the Albany licensing district, in accordance with the express wish of the electors of the poll taken on 30th of April last…

Mr Burt delivered the decision of the court, which was that the licenses of the Spencer Inn and the York Hotel must go. In doing so, he said: "Resolution C having been carried by a majority of the electors at the local option vote taken in this licensing district on 30th of April, 1921, it became the duty of this court to determine the reduction to be made in the number of existing licensees in the district, of the kind of which the vote applies, as provided by the licensing act, 1911."[49]

The court took into consideration a number of factors including the number of licence breaches and adverse police reports. The article went on to conclude: the court expressed its unanimous opinion that the two licenses which must cease to exist should be those of the York Hotel and Spencer Inn… [50]

Breweries

Brewing in King George's Sound was one of the earliest industries to gain some traction in the fledgling settlement. Given the easy access to spring water supply emanating from Mount Clarence that was of sufficient purity to suit the needs of those interested in pursuing brewery operations it was not surprising that several brewing companies began operating in Albany from the 1860s onwards. The earliest request for a license to brew at King George's Sound was made by John Ward in 1863. Ward had been able to purchase a failing flour mill operation that was then situated at the intersection of Earl, Short and Spencer Streets. This property was subsequently converted into a brewery by Ward who then applied for the necessary license to do so on 30th March 1868 for which he paid £10 for the privilege.

On 28th February 1871, Charles Gustavus Heinzmann also was granted a license to brew beer in Albany under the banner of the Southern Brewery Company. William Mumme had been an apprentice brewer in Hamburg Germany and fortuitously partnered with Gustav Heinzmann to begin this Albany brewing enterprise.[51] Mumme left shortly afterwards to take up a Perth business opportunity. The Southern Brewing Company continued to be operated by Heinzmann with John Ward (junior) as a brewer. This brewery was located at the intersection of York, Ulster and Middleton Roads, at the top end of town.

An article in *The Inquirer* of May 1879 was highly complementary of the beer that Heinzmann was brewing in Albany:

Colonial Beer
We have received from Mr Heinzmann a sample of his beer manufactured at his brewery at Albany… which compares favourably with the genuine article from the Stanley and Swan breweries.[52]

This enterprise was operating successfully according to *The Inquirer*, 14th May 1879 and in December 1881 it again commented on the quality of the product that was being produced in Albany:

Colonial Beer
Yesterday at the request of Mr Burke who represents Argents Albany Brewery, we sampled their product which would do credit to any part of Australia and was equal to any English beverage.[53]

The Southern Brewery Company, also trading as the Great Southern Brewery Company, operated throughout the period 1876 to 1905. James Meyers had been operating the Southern Brewery during the 1880s in partnership with William McKail and when the Southern Brewery amalgamated with the smaller

---

[49] *The Albany Advertiser.* 30th July 1921.
[50] Ibid.
[51] It is of interest note that Mumme subsequently moved to Perth as a brewer and became a partner of the Swan Brewery.
[52] *The Inquirer.* 14th May 1879.
[53] Ibid. 7th December 1881.

Crown Brewery operation in 1890 Meyers left to start his own brewery which he called the Lion Brewing Company.

Up until his departure from the company, there were various owners and partnerships associated with this company. James Meyers was involved in the company from 1883 and possibly one of the original lessees of the brewery property. Furthermore, in 1887 he was joined by McKail in a licence application. Nevertheless, in 1889 Meyers left the Southern Brewery Company to establish the Lion Brewery on the Perth Road and in that same year Heinzmann applied for and was granted the Southern Brewery licence that had now been vacated by Meyers.[54]

The *Australian Advertiser* of October in 1890 informed its readers of The Southern Brewery's transition into a Limited Company with several directors listed, including Christopher Heinzmann (Gustaf's son) and John Ward son of the first brewer who operated out of the old windmill. Ward was retained by the company more than likely due to his brewing knowledge.[55] Unfortunately, there was an acrimonious falling out among the directors of the company which led to some newspaper claims of issues relating to how the business operated.

James Meyers, who was a German immigrant, started the Lion Brewery on the Perth Road and later with his sons purchased the Southern Brewery and changed its name to Excelsior. Together they then built a new brewery plant along Middleton Road, and in 1906 the company's name was changed to the Albany Brewing Company. This company continued its operations until it closed on June 30th 1934.[56]

> THE
> SOUTHERN BREWERY COMPANY,
> LIMITED.
> YORK STREET & ULSTER ROAD,
> ALBANY.
> BREWERS & MANUFACTURERS
> BY STEAM POWER, OF
> Aerated Waters, Cordials, etc.
>
> JAMES MEYERS,
> THE LION BREWERY,
> PERTH ROAD, ALBANY,
>
> Having erected a very complete BREWERY AND AERATED WATER FACTORY and using only Prime Materials, is able to supply the best Ale, Stout and Aerated Waters in W.A.

Another brewery that was established in Albany between 1880 and 1881 was the Oriental Brewery. This was owned and operated by Bartholomew Argent and operated out of premises in Grey Street West (previously named Gordon Street). The Oriental was sold in 1890 and was purchased by Timothy Cullinane who changed the company's name to City Brewery and later the name was again changed to the Cambridge Brewery. The brewery was sold with Cullinane taking over the plant in 1897. John Ward (junior) continued the operation of this business until it closed operations in 1907.

Bakers

J.F.C. Greeve and Sons – the oldest reliable established bakery in Albany. Established in 1886.
Advertisement in the booklet, Alluring Albany.

In the later period of Nineteenth and early Twentieth Century there were reported a number of well-respected bakery's operating in Albany. The earliest reported bakery was that operated by Johann Ferdinand Christoff Greeve and Johann Muller. This bakery commenced operations out of a building situated in York

---

[54] For an extensive review of these early years of brewing in Albany refer to Spiller., G. *Tanglehead*. Published by the Albany Residency Museum 1999.
[55] The *Australian Advertiser*. Albany. 29th October 1890.
[56] The Albany Brewery was eventually purchased by a newly formed company Holland and Long whose main business was making cordial and aerated waters. It was later on sold to a partnership of Michael Bradly and James Clancy. The latter sold his share to Bradly's brother Bill. James Meyers junior was retained by the new company as a brewer.

Street in 1886. Diaries of visitors and the local newspaper indicate that this bakery was well regarded by both Albanians and visitors:

PREMIER BAKERY.

J. F. C. GREEVE & SONS
(Established 1886).
The Oldest Reliable Established Bakery in Albany.

We have the most Up-to-date Appliances and First-class tradesmen; therefore, we are able to supply nothing but the Best Goods.

Once Tried, always used—Satisfaction Guaranteed.

Our Carts deliver Bread and Small Goods to all parts of Albany at shortest possible notice. Wedding Cakes are decorated to suit any taste. Our small goods are the Cheapest in town— a glance at our windows will suffice.

Country Orders receive Our Strict and Prompt Attention.

If you are dissatisfied with your Baker, give us a trial, and you will be satisfied with your Baker.

Picnics and Other Parties Catered For.

Prices to Suit is Our Motto. A Trial Solicited.
Ring Up 'Phone 96 and you will get your Orders at once.

Malt and Milk Bread Every Day.

Approaching nearer we peep into the first window. This is filled with good things enough to make a thrifty housewife rejoice and suggests the ever-present Christmas cakes and puddings. But we are forgetting there is the realisation of our dreams in front of us in the shape of some delicious cakes, the production of Messrs. Greeve & Muller, confectioners and bakers. They are very tastefully iced with white icing, with the words "A Merry Xmas and a Happy New Year," in red across the top. These cakes are simply delicious in taste, and we are sure must be much appreciated by the good folk of Albany. But we have already lingered too long before one window, and must just take a glance at the next...[57]

The Greeve and Muller enterprise sourced flour from two locations. What was termed 'hard' wheat for the baking of bread was purchased from the Barossa Valley in South Australia while 'soft' wheat for the making of cakes was obtained from a flour mill in Katanning.

In 1887 an advertisement appeared in *The Albany Mail and King George's Sound Advertiser* indicating:[58]

Keen diarist Margaret Walpole made a passing remark relating to the fare for sale in the local bakery:

After breakfast, at which the Captain and the Harbour Master joined us, a little steam launch came puffing alongside to take us ashore and delighted at the thought of a ramble among the hills we were soon ready to start. The second mate, Mr Golding, the Miss Patersons, George [Dr George Walpole, formerly House Surgeon of the National Eye and Ear Infirmary, Dublin, practised his profession in Albany from his residence] and I made up a party and first of all, we went on an exploring expedition through the town. It is very small and oh, how small! No cabs or carriages or carts only, now and then, a butcher or baker's boy lazily cantering along on horse-back, basket on arm, lead us to remember that even here the ordinary everyday business of life was carried on...

During our excursion through the town, we found a little baker's shop and there were actually some penny tarts in the window; at once we went in and bought some and then we went off for our clamber up the hills.[59]

The arrival of a new baker's wagon in the town in 1889 was of particular interest to the town as this article from the local newspaper attests:

Yet another's Baker's Cart to be chronicled. The Bakers are always going in for new carts. This one is constructed by Mr H Permain and is a "thing of beauty" which we trust Mr Greeve, the happy proprietor, will find "a joy forever," or anyhow for as long as he uses a baker's cart. The peculiarities of its construction are first that it is fitted with a spring draught bar thereby easing the pull on the horse's shoulders. Second, it has an improved wheel lock, by means of which the driver by touching a handle locks the wheel thus doing away with the necessity of the old chain arrangement when the driver has to descend and leave his vehicle in the street. Third, the cart is hung on three springs, the rear one acting as a check on the others and avoiding a wobble when the trap jumps an Irish bridge or bad rut. The ventilation also, a great matter when carrying new hot bread, has well been looked after. Altogether, Mr Greeve conspicuous yellow conveyance promises to be a success.[60]

---

[57] *The Albany Mail and King George's Sound Advertiser.* 29th December 1886.
[58] Ibid. July 1887.
[59] Extracts from a typescript in the National Library of Australia of the original *Diary of Margaret Walpole* made in 1927. Published in Douglas R.G. Sellick. *First Impressions* Albany. Museum of Western Australia. Perth.
[60] Ibid. 22nd May 1889.

Greeve bought out Muller in 1889 and operated the bakery until November 1923 at which time the bakery site was leased to Edward Balston who later became Mayor of Albany. Issues with the lease resulted in the enterprise returning to Greeve in 1925 at which time it ceased operating as a bakery.

William John 'Jack' Day from South Australia, was an employee of Greeve and Muller:
He left South Australia the 14th July 1892 and as the local newspaper retrospective informed its readers:
> ...he sailed from Port Adelaide for Fremantle but on arrival of the steamer in Albany, Mr day was approached by the late Mr J.F.C. Greeve and offered the position of Forehand baker in his bakery, then the largest bakery in Western Australia outside the metropolitan area. After much consideration, Mr Day agreed to accept the job, and, taking his luggage, left the ship, and, agreeing to remain for twelve months... He is still here. [61]

Day left the Greeve and Son company to establish his own bakery with Charlie Phillips in December 1896. This business operated for a short time out of premises situated at the corner of Aberdeen and Grey Street with the oven located at the rear of the property. It then moved to a more prominent York Street frontage. The business continued to operate well into the Twentieth Century.[62] William 'Jack' Day also became a Mayor of Albany.

Transport

As far as Albany was concerned the world had changed significantly during the previous 100 years from Cantonment to a town ready to celebrate its centenary. The impact of global conflicts, particularly the threat of invasion and the influx of immigrants due to the gold rush saw a significant shift in the town's services in the later part of the Nineteenth Century.

Innovations in transport, exemplified by the establishment of the Great Southern Railway and the opening up of the Perth Road both made travel more accessible, albeit a still expensive proposition. Therefore, there remained a strong reliance on horse and cart and 'shanks pony' in the town.

As to be expected, there was a heavy reliance on horse-drawn carts for the portage of cargo along with the more sedate buggies and sulkies for everyday family use. Given the large amount of horse traffic in the town, several watering troughs were established along York Street and Stirling Terrace. A very insightful perspective of travel in and through the town was supplied by a local historian, Dennis Greeve:
> There were many horse-drawn carts and sulkies and even a four-wheel trap drawn by two horses. Most of these vehicles were owned by folk living along the King River Road. On a cold winter's day, you would be lucky to see a vehicle of any type in the Terrace. Customers entered these business houses through the back door, via Peel Place. The Terrace doors were kept closed.
>
> Owing to the number of horse-drawn vehicles in use, there were a number of watering locations for the horses to have a drink; known as Horse Troughs.
>
> Before the pumping station at Two Peoples Bay supplied Albany Town with water, the people relied on wells for their water and the horse troughs were located where water was close to the surface and each trough was built over a well and had a hand pump to draw the water up into the trough. When the water scheme was installed, the troughs were connected to it and the wells filled in. It was a requirement that Horses had to be shod; steel horseshoes nailed to their hoofs and the horse-drawn carts required their wheels rimmed with iron tires; a service provided by a Blacksmith. Albany had two Blacksmiths in the 30s; one located in a laneway next to the Royal George Hotel and another at the beginning of the old Perth Road.
>
> By the decade commencing 1920 onwards only those folk who were well off could afford to own a motorcar; therefore, motor vehicles were few and far between. The roads were poorly made right throughout the town. Stirling Terrace, York Street and odd sections of adjoining roads were the only sealed roads; the remainder were

---

[61] *The Albany Advertiser*. 6th July 1939.
[62] In 1950 the bakery passed to his son Lindsay Day who moved the enterprise to the newly formed area of Mount Lockyer at which time it was called Day Brothers Bakery. In 1987 it was sold to Tip Top Bakers.

gravel, and some were only sand. When I was 6 years old, I could count how many Albany folk owned cars with my fingers on both hands and my toes. There may have been 20 cars including two taxis, and I could add to that number with 4 motor trucks that transported goods into the town and two buses that carried people between Middleton Beach and the town.

The road to Perth had many miles of poorly made road and those who were brave enough to drive to Perth often bogged their vehicle in mud in the winter months and deep sand in the summer, making the trip a nightmare.

The train service to and from Perth provided the majority of country-folk the means of travel and the interstate shipping services provided for those travelling between the Eastern States and Western Australia. Because of these two means of transport, people arrived in Albany by train at the Railway Station or a ship at the Town Jetty and therefore Stirling Terrace being close to both arrivals, was at that time, the business centre of town; there was very little business carried out in York Street above Serpentine Road.[63]

The combination of excess runoff after a heavy rainfall and horse traffic often led to some amusing anecdotes being reported in the local newspapers. For example, as listed on the Municipal Council agenda, some correspondence was received and tabled concerning a local doctor:

From Dr Smith acknowledging communication from the Municipal Council warning him against jumping his horse over the drain in Stirling Terrace or riding along on the Municipal footpath and complaining that their order practically debarred him from using his horse: also asking for a bridge across the drain. A long discussion arose, and it was finally determined that a crossing should be at once made opposite Dr Smiths door and that eventually, when funds permit, that the whole drain be covered over.[64]

And another instance:

During the sitting of the local court on Thursday, an incident occurred which caused considerable amusement. While the Council were arguing some points of law, a buggy and pair of horses were seen from the windows of the Court House to dash down Stirling Terrace. As the runaway trap passed the corner everyone rushed out expecting to see a big smash. The public made for the door, the magistrates for one window and the lawyers for another. The dignity of the Court was completely upset by a runaway team, which appeared to have been perfectly satisfied with having gone so far and did not upset itself. Mr Roach was the driver, and he kept his horses well in hand, turned York Street corner very skilfully, and guided his team along Middleton Road, where the heavy sand soon bought them up. A serious accident might have been the result, but coolness and skill averted disaster, and at the same time taught a lesson to the horses, which are not likely to run away again.[65]

Unfortunately, as the town grew and its transport requirement by necessity also expanded there was an increase in cases of cruelty to animals highlighted regularly in the local press:

Cruelty to horses in Albany.
To the editor.

Sir,
Could not the SPCA or the police do something to prevent the cruel treatment of horses during the summer rush at Albany? At some sports recently two ponies were written [sic] with their sides bleeding from spur wounds… The police were requested by a lady to order the removal of the spurs, but they merely warned the boys that they were liable to prosecution. The same evening a cab-horse was driven until it could not go another step and passing the brewery it had to be taken out. Its distress was heartrending. Yet no one seems to know what action to take to bring those responsible to justice. Surely this was a case for police interference…[66]

And another letter along similar lines to The West Australian newspaper.

To the editor.

Sir,
I congratulate your correspondent upon drawing public notice to the need for the protection of animals, particularly horses at Albany…

---

[63] Private correspondence received from local Albany historian Dennis Greeve.
[64] *The Albany Mail and King George's Sound Advertiser.* 16th June 1888.
[65] Ibid. 17th July 1886.
[66] *The West Australian* 19th January 1912.

My attention was particular attracted to certain vehicles which conveyed pleasure seekers to and from one of the pleasure resorts. The horses were in poor condition and are obviously weary and the driver justice obviously in excellent practice with the whip. I made it my business on returning to Perth to personally interview the SPCA ….

My experience of this class of evil-doer who is so callous that he will drive a dumb, distressed creature to the last stage of exhaustion, is that mere remonstrance is wasted on him. The only effective argument is through the medium of the police court, and a magistrate fully alive to his duty, and the possibilities of the law in the way of punishment.[67]

First Aeroplanes to Grace Albany's Sky

In January 1919 a tiger moth, the first successful aeroplane venture to land in Albany had to use Middleton Beach as its runway. The pilot offered joyrides to residents, also entertaining the populous at large with some aerobatic manoeuvres. The excitement in this new form of travel captured the imagination of the town's inhabitants.

However, this was not the first aeroplane to grace the Albany's skies. There was a very keen local interest in aeronautics and a group of Albany businessmen were determined to develop their own plane unfortunately, as the newspaper reported, with very limited success:

Albany's First Aeroplane.

Spurred on by aerial progress in England and elsewhere, a number of local enthusiasts experimented with aircraft about the year 1912. In that year a machine built at Kalgoorlie earned considerable fame by flying to Perth. In 1913 Messrs Alex Fraser, Charles Leyton, and Bob Reynolds built an aeroplane at Albany.

The engine was a 24 HP three-cylinder Anzini, and the propeller was made by William Forsyth, a local built boat builder, now established at Fremantle. The frame was of Hickory, and, scorning superstition, the syndicate had it assembled at Mr Leightons undertaking and joinery shop. On its trial flight at the Albany racecourse, it crashed into a fence and broke off the carburettor. Not being daunted, the owners made the next attempt on the beach at the end of the town. This time the machine left the ground but came to grief in the sea. By this time the funds of the syndicate were getting low, so the machine was taken to bits, shared up and sold…[68]

In early February 1920 while on a visit to Albany with his aeroplane in tow Major Norman Brearley[69] conducted a number of aerial flights around the town which further stirred the public's interest. An article in *The Albany Advertiser* provided some insight into the way these flights were executed at this time:

The machine, one of the scout types used in the late war, was brought to Albany from Perth by train and assembled on the Ulster Road reserve, where arrangements had been made for garaging it. The flights for passengers were arranged to start from Middleton Beach, and a course at that place was made the principal rendezvous while a large number made Mount Clarence a vantage point. As it turned out the latter spot afforded the best view, as after landing on the beach it was found the sand was too soft and yielding to allow a satisfactory take-off, and recourse was made to the hard ground at Shelly Beach. Thus, the folk on the Mount saw the flights from the reserve to Middleton, fence to Shelly Beach and from there every trip of which there were 5 return home.[70]

A couple of days later Major Brearley offered to take local Albanians for joy rides over the town in his plane.

Major Brearly will carry out passenger flights this afternoon and tomorrow. Flying will commence at 2:30 pm on each day from the Town Beach, near the old loco sheds. This beach is within easy walking distance of the town, and those not wishing to walk and can catch a bus, which leaves the Church of England corner at 3 pm and 3:30 pm for 6p each way. All who have had the pleasure of viewing Albany from the clouds are loud in their praise of the scenery and surrounding country. Albany from the air is one of the most beautiful places in

---

[67] Ibid. 24th January 1912.
[68] *The Albany Advertiser.* 26th February 1929.
[69] Major Norman Brearley, DSO, MC.
[70] *The Albany Advertiser.* 4th February 1920.

> *the West, and those were thinking of flying should get in touch with Mr Cyril Pilley, Major Brearley's secretary, at the Royal George hotel.*[71]

Later that month the Governor of Western Australia, Sir Francis Newdegate visited Albany to review accommodation at the Government Cottage for the upcoming summer season and further, to ensure it was satisfactory in readiness for his wife Lady Newdegate in transit from England. While in Albany he was afforded an opportunity to participate in an aeroplane flight:

> *Sir Francis Newdegate first made the acquaintance of Albany in the course of a short spell ashore while passing through in a mail steamer 34 years ago. He was then impressed with the beauties of the place and came along today with pleasurable anticipations. His greatest hopes were, however, exceeded, for to use his own language, he has been privileged to exploit the attractions of the locality through the medium of three elements, earth, area and water. He arrived by train and spent the morning in company with Mr F. Palmer, Supervisor of Public Works, making an inspection of the Government Cottage in Grey Street. He filled in the time to lunch by motoring around Marine Drive and out to King River. Afterwards his Excellency became the guest of Major Brearley for a flight over the town. Sir Francis was motored to the beach at the Western end of the harbour, and there he was picked up by the aviator. Major Kerr Pearse ascended with his Excellency, and the party spent fully 20 minutes in the air, circling around the town and harbour and climbing out of sight well above the clouds which in part had obscured the sky. The landing was effected on the Ulster Road reserve. In coming to earth his excellently exclaimed: "That's ripping. I am sorry to come down." It was the first time either the governor or his aide-de-camp had been up in an aeroplane...*[72]

The Albany Baths

A consortium of businessmen formed the Albany Sea Bath Company in June of 1888. Initially there were five hundred £1 shares offered in the company. The Baths were to be situated on the eastern side of the town jetty and were began on 17th November 1888. Humphries was appointed the first lessee of the baths on 12th January 1889.

It was not long after the beginning of the first swimming season that attention was being drawn some behavioural issues that were becoming evident. *The Albany Mail* was the first newspaper to raise the issue of inappropriate social conduct at the baths:

> *We must draw attention of the Bath's lessee to the larrikinism that takes place in the Baths. The big boys duck the little ones, some of the little fellows being terribly frightened.*[73]

A few years later *The Australian Advertiser* also reported on a further complaint that:

> *Complaints again have been made of persons being allowed to bathe in the Albany Sea Baths in a nude state. The practice is very objectionable, as the bathers can be plainly seen from the jetty and should be stopped at once. One of the Sea Bathing Companies rules provides that men shall be clothed in a bathing costume. Who is to blame for the non-enforcement of this rule?*[74]

On 23rd November 1900 a feature article appeared in *The Albany Advertiser* that profiled the new lessee of the Baths, George Pazakos. The article indicated that he Pazakos had fully renovated the existing Baths structures and cleaned the facility to ensure that it was free from weeds. Separate hours for bathing were assigned for women only and the costs were threepence for adults and a penny for children.

Pazakos was, if his advertisements were to be believed, quite an exhibitionist in the art of swimming and diving, including one event where he ate a bunch of grapes while sitting underwater on an iron chair and table setting. He also operated a fresh seafood salon from the Baths. Previous to becoming the lessee of the Albany Sea Baths Pazakos had operated a store between the then White Hart and Royal Georges Hotels.

---

[71] Ibid. 7th February 1920.
[72] *The West Australian.* 21st February 1920.
[73]. *The Albany Mail.* 20th February 1889.
[74] *The Australian Advertiser.* 29th November 1895.

> *Albany Carnival.*
> *A swimming carnival was held under the auspices of the Albany athletic club, in the town baths, on Thursday, of last week. Mr G. Pasakos, the proprietor, financed the venture, which proved most successful in every way. A great novelty in the program was an exhibition of walking under the sea by Mr Pasakos who is an old diver. Armed with an iron bar, weighing 75 lb, he covered a distance of 190 feet and was one minute 39 seconds under the water.*[75]

The impact that a decline in shipping had on the Albany economy with the Port of Fremantle in full operation it was not surprising that the Municipal Council looked towards the tourism industry to alleviate some of the economic downturn being experienced in the town. In 1910, as part of an initiative to interest and hopefully accommodate potential visitors the Council made an offer to purchase the Albany Sea Baths venture and furthermore to construct tennis courts on the harbour front as well.

> *The Baths.*
> *The Mayor said that at the last ordinary meeting of the Council he and Mr Paton had been asked to interview Mr Dymes in regard to the Baths. The meeting has taken place and Mr Pazakos was present. Mr Pazakos had previously offered to sell his interest in the bath for £400 but at this interview he said he was prepared to take £300. Provided, however, the council undertook to keep him at seven years lease of the new bars at a rental of £100 per annum…*[76]

Nevertheless, an agreement on the sale could not be negotiated so the Municipal Council determined to construct its own Baths structure. In 1912 Albany could boast a new Municipal Council sea baths establishment. Furthermore, new tennis courts in the area were also developed in the vicinity. A range of amenities were on offer at the new Municipal Baths including a total of 34 bathing boxes, both meeting and café facilities, six enamel plunge baths (fresh hot and cold baths as well as seawater options). The original Albany Sea Baths were later sold by Pazakos in 1919 to Messrs Craigie and Blake, who had other commercial enterprises in the town. *The Albany Despatch* reported on a Municipal Council meeting at which time an agreement was reached to relocate and rejuvenate the Municipal Baths as part of a rebuilt town jetty Sea Bathing Company facility:

> *Reports.*
> *The parks, gardens and bars committee recommended that the Council accept the offer of the Sea Bathing Company (Ltd) as outlined in the letter of the 14/2/ 24. The Company offered their interest in the town jetty baths to the Council for the sum of £200, present lessees Messrs Craigie and Blake, to have a five-year lease of the new baths to be erected on the site of the town jetty baths, at a yearly rental list on £10 per annum of the capital outlay, but not to exceed £100 per annum.*[77]

In mid 1924 a resolution was taken by the Council to demolish the existing Municipal Baths and use the material from it to replenish the Albany Sea Baths structure.

> *The Municipal Baths.*
> *At the Town Council meeting on Monday evening last, the Baths Committee made the following recommendation: That the council be recommended to acquire the town jetty baths and reconstruct same, using old material from the Municipal baths, as suggested by Mr A. H. Jeffries. This was agreed to in the matter passed on to the finance committee, who will receive and estimate the expense and decide how the money is to be raised.*[78]

In 1951 it was reported in the local press that the Municipal Baths were in very poor condition. Consequently, the proposed swimming carnival for that year was in danger of being cancelled. Then in 1953 a strong gale had caused some damage to the facility:

---

[75] The Western Mail. 30th January 1904.
[76] *The Albany Advertiser.* 17th December 1910.
[77] *The Albany Despatch.* 28th February 1924.
[78] Ibid. 26th June 1924.

Gales Sweep State
Damage in Albany

A strong gale which swept the southern portion of the State during the week-end, did much minor damage in Albany. …

A trail of damage around the town marked the violence of the wind. Mostly the damage was minor, but in a few cases heavy loss was caused.

The south wall of the Municipal Baths enclosure was blown down when it caught the full fury of the south-west wind. Nearby electric poles on the jetty were blown down and live wires created a hazard till cleared up by linesmen.[79]

The following year the baths were demolished.

Albany Chamber of Commerce

A preliminary meeting of interested Albany businessmen was held in February 1892 to determine the feasibility and general interest in forming an Albany Chamber of Commerce. Among the attendees at the meeting there was acceptance of the idea subject to further exploration of a possible charter and a determination of what could eventually be the organisation objectives. A further meeting of the interested parties chaired by the Mayor; John McKenzie was held on 17th November 1892. The creation Albany Chamber of Commerce was formalised 11 days later on the 28th November 1892 in the Town Hall. The first meeting was again chaired by McKenzie until office bearers were elected.

A selection of advertisements from 1892 gives a perspective of the diversity of commercial interests in Albany at the time of the formation of the Albany Chamber of Commerce.

WILLIAM P. KINSELLA,
DENTIST,
GORDON STREET, ALBANY.
Artificial Dentures of the Best Material. Satisfaction guaranteed.
CONSULTATIONS FREE.

P. H. W. JOHNSON & CO.,
PHARMACEUTICAL and DISPENSING CHEMISTS,
ALBANY, W.A.
Prescriptions carefully dispensed with the purest Drugs and Chemicals. Sundries of all descriptions kept in Stock.
Special Preparations.
Cherry Cough Syrup, 2s. 6d.
Dysentery and Diarrhœa Drops, 2s.

KANGAROO SKINS.
WM. MOFFLIN & CO.,
YORK STREET, ALBANY, W.A.
AND AT FREMANTLE, LONDON, SYDNEY, MELBOURNE and ADELAIDE.
ARE PURCHASERS OF
KANGAROO, SHEEP AND WALLABY SKINS.
HIDES, HORSEHAIR, WOOL, GUM, ETC., ETC.
HIGHEST CASH PRICES GIVEN.
LIBERAL ADVANCES MADE.
W. D. MILLS, MANAGER.

"**JESSIE**," STEAM LAUNCH,
T. PLACE, PROPRIETOR.
Plies regularly between Mail Steamers and Jetty carrying
PASSENGERS AND LUGGAGE.
The "JESSIE" may be hired for Pleasure Trips when not otherwise engaged.

JOHN E. ANGOVE,
Stationer, Music Seller, News Agent, Fancy Repository.
Agent for Madam Weigel's Dress, etc. Patterns.
Native Curios, Views of Albany, Perth, Fremantle and West Australian Aboriginals.
ARGYLE BUILDINGS, Near Post Office,
STIRLING TERRACE, ALBANY.

DREW, ROBINSON & CO.
IMPORTERS, GENERAL MERCHANTS.
AGENTS FOR
The Imperial Fire Insurance Company.   Commercial Union Assurance Company, Limited.   Dunn & Co's Eclipse Roller Flour.   Burford's Signal Soap.
Buyers of Sandalwood, Kangaroo Skins and Produce.
ADVANCES MADE ON WOOL.
STIRLING TERRACE,
DREW, ROBINSON & CO.

---

[79] *The Albany Advertiser.* 19th May 1953.

The Albany Brothel Incident

As the Nineteenth Century was coming to an end Albany's development with a Victorian society paradigm in terms of acceptable customs and conventions were clearly highlighted in respect to the community backlash concerning the operation of a brothel in Spencer Street. At the council meeting held in January 1898 the following item was addressed in respect to a perceived public nuisance:

A letter was read from Mr H. Monaghan notifying that a deputation would wait on the Council asking them to remove a horrible and disgusting evil that existed on Spencer Road, namely, two houses occupied by Japanese for the practice of prostitution, causing an annoyance to the whole neighbourhood, and being detrimental to property holders in that part of the town.

The Town Clerk read also a petition from 21 residents couched in the same terms.
Mr Doig asked the Council to use their influence to put a stop to the nuisance complained of. It was, he said, dangerous after dark, for women or children to pass the neighbourhood where the homes complained of were situated.

Mr J. Kendrick said that on four occasions he had complained to the police of the nuisance. He regretted to say that a constable in plainclothes and visited the houses and enquired as to the terms, showing that they knew the character of the houses, and should have shifted the occupants. There were frequent rows in the houses complained of, and only recently a party of four had a quarrel and fought with billets of wood and knives…

Cr. Layton thought that it was the duty of the council to meet the wishes of the petitioners by all means in their power and if necessary to pay pass by law at once…[80]

Two months later the actions of the Municipal Council of Albany were able to achieve the desired outcome:

Colonial Secretary's Office,
Perth, March 10 1898.
His Excellency the Governor and Executive Council has been pleased to confirm the following By-Law made by the Council of the Municipality of Albany.
G. F. Elliot,
Acting Undersecretary.

Municipality of Albany.
By Law number. 24.
For suppressing the keeping of homes of ill fame within the Municipality of Albany.
Any person acting as proprietor, keeper, one having the control or management, or any person being the occupier of any brothel within the Municipality of Albany shall upon conviction, forfeit and pay a penalty not exceeding £20…
The foregoing By-Law was duly made and passed by the Council of the Municipality of the Albany this first day of February 1898.
W.G. Knight,
Mayor[81]

Nevertheless, in the end the by-law was not necessary as the local newspaper was able to report that the perceived nuisances had already left the colony:

Objectional Residents.
Sub-Inspector Lemon wrote stating that the Japanese, whose conduct had been recently placed before the notice of the Council had left the colony. [82]

Les Johnson, a local historian indicated that in 1896 there were some prostitutes plying their trade which included:

---

[80] Ibid. 6th January 1898.
[81] Ibid. 19th March 1898.
[82] Ibid. 3rd February 1898.

> *One lady of more than usually ill fame thanks to her all but unmentionable letting down of the White Australia principle by satisfying the needs of large parties of Chinese workers during daylight hours in a house of Spencer Street.*[83]

Garden (1977) relates a case of a young girl, the illegitimate niece of a local woman whose services as a prostitute were offered to all and sundry. She was subsequently rescued from this 'fate' by a family called Dunn and removed to a Porongurup farm that they owned for her well-being, much to her aunt's disgust who exclaimed that she was being deprived of a valuable source of income by this action[84] However, according to Garden this was not an isolated incident as the town was served by a number of women in similar circumstances.[85]

According to police records during the Nineteenth-Century prostitution was more a contained inhouse operation in the town than the very visible and quite tolerated Kalgoorlie experiences.

A similar but unfortunate issue that created quite a scandal in 1911 involved the visit of two ladies who were visitors to the town. On the advice of a visiting police officer the licensee of the White Star Hotel Charles Reddin was talked into refusing accommodation to two women en route from Fremantle to Melbourne travelling on the coastal steamer run. The policeman who raised the issue in question was holidaying in Albany and indicated to Reddin that judging from the attire that the ladies were wearing at the time that they had "*come from one of the low houses in Perth, and consequently they were no good.*" The girls were also refused lodging at the Weld Arms Hotel on the same advice from the policeman. They subsequently took their grievances to both the newspapers and to lawyers. *The Sunday Times* reported:

> *The case is certainly one calling for inquiry at the hands of the attorney general and the chief Commissioner of police. Even if the girls were what the police alleged against them… They ought not to have been treated in the way they were.*[86]

Albany Zoo

Hidden among the newspaper archives relating to Albany was an item concerning a little-known entertainment activity in the town around the turn of the century in the form of a zoo. The zoo was in reality a seasonal activity that involved animals from a circus being rested in Albany between travelling commitments. A feature article in *The Albany Advertiser* titled "Thirty Years Ago" provided insight into this little known aside:

> *How many Albany people remember the time when Albany had its zoo? The occasion was when the Fitzgerald Brother's circus animals were kept in Albany between the seasons. For a time, they were on exhibition either in the grounds or adjacent to the Weld Arms Hotel, of which Mr Jimmy Fowles was the licensee. Subsequently the animals were transferred to a farm behind Mount Melville and there were put through their daily exercise by their trainers.*[87]

Chinese Market Gardens

Although Albany census data of the time failed to identify the number of Chinese residents in the settlement during its first hundred years of existence, it is understood that a number were employed on both the boats and also as domestic servants. Chinese labour began to appear in the colony at around the mid 1840's. However, with the onset of the Coolgardie and Kalgoorlie Goldrush in the 1890's there was a steady influx of Chinese immigration into the town. Some like Ah Sam were well known and well respected for their market garden produce and general expertise:

> *Lands Around Albany*
> *Millbrook*
> *By Our Special Reporter*

---

[83] Johnson, L. *Love Thy Land*. Shire of Albany. 1982.
[84] Record of the event as reported in Donald Garden. *Albany: Panorama of the Sound*. Nelson. 1977.
[85] Ibid.
[86] "An Albany scandal: respectable girls classed as undesirables." *Sunday Times*. 17th December 1911.
[87] *The Albany Advertiser*. 23rd January 1930.

When a few weeks ago I visited the King River district I had no time to reach Millbrook, one of the oldest places in the district. I was besides more interested in seeing what the new settlers were doing. For years I had heard of Millbrook as one of the show places at the district to be visited, especially in the fruit season. My visit to Millbrook has well repaid me for it has shown what can be achieved with fruit in this district.

The name Millbrook comes from a stream of that name which runs all the year round. There are several selections now upon this brook and they are likely to be more. The most important of them is that of Mr Neuwman ... The place, Millbrook, lives about half a mile beyond Mr Neuwman's farm and it has been established for over 22 years. The first owners were Mr H.E. Warburton and said Thomas Campbell who established there a sawmill for Jarrah which was driven by a mill race down from the brook... I found Millbrook lying in the valley through which the brook was running strongly.

It seemed at first a large Homestead with a number of buildings of wood about it on the grassy bank of the stream, but most of the buildings I afterwards found were the remains of the old sawmill... The tenant of Millbrook is Ah Sam and excellent representative of the Flowery Land. For eight years Ah Sam has rented the place from Mr Warburton, but last year it was purchased by Mrs Patterson, of the Freemason's hotel who will enter into possession when Ah Sam's lease expires. It is understood that Ah Sam has made money at Millbrook, when you ask him the question, he shakes his head gleefully and says, "no money". However, he has recently brought his wife out from China and his son would have come to but for the recently passed law as to alien immigration...

He is the one Chinaman in the district for who everyone has a good word, and have a vote of the local people had been taken as to whether Ah Sam should have his son as well as his wife the vote, I believe would have been unanimous in his favour...

When Ah Sam took on Millbrook, I suppose there were few Europeans who cared to live in the wilds and earn a living off the soil. It is different now. There are plenty of people who are ready to tackle not merely established farms but to enter upon land presenting every difficulty to the Pioneer. Prior to coming to Albany Ah Sam was seven years at Fremantle... During the eight years he has been at Millbrook, Ah Sam has apparently done very well, and it is said the place, though there is only about 6 acres under cultivation, yields a profit of about £600 per annum...[88]

However, not all market gardens were viewed in the same light as Ah Sam's Millbrook venture. A letter published in *The Albany Advertiser* in 1896 was highly critical of an in-town Chinese market garden enterprise that was operating opposite the Town Hall in York Street at the time:

The Editor
Albany Advertiser

Sir,
Will you allow me space to expose a public nuisance in York Street, nearly opposite the Town Hall. The stench from the Chinaman's garden there is enough to cause a pestilence and it must be very unpleasant for the people living in that locality. I have heard several person's passing remarks on the same subject and asking if the nuisance cannot be abated.
Daniel Fitzgerald.[89]

Gold Find

With the gold find in the Eastern States in 1852 and later in several Western Australian regions it is not surprising that there was some general excitement throughout the colony seeking the next big strike.

The Western Australian gold rush began with the first discovery of gold in the late 1880s. News of the gold spread as fast and soon prospectors were arriving to try their hand at seeking their fortune. In Western Australia the most significant finds of the late Nineteenth Century were at Halls Creek in 1885, which

---

[88] Ibid. 15th September 1898.
[89] Ibid. 1896.

triggered the Kimberley gold rush; Southern Cross in 1887, which began the Yilgarn gold rush; Cue in 1891, resulting in the Murchison gold rush; Coolgardie in 1892 and then Kalgoorlie in 1893. As the finds grew and word spread about the riches being discovered an increase in population soon followed, many entering the state through the port of Albany.

It is not surprising, that initially Albany also had a period of fame in respect to a gold find when a possible early discovery of the metal was found in nearby Kendenup. In 1872 on the back of some less significant gold finds in Western Australia John Hassell, claimed that traces of gold were found on his Kendenup Estate and as a consequence he floated a company, The Standard Gold Mining Company.

While the samples that were initially assayed yielded some favourable initial returns, nonetheless, when machinery was erected at the site not enough gold was recovered to pay for the ongoing working of the mine. According to the 1890 edition of *The Albany Guide and Handbook of Western Australia* this was probably due to large aspects of the quartz recovered containing iron pyrites or alternatively not sufficient care being taken to ascertain in which portion of the reef the gold occurred. The guide was very optimistic however, indicating that:

> *The reef itself and many more in the neighbourhood are a very promising character, and there is not the slightest doubt they will be for long be again tested.*[90]

Nevertheless, the gold that was discovered by Hassell at his Kendenup farm in band of quartz that continued to be of insufficient quantity to make the endeavour worthwhile. Consequently, interest in his find petered out quite soon afterwards.

There was some initial newspaper reporting on the find, however, the Albany correspondent for *The Fremantle Herald* reported:

> *I don't know whether the report of finding gold down here has caused much excitement in the city and port, but down here numbers have got the yellow fever and are light-headed. It may not be uninteresting to trace the history of the report, which I trust will prove a reality. The first rumour of gold was raised by a man named Joe Foot, who, while digging a well for Mr G.T. Butcher, came upon some quartz, black and white. In the black quartz was found some shiny particles, which Joe at once pronounced to be gold. The specimens were shown round, and opinions – as is usual – differed. Some believed and other disbelieved. Joe, however, had firm faith in his find, and the sneers of those who declined to believe that "Cranky Joe" was the individual Providence would select to discover a gold-field and save the colony, did not shake his convictions or check his prospecting exertions and excursions.*
>
> *He was digging and delving everywhere, and loaded with specimens of every description of quartz, solicited all with whom he came in contact to examine and judge. Sooner or later luck comes to perseverance, and one day Joe had gone on board the P&O Steamer, where he met a person named Brown. Brown, I admit is common, but this Mr Brown was distinguished from the herd of common Browns by the sobriquet of Lucky Brown. Lucky Brown had been to the Victorian diggings, where his success had earned him the agreeable nickname applied to him, and he was no on his way to England to enjoy the fruits of his diligence and his luck. Lucky Brown saw Joe's specimens, and pronounced them to contain gold, made enquiries as to where they had been found, the quantity, and so forth, and declared had he had time he would have visited the spot from where they had been obtained. This favourable opinion given by such an authority as Lucky Brown, spurred Joe on to still greater exertions and produced a favourable opinion in the minds of others. A small quantity of quartz was at last sent to Victoria and the favourable report that was returned induced Joe to take out a digger's license and apply for the reward.*
>
> *So much for the first outbreak of gold fever. Now for the second. Notwithstanding that Joe's discovery was at first pooh-poohed, his subsequent slight luck in collecting specimens proved to cause muciferous excited interest and hope, and a sharp look out has been kept for any sign of gold-bearing quartz. The reef at Kendenup looked likely to turn out right, and Mr Hassell, the owner of Kendenup, sent away a small quantity to be tested and the result showed 1¼ oz to the ton. This news, so inexpressibly more favourable than the most sanguine dared hope for sent the good people of what you lively denizens of the Swan have been pleased to dub "Sleepy Hollow"*

---

[90] *The Albany Guide and Handbook of Western Australia.* Published by H. Pierssene, Albany. 1890.

half frantic with delight. A meeting was called to determine what was best to be done and how best to turn the discovery to account.

All things considered the prospects of this place are bright and encouraging in the extreme; and as the progress and prosperity of one part of the colony must benefit to a greater or less extent every other 'portion, you may join with us in our rejoicing that there is some sign of the "good time coming" and of the colony moving in the right direction this time.[91]

Interestingly later editions of the paper showed very little interest in the find:

Discovery of Gold at King George's Sound
From our own Correspondent

I have not much news to give you. Everything is very dull, notwithstanding the promising rumour of gold; but you know how long it takes to wake up an Albanian to anything beyond his own immediate interests.

…York Street is finished and is to be handed over to the Town Trust next week. This work reflects much credit on Mr Broomhall. I doubt much if anyone could improve on it. From all I hear, it is the best piece of road in the colony, and has been entirely under the direction and supervision of Mr Broomhall, who had to contend with and overcome many difficulties which a man not an engineer would have failed in.

Peter Rennison, a ticket-of-leave holder, was drowned on the 8th inst., in attempting to cross the Salt River. This is the only accident by the floods in this neighbourhood, although nearly the whole country has been under water from the heavy rainfall.[92]

Albany Woollen Mills

The concept of establishing a woollen mill in Western Australia was first proposed in 1920 after some strong advocacy from *The Albany Advertiser* and *The Albany Despatch* with both newspapers outlining the significant climatic, environmental and economic benefits of constructing a woollen mill in the town.

Albany Wool Scouring Works.
(By "Broke.")

Wool scouring works at Albany as suggested, is one move in the right direction which we. hope will yet be followed by another good move eventually that of manufacturing the wool into cloth. But while we persist in our determination to send the raw material away, it-is far better that we should scour the wool and save freights.

Our principal export of wool is in the greasy state, which contains a lot of dirt, that woolgrowers have always paid the shipping people for carting it away over the sea for them, and at the price of the freights and the dirt was dear but the Australian wool grower paid it.

Upon the wool's arrival at its destination, it had to be scoured. Consequently, we were not only paying freight for the cartage of dirt, but we have been consistently doing ourselves out of a job at home, as well as the grower out of more money…

The cost of wool, cost of transport for wool—and dirt, and cost of labour in England to scour and manufacture the wool, and the cost of transport back again to Australia, would assist materially in the forward movement for the establishment of our own woollen mills. Not only. would the woolgrowers gain, but the whole of the people of the State would benefit, and it would pay us (even' if we had to raise loan to do it) to bring the wool workers and their machinery out from England at the "expense of the State. Calculate the savings that would be effected all round and the money that would be kept in circulation in our own land.[93]

---

[91] The *Australian Town and Country Journal.* Sydney. 22nd November 1873.
[92] The *Inquirer and Commercial News*, Perth. 7th September 1870.
[93] The *Albany Despatch.* 29th January 1920.

In 1921 the Minister of Industry John Scadden who would later become the Premier of Western Australia announced that Albany had been chosen over competition from expressions of interested for the mill from Perth, Bunbury and Collie. The construction of the Albany Woollen Mills commenced in 1923 and they were opened in 1925.

[94]

Albany Woollen Mills.
The Only Establishment of Its Kind in the State.
To Albany falls the distinction of possessing the only Woollen Mill in the state of Western Australia. This is controlled by the West Australian Worsted and Woollen Mills Ltd and the chairman of the board of directors is Mr E. Lee Steere, a prominent figure in the pastoralists industry of the state. That Albany is proud of its mill, and appreciative of the excellent advertisement the town received thereby, goes without saying.

The mill was officially opened on February 5, 1925, by the State Governor Sir William Campion. Speaking on that occasion, the chairman of directors reviewed the initial efforts of the promoters, and declared that the scheme was launched not purely with the intention of making money, but because of the anomaly that although there were 40 or 50 mills in Australia, Western Australia could not claim possession of one…

A number of people desired the erection of the mills in the metropolitan area, but the promoters insisted on Albany as the site because the climate and other conditions were so suitable, and because of the claims of the centralisation… This state is a vast wool producer, and the establishment of the mill was a natural corollary of industry which is worth millions of pounds to the state annually.

The mills cover practically 2 acres of land and occupy and imposing site on the slopes to the south of Mount Melville… Many of the workers are locally born and have shown much aptitude for the work in which they are engaged.[95]

However, in 1926 just one year after the mill opened there were rumours that the whole enterprise was on the brink of closing. These rumours prompted the Chairman of Directors, Ernest Lee Steere to refute them in local newspapers maintaining the mill's ongoing viability. Nevertheless, the mill continued to make a loss for most of the early years. Unfortunately, the site chosen proved to be somewhat problematic as the noise and smoke that was emitted were constant problems for the town. Added to this issue the fact that the wool produced was too distant from markets also contributed to its effectiveness.

The Albany Woollen Mills continued to operate and gradually became a far more viable enterprise despite some lean times during the depression years. Disappointingly for Albany the woollen mills were placed into receivership in 1996 with the collapse of the Bell Resources Group which owned them at that time.

---

[94] Albany Woollen Mills 1919 photograph courtesy of Mark Saxton and Albany Historical Society.
[95] *Western Australia's Gem in a Granite Setting.* Albany Directory for Season 1928-1929.

Closing Remarks

In this work, it has been possible to only provide a sample of the many commercial interests that have evolved in the town due to space limitations. There is much to Albany's commercial development over the years leading up to its first Centenary Celebrations in 1927 that could have been included. There also have been several local business identities who have in their own way left a mark on the town, some of whom have gone on to accept Mayoral responsibilities over the years.

CHAPTER 18
BUILDINGS OF HISTORICAL SIGNIFICANCE

Overview

The early pioneer settlers to Albany were forced to initially construct their homes from whatever materials they were able to source within the locality of the Sound. It is not surprising that considerable ingenuity was shown in some of the building techniques employed during these early days of the settlement's existence. While some early settlers had the foresight to bring some building materials such as slate and prepared timber with them on their journey to Albany most others were forced to construct their homes using a rough timber framework, usually employing the local mahogany (jarrah) for this purpose and then filling the walls with branches plastered over with mud. This construction technique became known as wattle and daub.

By the end of 1827, the Cantonment included several buildings among which were the Commandants Residence, a simple hospital building, barracks and officer's quarters, a commissariat store as well as blacksmith and powder magazine facilities. Progress in the settlement was initially very slow due to the lack of a sufficiently large labour force and limited financial revenue. Consequently, the initial dwellings were small and rough built. With time and greater prosperity, stone and brick houses began to be constructed in the settlement. Over time a number of significant buildings were erected in Albany during the latter Nineteenth and early Twentieth Centuries.

The Octagonal "Chapel" – 1836 [1]

Albany's first "chapel" was built in a shape with octagon walls that were framed with jarrah and then covered over with wattle and daub.[2] The information available about the Octagon building to which this statement refers can be sourced from the private letters of several of the residents of Albany at the time. What can be ascertained is that the so-called Octagon "Chapel" or meeting place stood at the corner of Duke and Parade Streets and was built in 1835 through the philanthropy of a private citizen, Thomas Brooker Sherratt, a man of strong religious convictions and a prominent member of the then settlement. It was built as his "church" and 'bully pulpit'. It is reported that Sherratt with his own brand of religious fervour would preach in his "chapel" and was reluctant to let others do so unless they had gained special permission from him.[3] This situation changed with the arrival in town of The Church of England Archdeacon John Ramsden Wollaston who interestingly made only one entry in his journals about the Octagon "Chapel":

Hope to get up some plain singing at church (i.e., Octagon Chapel). All are musical in Perth but few here.[4]

The Octagon "Chapel" as a religious meeting place itself was not a great success, due in part to the later unsound mental state of its founder T.B. Sherratt and subsequently, it ceased operating as a chapel. The building was later demolished.

---

[1] The term Chapel is used here as this is a more correct usage of a non-consecrated place of worship. The Octagonal "Chapel" or meeting place had not been consecrated and so should not be referred to as a church.
[2] West, D.A.P. *The First Hundred Years. 1791-1891. Albany Advertiser.* 1932.
[3] Sketch of Octagonal Chapel from The Albany History Collection, Albany Town Library.
[4] Wollaston, J.R. *Wollaston's Albany Journals.* Vol 2. Perth. 1954.

The Church of St John the Apostle and Evangelist

Construction of St John's Anglican Church in York Street began in 1841 and took seven years to complete with finance for its construction raised through public subscription. The builders commissioned to undertake its construction were Gordon and Sinclair. On 8th July 1848, Archdeacon John Ramsden Wollaston became the Parish Priest even though the church was not fully completed at the time of his appointment. Wollaston was instrumental in overseeing the completion of the building. The granite stone used in the building was quarried from Mount Melville and Mount Clarence.

On the 25th October 1848, the Lord Bishop of Adelaide, the Right Reverend Augustus Short completed what was to be the first consecration of a church in Western Australia when he conducted the special service for that event at St John's.[5]

What became known as the Rectory (or Parsonage) was commenced a year later in 1849 and was able to be occupied by Archdeacon Wollaston by August 1850. A second story was built in 1880. The tower of St John's Church was added later in 1853 after Wollaston had received a government grant to help subsidise its construction.

Church of St Joseph - Roman Catholic Church and Convent

Although it was not the first Roman Catholic Church built in Albany, the current complex in Aberdeen Street was completed in 1878 and was officially opened on 28th April of that year. The foundation stone of the church was laid by Bishop Griver in 1877.

The convent building was subsequently opened in 1881. The first school borders were able to be enrolled and occupy the building from the 27th June of that year. Father Facundo Mateu was responsible for overseeing the construction of the church while it was the Sisters of the Order of the Apparition who superintended the construction of the convent and school.[6]

The sisters received a kind donation from Marie De Bourbon of a church bell in recognition of their assistance in nursing sick French sailors who had arrived at the Albany port during a typhoid epidemic. It was claimed that the bell was the largest in the colony of Western Australia at the time. Madam Bourbon had the bell inscribed:
> *'Manus Dominae Eductis Mae in Viam Australem.'*

Translated it says:
> *The hand of the Lord guided me to this southerly way.*

Government Cottage: "The Rocks"

One of the most impressive private dwellings in Albany is the old Government Cottage a building that is referred to locally as "The Rocks". It is located in Grey Street West on the south face of Mount Melville. The building has a commanding view of the harbour looking out over Princess Royal Harbour. It was originally built for the then Mayor of Albany William Grills Knight circa 1884.

---

[5] Sketch of the St John's Church by Joan Campbell and sourced from Albany History Collection, Town Library.
[6] Sketch of the Roman Catholic Church by E. Bracey and Joan Campbell and sourced from The Albany History Collection, Albany Town Library.

In 1913 the State Government purchased the property for use as a Vice-Regal summer residence for the Governor of Western Australia. During The Great War it was employed as a convalescent home for soldiers returning from service overseas.[7] After the war, it once again reverted to a Vice-Regal summer residence. Governors Sir William Campion, Sir William Ellison-McCartney and Sir Frances Newdegate availed themselves of its facilities during their respective tenures in office.[8]

The building was leased in 1937 to Miss Swan and Mrs Dawson for use as a residential college for girls and a co-educational school for day students. This school was named the "Park School". The building was later used as a boarding house for girls attending Albany High School. More recently has reverted to private ownership.

The Government Farm - Strawberry Hill

In 1827 the Cantonment's first area of land under cultivation became affectionately known as Strawberry Hill Farm. Originally it was referred to as The Government Farm, then later in its life it was simply referred to as the Old Farm. It was Captain Joseph Wakefield who initiated the first plantings of maize and some legume crops in an area that the farm would subsequently occupy. While the crop of maize initially failed, due mainly to poor ground preparation and a failure to understand southern hemisphere seasonal weather factors a start had at least been made to get an area within the settlement under cultivation.

When Lieutenant George Sleeman assumed the role of Commandant in 1829 after Captain Joseph Wakefield's departure the farm could boast close to 3 acres of land under cultivation. At this time the area was also supporting a small herd of sheep and cattle stock. It was late 1829 that the first significant vegetable crop from the farm was gathered for the Cantonment's use. In 1831 Captain Barker was to report that he was able to make a damper from the wheat that had been harvested at the farm.

A small cottage was later constructed on the farm in 1831 by the colony's first Resident Magistrate Dr Collie as accommodation for Governor Stirling and his wife Ellen for their vice-regal visit to the settlement. Nevertheless, on January 1st 1832, Governor Stirling ordered that the farm be either sold or leased. The farm allotment was eventually leased to John Lawrence Morley in June 1837. Unable to make his fortune with the British East India Company in India Morley had travelled to King George's Sound after first spending some time in the Swan River Colony. He had accepted a post as Assistant Commissariat Officer in the settlement. Morley retained the lease until 1833 when it was then on-leased to Sir Richard Spencer, the recently appointed Government Resident at King George's Sound.[9] It was subsequently purchased by him in 1834. Sir Richard Spencer then immediately set about refurbishing the farm buildings as well as introducing a variety of livestock to the area, including a flock of Merino sheep.

Like so many aspects of Albany's Historical Record, there is not a definitive attribution to the name Strawberry Hill for the farm. Dr Alexander Collie who had constructed the farm building in 1831 had remarked in a report to Governor Stirling that he had:
...*sent 100 strawberry plants* [to Perth] *and... I shall send many more.*[10]

It is in a report to the Lieutenant- Governor Captain James Stirling from Sir Richard that the first reference to Strawberry Hill Farm as an entity is attributed. He used the name in correspondence for the first time in early in 1833 and then again in November of that year at which time he indicated that he was:

---

[7] Sketch of The Rocks. The Albany History Collection, Albany Town Library.
[8] *The West Australian*. 1st July 1937.
[9] Chessell, G. *Richard Spencer*. University of Western Australia Press. 2005.
[10] *Alexander Collie Letters* (State Library of Western Australia).

"gathering a bushel of strawberries every day.[11]

From 1834 through to 1835, Sir Richard negotiated to have some further extensions made to the main farm house with a second story added to it. Furthermore, at this time several outbuildings were also constructed including some stables. Then in 1836 Spencer organised for a contract to be let for the supervision of the construction of a new more substantial residence for his family. The work was completed in December of that year.[12] For many years Strawberry Hill Farm occupied a significant place of honour within the town with many celebratory events held on the premises.

The Spencer family retained ownership of the farm until 1889 when after a period of significant neglect, it was finally purchased by architect Francis Bird for the sum of £1500. Bird immediately set about renovating the property and renamed it "The Old Farm". It remained in the Bird family until after the Second World War when it was sold in 1956 to the Albany Town Council for £2000 and they then transferred its ownership to the State Government and then later on to the National Trust thereafter.

Mechanics Institute and Town Library.

A new purpose-built Albany Mechanics Institute was completed in 1854. In its initial year of operation, the building was used during certain daytime hours as a school annexe. When the school was dismissed for the day, it reverted to both the town library and Municipal Offices.[13] Mr Thomas Matheson Palmer was the headmaster teacher at the school when it occupied this building. In 1857 the school annexe was relocated to Stirling Terrace to a building on the site of what would later become Albany's future courthouse. *The West Australian* newspaper provided a potted history of the institution:

The Albany Mechanics Institute was founded during 1852. At the public meeting in that year which brought it into being a collection towards the building fund realise some £20 (actually £27). At this meeting also the first office bearers were elected and comprised of men who in different spheres played a large and important part in the affairs of Albany of those days. They were president Lieutenant Grossmann, R.E.; deputy president G. E. E. Warburton; treasurer, the Venerable Archdeacon Wollaston; secretary and Arthur Trimmer. Pending the erection of a suitable building, the 'Octagon Chapel' was placed at the disposal of the Institute's committee by its owner, T.B. Sherratt. It was in this building that the Albany Mechanics Institute opened at a time when Albany only comprised some 50 buildings.

Later in 1853, the government of the day granted a block of land …. upon which the institutes building could be erected. In 1857 a portion of the building was used as a state school. By the year 1860 under the presidency of Captain John Hassell, it [the Institute] had attained a membership of 44 and a debt-free building. In 1866 the Institute was still functioning in a healthy manner, and on the recommendation of the Government resident Sir Alexander Campbell, the Government made a grant of £10 towards outbuilding improvements. When recommending the grant, the Government Resident wrote that a public reading room, furnished with newspapers and periodicals was open from 9 am to 9 pm…[14]

The Mechanics Institute continued to provide residents with a library facility that offered a selection of literature, magazines and newspapers along with access to the occasional lecture evening conducted on topics of local interest. The Great War had a significant impact on the membership of the Mechanics

---

[11] Chessell, G. *Richard Spencer.* University of Western Australia Press. 2005.
[12] The contract as let to William Diprose.
[13] Sketch of Mechanics Institute from The Albany History Collection, Albany Town Library.
[14] *The West Australian.* 17th December 1938.

Institute and in August 1916 both the building and its assets at that time were offered to the Albany Municipal Council. The offer was accepted and on March 1st 1917 the Albany Municipal Library was officially opened.

The Headmaster's House

The Headmaster's House located between York and Collie Streets was built circa 1880 as a private dwelling owned by John McKail. and before the purchase of 'The Rocks' as The Government Cottage, it occasionally doubled as the Governor's summer residence. The building was later acquired by the Education Department of Western Australia in 1902 for accommodation for the headmaster of the primary school that was situated at the corner of Collie and Serpentine Roads. Initially, the building was called Drew's house as it was previously inhabited by Charles Drew of the Drew, Robinson and Company. As the property was linked to McKail's merchandising firm which Drew had purchased in 1900 he also acquired the property as part of that business transaction.

The house was advertised for sale in *The Albany Advertiser* in 1901 and at this time it was purchased by the Government of the day and became the property of the Education Department of Western Australia. On 22nd October of that year a tender was issued to renovate the house[15]:

Tenders for Public-Works.
Albany P.W.A.D. Office
Harbour Master's Quarters. Albany School Master's Quarters.
Tenders for works will be received at the above office on Friday, October 25 1901, till noon.
The lowest or any tender not necessarily accepted.
By Order,
Francis Bird,
Inspector of Works

In 1978 a grant was obtained by the author to renovate the house and convert it into Education Department office accommodation and Resource Centre facilities. It fulfilled this role for about 40 years until it was acquired to be part of the Albany Campus of the University of Western Australia.

Commissariat Store/Her Majesty's Customs and Excise

Before the settlement of King George's Sound was transferred to the control of Governor Captain James Stirling in 1831 the Commissariat Store had been for the previous four and a half years occupied as a New South Wales Cantonment and controlled by Governor Ralph Darling from Sydney. The site of the first Albany HM Customs House was a location on the northern side of The Princess Royal Harbour bounded by a small promontory known as Residency Point. Following the transfer of the settlement to Governor Stirling's control the military guards, civilian staff and crown convict labour force returned to Sydney and were replaced by similar personnel except for the convict element from the Swan River Colony, Perth. Control of the settlement was vested in the newly appointed Government Resident and surgeon Alexander Collie.

The first ordinances regulating the duty on the sale by retail of spirits and fermented liquor in the new settlement were made in 1832. A month later, on June 9th regulations to impose certain duties on imported spiritual liquors were approved by the Government Resident. The Government Resident Collie purposed the first Commissariat Store as Albany's Customs and Excise warehouse in that year.

At the time of the appointment of Sir Richard Spencer the original Commissariat Store was found to be beyond repair and consequently, a trio of new buildings was planned by him for the growing settlement. Buildings to cater for a range of Government enterprises were constructed in what is now Lawley Park. They comprised a new Customs Office, a military barracks and a combined guardroom and hospital. This endeavour was such a significant undertaking that it was subsequently reported in *The Perth Gazette* of March 26th 1836:

---

[15] *The Albany Advertiser*. 22nd October 1901.

> *On Wednesday the ninth instant Lady and Miss Spencer laid the foundations of each of the new government buildings about to be erected in Albany under which were deposited medallions showing an excellent likeness to the present Majesties King William 1V and Queen Adelaide. On completion of the ceremony, three hearty cheers were given by the spectators amongst him with several offices of the HMS* Beagle *then anchored at Hanover Bay refitting.*[16]

At the time of the ceremony, Albany was served by McKenzie's Ship Inn, Sherrat's Family Inn and the Albany Hotel. Sir Richard appointed his eldest son, Hugh Seymour, as a wholesale merchant in the new Commissariat building.

Town Hall

Records indicate that a discussion on building the Town Hall commenced around 1875 but it was not until 1883 when a block of land was purchased and donated to the Municipality that discussions in earnest began for its construction. While in 1883 there was a perceived need for a Town Hall facility to service the community, the actual entity took some years to eventuate. Much of the success of the Municipal Council's endeavours in securing funding for the Town Hall venture can be attributed to the economic prosperity that had accompanied the Great Southern Railways construction, which further encouraged an increased investment and overall optimism in the town's future.

Once the funding had been secured the Town Hall venture still did not have a smooth gestation period. Issues relating to its proposed location in the town and difficulties obtaining suitable plans for the building dogged its early development phase. There were two sites favoured in the town for sighting the Town Hall, one overlooking Albany Harbour from Stirling Terrace, and the other at the top end of York Street.[17] While the past Resident Magistrate R.C. Loftie had moved for a site nearest Stirling Terrace and the new proposed railway station, the Mayor Counsellor William Grills Knight indicated that the Municipality had bought a site in York Street as the council intended to make this the principal Street of the town. His suggestion was widely applauded. Even though the specially convened public meeting held in May 1886 was tension-filled the York Street site was eventually determined for the Town Hall.[18] The meeting voted in favour of York Street 31 votes to 13.

The official commemoration of the laying of the foundation stone was well described in *The Albany Mail* of December 9th 1886 when the paper reported:
> *In accordance with the announcement that appeared in our issue of last Wednesday, the ceremony of laying the foundation stone of the Albany Town Hall by the Mayoress Mrs W. G. Knight took place at 3 o'clock on the site chosen for its direction, at the corner of Gordon (now Grey Street West) and York Streets.*[19]

The event was preceded at precisely 2 o'clock when a Bugle was blown sounding assembly and calling the Albany Defence Rifles to 'fall-in' for a parade. *The Albany Mail* reported the event in glowing terms:
> *A few minutes before the appointed hour numbers of Albanians could be seen winding their way in different directions to the building now in course of construction; a building which when finished will compete with any of its kind in similar districts of the Australian colonies.*[20]

A time capsule was placed into the cavity behind the foundation stone which contained several coins, a copy of The Albany Mail newspaper of the day and notice giving some of the details of the ceremony

---

[16] *Perth Gazette.* 26th March 1836.
[17] L. Johnson. *Heart of a Town.* Pamphlet. Undated.
[18] *The Albany Mail.* 8th May 1886.
[19] Ibid. 9th December 1886.
[20] L. Johnson. *Heart of a Town.*

including the name of the Mayor, the architects, the builders, Clerk of Works and Town Counsellors. It also acknowledged Queen Victoria in the 49th year of her reign.

The Albany Mail went on to describe how the Lady Mayoress, Mrs Knight, tapped the foundation stone with the handle of a ceremonial trowel three times in what was described as, "a first-class style" said:

> *I pronounce this stone to be well and truly laid. The Mayor then called for three hearty cheers for the contractors which was given a good style, the band playing 'old England still.*

Unfortunately, the actual opening of the Town Hall on June 1st 1888, was reported as being a very dreary day and the local newspaper indicated that the flag hung limply on the Town Hall's flagstaff saying:

> *It was loth to fly out, as she was ashamed of the weather.*[21]

The Clerk of Works, Mr Foreman, presented the keys to the hall to Mayor Knight, and the official party along with and those townsfolk who hadn't fled from the poor weather situation were "admitted at once for shelter" reported the newspaper. As to be expected, the opening of the Town Hall was well covered by the local newspaper:

Opening Ceremony.

> *Friday morning broke cold and wet, and the weather did not improve as the appointed time drew near for the opening ceremony. The decorative flags outside the building hung dark and listless, while the Union Jack clinging to its mast as if ashamed of the weather; it was loath to fly out. A considerable amount of delay occurred and getting things ready, and of course, any idea of a procession had to be abandoned. Mr Foreman, the Clerk of Works, gave the key to the building to the Mayor on the steps soon after 10 o'clock, and the public were admitted at once for shelter. A number of the ladies of Albany were then accommodated with seats on the stage at the end of the hall, where at about a quarter to 11 o'clock the Mayor and Counsellors also took their seats in front of the ladies. The acting Government Resident, Mr Hare the Hon. J.A. Wright, and Mr S. S. Young, Managing Director of the West Australian Land Company, also had seats in line with the counsellors. Shortly after these arrangements had been made the Mayor rose and read the following certificate from the Director of Public Works:*

> *... I do hereby grant to the Mayor of Albany this certificate to the effect that the Town Hall at Albany is properly constructed for use as a public building.*
> *Given under my hand at*
> *Albany this thirty-first day of May, eighteen hundred and eighty-eight.*
> *J. Arthur Wright.*
> *Director of Public Works.*[22]

The Mayor then took the opportunity to respond:

> *...the pleasing duty has been allotted to me to open the Albany Town Hall. I am proud, in response to the wishes of the council, to perform that ceremony.*[23]

The Governor of Western Australia was supposed to have performed this action but affairs of state prohibited his attendance at the event. However, he did send a message to the Mayor of Albany to be read out on this important occasion:

> *In expressing my regret at not being able to be present at the opening of your Town Hall, I wish to offer my heartiest congratulations to the Municipality and people of Albany on an occasion so important to the civil institutions and progress of the town. Pray read this telegram to the citizens and convey my best wishes for the health happiness and prosperity of all.*[24]

After the Town Hall was declared open there followed a banquet at 2 p.m. with more than 60 ladies and gentlemen in attendance. A ball that commenced at 9 pm completed the festivities. The evening event was up lit by both gaslight and candles and *The Albany Mail* newspaper tactfully reported:

> *Time will not allow us to note which looked the best, if such a thing were possible, for where are all are beautiful, who can profess to choose?*

---

[21] Ibid.
[22] *The Albany Mail and King George's Sound Advertiser.* 6th June 1888.
[23] Ibid.
[24] Ibid.

At this stage in its evolution, the Town Hall was still without a clock. Earlier on 20th April 1883, the Municipal Council had sought permission to auction off some land and use the proceeds from that sale for the purchase of a clock for the tower. [25] However, like other decisions relating to the Town Hall building processes the clock tower had been proposed sometime earlier but due to a lack of consensus among the Councillors as to the form it should take no progress on the idea had at this time eventuated. Eventually the tower to house the clock was completed and the clock for it was purchased from England from the firm of William Potts and Company and subsequently delivered to Albany on board the steamship *Nairnshire*. It was installed late in February 1891 with a formal ceremony starting the clock at 3 p.m. on 15th April.

Convict Depot and Goal

An old stone Gaol was built in 1836 was located at what is today, Lawley Park. As early as 1834 the settlers in Albany were asking for access to convict labour, but opinion in the colony was divided on the wisdom

of reintroducing convicts into the settlements. This position remained until it was realised that the labour force was required to better help establish the settlement. In 1851 Lieutenant William Crossman, Royal Engineer, bought the first gang of convict prisoners who were selected Ticket of Leave men, and they were immediately employed in initially building their own establishment, what was to become a convict hiring depot. Crossman who was stationed in Albany from 1852 to 1856 was responsible for the planning and construction of many of the town's public works including the Point King Lighthouse and the first bridges over the King and Kalgan Rivers.[26]

The Ticket of Leave convicts were drafted into work gangs and could be hired by settlers or employed on public works. A new location was determined for the Convict Hiring Depot, and it was subsequently built in 1851 and located at Point Frederick (at the corner of Stirling Terrace and Parade Street). The depot was briefly closed towards the end of 1855 because of the high demand most of the convicts were hired out to settlers. Furthermore, it was noted that the depot's continued running costs were making its operation less than profitable. Nevertheless, the depot reopened in January 1857. The maximum number of convicts at the one time in the community appears to have been in 1868 when there were 165 recorded.[27]

The building served as a Convict Hiring depot until 1868 at which time it was renovated with brick and consisted of 12 small cells and two rooms that were designated for the superintendent's quarters along with a general storeroom. An enclosed exercise courtyard that was built with high walls topped with broken glass to deter any planned escapes was included.

In 1868 Imperial convict transportation ceased and overtime numbers held in the depot greatly diminished with the building later being subsumed into a civic gaol. By the 1860s the small colonial gaol which was located at Lawley Park had become overcrowded and as a consequence, extensions were added to the convict gaol from 1872 to 1874 to accommodate these miscreants. In 1879 the Government Gaol closed

---

[25] Sketch of Town Hall and York Street from Mary Stuart Boyd. *Our Stolen Summer*. Blackwood Press 1900
[26] Sketch of the Convict Depot by E. Bracey and sourced from The Albany History Collection, Albany Town Library.
[27] Susanne Horton (Ed) *The History of the Albany Convict Goal, its Convicts, Gaolers and Warders*. Albany Historical Society. 2008

for good and in 1873 it became the civic or colonial gaol with warders in charge of prisoners. The convict hiring depot and settlement's early gaol is now a museum.

Cabman Shelter and Women's Refuge Built

There is an interesting background to the philanthropic provision of the Albany Cabman's Shelter that was built in 1909. As horse-drawn cabriolet services were for many inhabitants the only means of navigating in and around the town a special shelter arrangement was constructed at the corner of York Street and Stirling Terrace, which was then still the significant commercial end of town. The concept was to provide cab drivers with a place to shelter out of the weather whilst waiting for custom. The shelter was financed by a local businessman Frank. Dymes.[28] It was very popular and in 1926 the shelter facilities were expanded by public donation to accommodate a Women's Rest Centre as well:

> *The Women's Rest House, situated in Stirling Terrace West, is a lasting memorial to the social and charitable workers of Albany. The building was erected by public subscription, and cost in the vicinity of £1000. It is tastefully furnished and fitted and is much use by residents of the district when spending the day in town. The upkeep is derived from voluntary sources and social efforts. The caretaker is in attendance daily to assist visitors* [29]

The Residency

The original Commissariat Store that was located on what has now been termed Residency Point was later converted and further expanded into a domicile and offices for Government Residents and then later on for Resident Magistrates. During the period from the 1880s to the early 1900s, the Residency and its surrounding lawn and garden areas was an important focal point for community activities and social gatherings. It's fulfilled this role until 1953 at which time the building was used as a school boarding facility and later in 1975, it became a branch of the Western Australian Museum [Museum of the Great Southern].

Courthouse

The first government district constable was appointed to Albany was in 1836. However, as the population of the town grew, so did the need for a larger expanded police force. Consequently, by 1854 there were a total of seven in the police department at that time including a deputy superintendent, three mounted constables along with three native assistants.

Initially, the Convict Hiring Depot was used for the Albany Courthouse. From the late 1860s onwards, it operated from several locations in the town but primarily out of the recently constructed government offices that contained the Albany Post Office, HM Customs House and Bond Store structure on Stirling Terrace. Premises were rented for the police at this time as well and like the courthouse, facilities were considered unsatisfactory to meet the towns growing needs in respect to its law and order.

Extensive lobbying of the Government and the Legislative Council by the Chamber of Commerce eventually resulted in preliminary plans for a new building to be created. The site chosen was that occupied by the then Government School Building, soon to be redundant with new education facilities planned for

---

[28] Mr Frank Dymes was a local business-man and honorary United States of America Consul.
[29] *Western Australian Gem in a Granite Setting*. Season 1928-1929. Official Albany Directory.

Collie Street and Serpentine Road. The old school building was subsequently demolished and in 1896 the Public Works Department submitted final plans for the courthouse for Government approval.[30]

Of interest was the glowing description of the planned Courthouse structure provided to the general public:
> *The new courthouse and police station which it is intended to erect at Albany will be a somewhat pretentious structure and will be undoubtedly an ornament to the town. The building will face Stirling Street* [Terrace] *and will also have a frontage to a private thoroughfare at right angles to the street mentioned. The structure which will comprise two storeys will be built in a style savouring of the Romanesque. It will have a base of local granite, the rest of the building being a brick with cemented freeze. The scheme of the building provides for a well-appointed and commodious police station and various public offices on the ground floor, while the courtroom and attached rooms and offices are located on the first floor... The building will be roofed with a green Westmorland slate.*[31]

The local Public Works Officer Francis Bird supervised the construction of the Courthouse after tenders for the building were called in June 1896.[32]

The Chief Magistrate C. R. Loftie expressed "some disappointment" that the plans proposed did not include a goal facility which he claimed:
> *"was very much needed as I have frequently pointed out the last five years."*[33]

Existing lock-up facilities in the old gaol continued to be used for prisoner accommodation and it was not until the Public Works Department was charged with preparing plans for new lock up and quarters that were presented in May 1908, was there some action on the goal issue.[34]

The Albany Courthouse was officially opened on 7th February 1898 by the Acting Premier at that time who was Edward Horne Wittenoom. In opening the building, he remarked that it was:
> *...one of the best in the country and the people of Albany should be well satisfied with it. There were very few places in the colony that could boast better public buildings than the Albany Town Hall, Courthouse and Post Office.*[35]

Co-operative Society Building

The Albany merchants had held a monopoly on the trade-in foodstuffs and other essential items, including clothing and homewares during the early years of the settlement's growth. They were not shy in charging high prices for their imported products sold to the local inhabitants. This was a cause of general concern among the town's population, themselves barely managing in those early years of settlement to establish a firm financial foothold. The Albany Co-operative Store was an initiative aimed at breaking this merchant monopoly.

The Albany Co-operative Society was the first Co-operative society established in Western Australia, and one of the first in Australia. The building is associated with the P&O shipping company and was established by the local P&O agent William Clifton who sought to use a Co-operative facility for the benefit of the company's growing workforce. Under the inspiration of Clifton, a Co-operative store was open in the late 1860s, resulting from his concerns that employees were finding it difficult to get basic provisions in the town at a fair price. Existing town merchants were tending to charge high prices and make large profits from the merchandise that they imported from South Australia. They were selling these provisions in Albany to his employees at what he deemed to be at a prohibitive cost and his Co-operative initiative was designed to alleviate some of their financial burden accordingly.

---

[30] *Australian Advertiser*. 31st December 1896.
[31] *West Australian*. 25th May 1896.
[32] *Australian Advertiser*. 6th June 1896.
[33] Albany Courthouse Records, *State Records Office*, AN 17, ACC. Number. 346. In Albany Precinct Conservation Plan, Albany Town Library.
[34] Ibid.
[35] *The Albany Advertiser*. 8th February 1898.

The Albany Co-operative Society building was constructed in 1870, as a retail outlet and store that also included the manager's residence. It had moved to the newly constructed premises at the corner of Spencer and Frederick Street from its previous cottage location. [36]

Throughout the 1870s the Albany Co-operative Society's business was profitable, however, towards the end of that decade as business declined for the P&O Company's Albany operations and with manager Clifton's transfer, it was decided to downsize its operations. In 1885 the Co-operative Society ceased operations after the building was sold at auction to Alexander Moir who leased it to Edward Barnett from 1890. It became Barnett's Store for a short period before he moved his successful operations to a better location on Stirling Terrace.

Cottage Hospital

In 1886, after considerable agitation by the town's people Governor Broome acceded to a request to replace the existing, woefully inadequate hospital facilities that until this time had served Albany. The Albany Cottage Hospital was designed by the government architect George Temple Pool in 1887 however, the building was actually completed 9 years later in 1896 in Vancouver street. The hospital was primarily constructed of locally sourced granite and limestone. It replaced the rudimentary hospital facilities that had adjoined the barracks, guard room and commissariat store located in present-day Lawley park.

The Albany Cottage Hospital served as the Albany Hospital until 1962 when the first Albany Regional Hospital was constructed. After its use as a hospital, the building remained unoccupied for several years. In 1986 one hundred years after it was constructed it began its new life as Albany's Cultural Centre. Today it is named the Vancouver Arts Centre.

Matthew Cull House

Matthew Cull was originally employed on the wharf by the P&O company. He then left this employment to take on the role as The Verger at St John's Church in 1881, a position which he held until 1937. He had purchased an allotment of an acre block on Middleton Road next to Sir Alexander Cockburn-Campbell's property. Previously the land had been used as a market garden operated by Chinese Gardeners. He had selected the property because of the advantage it held in terms of soil fertility and an almost permanent water source near the house.

Initially, the house consisted of only two rooms with an external kitchen area. Over time Cull added to the house increasing bedroom and living area spaces to accommodate his large family needs. Eventually, he added a second story to the building.

Matthew Cull House.

Halfway along the road to Middleton Beach from the town of Albany is a quaint two-story house built by the late Matthew Cull, verger of St John's Church of England, Albany, for 56 years and also a foundation member and warden for 54 years of the Albany branch of the Manchester Unity Lodge. This house is unique as it was built entirely by Mr Cull himself. He was a good handyman, carpenter and bricklayer and tackled any job that came his way.[37]

Hillside House

Located in Cliff Street Albany, Hillside House was commissioned by Albert Young Hassell in 1886. He was the second son of a former Royal Navy Captain. Albert Young Hassell inherited his father's

---

[36] D. Bulbeck. (1969). The P & O Companies Establishment at King George's Sound 1850-1880 in Early Days. *Journal of the Royal Western Australian Historical Society*. Vol. V11, p. 105.
[37] *The Albany Advertiser*. 2nd October 1939.

Kendenup Estate in the late 1870s in 1878, he married Ethel Clifton who was the daughter of William Clifton, the P&O Agent for Albany. In August of 1886 an Adelaide architect Thomas English, of the English and Soward architectural firm, prepared the plans for Hillside Lodge.[38]

The Star of David insignia on the front gable of Hillside was placed there in deference to the Jewish origins of Ethel Hassell's mother. At the time the Hassell family moved into Hillside House they had five children. While occupying Hillside House Ethel Hassell conceived another five children, three of whom survived. The house was originally situated on four acres of land and comprised a complex that included several outbuildings. One of these was a small cottage occupied by Ah Kit, a Chinese shepherd originally employed at the Kendenup estate.

The Hassell family were prominent in politics and had a number of commercial enterprises in Albany and the wider community. Albert Hassell was a member of the local Roads Board, a Member of the Legislative Council [MLC] for Albany in the period 1871-74, the Member of the Legislative Assembly [MLA] for Plantagenet 1890-1904 and represented Western Australia at the Federal Convention 1897-8. He died in 1918 and Hillside House remained within the Hassell family until 1948.[39]

Pyrmont House

Pyrmont House was constructed in 1858 by Thomas Meadow Gilham a representative of the P&O Company and a prosperous merchant in the town. The name Pyrmont is thought to have been given to the house in honour of Queen Victoria's eighth son's wife's maiden name, she was Princess Helena of Waldeck and Pyrmont and was of German descent. The house was later sold to Robert Muir who became later the Mayor of Albany in 1891.

It was used as a private school from 1892 until 1898. Other owners of the property included George Hill a butcher and then Edward Barnett a local department store owner. In more recent years the house has undergone several significant iterations including a CWA Hall, a spare car parts store, reception centre and restaurant and currently as general office space.

Wollaston House

The house that now stands on the corner of Duke and Parade Street was originally constructed by the builder John Lawrence Morley. It was located on the shores of Princess Royal Harbour near Lawley Park. The house was named after Dr Henry Wollaston, the son of Archdeacon Wollaston. He had purchased the unfinished building from the estate of Morley who had drowned in a boating accident in King George's Sound when undertaking his duties as Harbourmaster.

Wollaston had purchased the original house built by Morley and had it dismantled and rebuilt at the foot of Parade Street. The property on which the building now stands was originally owned by the publican and businessman Diggory Sergeant Geake. It is purported that the block of land on which the house stands was transferred to Wollaston as payment for an outstanding medical debt.

After a time in private ownership, the house was for many years used as maternity home until it was sold into private hands in the 1920s.

Norman House

Norman House was originally the residence of George Cheyne who completed it circa 1858. Originally designed by Cheyne himself as his primary residence in Albany his departure from the town for England in 1860 left the house unoccupied until it was purchased by Captain John Hassell in 1865. The House was part of Hassell's estate and subsequently passed to the Dymes family as part of a family linked inheritance.

---

[38] Thomas English was Mayor of Adelaide in 1862.
[39] Heritage Council of Western Australia. Western Australian Government.
http://inherit.stateheritage.wa.gov.au/Public/Inventory/Details/fcfe7fea-cccd-4cd1-abcd-128d080a64f5

In later years Norman House was used as a hostel for boys attending Albany High School and was operated by the Methodist Church (Uniting Church today) and in 1962 the building was renamed for John Norman Jr. a Trustee of that church. Currently, the building is used for bed and breakfast accommodation.

Camfield House

Camfield House was built in 1852 for the then Government Resident Henry Camfield and his wife Anne on an allotment located at the corner of Serpentine Road and Crossman Streets on the northern side of Mount Melville. The house was later sold to a local merchant N.W. McKail in 1889 by Anne Camfield who had moved to Perth after her husband's death. However, in 1896 Father Mateu purchased it for the first iteration of a Christian Brothers College in the town. It is now privately owned.

The Mount

The Mount was at its time one of the most spectacular buildings in Albany. The house was built for William Clifton the Albany P&O agent and was constructed in 1867 six years after his arrival in the colony. When he left Albany in 1882 The Mount became a private hospital facility in 1899 with Dr Wardell-Johnson in attendance. Johnson was also one of the first qualified chemists in Albany. Later The Mount became a boarding house. Unfortunately, the building was bulldozed in 1976 to make way for the Albany RSL Stirling Club that now occupies the site.

Patrick Taylor Cottage

Patrick Taylor Cottage is of a typical wattle and daub construction. Originally it had a shingled roof that was later replaced by corrugated iron. The cottage as it stands today is a single storey residence. While the original building consisted of only two rooms under the main roof with a kitchen and veranda arrangement in an annexe, over time it was extended to include seven rooms. Then in 1846, it was further modified to form its current iteration of eleven rooms: an entry, dining room, bedroom, nursery, family room, sewing room, kitchen, laundry, box room, parlour and side veranda.[40]

The original building was constructed by John Laurence Morley a former employee of the British East India Company. Morley was for several years the Assistant Government Commissariat Officer a role he commenced in December 1831. A well-regarded builder Morley was also the builder of the nearby Wollaston House.[41] Morley sold the cottage to Patrick Taylor in 1835 for £400. When Taylor passed away in 1877 his wife Mary remained living in the building until she died in 1887. The property was inherited by Taylor's son and was still owned by the family in the 1950s.

---

[40] *The History of the Oldest Dwelling in Western Australia and Patrick Taylor*. Albany Historical Society Publication. 2019
[41] Sketch of the Patrick Taylor Cottage by E. Bracey and sourced from Albany History Collection, Albany Town Library.

Patrick Taylor Cottage is currently owned by the Albany Historical Society which uses it as a local interest museum.

A Snapshot of the Town From the 1840's to the Early 1900s.

An excellent Albany snapshot of key entrepreneurs is obtained from the 1936 memoirs of Captain James Sales who was for many years engaged in whaling and other maritime activities in Albany and along the South Coast in general. Extracts of his work include the following recollections:

Albany Along the Terrace Eighteen Forties to Early 1900s

I can best tell you about other residents of the town in those days by telling you something of the settlement and where the people lived... Mr Cheyne built a house where Miss Dynes now lives and that that house was the eastern extremity of the settlement. The next building in the Terrace to the west was the home of Mr James Dunn, a wooden structure. Mr Dunn kept a hotel and a store. The place immediately to the westward was Mr Alexander Moir's, who here kept a store. This was a better structure of two storeys. It was built of stone and stood about where the Royal George Hotel now is. The next place was a small lean-to wooden building in which Mr John McKail began a store. During the sixties, he built a store where the White Star Hotel now is, and in the seventies, he built another store where the National Bank now stands. Alongside this latter store of his, Mr McKail built a warehouse. Later Mr McKail was elected to the legislative assembly to represent Albany...

Further west along the terrace was a small building, a bakehouse, standing back from the street alignment. This was run by Mr Ward. Then came Captain Symer's house, a two-storey building. Four brothers... lived there. They were stock people and butchers... In the next place, a wooden structure, Captain Hassell, of Kendenup station, used to carry on butchering. He also built what we used to call Noah's Ark. Between Hassell's place and the corner of York Street and the Terrace, was a brick two-storey building owned by Mr Daniels. This was where part of the Freemason's Hotel now stands. Mr Daniels sold it to the government for Offices...

Later Mr John McKenzie acquired the property and kept a hotel there. The same block has retained the license ever since the early sixties. During the later seventies and the early eighties, nearly all the vacant spaces in the Terrace frontage were filled up. Mr John Moir's new store was built; the Argyle buildings were erected and the Royal George Hotel... Later came McKail's store, J. F. T. Hassell's store, Barnett's, Drew Robinsons and the Freemason's Hotel. At the corner of the Terrace and York Street, where the picture theatre now is, there was a store that belonged to Mr Stephen Knight, the first Postmaster at Albany. He operated the Post Office from his private house...

Further along the Terrace the recollections of Captain sale indicated:

Now we come to Sherratt's place. Old Captain Sherratt built extensive stone buildings, some two storeys, and kept merchandise acquired from American whalers. The Sherratt family consisted of 5 sons and two daughters. George Sherratt kept a hotel adjoining the residence on the beach. There were several other buildings further west, Mr John Robinson's, Mr Tom South's, Mr John Williams's, and a big boarding house called the Green House. Another building still further west was a stone structure built by Mr Lane who called it "The Sailors Rest."

I forgot to mention a very old house of the bungalow style erected by Mr Patrick Taylor sometime in the 40s between Mrs Cooper's house and Mr Geake's...

The greatest development of Albany took place in the last 60 years during which time buildings were pushed up York Street and along Brunswick Road and Middleton Beach Road. I remember a very old building erected in the 60s. It was a flour mill erected for a small company and the ingenious man who built it was Mr Metcalf. It was constructed with rushes and clay; the inside being plastered. The millstones were of granite. There was a small sawmill attached to it used mainly for the sawing of shingles. Later Mr Ward turns this place into a brewery. The beer they called "Tanglehead".

Mr Thomas Sherratt built a small octagonal building up near Davidson's house at the back of Mr Bradley shop. This was used for the courthouse, a church and an infant's school. There was proper seating accommodation at the back. There were two sets of stocks with armholes and leg holes. There they used to put men who miss conduct themselves and if we children did anything wrong, we used to be frightened by being threatened with being put in the stocks.[42]

Closing Remarks

With a Deep-Water jetty for shipping and the Great Southern Railway for transport Albany was thought to be looking forward to a prosperous future. Buildings were becoming more substantial and local amenities were enhancing the popularity of the town. In determining a permanent water supply the main difficulty that the Municipal Council had was predicting the probable increase in population in the future years.

A change in status in the town was bought about by the opening of the port of Fremantle and its now pre-eminent position as the gateway to Western Australia, along with the move of the Great Southern Railway workshops to Midland were significant impediments to the town's growth. The population almost halved at the turn of the century as townspeople tended to follow where there was the best chance of continued employment. This happened to be in the state's capital, Perth. Nevertheless, as the new century unfolded Albany was able to reinvent itself as a health resort and tourist destination.

---

[42] *West Australian.* 21st March 1936.

CHAPTER 19
CELEBRATIONS AND ENTERTAINMENT

Overview

It is important to place Albany's Historical Record for the first decades of the Twentieth Century within a global perspective.

The Twentieth Century commenced with the establishment of the Australian nation on 1st January 1901 when the six British colonies—New South Wales, Victoria, Queensland, South Australia, Western Australia and Tasmania formed the Commonwealth of Australia. The New Commonwealth Parliament was opened by the first Governor-General of Australia, Lord Hopetoun.[1] In that same year Queen Victoria died and was succeeded by her son as King Edward V11. On the scientific front, the Italian electrical engineer Guglielmo Marconi transmitted the first radio signals across the Atlantic Ocean and in 1903 the first powered and controlled flight of a heavier than air craft by the Wright Brothers at Kittyhawk North Carolina in the United States of America took place.

In 1905 Norway gained its independence from Sweden. The following year San Francisco in the United States of America was devastated by an earthquake and fire that killed over 3000 people.

1907 New Zealand became an independent Dominion within the British Empire. In 1910 Japan annexed the Korean Peninsula and in that same year China ended slavery. In April 1912 the 'unsinkable' passenger liner *Titanic* struck an iceberg off Grand Banks Newfoundland and sank on its maiden voyage across the Atlantic.

On the 28th of June 1914 the assassination of the heir to the Austrian throne triggered the start of Great War between the European powers of Germany, Austria-Hungry, and its allies and the Triple Entente which involved the British Empire, France, Russian, and their allies. In that same year Egypt and Cyprus were declared British Protectorates and the Panama Canal was opened between North and South America. In 1915 Italy joined the war against Germany and its allies, and Mahatma Gandhi returned to India to lead the non-violent resistance to British rule. Also, during 1915 the unsuccessful Gallipoli campaign involving a significant number of Australian and New Zealand troops unfolded across the Dardanelles Straight.

1916 in Europe saw the battles of Verdun, Jutland, and the Somme, which turned out to be some of the deadliest fighting of the Great War resulting in a significant loss of life. This was also the year in which Albert Einstein published his general theory of relativity.

The United States of America declared war on Germany, Hungry, and Austria in 1917 while in Russia Czar Nicholas 11 abdicated the throne. In October of that year the Bolsheviks seized power from the Provisional Russian Government. In 1918 the armistice was signed on 11th November to end the Great War and the Weimar Republic was established in Germany. The Treaty of Versailles, a peace agreement between the Allies and Germany was signed in 1919 resulting in territorial losses and significant other restrictions on the Weimar Republic.

1920 saw the League of Nations formed and the start of prohibition in United States of America resulting in widespread bootlegging operations being undertaken by the country's underworld. The Turkish Republic was founded by Kemal Ataturk in 1923.

In 1926 in the United States of America Robert Goddard launched the first liquid fuel rocket while in Scotland John Logie Baird an electrical engineer demonstrated the first workable television system.

---

[1] John Adrian Louis Hope, 1st Marquess of Linlithgow, 7th Earl of Hopetoun

Albany Week and The Albany Season.

> **Albany!!! Albany!!!**
> **Beautiful Albany!**
> The Health Resort of Australia.
> Where to spend the holidays! Spend them in
> the coolest summer climate in Australia.
> Summer heat from 70 to 80° in the shade.
>
> No hot winds. No hot nights. No mosquito pest.
> The Healthiest Town In Australia.
>
> **Attractions:** Magnificent scenery; Walks in the hills; the finest Marine Drive in Australia; Sea Bathing; Fishing; Trips by Launch or Buggy to Beautiful Picnic Resorts; Splendid Cycle Rides; Cycles and Boats for Hire.

Advertisement December 1898[2]

The mild weather characteristic of the summer months in Albany was referred to in the local press as the 'Albany Season'. Quite often the Governor and his entourage would move from Perth to the Governor's designated summer residence the Government Cottage later known colloquially as 'The Rocks'. His arrival always added to the Albany Season with a range of various events occupying the towns social calendar during his stay.

The Albany Season.

For twenty-one successive years the holiday fixture so long and favourably known as the Albany week, but now merged into the more ambitious season covering a period of four weeks, has been carried through by the residents of Albany. Started as it was to give residents living under less favourable climatic conditions in other parts of the state a respite from the arduous duties of everyday life, an opportunity to engage in a holiday at what is universally considered to be the premier watering place of the state, the movement has so grown in public favour that its recurrence is annually looked forward to by hundreds of regular patrons. Public men charged with the responsibilities of handling the State's affairs are glad to shelve their burdens for a brief period and join with the residents and others in participating in a round of popular outdoor sports and amusement. Said Mr Tucker, of the Y. A. L.: "Albany has the best tonic air in Australia. Appetisers are certainly not needed there. As compared with my experience with boys' camps in all parts of the Commonwealth, the food consumption at the January camp exceeded all others by twenty five percent."

The official opening of the season will take place at noon on Monday when his Excellency the Governor, Sir Harry Barron, K.C.M.G, C.V.O, will officiate. The opening will be preceded by civic reception tended to the Governor by the Mayor and Counsellors.
The Princess Royal Sailing Clubs annual regatta will be held on Monday and as the club has received good entries, including three boats from Perth, a fine day's sport in the harbour is assured. Golf will interest a great many of the visitors and the Middleton Beach golf links promise to be a centre of attraction or the week.

Social functions will engage attention on Wednesday, when the Mayoral at Home to the Governor will take place in the Town Hall, followed by children's plain and fancy-dress ball at night at which the Mayor and Mayoress will entertain the youthful population...[3]

A four-week period that was known as the Albany Season commenced during The Great War. The season had evolved from Albany Week, a calendar of festivities each year, itself a regular community celebration that was first mentioned in the colony's newspapers in 1892.

---

[2] *The Albany Advertiser.* 15th December 1898.
[3] Ibid. 31st January 1914.

Each year the minutes of the Albany Week planning committee were published in the local newspaper so that the community at large could understand what was contemplated in the way of activities for these celebrations:

The Albany Week.

Meeting of the executive committee appointed to make arrangements in connection with the proposed Albany week was, reports the local paper, held in the mayor's room on the 19th instant. They were present the mayor, Mr John McKenzie, the Hon J. A. Wright, MLC ... [et al.].

It was decided that the days of Tuesday, Friday and Saturday should be devoted to cricket and challenges to the Metropolitan Club would be sent forthwith. Mr Freeborn suggested the advisableness of making arrangements with the launch owners for marine excursions on the Monday of the Albany week. The suggestion was cordially received, as was also the proposition of Mr Keyser that the different Friendly Societies in Albany be asked to cooperate by holding their annual demonstration on the Tuesday.

Dr Robinson's proposition that the regatta committee be communicated with as the holding of rowing and swimming events on the Monday of Albany week was unanimously agreed to.

The Mayor informed the meeting that the council intended to welcome the Governor at the Town Hall on the morning of Monday.

Mr Wright suggested that a fireworks display be held on the Saturday of Albany week. The suggestion met with the approval of the meeting. Mr Freeborn suggested that a lawn tennis tournament we got up for the ladies with cordially approved off...
Suggestions were also discussed and entertained as to a rifle match and the secretary was instructed to communicate with the local volunteers as to a shooting contest at Albany in the Albany week.

Mr Wright said that the committee and people who had suggested Albany week which to work harmoniously with everybody in the town, and he felt sure that the cooperation and support of all citizens will be given quarterly to an invitation that would be for the best interests of colonists as a whole...[4]

The Albany Week celebration was indeed a very successful and well-patronised community event. It ran for 21 years until the outbreak of The Great War in 1914. Held in February each year Albany Week attracted many visitors from around the metropolitan area and other rural settings. As foreshadowed the week involved a calendar of several sporting and social events, including horse racing, sailing regatta's, swimming carnivals and assorted other competitions along with orchestral and social dance evenings and more often than not a Governor's Ball in the Town Hall.

The Albany Week
The program of festivities.
By Telegraph.
From our correspondent.

At the meeting of the general committee last night, the following program with adopted for the Albany Week: Monday - welcome to the Governor by the Town Council at noon. In the afternoon the Mayor will entertain all the children in the town to a picnic at the recreation ground. In the evening there will be an orchestral concert. Tuesday: the metropolitan cricketers will play the land companies team. There will be a united Friendly Societies gathering. A special launch will be charted to convey the Governor to the ground, where he will be presented with an illuminated address. In the evening the Governor will open the Presbyterian fancy fair in the Town Hall. Wednesday, the first day of the races: in the evening there will be a fancy fair. Thursday: the second day of the races. In the evening there will be a race ball in the Town Hall. On Friday there will be a cricket match, Metropolitan v Albany Club. There will also be a railway employees' demonstration on Saturday...[5]

After all the detailed planning, preparation and an agreed timetable of events Albany Week was conducted with much fanfare:

---

[4] *The Western Mail.* 22nd October 1892.
[5] Ibid. 31st December 1892.

Albany Week.

Albany week has become quite an institution, and during the seven days in February which each year are set apart for the festivities the usually quiet little town hardly knows itself. Bouts and parties, races, picnics, balls are indulged in, and thoroughly enjoyed, for Albany is supremely favoured in the matter of climate and anyone reading the weather reports will see that when Roebourne, Cue, Coolgardie, and Perth are sweltering in a temperature of considerably over 100° the maximum Albany ranges from 74° to 78°.

Letters from visitors there to their list favourite friends in Perth talk of thick dresses, and rain, and cold winds, things which the unfortunate Perthites have almost forgotten ever existed, and which are as difficult to believe in as the tiles which are bound among old travellers onboard a ship rolling heavily through the intense, unbearable heat of the Red Sea, of how last time they crossed that awful place they had to wear overcoats out into the cold weather they experienced.[6]

As an aside, it was interesting to note that newspaper reporting of Albany Week in 1893 provided significant insight into how some racial slurs were openly printed and were obviously seen as acceptable reporting practices by the population at large. For example, *The Western Mail* reporting of an instant at the 1893 Albany Week Turf Club events highlights the issue of racial insensitivity quite well:

The Albany Week
By Our Special Reporter
Albany, February 8

The races yesterday were not without amusing incidents. The clerk of the course had the usual number of dogs to run down, but towards the end of the afternoon a heathen Chinee [sic], who had evidently imbibed too muchee samshu [sic], got through the rails onto the course and refused to move on or off. He cared nothing for the official's formidable whip, and squared up to the clerk, and started punching the horses most vigorously. The clerk turned the business and his horse on to the aggressive Chinkee [sic] but the horse was altogether too pacific and would not kick worth a cent. Finally, a policeman came and removed the Chinkee... [7]

The newspapers of 1900 maintained an enthusiastic perspective in their reporting of the Albany Week festivities attributing much of the success of the event to the mild summer climates of the town:

The Visitors in The Week.

The Albanians, knowing the men are merriest when they are from home have for the last nine years held their annual week at the beginning of February, for at that time the town is filled with visitors, who, have nothing, in particular, to do, seize on any form of recreation which presents itself...

This year Albany was fuller than ever with visitors escaping from the heat of the other parts of the colony, and the committee of the week felt that, with a larger community, a thoroughly enjoyable time would be spent. They were right in their surmise as to the enjoyment, but it cannot but strike one with what indifference the visitors view these proceedings which are got up almost entirely for their amusement.[8]

As to be expected the Albany Season was well covered in the town's newspapers:

Albany Season.

The Albany season for 1917 was brought to a conclusion on Saturday, when the two chief attractions were the regatta and conclusion of the bowling clubs carnival. Despite the fact that the program of events has been much curtailed owing to the war the different functions have been well attended, while visitors have been given ample opportunity of seeing the various resorts provided around Albany.

Children's fancy dress ball.

The children's fancy dress ball, held in connection with Albany Season, took place in the Town Hall on Wednesday night, and proved to be a great success. Although not in such large numbers as previous years, the fancy costumes from a spectacular point were rich. During the evening the children were put through the grand

---

[6] Ibid.
[7] *The Western Mail.* 18th February 1893.
[8] Ibid. 17th February 1900.

march, under the direction of Mr Herbert Robinson, and the night was a picturesque one, the different manoeuvres being performed with credit to the children…[9]

Queens Victoria's Jubilee Celebration - 1897

Queen Victoria ascended to the throne of Great Britain in 1837 and in 1887 her reign of 50 years was commemorated throughout the British Empire and was celebrated as her Diamond Jubilee. The people of Albany marked the occasion in a number of ways, including the construction of a Rotunda in Stirling Terrace and the construction of The Queen's Gardens; the laying of the foundation stone for the new Albany Hospital and the planting of a trees, [the quite large tree located next to the Albany Library complex (previously the primary school yard) in York Street is an example], were just three such events undertaken by the town to commemorate this event. Notwithstanding these construction and planting elements to mark the commemoration, the people of Albany were very keen to celebrate the Queen's Jubilee in more a participatory style:

Jubilee Day at Albany, Western Australia.
The people of this important part of Australia are to be congratulated upon the enthusiasm displayed upon the occasion of the Queens Jubilee. Their manifestations of loyalty we are not excelled by any other Town in Australia. Both public officials and private individuals vied with each other in their determination to make the Jubilee celebrations successful…
The foundation stone of the new Albany Hospital was laid by the government president, in the presence of the leading inhabitants. The children were treated to many good things, amongst which was a find Jubilee pudding…[10]

The *Albany Mail and King George's Sound Advertiser* devoted much of its 25th June edition to a summary of the Queen's Jubilee celebrations:

The Queens Jubilee Celebration in Albany.
The weather has been so boisterous all the week that on Monday night the promise of a fine day for the Jubilee celebration appeared anything but hopeful. However, though cloudy and rather cold, no rain fell on Tuesday morning, and at 10 o'clock the children of the various schools in the town accompanied by their teachers were martialled at the courthouse; where the volunteers, commanded by Lieutenant Moir were also drawn up; Mr Loftie, the Government Resident, inspected the volunteers, and then the Mayor, after reading, handed him the following address, with the request that he would transmit it to his Excellency the governor to be forwarded – to her most glorious Majesty, Queen Victoria, Queen of Great Britain and Ireland, Empress of India &c.[11]

As to be expected there were many speeches delivered to mark this occasion which were also printed in the newspaper:

May it please your Majesty.
We, the Mayor and Counsellors, on behalf of the town of Albany and the district of Plantagenet, your Majesty's subjects in this distant part of your empire, beg to offer our humble, united, and earnest congratulations on the completion of the 50th year of your reign. We beg to assure your Majesty of the continued loyalty and devotion of your colonial subjects, and we humbly pray that your happy reign may be prolonged. We remain, with the profoundest veneration, your Majesty's most faithful subjects and dutiful servants.
Signed on behalf of the inhabitants of Albany.
W.G. Knight, Mayor.

In a few words the Government Resident expressed the pleasure he felt in performing the duty allotted to him and promised to forward the address as desired.
The Mayor then said: we have assembled today to celebrate her Majesty's Jubilee. We are proud of this opportunity of joining with our fellow colonists in celebrating that great festival, which the whole British nation throughout the Empire will be commemorating at this time. It is indeed a very rare festival that Queen Victoria is celebrating this year, as few monarchs have ever been permitted to reign half a century, but when we consider that in addition to this her Majesty, after so long reign, stands glorious, honoured, and beloved, the head of the

---

[9] *The Albany Advertiser.* 28th February 1917.
[10] *The Pictorial Australian.* Adelaide. 1st July 1887.
[11] *The Albany Mail and King Georges Sound Advertiser.* 25th June 1887.

largest empire the world has ever seen, and when we look back at the progress in peace, science and civilisation, that the British nation have made during her reign, we might well tender her our love and affection. May God Almighty grant her and her empire many, many years of peace, happiness, and prosperity, God bless our queen! I now ask you to get three hearty cheers for her Majesty...[12]

The *Albany Mail and King George's Sound Advertiser* continued its coverage:

As soon as the procession was formed it marched off up Stirling Terrace with the band playing, but the small legs of the younger children could hardly keep up at marching pace and the little one straggled considerably. About 350 started in the procession, but quite half as many more must have joined en route and there must have been at least 500 at the end of the match, which led along Stirling Terrace up York Street to the corner of the Town Hall, and so by Gordon and Duke Street then to the recreation ground. On arriving on the grounds some time was taken up in distributing the medals to the children, which was occupied by the public principally watching the volunteers, who completed business with pleasure by having a little marching drill. The Aborigines in the meantime were being taken care of by Mr Loftie who distributed a government present of cake and tobacco to each of them...[13]

As the celebrations wound down after a number of athletic and other sporting events had been conducted, the local newspaper then provided a summary of the day's celebrations:

...The consolation race, prize a rifle, was won by Martin. This finished one of the most successful days sports ever held in Albany. The weather was perfect, and all the proceedings went off without a hitch or dispute, and with the greatest harmony. If some of the events are not up to first-class time, we must remember the shortness of the period allowed for preparation, and no one had received any training. The Sports Committee worked manfully the whole day, and though the last few events had to be slightly hurried to save daylight, the programme was successfully carried out. A great deal of the success of the meeting was due to Mr Kelly, of the railway, who is an excellent member of any committee, and we hope to see is name often figure on them on future occasions. To the credit of Albany, let it be said that not a single unpleasantness or accident marred the two days enjoyment and a clean file at the police station recorded that two days of really "A1" amusement could be rationally enjoyed by a thousand men without the assistance of a police force.

In the evening at nine o'clock, the second night of the Jubilee Ball, the Court House was again well filled with dancers, and a pleasant termination was made of the festivities.

The music in the ball-room was excellent as it always is, when Messrs. Permain and Hartland are the musicians, and Mr Kelly made an admirable M.C. On the whole then, thought there have been many grander celebrations of Her Majesty's Jubilee throughout the world, we may claim that none have had a more satisfactory and all round pleasanter one than has been enjoyed in Albany.[14]

First Agricultural Show - 1889

Founded in 1889, this community organised event takes place annually in mid-November.
The West Australian indicated that apart from being one of the State's longest running country shows, the Albany Agricultural Society has been seen as setting a standard in organisation and innovation. In the March, 1890 edition, it provided a wonderful glimpse into that year's Albany Agricultural and Horticultural Society show:

Albany, March 14.
The great event of the week has been the agricultural and horticultural show, which has been a great success both in quantity and quality of the exhibits. Notwithstanding that an exhibitor from the capital brought a formidable array of fruit to compete against that growing in the district, it was credible and satisfactory that the most successful prize taken was Mr George Warburton, of the Gordon River. This gentleman's show of apples was particularly good, and his grapes were well flavoured as well as good looking as any that I have tasted grown in the colony. The care shown in the selection of Mr Warburton's exhibits and in the manner of their carriage

---

[12] Ibid.
[13] Ibid.
[14] *The Albany Mail and King George's Sound Advertiser.* 25th June 1887.

from the Gordon was most marked from the condition in which the various fruits appeared on the table after the long journey, the bloom on the grapes and plums as perfect as if they only been just picked from the trees.

Mr W Sounness upheld his reputation as a potato grower by the exhibition of some magnificent specimens, and in fact nearly all the fruit and vegetable showing would have received owner in any exhibition of a similar character held for a much larger district.

... The indefatigable secretary of the Agricultural and Horticultural Society must have been perfectly satisfied with the interest shown by Albanians in the exhibition, and he is to be congratulated on the excellent arrangement of the exhibits and the entire success of the whole of the proceedings.

"It has readily adapted to meet the changing needs of the community and to ensure the show remains relevant to the rural sector and the local community."[15]

Cinemas

King's Pictures

Kings Pictures began operating from the Town Hall in 1908 and ran four nights a week; Monday, Tuesday, Thursday and Saturday presenting as the newspaper advertising indicated:

Programs of extraordinary brilliance, charm and variety.

The proprietors of the King's Pictures were Passmore and Alan, and as this was the era of silent films the musical director was Otto W. Berliner who accompanied the silent films by providing them with a musical soundtrack.[16] King's Pictures ran for four years until 1912 until Empire Pictures opened in purpose-built premises in York Street.

Empire Theatre

Empire Pictures began screening regularly at the Princess Pavilion in 1906. This venue was also later used as a skating rink. In 1911, the theatre was managed through Perth by Thomas Coombe who announced his company's intention to build in Albany the state's first purpose-built cinema in a rural area which would be called the Empire Theatre. The buildings were constructed in 1912. As a young patron of the movies Dennis Greeve recollects the magic of these theatres:

There were two movie theatres in York Street, the Regent and the Empire. The Regent was beautifully appointed with the entrance lobby lined with marble. Saturday matinee for the youngsters was held in the Empire Theatre with a six-penny entrance fee. Short films made up the first part of the program followed by an interval of ten minutes then the main film was shown. Pass out tickets weren't issued at the interval period and although it was dishonest, we youngsters would sneak in and find an unoccupied seat. The theatre owner was aware of this, but there were so many youngsters in the 30s who could not afford six pennies and he turned a blind eye to it.[17]

---

[15] *The West Australian.* 19th of March, 1890.
[16] L. Johnson. *Heart of a Town.* Pamphlet.
[17] Private Correspondence with Local Albany Historian Dennis Greeve.

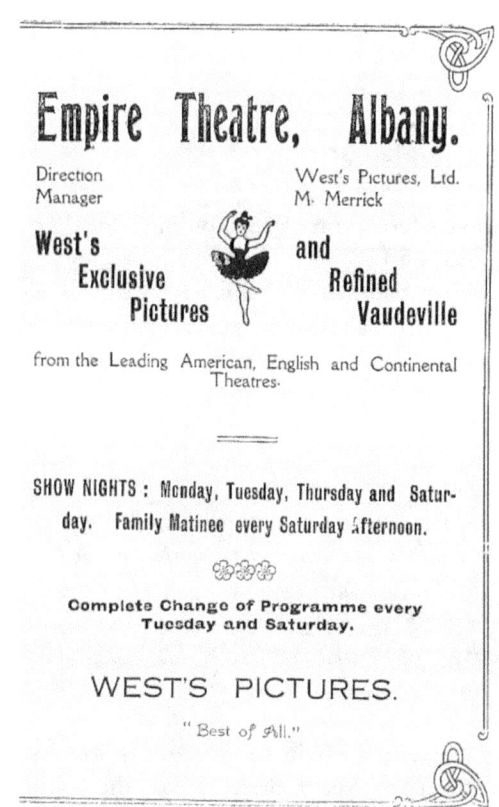

The Empire Theatre opened on 31st October 1912 and closed on 25th September 1963 with "Hatari!" the last film it screened. It was later used as a skating rink, a youth amusement centre, a live theatre, and then a nightclub. The theatre building now houses a number of commercial outlets. *The Albany Advertiser* often would help promote movie nights in the town:

A special programme has been arranged for in-night, when a benefit will be tendered to the Returned Soldiers' Association, the whole of the proceeds being donated to their furnishing fund. Two pictures, will, be screened, titled, "The Hillcrest Mystery," from the pen of Irene Castle, and "Naulakha," which features Antonio Moreno and Helen Chadwick. "The Hillcrest Mystery" is an exciting story of German espionage and intrigue, and the picture abounds in tense situations. "Naulakha" is a dramatisation of Rudyard Kipling's famous story, and in the touch of the impossibility of the East and West meeting in harmony is amply exemplified. A strong love pervades the picture, and it has abundance of plot material. The principal feature on to-morrow night's bill is "The Claim", which presents Miss Edith Stoney. A second is entitled "Her Good Name," while the "Australian Gazette," has an educational subject, and two comedies are also included.[18]

Besides the regular film events a number of community celebrations also were conducted in the spacious Empire theatre auditorium:

Royal Naval Concert at the Empire Theatre - 1919

The Queen Carnival funds benefited to a very large extent as the result of the entertainment given by the [visiting] members of the Royal Australian Navy at the Empire Theatre on Monday night. This is the second occasion on which this talented concert party has materially assisted the movement and the latest effort eclipsed anything of the kind yet held in Albany. Long before the hour appointed for starting crowds thronged the Empire Theatre and shortly after 7.30 only those patrons who had taken the precaution to reserve their seats were able to gain admission. Hundreds had to be turned away. Prior to the performance the ship's band rendered several selections outside. The programme submitted was a varied one and opened with a series of lantern sketches by one of the crew. Company songs, ragtime, solos, sketches, comic and sentimental songs, illustrated recitations, dances and band selections followed, almost every performer being recalled, with the result that it was close upon midnight before the audience dispersed. The whole performance terminated with the tableau, "Sons of the Empire" and a grand chorus. The accompaniments were played by Miss Bray and Mr. B. J. Griffiths. During the evening Mr. H. Robinson thanked the officers of the ship and the members of the company for the great assistance they had rendered during their stay in Albany.[19]

Regent Theatre

The Regent Theatre (Lambert's Pictures) opened inside the former St Alban's Buildings on York Street, just south of the intersection of Frederick Street on 5th February 1925. The Regent Theatre was closed and demolished in September 1969 and is now the site of Albany's **Totalisator Agency Board** Premises.

The building was designed along modern lines, with a seating capacity in excess of 1000 persons.

---

[18] *The Albany Advertiser,* 8th January 1919.
[19] *The West Australian,* 7th February 1916.

Entrance to the stalls was through doors on each side of a marble stairway leading to the dress circle. A landing half-way up the stairway served as a lounge for circle patrons. Designed essentially as a picture house, the theatre was fitted with a large stage, that allowed for the presentation of vaudeville turns.[20]

Albany Town and the Federation Issue

Australia's road to Federation was not a simple one with the first referendum of 1898 on the issue defeated with New South Wales voting against union. After the initial false start and with Queensland voting on the matter for the first time the second referendum held in 1899 on Federation was carried in the Eastern Colonies albeit without Western Australia's participation. There was much heated debate within the colony where there was dogged opposition from the Government members to the proposition of union with the other colonies, to the chagrin of the Eastern Colonies as was evidenced by the sarcastic and often caustic comments published in their newspapers:

Westralia's Hesitation.
From the Sydney Bulletin.
Westralia has referred the Federal question to a select committee of Parliament, with instructions to doze over it till not later than September 5. After that it will present the results of its deep sleep to Parliament, and Parliament will act or otherwise. There is no attempt on the part of the old sandgroping element, which still controls the Legislature that forms only a small portion of the community, to disguise the fact that it is against union. It doesn't like new things; it doesn't like to be disturbed; it loves to lie and sleep away the long languid days in the sun....[21]

A number of reasons were proffered by the Government for Western Australia's reluctance to join in the Federation of Colonies. A rapid growth in the colony's population and wealth derived from the goldrush in Coolgardie and Kalgoorlie along with a strengthening in agricultural production at a time when the Eastern colonies were experiencing an economic depression concerned Western Australia' parliamentary leadership, which maintained that the colony's economic and political power would be weakened if it agreed to join the union.

Consequently, the Government of Sir John Forrest delayed Western Australia's decision about Federation. The views of his Government were not widely shared outside of the Perth-Bunbury Coastal fringe with communities around the eastern goldfields and the port of Albany, expressing a strong inclination towards Federation believing that their regional interests would be better protected through a national union. The Federal League an organisation that was created to foster a Federation agenda was well supported in Albany and the Goldfields. In Western Australia, there were increasing tensions because of the different opinions and political indecision:

Federation.
Mr Leake to speak in Albany.
The joint secretaries of the Albany branch of the federal league received the following telegram from Mr Leake, yesterday: Can speak on Federation on Saturday. Can you arrange meeting. Asked Mayor to preside. Principal subject, Federation…
The Albany Advertiser. 17 August 1899.

The large increase in the general population brought about by the goldrush in Coolgardie and Kalgoorlie had a significant social and political impact on Western Australia and most significantly on Albany. The influx of prospectors and ancillary personnel to the colony were very much at odds with the perceived isolationist orientation of the Western Australian Government that was seen as dragging its heels in the move towards Federation. Consequently, with a sense of frustration towards the attitudes of those in government towards Federation a petition was organised and sent to Queen Victoria asking to separate the goldfields region from the rest of Western Australia the intention of which was to create a new state that would then become part of the new Commonwealth.

---

[20] *The Albany Advertiser.* 3rd September 1924.
[21] *The Albany Advertiser.* 17th August 1899.

Separation Movement.
Albany Branch.
Petition to the Queen.
To the Queen's Most Excellent Majesty.

We, your Majesty's most loyal and dutiful subjects residing in that portion of the Colony of Western Australia lying within the following boundaries… humbly approach your Majesty with every assurance of our loyalty and devotion to Your Majesty's Crown and Person and humbly entreating Your Majesties gracious consideration to this our petition.

The boundaries of the territory we desire to separate from Western Australia embrace about 8, 360, 000 acres, of which 75 per cent is most suitable for general agricultural purposes, with an estimated population of 5500.

1. We are unanimously in favour of adopting the Federal Constitution Bill recently passed by the other five Colonies of Australia.

2. The Government and Parliament of this Colony have refused to allow the said Commonwealth Bill to be submitted to the vote of the people.

3. A petition to Your Majesty is now being prepared by the inhabitants of this colony residing on the Eastern Goldfields, praying Your Majesty to grant them separation with Responsible Government, and we earnestly desire to be included in the territory of the proposed new Colony.

4. No constitutional method of carrying into effect our desire for Federation is open to us, other than the one for which we now humbly pray.

5. Your petitioners humbly submit that the Port of Albany, which is within the boundaries of the territory they propose shall be separated from Western Australia, as it is an important strategic position, both for Australia and the Empire at large, as shown by the fact that its present defences have been provided for by Your Majesty's Imperial and Colonial Governments, and that it is desirable in the interests of the Empire, and especially of Australasia, that it should be within the boundaries of Federal Australia, and its defences under the control of the Federal Navy and Military authorities.

We, therefore, humbly pray that Your Majesty may be pleased to include the territory within the boundaries here in before defined in the proposed new colony, with all the rights, privileges and responsibilities of Self-Government…[22]

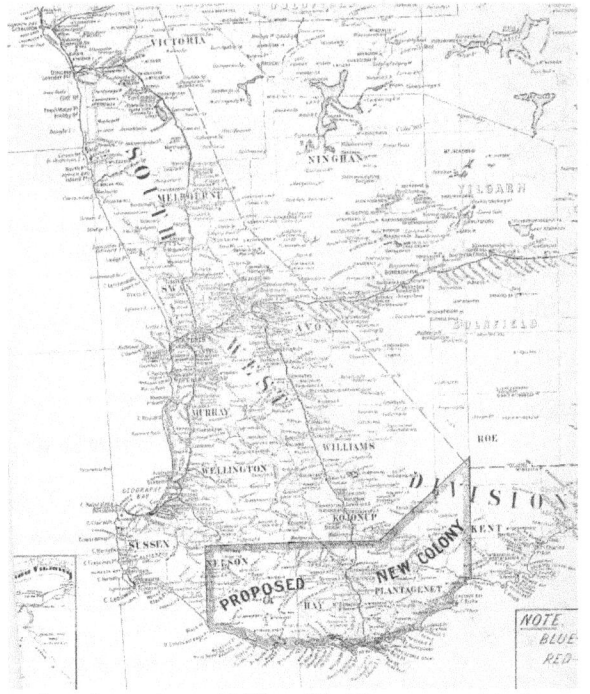

This action forced the then Premier of Western Australia Sir John Forrest to allow a referendum on the issue of Federation.

West Australian Separation League.
Albany Manifesto.
Add a public meeting held in Albany Townhall on Wednesday, January 3, 1900, resolutions in favour of separation for Federation were unanimously adopted and a committee of representative men was appointed to organise a lead to carry out that object. The committee has failed several meetings in this place itself in communication with the Goldfields separation league.[23]

The subsequent referendum was held in July 1900 and resulted in Western Australia accepting Federation. The issue of Federation had been dominated political discussions during the 1890's. The concept of all the Australian colonies becoming a Federated unit gained particular traction throughout 1897 to 98. However, with the separation movement underway on the goldfields with the intention of severing that region from the rest of the state the Forrest Government had to accept that the union of all colonies was inevitable especially after the July 1900 referendum was carried.

---

[22] *The Albany Advertiser.* 13th February 1900.
[23] Ibid. 15th February 1900.

Declaration of the poll.
The poll was declared in the lower Townhall which proved totally inadequate to accommodate the large crowd of electors who had gathered outside. When the door was open the scramble took place for the best positions in the room which was soon occupied. After returning Officer had declared the poll as above loud cherry and groans followed.[24]

It's interesting that the Albany District was very strongly in favour of Federation and had also supported the actions of those in the goldfields towards union.

The Advertiser.
Editorial.
Thursday, August 2, 1900.
The people of Western Australia have shown by their votes on the Commonwealth Bill that they are as ready for nationhood, for a wider political horizon and for higher ideals as were the people in the Eastern Colonies. They have been ready to step into line with the other colonies at any time during the past two years, but our peculiar political condition, in which the minority of the electors held absolute power through their representatives, held back the people. These constituencies, which are represented chiefly by supporters of the Government, have almost without exception cast a majority against Federation. When one comes to look at the returns it is easy to see how it happened that after declaring for Federation Sir John Forrest found it expedient to trim his sales. Had he not so trimmed he would've been cast out of power, and it is the Premiers aim to retain power, as he believes the Colony would go to wreck if he left office.

Among the towns in the coastal districts Albany heads the list of the Federal strongholds as we expected she would… The people on the whole ignored parliament altogether in their decision… It is a great victory for the Federal League and indeed for every consistent and ardent Federalist… In the press the Advertiser is the only newspaper in the coastal districts which has consistently, in season and out of season, advocated that this colony should enter the union, while on the Goldfields newspapers were all for Federation…

We are all Australians now, members of the newest and the most vigourous nation in the world; and nation of which much is expected. Nothing in the history of the world is more creditable than the peaceful and harmonious way in which the six colonies have come together in order that they might be the stronger for defence, the stronger to aid the mother country, and the better able to use and develop the resources of a great territory.[25]

As can be imagined the importance of the establishment of the Commonwealth of Australia was a most significant milestone in the nation's history. The commemorations that would be held to mark the event on the 1st January 1901 drew widespread British Empire participation with contingents of troops from all corners of the Empire asked to participate. A representative contingent from India arrived in Albany on its way to Melbourne for the Federation celebrations:

Indian Troops.

Arrival at Albany.
A representative contingent.
The steamer **Dalhousie** *of the Royal Indian Marine Service, with Indian troops on board for the Commonwealth celebrations, called in this morning for coal… The ship is manned by natives, who, by way of uniform, wear dark blue loose blouses and pyjamas, the latter being Indian terms for various forms of native leg dress… The native troops on board number exactly 100, half being native commissioned officers and the other half native non-commissioned officers.*

There are no privates. The request made by the Imperial Government to the Indian authorities was that 500 troops should be sent, but in view of the absence of many of the native regiments on active service in South Africa and China, the Viceroy decided on sending only 100. The troops selected authority representative of the different castes of natives throughout the whole of India, and all have seen service. They are physically fine a lot of men. The officers in charge are English, viz; Commanding Officer, Lieutenant-Colonel LS Peyton, 14th Bengal Lancers…

---

[24] Ibid. 4th August 1900.
[25] Ibid. 2nd August 1900.

Although the number of troops is limited to 100, there are in all 180 Indian natives on board, the 80 comprising the servants of the offices. They all came ashore at Albany. They bought with them live sheep, and first proceeded to the pilot station, where the animals were killed according to the rights of the different castes. The servants were then left behind to cook the meat, while the Offices and non-coms proceeded to the town. They strolled around and manifested great interest in all they saw... The majority wore khaki blouses with knee breeches, and either gaiters or puttees...

The steamer left Bombay on November 23rd and had a pleasant voyage. Captain Pifford came ashore and exchanged the usual courtesies with local officials.[26]

Celebrating British Empire Day

The first celebration of Empire Day occurred on May 24th 1904 but was limited to those living in the British Isles. Its history was outlined in an article that ran in *The Albany Advertiser*:

> *...Before proceeding further it may not be out of place to re-capitulate the history of Empire Day. As a very new institution there is a possibility that it may not be thoroughly understood. By way of explanation, therefore, the definition of its founder, Lord Meath, maybe taken as best outlining the object in view. "It is intended, he said, that the Empire Day celebration shall be but the outward and visible sign of an inner and spiritual awakening of the peoples who constitute the British Empire to the serious duties and responsibilities which lie at their door."*[27]

The general scope of Lord Meath's intentions was outlined in the letter which he addressed to the Governors and Prime Ministers of all British colonies on July 16th 1902. An extract from that correspondence is presented:

> *For years I have advocated the establishment throughout the Empire of a day to be called Empire Day, on which, by state regulation in each portion of the Empire, a holiday shopping given to all scholars attending schools entirely or partially maintained out of public funds, with the exception of a couple of hours in the morning, these to be spent by the children in exercises of a patriotic and agreeable nature and in listening to lectures, recitations, etc., On subjects of an imperial character. Such a holiday should be held on the same day throughout the whole of the dominions of the King Emperor; if possible, I would venture to suggest on May 24, the birthday of our late sovereign, Queen Victoria, Empress of India...*[28]

In Albany the first Empire Day was conducted on May 24th 1907. The following year the local newspaper enthusiastically provided a retrospect of the events of the 1908 celebrations:

> *As was the case last year, the celebration at Albany was made of an exceptionally impressive character through the enthusiastic efforts of the Mayor Mr C. McKenzie and Major Meeks. The fact that the anniversary fell on a Sunday made it necessary to separate the holiday side of the function from the more serious proceedings, and the cooperation of the different clergyman was secured in the arrangement of a monster open air patriotic service, which combined with an unusually brilliant military display serve to fittingly mark the great occasion. Glorious weather: the Queen's weather of tradition, prevailed and the largest gathering yet seen on the ground assembled on the Parade Street Recreation Reserve to participate in the programme. There must have been upwards of 1200 adults present...*
>
> *As a matter of fact, the whole of the residents of the town may be said to have taken an interest in the proceedings.*[29]

Centenary Celebrations - 1927

The Albany Centenary celebration was conducted on the 21st January 1927 exactly 100 years to the day after the official raising on the British flag at Residency Point for the second time in a ceremony led by Major Lockyer, Captain Wakefield and Lieutenant Festing. In raising the Union Jack and completing the other formalities of occupancy they were complying with Governor Ralph Darling's written instructions which read as:

---

[26] *The Inquirer and Commercial News*. 21st December 1900.
[27] Ibid. 27th May 1908.
[28] *The Albany Advertiser*. 27th May 1908.
[29] Ibid.

When the site is determined upon, you will display the colours, with which you are furnished for this purpose, cause the troops to fire a 'Feu de Joie' and observe all other formalities which are usual on such and occasion.[30]

On the 21st January 1827 with all crown convicts, soldiers and cargo discharged from *Amity* and the basic essentials of the future military camp established Governor Darling's instructions were then followed to the letter by Major Lockyer. On the 21st January 1927 a celebration of the first centenary of the Cantonment which had led to the development of the town of Albany was conducted. The Albany Centenary Committee issued a commemorative booklet to mark the occasion titled: *Centenary of Western Australia Albany 1827 - 1927*. The cover of the booklet remarked:

To Commemorate the First settlement of Western Australia by Major Lockyer, H.M. 57th Regiment, who hoisted the British Flag at Albany on 21st January, 1827.[31]

The official dinner.
Albany, January 23.
Glorious weather prevailed for Yesterdays Centenary celebration program. Albany is text to almost capacity point with visitors from every corner of the state and the utmost enthusiasm prevails. The big features of the day were the Princess Royal Sailing Club's regatta and the tennis championship finals. The regatta was conducted from the town jetty...

The setting was indeed beautiful. Hundreds of spectators lie on the jetty and upwards of 1000 views the sports program from the landing stage while the yacht race for the Centenary cup was in progress. The crew of the war vessel were active participants in the water events and contributed novelty items.

The Centenary dinner, held in the evening at the Freemason's hotel proved a memorable function. Guess to the number of 70 included the governor and his party. His Excellency made a happy speech and congratulated the committee on the success of their program to that stage. The crowning triumph of the efforts had been, he thought, the kindly worded message of greeting and remembrance forwarded by his Majesty the King to Albany citizens. The governor also reviewed Albany's past hundred years, paying a tribute to the pioneers. He urged the present and future generations to emulate the spirit of their forebears and their sleeve a worthy record of progress for the coming generations to celebrate on Albany's 200th birthday...

Albany in past years had enjoyed great prosperity, but it was this nothing to what would eventually accrue to it. As production from the land increased so would industries follow. He had filtered his duty to place the position before them as he saw it and he offered his remarks with humility and in the kindest possible spirit, and in return for the warm-hearted hospitality tent at himself and Lady Campion and family during their many visits to the town.

On Sunday morning the various churches held special Centenary services.[32]

Ceremony at Point Frederick.[33]
Re-enacted Yesterday.
Yesterday, 100 years afterwards, the scene was re-enacted to mark the Centenary of Western Australia. On exactly the same site Union Jack was unfurled and honoured in the presence of his Excellency the governor so William Campion. The ceremony was a simple as that perform so long ago but the company and surroundings were vastly different. In place of the few uniform figures that graced the original proceedings on a barren sure with thousands of people, men, women and children in holiday attire, who entered enthusiastically into the spirit

---

[30] *The Historical Records of Australia*, Series I, Vol. XII.
[31] *Centenary of Western Australia Albany 1827 -1927*. Issued by The Committee. 1927.
[32] *The Western Mail*. 27th January 1927.
[33] A typical myth concerns the Royal Duke whose title honours the City's name and main street: HRH The Prince Frederick, Duke of York & Albany. The frequent use in many local histories of Augustus as Prince Frederick's second Christian name is incorrect and should never be used. The Royal Archives at Windsor Castle indicated in private correspondence to Douglas Sellick:" ... the *Sergeant of the Vestry of the Chapels Royal has consulted the original Royal Register entry for the Duke of York's Baptism on September 14th 1763. It reads as follows: "This evening His Royal Highness the young Prince was christened at St. James's, by the name of Frederick: His Grace the Archbishop of Canterbury perform'd the Ceremony. Therefore, The Royal Archives can confirm that the use of Augustus as Prince Frederick's second Christian name is incorrect".*

of the celebration. The site, once open country, is now an enclosed space, cut off from the town by railway line. There so long as can be remembered was located the home for long line of government residence, the centre of official hospitality. It is him in on all sides but that facing the harbour. The beach, probably a little change, served are useful purpose yesterday in providing room for the crowd. Many persons that's moved over the grounds for the first time conscious its historic associations.

… after the march pass, his Excellency and filled the Union Jack and the band played the National anthem, while the assembled company stood at attention. The mail then spoke of the significance of the ceremony and ounce at the governor would address the people also in the importance of the occasion.

The Governor said, Mr Mayor, as you say this is perhaps the most important ceremony of Centenary week. I hope this moment performed the ceremony of unfurling the Union Jack which was unfilled the first time on this spot 100 years ago. First of all, imagine what the conditions were then compared to now. You see Albany established. You have telephones, railways, roads, etc but when Major Lockyer and 74 people with him first landed there was nothing but bush, and he knew practically nothing about the country. There were certain number of Americans engaged in the whaling and sealing industry, touching as far as shark Bay…

Lord Bathurst, the Secretary of State, was so alarmed that the French would occupy New Holland, which we now know as Western Australia, that he ordered Government Darling to send an officer to King George's Sound. Subsequently New Holland became Western Australia…

Today we fly the Union Jack which is the flag of the nation and is flown throughout the British Empire. We should be proud of that flag because that flag means British justice where-ever it is flown. Be true to that flag because it means one God, one King and one country. He was proud and pleased to be there that afternoon to take part in that ceremony and asked them to think what Australia might be in the next 100 years.[34]

Albany Citizens React to Western Australia's Centenary Celebrations

The 1929 celebration of the Western Australian State Centenary caused considerable ill feeling among many local Albany residents as this exchange illustrates:

State Centenary.
Albany Indignant.
A letter received from the premier's private secretary, through Mr A. Wainsborough. M.L.A. [to the Municipal Council]:
"With further reference to the Centenary celebrations, and your letter of the sixth instant, it appears that it would be desirable to organise the celebrations with a view to their being held in 1929. In1829 the first Governor of the state, Captain Sir James Stirling, arrived with the first party of settlers, and held in the commission of his Majesty the King to establish the settlement and undertake the Government of Western Australia. With this date in view ample time exists for the consideration of the means which should best be adopted for the celebrations of so important and event in the manner which will be of the widest interest and most practical benefit to the greatest number of people."

The meeting carried the following resolution:
"This committee having learned with deep regret the Government's suggestion to ignore the fact that Western Australia was first settled at Albany, and that it was at Albany the Union Jack was first flown on the western coast of Australia, enters its emphatic protest against such a step, which would delay for three years the obvious advantage that would accrue to the state from the celebrations of it Centenary.[35]

State Centenary.
Albany's Claim.
While not claiming any ancestral interest in the matter, a deputation from Albany, which waited on the premier Mr P. Collier, on Saturday morning strongly urged that the hundredth anniversary, next year, of the arrival of

---

[34] *The Albany Advertiser.* 22nd January 1927.
[35] *The Western Mail.* 10th September 1925.

Major Lockyer at Albany, to found a settlement, should be adopted for the purpose of Centenary celebrations in connection with the foundation of the state.

On consulting some Historical Records, the premier was able to show that Albany had been quite populous with parties of pioneer adventures before the advent of Major Lockyer, and he was not prepared to admit, offhand, that Captain Vancouver's arrival, in the Discovery, in 1791, Flinders landing in Investigator *in 1807, or even return the King's arrival in 1800, should be overlooked in favour of major lochia. Since the latter, he said, was by no means the first land at Albany, it might perhaps be desirable to take the date of the arrival of the first Englishman.*

Mr Catling of the Albany Advertiser suggested that perhaps that particular Englishman did not have any official right to landing to which the premier replied that any Englishman, on landing on unoccupied territory, could be relied upon to assert a claim to it, on behalf of his country. The premier was also not prepared to admit, offhand that the date of the founding of the Swan River settlement by Captain Stirling, in 1829, should not be taken as a basis of state Centenary celebrations. But he assured the deputation that the government had no feeling on the matter, one way or another, and that he would talk it over, impartially, with his Cabinet colleagues.[36]

Albany's 'Claim to Recognition' necessitated a response from the State Government. The response was forthcoming from the acknowledged historian and State Librarian Dr J. S. Battye who responded in some depth in an article published by *The West Australian*:

Some Historical Points.

Amongst the questions raised by the approach to the Western Australian Centenary is that of the date upon which it should be celebrated, due to the fact that a settlement existed at King George's Sound prior to the actual establishment of the colony (now State) of Western Australia.

Prominent amongst those who have urged the claims of Albany is Sir Nicholas Lockyer [son of Major Lockyer], who has made several statements which call for a reply from those who contend that there was no colony of Western Australia until Captain Stirling landed upon Garden Island with the first band of officials and settlers in June, 1829. And, as, in the course of his argument, Sir Nicholas Lockyer has taken me to task, I may perhaps be forgiven for traversing some of his statements. In the course of a communication forwarded by him to the Albany Centenary Committee, and published in the "West Australian" on April 19 last, he states: 'I gather it is considered that Major Edmund Lockyer hoisted the British flag at Albany on December 26, 1826. [It was really on January 21, 1827, that the ceremony took place] . . . It has been the custom to ignore the part that Albany has played, not only in the history of Western Australia, but in the history of the continent. It has also been the custom to refer to the first settlement as a convict settlement, and this is repeated in a recent book by Dr. Battye, who is inaccurate in other references to the period. A reference by Governor Darling to the proposed convict settlement, due to misreading his instructions, has probably led to this error. The fact, however, remains that Albany was never a convict settlement. The twenty convicts sent with the expedition in 1826 were merely sent as servants and laborers, and I find no record of convicts having been sentenced to transportation to Albany."

This view is further emphasised in a second letter to the Albany Centenary Committee, published in the "West Australian" on July 6. Three points worthy of discussion arise out of these communications - first, whether the settlement at King George's Sound was intended to be a convict settlement, and whether it was so regarded in the first place; second, the date of the foundation of the settlement at King George's Sound; and third, the claim of Albany that this early settlement shall be regarded as the foundation of Western Australia.

As to the first point—whether the settlement at King George's Sound was intended to be a convict settlement! At the beginning of March, 1826, Lord Bathurst instructed Governor Darling to take the necessary measures to procure correct information respecting the country adjoining Shark Bay, "in order that should it be deemed advisable to establish a penal settlement, to which those convicts may be sent whose offences might not require their rigorous confinement in Norfolk Island, his Majesty's Government might have been the means of

---

[36] Ibid. 15th October, 1925.

accomplishing that object." The idea was that Shark Bay should take the place of Moreton Bay, then used for that purpose; that Moreton Bay, in turn, should be used for the type of prisoner then stationed at Port Macquarie, and that Port Macquarie should be thrown open to general colonisation.

In a further despatch of the same date, after referring to the establishment of an open settlement at Western Port, Lord Bathurst mentioned that the establishment to be formed at Shark Bay was partly for a different object. Later in the same month Darling was instructed to first make a survey of the land around King George's Sound, as the Shark Bay country was deemed extremely barren, and it might be advisable to establish the settlement at King George's Sound. Replying to these despatches, Darling stated that he thought King George's Sound would be found totally unfit for the purposes of a penal settlement, and, in a later despatch described it as being too remote for the purpose. In view of that correspondence, it can scarcely be said that Darling in any way misread his instructions when he directed Major Lockyer to lose no time in selecting, after his arrival at King George's Sound, "such a site as may be most eligible for a penal settlement."

Sir Nicholas Lockyer cannot, therefore, it seems to me, maintain the position that it was not intended to make King George's Sound a convict settlement. He might say, however, that even if it were so intended such convict settlement was never actually established, and that the convicts were merely sent as "servants and laborers."

This leads us to consider "whether King George's Sound was ever regarded officially or otherwise as a settlement of that character. That it was officially regarded as such is evident from the estimates of annual expenditure in regard to convicts, forwarded by Darling to the Colonial Office in December, 1826. In that estimate King George's Sound is grouped with Port Macquarie, Moreton Bay, and Norfolk Island as a penal settlement. But it must have become apparent to Governor Darling that its retention as such was impossible owing to its distance from Sydney, as, in the quarterly return of prisoners in April, 1827, wo find it described merely as "A Government Establishment." It was not, therefore, at any time during its control from New South Wales a free settlement in the sense that Western Port was, where the convicts were merely sent to clear the ground and prepare the way for free settlers. A return, dated July 19, 1827, shows that the population of King George's Sound, at that date, consisted of 19 soldiers, three of whom were married and had four children amongst them, and 24 convicts (not 20 as Sir Nicholas Lockyer states, nor 23, the number given in Major Lockyer's diary). There was not, at the time, any free settler in the place, nor does it appear that any came there during the whole period that King George's Sound was occupied' by the soldiers and convicts from New South Wales. In fact, in reporting the withdrawal of the establishment in January, 1831, Darling gave it as his opinion that "free people would not be disposed to reside there." and Governor Stirling upon taking over control, reported that King George's Sound would be "speedily thrown open for location," and that several individuals were about to proceed there.

In view of those circumstance.!, it can scarcely he claimed that the convicts were merely sent as servants and laborers. Further, there is' no doubt that King George's Sound was generally regarded as purely a convict statin from 1826 to 1831. Major Irwin writing in 1835, in regard to the matter, said, "This settlement has been occupied some years by the Sydney Government it was subsequently banded over to the Western Australian and the convicts were withdrawn."

Colonel Hanson, of Madras, who visited the place in 1832, wrote: "It is strange to find that King George's Sound, though so long occupied as a penal settlement from Sydney, exhibits at this station hardly a vestige of man's work. What the convicts could have been about during the many years, they have been stationed there, it is difficult to imagine. Mr. Carew, the present commandant, declared that the most positive orders existed not to erect a single dwelling house or public work of any description beyond the miserable huts that were necessary for the cover of the party."

Hoisting the Flag.

As to the second point—the date of the foundation of the settlement at King George's Sound, Sir Nicholas Lockyer contends that the date should be January 21, the date upon which the flag was hoisted, as that ceremony represented "the first official claim to British dominion over the whole continent of Australia." That can scarcely be the case, as Major Lockyer was specifically instructed to "avoid any expression of doubt as to (he whole of New Holland being within this (i.e., British) government." The claim to Australia as a whole was really made when Governor Phillip took possession of Botany Bay, and any occasion on which the flag was hoisted thereafter, as in the case at Arthur's Head, by Captain Fremantle, on May, 2, 1829, was merely evidence of occupation.

With regard to the expedition to King George's Sound, it arrived there on December 25, 1826, and the first landing was effected on the following morning by Major Lockyer and Lieutenant Festing, in search of a satisfactory site for the settlement. They fixed upon the site provisionally, but spent the two following days in further exploration, so that the convicts and stores were not landed until December 29. The erection of shelters occupied some little time, and it was not until January 21, 1827, that a flagstaff was erected from which the flag was flown for the first time. In all probability this date was chosen because it happened to be Major Lockyer's birthday. Arguing from analogy, there seems to be every reason for fixing December 26 as the date of the foundation of the settlement, which, by the way, was called Frederick Town and not Albany—that name came later. It will be remembered that Governor Phillip. with the "First Fleet," anchored in Sydney Cove on January 26, 1788. and proceeded to land the convicts and stores. The proclamation establishing the colony was not read until February 7, but notwithstanding that fact no one has questioned January 26 as the foundation day of Australia.

Again, Captain Stirling, with the first band of colonists, arrived off Garden Island on June 1, 1829. The settlers were landed there on the following day, but it was not" until the 18th of the month that the proclamation establishing the colony was read simultaneously on Garden Island and upon the mainland. In spite of that June 1 has always been recognised without question as the foundation day of Western Australia.

With regard to the third point, that the foundation of the settlement at King George's Sound should be regarded as the foundation of Western Australia, there is ample evidence that the settlement at the Sound, whilst the convicts were there, was never within the colony of Western Australia. When Captain Stirling was sent to establish the colony, be was bound only by the regulations issued by the Colonial Office and by instructions issued under the signature of George IV. The one stated that no convicts should be sent to the colony, and the other simply gave him directions for government, but established no boundaries. The boundaries were not laid down until his commission was issued, and that commission was of issued until March, 1831, after the decision to remove the convict establishment from King George's Sound. That establishment cannot, therefore, in any sense he said to have been part of the colony of Western Australia.

In view of the evidence available, it may, therefore, be reasonably stated that King George's Sound was settled in the first place with the object of making it a penal settlement; that, the actual foundation of that settlement was effected on December 26, 1820, but that the colony (now the State) of Western Australia, was not brought into being until June 1, 1829.[37]

Outdoor Leisure Pursuits

Albany has always had a keen interest in outdoor sporting pursuits. With the overall increased economic prosperity that was evident in the town in the later decades of the Nineteenth Century it was not surprising to note that many sporting ventures and clubs were subsequently formed. As a response to the growing community interest in outdoor leisure activity in 1896 the Albany Town Council fenced an area of public open space that would later become The 1927 Centennial Oval. The oval became the centre of a number of the town's sporting and recreational pursuits. As *The Western Australian Gem in a Granite Setting* enthusiastically summarised in its report on the town:

Centennial Oval
A Well-Equipped Racecourse and Sports Reserve

Albany is fortunate in its possession of Centennial Oval, which is situated in Ulster Road to the north of the town. The Oval is vested in the Municipality and is controlled by an advisory board. By means of working bees organised by a band of patriotic citizens the Oval has been bought to its present high state of perfection. The efforts of the Albany Racing Club, one of the most progressive and flourishing provincial bodies in the state, also played a big part. The grandstand was erected by means of a Centenary grant of £500 from the State Government, supplemented by like amount from the Town Council. The racetrack of 6 ½ furlongs, was laid down and fenced by voluntary labour, and many of the fixtures were also erected at this time. The club had gradually added to these until today the course is one of the best equipped in the state and a big asset to the town as a holiday resort.[38]

---

[37] *The Western Mail.* 29th July 1926. Also reported in *The Albany Despatch.* 15th July 1926.
[38] *Western Australian Gem in a Granite Setting.* Season 1929. Official Albany Directory

At the turn of the century Albany could boast a number of sporting past-times that had become well developed including horse racing, sailing, football, athletics, rifle shooting, tennis, golf, bowls and swimming.

> *The other branches of sport; cricket football, hockey and cycling also use the Oval to advantage, and the cycling club members also displayed find spirit in laying down their own track. Albany is noted in the realm of sport and every section is catered for. The Rifle Club's range is situated near Centennial Oval and is well equipped. The annual matches of the Great Southern Rifle Union are held here during the summer season and attract a big entry. The game of tennis is also well catered for, as is in addition to the Albany's Clubs courts in Lawley Park, players can join up with St John's Church Club, the Methodist Church, and St. Joseph's Church Club. The Albany Bowling Club is a healthy body, with headquarters in Gairdner Street, near the Woollen Mills. The greens are well-kept, and every facility exists to advance the sporting and social aspects of the game.*
>
> *The Princess Royal Sailing Club is well established and during the season conducts weekly contests. The annual regatta in Princess Royal Harbour is a season feature. The Albany swimming club is established at the town jetty baths. During the season carnivals are conducted and Katanning and other great Southern clubs participate.*
>
> ### *Croquet Clubs.*
> *Lovers of the game of croquet are well catered for in Albany. St John's Croquet Club has its headquarters on the northern side of the picturesque old church of Saint John. The greens are spacious and every facility is offered to play. The club has an extensive membership list, and the social aspect is also well catered for. The Albany Bowling Club also has a croquet lawn set alongside and this is governed by the lady associates. The lawn is set in a pretty corner operate Street reserve. Throughout the season matches are arranged in the club has proved a splendid addition to the social life of the town.*
>
> ### *Albany Tennis Club.*
> *The six courts at the Albany tennis club are set in picturesque surroundings in the south eastern corner of Lawley Park, off Brunswick Road. The courts are all asphalt. The Hardcourt Championships are held here annually in January...*
> *The Albany Tennis Club is the best equipped body outside the metropolitan area and will compare with many of such in that locality. It has ladies and gentlemen's dressing rooms, shower baths, lavatories, etc. There is also a tearoom capable of seating 100 people at once from which a beautiful seascape of the harbour is obtained*[39]

Albany Turf Club

The Albany Turf Club had been formed in 1865 and its race meetings were always well attended. The Turf Club had always been well patronised however, the issue was always about securing thoroughbred horses to compete in the various events that the club staged. The newspapers related a series of issues with respect to the importing of horses into the settlement from the Eastern States.

> *Shipping horses to Albany.*
> *Glenview asked if I can let him know the cost of shipping horses from Sydney to Albany Western Australia, and also whether there is much danger of there being hurt or killed in transit. Answer: at the present time the steamship companies are asking 6 pounds per head for freight from Sydney to Albany. This may appear to you to be heavy, but it's not really so when the conditions are taken into consideration. There is always a certain amount of dangerous shipping horses and Schippers have to take this risk, although there is an opportunity of ensuring against accidents, at fairly heavy premiums. Of course, nearly everything depends upon the sort of voyage, and the conditions of the weather. He might happily have a good voyage, but you might very easily happen to meet weather conditions which might bring disaster to the horses.*[40]

The importation of livestock for horse racing in the town always provided excellent folder for the sporting section of local newspapers. And article relating to the arrival of a mare purchased by the then Mr Hare is a good example:

---

[39] Ibid.
[40] *The Farmer and Settler.* Sydney. 7th April 1911.

> *Arrival at Five Horses at Albany.*
> *By Telegraph*
> *Albany, December 1.*
> *By the SS Nemesis, which arrived at Albany from Adelaide this morning, Cleverley landed with Mr Hare's racing mare Gladness, by Emerald out of Young Welcome, there are also Mr Frank Craig's horses; the colt called Mount Zeehan, by Progress from Solid Silver, and the stud mare Violet, by Argus Scandal out of Lily, with a yearling filly by spark. These horses are in capital condition, as are also another batch of fifty-six.*[41]

Nonetheless, not every attempt at securing livestock from the Eastern States ended happily for the local racing entrepreneurs:

> **A Stormy Trip.**
> *25 Horses Lost.*
> *Albany, June 29.*
> *The SS Cornwall experienced the heavy weather that has delayed the arrival of all the vessels from eastward during the past week. The Cornwall was timed to arrive here from Sydney on Monday evening, but she did not put in an appearance to last evening. Captain Barter reports a trying passage. On the 22nd instant, an incident occurred to the condenser, and for 30 hours the vessel was heaving to while repairs were effected. A westerly gale was then blowing, with heavy seas, and the vessel was buffeted about at its mercy. There were 125 horses on board, and although the fittings remain secure, the animals suffered considerably from being knocked about. Nineteen horses were killed, and six others died from exposure. The weather moderated as Albany was approached.*[42]

An interesting article on the Albany Turf Club was provided by *The Albany Advertiser* in 1941 as part of the ongoing series dealing with town's people's memories of early Albany. One particular story relates to the period of the 'Russia' scare and the visit to the port of the Russian cruiser:

> *Early Albany Racing Memories.*
> *When horses were tough.*
> *The entry of Russia into the present war recalls instant in early Albany history of the "eighties". In 1886 a rush and warship, the* Vestnick, *visited the Albany and the offices and crew were present at a race meeting conducted by the Albany Turf Club. The main race of the day was the Plantagenet cup of 15 sovereigns, a weight for age event run over 3 miles. The race was won by the Clown, owned by the secretary of the Albany Turf Club, the late Mr 'Jockey" Hare.*[43]

Roller Skating Rink

A particular form of entertainment that local Albany inhabitants welcomed with great enthusiasm was roller-skating. At one time there were two roller skating rink's operating in the town. The sport catered for people of all ages. Initially roller-skating took place in the Albany Town Hall, although this was only made possible when the Municipal Council was forced to reverse a previous decision it had made:

> *Too Hasty*
> *The action of the municipal council in refusing the applications of the rinking club and Mr Brotheridge for the use of the Town Hall for rinking purposes demands further consideration. The reason assigned for the refusal was that the noise occasioned by the rinking would be a source of annoyance to any of the tenants of the offices of the ground floor who might require to use their offices on rinking nights. No other reason was assigned as far as The Observer has been able to ascertain, no other reason exists. The tenants of the offices expect and are entitled to receive every consideration at the hands of the council. They should not be subjected to any annoyance that can possibly be avoided, and if the noise of the rinking would seriously affect them the council was right, as a landlord, in refusing to let the large hall for the purpose. It is, however, a question whether the reason assigned was sufficiently weighty to make the action of the council appeared judicious.*[44]

Quite obviously the council reconsidered its position as the following article in the *Australian Advertiser* indicates:

---

[41] *The Inquirer and Commercial News.* 2nd December 1891.
[42] *The West Australian* 30th June 1900.
[43] *The Albany Advertiser.* 3rd July 1941.
[44] *The Albany Observer.* 22nd May 1890.

Rinking in the Town Hall.

On Wednesday evening rinking in the Town Hall which commenced for the season. The weather was very unpropitious and deterred a number of persons venturing out of doors but not withstanding this there was a fairly large attendance of young people who seem to enjoy themselves greatly. Judging from the enthusiasm displayed on Wednesday evening roller-skating as a past time it's fair to be the most popular in Albany this winter.[45]

Even with a relatively small-town population roller skating had quite a following eventually two purpose-built rinks were constructed for the purpose.

The Broadway Elite Roller-Skating Rink.

The Broadway elite roller-skating rink was open by invitation on Friday night. A large audience responded to the invitation issued and judging from the continuous laughter at the efforts and misfortunes of the novices, appeared to thoroughly enjoy themselves. In the earlier part of the evening but very few could be induced to put on the skates, but after witnessing the very grotesque capers that some of them or venturesome acquaintances were indulging in, they could no longer resist the temptation of trying to outdo them as it appeared to be very easy. Soon are very large number of novices were being spreadeagled all over the hall to the great amusement of the spectators, who were in continuous state of laughter. Some who in the old country had been adept in ice skating, soon managed to glide along, but others could not keep on their feet and were constantly attempting to kick the roof of the hall… We are requested to state that the afternoon is the best time for ladies to appear on the rink, and that Wednesday mornings especially set apart for ladies only, and that they will receive every attention and assistance from the proprietor in learning the art of roller-skating…[46]

And yet another roller-skating venture was commenced later on:

Albany Picture Gardens and Skating Rink.

The new skating rink at the corner of York Street and Stirling Terrace presented a brilliant and attractive appearance on Monday night when its official opening took place in the presence of a large assemblage of skaters in plain and fancy costume and of the general public. The rink is an open air one and has a large skating area and a new granolithic floor appear to give every satisfaction to those using it. The whole of the grounds were well lighted with numerous acetylene gas jets by mush more and company, rendering objects as visible as by daylight. The Albany brass band played incidental music throughout the evening and added considerably to the night's enjoyment. The judges of the various events with chosen from the spectators present…[47]

Unfortunately, in 1912 a large fire destroyed one of Albany's well supported entertainment venues, the Princess Skating Rink.

Destructive Fire.
Skating Rink Destroyed.

In the early hours of Thursday morning a fire broke out in the building known as the Princess Skating Rink, which was levelled to the ground. About 1:10 the alarm at fire was given to the fire station by Messrs A. Bruce and J. Gorman, who were returning from a dance, and saw the building a blaze, an Engineer Wright, who sleeps at the station, at once called Foreman Evans and Captain Paton and arouse members of the Fire Brigade living close to the station. The small manual engine was run to the scene, but it was soon apparent to Foreman Evans that there was no hope of saving the rink and efforts were then concentrated on the adjoining buildings. A strong south-west wind was blowing at the time, but fortunately for the surrounding properties this dropped when the fire broke through the walls of the rink…[48]

Golf Club

In 1899 work commenced on golf links adjacent to Lake Seppings and that same year the Albany Golf Club was established. In respect to this sporting venture, as the newspaper reports indicate, there was indeed

---

[45] *The Australian Advertiser.* 20th June 1890
[46] Ibid. 12th August 1889.
[47] *The Albany Advertiser.* 2nd February 1910.
[48] Ibid. 16th November 1912.

very little procrastination as had been evident in some previous Albany facility developments. The germ of an idea of a golf links for Albany was keenly pursued:

> *It will be seen that with the Bowling Green and the garden we have more to offer to visitors then in past years, but we consider that there is not the slightest reason why golf links should not be provided. We have gone carefully into this matter and are of the opinion that there would be no difficulty in providing excellent golf links for use during the coming summer. Nothing would have a greater influence upon the kind of people we desire to come to Albany than the announcement that golf links were available for the use of visiting players. Golf clubs are numerous on the goldfields whence come the majority of our summer visitors and there are also clubs at Perth while it is probable the players at Melbourne and Sydney would make the trip.[49]*

There was very strong advocacy for such a facility and support for the club from the local newspaper:

> *For some time, The Advertiser had been advocating the making of golf links Albany because of the great benefit they would be to the town in the summer months. Along with golfers Mr Keyser and others have inspected the sandhills behind Middleton beach and had been informed they would make ideal links. He had a plan of a nine-hole course prepared by Mr J Endo and he had found at 37 acres of clearing would be necessary…[50]*

The Albany Golf Club was subsequently formed:

> *The adjourned meeting of those interested in the formation of a golf club in Albany was held at the Freemason's hotel on Saturday evening. There was a large attendance. Dr Robinson accepted the chair.*
> *In the opinion of the committee the site suggested* [behind the sandhills of Middleton Beach] *is pre-eminently suited for golf links. Mr WH Angove kindly assist the committee by making a rough survey of the course, marking out the process proposed teeing grounds and putting greens. The length of the course Will be 1 ¼ miles and the area to be cleared it's approximately 35 acres. This will leave a clear space of 50 yards on either side of the direct line from teeing ground to the hole…[51]*

Progress was quite quick in not only developing the facilities but also in looking further afield to encourage attendance at its competitions:

> *Good progress is being made with the clearing operations at the golf links at Middleton beach. The potting green will be completed about the end of the week. Had a recent meeting of the Perth golf club, a letter was read from Dr Robinson Captain of the Albany Club informing them that members of Perth club visiting Albany would be made honorary members during their stay in town. The members received a letter with thanks and expressed the opinion that the establishment of a golf club would prove a great attraction to the town.[52]*

Bicycle Club

Another successful sporting activity that began to thrive in Albany was the local cycling club. The first annual meeting of the Albany Bicycle Club was held at the Royal George Hotel in October 1897. In the early years of its existence issues relating to members adhering to appropriate road rules and the provision of suitable cycling areas dominated the club's agendas:

> *Bicycle Traffic.*
> *A letter was received as follows from Mr F Doyle captain of the Albany Bicycle Club: I beg to acknowledge receipt of letter from the Town Clerk with reference to the laws of cycling, and I may state that every member of the club has been cautioned and we will endeavour to carry out the laws. Our club rules also provide the penalty be inflicted on any member disobeying the laws of the Municipality. I admit that all the races were held on the road, the police were asked for their assistance and every care was exercised prevent accident or interference with general traffic…*
> *In conclusion I, on behalf of the bicycle club, asked at the Council have a bicycle track made for the upcoming cycling season. Judging by the attendance of spectators at our recent road races, it would pay for itself within two years.[53]*

---

[49] *The Albany Advertiser.* 15th August 1899.
[50] Ibid. 26th August 1899.
[51] Ibid. 5th September 1899.
[52] Ibid. 26th September 1899.
[53] *The Albany Advertiser.* 22nd July 1897.

At the annual presentation evening for the Albany Bicycle Club the lack of women members was raised as an issue, so it was suggested that they form their own club:

Annual ball.

The annual ball in connection with your boat club was filled in the Oddfellows Hall on Wednesday evening proved a great success. It was a very large attendance and a good program of dances was gone through under the supervision of Mr W Beddin who filled the position of M.C...

Counsellor Reynolds, president of the club, I'm writing to present the prizes to the successful competitors at the Jubilee sports, said that cycling was very pleasant and healthy sport and hope before long the people of Albany would see a cycling track laid down as it was necessary for racing. One thing he noticed was that no lady cyclists had to receive prizes for which he was very sorry. It's a shame that ladies were not able to join the club. They should form one for themselves...[54]

The Princess Royal Sailing Club

In keeping with the local convention of sporting clubs meeting in a designated Albany hotel The Princess Royal Sailing Club was formed in 1909 at a meeting held at the White Hart Hotel:

The meeting convened by Mr CW Reddin to consider the advisableness of forming a sailing or regatta club took place at the White Hart Hotel on Wednesday night and was largely attended. Upwards of 50 were present and if the enthusiasm shown goes for anything success of the club formed is assured.

The Mayor resided and explained the objects of the meeting. He said he was pleased to see such a gathering as the formation of a club whereby sailing and rowing races and other aquatic sports could be carried out in a proper manner was another step towards the advancement of Albany as a pleasure resort. He considered that there was no better sport than yachting and rowing and such sport it would be interesting to the visitors as well as the citizens in the town...

It was decided that the name of the club should be the Princess Royal Sailing Club.[55]

By October subscriptions were being collected and the club office bearers selected:

Albany Regatta.
Albany Sailing Club.

A committing meeting of the above was held at the London Hotel on Thursday evening, when the mayor resided. There was a large attendance. The collector reported that the amount in hand and promised amounted to about £40. We've decided to send him to Denmark to canvas for further subscriptions... A general discussion then insured and great interest appear to be showed in the movement, and it was generally agreed that everything pointed to a successful regatta being held as large entries will probably be received from the various events and all that was needed was a fine day.[56]

Cricket Club

The Albany Cricket Club was established in 1889 and one of the main issues confronting the club members was who they could play against. Without a viable opposition team to play against difficulties were imagined in maintaining membership interest:

The first annual general meeting of the Albany cricket club was held in the courthouse on Tuesday evening. There was a large attendance of members.

Mr R.C. Loftie presided. Gentlemen he reported:

Your committee have great pleasure in reporting that the past cricket season has been most successful...

Your committee have had many difficulties to contend with among which one is due to the isolated position of Albany, it being difficult to arrange matches and keep up an interest in practice, without opposition teams visiting us. Now that the Great Southern Railway is open, we hope to receive the visits of teams from Perth, Fremantle and York and trust that before the present season closes, we should be able to send a team to beat them on their

---

[54] Ibid. 4th December 1897.
[55] *The Albany Advertiser.* 27th February 1909.
[56] Ibid. 16th October 1897.

own ground. The greatest difficulty your committee has had to content with is the cricket ground. A suitable spot cannot be secured in Albany and the recreation ground it is a disgrace to the town.[57]

Rifle Club

Attempts to establish the Albany Rifle Club did not proceed smoothly as the local commander of the Albany volunteers was unwilling to assist or allow the use of the Albany Volunteer Rifle facilities and equipment.

Albany Rifle Club
The Albany rifle club, which was inaugurated a few weeks ago with so much promise, it's already in a bad fix. Through no inherent fault, and by no mismanagement of its governing body, its progress has been suddenly arrested, and though it is to be hoped the check is only temporary, it is nevertheless most serious at the present stage. The commanding officer of the local volunteers has put his military heel down on the neck of the rifle club; and apparently intends keeping it there. He has refused the club the use of the butts and rifles on the grounds that he has no power to grant either. When the Oracle of the hirsute hat speaks is only proper that all should bend the neck and bow the knee. Upon pull matters military, from the time of a sword not to the conduct of a campaign, the opinion of the occasionally resplendent captain of our phantom volunteers as acknowledged to be indisputable...[58]

A call for assistance from Perth based Rifle Clubs was not forthcoming and the suggestion was made that the club's members affiliate with the local volunteer rifles:

Adjourned meeting of those interested in the formation of a rifle club in Albany met last night at the Freemason's hotel. There was a good attendance.
Information had been received in the form of a letter from Captain Cook: I duly received your letter of the 23rd instant and reply by return. The idea of forming a Rifle Association in Albany cannot, I understand, be carried through as the Association formed in Perth... What you should do is to form yourselves into a rifle club and affiliate yourself to the local forces by being sworn in as members of a rifle club willing to cooperate with the forces should they be called upon to defend the colony. By thus doing you are entitled to a grant annually from the government and permission to shoot on the range when not actually in use for drill purposes.[59]

Football Clubs

The first Albany football team following the Victorian Football League format was formed in Albany in 1890. The initial team was named the Albany Rovers Football Club. Initially, the club played matches against any group that could secure enough members to form a team. Football games were played on the Parade Street reserve bordered by a picket fence and were well attended and a great source of entertainment for the spectators. In the early days of football in Albany the Football Association meetings were held in a room at the rear of the Royal George Hotel.

In 1891 the Albany Football league was expanded to include the Mercantile Football Club which drew members from Albany to Katanning. In 1893 the league was further expanded to include teams from The Forts, The Volunteer Rifle, Plantagenet and Katanning.[60] An article in *The Albany Advertiser* of 1897 provides a wonderful insight into the approach to a game where the rules were still being negotiated:

Review of the Past Season.
The football season terminated last Saturday, and it was undoubtedly from every point of view the best season experienced in the town.

Following in the footsteps of the cricketers, the ward club system was adopted and worked with great success.

---

[57] *The Albany Advertiser.* 30th August 1889.
[58] Ibid. 12th August 1890.
[59] Ibid. 11th July 1890.
[60] Norman, G. *History of the North Albany Football Club.* Albany History Collection, Albany Town library.

The rules on many points were defective but these will probably be overcome with the advent of next season. The Association decided to adopt the point system, that is six points for a goal and one for a behind, and this system produced excellent results. The Association was not altogether a happy body, but this was probably due to the fact that it was composed almost wholly of players who were naturally biased in dealing with questions affecting their side. However, it is to be hoped that next season the association will be composed of non-players...[61]

Exciting matches were witnessed right throughout the season and many contests were one [sic] by less than a goal (six points). The matches aroused keen interest among the sport-loving public as may be judged by the large attendances each Saturday afternoon...The games for the most part were played in a friendly spirit and during the season only four players were reported to the Association for infringement of the rules.[62]

Closing Remarks

With increased economic prosperity in the town evident in the final decades of the Nineteenth Century residents were able to turn their attention to more leisurely pursuits. The Albany Turf Club had led the way when formed in 1865 and since then a large variety of alternative sport and leisure activities and clubs were formed. The Municipal Council had facilitated this growing interest in sporting ventures with the creation of Centennial Oval that fostered and catered for various sporting activities including cricket and horse racing. The Oval was particularly suited for summer sporting activities. At Lawley Park new tennis courts and other recreational facilities also began to be developed. There was a heightened view that the town was going places.

Unfortunately, the economic downturn caused by the loss of both the Royal Mail and its associated passenger and cargo ship visits to Fremantle as well as the Great Southern Railway workshop's relocation to Midland, along with the significant population decline that resulted from these decisions required a substantial rethink in the direction for the town. Fortunately, it was during the first decades of the Twentieth Century that Albany was able to very successfully reinvent itself as a prime Western Australian tourist destination. The Albany Week celebrations that had commenced in 1892 gradually evolved into an extended Albany Season. In later years *The Albany Advertiser* was able to look back on this time and capture the essence of this new-found enthusiasm:

It is not necessary to present any apology with the following summary of the attractions and possibilities of the Albany district. In most households, the business of planning the annual holiday is a serious business, involving consideration of a number of matters. First it is essential that the scene of the holiday should offer a change both of scenery and of climate. Second, it is desirable, from the point of view of the average family, that it should be easily accessible, by road rail or sea. Finally, it is necessary that the resort should offer reasonable facilities for enjoyment, both of sport and socially, without being so expensive as to place a sojourn beyond the reach of the family man...
When it is considered that over the greatest part of the State, from December to March, temperatures soar past the century in heat waves which may last for weeks on end, Albany then becomes an oasis of comfort, with its almost unfailing see breezes tempering the summer heat.

As to facilities for enjoyment, Albany offers them in abundance... Within the town boundaries are excellent golf links, tennis courts, bowling greens, croquet lawns and other sporting facilities... Fish are plentiful in all the south coastal waters, and game abounds in the bush. Bathing in surf and sheltered waters maybe indulged in any of half a dozen or more splendid beaches within easy distance of the town. For evening entertainment, there are talking picture shows, concerts by the Albany volunteer Fire Brigade, frequent dances and other social activities.
Two picture theatres, show the latest and best releases of all British and American studios and give performances nightly. Both theatres are very well equipped and comfortable...

---

[61] Albany Floaters Football Team circa 1902, courtesy of Albany Historical Society.
[62] *The Albany Advertiser.* 16th September 1897.

CHAPTER 20
CONCLUSION

There are indeed many thousands of articles, pieces of personal and government correspondence and the like that contribute to Albany's Historical Record. Sifting through these documents to elicit a narrative that unravels the development of the town has at times been most challenging. The methodology we have employed in this work has relied on retrieving original primary source material uncomplicated by the later interpretations of others to identify events and issues as they were contemporaneously presented; unadulterated by later use of interpretation. To this end we have ensured that a close scrutiny of available manuscripts has been undertaken with every attempt made to ensure that their perspective has been preserved without distortion. In unravelling The Historical Record of Albany many contributing sources have been assessed, dominant trains of thought presented and, where appropriate, those fabricated myths and inaccuracies that have existed in the public arena, challenged. The claim of historical accuracy has by necessity rested upon access to the fullest documentation and information. Little attention has been paid to personal reminiscences or family histories that post-dated the events being discussed unless they can be cross checked with more reliable primary sources.

We have noted Crowley's comment that, *"there is necessarily no particular method best suited to the work of collecting information nor one particular way of writing Australian local history."*[1]

We were keen to ensure that this work did not become a simple catalogue of dignitaries as is often the case when local history is attempted. A further initial methodological issue in presenting this local history was to determine whether or not to adopt a more traditional approach by employing a chronological treatment of events. Instead, we opted to develop the work along the lines of key themes and then within each of these present the material in a more chronological format. From the perspective of both the reader and The Historical Record this approach was identified as most useful.

Extensive use has been made of contiguous newspaper articles and autobiographies as a source of information with these being complemented by private and public records and reports, pamphlets and personal diaries, correspondence and manuscripts.

Early settlers bought with them whatever their home country of origin was able to provide to them and added to this foundation the fruits of their own labour and inventiveness. Perhaps not all of the early European visitors to King George's Sound and the settlers that have followed them are well known to many. It has been an aim of this research to bring to life the town's Historical Record to provide an insight into the people who went before, and by acknowledging their efforts, to help each and every one of us understand our town, its destiny and perhaps ourselves in the process.

This book has presented a history that is unique in form and format as it is drawn primarily from the words of those who saw it and those who made it. All the great events of the period from Captain Vancouver's initial possession through to the arrival and establishment of a New South Wales Cantonment in 1826 to the raising of the Union Jack flag and settlement in 1827 and on to the Centenary celebrations of the 21st January 1927 are all represented in this work.

What is presented in the documents we have selected consists of accounts of Albany's history from 1791 to 1927, as recorded in a variety of print sources. While early European and Menang Aboriginal interactions are dealt with at some depth, nevertheless the rich oral history of the original inhabitants of King George's Sound are best sourced from more current sites that are attempting only now to capture this rich history and mythology.

The reader is encouraged to wonder and to wander through these pages that represent but only a snapshot of the town's first hundred plus years of European settlement to gain an appreciation of its history and the foundation for growth that was facilitated by its early pioneers. Nevertheless, there will be moments when

---

[1] F.K. Crowley. *Problems in Local and Regional History*. Journal of the Royal Western Australian Historical Society. 1956.

the reader may encounter anomalies and or contradictions of events which may currently have currency in other published works. These may have been deliberately or mistakenly perpetrated through inaccurate interpretation of events or myth-making attempts which together create moments of contention. It is, for this reason, that we have relied upon primary sources as the main reference for comments made in this work.

While some events on The Historical Record are already quite well presented in most history texts nonetheless, there are also the many less obvious happenings that together form a narrative that captures the town's social history that has long been overlooked, yet now preserved in this Historical Record.

There is something special about this verdant southern town in Western Australia.

POSTSCRIPT

Speaking of the power of the past in justifying the present, leading Australian historian Peter Stanley wrote:
'Myths provide comfort and justification…fostered and embraced by those who seek not truth, but reassurance, even if it is based on falsehood or exaggeration.'

The Anzac tradition and the history through which it evolved is perhaps our most mythologised form of national reassurance. It provides a stirring narrative, an annual commemorative celebration and a network of memorials around the country, crowned by the ultimate cenotaph of the Australian War Memorial. It has a heroic central figure in the form of the larrikin 'digger', and it resonates through national, state and local communities, as well as the hearts and minds of many Australians. Together, this makes Anzac a mighty power, available to those who wish to use it, including politicians, the military, marketers, interest groups and everyday folk who may have Anzac ancestors and/or family and friends currently serving in the military. Like all mythologies, Anzac can be moulded and shaped to any number of sometimes contradictory purposes and ends.

Essential to all mythologies is a foundational legend of some kind. Where and when did it begin? In the case of Anzac there has evolved an influential narrative involving Albany and the actual and alleged activities of Padre White, particularly in relation to the dawn service. That intense prelude to Anzac Day events has long been considered the most potent, moving an authentic element of the commemorative Anzac mode. Steffan Silcox and Douglas Sellick have shown how inaccurate are most of the claims about White and the dawn service. They also puncture several other subsidiary elements of Albany's originary claim.

In doing this, they have done a great service, for which they will not necessarily be applauded. Not only Albanians, but many other Australians hold the myth dear. But myth is not history and although history can easily become myth, it is the sworn obligation of the serious historian to separate the two. Why? Because when we refuse the truth about the past, no matter how uncomfortable of confronting, we leave the present open to manipulation by special interests, often with agendas that are antagonistic to the genuine communal values of Anzac with which many identify.

We need our myths as much as we need our history. But we also need to be able to tell the difference between them for a clear-eyed consideration of the present and the future. At this moment in 2021 Australia has made some new strategic choices with momentous consequences. Understanding the relationship of Anzac history and myth, from its grassroots appeal to its political power, has never been more important. This excavation of the history of Albany's Anzac legendry is a vital contribution to a better understanding of who and what we are – and where we are going as a people.

Dr Graham Seal AM
Emeritus Professor
School of Media, Creative Arts and Social Inquiry | Faculty of Humanities
Curtin University

APPENDIX 1

A Short Chronology of the King George's Sound and the Albany Town to 1927

1627: Pieter Nuyts sailed at a distance off the southern coast of New Holland in the *Gulden Zeepaart*.

1791: August 28th: Captain George Vancouver, in the ship *Discovery* and Captain William Broughton, in *Chatham* arrive at the Sound. Vancouver names it King George's the Third Sound also The Princess Royal Harbour.

1800: August 27th: Two British whalers, Captain Dixson in *Elligood* and Captain Dennis in the *Kingston* replenish water supply at Emu Point while looking for whales.

1801: December 8th: Commander Matthew Flinders enters The Princess Royal Harbour. He climbed Mount Clarence and explored the King George's Sound hinterland.

1802: February 2nd: Frenchman D' Freycinet discovers the Kalgan River (*Riviere de Francais*) and meets the whaler *Union* from the USA at what became known as Two Peoples Bay.

1803: February 17th: French Captain Baudin arrives at King George's Sound in the corvette *Geographe*.

1815: The convict transport ship *Emu* arrives under the command of Lieutenant Forster. Most likely that Emu Point is named after this ship.

1818: January 20th: Lieutenant Phillip Parker King makes his first visit to King George's Sound in *Mermaid*. He is accompanied by surveyor J. S. Roe who explores around Oyster Harbour.

1821: December 23rd: King in *Bathurst* makes his second visit to the Sound. This time he makes observations of the natives at Emu Point.

1826: October 15th: The *Astrolabe* under the command of the French Captain d'Urville arrives at Vancouver Point in King George's Sound. He sets up an observatory and studies the area.

1826: December 25th: Major Edmund Lockyer and Captain Joseph Wakefield anchor in Princess Royal Harbour on *Amity* with Crown Convicts and a British Army detachment of 21 to establish a Cantonment.

1827: January 21st: Major Lockyer raises the Union Jack for the second time and celebrates the permanent establishment of a British military presence at King George's Sound.

1827: April 8th: Captain Joseph Wakefield takes command of the Cantonment. Lockyer returns to Sydney with Captain James Stirling and sells his army commission.

1828: December 28th: Lieutenant George Sleeman assumes command of the Cantonment.

1829: A makeshift hospital facility is constructed at Residency Point.

1829: January 29th: Doctor Braidwood Wilson and John Kent with the aid of Mokare begin their exploration of the settlement's hinterland.

1830: December 14th: Captain Roger Bannister leaves Perth overland for the Sound. Banister's party reaches King George's Sound on February 4th 1831 after getting lost on the way.

1831: January 29th: The settlement is placed under the control of the Swan River and Albany is named. Captain Collet Barker becomes Commandant.

1831: March 7th: Captain Collet Barker transfers Strawberry Hill Farm over to the Swan River Government.

1831: April: Dr Alexander Collie appointed as Resident Magistrate in the settlement. With Mokare he explores the Kalgan River and the settlement's hinterland.

1831: November 12th: Lieutenant-Governor Captain James Stirling second visit to King George's Sound on the brig *Sulphur*.

1832: January 21st: The settlement is officially named Albany by Stirling.

1832: February: Surveyor Hillman develops a town plan with a number of allotments for sale.

1832: July: G.M. Cheyne takes up 15,500 acres now known as Cheynes Beach area.

1833: September 13th: Sir Richard Spencer and his family arrive and move into Strawberry Hill Farm.

1834: December: The first honeybees are imported into the settlement by Mrs Mary Taylor (nee Mary Bussell).

1835: February: Thomas Booker Sherratt begins operating a whaling station at Doubtful Island Bay, north-east of Albany. He also builds the 'Octagon Chapel' as a meeting and church facility.

1835: The first Public and General Liquor license granted in Albany is issued.

1835: March: John H. Morley constructs building in Duke Street later to be known as Patrick Taylor Cottage.

1836: July: First survey for the Albany to Perth Road is completed. A survey map of Albany drawn by Alfred Hillman, Government Surveyor details properties allotted for specific use in the town, inclusive of burial ground.

1836: T.B. Sherrat commences whaling venture in Doubtful Island Bay.
1837: First Albany jetty is constructed. Middleton Road made on orders from Sir Richard Spencer to *"enable ships to land goods at Ellen Cove"*.
1837: September: Patrick Taylor marries Miss Mary Bussell.
1837: September: General agitation against foreign whalers in Albany's coastal waters.
1838: February: A report of natives spearing cattle in the Hay River area.
Two whaling companies established at Cheynes Beach.
1838: August: The West Australia Bank opens a branch in Albany.
1839: July 14th: Sir Richard Spencer dies.
1840: 31st December The Peninsular and Oriental Steam Navigation Company of London had is incorporated by Royal Charter and known now by its famous acronym P&O.
1841: April: Meeting held in Octagonal "Chapel" regarding to building a more substantial Church of England church in Albany.
1842: The Family Inn established by the Sherratt family.
1843: The Albany Town Trust is established.
1847: Chinese servants begin to be employed in Albany. Coal is discovered at the Fitzgerald River.
1848: July, Archdeacon John. R. Wollaston arrives in Albany.
1848: October, Church of St John's Church and the town's cemetery are consecrated by Bishop Short.
1848: Albany Town Trust is formed.
1848: *HMS Acheron* first steam ship to visit Albany.
1849: Mr and Mrs Knight operate a school for local children.
1850: After a scarlet fever scare Dr Henry Wollaston is appointed medical officer for the town.
1851: Albany is Incorporated as a town.
1852: First Royal Mail from Britain by the Royal Mail Steam Navigation Company's vessel *Australian*.
1852: First P&O steamer to visit Australia, *Chusan* with Royal Mail, passengers and cargo from Singapore.
1852: The Mechanics Institute is established and moves temporarily into old Octagon "Chapel".
1852: 'Annesfield' school for Aboriginal children opened by Anne Camfield in her house.
1853: P&O commenced its operations in the town.
1853: A foundation for the first Roman Catholic Church is made. This church is never completed.
1853: *Sir William Molesworth* arrives in the harbour with 20% of its crew with scarlet fever.
1854: The Point King Lighthouse is built. The first Upper King and Upper Kalgan bridges are constructed by Lieutenant Crossman.
1856: the Albany Convict Depot is closed, and the commissariat returned to Perth.
1857: Breaksea Lighthouse commences construction.
1861: First permanent Roman Catholic Church started. The Residency is built.
1862: Ex-convict Thomas Palmer opens first Government School.
1863: The second measles epidemic within the town.
1867: April: P&O Agent W. Clifton initiates plans for the formation of the Albany Co-operative Store
1868: The Post office building in Stirling Terrace commences construction.
1867: 21st June, First telegraph message from Perth to Fremantle.
1868: January: Albany Co-operative Store opens in house.
1868: Building commenced on post office, courthouse, municipal meeting rooms, and customs house.
1870: York Street development completed.
1870: Gaol at Parade Street is built.
1870: The Albany Co-operative Store Building opens.
1871: Albany gazetted a Municipality that incorporates the Plantagenet Region under Act.
1871: 'Annesfield' aboriginal school closes and remaining students sent to Perth.
1872: The first Albany School Board is formed.
1872: 26th December, Albany to Perth telegraph opened.
1873: 29th April, *SS Baroda* arrives in port with smallpox on board.
1874: Chancel of St John's Church built.
1875: The Albany to Eucla Telegraph line is started.
1875: Roman Catholic School run by lay teachers.
1875: Governor Weld officiates at erection of the first telegraph pole for the Albany to Eucla line.
1877: Patrick Taylor dies. The Telegraph line to South Australia is completed.
1878: Local volunteers form a local military force incorporated as the Albany Defence Rifles in 1885.

1879: The last recorded export of whale oil during the 19th century from the town is recorded.
1881: Prince George of Wales and Prince Albert Victor of Wales visit on *HMS Bacchante*.
1881: The building of the Roman Catholic Convent is commenced.
1881: *The Albany Advertiser* newspaper is printed by Hamel and Foster.
1881: Defence report proposed Federal fortifications for King George's Sound.
1883: The Albany Co-operative Store is wound up.
1884: The contract for the Great Southern Railway is let to Anthony Hordern.
1884: Fred Dymes store owner is appointed U.S.A. Consular Agent in Albany.
1884: 16th December, *SS Preussen* arrives with smallpox among passengers.
1886: Work commences on the Albany to Beverley railway line.
1886: May, A Russian warship *Vestnick* is moored in the port for close to a month.
1886: A meeting of the Federal Council of Colonies discuss the Defence of Albany.
1887: The Australian Colonies agreed to jointly fund fortifications at King George's Sound.
1888: June 13th: The Albany Town Hall is opened.
1889: The Albany to Beverly railway is open and ending Royal Mail horse coach services.
1890: Albany to Denmark railway is opened.
1890: Albany becomes a staging area for those travelling to the Coolgardie and Kalgoorlie goldfields.
1891: April 1st: The clock tower is added to the Town Hall and is started at 3 p.m.
1893: Fortifications on Mount Adelaide are completed.
1893: 3rd May. Run on the Albany Branch of the Union Bank due to National economic recession.
1895: The Albany telephone exchange operational – operated by Louise Parish and Charlotte Prideaux.
1895: Construction begins on an eighty-foot clocktower to the western end of the original Post Office
1895: Albany School in Collie Road completed. Boys and girls separated on the same site.
1896: Albany boasts 6 hotels. – Freemason's, London, Albany, Weld Arms, York, Royal George.
1896: Centennial Oval created by the Municipal Council.
1896: Post Office with a clock tower expansion made to original building completed.
1896: 27th November. A Branch of the Western Australian Bank is opened in Albany.
1897: 7th January, Government buys Great Southern Railway for 1 million pounds.
1897: Queen Victoria's Diamond Jubilee – Rotunda built, and Queen's Gardens created.
1897: Fremantle Port opens. Royal Mail steamers calling at Albany since 1852 now go there.
1897: Reverend W. Wardell Johnson last Colonial Chaplain resigned.
1897: Father Mateu secures Camfield House and establishes Christian Brothers Grammar School.
1898: Albany Courthouse built on the site of the old Government School.
1898: Albany Golf Links established.
1899: Boer War contingent of Australian troops sails from Albany for South Africa.
1900: Christian Brothers Grammar School closes due to lack of sufficient enrolments.
1901: Federation of the six colonies to create the Commonwealth of Australia.
1901: July. The Duke and Duchess of York and Cornwall arrives on *Royal Yacht Ophir*.
1905: First cargo and passenger service between Albany and Denmark.
1906: Movie nights held in Town Hall run by Kings Pictures.
1908: Albany hosts Great White Fleet of 15 United States Navy battleships.
1908: 13th May, Daisy Bates visits Albany on lecture tour.
1909: Albany Municipal Volunteer Fire Brigade established.
1909: Cabman's Shelter opened.
1909: Princess Royal Sailing Club established.
1910: Empire Pictures commence screening of films in new cinema in York Street.
1910: Lord Kitchener Commander-in-Chief of the British Army visits The Forts on Mt Adelaide.
1912: Government purchases 'The Rocks' for Governor's Summer residence.
1912: 27th October, Father A.E. White delivers his first Albany sermon at Evensong in St John's Church. He celebrates Holy Communion for the first time in Albany at the 8 am in St John's Church on Christmas day the following year.
1914: First and second ANZAC troop ship convoy depart for the middle-east.
1914: New Infants School built on Albany Highway (Perth Road).
1915: 28th October. Bank of Australasia opened for business in St. Albans Building York Street.
1916: Canon John Garland of the Church of England priest establishes the first ANZAC Day.
1916: Commemoration Committee is established in in Brisbane, Queensland.

1917: 25th April, The Western Australian Branch of the Returned Sailors and Soldiers Imperial League of Australia was officially charted.
1918: Albany High School co-located on the site of the Primary School in Serpentine Road.
1920: June. The Prince of Wales, later Edward VIII visits aboard *HMS Renown*.
1922: A Royal Commission was established by the Legislative Council to investigate hospital provision in rural areas of Western Australia.
1924: Albany High School built on side of Mt Clarence. Formally opened the following year.
1925: Woollen mills open. They close 1985.
1926: Cabman's Shelter extended through public subscription to include Women's Rest Centre.
1927: There are 4 substantial schools operating in Albany; 3 government and 1 Roman Catholic.
1927: January 21st: Albany Centenary celebrations.

APPENDIX 2
Military Commandants, Government Residents and Magistrates, and Governors

A summary of the office holders of either Commandant or the Government Residents for Albany or those holding Mayoral positions commencing from December 1826 to 1930.

Commandants:

Major Edmund Lockyer:	December 1826 to April 1827.
Captain Joseph Wakefield:	April 1827 to December 1828.
Lieutenant George Sleeman:	December 1828 to December 1829.
Captain Collet Barker:	December 1829 to March 1831.

Government Residents at Albany during the 19th century.

Alexander Collie:	1831 to 1832.
Lieutenant Donald McLeod (acting):	1832 to 1833.
Sir Richard Spencer:	1833 to 1839.
Captain George Grey:	1839 to 1840.
Captain Peter Belches (acting):	1840 to 1840.
John Randall Phillips:	1842 to 1847.
Henry Camfield:	1847 to 1860.
Sir Alexander Cockburn-Campbell:	1861 to 1871.
Gustavus Edward Cockburn Hare	1871 to 1881
Rowley Crozier Loftie	1882 to 1889
John Arthur Wright	1896 to 1908
Archibald Edmund Burt	1908 to 1934

Mayors of Albany

1885 William Finlay, the inaugural Mayor of Albany
1886 to 1888 William Grills Knight
1888 Lancel Victor de Hamel
1889 to 1890 John Moir
1891 Robert Andrew Muir
1894 to 1897 John Moir
1897 to 1899 William Grills Knight
1899 to 1907 Cuthbert McKenzie
1908 to 1912 Harry Sims
1913 to 1915 Herbert Robinson
1916 E.G. McKenzie
1917 A.F. Cuddihy
1918 to 1921 W.J. Day

1921-24 E. Balston
1925-26 P. Lambert
1926-31 C.H. Wittenoom (Also served in this role 1940-1952)

Governors of New South Wales and Western Australia and its dependencies from 1826 to 1931.

1826 – 1827 Lieutenant Governor Ralph Darling
1828 – 1839 Captain James Stirling
1839 – 1846 John Hutt
1846 – 1847 Lieutenant-Colonel Andrew K H Clarke
1847 – 1848 Lieutenant Frederick Chidley Irwin [Acting Governor]
1848 – 1855 Captain Charles Fitzgerald
1855 – 1862 Sir Arthur Edward Kennedy
1862 – 1868 John Stephen Hampton
1869 – 1875 Sir Frederick Aloysius Weld
1875 – 1877 Sir William Cleaver Francis Robinson
1878 – 1880 Major-General Sir Harry St George Ord
1880 – 1883 Sir William Cleaver Francis Robinson
1883 – 1889 Sir Frederick Napier Broome
1890 – 1895 Sir William Cleaver Francis Robinson
1895 – 1901 Lieutenant Colonel Sir Gerard Smith
1901 – 1902 Captain Sir Arthur Lawley
1903 – 1909 Admiral Sir Frederick George Denham Bedford
1909 – 1913 Sir Gerald Strickland
1913 – 1917 Major-General Sir Harry Barron
1917 – 1920 Sir William Grey Ellison-Macartney
1920 – 1924 Sir Francis Alexander Newdegate
1924 – 1931 Colonel Sir William Robert Campion

APPENDIX 3

THE 39th DORSETSHIRE REGIMENT OF FOOT IN AUSTRALIA

The 39th Regiment of Foot was a British Army regiment and was among one of the first to be stationed in Western Australia. Previously it had served in Sydney and then later at King George's Sound. The regiment was raised under a Royal Warrant dated 13th February 1702 in Ireland during the wars of Queen Anne and had seen service in many countries between 1704 and 1825, Gibraltar, Spain, Portugal, France, Minorca, Ireland, Jamaica, West Indies, India, Italy, Malta, and the United States of America.

An order was received on the 10th July 1825 for a detachment of the 39th Regiment under the command of Captain Joseph Wakefield to proceed to New South Wales. The first division left Cork on the 30th September 1825, consisting of one captain, [Captain Joseph Wakefield] one subaltern, one serjeant, and twenty rank and file soldiers. They embarked in the *Woodman* convict ship on the 4th November 1825, and proceeded to Van Diemen's Land and then on to Sydney. During the period the Regiment was employed in New South Wales, detachments were stationed at Van Diemen's Land, King George's Sound, and on the northern coast.

In 1826, Captain Joseph Wakefield proceeded [from Sydney] to assist in the establishing a Cantonment at King George's Sound on the southern coast of New Holland.

New Colours were presented to the 39th by General Ralph Darling, in the Barrack Square of Sydney, on the 16th May 1831. The ceremony of blessing was performed by the Archdeacon of Sydney, The Venerable

William Broughton, who later as the first and only Lord Bishop of Australia on a voyage to England, his ship briefly called at Albany.

The festivity consequent on the presentation of the Colours was damped by the melancholy intelligence of the death of Captain Collet Barker, who was murdered on the 30th April 1831, by the native tribes on the southern coast of New Holland, near the spot at which Captain Charles Sturt of the 39th Regiment had made the coast on his second expedition. Captain Barker had served in the 39th Regiment for a period of twenty-five years and was highly esteemed. At the time of his death, he was returning from King George's Sound, where he had been for some time Commandant, but which Settlement he had been ordered to deliver over to the new Government of Western Australia and had landed for scientific purposes near the spot where he was murdered.

On the 30th May 1831, a General Order was issued, acquainting the Regiment that it was destined to proceed to India and they embarked at Sydney on the 21st July 1832, in three divisions, and disembarked at Madras on the 22nd September, 10th and 14th of October. The remaining four companies embarked at Sydney on the 3rd of December, and arrived at Madras on the 21st February of the following year. The Regiment served with distinction all over the world until 1958 when it was amalgamated with the Dorset Regiment to form the Devonshire and Dorset Regiment.[2]

---

[2] Cannon, R. *Historical Record of The British Army comprising the History of every Regiment in Her Majesty's Service*. The Military Library, Horse Guards, London 1853.

INDEX

A

Aboriginal/s, 5-24, 34, 41, 45, 61, 69, 76, 81, 88, 98, 102, 107, 119, 123, 132, 134, 137, 139, 153, 159, 162, 174, 192, 196, 203, 349, 352
Aboriginal language, 10, 19, 23, 76, 88, 98
Acheron HMS, 155, 217, 352
Aeroplane, 298-299
Ah Sam, 303
Albany Advertiser, The History of, 280-281
Albany Baths, 299-300
Albany Bicycle Club, xx, see also Transport 344-345
Albany Centenary, 52, 335-338, 356
Albany Chamber of Commerce, 301-302, 317
Albany Defence Rifles, 233-234, 314, 354
Albany Hotel, 282, 287-289, 291, 314, 345
Albany Incorporated as Town, x-xi, 180, 352-353
Albany Infants School, 142-143
Albany High School, 143-144, 151, 311, 321, 354
Albany Municipal Council, 204-205, 210, 314, 353
Albany Naming, ii -iii 2, 69, 337
Albany Observer, The History of, 270, 365, 366
Albany Perth Road, 178-179, 191, 196, 351
Albany Primary School, 142
Albany Roads Board, 180-181, 289, 320
Albany Season, 325-327, 347
Albany Shire, 5, 367
Albany Town Council, 186, 207, 210, 211, 215-216, 246, 287-288, 300, 312, 326, 340, 367
Albany Town Hall, 3, 70, 157, 262, 270, 314-315, 318, 342, 353
Albany Town Library, 312-313, 366
Albany Trust, 80, 180, 306, 352
Albany Turf Club, 327, 341-342, 347
Albany Week, 249, 325-327
Albany Woollen Mills, 306-308
Agricultural Show, 329
Allouarn, F.A., 56
American Whalers, 32, 84, 127-130, 155-156, 225, 322
Amity, Brig, iii, 4, 8, 12-14, 43, 47-49, 51-52, 54-55, 57-59, 85, 115, 336
Anderson, Black Jack, 33, 75
Anglican Church: see also St Johns Church, 152, 154, 156, 269-270, 272, 274, 310
Angove River, 204, 208
Annesfield, 21-22, 137, 147, 352
Anzac Convoy, 3-4, 253-258, 269-272, 277, 354
Anzac Day, 2-3, 269, 273-274
Anzac Word Origin, 275-276
Arbour Day, 144

Arpenteur, 155
Astrolabe, 8, 11-12, 43-45, 50, 351
Australian, 193
Australian Royal Mail Steamship Navigation Company, 193, 217-219

B

Bacchante, 6, 93-96, 170, 266, 353
Baesjou, J. A. Dr, 199-200
Bakers, 294-296
Bald Head, 27-28, 35, 41, 53, 86, 89-90, 93, 105, 129, 169-171, 219, 247-248
Balston, E., 295, 355
Banks, J., 30
Bannister, T. Captain, 66-67, 178, 351
Barker, C. Captain, 8, 15, 24, 61-62, 64-65, 351, 354, 356
Barlee, F., 122-123, 163
Baroda, 162-163, 352
Bates, D., 23-24, 353
Bathurst, 10, 42
Bathurst, Lord, 47, 49-50, 56, 114, 337, 339, 351
Baudin, N., 9, 24, 25, 35, 37-43, 351
Baxter, J.,81-82
Baxter, W., 62
Beagle, 25, 89-90, 314
Bean, C. E. W., 272, 275
Belches, P. Captain, 117, 354
Bell, St Joseph's Convent, 310
Bengal Lancers, 333
Berliner, O.W., 149, 260, 330
Bird, F., 74, 312, 318
Bird, M., 75
Birdwood, W.R., 265-266, 275-276
Bland, R., 19-20
Boer War, 114, 161, 240-245, 252, 277, 353
Bombay, 217, 335
Bond Store, 191, 198, 317
Brady, J. Bishop, 134-135, 152, 157
Brassey, A., 167, 205
Brassey, T. Sir, 235-236
Breaksea Island, 27, 45, 86, 93-94, 97, 130, 168-173, 222, 236-238, 247, 268-269, 352
Breaksea Lighthouse, 168 -173, 177, 220, 352
Breweries, 292-294
British East India Company, 311, 321
British Squadron, 252, 267-268
Broome, F.N. Governor, 109, 171, 183, 189, 201-202, 232, 319, 355
Brothel Incident, 302-303
Broughton, W. Captain, 8-9, 26-28, 31-32, 47, 127, 350, 351
Broughton W. Bishop, 74, 154, 356

Bunbury, ii, 77, 138, 154-155, 157, 180, 191-192, 236-237, 270, 307, 332,
Bush Brotherhood of St Boniface, 3, 269-270
Busselton, ii, 180, 195,

C
Cabman Shelter, 316-317, 353, 354
Camfield, Mrs A., 21-22, 24, 109, 137, 139, 146, 352
Camfield, Henry., 21-22, 139, 155, 162, 354
Camfield House, 21, 137, 146-147, 321, 353
Campbell – Cockburn, A. 22, 139, 171, 193, 195, 199-200, 312, 319, 354
Campbell - Cockburn, T., 141, 184, 201, 206, 280-281, 304
Campion, W.R. Governor, 6, 144, 264, 307, 311, 336, 355
Candyup, 78-79
Cantonment, iii-iv, 4, 8, 14, 23, 25-26, 43, 47-50, 52, 56, 58, 84, 85, 111, 113, 115, 296, 309, 311, 313, 336, 348
Cape Arid, 225
Cape Chatham, 28, 47
Cape Leeuwin, 32, 56, 68, 93, 172, 238
Cape Howe, 27, 33, 36, 42
Cape Manypeaks, 53
Cape of Good Hope, 32, 41, 50, 61, 172
Cape Otway, 93, 95
Cape Riche, 82-83, 116-117, 225
Cape Town, ii, 30,
Cape Vancouver 169
Casuarina, 10, 37-39
Casuarina, Tree, 71, 83, 90
Catacombs, 197-198
Catholic Church, Roman, 93, 131-135, 151-152, 156-157, 159, 310, 352-353
Catholic School, 92, 134-136, 145-146, 151-152
Centennial Oval, 340-341, 347, 353
Chamber of Commerce, See also Albany, 279, 246
Champion, 77-79, 87, 127, 155
Chatham, 8, 26-29, 351
Cheesewright, 185
Chester, E., 77
Cheynes Beach Whaling Company, 127, 129, 351
Cheyne, G. Captain, 88, 129, 283, 320, 322, 351
Chinese Garden nuisance, 211-212
Chinese Market Garden, 304-305, 319
Chinese Workers, 220, 303-304, 320, 352
Church of England, 135, 153-155, 269-270, 274-275, 298, 309, 310, 319, 352, 354
Church of England Schools, 132, 135, 137, 147-150,
Chusan, steamship, 105-106, 193, 219-220, 352
Chusan Hotel, 289-290

Christian Brothers, 146-147, 321, 353
Cinemas, see also Empire and Regent Theatres and King pictures, 330-332
Clarke, A.K. Governor, 25, 33, 138, 355
Coaling Depot, 161, 167, 170, 179, 188, 217-220, 222-223, 228, 229, 232, 248
Coates and Company Gas Supply, 204, 212, 214-215
Collie, A. Dr, 8, 15-18, 78, 278, 311, 313, 351
Commercial Inn and Tavern, 282-283
Commissariat Store, 62, 78, 117, 132, 140-141, 143, 309, 311, 313-314, 317, 319, 321, 352
Cottage Hospital, 195, 202, 319
Convent, Roman Catholic, 146, 151, 157, 310, 353
Convict Depot, 316-317, 352
Convicts, 130, 142, 160, 168-169, 178-180, 191-192, 194, 202, 223, 313, 316-317, 336-340, 351
Convict Ships, 40, 355
Convoys, 253-258, 269, 271-272, 277, 354
Coolgardie, 100, 140, 228-229, 304-305, 327, 332, 353
Co-operative Society, 318-319
Co-operative Store, 225, 318, 354, 353
Courthouse,140-142, 157-158, 191, 194-195, 214, 248, 293, 312, 317-318, 345, 352, 353
Cricket, 94-95, 111, 161, 261, 291, 326, 341, 345, 347
Crimean War, 160, 219-220, 231, 290
Crossman, W. Lieutenant, 193, 316, 321, 352
Customs and Excise, 191, 193-195, 197-198, 222, 233, 313, 352

D
Dame School, 132, 141
Darling, R. Governor, iv, 12-14, 33, 47-52, 55-58, 68, 114, 241, 313, 335-339, 349
Darwin, C., 25, 89-90, 112, 235
Dawn Requiem 1930, 269-271, 274
Day, W.J., 296, 355
Deep Water Jetty, 227
Defence, 171-172, 177, 231-241, 244, 333, 353
Defence Rifles, 232-233, 314
De Freycinet, L., 24, 37-38, 55, 351
De Hamel, L.V., 167, 200, 280, 354
D' Entrecasteaux, B., 32, 38
De Saisson, 43-44
Denmark, 61, 63, 65, 157, 190, 242, 281, 345, 353
Discovery, 8, 26-30, 338
Drew Robinson and Company, 159, 216, 240, 313, 322
Duke of York, iv, 2, 52, 69, 96, 266, 336,
Dunn, J., 77, 225, 303, 322
D'Urville, J.S.C.D., 11-12, 43-45, 78, 351
Dymes, F.R., 291, 300, 317, 320, 353

E

Eales, J.H., 285-286, 288
Eclipse Island, 27, 41, 171-173
Education Act 1871, 131, 139-140, 145
Edward V11, 266, 276-277, 324, 354
Egerton Warburton, Margaret., 74-75
Elderslie, Ship, 166-167
Electricity, 212-216
Elleker, 61
Ellen Cove, 180, 224, 311, 352
Ellen, 69, 86
Elligood, 32, 35, 42, 351
Emden, 253-254, 258
Empire Day, 335
Empire Theatre, 330-331
Emu, 40, 351
Emu Point, 4, 39, 40, 351
Esperance, 32, 35, 37, 65, 82, 173, 226, 229
Esperance, 32
Esplanade Hotel, 285, 287-288
Eucla, 82, 173, 175-177, 352-353
Eyre, E.J., 78, 81-83, 107, 174

F

Federation, 166, 172, 177, 229, 235, 244, 277, 332-335
Festing, C., Lieutenant, 12-13, 51-57, 335, 340
Fish Ponds, 204-210
Fitzgerald, C. Governor, 21, 131, 136, 192, 355
Fitzroy, R., 90
Flinders, Captain M., 9-10, 24, 26, 34-37, 41-42, 53, 82, 338, 351
Football, 261, 341, 346-347
Forrest, J., 158, 175, 177, 189, 229, 243, 246, 332-334
Fortifications, 167, 172, 226, 231-240, 253, 353
Fowler's Bay, 34, 82-83, 174
France, 46, 50, 56, 74, 85, 100, 114, 160-161, 231, 255, 261-262, 263-264, 266, 273, 277, 324, 355
Frederick, Duke of York and Albany, xi, 2, 52, 69, 96, 266, 336
Fredericks Town, xi, 2, 52, 69, 150,
Freeborn, R., 147-148, 149, 151, 326
Freemason's Hotel, 258, 274, 285-287, 289, 292, 304, 322, 336, 344, 346, 353
Fremantle, ii, 3-4, 6, 48, 67, 69, 95, 103, 107, 111, 118-120, 138, 140, 154, 155, 158, 163, 168, 173-176, 180, 184, 188-189, 193-194, 195, 198, 205, 207, 217, 221, 229-230, 233-234, 238, 246-247, 252, 255-256, 266, 269, 278, 282, 286, 292, 296, 298, 300, 303-305, 323, 350, 351
Fremantle, C. Captain, 47-49, 339
French, i, 4, 7, 9-12, 25-26, 32-34, 37, 43-45, 47-51, 55-56, 60, 68, 70-71, 82, 85, 89, 106, 114, 116-118, 127-130, 145, 156, 184, 217, 231, 255, 257, 277, 310, 337, 351
Frenchman Bay, 4, 127, 130, 208, 222, 236
French River, 43, 60, 70-71
Freycinet, L., 24, 37-38, 55, 351
Furness, H, 85, 100

G

Gallipoli, 3, 257, 260-261, 265-266, 270-276, 324
Gaol i, 23, 25, 138-141, 147, 235-237, 261, 337, 365
Gas, 108, 204, 212-215
Geake, D.S., 102, 168, 282-283, 322
Geake's Island, 102, 164
Geographe, 9, 10, 34, 37, 40
Geographe Bay, 84
Glen Candy, 78, 81
Gold, 7, 118, 119-120, 136, 138, 149, 167, 175, 190, 216, 237, 242, 264, 285
Goldfields, i, 100, 111, 143, 228, 240, 332-334, 343, 351
Golf Club, 267, 341, 344
Golf Links, 208, 267, 325, 343-344, 347, 353
Government Cottage, 74, 144, 275, 299, 310-311, 313, 325
Government Farm, (Also referred to as Strawberry Hill and The Old Farm), 4, 74, 113, 311
Government Schools, 132, 138, 141-143, 145, 151, 212, 317, 352
Government Schools' Board, 140
Governor Phillip, 61
Grace, W.G., 111
Grammar Schools, 131, 133, 138, 144, 147-150, 353
Great Southern Railway, 182-197, 194, 198, 221, 227, 229, 281, 284, 289, 292, 296, 314, 323, 345, 347, 353
Great War, ix, 5, 130, 144, 208, 244, 252, 253-257, 261-263, 272-273, 275-277, 292, 311, 312, 324-325
Great White Feet, 245-252, 353
Green Island, 4, 29-30, 39, 43-44, 53-54
Greeve, J.F.C., 294-296
Greeve, D, 144, 208, 297, 330, 368
Grey, G. Captain, 24, 76-77, 354
Grey 2nd Earl, 7, 83, 114

H

Hackett, 279
Haggard, R. Sir., 274-275
Hampton, H.S., Governor, 121, 139, 193, 355
Hay River, 63, 65, 74, 352
Hay, R., 51, 57, 85

Harbour Master (Albany Port), 103, 169-171, 227, 250-251, 271, 295, 313
Hare. G.E.C., 186, 194, 205, 210, 315, 341-342, 354
Hassell, A.Y., 319-320
Hassell, A.Y.(Mrs), 4-5, 132, 141, 156
Hassell, J. 18-19, 95, 166, 212, 230, 285, 305-306, 312, 320, 322
Headmasters House, 313
Hen and Chicken Inn, 282-283
Hillman, A., 74, 178, 351
Hillside House, 319-320
Historical Record (The), ii, viii, x -xi 1-6, 22, 24-26, 32, 37, 47-48, 55, 58, 77, 103, 153, 156, 269, 276-278, 311, 324, 338, 348
Hoover, H., 100
Hordern, A., 182-190, 272, 353
Hordern Monument, 180
Horses, ix, 59, 67, 82-83, 94, 107, 116, 179, 193-194, 196-197, 207, 214, 253, 256, 296-297, 327, 341-342
Horse and Groom Hotel, 287
Hospital, 63, 162, 164, 167, 186, 199-203, 211, 227, 245-246, 254, 257-262, 309, 313, 319, 321, 328, 353
Hotels, 169, 179, 210, 282-293, 299, 353
Hügel Carl von., 86-89
Hutt, J. Governor, 19, 76, 134, 152, 355

I
Indian Ocean, ii, 3-4, 56, 85, 168, 172, 239, 249, 253-257
Indian Troops, 334-335
Ingoldby, F. Captain, 240, 243
Ile de France, (see also Mauritius), 74, 85
Infants School, 142-144, 151, 212, 354
Inspector of Nuisances, 204-205, 210-212
Inspector of Police, 197, 249, 303
Investigator, 9, 26, 34, 41, 338
Irwin, F. Governor, 19, 136-137, 161-162, 355

J
James Patterson, 77
Japan, 160, 239, 245-246, 277, 323
Japanese Prostitutes, 302-303
Japanese Naval Squadron, 246, 252, 256
Jarrah, (see also mahogany), 66, 108, 221, 304, 309
Jerramungup, 20
Jetty/Jetties. (see also Port Facilities), 106, 116, 118, 166, 176, 185, 193-194, 207, 212-213, 220-221, 224-228, 243-244, 248-249, 252, 259, 267, 283-284, 297, 301, 323, 336, 352

K
Kalgan River, 30-32, 42-43, 60, 63, 73, 78, 89, 193, 208, 225, 268, 316, 351
Kalgoorlie, ix, 100, 140, 147, 228, 298, 303-305, 332, 353
Kangaroo Island, 33-34, 45, 55, 58, 172, 219-220, 223, 270
Katanning, 182, 190, 295, 341, 346
Kendenup, 19, 62, 98, 305-306, 319-320, 322
Kerosene Lighting, 204, 210, 212-215
King Edward V11, 277, 324
King Edward V111, 266
King George 1V, 47
King George V, 96, 253, 265-266, 273-274
King, P.P. Lieutenant, 10, 18, 40-42
King River, 30, 62-63, 72-73, 117, 193, 208, 225, 240, 258, 296, 299, 304, 316
King, Tommy, 22-23
King William 1V, 314
Kingfisher, 218-219
Kings Pictures, 149, 353
Kingston, 32-33, 351
Kipling, R., 110
Kitchen, A., 257-258
Kitchener, Lord., 255-256, 354
Knight, L., 132, 141, 154, 352
Knight, S., 132, 141, 180, 225, 322, 352
Knight, W.G., 135, 141, 155, 205, 225, 303, 310, 314-315, 328, 354, 355
Kojonup, 20, 191

L
L'Uranie, 55
La Perouse, 32
Larkins, 218, 226
Lawley Park, 3, 132, 140, 141, 143, 156, 225, 248, 266, 313, 316, 319, 320
Lawson, H., 97-99, 204, 221, 278
Legislative Assembly, 235
Legislative Council, 21, 24, 120, 131, 140, 142, 152, 161, 172-173, 179, 182-183
Le Havre, 38-39, 83, 85
Le Heroine, 156
Lewis and Clark, 25
Lighthouses, See Breaksea, Eclipse and Point King, 93, 101, 160, 168-173, 222, 238, 316, 352
Lime, 283
Limeburner's Creek, 207-208
Little Grove, 261
Lockyer, E. Major, ii-iii, 4, 8, 12-14, 26, 43, 45, 47-60, 62, 114-115, 127, 224, 296, 335, 340, 350, 351, 354
Loftie, R.C., 93-95, 168, 200, 234, 314, 318, 328-329, 345, 354
London, ii- iv, 61, 76, 90, 108, 126, 132, 160, 171-172, 183-185, 188, 206, 212, 215, 217, 210,

224, 231-232, 235, 254, 255, 262, 269, 273-274, 349
London Hotel, 263, 289-290, 292, 345
Lyttleton, S., 191

M
Macleay, A., 58-60
MacKillop, Sister M., 92
McKail and Co., 159, 313, 322
McKail, J., 131, 288, 290, 322, 313
McKail, N.W., 146, 293, 321, 322
McKenzie, H., 283, 301
McKenzie, J. 158, 225, 283-286, 314, 326
Mail Coach, 192, 194, 196-197
Manby, T. Midshipman, 29
Mauritius, 74, 85, 172, 220, 225
Mass Rocks, 156-157
Mateu, F. Father, 145-146, 157, 310, 321, 353
Matthew Cull House, 319
Mechanics Institute, 142, 312-313, 352
Melbourne, 146, 158-159, 161, 165, 169, 174, 222, 235, 236, 238, 244, 249, 255-257, 270, 274, 277-278, 303, 334, 344
Menang, 7-9, 16-17, 22, 24, 69, 348
Menzies, A., 26, 28, 30-32
Mermaid, 10, 40-41, 351
Methodist (Wesley) Church., 158-159, 320, 341
Meyers, J., 293-294
Michaelmas Island, 13, 14, 53-54, 57, 68, 86, 248
Middleton Beach, 11, 74, 95, 128, 151, 208, 224, 237, 239, 247, 261, 268-269, 287-288, 297, 298, 319, 322, 325, 344, 352
Military Wedding, 260
Mississippi, 82, 83
Mokare, 8, 15-17, 24, 61-65, 69-72, 351
Morley, J., 77-78, 88, 311, 320-321, 351
Movie Theatres, See Cinema
Motorcar., 296
Mount Adelaide, 3, 238, 240-241, 253, 353
Mount Barker, 19, 178, 182, 190, 274
Mount Clarence, 3, 70-72, 86-88, 97-98, 143, 180, 208-209, 222, 269, 271-272, 293, 298, 310, 351
Mount Gardner, 38, 55, 170
Mount Melville, 13, 61, 72, 204-205, 208, 304, 309, 321
Municipality Institutions Act 1871, 180-181
Museum of the Great Southern, 219

N
Nakina, 17
Napoleon, 25, 29, 74, 86, 231
Naturaliste, 9, 10, 37, 40
Neuwman, C.M., 304
New Holland, ii, 9, 12, 17, 25, 26, 30, 32, 33, 40, 43, 47, 48, 52, 56, 63, 87-89, 244, 337, 339, 351

Newspapers, See full list in Bibliography
New South Wales, ii-iii, 9,11, 12, 25, 34, 37, 42, 43, 47-48, 50-51, 52, 57, 58, 61, 64, 68-69, 81, 86, 91, 99, 114-115, 165, 187, 220, 229, 272, 277, 313, 324, 332, 339, 355
New Zealand, 2, 3, 33, 56, 114, 160, 172, 217, 231, 241, 253, 255-257, 275-276, 277, 280, 283, 324
Night School Classes, 144, 150
Nind. I.S., 12-15, 24, 52-53
Norman House, 320
North German Lloyd Line, 217, 227
Northumberland, 169
Nuyts, P., 26, 92, 351

O
Octagon "Chapel", 142, 153-154, 309, 312, 351,
Old Farm, See Government Farm and Strawberry Hill farm, 311-312,
Old Gaol, 283, 318
Ophir, Royal Yacht, 96, 353
Order of St Josephs, 92, 145, 146
Orient Line, 172, 222, 223
Otway, 195, 221
Oyster Harbour, 4, 25, 27, 29, 30, 31, 34, 35, 37-43, 53-55, 63, 70, 86, 88-89, 95, 110, 236, 351

P
P&O, 162-163, 168-169, 171, 176, 179, 185, 193, 195, 217-230, 305, 318, 319, 320, 321, 352
P&O Floating Dock, 226
Parade Ground, 4
Parade Street, 13, 56, 111, 224, 285, 309, 316, 320, 335, 346, 352
Parish Pilgrimage, 269, 271
Parmelia, Ship, 171
Patrick Taylor Cottage, 78, 321, 351
Pavlova, A., 110-111
Pazakos, G. 259, 299-300
Peninsula and Orient Company, see P&O.
Perth, 111, 115, 120, 122, 124, 128, 133, 134, 136, 139, 142-143, 146, 158, 167, 168, 173-176, 178-179, 180, 182-183, 188-189, 191-197, 205, 221, 229, 234, 241, 274, 279, 293, 297, 313, 323, 325, 330, 332, 349
Perth-Albany Road, 178-179, 191, 196, 351
Phillip, A., Captain, 234
Phillips, A.C., 80
Phillips, J.R., 76, 180, 354
Plantagenet, 43, 44, 61, 69, 120-123, 140, 180-181, 281, 320, 328, 342, 346, 349, 352
Point King, 95, 168-171, 173, 221, 239, 247, 268, 352
Point Frederick, 316, 336
Possession, ii, 26-30, 47-48, 56, 115, 339, 348
Point Possession, 27-31, 35, 43, 93, 218, 221

Police, 115-120, 123-125, 142, 166, 192, 194, 196-197, 249, 298, 303, 317-318, 327, 329
Porongerup Range, 61, 303
Port Jackson, 9, 35, 41, 45, 50, 52, 84, 91
Postmaster, 101, 137, 191-192, 195, 225, 230, 284, 322
Post Office, 157, 175, 177, 191, 193-198, 207, 221, 227, 230, 283-284, 317-318, 322, 352, 353
Post Office Alcove, 197-198
Premier Hotel, 289-290, 292
Presbyterian (Scots) Church, 149, 157-158
Pretious, W. Captain, 120, 171
Preussen, 165, 353
Prideaux, C., 178, 353
Prince Albert Victor of Wales, 93-94, 96, 170, 353
Prince Edward of Wales, 266, 276
Prince George of Wales, 93, 96, 170, 353
Princess Royal Harbour, The, xi, 2, 4, 12, 27, 29-30, 32, 35-36, 43-44, 47, 52, 68, 164, 184-185, 189, 194, 217-218, 229, 237, 241, 246, 256-257, 271, 276, 280, 282-283, 350
Princess Royal Sailing Club, 325, 336, 341, 345
Proclamation, xi, 47-49, 64, 161-162, 340, 350
Prostitution, 302, 303
Pyrmont House, 151, 320

Q
Quarantine, 160-168
Quarantine Station (Quaranup), 94, 164-168, 222
Quoy, Midshipman, 12, 43, 44, 45
Queen Victoria, xi, 114, 161, 201, 245, 277, 314, 320, 324, 328, 332, 335, 350, 351
Queen Victoria's Jubilee, 201, 215, 328

R
Railway, (see also Great Southern Railway), iv, 114, 161, 182-190, 195-196, 200, 204, 206, 214, 216, 230, 253, 280, 289, 337, 345, 347, 353
Railway Hotel, 288-289
Railway Workshop, 189, 229, 323, 347
Rangatira, 93, 104, 162, 258
Rectory St. John's, 148, 260, 310
Regent Theatre, 330-332
Renown, 266-267, 354
Residency, 4, 168, 244, 317
Residency Point, ii, 4, 6, 52, 56, 199, 201, 313, 317, 335, 350, 351
Returned and Services League, (R.S.L), 3, 271, 274
Returned Soldiers and Sailors Imperial League of Australia, 262-263, 270
Rinking, 342-343
Roads Board Act 1888, 180
Robinson, H., 159, 215-216, 327, 330, 343, 355

Robinson, W.C.F. Governor, 22, 139, 231, 355
Roe, J.S., 40-41, 69, 73, 113, 351
Rogers, C. Dr., 94, 234
Roller Skating, See Rinking
Rood Screen, St John's Church, 264-265
Roosevelt, T. U.S.A. President, 245-246, 250
Rossiter, T. Captain, 82-83
Royal Commission 1922, 203, 354
Royal Geographical Society, 18, 74, 99
Royal George Hotel, 240, 288-289, 322, 344, 346, 353
Royal Mail, 105, 109, 176, 191-194, 196, 198, 217-220, 347, 352-353
Royal Western Australian Historical Society, 48, 291, 348
Royal Yacht, (see also Ophir), 96, 353
Russian Scare, 97, 177, 226, 233-236, 291

S
Sainson, L.A. Draughtsman, 12, 43-45
Sandalwood, 188-189, 221
Sale, J. 22, 77, 185, 220, 322
Salsette, 162
Sanitary, 204-205, 209-212, 288
Sanitation, 201, 209, 211
Scadden, J. Premier, 208, 259, 307
Scarlet Fever (Scarletina), 161-162, 166, 354
Saw, L.E. Charge Nurse, 261
Schools: 131-152
　Aboriginal: see also Annesfield, 139, 352
　Christian Brothers: 146-147
　Dame: 132
　Government: 134, 136-138, 140-144, 312-313, 317, 320, 352
　Private: 134, 150-151, 320
　Grammar: 133, 138, 147-151, 353
　Roman Catholic: 92, 134-135, 139, 145-146, 310-311, 353
Scots Church, See Presbyterian Church
Scratchley, P.H., 232, 235-238
Secret Instructions, 50-51
Seal Island, 27, 29, 32, 35, 37-39, 41, 42, 45, 73, 86
Sealers Oven, 127
Sealers, 4, 7, 14, 17, 52-53, 54-55, 57, 60, 65, 68, 127-130, 221
Sesquicentennial Celebrations, 6, 156
Sherratt, T.B., 128, 129, 132, 153-154, 166, 284-285, 309, 312, 314, 322, 351, 352
Sherratt Family Inn, 284-285
Ship Inn, 225, 282-284, 314
Short, A. Bishop, 154-155, 310, 352
Singapore, 193, 217, 219, 220
Sir William Molesworth, 162, 352
Skating Rink, see Rinking

Sleeman, G. Lieutenant, 4, 5, 60-63, 65, 115, 311, 351, 354
Smallpox, 100, 161-165, 353
South Australia, 3, 23, 34, 65, 81-82, 91-92, 99, 103, 107, 114, 124, 124, 143, 165, 171, 173-177, 187, 192, 196, 224, 238, 242, 295-296, 318, 324, 353
Southern Brewing Company, 293-294
Spanish Influenza, 168
Southern Ocean, 251, 257
Spencer, A., 132, 350
Spencer, E., 173, 180, 191
Spencer, Eliza, 76
Spencer Gulf, 33-34
Spencer Inn, 291
Spencer, S., 153
Spencer, R., 73-77, 85, 87, 89, 133, 153-154, 180, 191, 282-283, 311-313, 350, 351, 352, 354
St John's Church of England, 23, 148, 151, 153-154, 156, 159, 264, 273, 274, 310
St. Joseph's Church, 157, 341
State Aid to Schools, 134-135, 139, 145
State Assisted School's Act 1895, 139, 159
Stirling, E., 279
Stirling, J. Governor, 2, 47, 48-50, 52, 56, 64, 66-67, 68-69, 74, 113, 127, 132-133, 161, 182, 278, 284, 311, 313, 337-340, 351
Stirling Range, 60, 88
Strawberry Hill, (see also Government Farm), 11, 74, 76, 89, 311-312, 350, 351
Street Crossing Issue, 189
Street Lighting, 204, 212-216
Strickland, W, 285
Success, 50, 52, 68
Sulphur, 69, 161, 282, 351
Swan River, 33, 48, 55, 57-60, 62, 73, 84, 86-88, 284
Swan River Colony, 14, 48, 56, 64, 68, 69, 77, 80, 84, 86, 89, 107, 113, 131, 133-134, 153, 159, 161, 172, 178, 180, 182, 199, 278, 282, 284, 311, 313, 338, 351
Swimming Baths, See Baths
Sunbeam, Yacht, 167
Sydney, ii-iv, 2, 7, 33-35, 37, 48-50, 52, 54-59, 65, 68-69, 74-75, 86, 98, 105-106, 108, 134, 146, 154, 164-165, 182, 218-219, 230, 249, 313, 339, 341, 349, 351, 355-356
Sydney, 254-256

T
Talbot House, 263-264
Tasmania, (see also Van Diemen's Land), 90, 99, 160, 166, 242, 324
Taylor, E., 148-149, 352
Taylor, M., 77-78, 351
Taylor, P. 77-81, 180, 199, 217, 287, 321-322

Telegraph, 96, 98, 104, 107, 114, 160, 163, 172, 173-177, 181, 189, 195, 196, 202, 222, 224, 230, 255, 257, 275, 278, 352-353
Telephone, 177-178
Tennis Courts, 141, 267, 300, 326, 336, 341, 347
Teresa, Sister, 146
Terra Australis, 9, 26, 29, 34-35, 43
Ticket of Leave Men, 115, 118, 143, 192, 316
The Forts, 240-242, 244, 247-248, 252-253, 255, 287, 346, 354
The Mount, 96, 298, 321
The Rocks, 144, 259, 261, 275, 310-311, 313, 325, 354
Thirty Ninth (39th) Regiment of Foot, ii -iv, 13, 47, 60-61, 350, 355-356
TocH, See Talbot house, 262-264, 271, 283
Town Jetty, 193-194, 207, 212-215, 221, 224-225
Town Improvement Act 1841, 79
Town Trust, 79
Transport, (see also Railway, Bicycle, Horses and Aeroplane), 296-297
Trimmer, A., 312
Trimmer, Miss., 22
Trollope, A., 91-92, 180
Turf Club, 327, 341-342, 347
Two People's Bay, 37, 128-128, 204, 296, 351
Typhoid, 100, 161, 165, 167-168, 204, 206, 209, 211, 310

U
Union, 37, 351
United States of America, 37, 99, 100, 114, 132, 160-161, 245-246, 248, 249, 250, 251, 252, 277, 317, 324, 353, 355
Union Jack, 6, 226, 315, 336-337, 348, 351

V
Vancouver Arts Centre, 319
Vancouver, Cape, 169
Vancouver, G. Captain, ii-iv, 8-9, 17, 24, 25-29, 30-31, 32, 35, 37-39, 41, 43, 47, 101, 127, 338, 348, 351
Vancouver Peninsula, 4, 89
Vancouver's Well, 4
Van Diemen's Land, (see also Tasmania), 7, 32-33, 34, 45, 55, 57-58, 69, 86, 287, 356
Van Zuilecom L. Captain, 226
Vasse River, 19, 180
Victoria, State, 52, 91, 99, 101, 107, 114, 148, 157, 159, 165, 176, 187, 212, 238, 240, 242, 264, 277, 306, 324
Volunteers, 96, 128, 186, 233, 240-242, 244, 326, 328-329, 346, 353

W
Wakefield, J. Captain, 13, 47, 51-54, 56, 58-60, 62, 115, 224-225, 311, 335

Walpole, M., 108-110, 295
Water Supply, 11, 168, 204-209, 293, 323, 351
Waterman's Arms Inn, 282
Waychinnicup, 127
Weld, F.A. Governor, 76, 131, 139, 152, 175, 195, 353, 355
Weld Arms Hotel (Tavern), 285, 287, 291-292, 303, 353
West /Australian Land Company, 205, 227
Western Australian Centenary, 337-338
Whalers and Whaling, 4, 7, 14, 17, 29, 30, 32-33, 37, 44-45, 54, 55, 65, 83-86, 101, 116-118, 127-130, 213, 221, 223-225, 284, 322, 351, 352
Wheat, 74, 274, 295, 311
White, A.E. Padre, 260, 263, 269-272, 351, 354
White, A.C. 263
White Star (Hart) Hotel, 251, 288, 289, 299, 303, 322, 345
White Star Liners, 217, 227, 229, 250, 288
White Swan Hotel, 287
Wilson, T.B., Dr, 8, 15-16, 24, 61-65, 67, 115, 351
Wilsons Inlet, 69, 94
Wilsons Prominentary, 105, 219,
Wittenoom, C.H., 355
Wittenoom, E.H., 318

Wittenoom, J.B. Reverend, 119, 131, 133-134
Wollaston, J.R. Archdeacon, 80-81, 137, 152, 153-156, 217, 309-310, 312, 320, 352
Wollaston H. Dr, 320, 352
Women's Rest Centre, See Cabman Shelter. 316-317
Wool, 306-307
Woollen Mills, 306-308, 341, 354
World War 1, See The Great War, 3, 100, 231, 258, 263, 265, 269
World War 11, 187, 245, 271, 284, 312
Wreath Laying Custom, 3, 269, 271
Wylie, 81-83, 174

X
Xenophon, ship, 34

Y
York, 19, 138, 178, 180, 183
York, Duke, See Duke of York, ii-iv, 2, 52, 69, 96,
York Hotel, 292-293, 355

Z
Zoo, 303-304

BIBLIOGRAPHY.

Newspapers

First editions of relevant newspapers were accessed through the National Library of Australia, General Catalogue Collection and that were deemed pertinent for the period that was being reported upon are listed below. They have been extensively accessed through the Trove Online resource available to researchers and the public alike. These following newspapers have been extensively cited throughout the work.

The Perth Gazette and Western Australian Journal.
The Port Phillip Patriot and Melbourne Advertiser.
The Inquirer and Commercial News. Perth.
The Albany Observer.
The West Australian, Perth.
The Albany Advertiser.
The Colonial Times. Sydney.
The Observer London.
The Sydney Gazette and New South Wales Advertiser. Sydney.
The Perth Gazette. Perth.
The Colonist. Sydney.
The Daily News. Perth.
The Australasian Chronicle. Sydney.
The Adelaide Chronicle and South Australian Record. Adelaide.
The Albany Banner.
The Perth Gazette and Independent Journal of Politics and News.
The Sydney Morning Herald.
The Leader Melbourne,
The Albany Despatch.
The Adelaide Observer.
The Perth Gazette and West Australian Times.
The Albany Mail and King George's Sound Advertiser.
The Hobart Gazette.
The Western Mail. Perth.
The Government Gazette. Perth.
The Fremantle Herald.
The Australian Advertiser. Albany.
The Fremantle Herald.
The Port Augusta Dispatch and Flinders' Advertiser.
The Express. Fremantle.
The Western Australian Times. Perth.
The New York Times, Manhattan, New York City.
The Albany Wizbang.
The Argus, Melbourne.
The Fremantle Journal and General Advertiser.
The Esperance Express.
The Albany Mail.
The Australian Town and Country Journal. Sydney.
The Call. Perth.
The London Gazette.

Journals and Periodicals

Collie, A. *Letters with Respect to the Early History of the Swan River Settlement 1829 - 1835*. Parliamentary Library of the Commonwealth, London, 1912.

Early Days. Journal of the Royal Western Australian Historical Society, Nedlands.

Hanson, Lt. Col. *A Voyage from Madras to the Swan River, King George's Sound, and Van Diemen's Land in. The Years 1831 and 1832*. Guildford, 1833.

Hassell, A.Y. *Early Memories of Albany*. Printed privately, 1910.

Horton, S. (Ed). *The History of the Albany Convict Gaol, Its Convicts, Gaolers and Warders*. Albany Historical Society, 2008.

Lockyer, E. *Journal of Major Edmund Lockyer. Commandant of the Expedition Sent from Sydney in 1826 to Found a Settlement at King Georges Sound Western Australia*. Library of News South Wales, 1827

Manby, T. *Journal of the Voyages of the HMS Discovery and Chatham*. London, 1798.

Steere, F.G. *Bibliography of Books, Articles, and Pamphlets Dealing with Western Australia*. Perth, 1923

The Albany Advertiser Holiday Number. 1936.

The Albany Advertiser Holiday Number. 1938.

The Western Mail Centenary Number. Perth, 1929.

Books and Other Publications.

Albany's Nineteenth-Century Buildings. Albany Historical Society, 1988.

Australian Dictionary of Biography 1788-1939. University of Melbourne Press, 1996.

Australian Encyclopaedia. Angus and Robertson, Sydney, 1927. The Grollier Society of Sydney, 1963.

Australians: A Historical Library. In 11Volumes, The National Library of Australia .1987.

Aveling, M. (ed) *Westralian Voices*. Documents in Western Australian Social History. University of Western Australia Press, Perth, 1979.

Bartlett, J. *Built to Last. A History of the Anglican Church of Saint John the Evangelist Albany WA 1948 to 1998*. Printed privately, 1998.

Battye, J.S. *Western Australia. A History from its Discovery to the Inauguration of the Commonwealth*. University of Western Australia Press, Perth, 1978.

Battye, J.S. *The Cyclopedia of Western Australia in Two Volumes*. 1912. Hesperian Press, Perth, 1985.

Berryman, I. *The Swan River Letters*. Swan River Press, Perth, 2002.

Municipal Heritage Inventory. Review for the City of Albany. Heritage Today, Mount Lawley, 2000.

British Parliamentary papers: Select Committee Report and other Reports and Papers Relating to Australia. with Minutes of Evidence and Appendix 1890. Irish University Press, Dublin.

Bodycoat, R. & Sellick, D.R.G. *Memorial Park Cemetery, Albany, Western Australia: Conservation Plan*. Local History Collection. Albany Town Library. 2005.

Bodycoat, R. *St John's Church, Rectory and Hall, Albany, Western Australia: Conservation Plan*. Local History Collection. Albany Town Library. 1998.

Bodycoat, R. *Major Lockyer Precinct, Albany, W.A. Policy for Conservation*. Local History Collection. Albany Town Library. 1992.

Clark, M. *Sources of Australian History*. Oxford University Press. London 1957.

Colebatch, H. *A Story of a Hundred Years: Western Australia 1829-1929*. Perth. 1929.

Cottesloe, L. *Diary & Letters of Admiral Sir C.H. Fremantle*. Fremantle Arts Centre Press, 1985.

Cross, J. *Journal of Several Expeditions Made in Western Australia…1829,1830, 1831 & 1832*. London, 1833.

Crowley, F.K. *A Documentary History of Australia.1788-1840*. Vol.1. Nelson, West Melbourne, 1980.

Dictionary of National Biography, 1885-1900. Oxford University Press, London, 1990.

Dowson, J. *Old Albany: Photographs 1850- 1950*. National Trust of Western Australia, Perth, 2008.

Dowson, J. *Off to War 1914 -1918*. Fremantle, 2014.

Erickson, R. *Bicentennial Dictionary of Western Australians. Pre-1829-1888*. Perth, 1988.

Ferguson, J. *Bibliography of Australia*. Sydney, 1941.

Garden, D.S. *Albany. A Panorama of the Sound from 1827*. Nelson, Melbourne, 1977.

Garden, D.S. *Southern Haven. A History of the Port of Albany*. Albany Port Authority, Albany, 1978.

Giuseppi, M. S. *A Guide to the Manuscripts Preserved in the Public Record Office*. HMSO, London, 1923-1924.

Greeve, D. *The York Street Gully*. Local History Collection. Albany Town Library. 2000.

Historical Records of Australia. Series 1 to IV. Library Committee of the Commonwealth Parliament, Sydney, 1914-1925.

Historical Records of New South Wales. Volumes 1 to VII. Government Printer, Sydney, 1901.

Johnson, L. *The Heart of the Town*. (undated)

Johnson, L. *Love Thy Land*. Albany Shire Council, 1982.

Johnson, L. *More than a House. The Old Farm on Strawberry Hill*. 1984.

Kieza, G. *Banks*. Harper Collins, 2020.

Marshall, J. *Royal Naval Biography*. London, 1830.

Mossenson, D. *State Education in Western Australia. 1829-1960*. University of Western Australia Press, 1972.

Mulvaney, D.J. & Green, N. *Commandant of Solitude. Journals of Captain Collet Barker 1828-1931*. University of Melbourne Press, 1992.

Neal, W.D. (Ed). *Education in Western Australia*. University Of Western Australia Press. 1979.

O'Byrne, O. *A Naval Biographical Dictionary*. John Murray, London, 1849.

Ogle, N. *The Colony of Western Australia*. 1839. John Ferguson Pty. Ltd, 1977.

Pierssene, H. *The Albany Guide and Handbook of Western Australia*. Albany, 1890.

Report from the Select Committee on the Western Australian Constitution May 1890. Hansard, London.

Saggers, T. *Crossing the Kalgan*. Tangee Publishing. 2007.

Sellick, D. R. G. *First Impressions: Travellers' Tales, Albany's 1791-1901*. Western Australian Museum Press, Perth, 1997.

Spearritt, P. *The Heritage Significance of Albany – A Cultural Tourism Strategy – Prepared for the Albany City Council*. Albany City Council, 1994.

Stannage, C.T. *A New History of Western Australia. Perth 1981 & The People of Perth: A Social History of Western Australia's Capital City*. University of Western Australia Press. Perth 1979.

Stratham, P. *Dictionary of Western Australians 1829-1914. Vol.1. Early Settlers*. University of Western Australia Press, Perth, 1979.

Statham-Drew, P. *James Stirling: Admiral & Founding Governor of Western Australia*. University of Western Australia Press, Perth, 2003.

The History of the Oldest Dwelling in Western Australia. Albany Historical Society, 2019

Kemp, P. *The Oxford Companion to Ships and the Sea*. Oxford University Press. London, 1976.

Trollope, A. *Australia*. First Published in 1873. Reprint University of Queensland Press. 1967.

Wollaston J.R. *Wollaston's Albany Journals. 1848 to 1856*. Collected by Canon A. Burton and Edited by Canon P. U. Henn. Volume 2. Patterson Brokensia, Perth, 1954.

West, D A. P. *Albany: The First Hundred Years 1791 -1891*. Printed Privately, 1932

West, D. A.P. *The Settlement on The Sound*. Albany Historical Society. 1976.

Who Was Who? 1897-1960. A & C Black, London, 1981.

Acknowledgements

Our first order of gratitude must go to those people who have encouraged and fostered the collaborative effort that has bought this historical research to a successful conclusion. Cheryl 'Joe' Silcox, Beejay Silcox, Daniel Hatch, Sam Allen, Levi Silcox and Jeannie Stead. Margaret Ytting, The Revd. Dr. John A. Moses, Scott Parsons, Chloe Bird Mauger & Carla and Anita Onions have been to the forefront in this regard.

It has been a stroke of good fortune in developing this manuscript to have access to original reports, correspondence, diaries, journals and newspaper articles covering the period 1791-1977. In this regard we acknowledge the Australian National Library through its online access program Trove, The Battye Library of Western Australia, The State Library of Western Australia, The Albany History Collection housed in the Albany Town Library and the Albany Historical Society photographic collection.

While local histories are a valuable source of primary reference material and use has been made of these avenues for research accordingly, it has been through the National Library of Australia and in particular its online Trove program that most of the significant material for this historical record has been obtained. The reason for this is because Trove sheds light on the key resources available to help broaden our understanding of Australian History in general. The National Library collection, specifically its general catalogue has extensively been used due to the ease of locating key information. We therefore wish to formally acknowledge those responsible for archiving this wonderful resource.

We also would like to acknowledge local identity and historian Dennis Greeve, Professor Graham Seal, Professor Peter Spearritt and Professor Stephen Foster not only for their contribution to this work but also their support as peers in its development. Their guidance, review of material presented and contribution has been most welcomed. Appreciation is also afforded to Dr Neil MacNeill and Mr Peter Bridge for their editing efforts and overall encouragement of our endeavours with respect to this manuscript.

A vote of thanks is extended to Sue Lefroy and Ryan Dowell librarians with the Albany Town Library with responsibility for co-ordinating and archiving the Albany History Collection. Their endeavours in helping us locate some key pieces of information has been appreciated.

Finally, we owe a great debt to the many visitors and early settlers in the town whose journals, reports and diaries have provided insightful historical evidence that has supported and at times underpinned the reconstruction of Albany's Historical Record. It would be remiss of us not to include in this respect those reporters and editors employed by the early newspapers that serviced the town, with a special mention to the outstanding efforts over time of the town's current local newspaper, *The Albany Advertiser*. Much of Albany's history can be distilled from the pages of these publications.

We would be remiss in not giving a particular shout out to Milli and Indi our loyal companions throughout this endeavour.

About the Authors

Dr Steffan B. Silcox

Dr Steffan Silcox had an eclectic career in education and performed several roles while working for the Western Australian Department of Education, including Principal of Secondary School, District Superintendent, acting Executive Director of the Department of Education and District Education Director. He co-authored a book on education titled *Renewing Educational Leadership* which gained international attention. He was also a lecturer at Curtin University before turning his attention to historical research. Dr Silcox was a Councillor on the Albany Shire Council before it became integrated with the Albany Town Council.

Dr Silcox gained his PHD from Curtin University with ground-breaking research on Leadership and Organisational Management. His other qualifications include a master's degree from the University of Western Australia and several degrees in the Social Sciences specialising in history and politics along with an education degree and other qualifications. He was awarded recognition for his research and leadership in Western Australian education with both state and national fellowships and was subsequently named Western Australian Secondary Principal of the year and in 2012. His mantra is that he would rather be a leader among leaders than a leader of followers.

Mr Douglas R. G. Sellick

Douglas R. G. Sellick is an internationally recognised history and literary researcher and anthologist. Educated in Albany and later at the London Bishopsgate Institute, Centre for the History of the Fine and Decorative Arts in conjunction with the Courtauld Institute of Art. Mr Sellick was awarded a prestigious Churchill Fellowship in 1974. After a significant career in shipping with the P&O and British India shipping lines later he worked variously in book and magazine publishing in London, New York, San Francisco, and Sydney. Mr Sellick was a Research Assistant at the Research School of Social Sciences at the Australian National University where he was also instrumental in undertaking key research for *Australians: A Historical Library* for the Australian National University. Later he became the Chief Librarian for Fairfax Publications in Sydney. He was a member of the working party for the 1988 Australian Bicentennial Authority Historic Records Register which is now housed in the National Library of Australia.

Mr Sellick has compiled a number of anthologies on Australian, Maritime and Albany history. For a number of years he was the Local Studies Officer with the Albany Town Library and Curator of Military History at The Princess Royal Fortress.

Douglas Sellick is committed to ensuring the accuracy of Albany's Historical Record.

www.ingramcontent.com/pod-product-compliance
Lightning Source LLC
Chambersburg PA
CBHW080855010526
44107CB00057B/2581